T5-CVM-275

Wissenschaftliche Untersuchungen
zum Neuen Testament · 2. Reihe

Begründet von Joachim Jeremias und Otto Michel
Herausgegeben von
Martin Hengel und Otfried Hofius

31

The Johannine Approach to Mission

A Contextual Study of John 4:1–42

by

Teresa Okure

J.C.B. Mohr (Paul Siebeck) Tübingen

Published with the aid of the Institute of Missiology Missio, Aachen (W. Germany)

BS
2615.2
.O38
1988

CIP-Kurztitelaufnahme der Deutschen Bibliothek

Okure, Teresa:
The Johannine approach to mission: a contextual study of John 4:1−42 / by Teresa
Okure. − Tübingen: Mohr, 1988.
  (Wissenschaftliche Untersuchungen zum Neuen Testament: Reihe 2; 31)
  ISBN 3-16-145049-3
  ISSN 0340-9570

NE: Wissenschaftliche Untersuchungen zum Neuen Testament / 02

© 1988 by J. C. B. Mohr (Paul Siebeck), P.O. Box 2040, D-7400 Tübingen.

This book may not be reproduced, in whole or in part, in any form (beyond that permitted by copyright law) without the publishers's written permission. This applies particularly to reproductions, translations, microfilms and storage and processing in electronic systems.

Typeset by Sam Boyd Enterprise in Singapore; printed by Gulde-Druck GmbH in Tübingen; bound by Heinrich Koch KG in Tübingen.

Printed in Germany.

The Mother of Jesus
(Jn 2:1−11)

Preface

The title of this work will, perhaps, come as little surprise to the reader when he or she realizes that the author hails from a "mission" country. My interest in mission dates back to my childhood days, and was inspired by my living experiences of mission in the African context. I was often struck by the contrast between certain statements of Jesus found mostly in John's Gospel concerning his mission from the Father and the actual conception and exercise of mission which obtained in my context. This contrast belonged mostly in the order of the attitude of the missionary to the work and the people, and of method in the exercise of mission. The whole experience raised for me a number of unanswered questions concerning the relationship of the mission exercised in my context to the mission of Jesus.

In the course of my biblical studies, however, I had completely forgotten that I had had these questions. The choice of the topic for this work was therefore not consciously connected with them. This was due largely to the orientation of the biblical discipline itself which, like most theological disciplines of this century was, and to a large extent still is, literary and academically oriented, not designed to address real life issues. It was only afterwards, indeed as I was reflecting on a suitable preface for this book, that I remembered that I had had these questions, and that here in the pages of this book I had finally found personally satisfying answers to them.

The contents of this book were first submitted as a doctoral dissertation on September 21, 1984 to the Faculty of Theology of the Graduate School of Arts and Sciences at Fordham University. Apart from minor alterations made mostly for greater clarity, the work from chapters one to eight appears here as it had originally been submitted. In its conception and execution, the work is entirely my responsibility. Hence I stand to blame for any weaknesses or flaws it may embody.

But as is well known, nobody undertakes and completes a major academic project, let alone a doctoral thesis, without the help of others. My profound gratitude goes to Professor C. H. Giblin, S.J., the moderator of this dissertation. The confidence that he showed right from the start, in my ability to handle this topic the way I had designed it, even when it seemed that this topic was not viable, proved a constant source of encouragement throughout the period of research. During my two years at the Ecole Biblique, Jerusalem (1981—83), he showed a sustained interest in the work by writing regularly, reading skillfully and promptly the scripts submitted by mail and drawing my attention to any publications that were relevant to my topic. He also arranged his own sabbatical at the Biblicum in 1983/84 in such a way that he could be available at Fordham for consultation during the Christmas and Easter vacations. His personal delight at the outcome of the work was manifested in the sumptuous party which he threw in its honor on the day of the defence. Two other members of Fordham also served on the dissertation committee. Dr. J. M. McDermott, S.J. willingly stepped in as a reader when unavoidable circumstances made it impossible for Dr. M. Callaway to continue to do so. Rev. Dr. R. J. Dillon functioned as the sustained "devil's advocate" of the project.

My two years at the Ecole Biblique were years of special grace. The atmosphere of simplicity, love and friendship as well as of serious academic research which I experienced in this august institution from both professors and colleagues helped in no small way to build up my inner resourcefulness and academic confidence. The multi-dimensional approach to biblical research (literary, archaeological, geographical, historical, etc.) which characterizes the Ecole, and the exceptionally easy access to its rich library resources have left their distinctive imprint on this work.

Professors M.-E. Boismard, O.P., and Jerome Murphy-O'Connor, O.P., in particular, read the first four chapters of this work and offered encouraging and challenging criticisms. I am specially indebted to Professor Boismard who, though my methodology was clearly distinct from, if not opposed to his own, treated my approach with great and most edifying (in the etymological sense of the word) respect. Professor J. Murphy-O'Connor often drew my attention to material that might support or challenge my position at some controversial points in the discussion. During his term as visiting professor here at the Catholic Institute of West Africa in 1986, Professor Johannes Beutler, S.J., also read the original manuscript of this book and made perceptive criticisms which helped me to further clarify my position in the relevant areas.

My studying at the Ecole Biblique would not have been possible in the first place without an initial grant from the Institute of Missiology (MISSIO) Aachen. This Institute also financed the last phase of the research at Fordham University in 1983/84 and finally granted the printing subsidy to this present publication. MISSIO thus contributed in a significant way by providing the necessary financial support for a good portion of this work.

I express my sincerest gratitude to Professors Dr. M. Hengel and Otfried Hofius, the editors of the WUNT series, for accepting this work for publication in this series. Professor Hengel, in particular, showed a most encouraging personal interest in the work from the moment he received the first installment of the manuscript. I am also deeply grateful to him for spontaneously undertaking to write an editorial foreword to this book. The publishers, J.C.B. Mohr (Paul Siebeck), have been remarkably understanding and patient with me in the preparation of this manuscript. My manifold engagements caused exceptionally long and unforeseen delays in the proof-reading of the manuscript and the preparation of the indexes, and ultimately in the publication of the book. This situation would have been enough to cause the despair of any publishers, but not of Mohr-Siebeck. I am also grateful to them for footing all the cost of this publication beyond the printing subsidy granted by MISSIO.

It will be impossible to mention all the people who helped in different ways in the execution of this work. Throughout my course of study, the Jesuit communities at Fordham provided a general atmosphere of acceptance which greatly enhanced my work. Professor R. F. Smith, my one time head of department, who also served on the examining board of the dissertation, greatly encouraged my desire to see this work published and made fruitful suggestions to this effect. Many members of my religious congregation, the Society of the Holy Child Jesus, particularly Catherine Hallahan, Jean Adams, Catherine Murphy and the members of the African Province gave me their abiding moral and human support. Teresa Mee, the Vice-provincial of the then West African Vice-Province at the inception of this study, deserves a special mention for having had the vision to mission me to undertake doctoral studies in Scripture even though the usefulness of such a course for a "Third World" country was then contested. Nor must I forget my loving parents, Chief B. U. and Mme Paulina Okure, and the members of my family who prayed without ceasing for God's unfailing protection of me and guidance in my work. Their prayers were abundantly answered.

This litany of acknowledgements would be incomplete without the special mention of Jesus. The statement of the Psalmist applies most aptly in my case: "If the Lord had not been my help," this work would never have seen the light of day (Ps 94:17). Jesus' unfailing help sustained me most tangibly throughout my entire course of study in ways that might be described as miraculous. His sustaining companionship was felt not only in the academia, but in respect of the human and physical conditions which proved particularly trying during the last year of the research. For the schooling in trust which he provided for me through these trying circumstances, I am deeply grateful to him. It is but a small token of gratitude that I should dedicate this book to his Mother on this feast of her birthday, September 8, as her birthday present.

I also thank the Mother of Jesus herself, who with a motherly concern constantly encouraged me, and on occasions when my supply of wine seemed to have completely dried up, exhorted me to trust Jesus and do whatever he tells me. If somewhere, anywhere in this book the reader should feel that the best wine had been kept until now, he or she should give the glory to God in Jesus who in this way continues to work his signs among us, so that we, too, may see his glory and learn to believe in him.

Port Harcourt   Teresa Okure, S.H.C.J.
September 8, 1987

Foreword of the Editor

Time and again in recent years we have heard the cry of Cassandra that the era of "western theology" is drawing to a close. If the emphasis here is on the questionable geographical adjective, "western", then such proclamations need disturb us but little: the Christian faith is neither restricted to a relatively small region of the globe, nor the private domain of "white" people. The New Testament already speaks of the "oikumene" and includes therein all humanity. If, however, by this announcement is meant the end of a theology that is both critically responsible *and* grounded on biblical truth, then indeed we are dealing with false prophecies. In John 8:32 the Johannine Christ promises, "the truth shall make you free". These words can be read above the entrance to the University of Freiburg, and ought especially to be borne in mind by our generation in church and theology since the accent here lies on the word "truth" — truth identical with the person and work of Christ. The promise presupposes that this truth itself knows how to retain its inherent freedom, its liberating power, beyond the passage of time and changing populations, and that "*it* will overcome". This is also valid for a biblical exegesis that serves this truth: it is not bound to continents, countries or clans.

Six years ago in a foreword to the first critical study from the so-called "third world" in the WUNT, *The Origins of Paul's Gospel* (1981; [2]1984), by the Korean, Seyoon Kim, I pointed out that "the first 'Gentile Christian' . . . — even before the Roman Cornelius — (was) an African, the minister of Queen Candace from what was then Ethiopia, the kingdom of Mroe on the upper reaches of the Nile". Now, introducing the impressive study on John by an African, Dr. Teresa Okure, S.H.C.J., from Nigeria, I could add that the two most important commentaries on John from the early Church were written by Africans. Origen began his exposition on John while still in Alexandria and after a long interruption finished it on Palestinian soil; Augustine composed his *In Iohannis Evangelium Tractatus CXXIV* as Bishop of Hippo in the years between 413 and 418. Indeed, a glance at the early Church reveals the original breath of the missionary effectiveness of the Gospel, from Spain to India and from Ethiopia to Germania and Brittania, in which the most important centers of Greek and Latin theology, Alexandria and Carthage, lay on African soil. No less a figure than the great African politician and philosopher Leopold Senghor emphasized these "ecumenical" facts in a speech at the occasion of his receiving the Dr. Leopold Lucas Prize from the Evangelical Theological Faculty at Tübingen.

Sister Teresa Okure teaches at the Catholic Institute of West Africa in

Port Harcourt, Nigeria. She wrote her dissertation, "The Johannine Approach to Mission. A Contextual Study of John 4:1–42", under the direction of the Rev. C. H. Giblin, S.J., at Fordham University, New York. This refreshing and often provocative study with its clarity and inner consistency represents a significant scholarly achievement from which the editor has profited, and to which he is grateful for stimulus at a number of points — not least where, while holding a somewhat different view, he gladly concedes that the author supports her opinion with arguments that command attention. Especially gratifying is the concentrated energy with which she insists on the question of *christological truth*, over against, for example, the overvaluation of religio-historical conclusions. Here lies the true heart of Johannine theology that we must always keep in view. To that end I hope this study will find many dedicated readers who will allow themselves to be infected by its inner passion and open themselves to the spirit of the Johannine Corpus, and in that spirit experience that truth of John 8:32.

It is certainly no accident that the author has chosen as her topic the frequently neglected question concerning mission in the Fourth Gospel, taking as her paradigm the story of Jesus and the Samaritan woman in John 4:1–42. Here it is clear that personal, existential involvement and exact philological-historical exegesis need not be kept separate from one another. Rather, it is only a combination of the two that can lend to a critical-theological exposition that deep dimension that gives the biblical texts voice and discloses their claim upon us.

That the author is able to criticise constructively a sated and self-satisfied "western" theology is shown by her remarks (p. 296, n. 11) on the common misunderstanding of today that mission is by and large only economic and social "foreign aid". This overlooks how much we in Europe and North America, at the end of the twentieth century, are in need of "spiritual" foreign aid, and how much our own countries have become mission fields, dependent on a renewed practice of the Christian faith. One hopes that other studies of similar quality will follow from this African theologian.

M. H.

Contents

List of Charts and Illustrations

List of Abbreviations

The system of abbreviations used in this study is the standard one comprehensively compiled in the *Journal of Biblical Literature* (= *JBL*) 95 (1976) 331–346 and in the *Catholic Biblical Quarterly* (= *CBQ*) 38 (1976) 437–454, also reprinted in the *CBQ* 46 (1984) 393–408. It is assumed that the reader is familiar with this system, and if necessary will have ready access to the list compiled in these journals. Accordingly, the list given below contains only those very few entries which are not included in these journals.

BD	The Beloved Disciple
IrBibSt	Irish Biblical Studies
JSNT	Journal for the Study of the New Testament
MM	The Memar Markah
SQ	The Semeia Quelle
RechSR	Recherches de Science Religieuse
RQ	The Offenbarungsreden Quelle

Introduction

Biblical scholarship in recent years has witnessed a revival of interest in mission. This interest is inspired for the most part by the changing situation in the so-called mission lands where previously silent and passive recipients of the mission have now become its active agents either in their own countries or in other lands[1]. These recipients have also claimed the right to re-tell the story of the missionary endeavors from their own perspectives, even as the missionaries previously told it from theirs[2].

This new situation highlights the need to reappraise the whole notion of mission and some of its key aspects, in particular, the constitutive role of Jesus in the missionary enterprise, the relationship between the evangelizer and the evangelized, method in the exercise of mission, and the contribution of the audience in the missionary endeavor with respect to both its content and method. The emphasis on the role of the audience in particular may be seen as closely connected with the current concern among women and peoples of the Third World that Scripture and theology be done from their own perspectives too as subjects, who until now have been but passive objects of these disciplines. Thus the new trend in studies on mission forms part of a wider movement which requires that attention be increasingly paid to the hitherto neglected perspectives in the biblical and theological disciplines. The purpose of this whole exercise is to promote a more universal comprehension of the gospel message itself and, ultimately, to bring about the realization of a fuller humanity for all in Christ.

The present study constitutes an attempt to address some of these key missionary issues from the specific standpoint of John's Gospel. Though not expressly so marked, the work is organized in three parts. Chapters one to two (part I) deal with mission as an issue in John's Gospel with reference to its internal and external evidence. Chapters three, four and five (part II) are devoted to an examination of the basic text on mission (Jn 4:1—42) chosen for this study; chapters six and seven (part III) deal with

---

[1] The Nigerian Church, for instance, has embarked upon a "new era of evangelization" aimed at consolidating the faithful in their Christian belief and making the Gospel more firmly rooted in the cultures of the people. It has also undertaken extensive work in foreign missions through the religious congregations, mostly of women, and the National Missionary Seminary of St. Paul, Iperu.

[2] See, for instance, G. H. Anderson and T. F. Stransky, *Mission Trends No. 3: Third World Theologies* (Paramous, NJ: Paulist, 1976); S. Torres and V. Fabella, eds., *The Emergent Gospel: Theology from the Underside of History* (Maryknoll: Orbis, 1978); *Irruption of the Third World: Challenge to Theology* (Maryknoll: Orbis, 1983); and K. Appiah-Kubi and S. Torres, eds., *African Theology en Route* (Maryknoll: Orbis, 1979).

the context, both Gospel and social, of the missionary issues raised in the basic text; and chapter eight offers the summary and conclusion of the entire study and highlights new directions for further research.

A detailed plan of the study, a description of the contextual method applied and the rationale for adopting it are set forth in chapter two. In addition, each chapter and major sections thereof introduces the task to be performed and offers a summary of the major conclusions reached. This approach inevitably carries with it a certain degree of repetition. Looked at positively, these repetitions are designed to facilitate the work of the reader and to involve him or her more closely in the process of the work so that he or she can be in a better position to evaluate the conclusions reached.

The contextual method employed calls for some description (pp. 50—51) not only because it is relatively new in contemporary NT studies, but because the consistent results it yields radically challenges some of the cherished conclusions previously arrived at and almost universally accepted as normative interpretations of the Johannine position. This is true with regard to the notion of mission in the Gospel in general and to the interpretation of Jn 4:1—42 (chapters four and five) in particular.

A crucial aspect of the context is the world of thought and ideas (*Weltanshauung*) which the Evangelist and his immediate audience shared with their contemporaries. This larger socio-cultural context becomes important for our understanding of the manner in which the missionary issues are raised in the Gospel, that is, of the Evangelist's own approach to mission. The hortatory persuasive nature of the Gospel (20:30—31) further demands that special attention be paid to the techniques of convincing preaching employed in the Gospel, as these were operative at the time of the Evangelist and his contemporary audience. Thus the work of Jewish rabbis and Hellenistic-Greek rhetoricians of the NT era consistently offer special insight into the overall rhetorical style of the Evangelist, hence to our better understanding of his meaning and purpose. The importance of both the contextual and the rhetorical methods for Johannine studies are underlined in this study (pp. 297—306, 306—311). But both need to be further experimented with so that their value for Johannine studies can be more solidly ascertained and appreciated.

The reader will perhaps find irksome the tendencies in this study to be exhaustive on the one hand and to detect flaws in previous works on the other. Again there were contextual reasons for this. From the inception of the work to its completion, and beyond, the reactions of almost all who heard of its topic invariably took two forms: While the majority doubted that John's Gospel had anything to do with mission understood, of course, from the twentieth century perspective of outreach to "pagans" in Third World countries, the few who were prepared to concede that the Gospel did have something to do with mission wondered what more I could possibly say on the subject after the works of such eminent scholars as Bultmann and John McPolin. Yet a third group of scholars took strong exception to my designing and applying the contextual method when in their view redaction criticism was now *the* established method for any *scientific* biblical research. From the outset of the study, therefore, and thoroughout its entire duration, I was constantly forced to hold my own against a crowd of eminent Johannine scholars and NT critics. It became necessary to demonstrate persuasively to the ones, that John's Gospel did have something to do with mission, to the others, that the last word had not been spoken on mission in the Gospel, and to the others again, that no methodology, no matter how universally accepted it may be, can have the absolute monopoly in *scientific* NT research at any one point in history. To hold otherwise is to deprive the researcher of his or her freedom to experiment with new methods which could lead to new discoveries of meaning. In this respect, even though I have argued strongly and with cogent reasons for my own contextual method (pp. 297–306), I do not see this method as *the* norm in Johannine studies.

When seen, therefore, against the background of contention in which this work was executed, both the tendency to exhaustiveness and the markedly critical stance to previous works emerge as a survival strategy, a claiming of the right to be heard. This whole experience goes to prove how much the context does colour our undertakings even today as it did in the time of our Evangelist. Its reflection in this work also stands as an abiding plea to older and more experienced scholars to refrain from adopting measures which could stifle the genuis of new comers.

As regards the criticism of previous methodologies in general, the perceptive reader might be led to read this as yet another example of the reaction of Third World theologians to the inadequate theological methodologies employed by First World scholars[3]. The editorial foreword by Martin Hengel already points in this direction (pp. viii–ix). True as this may be in retrospect, this study was not consciously designed as a critique of First World biblical scholarship. The basic assumption is that whether the scholar hails from the First or Third World, he or she must needs address the issue of meaning, or of relevance for life, of his or her theologizing, insofar as such theologizing claims to be Christian. A methodology that empties the text of its meaning through over-concentration on its "archaeological" developments defeats its own purpose and can result in the destruction of the faith of the unskilled reader, if not of the researcher himself or herself. Biblical scholars and theologians have a heavy responsibility in this regard to their "lay" audience.

This search for meaning is particularly relevant in respect of John's Gospel whose expressed purpose is to inculcate in the reader a life-giving faith-response to Jesus. My view is that an interpretation of the Gospel which does not take seriously into consideration this faith-dimension of

---

[3] See, for instance, the critical summary of these theologies by Per Frostin, "The Hermeneutics of the Poor – The Epistemological 'Break' in Third World Theologies", *Studia Theologica* 39 (1985) 127–150.

the Gospel risks missing a vital key to the Johannine meaning (p. 311). The issue of the relationship between methodology and meaning in the doing of theology constitutes one of the greatest challenges facing biblical scholars and theologians today[4]. For Johannine scholars, this challenge is particularly pressing, since the methodologies currently employed and the assumptions behind them may be largely responsible for the continued "enigma" of the Gospel.

Of the original insights offered in this study, those that emerge in the interpretation of Jn 4:1—42 are likely to be judged by the reader as the most tenable. The interpretation of this passage forms the pivot of my thesis on the Johannine approach to mission. Conversely, the interpretation given concerning the situation of the Johannine community is likely to emerge as the most controverted of the study, especially since it runs counter to the views of prominent Johannine scholars. Studies on Jn 4:1— 42 and on the Johannine style which have appeared since the completion of this work tend to follow the line of interpretation given in this study. There is, for instance, a growing appreciation of the rhetorical features in the Gospel and an awareness that the Johannine narrative technique itself constitutes an integral part of the Evangelist's meaning[5]. By their cumulative evidence, these more recent and independent studies lend support to the main line of interpretation sustained in this study.

As regards the situation of the Johannine community, Stephen Smalley's commentary on the Johannine Epistles published in 1984, the same year in which this study was completed, calls for a brief examination[6]. On one key point, Smalley's position agrees with mine (pp. 256—261, esp., 260— 261) that a section of the Johannine *Christian* community found it difficult to accept the messiahship of Jesus (p. xxiii). This is clearly a departure from previous theories which saw those who rejected the messiahship of Jesus as die-hard synagogue Jews. But Smalley's position differs widely from mine on a number of other key issues. First he posits four groups within the Johannine community — the orthodox or truly Johannine

---

[4]Systematic theology is facing up to this challenge through the emergence of liberation, black and Third World theologies. In the field of Scripture, Elizabeth S. Fiorenza's *In Memory of Her: A Feminist Theological Reconstruction of Christian Origins* (New York: Crossroad, 1983), constitutes a seminal attempt to address the issue of the relationship between meaning and method. The quest for new methodologies which will best enable the interpretation of the Gospel message to address the questions raised by different groups of people today constitutes a challenge which biblical scholarship must needs face prayerfully and courageously.

[5]Worthy of note among these studies are: F. Genuyt, "Exégèse de Jean. L'entretien avec la Samaritaine (4, 1—42). Analyse sémiotique," *SémiotBib* 36 (1984) 15—24; J. S. King, "Is Johannine Archaeology Really Necessary?" *EvangQuart* 56 (1984) 203—211; A. Lenglet, "Jésus de passage parmi les Samaritains (Jn 4, 4—42)," *Biblica* 66 (1985) 493—502; F. Manns, "Exégèse rabbinique et exégèse johannique," *RevBib* 92 (1985) 525—538; M. Pamment, "Focus in the Fourth Gospel," *ExpTim* 97 (1985) 71—75, and Gail R. O'Day, "Narrative Mode and Theological Claim: A Study in the Fourth Gospel," *JBL* 105 (1986) 657—668.

[6]Stephen S. Smalley, *1, 2, 3 John* (Word Biblical Commentary, 51; Waco, Texas: Word Books, 1984).

group, two heretically inclined groups, one of Jewish origin who held a low christology and found it difficult to accept the divinity of Jesus, the other of Hellenistic/pagan origin who held a high christology and found it difficult to accept the humanity of Jesus, and finally a fourth group, the sessesionists proper. Secondly, he maintains that while the Jewish group emphasized the importance of the law, the Hellenistic/pagan group tended to regard "righteousness" as unimportant (p. xxiv). The aim of the Gospel and 1 John then is primarily to "provide a balanced christology" for both groups, and secondarily to deal with the ethical problems of each (p. xxvi).

My position which rests principally on the evidence of 1 Jn 1:18—19 posits two, not four groups within the community, namely, the sessesion-ists or heretical group, and the Johannine or "orthodox" group to whom the Gospel and 1 John are addressed (pp. 256—258). The same heretical group, of Jewish origin, deny the divinity and messiahship of Jesus, while some members of the "orthodox" Johannine group, tend to neglect the importance of brotherly love modeled on Jesus' own love for them (1 Jn 3:16; cf. Jn 13:34). This tendency on the part of the "believing" disciples, I have argued, arose out of a mistaken notion of charismatism similar to that of the Corinthians (pp. 276—277).

Moreover, there is no visible evidence in the Gospel or Epistles that the humanity of Jesus constitutes a stumbling block to the Johannine audience. I have discussed at length the only passages which might give rise to this interpretation, namely, 1 Jn 4:2; 2 Jn 7 (pp. 246—248). In these passages as in the highly controversial 1 Jn 5:6—8, the issue in my view is the divinity of Jesus revealed in human form, not the humanity of Jesus divinized. People of Jewish background were familiar with divinizations of human beings (cf. Jn 10:34—35; Ps 86:2; Exod 7:1) not with the incarnation of God. That the issue in 1 Jn 5:5—9 in particular is not the humanity of Jesus *per se*, is indicated by the statements about the divine witness to Jesus as "his Son" (1 Jn 5:9—12). Furthermore, the coming in "water and blood" signifies not primarily the humanity of Jesus proved by his death on the Cross, but this divine humanity seen as the medium of salvation. "Water and blood", as most scholars agree, symbolize the sacraments of baptism and the eucharist through which the believer is ordained as a full-fledged Christian and can be said to overcome the world (1 Jn 5:5). Jesus' coming "in water and blood" thus refers primarily to his role as God's Messiah and agent of salvation; in short, the reference in this passage is primarily soteriological. But it is only as ontological Son of God that, in the Johannine perspective, Jesus is the Messiah, Saviour. That is why I regard 1 Jn 5:5—8 as yet a different formulation of the one question at issue in both Gospel and Epistles, namely, Jesus' divine messiahship which is denied by the sessesionists.

Moreover, the consistency with which this issue is formulated, "the Christ, the Son of God", leads me to see this as one, not two problems, posed for one, not two groups of people. Were it otherwise, the formula-tion would have read "the Christ *and* the Son of God" where the copulative "and" would have established a different relationship between the two terms than the present one of apposition. The protracted debate between Jesus and the Jews in Jn 5—10 supports this interpretation. Here the same group of Jews know Jesus' humanity so well (6:42; 7:27; 8:57) that they cannot but see his claim to divinity as blasphemy (5:18; 6:42b, 66; 8:58—59; 10:31—39). The same unity characterizes the treatment of the issue in the Epistles (pp. 254—255).

Smalley's contention that the emphasis on "law" in the Epistles is a later development of the heretical group of Jewish origin also strains credibility. A distinction missing in his analysis needs to be made between Torah-inspired observances and the commandments emphasized in the Gospel and Epistles. Here these commandments boil down to two: believing in Jesus as God's Son and Messiah, and loving as God and Jesus love (Jn 6:29; 13:34—35; 1 Jn 3:16—18, 22—23; 4:10—11). Both commandments have a christological, not Torah origin. Both are also intrinsically, centrally related to the Johannine understanding of discipleship. In this understanding, one cannot be a disciple unless one believes in Jesus and keeps his new commandment of love. In the Gospel, on the contrary, the Law (Torah) functions not in terms of ethical observance, but as a reliable source of revelation which provides valid criteria for testing Jesus' claim to messiahship (7:42) and as an instrument of salvation pitted against Jesus (9:28—29). Here, too, the Johannine contention is that Jesus transcends the Law both as a source of revelation and as an instrument of salvation. It is on the basis of this transcendence that he gives the new commandment of love.

Finally, unlike Smalley, I do not consider the Johannine "orthodox" group to be uniformly saintly, but as having complex moral problems (pp. 252—254). For though by baptism they may have been without sin (1 Jn 3:6, 9; 5:18), in practice they were all sinners (1 Jn 1:8—9; 3:10—18). That is why it became necessary, especially during the crisis situation when relationships would have been particularly strained, to exhort the group to be in truth and deed what they professed in word (1 Jn 3:8; cf. pp. 252—253). Brotherly love holds the key to this holiness, understood as a sharing in the life of God (1 Jn 1:6; 2:6—11; 4:11—12).

My examination of Smalley's position, therefore, does not lead me to modify my position concerning the situation of the Johannine Community on the points on which we differ. This stance is based principally on the internal evidence of the Gospel and Epistles and on the unified manner in which the central issues raised are treated in both works. This stance, of course, is open to dispute. It is, therefore, hoped that the arguments set forth in the pages of this book will generate a rich and enriching discussion among us Johannine students. It is hoped, above all, that such dialogue will send us all back to the texts, to an ever closer reading and listening to the texts, and that the ultimate purpose of this exercise will be the desire to understand better and adopt within our own contexts the Johannine approach to mission.

Chapter I

The State of the Question

A. The Johannine Data for His Notion of Mission

The precise meaning, nature and scope of mission in John's Gospel are subjects of perennial debate[1], but that mission itself is a leitmotif or "foundation theme" of the Gospel is hardly a matter for dispute[2]. Though the word "mission" is not actually used, a sense of it pervades the Gospel[3]. Jesus characteristically designates his Father as "the one who

[1] See the survey below, pp. 7–34. Further discussion on these topics can also be found in R. Kysar, *The Fourth Evangelist and his Gospel: An Examination of Contemporary Scholarship* (Minneapolis: Augsburg Publishing House, 1975) 147–165; A. Wind, "Destination and Purpose of the Gospel of John," *NovT* 45 (1972) 26–69; J. McPolin, "Studies in the Fourth Gospel: Some Contemporary Trends," *IrBibSt* 2 (1980) 2–26; R. Schnackenburg, *Das Johannesevangelium* I (Freiburg: Herder, 1965) 136; W.G. Kümmel, *Einleitung in das Neue Testament* (17. Aufl.; Heidelberg: Quelle and Meyer, 1973) 194–200.

[2] Thus, for Bultmann ("Die Bedeutung der neuerschlossenen mandäischen und manichäischen Quellen für das Verständnis des Johannesevangeliums," *ZNW* 24 [1925] 100–146) the "centrale Anschauung" or "Grundkonzeption" of the Gospel is that Jesus is "der Gesandte Gottes . . . der Offenbarung bringt durch Worte und Taten" (p. 102). McPolin ("Mission in the Fourth Gospel," *ITQ* 36 [1969] 113–122, esp. p. 114; and *John* [NT Message 6; Wilmington: Michael Glazier, 1979] 75, 97) praises this view. Ernst Haenchen ("'der Vater der mich gesandt hat,'" *NTS* 9 [1963] 208–216) sees the expression, "der Vater der mich gesandt hat," as the core of the Johannine "Offenbarungslehre" and the "Lieblingsformel" of the Gospel (p. 208); similarly, Werner Bieder, *Gottes Sendung und der missionarische Auftrag nach Matthäus, Lukas, Paulus und Johannes* (Theologische Studien 82; Zurich: EVZ-Verlag, 1965) 40. Joseph Kuhl (*Die Sendung Jesu und der Kirche nach dem Johannesevangelium* [Studia Instituti Missiologica Societatis Verbi Domini; St. Augustin: Styler, 1967] 1) also notes that the "Sendungsidee" constitutes an essential aspect of Johannine theology.

Other scholars who do not specifically emphasize the predominance of the mission theme in the Gospel do, nonetheless, recognize the centrality in the Gospel of Jesus' self-revelation and salvific work. See, for instance, Rudolf Schnackenburg, "Die Messiasfrage im Johannesevangelium," *Neutestamentliche Aufsatze. Festschrift für Joseph Schmid zum 70. Geburtstag* (ed. J. Blinzler, O. Kuss, and F. Mussner; Regensburg: Friedrich Pustet, 1963) 240–264 and *Johannesevangelium* I, 136–137; R.E. Brown, "The Kerygma of the Gospel According to John: The Johannine View of Jesus in Modern Studies," *Interpretation* 21 (1967) 387–400, esp. 389–392.

[3] The absence of the word "mission" perhaps explains the general reluctance of scholars to employ the term when discussing the life and work of Jesus. Thus, the idea of "sending" rather than of "mission" dominates the following important studies: Bultmann, "Die Theologie des Johannes Evangeliums: Die Sendung des Sohnes," *Theologie des Neuen Testaments* (3. Aufl.; Tübingen: Mohr, 1958) 385–392; see also pp. 393–422; J.P. Miranda, *Der Vater der mich gesandt hat* (EHS

sent me" (ὁ πέμψας με πατήρ). This insistently repeated motif occurs in different forms forty times in the Gospel, twenty-five times with the verb πέμπειν and nineteen times with ἀποστέλλειν[4]. To these passages which deal with the Father's sending of Jesus may be added those which deal with his sending of John the Baptist (1:6, 33; 3:28) and the Holy Spirit (14:26). This makes a total of forty-four explicit references to the sending activity of the Father in the Gospel[5].

While the terminology of sending emphasizes the role of the Father as "the sender," the Johannine notion of mission is equally embodied in the person on whom the Gospel narrative centers. Jesus himself is "the one sent." Though the actual expression ὅν ἀπέστειλεν occurs only four times in the Gospel (3:34; 5:38; 6:29c; 17:3 [= ὅν ἀπέστειλας]), the motif is present each time it is stated that the Father sent Jesus (see note 4 below). Jesus' self-understanding as "the one sent by the Father" thus constitutes his most fundamental self-definition in the Gospel. The other dominant titles by which he personally designates himself, namely, "the son of man" (3:13, 14; 5:27), "the Son" (3:16; 6:40; 8:36) and "the Son of God" (10:36), are all viewed from the specific standpoint of his mission[6].

23/7; Frankfurt a/M.: Herbert and Peter Lang, 1972); J.A. Bühner, *Der Gesandte und seine Weg im 4. Evangelium: Die Kultur- und religions-geschichtlichen Grundlagen der johanneischen Sendungschristologie sowie ihre traditions-geschichtliche Entwicklung* (Tübingen: Mohr-Siebeck, 1977); and the works of Kuhl, Haenchen, Bieder and McPolin cited in note 2 above. M. -E. Boismard and A. Lamouille (*Synopse des Quartre Evangiles III, L'Evangile de Jean* [Paris: Cerf, 1977]) and Martin Hengel ("Die Ursprünge der christlichen Mission," *NTS* 18 [1971] 15–38) are notable exceptions here.

This reluctance of scholars to use the word "mission" reflects a fidelity to the Johannine terminology which in itself is commendable. Yet it is to be noted that the word "mission" occurs nowhere in the NT. The word ἀποστολή (Gal 2:8) which the RSV translates "mission" means rather "apostleship" or "the office of an apostle" as it does in its only other three occurrences in the NT: Acts 1:25, 1 Cor 9:2 and Rom 1:5 (see *BAG* 99; *LSJ* 820; and Rengstorf, *TDNT* 1, 446–447); secondly, the Gospel, as indeed the whole of the NT, uses the same basic terminology (πέμπειν and ἀποστέλλειν; OT, שׁלח) to describe the sendings of the Baptist, the Holy Spirit and the disciples. If, then, these other "sendings" can freely be regarded as mission, there seems to be little justification for begrudging the same term to the idea of sending which permeates the Gospel and which applies primarily to Jesus' "sending" by the Father. Besides, if, as already noted, Jesus' mission is constitutive of all the other missions in the Gospel, then these latter can be termed "mission," only because the former is already mission. Hengel ("Ursprünge," 35–37) is surely right that if anybody deserves the term "Urmissionar" it is Jesus himself.

[4]With πέμπειν all in participial forms used as a substantive: 8 times in the nominative: 5:37; 6:44; 7:28; 8:16, 18, 26, 29; 12:49; 7 times in the accusative (5:23; 7:33; 12:44, 45; 13:20; 15: 21; 16:5); once in the dative (5:24); and 7 times in the genitive (4:34; 5:30; 6:38, 39; 7:16; 9:4; 14:24). With ἀποστέλλειν all in the indicative forms: ἀπέσταλκεν (5:36; 20:21); ἀπέστειλας (11: 42; 17:3, 8, 18, 21, 23, 25); ἀπέστειλεν (3:17, 34; 5:38; 6:29, 57; 7:29; 8:42; 10:36). It is not evident that a different shade of meaning is intended in the use of each of these two verbs.

[5]Bultmann (*Theologie*, 386) cites 25 occurrences; but his list is based only on πέμπειν. The present list is based on A.Q. Morton and S. Michaelson, eds., *A Critical Concordance to the Gospel of John* (The Computer Bible, Vol.V; Bible Research Associates, 1974).

[6]See, for instance, 3:13–19 where all three titles are developed in connection with the "sending" (3:17), "giving" (3:16) and "coming" (3:19) of Jesus into the world; and in particular 8:36. The references given here and in the rest of this section are by no means exhaustive.

At another level, Jesus is described in the Gospel as "the one who has come into the world" in the Father's name. Most frequently, this "coming" is expressed by Jesus himself in the first person perfect, either positively ἐλήλυθα (5:43; 12:46; 16:28; 18:37) or negatively οὐκ ἐλή-λυθα (7:28; 8:42). The positive instances are always invariably followed by a statement indicating the benefit for humanity of the purpose of his coming into the world, for example, as "light" (12:46), as fulness of life (10:10), or "not to judge the world" (12:47); or they emphasize the fact that Jesus comes "in the Father's name" (5:43). The negative statements, on the other hand, are always followed by an adversative ἀλλά and, like the ἀποστέλλειν and πέμπειν passages, they also draw attention to the sending activity of the Father (7:28; 8:42)[7].

Jesus' coming into the world is also mentioned by the Evangelist (1:9, 11; cf. 1:5, 10), by John the Baptist (1:15, 27, 30; 3:31a,c), by Nicodemus (3:2) and by Martha (11:27). His coming into the world as the Messiah constitutes the subject of debate among his Jewish audience in Jerusalem (7:27b, 31b, 41b, 42b), it is declared by his Galilean audience (6:14) and by the crowd on the occasion of his triumphal entry into Jerusalem (12:13, 15), and is mentioned in connection with the messianic expectation of the Samaritan woman (4:25a—26). The statements about Jesus' coming to the "hour" (12:27) and of the coming of his "hour" (7:30; 12:23; 13:1; 17:1) are also intrinsically connected with his mission, with the Father's glorification of him in this mission. Thus the terminology of sending/coming not only focuses attention on the Father and Jesus, it emphasizes the intimate and exclusive relationship which exists between them in this missionary enterprise.

The task for which Jesus is sent into the world by the Father receives a twofold description in the Gospel, viewed from the standpoint of the Father and that of the audience. From the standpoint of the Father, his missionary task is described variously as to do the Father's work (4:34; 17:4) and will (5:30; 6:38), to witness by his word and deed to the things he has seen and heard from the Father (3:11, 32 ; 5:19; 8:26, 28b, 38, 40) or personally to report concerning the Father (1:18; 14:9). From the standpoint of the audience, this task is described summatively as to save the world (3:17; cf. 1:29; 4:42), not to judge the world (8:15; 12: 47) or to give eternal life to those who believe in him (3:16; 4:10, 14; 10:10; 17:2; 20:30—31).

Strikingly, the statements on "witness" in the Gospel focus less on Jesus' witnessing activity to the Father and more on the Father's own wit-

---

[7]In addition, the forms ἔρχομαι (8:41) and ἦλθον (8:14a; 9:39; 10:10b; 12:27, 47; 15:22) are also found on the lips of Jesus. Once he speaks of his "coming" in the third person as "the light" (3:19). In contrast to the "sending" terminology, that of "coming" tends to emphasize Jesus' willingness to be sent and his active participation in the missionary enterprise (cf. Heb 10: 5—7, 9; Ps 40:7—9). A similar openness is suggested on the part of the audience who come to him with the desire to believe in him (cf. 1:46; 3:2 [?] ; 4:29, 39—42; 6:37, 44, 65; 12:21).

ness to Jesus (8:18; 5:32 [?]) and on the witness which others bear to Jesus himself: that of John the Baptist (1:6, 15, 19–36; 5:32–35), of the Holy Spirit and the disciples (15:26, 27), of the Beloved Disciple (19: 35; 21:24), of the Scriptures (5:39), of Moses (5:45–47), of Jesus' own works (5:36; cf. 10:25, 37–38; 14:11; 15:22–24) and even of Jesus himself (8:14, 18). A distinction is further made between the witness which Jesus bears to the Father and the witness which others bear to Jesus himself. For while Jesus' witness to the Father is synonymous with his revealing the Father (1:18) and is borne out by his entire life and work (8:46; 10:37; 14:8–11), the witness which the Father, others and Jesus' own works bear him means giving convincing evidence to his unique identity as the Father's sole salvific agent[8].

The question of Jesus' identity or credentials as the Father's envoy, thus constitutes an important aspect of the missionary data in the Gospel. For the insistent claim that Jesus is sent by or comes from the Father appears to be matched by an equally strong denial of this claim on the part of his Jewish audience, particularly, the leaders (5:18; 7–10). Thus an atmosphere of debate surrounds the whole projection of Jesus as "the one sent by the Father."

The Gospel also presents other important characters in the Gospel primarily from the standpoint of mission: John the Baptist (1:6–8, 15, 19–36; 3:26–36), the Holy Spirit (14:26; 15:26; 16:7–15) and Jesus' own disciples (4:38; 15:27; 17:18; 20:21). All these missions are shown to derive from Jesus' own mission, and to be in function of it as its witness (1:7–8, 19, 34; 3:26–28; 5:33; 15:26, 27). The Pharisees are also portrayed as "senders" to John the Baptist (1:19–28; cf. 5:33), to Jesus himself (7:32, 45–52) and to the parents of the man born blind (9:18–23). Their sending activity is negatively viewed in the Gospel and appears to be intended as a contrast to Jesus' life-giving mission from the Father. Similarly, Jesus' coming to give life to the full (10:10) is contrasted with the destructive coming of thieves and brigands (10:8, 10a), of the prince of this world (14:30) and of those who come in their own name and are well received (5:43). Thus the Gospel appears to contain an implicit criticism of false missionaries set against Jesus and typified by these negative figures, especially the Pharisees. This implicit criticism is heightened by Jesus' two statements addressed to the disciples concerning the relation of an ἀπόστολος to his sender (7:18; 13:16) and by such overtly polemic passages as 4:38, 42 and 15:16.

The focus on mission in the Gospel is not limited, however, to indicating the roles of the Father and the Son or the relationship in the missionary enterprise between the senders and the ones sent (1:33–34; 5:17, 19; 8:28–29; 15:16) or that between the various missionaries themselves

---

[8]See further Johannes Beutler, *Martyria: Traditionsgeschichtliche Untersuchungen zum Zeugnisthema bei Johannes* (Frankfurt a/M.: Josef Knecht, 1972) esp. 360; and Strathmann, μαρτυρεῖν, μαρτυρία, μαρτύριον, *TDNT* IV, 474–508, esp. 492, 500.

(1:15, 27, 30; 3:26—36; 4:38, 42 ; 15:16). Rather strikingly, a twofold emphasis is placed throughout both on the purpose of the mission, viewed primarily from the standpoint of the audience to whom it is directed, and also on the faith-response which this mission requires of its hearers[9]. This double emphasis is articulated in the ἵνα -clauses, of which 3:16 is the key text[10]. These clauses draw attention to the interaction necessitated in the missionary dialectic between the one sent and his living audience.

Thus all the major statements on mission in the Gospel have or presuppose a purposeful ἵνα -clause: Jesus is sent by the Father "so that" those who believe in him may have eternal life (3:15, 16) or "so that" the world may be saved through him (3:17); he comes "so that" all may have life to the full (10:10). John the Baptist is sent "so that" he may bear witness to the light (1:7a, 8), that Jesus may be revealed to Israel (1:31) and that all may believe through him (1:7b). Though no purposeful clause is explicitly attached to the missions of the Holy Spirit and of the disciples, it is understood that the whole purpose of their witnessing mission to Jesus (14:26; 15:26, 27) is "so that" the world may believe that the Father sent Jesus (17:21, 23; cf. 16:13—14; 17:17—20). Moreover, since their mission is portrayed as an integral aspect of Jesus' own mission, both necessarily share the same purpose.

This point is amply elaborated in the farewell discourses (13—17) where Jesus' accomplished mission is portrayed as constitutive of the mission of the disciples and as inclusive of it (Jn 17). It is further underlined in 4:36 where "rejoicing together" is seen as the one ultimate goal for all who are engaged in the missionary enterprise, whether they be sowers or reapers. Indeed, the purposeful clauses are also viewed from the standpoint of the audience's response to Jesus (5:34; 9:39; 10:38; 11:52; 12:47; 14:29). Not only is Jesus' mission from the Father solely for the benefit of his audience, this mission seeks a living response from this very audience[11].

---

[9]McPolin ("Mission in the Fourth Gospel," 114) sees the personal relationship between the one sent and his sender as that which "defines the internal aspect of mission," while the purpose constitutes "the external aspect." But McPolin's entire assessment takes little account of the role of the audience other than to say that a faith response is expected of them.

[10]Jn 3:16 is "the key text" on mission in the Gospel because it states summatively all the basic elements embodied in the notion of mission in the Gospel: the Father is the origin and source of the missionary enterprise; Jesus, his uniquely beloved Son, is his agent; the mission field is the world; the purpose of the mission is to give eternal life to humanity; and the audience relates to this mission by personally making a response of faith in Jesus as the Father's envoy. The whole undertaking rests on God's surpassing love for the world, his desire to prevent human beings from perishing. So it is all a "gift" (ἔδωκεν), and a "grace" (cf. 1:12—13, 17).

[11]Harald Riesenfeld ("Zu den johanneischen ἵνα-Sätzen," *ST* 19 [1965] 213—220) holds that these purposeful clauses originated from catechetical instructions within the Johannine community. In his view, therefore, these clauses do not indicate a missionary purpose on the part of the Evangelist (p. 218). Riesenfeld's position rests on his presupposition that mission means only "outreach to non-believers." This research will test whether such a view is indeed grounded in the Gospel itself or whether Bultmann (*Theologie*, 388) is closer to the Johannine position when he states

This focus on purpose and on the interaction necessitated in the missionary dialectic between the audience and the one sent reaches its climax in 20:30–31. This "closing text" proves to be important, not only because it explicitly states the purpose of the Gospel in evangelistic terms, but also because by recalling the foundational text on mission (3:16), it conclusively defines the whole purpose of the Gospel pregnantly in terms of mission[12]. Although the phrasing in 3:16 and 20:30–31 is not exactly identical, both passages clearly have the same end in view, namely, to evoke in the hearer/reader a life-giving faith in Jesus, the Father's envoy[13].

Together with the other evidence cited above, 20:30–31 makes it inevitable to conclude (1) that the Gospel derives its existence from mission, the mission of Jesus from the Father (3:16–17) which is the subject of "this book" (20:30), and (2) that it exists for mission, the same mission of Jesus as it was executed before the disciples (15:27; 20:30) and was understood by the Beloved Disciple (21:24), the witness who transmits this Gospel (21:24–25)[14]. Indeed, the so-called epilogue of the Gospel, Jn 21, appears to be closely connected with the missionary issues raised in the Gospel. It addresses specifically the issue of the disciples' relationship with Jesus in the missionary task.

---

that these purposeful clauses express "der Zweck seines [i.e., Jesus'] Gesandtseins oder Kommens" into the world.

[12]The sustained debate on whether John 20:30–31 or 21 constitutes the Evangelist's conclusion to the Gospel has most recently been treated by Minear, "The Original Functions of John 21," *JBL* 102 (1983) 85–95. It is not our intention here to engage in this debate; we hope that this research will throw some light on this whole issue. But whatever its origin and original placement in the Gospel, the significance of 20:30–31 for the understanding of the missionary character of the Gospel cannot be disputed. Indeed, the weight which this particular passage carries for the interpretation of the Gospel as a whole has been noted by Schnackenburg, *Johannesevangelium* I, 135 and "Messiasfrage," 240–264. See also the critical survey by Wind, "Destination and Purpose," 26–69, and our own survey of the discussion on the missionary character of the Gospel based on this passage, pp. 9–16 below.

[13]We may compare in particular 3:16b and 20:31:

3:16b: ἵνα πᾶς ὁ πιστεύων εἰς αὐτὸν ⎫   ἔχῃ ζωὴν αἰώνιον
              μὴ ἀπόληται ἀλλ᾽ ⎭

20:31:   ἵνα πιστεύ[σ]ητε ὅτι Ἰησοῦς ⎫   ζωὴν ἔχητε ἐν
              ἐστιν ὁ χριστὸς ὁ υἱὸς τοῦ ⎬   τῷ ὀνόματι αὐτοῦ
              θεοῦ καὶ ἵνα πιστεύοντες ⎭

Obviously, "to have eternal life" (3:16b) means the same as "to have life in his name" (20:31). This is a theme which runs through the Gospel and is developed in terms of "new birth" (3:1–21), "living water" (4:10–15; 7:37–39), "passing over from judgment to life" (5:24–29) and "bread of life" (6:26–58). See further 10:10, 28; 11:25 and 17:2.

[14]M. de Jonge (*Jesus, Stranger from Heaven and Son of God: Jesus Christ and Christians in the Johannine Perspective* [Missoula: Scholars Press, 1977] 118–119) sees in 20:30–31 the Evangelist's declared intention to transmit Jesus' mission; so, too, Brown, "Kerygma," 387–400; and Kümmel, *Einleitung*, 194–200, and *Die Theologie des Neuen Testaments nach seinen Hauptzeugen* (Grundriss zum NT; Göttingen: Vandenhoeck und Ruprecht, 1969) where he writes: "Diese Verkündigungsabsicht [i.e., of 20:20–31] wird aber nicht durch Predigt oder Lehre, sondern im Rahmen eines 'Evangeliums' ausgeführt" (p. 233).

The Gospel itself thus furnishes ample grounds for this present undertaking the purpose of which is to highlight the manner in which mission is conceived in the Gospel. The peculiarity of the missionary features highlighted in this data-survey calls for special attention and demands some explanation. From the standpoint of Jesus, these features embrace the dispute over his identity and credentials as the Father's agent of salvation, his insistent claim that he was sent by the Father, and the denial of this claim by some of his audience. They concern, too, the emphasis on the centrality of his mission, the consequent presentation of all other missions in the Gospel as derivative of his and in function of it and the obviously related polemic treatment of false envoys in the Gospel. From the standpoint of Jesus' audience, these features embrace the emphasis that Jesus' mission is for its sole benefit and the repeated appeal to this audience to believe and find life in Jesus as the Father's agent of salvation, or "the Christ and Son of God" (20:30—31). Are these features in any way related and is there a possible explanation for the predominantly polemic and disputative approach to Jesus' mission in the Gospel? And, most fundamentally of all, can we say in the light of these features that the Gospel is concerned with mission? What, indeed, is the Johannine notion of mission?

B. A Survey of Major Approaches to Mission in John's Gospel in the Twentieth Century

Contemporary literature on mission in John's Gospel strikes one as rich but bewildering. As yet one cannot, however, furnish a *Forschungsbericht* with respect to the particular topic of this present research, the Johannine approach to mission. For no systematic study has so far been worked out regarding the particular manner in which the Evangelist handles the topic of mission in the Gospel, even though studies exist concerning his style generally[15]. The following survey, therefore, does not

---

15 For the most part these studies on Johannine style are geared towards determining the unity of authorship of the Gospel. See, in particular, Eugen Ruckstuhl, *Die Literarische Einheit des Johannesevangeliums: Der gegenwärtige Stand der einschlägigen Forschung* (Freiburg in der Schweiz/Paulusverlag, 1951). This study is an "Auseinandersetzung" with Bultmann's three-level theory on the composition of the Gospel: the original *SQ* and *RQ*, the work of the Evangelist and that of the ecclesiastical redactor (*Commentary*, 6—12). In "Johannine Language and Style: The Question of their Unity," *L'évangile de Jean, sources, rédaction, théologie* (ed. M. de Jonge; BETL 44 [henceforth *BETL* 44]; Leuven University, 1977) 125—147, Ruckstuhl discusses in particular the reconstructions by Fortna (*The Gospel of Signs*, 131—145) and Nicol (*Semeia*, 145—147). See, too, Eduard Schweizer, *EGO EIMI: Die religionsgeschichtliche Herkunft und theologische Bedeutung der johanneischen Bildreden, zugleich ein Beitrag zur Quellenfrage des vierten Evangeliums* (FRLANT 56, NF 38; Göttingen: Vandenhoeck und Ruprecht, 1939). Boismard ("Un procédé rédactionnel dans le

pretend to be exhaustive. It is intended simply to outline the major contemporary trends in studying the topic of mission in John's Gospel.
Outlining these trends will highlight what is distinctively new about this
present undertaking and its dialectical relationship to previous studies.

The survey focuses on issues rather than on authors. These issues, of
course, are interrelated. For even a given author treats more than one issue
in offering his or her synthesis. The following schematization, then, attempts to analyze key standpoints. Citing an author in connection with a
particular issue is intended to acknowledge that that author has significantly contributed to the discussion of the issues in question or else to
illustrate the wide range of those supporting a typical viewpoint.

The ensuing survey is rather lengthy for a number of reasons. First
because despite the widely recognized centrality of mission in the Gospel,
existing surveys of Johannine literature to date do not specifically focus
on this issue. The one exception, perhaps, is Kysar, *The Fourth Evangelist
and His Gospel*[16]. But even here the studies on mission which the author
cites are treated only as side issues of much wider topics. Thus "The mission in Samaria" is treated only as an aspect of "The Situation and Purpose of the Evangelist" (pp. 160–163), "The mission of the Church"
only as an aspect of "The Church" (pp. 244–245), while the studies by
Miranda, Borgen, Haenchen and Kuhl on the sending of the Son are buried
in "The Indivisibility of Flesh and Glory," itself only an aspect of "Christology" (pp. 195–198). Thyen's survey completed by Becker focuses
even less on studies on mission in the Gospel. Malatesta's earlier bibliography contains very few listings on the topic[17]. The general impression
given, then, is that studies on mission in the Gospel are not important
enough to receive attention of their own. Hence the need for the present
survey.

Contemporary discussions on mission in John's Gospel may best be
grouped as four main categories: (1) those that debate about the missionary character of the Gospel, (2) those that search for the possible models
which could have inspired the Evangelist's portrait of Jesus as "the one
sent," (3) those that focus on the theological and Christological aspects
of mission in the Gospel, and (4) those that debate about the missionary
stance of the Johannine community.

---

quatrième évangile: la Wiederaufnahme," *BETL* 44, 235–241) illustrates from the use of the
technique of "reprise" the presence of compositional layers in the Gospel. Finally, Herbert Leroy
(*Rätsel und Missverständnis: Ein Beitrag zur Formgeschichte des Johannesevangeliums* [BBB 30;
Löwen, 1967]) and D.W. Wead (*The Literary Devices in John's Gospel* [Basel: Friedrich Reinhardt
Kommissionsverlag, 1970]) both emphasize the literary forms as bearers of theological meaning.

[16]See note 1 above.

[17]Hartwig Thyen, "Aus der Literatur zum Johannesevangelium," *TRu* 39 (1975) 1–69, 289–
330; 42 (1977) 211–270; 43 (1978) 328–359; completed by Jürgen Becker, *TRu* 47 (1982)
279–301; Edward Malatesta, *St. John's Gospel. 1920–1965: A Cumulative and Classified Bibliography of Books and of Periodical Literature on the Fourth Gospel* (AnBib 32; Rome: Pontifical
Biblical Institute, 1967) 149–150. This survey covers almost half a century, yet not more than
six works are listed under "mission," about half of which are articles or small booklets.

1. The Missionary Character of the Gospel

The discussion concerning the missionary character of John's Gospel is rooted in the importance accorded to the declared evangelistic thrust of the Gospel (Jn 20:30–31)[18]. The variant reading, however, raises a problem concerning the specific nature of this missionary thrust and of the audience addressed: Was the Gospel addressed to those already converted in order to strengthen their faith in Jesus (ἵνα πιστεύητε, present subj., "that you may continue to believe")? Or was it addressed to non-believers in order to win them to faith in Jesus (ἵνα πιστεύσητε, aor. subj. "that you may begin or come to believe")[19]? The latter reading gives rise to the view that the Gospel was a missionary document (*eine Missionsschrift*) designed to win converts; the former supports the view that the Gospel primarily served as a community document (*ein Gemeinde-Evangelium*) designed to meet the needs of those who already believed.

Eine Missionsschrift

Bornhäuser and Oehler were the first in this century to argue that John's Gospel was a missionary tract written in order to win converts[20]. For Bornhäuser those potential converts were Palestinian Jews ("für Israel," "für die Mission unter Israel"); for Oehler, they were Gentiles ("für Heiden, besonders für Griechen"). Strangely enough, both authors cite in support of their opposing views the same features in the Gospel, for example: the Logos concept, the polemic motif and the "signs" which Jesus worked[21]. T. C. Smith, W. C. van Unnik and J. A. T. Robinson later

---

[18]See n. 12 above. Indeed only Barrett (*The Gospel According to St. John* [2nd ed.; London: SPCK, 1978] 134–135) seems to think that 20:30–31 is of no importance, that the Evangelist wrote in order to please himself and never intended his work to be published.

[19]The witnesses for the first reading given in NA[26] include p66vid ℵ* B Θ 0250 892ˢ, and for the second reading, ℵ[2] A C D L W Ψ 0100 f[1.13] 𝔐. According to Bruce Metzger, (*A Textual Commentary on the Greek New Testament* [3rd ed.; London: United Bible Societies, 1975] 256) both readings have the support of early witnesses. The problem cannot, therefore, be resolved on the basis of witnesses alone but on the general thrust of the Gospel.

[20]Karl Bornhäuser, *Das Johannesevangelium: Eine Missionsschrift für Israel* (Gütersloh: Bertelsmann, 1928); Wilhelm Oehler, *Das Johannesevangelium: Eine Missionsschrift für die Welt* (Gütersloh: Bertelsmann, 1936) and *Zum Missionscharakter des Johannesevangeliums* (BFCTh 42; Gütersloh: Bertelsmann, 1941).

[21]Bornhäuser, *Missionsschrift*, 158, 172; Oehler, *Missionsschrift*, 11. For Bornhäuser the logos concept stems from the OT Wisdom traditions concerning the Torah and from Philo (pp. 5–14), while for Oehler they derive from the Greek, Stoic notions of logos *prophorikos* and *endiathetos* (expressed and immanent logos) (pp. 23–25). For Bornhäuser, the polemic struggle indicates the importance to both Jesus and the Jews of the issues raised (pp. 34–64); for Oehler, though the polemic and the parenetic are not mutually exclusive, the polemic against the Jews arises from the need to explain to the Gentiles how Jesus came to the cross (pp. 30–31). Finally, for Bornhäuser Jesus' "signs" serve to prove to the Jews that he is the Messiah; for Oehler, they serve to attract the Greeks by demonstrating his extraordinary powers as the *theios anēr* (pp. 23–27). The joint witness of both authors thus seems to prove that John's Gospel could appeal to *both* Jews *and* Greeks.

supported Bornhäuser's position but with the modification that the Jews addressed were those of the Diaspora, not of Palestine[22]. Oehler, in turn, found support from Dodd[23].

Today, the view that John's Gospel is a missionary tract whether for Jews or Gentiles is universally rejected and considered as closed, the main argument being that the gospel form belongs within the believing community[24]. Yet it must not be overlooked that the theory has in recent years been revived in a new form by those scholars who discern a special interest in Samaria and Samaritanism in the Gospel. Thus in 1958, John Bowman advanced the view that the Gospel perhaps sets out the teaching of Jesus "in a way that would make it more attractive to Samaritans," and that its purpose is possibly to create a bridge between the Samaritans and the Jews in Christ[25]. His suggestion was taken up and developed more positively by Edwin Freed in two articles where he argues that the Gospel was written to appeal to probable Samaritan converts, and to win Jews as well. Freed, then, believes that the Gospel has a missionary interest[26].

Meeks also contends that the secondary aim of the Gospel is to win Samaritan converts, the first being to replace "Moses piety" with Christology. Accordingly, he sees the Gospel as emphasizing Galilee as the place of Jesus' acceptance. Judea figures as the place of his rejection, whereas Jn 4:31–38 possibly hints at the Christian Samaritan mission[27]. Buchanan,

---

[22]T.C. Smith, *Jesus in the Gospel of John* (Nashville: Broadman, 1959); W.C. van Unnik, "The Purpose of St. John's Gospel," *SE* 1 (= *TU* 73, 1959) 338–350; J.A.T. Robinson, "The Destination and Purpose of St. John's Gospel," *NTS* 6 (1959–1960) 117–131, and *Redating the New Testament* (London: SCM, 1976) 292–294. Robinson's view is heavily criticized by J.W. Bowker, "The Origin and Purpose of St. John's Gospel," *NTS* 11 (1965) 398–406. For a more comprehensive survey of this whole question see Wind, "Destination and Purpose," esp. pp. 27- 32, 39–48; and Kysar, *The Fourth Evangelist,* 147–165.

[23]C.H. Dodd, *The Interpretation of the Fourth Gospel* (Cambridge: University Press, 1960) 9.

[24]See, for instance, Riesenfeld, "ἵνα-Sätzen," 414–216. Schille ("Bemerkungen zur Formgeschichte des Evangeliums, III: Das Evangelium als Missionsbuch," *NTS* 5–6 [1958–1960] 1–11) holds, on the contrary, that precisely because the Gospel is the book for believers, it is *ipso facto* "das Buch des Missionars." Dotty (*Contemporary New Testament Interpretation* [Englewood Cliffs: Prentice Hall, 1972] 667–68) holds a similar view. Hahn (*Das Verständnis der Mission,* 120–125, and 135–145 on John's Gospel and Epistles) for his part, believes that after the departure of the apostles, the Church shifted its focus from missionary outreach to non-believers to consolidation of the believing community itself. One gets the impression, however, that for him this work of consolidation is not really mission work. Oehler (*Missionsschrift,* 31–35) warns that "Missionspredigt" and "Gemeindespredigt" are not mutually exclusive.

[25]John Bowman, "Samaritan Studies. I: The Fourth Gospel and the Samaritans," *BJRL* 40 (1958) 295–308.

[26]Edwin D. Freed, "Samaritan Influence in the Gospel of John," *CBQ* 30 (1968) 580–587, and "Did John Write His Gospel Partly to Win Samaritan Converts?" *NovT* 12 (1970) 241–256, esp. pp. 242, 256.

[27]Wayne A. Meeks, *The Prophet-King: Moses Traditions and the Johannine Christology* (NovTSup 14; Leiden: Brill, 1967) 313–319; "Galilee and Judea in the Fourth Gospel," *JBL* 85 (1966) 159–169, esp. p. 169; "'Am I a Jew?' Johannine Christianity and Judaism," *Studies in Judaism in Late Antiquity 12: Christianity, Judaism and Other Greco-Roman Cults, Part I. Studies for Morton Smith at Sixty* (ed. Jacob Neusner; Leiden: Brill, 1975) 163–186; esp. p. 178.

however, goes a step further by emphatically affirming that "the Gospel attributed to John came from the Samaritan Christian Church," a thesis which he states rather than proves. Purvis, on the other hand, believes that Samaritanism reveals "the heterogeneity of Palestinian intellectual history during the Roman period," out of which matrix the Johannine Christianity seems to have emerged[28]. Last, but not least, is the thesis which Cullman has sustained over the years that John's Gospel was written from the standpoint of the Samaritan Christian mission begun by the Stephen-Philip group[29]. Similarly, Scobie finds it "an attractive thesis that the origins of the Johannine traditions are to be found in the community or communities which stemmed from the Stephen-Philip group"[30].

Whatever the merit of these highly speculative theories, the view that John's Gospel was written from the standpoint of the Samaritan Christian mission is fast gaining ground. It has won the support also of Brown and Olsson[31]. Again it will be noted that while some see the Gospel as written to win Samaritan converts, others believe that it was written from the standpoint of the Samaritan Church, that is, from the standpoint of those who already believed. This strong record of survival over the years of the question whether or not John's Gospel was written for believers or to win converts would seem to indicate that the issue is not closed, but rather needs critically to be re-examined.

Ein Gemeinde-Evangelium

Wilkens, Fortna and Nicol believe that the primitive *Grund-Evangelium,* "Gospel of Signs" or *SQ* was essentially a missionary document, designed

---

[28]George W. Buchanan, "The Samaritan Origin of the Gospel of John," *Studies in the History of Religions: Religions in Antiquity. Essays in Memory of Edwin R. Goodenough* (ed. Jacob Neusner; Supplements to Numen 14, Leiden: Brill, 1968) 149—175, esp. p. 175; J.D. Purvis, "The Fourth Gospel and the Samaritans," *NovT* 17 (1975) 161—178.

[29]Oscar Cullmann, "La Samarie et les origines de la mission chrétienne. Qui sont les ΆΛΛΟΙ de Jean iv, 38?" *Annuaire de l'Ecole Pratiques des Hautes Etudes* (Paris, 1953—1954) 3—12; also "L'opposition contre le Temple de Jérusalem motif commun de la théologie johannique·et du monde ambiant," *NTS* 5—6 (1958—1960) 157—173, reprinted as "Samaria and the Origin of the Christian Mission. Who are the ΆΛΛΟΙ of Jn 4,38?" in his *The Early Church* (London: SCM, 1956) 183—192; *Der johanneischer Kreis: Sein Platz in Spätjudentum, in der Jüngerschaft Jesu und im Urchristentum. Zum Ursprung des Johannesevangeliums* (Tübingen: Mohr/Siebeck, 1975) esp. pp. 49—57, see also 12—19 on the intention of the Evangelist; and "Von Jesus zum Stephanuskreis und zum Johannesevangelium," *Jesus und Paulus: Fs. für Werner Georg Kümmel zum 70. Geburtstag,* eds. E.E. Ellis and Erich Grässer (Göttingen: Vandenhoeck und Ruprecht, 1975) 44—46.

[30]Charles S. Scobie "The Origins and Development of Samaritan Christianity," *NTS* 19 (1972—1973) 390—414; and "The Use of Source Material in the Speeches of Acts III and VII," *NTS* 25 (1978—1979) 339—421, esp. 421.

[31]Supporters of this view include John MacDonald, *The Theology of the Samaritans* (NT Library; London: SCM, 1964) 32—33; Brown, *The Community of the Beloved Disciple,* esp. pp. 36—40 and 166—167; Olsson, *Structure and Meaning,* 254—256; A.M. Johnson, "Philip the Evangelist and the Gospel of John," *Abr-Nahrain* 16 (1975) 53—54; and Philippe de Robert, "Les Samaritains et le Nouveau Testament," *ETR* 45 (1970) 179—184.

to win Hellenists (Wilkens), Jews (Nicol), or both Jews and Gentiles (Fortna); but they affirm that in its present form the Gospel was intended to serve the needs of the community which produced it[32]. Indeed, it was the failure of the initial missionary effort which turned the present Gospel into both a polemic weapon directed against outsiders and an instrument of service for the community itself. This view is shared by a vast majority of scholars and can indeed be tagged "the accepted view" concerning the primary purpose of John's Gospel.

The range of suggestions concerning the needs of the community which the Gospel was destined to meet varies widely and can be classified in three broad categories: apologetic, polemic and parenetic. Of these three, the polemic and the parenetic are the most widely discussed. The apologetic is adduced merely to show how the members of the Johannine community defended their faith before unbelievers and/or other Christian groups who questioned their high Christology and their practices generally[33].

Since Irenaeus of Lyons first stated that the Gospel was written as a polemic against Cerinthus, a whole range of targets has been suggested as the goal against which the polemic in the Gospel is directed[34]. The most prominent of these is the anti-Baptist (first advanced by Michaelis), anti-Jewish (made popular by Grässer) and anti-world (emphasized by those who see the Gospel as a closed sectarian document)[35]. Other impor-

---

[32]Wilkens, *Entstehungsgeschichte,* 171; Fortna, *Gospel of Signs,* 225 (and also pp. 228–234 where he speaks of the Source's "wholly missionary emphasis on the christological question" [p. 233]); Nicol, *Semeia,* 77–79. Though Nicol denies that the Gospel is a missionary tract, he nevertheless believes that the present Gospel "does have some Jews in mind who are still members of the synagogue" (p. 146). This tallies with the view of Schnackenburg who believes that the present Gospel does have a missionary perspective; see n. 47 below.

[33]Hahn, *Das Verständnis der Mission,* 123, n. 2; Heinrich Weinel, *Grundriss der theologischen Wissenschaften. Biblische Theologie des Neuen Testaments* (Tübingen: Mohr-Siebeck, 1928) 411; Fortna, *Gospel of Signs,* 224, 229–231; Nicol, *Semeia,* 145; Meeks, "The Divine Agent and his Counterfeit in Philo and the Fourth Gospel," *Aspects of Religious Propaganda in Judaism and Early Christianity* (ed. E. Fiorenza; Notre Dame: University of Notre Dame, 1976) 43–67, esp. p. 44 (Meeks also believes that the apologetic sections in John serve a sectarian purpose [p. 54]); N.L. Geisler, "Johannine Apologetics," *BibSac* 554 (1979) 333–343.

[34]Irenaeus of Lyons, *Adv. Haer.* III, 11.7; Fritz Neugebauer, *Die Entstehung des Johannesevangeliums* (Arbeiten zur Theologie, 1/36; Stuttgart: Calwer Verlag, 1968) 28–39.

[35]J.D. Michaelis, *Einleitung in das Neue Testament* II ([4]1788) 1140 – cited in Kümmel, *Einleitung,* 185, n. 105. It is understood, of course, that the polemic is directed, not against John the Baptist himself, but against his followers who claim that he, not Jesus, is the Messiah. Erich Grässer, "Die antijüdische Polemik im Johannesevangelium," *NTS* 10 (1964–1965) 74–90; Meeks, "'Am I a Jew?'" *passim*; Neugebauer, *Entstehung,* 14; Georg Richter, "Die Gefangennahme Jesu nach Johannesevangelium," *BibLeb* 10 (1969) 26–39; Schnackenburg, *Johannesevangelium* I, 146–148; Brown, *John* I, lxx–lxxv. The most comprehensive study of the anti-Jewish question in John is offered by Reinhold Leistner, *Antijudaismus im Johannesevangelium? Darstellung des Problems in der neueren Auslegungsgeschichte und Untersuchung der Leidensgeschichte* (Bern & Frankfurt/Main: Herbert Lang, 1974). His survey covers the period from Bauer through the German ideologists to the time of the book's publication. On polemic in general in the Gospel see also Kysar, *The Fourth Evangelist,* 149–165; Wind, "Purpose," 31–32.

tant targets mentioned include an anti-docetic polemic (Wilkens), anti-Gnostic polemic (Bultmann, Schulz, Borgen), anti-Moses piety polemic (Meeks), anti-Great Church polemic (Käsemann, Brown), and even a polemic against some of the members of the Johannine community itself[36]. Thus the polemic in the Gospel has been judged to be directed against everybody.

Of the various reasons suggested for the parenetic motif, the need to strengthen the faith of the believing community, one emerges as the most widely accepted. This is the thesis developed at length by Martyn that the present Gospel was written to console and strengthen the faith of the Johannine community after the trauma of its ejection from the synagogue following the promulgation of the *Birkat ha-Minim* (a curse on the heretics) introduced by R. Gamaliel II at the Council of Jamnia (ca. A.D. 90)[37]. Strong supporters of the view include Brown, Kysar, Painter, Beutler, Schnackenburg, Lindars and Boismard-Lamouille[38]. But substantial criticism has been leveled against it by Robinson, Hare and, in particular, by Kümmel, who believes that Martyn's thesis is not proved, and Cohen, who questions the whole interpretation of the Jamnia de-

---

[36]Wilhelm Wilkens, *Zeichen und Werke: Ein Beitrag zur Theologie des 4. Evangeliums in Erzählungs- und Redestoff* (AThANT 55; Zurich: Zwingli, 1969) 167–168; Bultmann, *Commentary*, 9 (where he speaks of "a pointed anti-Gnostic theology" of the Gospel), and "Die neuerschlössenen Quellen," *passim;* Siegried Schulz, *Das Evangelium nach Johannes* (Göttingen: Vandenhoeck und Ruprecht, 1972) and *Komposition und Herkunft der johanneischen Reden* (BWANT 81; Stuttgart: Kohlhammer, 1960) 28–187; Borgen, *Bread from Heaven*, 148; Meeks, *Prophet-King*, 318–319, 297–301; Käsemann, *Jesu Letzer Wille nach Johannes 17* (3rd ed.; Tübingen: Mohr-Siebeck, 1971). For Käsemann the anti-Church polemic of the Gospel reveals itself in its "anti-sacramental" character (pp. 65–117); for Brown (*Community of the Beloved Disciple,* esp. pp. 81–88) it lies in the reaction to the "low christology" of "the Great Church." D.B. Woll ("The Departure of 'The Way': The First Farewell Discourse in the Gospel of John," *JBL* 99 [1980] 225–239 and *Johannine Christianity in Conflict: Authority, Rank and Succession in the First Farewell Discourse* [SBLDS 60; Chico: Scholars, 1981] 128, 176, n. 79) believes that the emphasis on the centrality of Jesus is directed as a polemic against Christian prophets who claimed to be Christ as in Mk 13: 5–6. See also Kysar's survey on the anti-Gnostic polemic, *The Fourth Evangelist,* 104–146.

[37]Martyn, *History and Theology*, esp. p. 18–41; "Glimpses into the History of the Johannine Community. From Its Origin through the Period of Its Life in which the Fourth Gospel Was Written," *BETL* 44, 147–175. Martyn's thesis relies heavily on the three occurrences in the Gospel of the term ἀποσυνάγωγος (9:22; 12:42; 16:2) and on the external evidence of the introduction of the *Birkat ha-Minim* into the *Shemoneh Esreh*. On the history of these two concepts and the problems they pose see Nicol, *Semeia*, 144–145.

[38]Brown, *Community*, 40–42 (Brown, however, believes that the situation was perhaps "more complex" than Martyn presents it); Kysar, "Community and Gospel: Vectors in the Fourth Gospel Criticism," *Interpretation* 31 (1977) 355–366; and *The Fourth Evangelist*, 149, 151; John Painter, "Glimpses of the Johannine Community in the Farewell Discourses," *AusBR* 28 (1980) 21–38; and "The Farewell Discourses and the History of the Johannine Christianity," *NTS* 27 (1981) 525–543; Beutler, *Martyria*, 345; Schnackenburg, "Zur Herkunft des Johannesevangeliums," *BZ* 14 (1970) 1–23; Lindars, *John*, 37 (but note that for Lindars, the Gospel was begun and finished before the introduction of the *Birkat ha-Minim*); Boismard-Lamouille, *Synopse III*, 59, 207–209, and *passim*. See further D.M. Smith, "The Presentation of Jesus in the Fourth Gospel," *Interpretation* 31 (1977) 367–378.

cree[39]. A variation of the same theme is that of Meeks who thinks that the Gospel was written long after the trauma of separation from the synagogue, and that this situation brought about not only a crisis of faith but also that of social identity which the Gospel seeks to meet[40].

The question raised, then, is whether these efforts to meet the various needs of the community can be considered as missionary work. In other words, do the apologetic, polemic and parenetic motifs serve a missionary purpose? Or does outreach to pagans constitute the exclusive meaning of missionary work? Wind and Hotlzmann believe, on the analogy of Justin's *Dialogue with Trypho,* that the apologetic motif does serve a missionary purpose[41]. Like Wind and Hotlzmann, Riesenfeld acknowledges that Justin's *Dialogue* serves a missionary purpose among Jews, but argues consequently that if the Evangelist had wanted to write a missionary tract, he would have written a work similar to that of Justin, and not a gospel. In his view we have no evidence in ancient literature that a gospel ever served a missionary purpose[42]. One wonders, however, whether Riesenfeld is not hereby begging the question. For might not John's Gospel be the one exception in ancient literature where *Missionsschrift* and *Evangelium* are wedded?

A few scholars also admit that the polemic motif serves a missionary purpose, in the sense of being a warning to others[43]; but the majority of scholars oppose this view. Indeed, the polemic element is cited as the single most important reason why the Gospel cannot be seen as a mis-

---

[39]Robinson (*Redating,* 272–275) describes Martyn's thesis as "highly imaginative"; Douglas R.A. Hare (*The Theme of Jewish Persecution of Christians in the Gospel According to Matthew* [SNTSM 6; Cambridge University, 1967] 48–56) questions the historical and exegetical foundations of the whole theory; Kümmel, *Einleitung,* 197; Shaye J.D. Cohen ("Yavneh Revisited" [SBLASP 21, 1982] 45–61) considers the whole theory to be historically unfounded on the basis of available Rabbinic sources relating to the Jamina era. Our own evaluation of this issue will emerge in the course of the study (see below, pp. 206–207, and 260–261).

[40]Meeks, "The Man from Heaven in Johannine Sectarianism," *JBL* 91 (1972) 44–77, esp. pp. 68–72; and "Divine Agent," 59.

[41]Wind, "Destination and Purpose," 43 (where he quotes van Unnik, "Purpose," 398–403) and 65 (where he agrees with the latter that the expression "Jesus is the Christ," has its roots in the Christian mission among the Jews as exemplified in Justin's *Dialogue* or in the works of Hegesippus and the Christian apologists of the second century; cf. Eusebius, *H.E.* 2.23.8–10); Oscar Holtzmann, *Das Neue Testament nach dem Stuttgarter griechischen Text übersetzt and erklärt II: V Das Evangelium des Johannes* (Giessen: Alfred Töpelmann, 1926) 961. Here Holtzmann argues that John depended on Justin's *Apology* and compares Apology 1.61.4–5 with Jn 3:4 and Apology 1.32.8–18 with Jn 1:12–14.

[42]Riesenfeld, "ἵνα -Sätzen," 215.

[43]Oehler (*Missionsschrift,* 29) holds that "Werbeschrift und Streitschrift schliessen sich nicht aus, gehören vielfach zusammen"; hence his belief that the primary purpose of the Gospel is not polemic against the Jews but the awakening of faith (p. 30); Kümmel (*Einleitung,* 197): "Ist also das Joh geschrieben, um den Glauben der Christen zu fördern und durch polemische Abwehr zu festigen." For Grässer ("Die antijüdische Polemik") the polemic functions positively only indirectly, for though it is directed against the Jews, it serves to strengthen the community of believers which must see itself as the new Israel.

sionary document. Meinertz is quite emphatic on the subject. In his view, the polemic against the Jews so pervades the Gospel that in no way can it (the Gospel) be considered "als eine Missionsschrift für Israel." Yet it is to be noted that throughout this work, Meinertz stresses the missionary thrust of the Gospel. For instance, John's portrait of Jesus stems from what he himself experienced of the divine redeemer and of his astonishing effect on the growing Christianity "in aktivster Missions -und Seelsorgetätigkeit"[44].

The same negative response applies in the case of the parenetic motif. Conzelmann rejects outright the view that the Gospel could possibly serve as a missionary document whether it be for Israel or for the world: "ist festzustellen, dass das Buch keinen missionarischen Charakter hat," since in Johannine thought, Israel and the world are "keine Alternative." It follows then that "Dem johanneischen Kirchengedanken entspricht nicht der Gedanke der Mission, sondern das 'Zeugnis', die Stärkung des Glaubens"[45]. It is most strange that Conzelmann should so emphatically deny the missionary value of witness in John's Gospel. The reason, as already seen, lies in the fact that "mission" is viewed primarily as outreach to non-believers. Allegedly, it was the failure of this missionary effort which led the community to turn in upon itself in an attitude of antagonism towards the world and the synagogue[46].

Despite these negative responses, some scholars maintain for different reasons that the Gospel in its present final form does have a missionary perspective. Such, for instance, is Schnackenburg's position. Similarly, Boismard-Lamouille's reconstruction of the literary stages of the Gospel shows not only that Document C had a missionary focus, but also that the Evangelist, John II (A and B) developed further the missionary emphasis in the Gospel. Furthermore, the most significant statements on mission in the Gospel (Jn 3:16—17; 4:38) are to be attributed to John III, the final redactor of the Gospel[47]. The net-result of their literary criticism, then, is. that a missionary focus permeates every redactional phase of the Gospel. Finally, though Hahn strongly maintains that the Gospel is "keine Missionsschrift," because among other things it contains very few "Missionsaussagen," he nonetheless believes that the "Sendungsaussagen" in the Gospel can only be understood from the perspective of mission. Indeed, the missionary element is the "Gesamtkonzeption" of both the Gospel and the Church[48]. Hahn's chief difficulty in this entire work lies in that mission for him, as for many others, means primarily the activity of the

---

[44]Meinertz, *Theologie des Neuen Testaments II* (Bonn: Peter Hanstein, 1950) 268, 313.

[45]Hans Conzelmann, *Grundriss der Theologie des Neuen Testaments* (München: Chr. Kaiser, 1967) 362.

[46]Nicol (*Semeia*, 143) believes that the author of the Gospel "lived in a town where the Synagogue was too hostile for missionary work."

[47]Schnackenburg, "Messiasfrage," 246; Boismard-Lamouille, *Synopse III*, 48—50.

[48]Hahn, *Das Verständnis der Mission*, 135—140.

disciples: "erst dort, wo die Jünger sich ihres Gegensatzes zur Welt bewusst sind und daraus die nötigen Konsequenzen gezogen haben"[49].

To sum up, the whole discussion on the missionary character of the Gospel thus reveals that only with great difficulty can one dismiss the question of the missionary thrust of the Gospel. It is evidence such as this which leads Wind to conclude that the problem, missionary or church, is a false one that should be dropped, even though he himself favors the view that the Gospel was written to win converts[50]. Dropping the distinction, however, is only a partial solution to the problem. It is to recognize that the Gospel has a missionary purpose, but it does not define the specific nature of this missionary purpose nor does it account for the peculiar features of the Johannine data on mission surveyed earlier. The real issue, then, would be to determine what the Evangelist himself understands by mission, irrespective of whether his missionary field be Palestine, Samaria, or the Hellenistic world at large or whether his audience be prospective believers, crypto-Christians or public believers facing a crisis of faith and of social identity.

Secondly, since the whole debate seems to hang on the tense of the verb πιστεύειν (20:31), though Kümmel rightly maintains that the solution is not to be sought in the tense but in the whole thrust of the Gospel[51], the critic needs to determine what believing in Jesus means in the Gospel. Is this an act performed once and for all, or is it something which the disciple stands in need of all through life? Finally, concerning the polemic motif itself and the theory of withdrawal in face of persecution, the question needs to be asked whether from the evidence of the literature we have (e.g., Mt 10; Acts 7–8), the appropriate Christian response in face of persecution was one of turning in upon self or whether, on the contrary, this persecution gave rise to a missionary impetus. Also from the Johannine perspective, might not the polemic element itself be explained in terms of the rhetorical, persuasive, even missionary thrust of the Gospel suggested by Jn 20:30–31? How, in fact, does this polemic element function in the Gospel and in relation to the Evangelist's own method?

2. The Quest for Models

The quest for the possible models which could have inspired the Johannine portrait of Jesus as God's envoy is by far the most systematically conducted area of research on mission in the Gospel. Bultmann's pioneer-

---

[49]Hahn, *Das Verständnis der Mission*, 142.

[50]Wind, "Destination and Purpose," 65.

[51]Kümmel, *Einleitung*, 194; similarly, Barrett (*John*, 134, 575) holds that even a solution of the textual problem would not resolve this issue, "since John may have used his tenses inaccurately."

ing article on the subject (1925) was soon followed by Odeberg's *The Fourth Gospel*[52]. But since then the topic has been explored in a number of doctoral dissertations mostly from the German school: Kuhl and Meeks (1967), Miranda and Beutler (1972), Appold (1976) and Bühner (1977), in the important articles by Schweizer and Borgen, and among the commentaries by Schnackenburg, Dodd and Schulz[53].

The basic impetus motivating this quest is contemporary interest in the history of religions (*Religionsgeschichte*). The underlying, even if not always the explicitly-stated, concern is to discover the religio-cultural background of the Evangelist. Quite often a new model is proposed from the standpoint of *Auseinandersetzung* with those previously set forth. Some of these studies approach the subject by examining relatively contemporary ideas in both the Jewish and Hellenistic contexts concerning the general notion of the one sent; others focus on a particular aspect relating to the envoy: the sending formula (Miranda, Schweizer, Kuhl), witness (Beutler), the oneness of the envoy with the sender (Appold), and "the way of the one sent" (Bühner).

The method of research, especially in the monographs, follows a common pattern which consists basically of the following: (1) an examination of the data outside the Gospel, (2) a study of the corresponding data within the Gospel, (3) highlighting the similarities or differences between the two, and (4) citing in conclusion the model which the author believes to have exercised the greatest influence on the Evangelist. The different models proposed can again be grouped into three major categories: Gnostic, OT-prophetic and Hellenistic-Jewish.

---

[52]Bultmann, "Die neuerschlossenen Quellen," 104; and *Commentary*, 64-66; Hugo Odeberg, *The Fourth Gospel Interpreted in Its Relation to Contemporaneous Religious Currents in Palestine and the Hellenistic Oriental World* (Uppsala: Almqvist & Wiksells, 1929). Originally planned to appear in three parts, only the first part (on Jn 1:19–12:50) was ever completed.

[53]Kuhl (*Die Sendung*, 3–52) focuses on the theology of mission in the Gospel (cf. p. 1); Meeks (*Prophet-King*) states the goal of the research on p. 1; Miranda (*Der Vater der mich gesandt hat*) devotes the entire work to this issue. See also his *Die Sendung Jesu im vierten Evangelium: Religions- und theologiegeschichtliche Untersuchungen zu den Sendungsformeln* (SBS 87; Stuttgart: Katholisches Bibelwerk, 1977) which offers a revised synopsis of his dissertation based on reviews of the latter; Beutler, *Martyria*, esp. "Teil I. Der Hintergrund," pp. 43–205, and pp. 339–351; Appold, *The Oneness Motif in the Fourth Gospel* (WUNT 2/1; Tübingen: Mohr-Siebeck, 1976). Though Appold relates his study to the various theories proposed on the background of the Gospel, his basic aim is to examine the "uniqueness" of the Johannine "oneness passages" (p. 8); Bühner (*Der Gesandte und sein Weg*) gives extensive surveys of both the secondary (pp. 8–86) and primary sources (pp. 87–341); Eduard Schweizer, "Zum religionsgeschichtlichen Hintergrund der 'Sendungsformeln', Gal 4,4f. Rm 8, 3f. Joh 3,16f. I Joh 4,9," *ZNW* 57 (1966) 119–210; also in *Beiträge zur Theologie des Neuen Testaments* (*NT Aufsätze* 55–70; Zurich: Zwingli, 1970) 83–95; Borgen, "God's Agent in the Fourth Gospel," *Religions in Antiquity*, 137–148; Schnackenburg, *Johannesevangelium* I, 101–134; Dodd, *Interpretation*, 10–130; Schulz, *Komposition und Herkunft*, especially the second and third parts of the study (pp. 28–187) and *Johannes*, 10–12.

The Gnostic Revealer model

First proposed by Wrede, this model was made popular by Bultmann. His contention is that the Gnostic redeemer myth (*Erlösermythos*) as found in the Hermetic corpus constitutes the background against which the Johannine *Jesusgestalt,* his *Bild des Gesandten* is to be understood. Not only his long article, mentioned earlier, but Bultmann's entire commentary is written from this basic standpoint. His view, shared by Käsemann and Dodd, is that John evangelized the gnostic ideas he found in his sources (*Offenbarungsreden*). Schulz and Schottroff go further in attributing the gnosticizing tendency to the Evangelist himself[54].

The main reasons for proposing the Gnostic model include the idea of the pre-existence of the messenger, the descending/ascending motif or his "whence and wither" and the use of the dialogue as a mode of revelation. Bultmann, for instance, found twenty eight parallels between the Johannine portrait of Jesus as the one sent and that found in the proposed sources, though even he admitted that there are also important differences, for instance, the idea of the "saved-savior" missing in John. Today the Gnostic model is almost completely discarded, though a few still believe in some form of Gnostic influence on the Gospel. The greatest criticism leveled against Bultmann's approach is that of circular argument. Meeks points out, for instance, that all the twenty eight parallels proposed by Bultmann are found only in John's Gospel[55].

---

[54]W. Wrede, *Charakter und Tendenz des Johannes-Evangeliums* (SVG 39, 1903) 29f; Bultmann, "Quellen," 100 (where he specifically denies that the Gospel has any links with the Synoptic Palestinian Christianity, the Hellenistic Pauline Christianity or the Hellenistic-Jewish Christianity of I Clement, Hermas, Hebrews or Barnabas); similarly, *Commentary*, 250–251 (where he rejects the OT-prophetic influence on the Gospel); Käsemann, "Ketzer und Zeuge," *ZKT* 48 (1951) 292–3, also in *Exegetische Versuche und Bessinungen* I (Göttingen: Vandenhoeck und Ruprecht, 1960) 169–187, esp. pp. 169, 186; Dodd, *Interpretation,* 109, 114, and his analysis of the "Leading Ideas," p. 133–285; Schulz, *Johannes,* 10, 63–64, 211, and *Untersuchungen zur Menschensohn-Christologie im Johannesevangelium* (Göttingen: Vandenhoeck und Ruprecht, 1957); Luise Schottroff, *Der Glaubende und die Feindliche Welt: Beobachtungen zum gnostischen Dualismus und seine Bedeutung für Paulus und das Johannesevangelium* (WMANT 37; Neukirchen-Vluyn: Neukirchener-V, 1970) esp. pp. 229–245, 295–296.

[55]For Bultmann's twenty eight parallels see "Quellen, 104–139; Kuhl (*Die Sendung.* 50–52) reduces these twenty eight parallels to twelve. Borgen's counter study of the Jewish halakhic traditions yields six parallels (a–f): the identity of the agent with his sender in judicial matters, his obedience to his sender in the execution of his mission, the forensic setting of the agent's mission, the agent's reference to his completed work and to his return to his sender, and his appointing others to continue his work upon his return to his sender ("God's Agent," 138–143). While for Borgen the basic principle is the equality between the agent and his sender, for Bultmann, the "myth" is the primary. Schweizer (*Beiträge* I, 85) contends that the Hellenistic parallels know of no real pre-existence and that in these works, the descent-ascent motif serves only a soteriological function.

Those who reject Bultmann's idea of model yet believe that the Gospel had some form of contact with Gnosticism include Schnackenburg, "Der Menschensohn im Johannesevangelium," *NTS* 11 (1964–1965) 135–137 and *Johannesevangelium II* (where he holds that the Son's way of speaking reflects the Christian response to some form of Gnostic redeemer thought); Miranda (*Der*

The OT-prophetic model

According to the reconstructional theory of Boismard-Lamouille, the distinctive characteristic of Document C (and John II-A) lay in the presentation of Jesus implicitly as "a prophet like Moses" especially with regard to his works (7:3; Num 16:28), his "signs" which prove that he is sent by God (2:1—11; 4:46—53; 21:1—6; Exod 4:1—9) and the judgment pronounced by God on those who reject his works (12:48; Deut 18:19). John II-A resumes and completes this idea of Jesus as God's envoy. He is not only "a prophet like Moses," but *the* prophet announced in Deut 18: 18. His "signs" authenticate his mission from God and their purpose is to incite men to believe in his mission. Thus for John II-A as for Document C, Jesus' "signs" have "une valeur apologétique,' they are presented as the reason for believing in Jesus. John II-B goes a step further and takes into account the entirety of Moses' mission, his work as revealer which the Evangelist views as an echo of Jesus' work and mission. Jesus is the new Moses, he far surpasses the OT Moses (1:17) because he abides in the bosom of the Father (1:18) and has been sanctified and sent into the world (10:35—36). But contrary to Document C and John II-A, John II-B emphasizes Jesus' words, not his "signs" as that which should elicit faith. Finally, in his efforts to mitigate the anti-Jewish and anti-world attitude of John II (the Evangelist), John III, the final editor, introduces such overtly missionary passages as Jn 3:15, 16a—17, 18b, 4:22—24, 37—38, and 17:20—21)[56]. Though the redactional theory of these authors is highly disputed, and rightly so, the value of their analysis lies in their showing that a missionary focus underlies every phase of the Gospel's redaction.

The OT models studied, however, include not only the prophets but also all those who were given a mission from God: kings, the ʿebed Yahweh and Israel itself[57]. Meeks holds that the inter-relationship of the two terms in John, "prophet" and "king," is best understood against the background of Moses-typology seen as God's commissioned agent (šalîaḥ) and set within the context of the Sinai theophany. The Christology of the Gospel is thus conceived polemically against these Moses traditions as held by a hostile Jewish group. The specific issues addressed include the mystical ascent and descent of Moses, his role as revealer, witness, giver of the Torah and of bread from heaven and as the good shepherd.

Vater der mich gesandt hat, 306) sees a possible gnosticizing interest in the motif of Jesus' "descent/ascent" (3:13) and of his whence and whither (7:17; 8:14; 9:29). McPolin ("Studies in the Fourth Gospel — Some Contemporary Trends," *IrBibSt* 2 [1980] 3—26) calls for a reassessment of "gnosis" as a possible element in the background, vocabulary and language of the Gospel.

[56]Boismard-Lamouille, *Synopse III,* 48—50 (for John II-A) and 44, 121, 129, 393 (for John III).

[57]Meeks, "The Man from Heaven," 54; see also Barrett, *John,* 40—42; Cullmann, *Johanneische Kreis,* 31—40; George MacRae, "The Ego-Proclamation in Gnostic Sources," *The Trial of Jesus* (ed. Ernst Bammel; London: SCM, 1970) 123—139; and Erich Fascher, "Christologie und Gnosis im vierten Evangelium," *TLZ* 93 (1968) 721—730, esp. p. 725.

Even the forensic character of Jesus' revelation, the judicial aspect of his mission, is to be understood against the background of "Moses piety" which the Evangelist seeks to replace with his Christology[58].

By comparing the sending formula in John with that of the literature of the period, Miranda comes to the conclusion that the OT-prophetic model, not the Gnostic one proposed by Bultmann, is that used by the Evangelist. The same position is held by Bruce Vawter, F. M. Braun, Fascher, and others. Similarly, Kuhl holds that the prophetic type of sending (Moses, the prophets, the Servant of Yahweh in Deutero-Isaiah) offers the closest parallel to the Johannine and NT idea of the one sent by God; but he also notes that in spite of these similarities important differences exist[59].

The Hellenistic-Jewish model

This heading is a blanket term for all the models proposed which cannot be classified under the OT-prophetic or the specifically Gnostic models, whether as found in the Hermetic corpus or in the Christian Gnostic literature (the *Gospel of Truth, Epsitles of Jacob, Apocryphon of John,* and the *Odes of Solomon*). Included in this category are the notions of sending found in the Wisdom literature concerning the descent of the *sophia-logos* to reveal divine truths to obedient men (Sir 24; Wis 7:7−9:18); in Jewish apocalyptic, particularly in the notion of the Son of Man (Dan 7; Ethiopic Enoch 42:37−71; 4 Ezra 13; cf. Baruch 3:37); in the Qumran Testimonia and Hodayoth concerning the *maskil* seen as the spokesman and revealer of God (1QH); in rabbinic literature (the Targums and the Halakhah) and in Hellenistic-Jewish Merkabah mysticism concerning the halakhic agent; and finally in the reinterpretations of the OT sending concept as found in Philo and Josephus[60].

---

[58]Meeks, *Prophet-King*, 287−319, esp. his conclusion, pp. 318−319.

[59]Miranda, *Der Vater der mich gesandt hat,* 372−386 (where he focuses particularly on the call and sending of the prophets); and *Die Sendung Jesu,* 46−70; Bruce Vawter, "Ezekiel and John," *CBQ* 26 (1964) 450−458; F.M. Braun, *Jean le théologien II. Les grandes traditions d'Israël et l'accord des écritures selon le quatrième évangile* (Paris: Gabalda, 1964) 49−152; Fascher ("Christologie," p. 729) makes the important observation that Jesus is fundamentally different from the prophets since he demands not only belief in his words but also in him; Brown (*John I,* LIX− LX) focuses on the missions of Moses and of the Servant in Deutero-Isaiah); Kuhl, *Die Sendung Jesu,* 14−16.

[60]See Günther Reim, *Studien zum alttestamentlichen Hintergrund des Johannesevangeliums* (Cambridge: University, 1974) 93−96, 188−189, 231−232, 282; Schweizer ("Sendungsformeln," 93) opts for a strong influence on John of the Hellenistic-Jewish Wisdom motifs in their mystical form; Herbert Braun (*Qumran und das Neue Testament* [2 vols.; Tübingen: Mohr-Siebeck, 1966]; I. 96−138) gives a synthesis of comparative studies between John's Gospel and the Qumran literature; see also II. 54−74, 75−84 and the bibliography, I. 1−6, II. v−x; James L. Price, "Light from Qumran upon Some Aspects of Johannine Theology," *John and Qumran* (ed. J.H. Charlesworth; London: Geoffrey Chapman, 1972) 9−37, esp. 25−37 (where he compares "the teacher" as priest and prophet to Jesus); Martin McNamara, "The Targums and Johannine Literature," *Targum and*

This is not the place to embark on even a cursory discussion of these models and the reasons given for proposing them. In addition to the individual works mentioned in the last footnote, critical surveys of these theories are offered by Kysar, Schnackenburg, Kümmel, Barrett, Brown, in the states of the question presented in the dissertations of Meeks, Kuhl, Beutler, Miranda, Appold and Bühner and in the more generalized background Studies by Percy, Dodd and Schlatter[61]. The research, however, reveals a growing consensus on two points concerning these different theories: (1) that the background for the Johannine portrait of Jesus as the one sent is essentially heterodox and syncretistic (Beutler, Schweizer and Kysar)[62], and (2) that the Evangelist encountered this syncretistic framework in a specifically Hellenistic-Jewish, rather than in a nebulous Hellenistic/Gnostic context. This view is strongly advocated by Borgen who holds that Philo and the early stages of the Merkabah mysticism offer concrete examples of the unification of the Jewish and Hellenistic tendencies of the period[63]. It is also shared by Bühner, the most recent major author on this subject. His research led him to the conclusion that the Jewish rabbinic and esoteric speculation on the connection between the OT-prophetic (the *šaliah* of God) and the angel messenger (the *mal'āk* seen as the *šaliah*) constitutes the basic history of religion's background underlying the Johannine conception of "the way of the one sent"[64].

Testament: Aramaic Paraphrases of the Hebrew Bible, A Light on the New Testament (Shannon: Irish University, 1968) 142—159; *The New Testament and the Palestinian Targum to the Penta-teuch* (AnBib 27; Rome: Pontifical Biblical Institute, 1966) 145—149; and "The Ascension and the Exaltation of Christ in the Fourth Gospel," *Scripture* 19 (1967) 65—72.

[61] Kysar, *The Fourth Evangelist,* 102—146; Schnackenburg *Johannesevangelium I,* 107—117, 131—135; Kümmel, *Das Neue Testament im 20. Jahrhundert: Ein Forschungsbericht* (SBS; 50; Stuttgart: KBW, 1970) 45—51; Barrett, *John* 27—41; Brown, *John* I, lii—lxiv; Kuhl, *Die Sendung Jesu,* 3—52; Beutler, *Martyria,* 106—168; Miranda, *Der Vater der mich gesandt hat, passim*; Appold, *Oneness Motif,* 2—8 (see also his excursus on the "Religio-historical Profile," 163—193); Bühner, *Der Gesandte und sein Weg,* 8-86; Ernst Percy, *Untersuchungen über den Ursprung der johanneischen Theologie. Zugleich ein Beitrag zur Frage nach der Entstehung des Gnostizismus* (Lund: Gleerup, 1939), *passim*; Dodd, *Interpretation,* 54—96; Adolf Schlatter, "Die Sprache und Heimat des vierten Evangelisten," *Johannes und sein Evangelium* (ed. Karl H. Rengstorf; Wege der Forschung 82; Darmstadt: WB, 1973) 28—201.

[62] Beutler, *Martyria,* 305—306, 338; Schweizer, "Sendungsformeln," 92—93; Kysar, *The Fourth Evangelist,* 119. MacRae ("Ego-Proclamation," 139) also holds that the Evangelist deliberately made use of his syncretistic background for his interpretation of the meaning of Jesus.

[63] See note 66 below on our evaluation of Borgen's approach.

[64] Borgen's thesis is developed fully in his "God's Agent"; but this thesis persists in most of his studies about John's Gospel, namely, *Bread from Heaven;* "Observations on the Midrashic Character of John 6," *ZNW* 54 (1963) 232—240; "Some Jewish Exegetical Traditions as Background for the Son of Man Sayings in John's Gospel (Jn 3, 13—14 and context)," *BETL* 44, 243—258; and "The Use of Tradition in John 12, 44—50," *NTS* 26 (1970) 18—35; Bühner, *Der Gesandte und sein Weg,* especially part three of the dissertation where he studies the prophet and מלאך (270—271, 341—373), the prophet as שליח (271—315), the מלאך as שליח (316—341), the Johannine Christ as a prophetic מלאך (374—399), the origin and nature of the Johannine sending Christology (402—414) and his final conclusion (422—344). Borgen's and Bühner's studies

The *general appraisal* of these theories which seek to discover the
underlying background/model for the Johannine portrait of Jesus as the
envoy of God is twofold: On the positive side, by collecting and inves-
tigating an impressive amount of data, they project a rich and stimulating
picture of the different conceptions of mission that were held in the last
centuries B.C. and first centuries A.D. On the negative side, the major
criticism of the *religionsgeschichtliche* approach are as follows: Firstly,
because it abstracts ideas and terminology from the texts examined, it
pays inadequate attention to the contexts of these texts, Johannine or
otherwise. Miranda's study, for instance, offers little exegesis of the
Johannine passages cited. In consequence, these studies contribute little
to our understanding of the Evangelist's own distinctive approach[65].
Kuhl's fundamentally theological approach is a possible exception to this
rule. Not surprisingly, he speaks of parallels between John and the literature cited rather than of models supposedly used by the Evangelist.

Secondly, the whole approach is highly speculative and subject to
circular thinking. As de Jonge points out in his review of Bühner's work,
little attention is bestowed on determining either the exact chronology
or the provenance of some of these traditions which are said to have influenced the Evangelist. Borgen, for instance, holds against Odeberg and
Bultmann that the Gnostic presentation itself was influenced by the
Merkabah mysticism, the basic principle of which is that the agent is in
every way like the one who sent him[66]. Thirdly, from the perspective of
this present research, it needs to be noted that an important aspect of
mission in the Gospel concerns the living interaction between Jesus,
God's envoy, and his variety of audiences; yet this aspect so vivid in the
Gospel receives little attention in these comparative studies. More intriguing, too, than the question of the specific model used by the Evangelist is the more fundamental question why, in the first place, he chose to
present Jesus' life and work from the primary standpoint of mission.

---

thus furnish further support for the growing view of modern scholars that "the evangelist and his
traditions had firm roots in some form of Jewish milieu" (Kysar, *The Fourth Evangelist,* 107; see
also, pp. 111, 122, 127, 132, 136, 137; 144—146).

[65]For instance, in his conclusion to his survey of contemporary Johannine literature on this
particular area, Thyen ("Aus der Literatur zum Johannesevangelium," *TRu* 39 [1975] 59—69)
notes that individual motifs and ideas which are derived from the "sogenannten 'traditions-ge-
schichtlichen' Studien" help to illuminate the development of religious thought at the time of the
Evangelist, but are quite worthless as far as the interpretation of the Gospel is concerned unless it
has first been established with absolute certainty that the Evangelist intended to co-opt the values
embodied by these ideas into his own work.

[66]See for instance, de Jonge's review of Bühner in *NedTheolTijd* 32 (1978) 318—325 (this
review is in Dutch; cf. *NTA* 23 [1979] 157); Borgen, "God's Agent," 138. It is to be noted, however, that nowhere in this entire discussion does Borgen himself date any of the material he cites,
beyond stating that they belong to "the early period of the Merkabah mysticism," about which
very little is known.

3. The Theologico-Christological Approach

The discussion on the theological and Christological aspects of mission in John's Gospel is found naturally in the Theologies of the New Testament and in New Testament Introductions. It is also the primary focus of Haenchen's "'Der Vater der mich gesandt hat,'" of McPolin's "Mission in the Fourth Gospel," and of Kuhl's *Die Sendung Jesu und der Kirche*. Scattered treatments are also found in the commentaries and in the more general works on the Gospel, including some of those already cited in this study[67]. The two major issues discussed in this area concern the role of the Father in the missionary enterprise and the different aspects and meaning of the mission of the Son. Chief among these aspects are Jesus' relation to the sending Father, to his audience and to other missionaries, his consciousness of himself as the one sent, and the means by which he accomplishes his mission. Again, given the major focus of this present undertaking, we can do no more at this point than depict in broad outlines the major contours of the discussion.

The role of the Father

The discussion on the role of the Father in the missionary enterprise takes its point of departure from 3:16. On the basis of this key text, the Father is seen as the origin or initiator of mission in the Gospel. His sending of his "uniquely beloved Son" reveals his supreme love for humanity. The *Heilswerk* which he initiates aims at the salvation of all peoples without exception. His sending activity also constitutes his legitimization and authorization of the Son in whom he works and through whom he requires unconditional obedience and faith from humanity.

The goal of his sending the Son is "damit dieser den Menschen Kunde von ihm bringe und sie in seine Einheit und Gemeinschaft mit der Vater hineinziehe"[68]. In brief, the Father is the origin and goal of the missionary enterprise, the unsent sender of the Son, of the Holy Spirit and of John the Baptist. McPolin sums it all up by calling him "the mission center, the source from which all missions derive"[69]. However, in the

---

[67]See, for instance, Bultmann, *Theologie*, 385–422; *Commentary*, 203–391; Conzelmann, *Grundriss*, 373–383; Kümmel, *Theologie*, 237–256; Braun, *Jean le théologien* III, 57–75; Blank, *KRISIS*, esp. chapters 2–7; Feine, *Theologie*, 312–316. For the commentaries see especially under Jn 3; 4:31–38; 5–10.

[68]For a fuller discussion on the Father's role in the missionary enterprise see Feine, *Theologie*, 313; Conzelmann, *Grundriss*, 372 (his comparison of Jn 3:13 to Rom 8:32, 39); Haenchen, "'Der Vater der mich gesandt hat,'" 211 (who holds that in sending Jesus it is the Father himself who "in Jesu Worten zu Wort kommt" and who in Jesus' words reveals his heart to us). Similarly, Bieder (*Gottes Sendung*, 40) holds that the sending passages emphasize the presence and activity of the Father in Jesus. See further, McPolin, "Mission in the Fourth Gospel," 114; for the commentaries see in particular the discussion on Jn 1:6; 3:16–17; 4:23; 6:44; 12:28b (cf. 8:54; 17:4); 15:1–2.

[69]McPolin, "Mission in the Fourth Gospel," 114, 121; and *John*, 35.

light of such passages as Jn 4:23; 5:17, 19, and 15:1—2, one must admit that the role assigned the Father in these discussions is rather static and remote by comparison to that assigned him in the Gospel itself.

The mission of the Son

As with the missionary role of the Father, the discussion on the mission of the Son consists for the most part, especially in the Theologies of the New Testament, in culling ideas from the Gospel itself. The ever-recurring expression, ὁ πέμψας με πατήρ is seen as the key to the Son's understanding of his mission. The expression reveals his self-consciousness as one sent. Because of this consciousness Jesus does not his own will but the Father's (5:30), seeks not his own glory but the Father's (7:18; 8:50, 54), and is so dependent on the Father that he can do nothing of himself (5:19, 30). His mission is to reveal the Father and thus bring life, light and knowledge to those who believe in him. Thus, as one authorized and commissioned by God, the Son demands an unconditional response of faith. His coming marks the eschatological event of judgment and separation, since the salvation he brings offers humanity the final chance to choose between life through faith or death through a refusal to believe[70].

In relation to the other missions mentioned in the Gospel, Jesus' mission is seen as central and normative. All the other missions derive from and are in function of his: John the Baptist prepares the way for him, and the disciples continue his mission in the world while their mission is made possible by the Holy Spirit who also leads them to faith in Jesus[71]. However, as already noted, the prevailing tendency in the literature examined is to limit "mission properly so called" to the post-Easter activity of the disciples and, in the case of Olsson and Lindars in particular, to understand the mission of Jesus himself as mission only when viewed from the standpoint of the mission of the disciples[72].

---

[70]Apart from Bultmann's *Theologie*, 385—445, the single most comprehensive theological work on the mission of the Son in recent years is Kuhl's *Die Sendung Jesu und der Kirche*. The basic aim of the work is to study the theology of mission in the Gospel, namely, "die Sendung der Jüngergemeinschaft in der Zeit des Heiligen Geistes" (p. 1). But since the mission of the disciples and of the Holy Spirit derives from that of Jesus, Kuhl devotes a great part of the dissertation to the sending of Jesus (chapter 1, 58—129). The second chapter deals with the sending of the Holy Spirit and of the disciples to complete Jesus' work (130—159); the third chapter treats the issue of the "whence" and "whither" of Jesus' mission and of the disciples (160—229); while the concluding chapter compares the Johannine idea of sending with those of the OT, Jewish and Gnostic literature (230—233). See further the literature cited in n. 67 above.

[71]In the discussion of the relation of the mission of Jesus to the other missions mentioned in the Gospel, greatest attention is given to the joint mission of the Holy Spirit and of the disciples, though McPolin ("Mission in the Fourth Gospel") and the commentaries also treat the mission of the Baptist. See in particular, Felix Porsch, *Pneuma und Wort: Ein exegetischer Beitrag zur Pneumatologie des Johannesevangeliums* (Frankfurt am/M: Joseph Knecht, 1974) 341—404; de Jonge, *Jesus: Stranger from Heaven and Son of God* (SBLSBS 11; Missoula: Scholars, 1977) 3—12; Meinertz, *Theologie*, 192; Bieder, *Gottes Sendung*, 45—46, 50.

[72]Olsson, *Structure and Meaning, passim;* Lindars, *John*, 175, 193, 195. A fuller appraisal of

On the more theological level, the discussion on the mission of the Son seems to center on three issues: First, how is the oneness of the Son and the Father to be understood? In the light of Jn 10:30, for instance, is this oneness ontological (*Wesensidentität* or *Wesenseinheit der Gottesnatur*) or is it a oneness in *mission ad extra*, a "congruency in action" (*Deckungsgleichheit in der Aktion*), such that Jesus alone is the perfect representative of the Father[73]? Meinertz, Zahn, Lütgert and Feine argue in the light of Jn 1:1c and 20:28 in favor of ontological unity, a unity which is not simply one of office. Conzelmann, Miranda, Braun and, to some extent, McPolin opt, on the contrary, for a unity of mission. Borgen's halakhic principle would support this option[74]. Meinertz's reminder that the Evangelist does not theologize or philosophize concerning the inner life of the Godhead is, however, worth heeding[75]. This calls for the need to distinguish between the Evangelist's own concerns and the interpretation which twentieth century readers might bring to the Gospel in the light of twenty centuries of the development of Christian dogma[76].

The second important issue discussed concerns the event which constitutes the mission of Jesus: is it his incarnation/sending, his passion/departure or the period in between the two? Zahn, Braun and Bultmann tend to see the incarnation as the mission event, because for Bultmann in particular it is the *Wortcharakter* of the revelation which counts[77]. Conzelmann on his part emphasizes the passion/departure, because this is the moment of fulfilment, the presupposition for the actualized relationship between God and human beings. For Hahn, sending means Jesus' coming down from heaven and his return thither (6:38; 16:28); in his view John is not interested in what Jesus actually does on earth nor in how he does it, as in Phil 2:6—11. What counts is the authority (*Vollmacht*) given him. In McPolin's view, "Christ's mission on earth, his self-revelation and his communication of life" are all "fulfilled through his return to the

---

the position of these authors is undertaken below in the discussion of 4:1—42 in modern scholarship, pp. 69—72.

[73]For the two contrasting German phrases cited here see Meinertz, *Theologie*, II, 275 and Miranda, *Die Sendung*, 90.

[74]Meinertz, *Theologie* II, 274; Theodor Zahn, *Grundriss der neutestamentlichen Theologie* (Leipzig: D. Werner Scholl, 1920) 28; Lütgert (*Die Liebe im Neuen Testament. Ein Beitrage zur Geschichte des Urchristentums* [Leipzig: A. Deichert, 1905] 139) holds that though the Father's love for the Son may express itself in the works which he gives to the Son to do, it does not consist in these works; Feine, *Theologie*, 312 (cf. 33f); Conzelmann, *Grundriss*, 372 ("ihre Einheit ist die Einheit des Heilswerks"); Miranda, *Die Sendung*, 90; Braun, *Jean* III, 57—58; McPolin, *John*, 98; Borgen, "God's Agent," 138.

[75]Meinertz, *Theologie* II, 273; similarly, Bultmann, *Commentary*, 249.

[76]Though the Evangelist's focus may have been different, evidence such as Jn 5:17—18, and 10:33, 36 would lead one to conclude that Jesus' oneness with the Father is also ontological, and that the unity in *mission ad extra* results from this ontological unity (cf. 1:1c).

[77]Zahn (*Grundriss,* 27) states: "Jesu Eintritt in das irdische Leben ist seine Sendung"; Braun (*Jean* III, 71) holds that Jesus' incarnation and his sending are "une seule et même chose"; Bultmann, *Theologie*, 412—422, 422—426.

Father"[78]. Thus, there is a clear tendency to divide Christ's life and work into compartments, and to select one of them as that which explains the notion of mission, instead of viewing the whole of his life from the standpoint of mission (3:16). Hahn's view that the Evangelist is not interested in what Jesus actually does on earth is particularly odd, given the fact that the Gospel narrative centers almost exclusively on this part of Jesus' life.

The third and final, and, for our purposes, the most important theological issue in this discussion concerns Jesus' attitude in the exercise of his mission. Does the use of such expressions as ὁ πέμψας με πατήρ and ἀφ᾽ ἐμαυτοῦ οὐκ, κτλ., indicate the Son's humility and obedience *vis-à-vis* the Father in the exercise of his mission or does it refer to his claim to authority as Revealer? Haenchen clearly sees these expressions as having a reference to Jesus' humility and dependence on the Father. The force of his mission is that by desiring to be nothing else but the hand and voice of the Father, he serves as an example for a world turned in upon itself and closed to God, an example which he also commends to his disciples[79]. Bultmann, on the contrary, states very emphatically that these expressions refer, not to Jesus' humility, but to his claim to authority as Revealer, in much the same way as the OT prophets had to speak God's word, even when they did not want to. His position is grounded in his belief that Jesus' words as Revealer "transcend the human possibilities of pride and humility." Such passages as Jn 5:17, 19, for instance, are "intended to lay bare the grounds of the equality of his work with the divine work, and not to show his subordination to the Father"[80].

Bultmann does acknowledge, of course, that "to be sent is to be dependent," but this dependence only serves as the basis of Jesus' equality with the Father in the missionary enterprise, not as his personal virtue. Bultmann's obvious difficulty in reconciling Jesus' humility as one sent with his claim as Revealer stems from his basic persupposition that the Johannine Christ is modeled wholly on the Gnostic Redeemer/Revealer figures[81]. Almost all his assertions about Jesus' mission: that as Revealer he reveals nothing other than that he is the Revealer, that the content of his mission is not the *Was* but the *Dass*, and that his mission of revelation is to be understood summarily as *die κρίσις der Welt*, a view which is strangely supported by Blank, all stem from the basic Gnostic standpoint from which he interprets the Gospel and Jesus' mission in particular[82].

---

[78]Conzelmann, *Grundriss*, 372; Hahn, *Das Verständnis*, 140; McPolin, *John*, 75. It is not clear whether by "fulfilment" here McPolin means "brought to completion" or "actualized."

[79]Haenchen, " 'Der Vater der mich gesandt hat,' " 210–212.

[80]Bultmann, *Commentary*, 247–250; quote, 248.

[81]*Commentary*, 248–250; cf. *Theologie*, 419: "Im gnostischen Mythos, dessen Sprache für Johannes das Ausdrucksmittel ist." Though Bultmann is forced at times to recognize the prophetic overtones in the Johannine portrayal of Jesus' mission, he nevertheless insists that the Evangelist's conception is formed under the Gnostic, not OT, influence.

[82]Bultmann, *Theologie*, 418–419 (on the "content" of Jesus' revelation), 385–422 (on Jesus' mission as "Die κρίσις der Welt"); similarly, *Commentary*, 203–285 (where he studies in particular

Bultmann's entire approach thus gives the impression that Jesus is a divine being in human form who strides over but barely touches the foreign territory, the earth, accomplishes his eschatological mission of revelation as judgment and leaves his hearers to take or leave it at their own peril. Thus in the words of Wrede cited by Bultmann, the Johannine Christ is "ein göttliches Wesen, das wie ein Fremder majestätisch über die Erde dahinzieht"[83]. Such a portrait is irreconcilable with humility in any sense of the word, and the tension which Feine recognizes in the Gospel's portrayal of Jesus as both dependent on and equal to the Father is eliminated[84].

A striking feature of Bultmann's projection is the impression that for him Jesus' hearers do not really count. Hahn's position also implies the same. What matters is the Revealer and his revelation, this despite Bultmann's constant reiteration that the audience is called to believe in Jesus. Indeed, his Gnostic view of the Johannine Christ constitutes the basis of the popular view that Jesus' interlocutors in the Gospel are no more than foils. Even a cursory glance on the section where Bultmann discusses the mission of the Son in Jn 5—8 confirms this impression: the only verses which Bultmann singles out for elucidation are those spoken by Jesus. The responses, or in Dodd's view, "interpellations," of the audience do not seem to count[85].

The *general evaluation* of these studies which deal with the theological and Christological approaches to mission in the Gospel may be sketched briefly as follows. On the positive side, these studies contribute much towards the understanding of the roles of the Father and the Son in the missionary enterprise, and of the rich dimensions of the Son's mission, even if at times there is a tendency to project the reader's twentieth century concerns into the Gospel. On the negative side, these studies tend to overlook the actual method by which Jesus executes his mission, the particular ways by which he interacts with his audience, his majestic stature not withstanding. Moreover, given the fact that the Evangelist chose to present Jesus' self-revelation in the form of dialogues and discourses, the question needs to be asked to what extent, if any, these dialogues reflect the contribution or standpoint of the given audience, even if the initiative of the encounter comes from Jesus. Finally, it is worth examining in the light of the Gospel's total conception of mission whether

---

Jn 4:43—6:59; 7:14—24; 8:13—20, all passages where Jesus' mission and identity are the subject of public debate); Blank, *KRISIS*, 231—263, 279—315.

[83]Bultmann "Quellen," 102, n. 2, citing Wrede, *Vorträge und Studien*, 207.

[84]Feine (*Theologie*, 313) cites 14:28 as evidence of Jesus' subordination to the Father, and 10: 30 as proof of his equality. It is to be noted, also, that the whole context of 10:30 makes it clear that Jesus' claim here cannot be understood simply in terms of equality in mission. In 10:33 his interlocutors distinguish between his works and his making himself God.

[85]Bultmann, *Commentary*, 203—285. Indeed, the same selective principle governs Bultmann's entire approach to the Gospel. See, for instance, pp. 140—166 (on Jn 3:1—21), 285—391 (on Jn 7—10) and 522—631 (on the farewell discourses). Dodd, *Tradition*, 320.

Bultmann is right against Haenchen that the Johannine Christ does not
condescend to plead with his audience, or that humility is not a feature
of his mission. The solution to these problems may yet lie in the proper
understanding of the Evangelist's own style and of the rich dimensions of
his rhetorical approach.

4. The Johannine Community's Interest in Mission

It is a curious phenomenon in Johannine studies that while the centrality of mission in the Gospel is universally recognized, and while there is
a clear tendency to interpret this mission thought primarily from the
standpoint of the mission of the disciples, there is nevertheless a serious
and sustained debate as to whether the Johannine community, the group
of disciples from whom and for whom the Gospel was written, was itself
interested in missionary activity[86]. The issue is closely linked, on the one
hand, with the discussion on the missionary or non-missionary character
of the Gospel already discussed, and, on the other, with the question of
the redactional levels of the Gospel and the correspondence between these
levels and the different historical situations of the community. The best
that can be done here is to present briefly but schematically the different
and often conflicting scholarly views on the subject[87].
We begin by recalling the different positions of scholars already discussed. First, those who see the Gospel in its present final form as a *Missionsschrift* written to win Jews, Samaritans or Gentiles obviously believe
that the community which produced the Gospel was missionary minded.
Included among them are Bornhäuser, Oehler, Smith, Robinson, Freed,
Wind, Dodd and Cullmann. To this list may be added Fridrichsen, who
believes that the entire Gospel was written from the standpoint of a very
successful Christian mission[88]. Next, there are those who hold that though
the present Gospel is not a *Missionsschrift* but a *Gemeinde-Evangelium*
it does nevertheless have a missionary perspective as a sub-theme. Included
among them are Schnackenburg, Kümmel and Meeks. These scholars
imply that while the community was preoccupied with its own internal

---

[86]For the discussion on the centrality of Jesus' mission in the Gospel, see n. 2 above, and for
the tendency to see the mission of Jesus in terms of that of the disciples, see n. 72.

[87]In addition to the literature cited below on the missionary situation of the Johannine community, see, for instance, Cullmann (*Joh. Kreis*, 49—52) who believes that the group which stands
behind the Gospel had "ein starkes missionarisches Interesse" in Samaria (p. 49); Schweizer,
"Der Kirchenbegriff im Evangelium und den Briefen des Johannes," *SE* 1 (= TU 73; 1959) 363—
381 (where he states, "Diese Gemeinde treibt keine Mission" [p. 379]); Wolfgang Wiefel, "Die
Scheidung von Gemeinde und Welt im Johannesevangelium auf dem Hintergrund der Trennung von
Kirche und Synagoge," *TZ* 35 (1979) 213—227.

[88]Anton Fridrichsen, "La pensée missionaire dans le quatrième évangile," *Arbeiten und Mitteilungen aus dem neutestamentlichen Seminar zu Uppsala*, VI (ed. A. Fridrichsen; Uppsala, 1937)
39—45. Fridrichsen bases his argument on such passages as 10:16 which he sees as a parallel to 4:
35—38.

problems, it never completely lost sight of missionary activity. Thirdly, there are those (Schille and Hahn) who believe that mission is constitutive of the Church and regard its very existence as serving a missionary purpose. In this connection may be mentioned those who see brotherly love in community as serving a missionary purpose: Lütgert, Bieder, Neugebauer and Conzelmann[89]. These three groups thus believe, though with varying degrees of conviction and for different reasons, that the community which produced the final Gospel was interested in mission.

The next group to be considered concerns those who approach the Gospel and its community through redactional studies. The common position is that in its early stages the Johannine community was interested in mission. This is the community to which belonged the *Grundschrift*, *Semeia-Evangelium*, Document C and John II-A. But in the view of these scholars, among whom are Wilkens, Fortna and Nicol, the community of the final Gospel was no longer interested in missionary outreach. Its major concern lay in its efforts to help its members cope with the crises of religious and social identity caused by ejection from the synagogue, suspicion by the Greater Church and rejection by the world. To this end, the community intensified its sectarian tendency and developed an all-round polemic against the enemies of the community[90]. The positions of Brown and Boismard on this whole question deserve special attention.

Brown's *Community of the Beloved Disciple* is particularly useful not only because the book largely offers a synthesis of contemporary theories on the situation of the Johannine community, but because it also gives good summaries of the positions of a number of modern scholars on the subject[91]. Brown himself postulates four phases in the history of the development of the Johannine community. In *the first phase,* the pre-Gospel, the community which consisted of members drawn from the followers of John the Baptist won converts from Jews with anti-temple views and from Samaritans with a "high Moses piety." The "high Christology" which developed as a result of the ideas brought by the new arrivals made the community "obnoxious to more traditional Jews" (p. 39) and finally led to the ejection of the community from the synagogue.

In *the second stage,* at the time the Gospel was written, the community may have moved from Palestine to the Diaspora to teach the Greeks, and

---

[89]Lütgert, *Die Liebe,* 137–167; Bieder, *Gottes Sendung,* 41–43; Neugebauer, *Entstehung,* 12; Conzelmann, *Grundriss,* 387. Conzelmann's position here contradicts his view mentioned earlier that "Dem johanneischen Kirchengedanken entspricht nicht der Gedanke der Mission."

[90]Studies which emphasize the sectarian character of the Johannine community include Robin Scroggs, "The Earliest Christian Communities as Sectarian Movement," *Studies in Judaism* 12, 1–23; Meeks, "The Man from Heaven"; Schweizer, "Kirchenbegriff"; de Jonge, *Jesus, Stranger,* esp. 99ff.; Nicol, *Semeia,* 146; F.F. Segovia, "The Love and Hatred of Jesus and Johannine Sectarianism," *CBQ* 43 (1981) 258–272; Béda Rigaux ("Les destinataires du IVe évangile à la lumière de Jn 17," *RTLov* 1 [1970] 289–319) sees the Johannine group as an "elite" community; see also his "Die Jünger Jesu in Johannes 17," *TQ* 150 (1970) 203–213.

[91]Brown, *Community,* Apendix I, 171–182.

so won converts from them. In *the third stage*, the defensive stance on
its Christology which the community took against Jews and Jewish Christians led to a split within the community itself, despite its earlier development of a theology of *koinōnia* to compensate for its ejection from the
synagogue. The Epistles were written at this stage to buttress the faith of
the few remaining members against the deception of the secessionists. In
the fourth and final stage, the secessionists, by far the majority, turned
towards various forms of Gnosticism, and the remnant, unable to survive
in isolation, joined the Great Church[92].

Thus, in Brown's view, the community was definitely active in missionary work in stage one, and to some extent in stage two, unless the
"opening to the Gentiles" which began towards the end of phase one was
completed before the Gospel was written[93]. In phase three, one could also
speak of missionary activity to the extent in which each of the divided
parties sought to win members for its group. In phase four, not only is
missionary activity out of the question, but the community itself is li-
quidated as a result of its own internal divisions.

This is not the place to engage in a review of Brown's book which is
so clearly written. For our present purposes, the following observations
need to be made. First, Brown's whole reconstruction is far too neat and
schematic to be true to life, and hence convincing, both in respect to the
development of its Christology and to the allegedly linear procedure by
which it acquired members: followers of the Baptist, Jews with anti-
temple views, Samaritans and then Gentiles. What strikes one as particularly odd is that Brown seems to attribute little or no theological importance to the disciples' own experience with Jesus. It would seem that
they learnt no Christology from the "teacher" even though they had
been with him from the beginning (15:25; cf. 1 Jn 2:25, 27; 2 Jn 9).
Moreover, the whole discussion seems to take it for granted that a Johannine community did exist, that it alone had a "high Christology," that it
alone was ejected from the synagogue and that there were no persecuting
Jews whither it moved to teach the Greeks. For Brown's theory to be convincing, these issues would need to be addressed, not presumed.

The position of Boismard-Lamouille is somewhat more nuanced than
that of Brown even though they, too, posit four stages in the history of
the Gospel. It needs to be noted from the outset that these authors do not
directly discuss the issue of the Johannine community or of its interest in
mission. Their position presented here is derived solely from their theories
concerning the four redactional levels of the Gospel. *First*, the community to which *Document C* belonged was definitely engaged in missionary
activity. The presentation of Jesus in this Document as a prophet from

---

[92]Brown's discussion of the different phases of the community is concentrated on pp. 25—164;
see also his summary chart, pp. 166—167.

[93]Compare the end of his chapter one (57—58) and the beginning of his chapter two (59—60)
with Chart One, 166.

God and the apologetic value attributed to his "signs" all aimed at leading the listener to believe in him. In *the second stage, John II-A* defined even more clearly the object of Jesus' mission and developed further the apologetic value of the "signs" showing how they should "inciter les hommes à croire en la mission de Jésus"[94]. In *the third stage, John II-B,* who is responsible for the bulk of the Gospel as we now have it, remained essentially within the line of thought developed by Document C and John II-A (his first redaction of the Gospel), except for his radical substitution of "witness/word" for "signs" as that which should "mener les hommes à la foi en Jésus"[95].

The whole idea of "leading to faith in Jesus" implies that the community to which John II-B belonged had a missionary interest, even if the poor responses received from both Jews and Gentiles led him to develop a polemic stance against these groups. For John II-B did not only attack feeble Christians, who like Nicodemus and the Jews in Jn 9 were incapable of breaking with the synagogue, and wrote the Gospel to encourage believers. By rewriting the Gospel after his move from Palestine to Ephesus at the end of the first century, he sought to win followers from this new region. In *the fourth and final stage, John III,* the final editor of the Gospel, clearly had a missionary interest in view: "ne tend-il pas la main à certains judéo-chrétiens qui s'étaient séparés du christianisme?" John III, then, did not only mitigate the anti-Jewish, anti-world attitude of John II, the Evangelist, he also gave the Gospel its most precious, universal and unequivocal statements on mission[96].

Thus, though the question of the relation of the Evangelist to the community is never directly addressed, the net-result of the Boismard-Lamouille reconstruction is that at least one person in the Johannine community never lost sight of the importance of missionary activity at any given stage of the community's development. Besides, it is not to be forgotten that John II-A and II-B are one and the same person[97]. Further-

---

[94]Boismard-Lamouille, *Synopse III,* 49.

[95]Boismard-Lamouille, *Synopse III,* 50.

[96]*Ibid.,* 59. For a fuller discussion on the activities of the different redactors see pp. 48–50, 58–59; for John III in particular, pp. 124–125, 266. Note that the anti-Jewish/anti-world attitude of John II-B itself results from his disappointment because of the refusal of both Jews and Gentiles to believe in Jesus (p. 400).

[97]The question of the relation of the community/audience to the author in the shaping or re-shaping of the tradition is one that is hardly raised in the discussion, least of all by redactional studies. Yet it is an important one. Did the authors have exclusive rights to the traditional material such that they could change, add, delete or manipulate it any way they wanted without being in any way accountable to the group of believers to whom these traditions ultimately belonged? In John, for instance, while the BD stands as the revered witness of the traditions, the Gospel also makes it clear that the "signs" of Jesus recorded in the book were worked before "his disciples" (20:30) who collectively are designated as his witnesses (15:27; cf. 1 Jn 1:1–5). Moreover, if it is true, as is generally held, that 21:24b–25 constitutes the community's response to the witness of the BD, namely, the Gospel, then the question needs to be asked how this community knows that the witness of the BD is true. This question is important since ultimately it was the commun-

more, it is the Evangelist, who on his second redaction of the Gospel as John II-B transforms the primitive account of a miraculous catch of fish recorded by Document C into a missionary pericope, showing that "ce sont tous les disciples de tous les temps" that Jesus calls to become "des pêcheurs d'hommes"[98]. When, therefore, John III sharpens the missionary focus of the Gospel, he is only following to its logical conclusion the fundamental missionary thrust of Document C and of John II, the Evangelist.

The final and more recent theories concerning the missionary interest of the Johannine community are those of Schnackenburg and Painter. Both these authors distinguish between the Evangelist and his community. In Schnackenburg's view, the redactional passages, Jn 17:20 and Jn 21, show that the Johannine school was more interested in missionary activity than was the Evangelist, even though the latter's missionary outlook cannot be entirely denied, given Jn 10:19 and 11:52[99]. Painter argues, on the contrary, that the Evangelist was more interested in mission than the community. The third redaction of his farewell discourses (Jn 16:4b—33) was intended to counteract the "withdrawal symptoms" of the community which turned in upon itself after its ejection from the synagogue.

This he did by directing the attention of the community to the world mission and to the relation of the Paraclete to the world. He succeeded so well that the many Gentiles won by the community as a result of his encouraging them to missionary activity later became a danger to the community itself. For this community tended to assimilate the worldly ways of the new converts, and as a result became so internally divided that the Evangelist was forced to write Jn 17 to ward off schism and to stress the missionary importance of love in community. Only when all his efforts to ward off schism failed did he drop the theme of mission; then in the First Epistle he focused exclusively on the orthodoxy of tradition and on its correct theological interpretation. But this happened only *after* the Gospel had been written[100].

---

ity which decided which books it would retain as canonical and which it would reject as being untrue records of its faith in Christ.

[98] Boismard-Lamouille, *Synopse III*, 485; for the redactional activities of John II-B in Jn 21, see pp. 476—489.

[99] Schnackenburg, "Der Missionsgedanke des Johannesevangeliums im heutigen Horizont," *Festgabe J. Glaike und B. Willeke* (ed. H. Waldenfels; Einsiedeln, 1978) 53—65; also in *Das Johannesevangelium IV: Ergänzende Auslegungen und Exkurse* (HTKNT IV/4; Freiburg: Herder, 1984) 58—72.

[100] Painter, "Farewell Discourses," esp. pp. 536—541. Note that Painter distinguishes between the Evangelist, the Johannine school and the Johannine community. In his view, the redactional Jn 21 proves that the Johannine school shared the missionary zeal of the Evangelist. Painter's reconstruction does not make it clear, however, when this school became active, especially if, as he believes, the Evangelist wrote the non-missionary First Epistle. Painter's theory as a whole is built upon that of Brown which he accepts as being "generally convincing," though he rejects Brown's attribution of the "high Christology" to a late stage in the community's development (pp. 525—526).

We may now attempt to *sum up* our discussion on the missionary situation of the Johannine community, even though the data reveals the complexity of modern theories concerning the missionary situation of this community. First, there is a unanimous agreement that the community in its early stages was keenly engaged in missionary activity. How long these early stages lasted and whether or not they witnessed to any of the written forms of the Gospel are, however, disputed[101]. Concerning the community of the final Gospel there is very little agreement. On the one hand, those who see the Gospel as a missionary document believe that the community was actively engaged in mission, while others'emphasize that the community was missionary by its very existence. On the other, Brown, Martyn and their group who believe the Johannine community was a closed sectarian group struggling to recover from the trauma of the *Birkat ha-Minim,* deny that his community had any interest in missionary outreach. The Boismard/Lamouille reconstruction offers a third alternative, namely, that one person in the community, at least, never lost sight of the importance of mission. Their position finds support partly from Painter and partly from those who hold that the Gospel has a missionary perspective as a sub-theme.

The question, then, whether or not the Johannine community was interested in mission calls forth a series of other questions: which Johannine community, and what is meant by mission in this context? Furthermore, is it necessary to distinguish between the stand of the Evangelist and that of his community on this issue of mission? Put differently, to what extent does the conception of mission in the Gospel reflect the personal stance of the Evangelist or that of his community or school? Are the Evangelist's community, school and audience one, two or three separate entities?

Since this research is concerned with the approach to mission in the finished Gospel and as it relates to the historical situation of the Evangelist and his audience, it will be our task to examine which of the hypotheses advanced concerning the missionary situation of the Johannine community at this finished Gospel level best corresponds with the conception of mission projected in the Gospel itself. If the Gospel is not a missionary document, that is, if the community to which the Gospel in its final form belongs was not interested in mission, how then is its undeniable focus

---

101 For Boismard-Lamouille, the first stage would stretch from about A.D. 50—56, covering the activities of Doc C and John II-A (pp. 67—70). But for Brown, the first phase is clearly the "pre-Gospel" phase (ca. 50's to 80's). The Gospel was first written only after the *Birkat ha-Minim* (ca. A.D. 85), most probably ca. A.D. 90 (p. 23). It is to be noted that unlike Boismard-Lamouille, Brown accepts only two, not four, stages of the composition of the Gospel, namely, "the Gospel mostly written," and the work of the redactor from the Johannine school who added Jn 21, for instance (pp. 20, n. 25; 22—24; cf. *John* I, xxxiv—xxxix). Why the Johannine school, which in Brown's reconstruction belongs to the non-missionary phase of the community would feel the need to add Jn 21 which clearly deals with the mission of the disciples is a question which Brown does not address in this study.

on mission (both that of Jesus and of the disciples) to be understood, especially since the overtly missionary passages (e.g., 3:16; 4:31–38; 17: 20; 21) are assigned to the final redactional layers of the Gospel (e.g., 4: 31–42; 13–17; 21)[102]? Does the answer to the question lie ultimately in the distinctions made by Painter and Schnackenburg between the attitude of the Evangelist and that of his school and community with regard to missionary outreach? Only the corroborative evidence of the Gospel and of contemporary NT literature can provide a solid basis for the answers to these questions.

C. Summary and Conclusions from the Data and Survey

The variety of approaches to mission in John's Gospel surveyed above testify both to the great importance attached to the issue of mission for the understanding of the Gospel and to the complexity of the elements involved in this issue. The survey also reveals that while a variety of aspects of this issue has been discussed some fundamental questions still remain to be asked. Each major approach surveyed gave rise to a different set of questions which we now summarize below.

1. The debate on the missionary or non-missionary character of the Gospel revealed that the problem is not unconnected with the modern understanding of mission primarily in terms of the post-Easter activity of the disciples. The question, however, is whether this in fact is how the Evangelist himself understands mission. And so the situation calls for the need to determine *what* the Evangelist himself understands by mission irrespective of the nature of his audience, the geographical setting of his missionary activity and the meaning that might be attached to mission in the twentieth century.

2. The discussion on the models which could have influenced the Evangelist's portrayal of Jesus as God's envoy revealed a general trend in favor of the OT and heterodox Jewish background as that which most influenced the Evangelist. But the approach also raises the more fundamental question *why,* in the first place, the Evangelist chose to present Jesus' life and work from the primary standpoint of mission. Is this choice in any way influenced by the missionary situation of the Evangelist and of his community? Or did he write simply out of a desire to experiment with existing missionary models?

3. On the theological and Christological levels, the survey revealed that while the role of the Father, the meaning of the mission of the Son, its relation to other missions in the Gospel and its soteriological and es-

---

[102]Other passages which explicitly mention the mission of Jesus and of the disciples include 4:1–2; 5:36; 10:10, 16; 11:52; 12:32; 15:27; 17:18; 20:21.

chatological significance for his audience have been discussed, the approach tends to obscure the dialogical aspects of mission so vividly present in the Gospel: the manner by which Jesus actually carries out his mission, the interaction between him and his living audience and the possible role played by this audience in the Johannine portrayal of Jesus' mission from the Father. These significant omissions spell the need to examine *how* the Evangelist understands mission. Why, for instance, does he choose to present Jesus' interaction with his audience in the form of dialogues and discourses? Is this choice determined by the missionary thrust of the Gospel itself, the need to engage and convince the audience to believe in Jesus (20:30–31) or is the feature to be attributed solely to the influence of the *Offenbarungsreden* source allegedly used by the Evangelist?

4. Concerning the discussion on the missionary interest of the Johannine community, lack of agreement became quite evident, except with regard to the first stage of the community which all agree had an interest in mission. Furthermore, contradictory theories were advanced concerning the later stages of this community. On the one hand, it was held that the Evangelist, not the community, was interested in missionary outreach, and on the other, that the redactor/Johannine school, not the Evangelist was so interested. Again while others held that the Johannine community in its last phases was a closed, sectarian and inward looking community whose relationship with the outside world consisted of a polemic tirade against its enemies, others held, on the contrary, that the Gospel reflects the situation of a community which had a very successful Gentile mission. All these theories need to be tested against the concrete evidence of the Gospel itself, set in the wider context of contemporary NT situations.

Obviously the problems here highlighted are too closely related to be treated as isolated topics. Basically, they all seem to be related to the way in which the Evangelist understands and presents Jesus' mission from the Father and the possible ways in which this presentation impinges on the actual missionary situation of the Evangelist and his audience. A proper treatment of these issues, therefore, calls for a method which will view them in a unified perspective, rather than through one-sided or either-or approaches. Hence the rationale for the choice of both the present topic of our research, the Johannine approach to mission, and of the method of text/contextual analysis adopted for this investigation. A description of this method and of the dimensions of the Johannine approach as well as the design for this study will be considered in our next Chapter.

The ultimate aim of the enquiry will be to come to a better understanding of the Evangelist's own conception of mission, through a careful attention to the different aspects of his approach to the subject. It is also hoped that the enquiry will throw some light on the important issue of the missionary situation of the Evangelist and of his audience and on the possible relation of this Johannine historical situation to the wider Christian missionary situation of the NT era.

Chapter II

The Scope of the Present Research and the Issue of Methodology

In this Chapter we shall discuss more fully the scope of the current research and the various methodological questions involved. To this end we shall organize the discussion under the following three topics: the dialectical relationship between the survey in Chapter one and the thesis topic, the dimensions of the Johannine approach and the methodology of the current research.

A. The Dialectical Relationship between the Survey and the Thesis Tropic

The rich Gospel data on mission and the variety of approaches to the subject surveyed in the previous Chapter testify to the great importance which mission holds for understanding John's Gospel. Although the survey showed that many aspects of the subject have been discussed, it also disclosed, on the one hand, that none of the issues raised has been conclusively resolved, and on the other, that some fundamental questions still remain to be raised. Moreover, it showed that not a few of these unresolved or still-to-be-asked questions bear on the Evangelist's own approach to mission. Accordingly, a proper understanding of this approach may in turn help illumine some of these unresolved questions which we list again for easy reference.

First, why did the Evangelist choose the concept of mission as the fundamental hermeneutic for interpreting the life and work of Jesus, using the gospel genre? In other words, why is there so much insistence in the Gospel that Jesus is sent by the Father and why are all other characters in the Gospel viewed from the exclusive standpoint of his mission? Has this emphasis any bearing on the missionary *Sitz-im-Leben* of the Evangelist and of his community?

Secondly, given the declared persuasive thrust of the Gospel (20:30—31) underlined throughout by the ἵνα-clause, how does the Evangelist present his material so that his audience can understand his message and so be led to make the appropriate response of life-giving faith in Jesus?

For the likelihood that the Gospel message or the claims made by Jesus might be rejected (5:43; 6:60; 8:59; 15:22) does not invalidate the need to present this message in ways which the audience can understand. Rather, it makes this need all the more imperative, especially if the Evangelist's declared intent that he wishes to persuade his audience to a faith-response is to be taken seriously (20:30–31).

Thirdly, concerning the audience itself, and still from the perspective of 20:30–31, does it play any essential role in the missionary enterprise such that its involvement and viewpoint constitute integral aspects of the missionary dialectic? Or do Jesus' interlocutors in the Gospel merely serve as "foils" for him or the Evangelist to expound his theological meaning[1]? Of what significance, if any, is Jesus' use of dialogue in the execution of his mission? Is the usage called for by the nature of the task itself, the need to engage the audience, or does it arise purely from sources allegedly used by the Evangelist?

Fourthly, from the point of view of method, what is the relation between the audience *in* the Gospel (Jesus' interlocutors) and the audience *of* the Gospel directly addressed in 20:30–31? or between Jesus' method of persuading his audience and that of the Evangelist?

Fifthly and finally, what does the total approach to mission in the Gospel tell us about the Evangelist's theology and conception of mission, and what possible bearing might this conception have on his own historical missionary situation?

The *aim of this research,* then, is twofold: first, by examining the Evangelist's method of approach to mission to highlight new aspects of mission in the Gospel. This will be done in dialogue with previous discussions highlighted in Chapter I, but most especially by paying close attention to the peculiar features of the Johannine data itself, using the method of text/contextual analysis. It is hoped that this contextual approach will lead to a fuller comprehension of the conception of mission in the Gospel. Secondly, from this comprehensive view of the Evangelist's approach to mission we hope to initiate a new inquiry into the missionary situation of the Evangelist with reference to the relevant literature of the period.

Clarification of Terms

To attempt to give a definition of mission at this point of the research would be tantamount to furnishing conclusions before the enquiry is even undertaken. For the whole point of the research is precisely to discover

---

[1]The classic position here is stated by Dodd in his description of the *dramatis personae* of the Johannine discourses: "In the main, at any rate, their role is passive and they serve as foils. . . . The interlocutor plays an essentially passive part; his interpellations do no more than provide the teacher with an occasion to elaborate his thought." *Historical Tradition,* 318. Dodd's view constitutes the universally accepted view concerning the characters of John's Gospel. See further Brown, *John,* 176 and n. 16 below.

what the Evangelist himself understands by mission. Nevertheless, from the joint evidence of the Johannine data and contemporary approaches to the subject surveyed in Chapter I, it is possible to define negatively what mission does not mean in the Gospel, and more positively, to point out the directions in which this meaning is to be sought.

First, it is evident from the discussion in Chapter I that the term "mission" in the Gospel perspective does not carry the primary meaning, as it does in the modern conception, of "outreach to non-believers," especially in foreign countries. Nor does the term "missionary" refer to the person who engages in this type of missionary outreach or to the activities thereof. However, even if this criterion were to be pressed, one would have to concede that in Johannine terms, Jesus is the missionary *par excellence*, since he is said to have come from the Father into this foreign, hostile world (1:9—10; 16:28a), to make him known (1:18; 12:· 45; 14:9—10), a world he subsequently leaves when his mission is completed (16:28b; 17:4, 6—8, 11a)[2]. Finally, the term "mission" does not refer primarily to the post-Easter activity of the disciples or of the Church as is often assumed in Johannine studies, though scholarly usage here is not always consistent[3].

On the positive side, the Johannine notion of mission is rooted in the two key statements of the Gospel, that God, out of love, sent his Son into the world to give eternal life to those who believe in him (3:16—17) and that subsequently, the Evangelist wrote his Gospel in order to make Jesus' mission present to his own readers and so inculcate in them the same response of life-giving faith in Jesus (20:20—31)[4]. The Johannine conception of mission thus embraces the whole spectrum of activity which results from Jesus' "sending/coming" into the world. It covers the role of the sending Father who authorizes (3:16—17; 4:10; 17:2), sustains (4:23; 5:19—23; 6:44; 14:10—11) and perfects (8:54; 12:28; 17:1) the mission, that of the Son who visibly executes this life-giving mission (4: 34; 17:4) by both his words and deeds (5:20, 36; 10:32, 38; 15:3, 22, 24;

---

[2]The "Apostolic Exhortation" of Paul VI, *Evangelii Nuntiandi* (*AAS* 68 [1976] 1—76) describes the whole of Christ's life as mission work (see in particular no. 6, p. 9). Consequently it sees all aspects of the life of the Church as having a missionary scope. This is a marked progress from the earlier documents of Vatican II (e.g., *De Ecclesia,* 19; *On the Ministry and Life of Priests,* nos. 3, 5, 7), which all distinguished between "the mission of the Church" and "missionary preaching to non-believers." Though the theology of mission in these latter documents was said to be rooted in John's Gospel, it is doubtful that the distinction they made has a basis in the Gospel itself.

[3]Thus Joseph Kuhl (*Die Sendung,* 1), whose dissertation is devoted to the study of the theology of mission in John's Gospel, asks: "Was lässt sich aus dem vierten Ev entnehmen über die Mission, d.h. über die Sendung der Jüngergemeinschaft in der Zeit des Heiligen Geistes?" It remains to be seen whether this generally accepted view corresponds with the Evangelist's own understanding of mission.

[4]In McPolin's view ("Mission in the Fourth Gospel," 33) "mission for him [i.e., the Evangelist] means that God the Father or his Son or both send representatives into the world to help in the divine saving work." But though he states further that "all these missions are accomplished in the world" (p. 114), his definition does not sufficiently take into consideration the role of the audience.

17:6a, 8a; 19:30; cf. 12:24)[5], and that of the hearers who are called to respond to this mission both by personally believing in Jesus as the Father's agent (3:16b; 5:24; 8:24; 17:3; 20:31) and by making known to others the reality of his mission (4:38; 13:34–35; 15:27; 17:18, 20; 20:22–23, 30–31).

"Approach to mission" in this study thus refers to the whole manner in which the Evangelist understands and presents Jesus' mission from the Father in the Gospel. It dyes both the method by which Jesus communicates his life-giving message to his audience and the bearing which this whole presentation has on the living interaction between the Evangelist and his own audience.

B. Dimensions of the Johannine Approach: The Key Significance of Jn 20:30–31

Jn 20:30–31 furnishes the key not only to the evangelistic purpose of the Gospel but also to its essentially rhetorical character: it sets out to persuade and convince its audience to believe that Jesus is the Christ, the Son of God. A comparison with contemporary Hellenistic and rabbinic literature makes it possible to see Jn 20:30–31 as a formal rhetorical statement which provides the key as to how the material contained in the Gospel is to be read.

First, the reference to the selective nature of the Gospel material (20:30; 21:25) may be compared with Cicero's dictum that the law he gives are not exhaustive but only representative and all-inclusive. Quintilian further underlines that the selectivity of the written material is called for by the need of the audience, not that of the author: so that the student/reader may not get lost in a maze of information and so lose courage. On the rabbinic side, one may recall the Hillel legend, that in order to teach a Gentile the entire Torah while he is standing on one foot he reduced it to "What is hateful to you, do not to your fellowman," adding that the rest is interpretation (*b. Šabb.* 30b)[6].

---

[5]Bultmann ("Quellen," 145–146; *Johannes*[11], 103–104 and *Theologie*[3], 393–394) holds that Jesus reveals nothing other than that he is the Revealer. His view was heavily criticized from the outset. The review of his *Theologie* in *ExpT* 67 (1956) 97–98, for instance, regards his view as "a serious misrepresentation of John's thought at a cardinal point in his theology." Basic to this theology is the revelation of the Father's love for humanity (3:16) and the new commandment to love one another as Jesus and the Father love us. See further, "The Bultmannian Debate," *NTA* 1 (1956) 213–235.

[6]Cicero (*De Leg.* 2.7.18) writes: "Leges a me edentur non perfectae – nam esset infinitum – sed ipsae summae rerum atque sententiae." Quintilian, *Inst. Or.* V.x.100–101. For the NT parallels to the rabbinic tradition see Mt 7:12; 22:39–40; Gal 5:14; Rom 13:8–10.

Whether Jn 20:30—31 is to be regarded as the conclusion to the *Semeia-Evangelium* (so Bultmann, Wilkens, Fortna and Nicol), or whether it is to be seen as composed by the Evangelist (John II-B) for the bulk of the Gospel as we now have it (so Boismard and Lamouille) does not diminish its value[7]. On the contrary, the fact that at each successive stage of the Gospel's development the author(s) of the Gospel felt the need to retain this passage argues rather for its key signifiance for understanding the Gospel. It would, of course, be unacceptable to conclude on the basis of 20:30—31 alone that the whole Gospel is written from an essentially rhetorical standpoint. For the assertion to be valid, other formal rhetorical devices must be shown to be present in the body of the Gospel. This will form a correlative task of the present research[8].

We are not hereby suggesting that the Evangelist is writing rhetoric for its own sake, any more than did the Hellenistic rhetoricians[9]. The rhetorical framework appears rather to be at the service of his declared evangelistic and persuasive thrust. Once the formal rhetorical import and key character of 20:30—31 are recognized, it becomes possible to deduce from these verses three basic guidelines for the study of the Johannine approach to mission, namely, the selective and interpretative nature of the material itself (or the rhetorical dimension), the view of the work as "a book" (τῷ βιβλίῳ τούτῳ, 20:30) (or the historico-literary dimension), and the hermeneutical principles which governed his choice of the "signs" narrated (or the socio-cultural dimension).

---

[7]Bultmann, *Johannes,* 541; Wilhelm Wilkens, *Die Entstehungsgeschichte des vierten Evangeliums* (Zollikon: Evangelisher Verlag, 1958) 171 (note that Wilkens does not subscribe to the theory of the *Semeia Evangelium,* but proposes instead an original Johannine *Grundevangelium,* which contained a journey account of Jesus from Galilee to Jerusalem and which the Evangelist developed by adding the discourses, p. 30—31). Cf. Robert Fortna, *The Gospel of Signs: A Reconstruction of the Narrative Source Underlying the Fourth Gospel* (SNTSMS 11; Cambridge: University, 1970) 197—198. W. Nicol (*The Semeia in the Fourth Gospel; Tradition and Redaction* [Leiden: Brill, 1972] 9—14) gives a historical survey of the whole discussion on the theory of the "Semeia-source" from Wellhausen and Schwartz (1908) to J.L. Martyn (1970). See also Boismard-Lamouille, *Synopse III,* 474—475.

[8]For a fuller description of these different devices and NT examples of each see Daube, *The NT and Rabbinic Judaism,* 141—195. Meinertz (*Theologie* II, 268) states that forms and ideas of the epoch must help to interpret the Gospel. Similarly, Lindars (*Behind the Fourth Gospel,* 42, 61) praises the "rhetorical skills" of the author.

[9]That the ancient authors never aimed at writing purely aesthetic work is common knowledge (cf. Daube, "Hellenistic Rhetoric," 249—250). Thus even in his *Rhetoric,* Aristotle proves to be a thorough-going moralist. Not only does he insist that moral proofs should take precedence over objective and logical ones (1.13556a.20—30), but his *Rhetoric* itself is the outcome of his *Ethics* (see *Aristote, Rhétorique,* I, text and translation by Médéric Dufour [Paris: Les Belles Lettres, 1938] 47). Topics treated in the *Rhetoric* include "good reputation" (1.136a.20—30), and "virtues" (1.1356a, 1361b). See further Quintilian, *Inst. Or.* V.xii.2. For the rabbinic equivalent of "rules for good conduct" (*derek ʾereṣ*) see *The Minor Tractates of the Talmud* (2 vols.; London: Soncino, 1965, 1971), 2. 529—577.

1. The Rhetorical Dimension

The recognition of the selective and interpretative nature of John's Gospel is as old as Clement of Alexandria[10]. It is well attested to in the Gospel itself: Jesus is described as the Father's interpreter and revealer (1:18; 12:45; 14:9); the task of the Holy Spirit is to make plain to the disciples all that Jesus taught and wishes to teach them (14:26; 16:13); and the Gospel itself is a record of these events as it was understood and transmitted by the Beloved Disciple for the benefit of the audience (19:35; 21:24). There is, too, a criticism of the lifeless Scripture-searching of the Pharisees (ἐραυνᾶτε, 5:39; Hebr. דרש) which is contrasted with the life-giving revelatory activity of Jesus (5:40; 17:2—3, 6, 8). What is significant, however, is the conclusion to be drawn from this interpretative nature of the Gospel for its comprehension.

First, though the Evangelist believes in the historicity of the events recorded, "the signs which Jesus worked," events which also have eye-witnesses (15:27; 20:30), he is clearly not writing history for its own sake, nor is he necessarily recording the selective events in the chronological order in which they occurred. Rather the presentation is governed by the known order of the gospel genre itself — origin, ministry, and passion/glorification of Jesus — and secondly, according to the norms of rhetoric, by the need to persuade and convince the reader to take a faith stance towards Jesus[11].

From this it should follow that the techniques of "convincing preaching" or of "pastoral (*seelsorgerliche*) pedagogy" are not to be lightly dismissed as unimportant, but should rather be approached as an important aspect of the Evangelist's persuasive purpose[12]. Moreover, it should

---

[10]Clement of Alexandria, "Hypotyposeos VI" (Eus. *H.E.* 6.14.7); cf. Maurice Wiles, *The Spiritual Gospel: The Interpretation of the Fourth Gospel in the Early Church* (Cambridge: University, 1960), particularly the discussion on "The Fourth Gospel and the Synoptics," pp. 13—40.

[11]Indeed for Aristotle (*Rhét.* 1.1356a.5—10, 19) the "art" of the orator is the most important part of rhetoric. Quintilian (*Inst. Or.*) considers the "arrangement" (*dispositio*) to be so important that he devotes a whole book (VII) to it, holding that "however abundant the matter may be, it will merely form a confused heap unless arrangement be employed to reduce it to order and to give it connection and firmness of structure" (*Praef.* 1).

[12]Thus Schnackenburg (*Johannesevangelium* I, 456) maintains against Windisch, Lindars and others in the discussion of 4:1—42 that "Dem Evangelisten geht es nicht um eine pädagogisch-seelsorgerische Einwirkung Jesu auf die Frau, sondern um die stufenweise Selbstoffenbarung Jesu." This view is a criticism of Hans Windisch ("Der johanneische Erzählungsstil," ΕΥΧΑΡΙΣΤΗ-ΡΙΟΝ: *Studien zur Religion und Literatur des Alten und Neuen Testaments. Fs. Hermann Gunkel zum 60. Geburtstag* [Göttingen: Vandenhoeck und Ruprecht, 1923]174—213) who was the first in this century to praise the pastoral and pedagogical techniques of the Evangelist. Others who with Windisch see the Evangelist as a "good pedagogue" include Brown, *John* I, I—XII; Olsson, *Structure and Meaning*, 249—250. Others emphasize the "dramatic" qualities of the Evangelist's style. For instance, Martyn (*History and Tradition*, esp. pp. 5—16) who sees the Gospel as developed on the basis of a two level drama; Dodd, *Interpretation*, 311; John Bligh, "Jesus in Samaria" *HeyJ* 3 (1962) 329—346; and the commentaries.

follow that these persuasive techniques are important, not only in the macrocosm of the Gospel but in the microcosm of individual pericopae in so far as each of Jesus' encounters with his audience aims at persuading the audience in question to believe in him[13].

A major methodological issue which arises in this connection is the relation between Jesus' method of persuading his audience and that of the Evangelist. If, as is generally maintained, Jesus' interlocutors serve as paradigms of response for the audience of the Evangelist, can Jesus' persuasive style be seen, in turn, as the style of the Evangelist[14]? It is generally held that the dialogues and discourses of Jesus were in effect composed by the Evangelist and that all the characters in the Gospel speak the Johannine language[15]. Therefore, to discover Jesus' techniques of convincing preaching is also to discover those of the Evangelist. But the Evangelist's own method is further amplified by the use of the narrative technique through which he brings his reader to become personally involved in the interaction between Jesus and his audience, to identify with the appreciative audience and so come to the appropriate personal decision for Jesus.

An important question to be addressed in this whole connection, then, is whether the generally recognized rhetorical and literary devices used in the Gospel — parallelisms, *double-entendre,* asides, even the dialogue form itself — function merely on the literary, aesthetic level. Do they merely move the story forward, allow for a side comment, effect a variation in style, or are they called for by the missionary thrust itself and by the need to engage the interlocutor? The question is important in view of the opinion mentioned earlier that what matters is the Revelation and that Jesus' interlocutors serve mainly as "foils"[16].

2. The Historico-Literary Dimension

The second guideline for the understanding of the Johannine approach is that the Evangelist consciously describes his work as "a book." The

---

[13]The individualistic approach to the different characters of the Gospel is particularly emphasized by C.F.D. Moule, "The Individualism of the Fourth Gospel," *Essays In New Testament Interpretation* (Cambridge: University, 1982) 91–101.

[14]See, for instance, R.F. Collins, "Representative Figures in the Fourth Gospel," *Downside Review* 94 (314, 1976) 26–48, 118–132; Xavier Léon Dufour, "Towards a Symbolic Reading of the Fourth Gospel," *NTS* 27 (1981) 439–456, esp. p. 444; E. Kraft, "Die Personen des Johannesevangeliums," *EvT* 16 (1956) 18–32. Kraft argues strongly that the Johannine characters are purely symbolic.

[15]See in particular, Felix Porsch, *Pneuma und Wort,* 2; for Olsson (*Structure and Meaning,* 250) "Even the Samaritans speak in Johannine terms."

[16]See n. 1 above, and, besides the commentaries, Porsch, *Pneuma und Wort,* 82–83; M. Michel, "Nicodème ou le non-lieu de la vérité," *RevSR* 55 (1981) 227–236. Martyn (*History and Theology,* 110) holds that these characters are foils "only as far as it goes"; van den Bussche (*Jean:*

complete picture of his approach to mission, therefore, lies in the perspective of the whole work, in the cumulative effect of the entire book, rather than in isolated passages. In what way does the general plan of the Gospel serve to highlight the Evangelist's conception of mission? It is understood, of course, that the book underwent different levels of composition before it reached its present final form[17]. It is also generally recognized that even old material takes on new meaning when placed in a new context. Hence, whatever legitimate meaning the different contents of the Gospel material may have had in their previous contexts[18], their meaning in this present Gospel context, put together by the final Evangelist or his redac-

---

Commentaire de l'Evangile Spirituel [BVC, Brugis: Desclée de Brouwer, 1967] 178) prefers to see them as types.

[17]Theories on the composition and redaction of the Gospel are legion. See, in particular, the surveys by H. Teeple (*The Literary Origin of the Gospel of John* [Evanston: Religion and Ethics Institute, Inc., 1974]) whose research covers the period "from 1796 to the present day" (p. 1); Lindars, *Behind the Fourth Gospel*, 11–60; Kysar, *The Fourth Evangelist*, 9–78; Thyen, "Aus der Literatur," 39, 289–326. The most recent comprehensive individual study by Boismard-Lamouille (*Synopse III*) discerns four redactional levels in the composition of the Gospel: 1) Document C, a pre-Johannine source, written in Aramaic in Palestine (ca. A.D. 50) by the BD; 2) the first redaction of the Gospel by the Evangelist (John II-A), also written in Palestine (ca. A.D. 60–65); 3) the second redaction by the same Evangelist (John II-B) written in Ephesus (ca. A.D. 90) and 4) the final redaction by a Jewish Christian of the Johannine school, also in Ephesus (ca. early second century A.D.). The theory of these authors thus compares with that of Lindars (*Behind the Fourth Gospel*, 59–60) who posits that the Gospel was developed by the Evangelist in four successive stages (between the 80's and 90's): 1) the traditional material mainly story items and sayings from the Jesus-tradition which the Evangelist (2) first developed as homilies, then (3) committed into writing in the form of a gospel at the request of his hearers and (4) subsequently revised and expanded in a second edition.

It is most striking, however, that despite the seriousness with which this issue has been discussed in the course of the centuries, the research has yielded nothing approaching a universal consensus. This is mainly because of the disagreement over the criteria used to isolate the different sources and levels of redaction and also because the phenomena often attributed to redactional levels can be equally explained by the dialectic dimension of the Evangelist's own style. Thus the Gospel itself seems to defy the attempts to break it into redactional units (the diachronic approach). As a result, many scholars are increasingly advocating a return to the synthetic approach to the Gospel. See, for instance, Teeple, "Methodology in Source Aanalysis of the Fourth Gospel," *JBL* 81 (1962) 279–286; D.A. Carson, "Current Source Criticism of the Fourth Gospel," *JBL* 97 (1978) 411–439; and the reviews of *Synopse III*. Kysar (*The Fourth Evangelist*, 279) contends that the key to the enigma of John's Gospel may yet lie "in a more intense investigation of the literature we now have at our disposal." In our view, John's Gospel itself, in its present final form, must be given a priority rating among this "literature we now have."

[18]Suggestions of the possible forms in which some of the Gospel material could have existed independently before being incorporated into the present Gospel include "a collection of miracle stories" (the *SQ* or Document C) (Bultmann, Fortna, Nicol and Boismard-Lamouille), a "Reisebericht" of Jesus from Galilee through Samaria to Jerusalem (Wellhausen, Schwartz, Wilkens), "homilies" (Lindars, Schnackenburg, F.M. Braun, Barrett, Sanders) and "catechetical instructions" (Riesenfeld, Lindars). Some passages are also regarded as dominical sayings (3:3; 4:34) or as proverbs (4:35, 37). A technical description of the pre-Gospel forms of the Gospel material can be found in Martin Dibelius, *Die Formgeschichte des Evangeliums* (Tübingen: Mohr/Siebeck, 1919, 1933); Bultmann, *History of the Synoptic Tradition* (Oxford: Basil Blackwell, 1968); see in particular his index references to John (p. 641).

tor and addressed to its final audience in a new life-situation, deserves special attention[19].

An important consideration which arises from this literary dimension is that the Gospel, if not the Evangelist himself (cf. 19:35; 21:24), and his audience stand removed in time and space from the actual occurrence of the events narrated[20]. Yet there is a certain telescoping of the "then" of the time of Jesus and the "now" of the time of the audience of the Gospel (cf. 4:38). The most striking aspect of this telescoping is that Jesus is made vividly present to the audience of the Gospel by means of the dialogues and discourses[21]. Important as the audience of Jesus is, how-

---

[19]In the OT field, the importance for exegesis of the canonical shape of Scripture has received much attention in recent years because of the works of James A. Sanders, *Torah and Canon* (Philadelphia: Fortress, 1972); "Text and Canon: Concepts and Method," *JBL* 98 (1979) 5—29; and Brevard Childs, *Introduction to the Old Testament as Scripture* (Philadelphia: Fortress, 1979); "The Exegetical Significance of Canon for the Study of the Old Testament," *Suppl. VT.* 29 (Congress Volume; Leiden: Brill, 1978) 66—80. Unfortunately, there is no exact parallel to these studies in the NT field; but see the collection of essays edited by Käsemann, *Das Neue Testament als Kanon: Dokumentation und kritische Analyse zur gegenwärtigen Discussion* (Göttingen: Vandenhoeck and Ruprecht, 1970), especially the essays by Herbert Braun (pp. 219—232) and Willi Marxen (pp. 233—257).

While Sanders emphasizes the canonical process, Childs focuses almost exclusively on the "canonical shape" of the biblical text, and holds that understanding the canonical shape "requires the highest degree of exegetical skill in an intensive wrestling with the text" (*Introduction,* p. 73). Again, he sees the final form of the Bible as that "which alone bears witness to the full history of revelation" (pp. 75—76). Whatever may rightly be said about the tendency to rigidity in Child's general approach to the problem, his point about the normative value of the final text cannot lightly be dismissed. Nor can his view that the canon exercises in respect to the earlier stages of the literature's formation "a critical function" which includes "rearranging, selection, expansion" (p. 76).

This "critical function" certainly applies in the case of John's Gospel, as the redactional studies themselves admit. In the Boismard-Lamouille's hypothesis, for instance, not only did the Evangelist, John II-B undertake a radical rewriting of his earlier version of the Gospel (John II-A), but the final redactor, John III, deliberately changed the theology of the Evangelist on a number of key issues: he toned down the "high **Christology**" of the Evangelist and sought to mitigate his anti-Jewish, and anti-world attitudes (*Synopse III,* 48).

[20]We emphasize "the written Gospel" rather than "the Evangelist" because the debate on the identity of the author of the Gospel, an issue which is closely related to that of its composition and redaction, is still unresolved. While this is not the place to discuss the issue, it needs to be noted that the emphasis and great significance attached to the "eyewitness testimony" of the BD cannot be lightly dismissed as having no historical significance. The question of the identity of the BD (13:23, 25; 19:26, 20:2, 8; 21:7, 20, 24), namely, whether he was John the son of Zebedee (tradition), the presbyter of 2 and 3 John (Thyen) or Lazarus (Boismard-Lamouille), must not be confused with that of the historicity of his existence. For further discussion on the subject see Brown, *Community,* 31—34; Schnackenburg, *Johannesevangelium* I, 60—68; and Robinson, *Redating,* esp. 298—311.

[21]Since the narrative form is basic to the gospel genre, the Evangelist could just as well have given narrative and indirect discourses instead of narrative, dialogue and direct discourses. Or, as Amos N. Wilder (*Early Christian Rhetoric, The Language of the Gospel* [Cambridge: Havard University, 1974 = SCM: Harper and Row, 1964] 30) points out, he could have produced a work like the Coptic Gospel of Truth, "a meditation on the Incarnation of the Word or the visit to this world of the heavenly Revealer." The dialogue form, then, not only makes Jesus dramatically

ever, the primary audience of the Gospel is the Evangelist's own readers, for whose sole benefit the "signs" of Jesus and his interaction with his audience are recorded or replayed (20:31).

An examination of the Johannine approach, then, demands that paticular attention be paid to the possible ways in which this audience could have understood the Gospel message from its own historical perspective. It further dictates the need to look for the possible levels of meaning: the literary and the doubly historical, the theological and the paradigmatic, and their points of intersection, at least as much as we look for its levels of composition and redaction. This proves to be particularly necessary when dealing with such problematic passages as 4:38.

3. The Socio-Cultural Dimension

The final guideline for the study of the Johannine approach to mission concerns the hermeneutical principles which governed the Evangelist's selective interpretation of the "signs which Jesus did," which hermeneutical principles he may also have shared with his contemporary readers. In order to determine this accurately, we would need to know for certain the sources used (whether these were oral or written) and the authorship (whether there were many or one), and if there were more than one author whether they all had the same end in view in each of their successive redactions of the Gospel[22]. Since there are no universally acceptable criteria for resolving these questions, we are forced to look into the internal evidence of the Gospel itself and to contemporary Hellenistic and rabbinic literature for possible clues as to what some of the generally held hermeneutical principles might have been.

The external clues are to be sought in the rhetorical guidelines for writing and interpreting the law developed at length by the Hellenistic rhetoricians such as Cicero and Quintilian, and from Jewish sources in the seven hermeneutical norms of Hillel (ca. 10 B.C.–A.D. 10) later expanded into thirteen by Rabbi Ishmael (d. A.D. 135)[23]. Quintilian is

---

present (for this a direct speech in the first or third person would have been sufficient as in ancient historiography), but it also engages the personal response or participation of the audience.

[22]For further discussion of these issues see Kysar, *The Fourth Evangelist,* 277–281. Kysar himself criticizes works like Pierre le Fort's *Les structures de l'église militante selon saint Jean* (Genève, Labor et Fides, 1970) which in his view presume a unity of authorship for the Gospel and Johannine Epistles (p. 245). But Kysar's own strong stand (p. 246) based on Martyn's thesis (*History and Theology*), that the only enemies against which the church fought were synagogue Jews, not enemies from within the church itself, is equally debatable. We know as early as Paul's Galatians that a threat to faith from within the ecclesial communities themselves did exist. So a polemic within the Johannine community itself cannot be completely outruled. Besides, a number of critics maintain against Kysar a unity of authorship for the Gospel and Epistles. See for instance, Riesenfeld, "ἵνα -Sätzen," 217–220; Boismard-Lamouille, *Synopse III,* 69, 491 (Apendix I); Morton *et al, Computer Concordance, e*; and our own discussion of this subject in Chapter VII below.

[23]Cicero's theories are developed mainly in his *De Inventione* and *De Oratore*. On the seven

particularly important as an external source for our enquiry not only because he is a contemporary of the NT era (his years span from about 34 to A.D. 100) but also because his *Institutio Oratoria* builds on and comments copiously on the earlier works of the Greek and Roman rhetoricians[24]. We are not, of course, suggesting that the Johannine author(s) slavishly followed the norms set by the Greek rhetoricians or the Jewish rabbis. Rather, these examples from both Hellenism and Judaism are more apt to give us a keener insight into the kind of mental climate which nourished the hermeneutical outlook of the Evangelist and of his audience (whether these were Jews or Gentiles), than does our own twentieth century technological outlook[25].

The contemporary Hellenistic and Jewish evidence bears on both the attitude to the material itself and the norms used in interpreting the material. Most important for our purposes is the recognition that the interpretation of a text carried the same authority as the text itself. Respect for "the tradition of the Fathers" (*Tg. Job* 15:18), for "the oral and the written Torah," (Hillel's "two Toroth," *b. Šabb.* 31a) stems from and testifies to this fact[26]. Indeed, since among the Graeco-Romans the law was supposed to be by nature concise, dealing only with the basics and the representative, it was only the interpretation, deliberately foreseen by the lawgiver, which gave it its complete meaning[27]. Furthermore,

---

hermeneutical norms of Hillel, see in particular *ARN* 37:10 (32a–32b), *t. Sanh.* 7:11, and *Sipra* Intro. 1:5; on R. Ishmael see *Sipra* Intro. 1:5; also "Hermeneutics," *Judaica* 8 (1971) 366–367 (on Hillel) and 367–370 (on Ishmael). Ishmael simply expanded Hillel's seven norms to 12 and added a thirteenth (cf. *Sipra* 1:7).

[24]In this research we shall, therefore, limit most of our references to Quintilian.

[25]On the influence of Hellenistic rhetoric on rabbinic and NT exegesis, see in addition to the literature cited in n. 9 above, M. Hengel, *Judaism and Hellenism, Studies in Their Encouter in Palestine during the Early Hellenistic Period* (2 vols.; Philadelphia: Fortress, 1974), esp. the sections on the influence of Greek Education on Judaism, 1. 65–73, 107–254 and the corresponding footnotes in vol. 2. Herman L. Strack, *Introduction to the Talmud and Midrash* (New York: Atheneum, 1974) 95; Joseph Bonsirven, *Textes rabbiniques des deux premières sciècles chrétiens: Pour servir à l'intelligence du Nouveau Testament* (Rome: Pontifical Biblical Institute, 1955); J.W. Doeve, *Jewish Hermeneutics in the Synoptic Gospels and Acts* (Assen: van Gorcum, 1954) and the bibliography given on pp. 208–214; and Asher Finkel, *The Pharisees and the Teacher of Nazareth* (AGSU IV; Leiden: Brill, 1964).

[26]On the "tradition of the Fathers" (πατέρων διαδοχή or παράδοσις τῶν πατέρων) see further Jos. *Ant.* 13.10.6; Mt 15:2; Mk 7:3, 5. Daube ("Rabbinic Methods," 242–243) holds that this respect is indebted to Plato's praise of "ancestral customs, which if well established, form a cover around the written laws for their full protection" (Plato, *Laws* 7.793B).

[27]See, for instance, Cicero, *De Inv.* 2.50.150–152; *Auctor ad Herennium*, 2.10.14; 2.12.18; Aristotle, *Rhét.* 1.13.13; Plato, *Statesman* 298Af.; Quintilian, *Inst. Or.* V.x.100–101; VIII. *Praef.* 3; Julian, *Digest* 1.3.10; and for rabbinic sources, *m. Ed.* 1.12. The belief that the oral Torah also came from Sinai is yet another convincing evidence that the rabbis did accept the principle that interpretation itself was foreseen by the lawgiver.

Since most of the examples cited above deal with Hellenistic-Roman jurisprudence and were adapted for the interpretation of the Torah by Hillel and his successors, the question needs to be raised whether John's Gospel does see Jesus and the Jesus-traditions which he interprets as having the same weight as the Torah. Put this way the answer is certainly positive: Not only does Jesus

since the interpretation was based on material already known to both the interpreter and the audience, it was acceptable to rearrange when necessary the sequence of events in order to bring out their true meaning[28].

Once these facts are recognized, it becomes less problematic that the Gospel attributes to Jesus and other characters speeches which in their present Gospel form are composed by the Evangelist himself, even though they are based on general traditions about Jesus (cf. the Johannine flavor of the Q saying used in Lk 10:22; Mt 11:27). These interpreted traditions can still be called "gospel," however recognizably different from the Synoptic accounts of Jesus' life they may be. Similarly, the current debate on whether Jesus of Narazeth spoke like the Johannine Christ, and if not, whether the Fourth Gospel is historically reliable also loses much of its force, being essentially a twentieth century problem, not that of the Evangelist or his contemporary audience. The whole issue of the relationship between John and the Synoptics also assumes a new dimension. The real issue then becomes, not whether or not John knew the Synoptics (or for that matter the Pauline traditions), but in what distinctive ways or by what new categories he reinterprets these known Jesus-traditions, at times supplementing, expanding and even correcting them, and, most importantly, for what purpose[29]? The role of the author of the Fourth Gospel as both Evangelist (a narrator of facts) and interpreter thus deserves a more positive evaluation[30].

---

have the same authority as the Torah, he indeed fulfils and *transcends* the Torah: the Law was given through Moses, but grace and truth came into being through Jesus Christ (1:17); Moses, the Lawgiver, and Scripture itself are only mere witnesses to Jesus (cf. 5:39—40, 54—47). Indeed, Scripture itself becomes credible only because of the words which Jesus had spoken (2:22). Finally, Jesus as God and Logos (1:1) is contrasted in an *a minori ad maius* argument with those to whom the word of God was merely addressed (10:34—36).

[28]Cf. Aristotle, *Rhét.* 1.1357a.1—7; while Cicero (*De Or.* 2.8.30) argues that art, not rhetoric, deals with what is known, Quintilian (*Inst. Or.* II.xvii.41—43) argues that rhetoric itself is an art, hence it deals with what is known. In his view, the subject of rhetoric covers both public matters and private affairs (II.xxi.4—6).

Indeed, the whole concept of interpretation itself presupposes known facts. Rabbinic exegesis with its eclectic style presupposes sound knowledge of the Scriptures. A homily in the synagogue service is based on a text which is first read (cf. Lk 4:16—22; Acts 13:15—41). Moreover, the very need to persuade the reader to the author's view-point, that Jesus is the Christ, the Son of God, means that the reader in question is capable of drawing an opposite conclusion from the one proposed by the Evangelist. In this context, the arrangement of the material, the *dispositio*, becomes very important as a persuasive strategy. That John's Gospel presupposes in his readers a basic knowledge of some, at least, of the Jesus-traditions is evident in such passages as 1:15, 30 (cf. Mt 1:3). De Solage (*Jean et les synoptiques* [Leiden: Brill, 1979] 170) believes that John not only cites few Synoptic material but that he deliberately avoids repeating them when he has no special reason to do so. See further, Smalley, *Evangelist and Interpreter*, esp. 150—242.

[29]On the relation between John and the Synoptics see, Boismard-Lamouille, *Synopse III*, 69; De Solage, *Jean*, 172—185; Moule, *Essays*, 104; Frans Neirynck, *Jean et les synoptiques, examen critiques de l'exégèse de M.-E. Boismard* (*BETL* 49; Leuven University, 1979); Josef Blinzler, *Johannes und die Synoptiker: Ein Forschungsbericht* (SSB 5; Stuttgart: Katholisches Bibelwerk, 1965); and Becker, "Aus der Literatur zum Johannesevangelium," 289—290.

[30]Redaction criticism has shown that the first three Evangelists were also interpreters. But it

The norms of interpretation include not only the seven rules of Hillel later expanded by Rabbi Ishmael[31], but also, as Daube amply demonstrates, various techniques and settings which served as conventional contexts for interpretation[32]. The following techniques and norms are particularly pertinent for our examination of the Johannine approach: the forensic variety of the halakhic type for which the setting in life is public attack and refutation of charges[33], the philosophical variety of the haggadic type, based on spontaneous inquiry, the odd gesture-question-pronouncement defined by the καθώς, καί motif (cf. Jn 13:1–17) all of which function in the context of instruction, arguments *a fortiori, a minori ad maius* (the *qal waḥōmer*) and by inference and analogy. The presence of some of these techniques in John's Gospel has already been noted, for instance, the halakhic elements by Borgen[34]. They offer a new insight, however, for understanding the Gospel when they are viewed as part of a recognizable system of interpretative techniques which underlie the Gospel, techniques which the Evangelist shared culturally with his contemporaries and which he musters in his efforts to persuade his contemporary readers to believe that Jesus is the Christ, the Son of God (20:30–31).

The internal clues to the Evangelist's hermeneutical principles are to be derived mainly from the key he furnishes to the reading of his "book,"

---

is also generally recognized that John's Gospel is the most interpretative of the four gospels. The declared interpretative thrust (20:30–31) which is missing in the Synoptics is itself evidence of this. A good example of the interpretative thrust of the Gospel lies in the Johannine approach to the sacraments. While the Synoptics tend to emphasize their institution (baptism, Mt 28:16–20; cf. *Didache* 7:1–3; the Eucharist, Mt 26:26–29; Mk 14:22–25; Lk 22:15–20) John, on the contrary, focuses on their meaning for the individual: baptism means "birth from above" which results in a new kind of life (3:3–8, 20–21), and the Eucharist, the bread of life (6:31–59), becomes a true remembrance of the Lord when it is lived out as self-sacrificing love after his own example (13:1–17, 34–35; 15:9–17). Moule, (*Essays*, 104) is right when he holds that "perhaps the Evangelist is consciously and deliberately interpreting the sacraments themselves in terms of other categories rather than interpreting other categories by means of the sacraments."

[31]On the role of these two men as founders of rabbinic exegesis see *b. Sukk.* 20a; *Sota* 48b (where Hillel is compared to Ezra) and *b. Sabb.* 116a (which describes Ishmael as the leading haggadist).

[32]For a fuller description of these techniques and some examples see Daube, *NT and Rabbinic Judaism*, 151–157, 175–183, 325–329.

[33]For a fuller description of the forensic type of rhetoric see Aristotle, *Rhet.* 1.2.26, 2.13; Quintilian, *Inst. Or.* III.ix.1–9, x; VIII.*Praef.*11; Cicero, *De Or.* 1.56.240; Julian, *Digest* 1.2.2,5; *b. Pesaḥ.* 66a; *y. Pesaḥ.* 33a (Hillel on trial before the Bene Bathyra).

[34]Peder Borgen, *Bread from Heaven: An Exegetical Study of the Concept of Manna in the Gospel of John and the Writings of Philo* (Leiden: Brill, 1965), and "God's Agent." Borgen's thesis is that Jewish halakhic principles, not Gnostic ones as Bultmann maintains, color the Johannine re-presentation of Jesus as the messenger from heaven. His focus, therefore, differs from that proposed in this study, which entails seeing the halakhic approach itself as part of a wholly different system of hermeneutics with firm roots in the Hellenistic-Jewish culture.

namely, in 20:30—31. These principles are basically two. It is in his statement of both that we meet his own distinctive departure from contemporary Jewish and Hellenistic concerns and encounter what transforms his work from a predominantly rhetorical/literary endeavor into a Gospel of "grace and truth" (cf. 1:17): First, 20:31 presupposes that, to the audience addressed, the categories "Christ, Son of God," "believing" and "eternal life" were meaningful concepts. A major concern of the Gospel, then, is to show convincingly that Jesus is indeed the Christ, the Son of God and giver of eternal life. If this portrayal is done from the standpoint of mission, as suggested, it is done in terms of what this portrayal means for the reader, not in terms of dogmatic treatise. Fundamental, therefore, to the understanding of the Johannine approach is that his Christology is pastorally functional. Questions asked of the Gospel on the level of exegesis must needs stay within this soteriological frame of reference.

Second, John's hermeneutical principle also operates within a faith context, both as its starting point (the faith of the Evangelist and of his fellow disciples who witnessed Jesus' mission, 15:27; 17:8; 20:30), and as its desired goal (the faith which he hopes to evoke in his intended audience, 20:31). Thus just as the Gospel is written from the standpoint of Jesus' mission seen as a gift (3:16), and for a missionary purpose, the constant human response which it seeks to evoke from its readers is that of faith generated by faith (3:16b, 20:31). The faith dimension of the Gospel emerges, then, as one of the basic hermeneutical principles of which one must never lose sight of, even if one does not share the Evangelist's own faith stance[35].

To sum up, these then are the three major aspects of the Johannine approach which will guide our enquiry into his conception of mission: the selective and interpretative nature of his material, the progressive and cumulative effect of the book which records events for the benefit of a non-eyewitnessing audience, and the hermeneutical principles at work in this portrayal of the past events of Jesus' life. All three aspects derive from and are in function of the hortatory/persuasive thrust of the Gospel. Therefore, by highlighting the presence of these different techniques in the Gospel and paying particular attention to the use the Evangelist makes of them in view of his readers, the research hopes to arrive at a more unified appraisal of his conception of mission. The underlying task again will be to determine the kind of situation which would have called for this hortatory/persuasive approach to the traditions concerning the identity and mission of Jesus, the Christ and Son of God.

---

[35]Cf. Juan Leal, "El clima de la fa en la Redaktionsgeschichte del IV Evangelio," *Estudios Biblicos* 22 (1963) 141—177.

C. The Methodology of the Present Research

1. The Contextual Method

Given this investigation's focus on the way the Evangelist handles the topic of mission, and the lack of established or universally accepted norms by which to control Johannine redactional activity, contextual study offers the method best suited to the exegetical task[36]. Contextual study may be described as a method which combines rhetorical and literary analysis in the quest for theological meaning viewed from the standpoint of the Evangelist and of his intended audience. The characteristics of this method may be briefly outlined as follows:

First, while not denying, and even while positively dialoguing with current theories on the composition and redaction of the Gospel and its individual contents, contextual study emphasizes the canonical text in its final redaction as both the final author and his audience would have understood it. Since the total context of the Gospel includes the work seen as "a book," one passage is used to highlight another and the relationship of the different parts are stressed[37]. The *Sitz-im-Leben* is also that of the Evangelist and of the audience of his final published work[38].

Second, in determining meaning, especially in controversial passages, contextual study gives logical priority to the viewpoint of the author and the order established by him in the text. This states what is obvious. Nevertheless, the point needs to be stated; it has even been stressed by Schnackenburg, Brown and others[39]. Accordingly, instead of readily resorting to theories of redaction and composition to explain what is deemed as contradictory passages, contextual study pays attention first to the possible dialectic, an aspect of the basic rhetorical mode in which the Gospel is cast, and which may inform the given passage.

---

[36]Critical surveys on the state of Johannine redaction can be found in Kysar, *The Fourth Evangelist*, 67–76; Thyen, "Aus der Literatur," 289–291; and Boismard-Lamouille, *Synopse III*, 9–70.

[37]On the need to emphasize the relationship of the different parts in interpreting the Gospel see, in particular, Teeple, "Methodology," 282–286; Cullmann, *Johanneische Kreis*, 10; and Thyen, "Aus der Literatur," 48–50 (where he stresses the importance of works "die also alle Details als Strukturmomente des Ganzen zu begreifen und ihren Funktionswert innerhalb des einheitlichen Systems zu bestimmen suchen" [p. 49]).

[38]It is generally held that each redaction of the Gospel was destined to meet the special needs of the community addressed. Cf. Kysar, *The Fourth Evangelist*, 81. The different reconstructions of the different stages of the Johannine community are also based on this principle. If such is the case, then the missionary emphasis which shall emerge from this research needs to be related to the missionary needs of the community to which the Gospel in its final form was addressed.

[39]Schnackenburg, "Das Johannesevangelium als hermeneutische Frage," *NTS* 13 (1966–1967) 197–210, esp. pp. 204–210. (Note that the pages in this issue of *NTS* are wrongly numbered.) See also Brown, "The Johannine Sacramentary Reconsidered," *TS* 23 (1962) 183–206, esp. 192, 195; Dodd, *Interpretation*, 290; Teeple, "Methodology," 297–282; Thyen, "Aus der Literatur," 49–50.

The aids given in the Gospel itself for determining the viewpoint of the author include: 1) knowledge which he attributes to or presupposes in his characters and the way in which these characters understand and interpret the events of which they are a part; 2) the structural order and context in which the events are placed (for instance, if, as is maintained, Jn 4:8, 27, 31–38 taken together is a late interpolation into an already existing story of Jesus' encounter with the Samaritan woman, why was this particular episode inserted into this particular story and in its present order?); and 3) the Evangelist's own interpretations given either as asides (4:9) or by the use of the interpretative formula ὅ ἐστιν μεθερμηνευόμενον (1:41; cf. 4:25)[40]. In brief, the contextual approach pays attention to possible ways in which the Evangelist might have employed or adapted any of the hermeneutical and rhetorical modes, both Jewish and Hellenistic, outlined above.

Third, where the precise meaning of individual words and concepts are disputed, and unless there is strong evidence to the contrary, contextual approach works on the presupposition that the Evangelist is reasonably consistent in his use of terminology, and so looks for his meaning in the disputed passage both in the immediate context and by having recourse to his usage in other parts of the Gospel. This will prove to be particularly necessary when discussing the meaning in context of such words as κοπιᾶν (4:6, 38), λαλεῖν/λαλιά (4:26, 42; cf. 9:37; 15:22) and μαρτυρεῖν (4:30; cf. 1:29, 34; 5:31–33; 15:27)[41].

Contextual study may thus be summatively described as a "listening approach" in that it lets the Gospel dictate its own hermeneutical principles and pays attention to the different levels of Johannine rhetoric briefly surveyed above. Thus, the method fosters attention not only to what is being said in the text, but, most importantly, to how and, ultimately, to why. The "why" belongs on the level of speculation and can only be inferred from the "what" and the "how" in corroboration with other possible contemporary evidence which may lie outside the Gospel itself. In the last analysis, therefore, the contextual method is essentially a synchronic approach since it seeks to coordinate the different levels of meaning, the literary and the theological, the historical and the hermeneutical, with a view to offering a unified interpretation of the Evangelist's conception of mission[42].

---

[40]See further, Teeple, "Methodology," *passim.*

[41]This point is important because there is a tendency in exegetes arbitrarily to assign different meanings to the same concepts in different parts of the Gospel, for instance, the "witness" of the woman in 4:28–29, 42. Quite often, this tendency reflects more our twentieth century theological presuppositions than the Evangelist's own concerns.

[42]To the extent in which contextual method seeks to come to grips with the viewpoint and message of the final text, it can be compared with redaction criticism in so far as this latter also seeks to delineate the distinctive voice of a given author (Matthew, Mark, or Luke) from that of his sources and traditions. But the basic difference lies in the fact that in John we have no universally recognized sources or proven methods by which to separate his redaction from his traditional mat-

2. Criteria for the Selection of Texts

The widely held view that mission is the leitmotif of the Gospel, or, in our view, the basic hermeneutic at work in the Evangelist's mind, means that the entire Gospel can be interpreted from the standpoint of mission. Moreover, since the *dispositio* constitutes an important aspect of meaning in any rhetorical work, a comprehensive treatment of the Johannine approach would require a systematic analysis of the entire Gospel, "the signs which Jesus worked" (20:30), since it is through the entire presentation that the Evangelist seeks to persuade his reader "to believe that Jesus is the Christ, the Son of God" (20:31)[43]. But since it would be impractical, beyond the scope of a dissertation, to undertake an analysis of the entire Gospel material, it becomes necessary to reduce the enquiry to workable proportions, but to do so in such a way that the material selected will be broad enough to encompass the central missionary issues raised in the Gospel, yet narrow enough to permit a close observation of the Evangelist at work. This raises the methodological question of the criteria for the selection of texts. What determines such criteria?

First, *the terminology of sending* comes readily to mind; the basic vocabulary of mission in the Gospel has already been documented in our initial survey of the Johannine data. But the vocabulary of mission in the Gospel is much wider than the verbs πέμπειν, ἀποστέλλειν and ἔρχεσθαι or those studied by Kuhl, Miranda, Rademarkers, Moule and others[44]. These lists tend to focus exclusively on the "sending/coming" of Jesus to the point of overlooking the importance of his living interaction with his audience and the terminology which this interaction carries with it. In our view, therefore, a more complete list of the Johannine terminology of

---

erial. Hence we have no way of measuring satisfactorily his redactional activity. In the last analysis, however, is it absolutely essential to have Mark's version of a given pericope before we can hear what Luke is saying in the same pericope? Comparisons help to illumine meaning but they do not constitute a *sine qua non* for hearing what any given passage says in its own right. See further Lindars, *Behind the Fourth Gospel,* 60–61.

[43]Different structures proposed for the Gospel include that of Kümmel (*Einleitung,* 160): Jesus' work in the world, 1:19–12:50; his return to the Father, 13:1–20:29; a prologue, 1:1–18; and a postscript 20:30–21:25. The more popular division is that of Brown, (*John* I, cxxxviii–cxxxix): "Prologue," 1:1–18; "The Book of Signs," 1:19–12:50; "The Book of Glory," 13:1–20:31; and Epilogue, 21:1–25. This division runs into conflict with the fact that the "signs" reveal Jesus' glory (2:11; cf. 2:23–25) and that the resurrection itself is seen as the summit of Jesus' "signs" (2:18–22; 8:28; 12:16). Van den Bussche, (*Jean,* 53, 59) also proposes a bipartite structure: Première partie, le jour de Jésus, sa vie publique, révélation voilée de sa gloire (ch. 2–12); Deuxième partie: L'heure de Jésus, la révélation de sa gloire (chs. 13–20). But his subsequent division of the Gospel into five books is an implicit admission that the Gospel cannot be divided into two clear-cut parts.

[44]Kuhl, *Die Sendung Jesu,* 53–57, 130–133; Miranda, *Der Vater der mich gesandt hat,* 8–18 (ἀποστέλλειν), 29–31 (πέμπειν), 39–43 (ἔρχεσθαι), 52–57 (καταβαίνειν), 82–87 (φανεροῦν), 100–104 (φωτίζειν and φαίνειν), 123–124 (διδόναι) and his synthesis, 129–307; Radermakers, "Mission et apostolat," esp. 100–112; Moule, *Essays,* 105–109 (on the coming, going and returning of Jesus); cf. Rengstorf, *TDNT* I, 398–447.

mission would be expanded to include: 1) *from the perspective of the Father*: the terms διδόναι (3:16), ζητεῖν (4:23c), ἑλκύειν (6:44), ἐργάζεσθαι (5:17), ζωοποιεῖν (5:21), δοξάζειν (12:28), ἔργον (4:34) and γεωργός (15:1); 2) *from the perspective of the Son:* καταβαίνειν (3:13), λαλεῖν (3:11, 34), κοπιᾶν (4:6, 38), κρίνειν (3:19; 5:27; 9:38), ἀκούειν (5:30), ζωοποιεῖν (5:21), τιμᾶν (8:49), and ποιεῖν / τελεῖν (4:34; 5:36; 17:4); and 3) *from the standpoint of the audience:* πιστεύειν (3:16, 17; 20:31); ἀκούειν (5:24), ἔρχεσθαι (5:40, 43), τιμᾶν (5:23), λαμβάνειν (1:11; 5:43), and θερίζειν (4:38).

The list is by no means exhaustive but it highlights two important facts: first, that terminology itself is just as expansive as the Gospel material, even though there appears to be a marked concentration in the dialogue sections of the Gospel (3—12)[45]; and second, that, as McPolin rightly observes, terminology is only an aspect of mission[46]. To use terminology, then, as the basic criterion for the enquiry would be to confine the study to the realm of ideas and abstractions, as is particularly the case with Miranda's dissertation[47]. This would defeat the whole purpose of this investigation which is to examine, not only the movement from the sender to the one sent, but most specifically the execution of the commission connected with the sending, the living interaction between the agent and his audience. Terminology makes full sense only when studied within this context of living interaction or as an aspect of this total conception of mission.

Given, then, the emphasis on mission in the Gospel as a living interaction between Jesus and his audience, those passages which treat the subject in the context of living encounter offer the most appropriate basis for our enquiry. These passsages are the dialogue sections in 3—10. These are also the passages in which the vocabulary of mission is most heavily concentrated and which receive most attention in studies on the mission of the Son[48]. In addition, the Gospel also portrays the mission of the Baptist as actually taking place within the context of Jesus' mission.

---

[45]This is true not only of the verbs of sending, but also of the whole discussion on Jesus' works. The only other section in which there is a concentration of terminology of mission is in chapters 13—17, where the missionary issues discussed in the dialogue sections are recapitulated, and where the missions of the Holy Spirit and of the disciples are described on the analogy of that of Jesus. Cf. 4:34; 5:30 and 17:4; or 5:20, 26; 7:3, 21; 10:25, 32, 33, 37, 38 and 14:10, 11; 15:22.

[46]McPolin, "Mission in the Fourth Gospel," 114, n. 5.

[47]Miranda, *Der Vater der mich gesandt hat,* esp. the summary of his analysis based on terminology, pp. 305—307.

[48]Jesus is not received, even though he comes in his Father's name (5:38, 43, 44); his works are the works of the Father and they bear witness to him (5:20, 36; 7:21; 10:25, 32, 37, 38); he comes from God but not to judge the world (3:2; 5:24, 40, 43); his audience debate whether or not he is the expected Messiah (7:27, 31); in contrast to his audience, Jesus knows his whence and whither (7:34, 36; 8:21). Bultmann's discussion of the mission of the Revealer as "the judge," for instance, centers on 5:1—47; 7:15—24 and 8:13—30 (*Commentary*, 237—284); and that of the hiddenness and contingency of revelation on 7:1—14, 25—52; 8:48—50, 54—55.

Hence, those passages which deal with his mission should also receive special attention: 1:6—8, 15, 19—37; 3:22—36; 5:31—36.

Though the farewell discourses and Jesus' departing prayer (13—17) obviously form an integral part of his mission, they add nothing essentially new to the fundamental conception of mission dramatically portrayed in the dialogue section. Rather they can be seen as a resume of the meaning of Jesus' mission, the aim of which is to explain more fully to the disciples the full meaning of this mission and its significance for them personally both as those who respond to and benefit from it themselves (15:1—18) and who are to become its living witnesses to others (15: 27; 17:20). The peculiar relationship between Jesus and his disciples in the execution of mission is underlined in these discourses by the dominance of the καθώς, καί motif[49]. In the general opinion of scholars, these discourses reflect in a special way the *Sitz-im-Leben* of the Evangelist and of his community. The missionary issues underlined in them should, therefore, serve as further guide to our understanding of the missionary issues alive in his community.

It is obvious that a detailed exegesis of the dialogue passages (3—10) would still not be feasible within the scope of a dissertation. A valid methodological procedure, then, is to select from among them for detailed analysis one passage (the basic text) which best demonstrates the interaction between Jesus and a variety of audiences as well as the different missionary moments present in the Gospel. Once the major issues and characteristics of the Evangelist's approach have been highlighted in this basic text, the other passages should be examined using as guidelines the results obtained from the analysis of the basic text. This wider contextualization should, in turn, test the results of the basic text, whether or not the issues highlighted can validly be considered as representative of the missionary concerns in the entire Gospel, or whether they are limited to the isolated passage.

Jn 4:1—42 best meets this criterion of basic text for the following internal and external reasons. On *the internal level*, the passage mentions

---

[49] In the earlier part of the Gospel, notably in the dialogue with the Jews, the καθώς, οὔτως or ὧσπερ, οὔτως motif defines Jesus' relationship with the Father in his capacity both as Son by virtue of which he does the exact same works as the Father (e.g., 5:19—23, 26—27) and as one sent by virtue of which he carries out his mission in complete dependence on and obedience to the Father (5:30; 8:28b). In the farewell discourses, on the contrary, the motif draws attention to the exemplary function which Jesus' whole method and attitude in the execution of his mission holds for the disciples, in particular, to the need for the disciples to be humble in the exercise of their mission both in regard to their mutual service (13:1—17) and to their complete dependence on Jesus or in obedience to him their sender (15:9—10; 20:21). Thus, as it applies to the disciples, the motif nowhere refers to their equality with Jesus in the missionary enterprise, except, perhaps, to the extent that they are to expect from their own audience the exact same rejection which Jesus himself experienced, because ultimately, such a response is a response to his, not to their mission (15:18—16:4). The discussion on the relationship between Jesus and the disciples in the exercise of mission will form an integral part of this research.

all the important characters involved in the missionary enterprise: the Father who sends and to whom the entire missionary work belongs (v 34), Jesus the one sent who does and completes this work of the Father (v 34), and the human audience for whose benefit the mission takes place, both non-believers (the Samaritan woman and the Samaritans) and prospective missionaries (the disciples, vv 31–38; cf. 42). The passage also mentions the Holy Spirit who enables believers genuinely to worship the Father (v 24). Discussed also are the important issues of Jesus' messiahship (vv 25–26), his life-giving mission (vv 10–15), and the relationship to Jesus' mission of the mission of the disciples (vv 31–42). In addition, the whole encounter takes place in a foreign country, for Jesus is neither a Samaritan nor from Samaria (vv 4, 9, 20, 22). In terms of the evangelistic thrust of the entire Gospel, the passage presents a complete process whereby the revelation of Jesus leads to faith in him (vv 29–30, 39, 42).

On the level of style, the passage contains narrative, dialogue and a didactic section which resembles very closely the style of the discourses, also addressed directly to the disciples (vv 31–38). Nor, finally, is the passage lacking in the terminology of mission as it applies to the Father: διδόναι (v. 10), ζητεῖν (v 23c), ἔργον (v 34a); to Jesus: κοπιᾶν (vv 6, 38), ποιεῖν / τελεῖν (v 34); and to the audience: ἔρχεσθαι (v 30) πιστεύειν (vv 39, 42) and θερίζειν (v 38).

On *the external level*, Jn 4:1–42 is the one passage in the Gospel which is most widely recognized as being indisputably concerned with mission, even if this mission is understood primarily as the mission of the disciples[50]. Thus both the internal and external reasons justify the choice of 4:1–42 as a solid basis for an enquiry into the nature of the Johannine approach to mission. In many ways, the passage proves to be a miniature of the whole Gospel.

3. The Design of the Study

In the light of the methodological principles outlined above and in keeping with the characteristics of both the Johannine approach and the contextual method described earlier in this chapter, this investigation will now proceed as follows: Part II of the study (made up of three chapters, III–V) will be devoted to a careful exegesis of the basic text (4:1–42) and Part III to a consideration of the contexts, both Gospel (Chapter VI) and social (Chapter VII), of the missionary issues highlighted in the analysis of the basic text. The scope of the individual chapters will be as follows:

---

[50]John Bligh, "Jesus in Samaria," 329–346; Olsson, *Structure*, 239–257; Roustang, "Les moments de l'acte de foi et ses conditions de possibilité," *RechSR* 46 (1958) 344–378; Cullmann, "Samaria and the Origins of the Christian Mission," *The Early Church*, 183–192; Dodd, *Interpretation*, 316.

Chapter III will be devoted to an examination of contemporary discussion on 4:1–42, with regard both to the problems posed by literary criticism for the interpretation of the text as a unified whole and to the specifically missionary interpretations of the text. This chapter (which will necessarily be short) will highlight the methodological problems involved in Johannine studies of which 4:1–42 is only an example. At the same time the discussion should pinpoint the problematic or unresolved areas with which this present exegesis needs to reckon.

Chapter IV will be devoted to the exegesis of vv 1–26, namely, Jesus' encounter with the Samaritan woman. The analysis will focus on the missionary features of the passage, the level of interaction between Jesus and the woman, as well as on the methodological procedures adopted by the Evangelist in his narrative dialogue. The exegesis will thus try to highlight the relationship between the content of the dialogue (what is being said) and the manner in which it unfolds, all viewed from the standpoint of mission.

Chapter V will set forth the analysis of vv 27–42, paying special attention to its different levels of meaning and to its literary and theological relationship to vv 1–26. The ultimate goal of the analysis of 4:1–42 will thus be to determine whether the whole of 4:1–42, not just the generally recognized vv 31–38, can be interpreted from the standpoint of mission.

Chapter VI will attempt to place within the context of the entire Gospel the major missionary issues highlighted in Part II. By placing the results of the analysis of 4:1–42 within the general framework of the Gospel, this Chapter will serve both as a control and as a further elucidation of the features of the Johannine approach. The joint evidence of both the basic text and the Gospel as a whole concerning the features of the Evangelist's approach should serve as a sound basis for our enquiry into the missionary *Sitz-im-Leben* of the Evangelist's community.

Chapter VII will initiate a discussion on the missionary situation of the Evangelist and of his audience, based on the results of the Gospel evidence concerning the distinctive features of the Evangelist's approach. Thus this Chapter will attempt to discuss the "why" of this approach. In other words, it will seek to establish the relationship between the missionary emphases present in the Gospel and the factors in the living situation of the Evangelist and of his audience which could have shaped his conception of mission. To what extend does the portrayal of mission in the Gospel reflect the missionary concerns of the Evangelist and of his community at the time the present Gospel was written? For instance, can we say on the basis of the Gospel evidence that the audience addressed consisted of would-be converts, crypto-Christians, the Christian missionaries themselves or all of these combined? The choice of NT works to be examined in this connection will be determined by the results of the analysis of the Gospel material. But in keeping with our contextual approach we will progressively seek for the evidence of the missionary situation of the Evangelist first within the Gospel itself, in dialogue with views previously advanced, especially in connection with the farewell discourses, then within the Johannine Epistles and finally within any relevant NT works.

Chapter VIII will summarize the conclusions of the research by drawing together the salient features of the Johannine approach as it relates to the living inspirational context of the Evangelist's work. It will also highlight the significance which this research holds for future Johannine studies. In particular, it will offer reflections on both the value, if any, of the contextual method and on the rhetorical significance of the Evangelist's own approach.

Chapter III

John 4:1–42 in Contemporary Scholarship

The present investigation, it has been noted, emphasizes the Gospel in its present final form. Nevertheless, the questions raised by the results of literary criticism concerning the unified meaning of 4:1–42 appear to be too significant for the comprehension of its mission theme to be completely overlooked. Connected with the problem of the literary history of the passage are the issues of its structural and thematic unity, of the relationship between its two generally recognized major sections: vv 1–30, 39–42 and 31–38, of the structural and thematic unity of each of these major sections and of the function of 4:1–42 in the Gospel as a whole. The methodological importance attached in this study to 4:1–42 as our basic text demands that we review in some detail the position of contemporary scholarship on these fundamental issues, since the results of previous studies may have serious consequences (both positive and negative) for our synthetic approach. Such a review should indeed provide an illuminating background for the particular orientation of the present exegetical focus. We will discuss first the question of the literary history of 4:1–42, then review the different approaches to its meaning and function within the context of its missionary perspective. On the basis of the results of this discussion we will formulate a working hypothesis for our exegesis of the passage[1].

A. The Literary History of 4:1–42

The debate on the literary history of 4:1–42 follows two diametrically opposed lines of argument. On one side are scholars like Brown, Bligh, Roustang and Schnackenburg who praise the artistic unity of the passage, consider it as one of the most skilfully written in the Gospel and attri-

---

[1] The literary critical analysis given below may be supplemented with that of Olsson, *Structure and Meaning*, 115–119. Olsson's study of the state of the question on 4:1–42 centers on the four models of interpretation (pp. 119–123); this present study, however, focuses on the mission theme in particular, and on the difficulties raised by previous studies concerning the integration of vv 31–38 into the rest of the passage.

bute it to one and the same author[2]. On the other are Schwartz, Bultmann, Wilkens, Fortna, Schulz, and Boismard-Lamouille, to name but a few, who detect in the passage the presence of joints, aporias and thematic incompatibilities which they hold testify to the presence of many hands in the composition of the passage[3]. The first group of scholars do not, of course, deny that the Evangelist used sources, except, perhaps, for Bauer and Lindars[4]. They simply argue that whatever sources the Evangelist may have used have been so completely rewritten that it would be impossible to isolate these sources from his own redaction.

The literary discrepancies noted by the latter group include the ungainly repetition of Ἰησοῦς in v 1, the apparent correction of v 1 and 3:22 by v 2, the interruptive nature of vv 8, 27 and 31–38 and the awkward transitional verses (27–30, 39 and 1–3, 43, 45) which link, on the one hand, vv 31–38 to the main story of Jesus' encounter with the Samaritan woman and the Samaritans and, on the other, the whole of 4:1–42 to the rest of the Gospel[5]. Furthermore, it is noted by Fortna and Boismard-Lamouille, for instance, that vv 31–38 is a patchwork of unrelated themes[6]. Similarly, the main story of Jesus' encounter with the Samaritan woman is reportedly made up of two or three independent themes: the theme of "living water" (vv 10–15), that of "true worship" (vv 20–24) and that of Jesus' messiahship (vv 25–26), while vv 16–19 are regarded as awkward transitional verses artificially contrived as a link between the unrelated themes of "living water" and "true worship"[7]. In addition, Bultmann and Schottroff regard vv 5–7 and 16–19 as a plain contradiction of vv 10–15; Bultmann and Wilkens again note the incompatibility between

---

[2]Brown, *John* I, 176, 180–181; Bligh, "Jesus in Samaria," 329; Roustang, "Les moments de l'acte de foi," 345; Schnackenburg, *Johannesevangelium* I, 455. Others include Dodd, *Interpretation,* 317; Barrett, *John,* 228; Hoskyns, *John,* 248; Ruckstuhl, *Literarische Einheit,* 114, 206; Leidig, *Jesu Gespräch,* 266.

[3]Bultmann, *Johannes,* 127–128. See further the reconstruction of his theory by D.M. Smith, *Composition and Order,* 39f.; Wilkens, *Entstehungsgeschichte,* 135–138; Fortna, *Gospel of Signs,* 189–195; Schulz, *Johannes,* 73–78; Boismard-Lamouille, *Synopse III,* 128–129. See further Nicol, *Semeia,* 40; and among the older commentaries, Wellhausen, *Johannis,* 20–23; and Spitta, *Johannesevangelium,* 98–106.

[4]Bauer (*Das Johannesevangelium* [2 Aufl.; HNT 6; Tübingen: Mohr-Siebeck, 1933, first published 1929] 75) describes the scene "als Ganzes literarisches Produkt des Evangelisten"; Lindars (*John,* 192) believes the traditional material was only "a peg" on which the Evangelist hung his themes.

[5]The reading κύριος in v 1 is given in P[66.75] A B C L Ws Ψ 083 f[13] and others, while other texts, ℵ D Θ 086 f[1] al lat sy[c], etc., have Ἰησοῦς in both instances. Since the latter is the *lectio difficilior,* it is naturally regarded as the original reading. Vv 43, and 45 are regarded as a "reprise" of v 3 which announces Jesus' departure for Galilee. This makes the whole of vv 4–42 look like an interruption of the journey narrative, or an insertion.

[6]Fortna (*Gospel of Signs,* 190) posits as the two themes of this section (vv 31–38) Jesus' food and Christian harvest; for Boismard-Lamouille (*Synopse III,* 134) the themes are Jesus' mission (vv 31–34), the evangelization of Samaria (vv 35–36) and polemic against certain Gentile Christians who held that revelation began only in Christ (vv 37–38). For a fuller presentation of their position see below, p. 72.

[7]See, for instance, Boismard-Lamouille, *Synopse III,* 134, 135; Fortna, *Gospel of Signs,* 190.

vv 39 and 40; finally, it is pointed out that v 39 ignores the coming of
the Samaritans in v 30 but appears to be called for by vv 29, 41—42. With
regard to the structural relationship of 4:1—42 to the entire Gospel, the
Wiederaufnahme of v 3 and 40 by v 43 is regarded as evidence that the
whole of the Samaritan episode is a later insertion (Wilkens and Spitta)[8].
Others again believe that the conclusion to the whole episode has been
completely rewritten[9].

The important conclusion drawn from these literary anomalies and
thematic incompatibilities, then, is that they argue strongly against the
attempt to interpret the passage as a unified whole. Hence, the best way
to comprehend the episode is to isolate the different historical layers each
with its own distinctive level of meaning, and, to respect the meaning
intended in each layer. Any other approach, it is held, betrays the intention of the different authors and of their sources[10]. The reconstructions
of the different historical layers proposed are far too complex to be discussed here in detail. Extensive studies of these theories are given in the
dissertations of Olsson and Leidig[11]. Here we can only indicate the general trends in the discussion.

---

[8]Bultmann, *Commentary,* 175 and n. 3; Luise Schottroff, "Johannes 4,5—15 und die Konsequenzen des johanneischen Dualismus," *ZNW* 60 (1969) 119—214; Wilkens, *Entstehungsgeschichte,*
136; cf. Spitta, *Johannesevangelium,* 101.

[9]See, for instance, Wellhausen, *Johannis,* 22; Bultmann, *Commentary,* 175; Fortna, *Gospel of
Signs,* 192; Spitta, *Johannesevangelium,* 111—112; Schulz, *Johannes,* 78.

[10]All efforts aimed at reconstructing the different historical strata of the passage, and indeed
of the entire Gospel, derive their basic impulse from this view. As already noted, one cannot deny,
or for that matter prove conclusively, that the Gospel material underwent different stages of composition and redaction. To insist, however, that only that interpretation is really valid which emphasizes the different meanings of the different, and in the last analysis, hypothetical layers, is to
undervalue the "creative" work of the final author, the canonical and critical role of the final redaction (cf. Childs, *OT as Scripture,* 75—76, n.19, p. 44 above) and also the importance of the final
audience for whose benefit the final redaction was undertaken.

Moreover, one cannot but question the value of so much effort spent in reconstructing (for
better comprehension, we are told) the different historical layers of a story of which we are finally
told that "it is, of course, not possible to reconstruct the original story." (Bultmann, *Commentary,*
179; cf. Fortna, *Gospel of Signs,* 190); and so one resorts to undated Buddhist parallels. It is to be
noted, also, that after isolating the different layers, Bultmann, like most of the literary critics,
proceeds to offer the interpretation of the passage as a unified whole (cf. pp. 176ff.). Boismard-
Lamouille's approach is a possible exception here since these authors endeavor to give a systematic
interpretation of the theology of the different levels which they discern. Even here, despite the ad-
mirable skill and application demonstrated by these authors, the results remain unconvincing. For,
among other things, as Xavier Jacques points out in his review of *La vie des évangiles. Initiation à
la critique des textes* (Collection "Initiation;" Paris: Cerf, 1980), a popular version of *Synopse III,*
the features attributed to different sources could equally be explained on stylistic or other grounds:
"On notera que, plus d'une fois, l'explication par un remaniement, pour vraisemblable qu'elle
paraisse, ne s'impose pas comme la seule possible," *NRT* 103 (1981) 891—892. See further Boers,
"Interpretation of Texts," 170.

[11]Olsson, *Structure and Meaning,* 115—119; Leidig (*Jesu Gespräch*) devotes the first 77 pages
of her dissertation to the different source theories proposed in contemporary literature: *SQ* (2—
14), *RQ* (14—19), other sources (20—24), the Johannine redaction (24—40), the post-Johannine
redactions (40—75), and the conclusion of her survey (76—77).

In the beginning of the century, the tendency with Wendt, Schwartz, Wellhausen and Spitta was to attribute most of the pericope to the *Grundschrift* (Wilkens' *Reisebericht*) and to see the work of the Evangelist as mostly editorial in nature. For instance, he wrote the introduction (vv 1–3) in order to bring the Johannine account in line with the Synoptics which nowhere mention the baptismal activity of Jesus and, also introduced the disciples into the story (vv 8, 27, 31–38). But even here disagreements occur[12]. Since Bultmann, however, the pendulum has swung in the opposite direction. Of the three principal layers isolated: pre-Johannine, Johannine and post-Johannine, most of the material in the passage is attributed to the Johannine level (that is, to the Evangelist). We present in chart form below a sample of the reconstructions proposed by eight representative scholars from Bultmann (1941) to Boismard-Lamouille (1975)[13].

Proposed Literary Layers in Jn 4:1–42

1. Pre-Johannine: Vorlage, Document C

Bultmann 1941	5(4)–7	9(10)	16————————26	28–30	40
Wilkens 1958	1, 3 5———7	9—————————26		28–30	40
Schenke 1958	5———7	9ab	16——22(23) 20–23——→Urform←—35–36a	28–30	40
Schottroff 1969	5———7	9ab	16–18 (independent story)		
Fortna 1970	4———7	9	16————19 25 26	28–30	40 42
Nicol 1972	5———7	9	16——————————30		40
Schulz 1972	5———7	9	16————19	29	40
B-L, 1977	5———7	9	16–18	28–30	(40)

[12]Wendt (*Das Johannesevangelium. Eine Untersuchung seiner Entstehung und seines geschichtlichen Wertes* [Göttingen: Vandenhoeck und Ruprecht, 1900]) assigns to the source vv 4–14 (except parts of vv 10, 11), vv 15, 19–25 and 27, 31–38; Schwartz, "Aporien im vierten Evangelium," *Nachrichten von der Königlichen Gesellschaft der Wissenschaften zu Göttingen* (Berlin: Georg Reimer, 1907) 342–374; (1908) 115–118, 479–560, esp. 504ff.; Wellhausen (*Johannis*, 20–23) assigns all to the *Grundschrift* except vv 1–3, 8, 27 and 37–38. He believes, further, that originally it was the Samaritans who brought Jesus food to eat; hence vv 31–36 were addressed to them, not to the disciples; Spitta (*Johannesevangelium*, 105–106) disagrees with Wellhausen that vv 31–36 belong to the *Grundschrift*, but rather sees these verses as introduced by the Evangelist (the *Bearbeiter*) from an unknown Gospel collection and inserted into the story by means of vv 8, 27, the probable reason being that in the original collection the story dealt with an event which took place in Samaria. Thus Spitta sees Samaria rather than mission as the link between the two parts of the episode; in his view mission begins only after the resurrection (p. 105).

[13]The page references for the authors surveyed in the ensuing chart are as follows: Bultmann,

2. Johannine: Evangelist, John II-A, II-B

Bultmann		8	(10)11–15	20		27 31--38	39-----42
Wilkens	4	8				27 31--38	39-----42
Schenke	(1) 3–4	8	10-----15	(23)24–27	31–34		
					36b 39	41–42	
Schottroff		8 9c	10-----15	19--26			
Fortna	1–3(4)	8 9c	10-----15	20–24 27	31------39	41 (42)	
Nicol	1–3		10-----15	20--26	31------39	41 (42)	
Schulz	1--4		10-----15	20----27	31-----39	41 (42)	
B-L, II-A		8	10.--14		27 31–34		
II-B	1, 3–4		10-----15	19–21	35–36 39-----42		

3. Post-Johannine: Eccl. Redactor, John III

Bultmann	1–3(4)			
Schenke	(1) 2	9c		37–38
B-L			22–24	37–38
(Odeberg 1929)				35--38

This survey chart which spans almost four decades of research on the composition and redaction of 4:1–42 is highly revealing as regards both the areas of consensus and of disagreement. First it is to be noted that Schenke recognizes an *Urform* which is anterior to the pre-Johannine level. For Wilkens, too, the pre-Johannine material existed independently of the *Reisebericht* but was later introduced into this journey account by the Evangelist who also added vv 4 and 43 to effect this insertion (p. 136). Since Schottroff is concerned mainly with vv 5–15, her reconstruction is incomplete, but she, too, believes that the pre-Johannine material (vv 16–18) existed as an independent story together with vv 5–7, 9 before it reached the Evangelist (p. 204). Schulz, it will be noted, is not very particular about assigning all the verses to the different levels.

In general, all eight scholars assign to the pre-Johannine level mostly the setting (vv 4/5–7, 9) and the transitional verses (16–18/19, 28–30, 40). With the exceptions of Wilkens, Fortna and Nicol who tend towards

Johannes (11 Aufl., 1950) 127–128; Wilkens, *Entstehunsgeschichte*, 135–136; Schenke, "Jakobs-brunnen-Josephsgrab-Sychar. Topographische Untersuchungen und Erwägungen in der Perspektive von Joh 4,5.6," *ZDPV* 84 (1968) 159–184, esp. 159–162; Schottroff, "Johannes 4,5–15," 200–201, 204, 206; Fortna, *Gospel of Signs*, 189–195; Nicol, *Semeia*, 40; Schulz, *Johannes*, 73–78; Boismard-Lamouille (= B-L) *Synopse III*, 128–144; Odeberg, *Fourth Gospel*, 190, n. 1. The numbers in parenthesis indicate verses which are assigned in part to the levels indicated. A straight line joining numbers indicates continuous verses. For a more exact distribution of verses in the Boismard-Lamouille reconstruction see *Synopse III*, 128–129.

the earlier view of the *Grundschrift,* all attribute to the Evangelist the main themes in the story of Jesus and the Samaritan woman: living water (vv 10—15, unanimous agreement), worship (vv 20—24, near unanimous agreement), and the revelation of Jesus' messiahship (vv 25—26) as well as the conclusion (vv 39—42 or 39, 41—42)[14]. Furthermore, as in the earlier theories of Wendt, Wellhausen and Spitta, all scholars agree that the episode concerning the disciples (vv 8, 27, 31—38) stems from the Evangelist. Only Odeberg, Schenke and Boismard-Lamouille assign the explicit mention of the mission of the disciples (vv 37—38) to the post-Johannine level.

Furthermore, only Schenke distributes the entire material concerning the disciples to all three levels while Boismard-Lamouille are alone in maintaining that the Evangelist developed vv 31—36 in two successive stages (see chart). Similarly, the introductory verses (1—4) and v 9c are distributed by different scholars to all three levels, though the majority attribute vv 1—3/4 to the Evangelist as did also Wendt and the earlier critics. Fifthly and finally, the most striking result of the survey is how few are the verses attributed to the post-Johannine level and how few scholars so assign these verses. However, despite their other disagreements, all scholars unanimously assign the overtly missionary section (vv 31—38 or 35/37—38) to the final redactor whether this final redactor be seen as the Evangelist (so the majority) or as the post-Johannine editor (so Odeberg, Schenke and Boismard-Lamouille).

The result of the survey thus emerges as follows: of the forty-two verses of the pericope only eleven (vv 5—7, 16—19, 28—30, 40) are assigned in part or in full by wide consensus to the pre-Johannine level, while the remaining thirty-one verses are assigned to the Evangelist himself. Put differently, if we omit the verses attributed to the Evangelist by unanimous or majority consensus, we are left only with vv 5—7, 16—19, 28—30 and possibly 40 as non-Johannine. The survey thus tends to reinforce the position of those scholars who argue in favor of the literary and artistic unity of the passage. By the same token, it lends great support to our own synthetic approach to the passage. Besides, it is stated by Bultmann and many of the other literary critics surveyed that the Evangelist freely rewrote the conclusion of the story, and, in the view of Boismard-Lamouille, even some of the original material[15]. If he left other verses unchanged, the only reasonable conclusion one can draw is that these unchanged verses must have suited well his purpose[16].

---

[14]Wilkens, *Entstehungsgeschichte,* 136; Fortna and Nicol are interested mainly in isolating the *SQ* from the rest of the passage. For Fortna (p. 190) the *SQ* automatically excludes all the dialogues, since the source contained only narrative. In contrast to Bultmann and Fortna, Nicol (*Semeia,* p. 40) sees no infallible eivdence that the source was necessarily a "semeia source."

[15]For Bultmann and others see n. 9 above; Boismard-Lamouille, *Synopse III,* 128f. esp. the different insertions by John II-A and II-B into the primitive account of Document C.

[16]This applies not only to the way the Evangelist handled the traditional material or Document C, but also to John II-B's radical re-writing of his own earlier version of the Gospel (John II-A).

The task of the exegete, then, is to explore the ways in which these unchanged pre-Johannine materials could have served the purpose of the Evangelist by paying close attention to how the problematic transitional verses may possibly function in the Gospel narrative as it now stands. The key to discovering the purpose of the Evangelist (who in our view is the author of the passage as we now have it) might, therefore, lie in the discovery of the relationship which he establishes between this overtly missionary pericope and the rest of the passage. We thus come to our next topic, the contemporary discussion on the missionary character of 4:1–42 and of its function both in the Gospel and in the life-situation of the Evangelist.

B. The Missionary Character and Function of 4:1–42

The research reveals that contemporary discussion on the mission theme in 4:1–42 centers on vv 31–38 which refers explicitly to the sending of the disciples and to "others" who labored before them (v 38). The discussion also invariably links vv 31–38 to the conversion of the Samaritans (vv 39–42). Mission, then, in this context means primarily, if not always exclusively, the post-Easter missionary activity of the disciples, with particular reference to the Samaritan mission (Acts 8:4–25)[17], and by extension, to the world mission of the church[18]. Lindars, for instance, denies that the story has any basis in the historical circumstances of Jesus' earthly life and holds that the Evangelist composed the story "on the basis of the mission that was actually undertaken there [i.e., in Samaria] in the years following Pentecost." The Evangelist then uses his knowledge of this successful Christian mission to make a point about the universal mission as he does concerning the coming of the Greeks in 12:20–26[19].

Even if John III is an incompetent who butchered the work of John II-B (boulverser . . . de façon assez déconcertante, en insérant tel ou tel logion sans qu'il offre de lien apparent avec le contexte," 48), he nevertheless had a goal in view, namely, to reconcile the Jews and rehabilitate the world by showing that "Jésus a été envoyé par Dieu" (p. 59).

[17]See Bauer, *Johannesevangelium*, 76; Wendt (*Johannesevangelium*, 119–120) holds that the reference is not to the *damaligen Erfolg*, but to a later time after Jesus' departure when the disciples enter into his work; Wellhausen, *Johannis*, 22; Spitta, *Johannesevangelium*, 205; Brown, *John*, I, 183–184; Schnackenburg, *Johannesevangelium* I, 455; Cullmann, *Johanneïsche Kreis*, 16 and *passim*; Olsson, *Structure and Meaning*, 239 and *passim*.

[18]Barrett, *John*, 229; J.A. Bailey, *The Traditions Common to the Gospels of Luke and John* (Nov TSup VII; Leiden: Brill, 1963) 105; Haenchen, *Johannesevangelium*, 247–248; Dodd, *Tradition*, 341–400; Leon Morris, *Studies in the Fourth Gospel* (Grand Rapids: Eerdmans, 1969) 280; Cullmann, *Johanneische Kreis*, 16–17 (where he refers to 10:16 and 12:20–32).

[19]Lindars, *John*, 192; cf. p. 176. Similarly, van den Bussche (*Jean*, 197) sees in this first missionary journey of Jesus outside Israel a prelude to the evangelization of Gentiles throughout the world.

Dodd, on the other hand, construes the setting in life as "the missionary Church occupied with the work of evangelization in the world"[20].

· Various suggestions are offered for the purpose of the story in this historical setting of the Evangelist. According to Cullmann, the purpose of the story in this setting is to claim dominical authority for extending the mission to Samaria. Wellhausen likewise believes that it is for this reason that Jesus is presented as the founder of the Samaritan Christian community; the title "Savior of the world" (v 42) indicates this. Lindars and Bailey hold that the story functions as a polemic against those who object to the Samaritan Christian mission on the basis of the prohibition in Mt 10:5 and Lk 9:51—56. For Schottroff, the story may have been used by the Samaritan Christians themselves to justify their existence before Jewish Christians; it functions, therefore, as a polemic against Jews who do not mix with the Samaritans[21]. From the perspective of the world mission, the story serves to inspire the disciples with an urgent sense of mission: they should not delay while others are so far ahead that they are already receiving their wages (Morris). For van den Bussche the story serves to alert the disciples to "l'avènement des temps messianiques"; for Haenchen, it shows that the missionary should be conscious of other workers[22].

Although scholars see a clear and strong emphasis on the post-Easter missionary activity of the disciples or of the church, they evidence a corresponding reluctance to see Jesus' work in Samaria as missionary activity. This reluctance, in our view, stems from the tacit agreement that mission refers only to the post-Easter activity of the disciples (as it does in modern terminology). Thus while it may sound like a major contradiction in this present research to present, on the one hand, a discussion on the mission of the Son in the Gospel (pp. 24—28 above), and on the other to state that scholars deny or are reluctant to see Jesus' work as mission, this is, nevertheless, an accurate description of the state of modern research on mission in John's Gospel as the concrete examples cited indicate. The situation is, therefore, clearly ambivalent. The apparent confusion in our presentation can be cleared by identifying the type of literature concerned in each case.

The works cited in the discussion on the mission of the Son are mainly *theological* in nature. They deal with the theology of mission in the Gospel on a more abstract/philosophical level. Conversely, those studies which tend to deny that Jesus' work on earth is missionary work, except when it is viewed from the post-Easter perspective, are primarily exegeti-

---

[20]Dodd, *Tradition*, 400.

[21]Cullmann, *The Early Church*, 192; Wellhausen, *Johannis*, 22 ("Jesu selber gilt also hier als der definitive Gründer der samarischen Christengemeinde"); Lindars, *John*, 175—176; Bailey, *Traditions*, 107; Schottroff, "Joh 4 5—15," 202—203. Schottroff, however, believes that "Samaria-mission" is hardly the issue here (pp. 203, 204).

[22]Morris, *Studies*, 280; van den Bussche, *Jean*, 196; Haenchen, *Johannesevangelium*, 247—248.

cal and historical in nature. Bultmann is a striking exception since his approach is both theological and exegetical. The only satisfactory explanation one can find for this phenomenon is that unconsciously exegetes are influenced by the twentieth century understanding of mission. It is this situation that makes the present study necessary[23].

Another striking result of the telescoping of the twentieth century understanding of mission with that of the Evangelist, or perhaps the cause of it, is that exegetes nowhere explicitly raise in terms of mission the structural and thematic relationship of vv 31—38 to the whole of vv 1—30, 39—42. Fortna and Schulz even categorically deny this relationship[24]. Yet this question proves crucial for our full comprehension of the passage. A close examination of the positions of Bultmann, Schnackenburg, Lindars, Olsson, Boismard-Lamouille and Leidig, each of whom adds a different dimension to the discussion on the missionary perspective of 4:1—42, will make this clear.

Bultmann recognizes an original story (vv 1—30) with a conclusion (vv 39—42). The Evangelist uses this conclusion to add two further ideas: Jesus and the disciples or "the task of mission" (vv 31—38) and Jesus and the Samaritans or "first- and second-hand faith" (vv 39—42). Both these sections are linked with the internal problem of mission. In particular, the sending of Jesus (vv 31—34) explains by analogy the sending of the disciples (vv 35—38), whose ministry is a continuation of the eschatological event begun in Jesus. Vv 39—42 then explain concretely the point made in the first section (i.e., in vv 31—38), namely, that the one sent is nothing of himself. For, important as the role of the woman is in leading the Samaritans to Jesus, the faith of the Samaritans rests ultimately not on her word but on the word and authority of Jesus[25].

Concerning its function in the Gospel, Bultmann holds that 4:1—42 forms a diptych with 3:1—21. For, just as Jesus' self-revelation is paralleled by the Baptist's witness to him (3:22—30), so here Jesus' self-witness (vv 1—30) is paralleled by the believers' witness to him (vv 31—42)[26]. Bultmann's whole interpretation is shared by Wilkens. The latter, however, finds the real link between 4:1—42 and 3:1—21 in the mention of the Spirit. For in Jn 3 Jesus speaks of birth through "water and the Spirit;" but in Jn 4 he speaks of "worship in Spirit and in truth." Both

---

[23]The basic question is whether the Gospel itself considers Jesus' work on earth as mission on all levels: historical, theological and exegetical, even if the Gospel was written from the post-Easter standpoint.

[24]Fortna, (*Gospel of Signs,* 189—190) believes that vv 8, 27, 31—38 have "only incidental ties to the story proper," and that when all the other dialogues are removed, "a coherent story, with only slight Johannine touchings, remains." Furthermore, even if the presence of the disciples was implied in the story's context in the source, "they fade into the background during this story" (p. 190). Schulz (*Johannesevangelium,* 77) believes that vv 31—38 introduce "eine ganze andere Szene mit völlig neuer Thematik."

[25]Bultmann, *Commentary,* 175, 195—200.

[26]Bultmann, *Commentary,* 131.

chapters, which in Wilkens' view are oriented towards baptism, thus under-score the point made in 3:22—30 that Jesus' baptism is greater than that of the Baptist[27].

Though Bultmann is right in emphasizing the essentially relative and dependent role of the disciples in the missionary enterprise, he obviously does not explore the missionary significance of 4:1—30. Moreover, it is not at all clear in what sense vv 35—38 or even all of vv 31—38 can be seen as "the believers' witness to Jesus" on the analogy of 3:22—30. If any-thing, vv 31—38 reveal, not the believers' witness to Jesus but the lack of it; the didactic nature of the whole section underscores this point. Also, the structural interpretation of the passage proposed by Bultmann (vv 1—30 and 31—42) greatly obscures the different functional significance of both vv 31—38 and 39—42 in their relationship to the story of Jesus' en-counter with the woman (vv 1—26).

Schnackenburg emphasizes the unity of the passage and believes it has a basis in history. He recognizes in it two dominant themes: the revelation of Jesus' identity (vv 1—26) and faith (vv 39—42). Mission (vv 35—38) constitutes only a third sub-theme underlying the passage, the other two being "living water" (vv 10—14) and "worship" (vv 20—24). But though suggested by the narrative itself, work in Samaria, this mission sub-theme has no real bearing on the story proper, being developed "nur in seiner Perspektive." It must, therefore, not be allowed to overshadow the main theme *(Hauptthema)* of the passage which is "die Selbstoffenbarung Jesu"[28].

Structurally, vv 31—38 (das missionarische Zwischengespräch) interrupt the flow of the story and serve mainly to fill up the time of waiting for the arrival of the Samaritans. They also help to heighten the conclusion of the story (though exactly how they do so Schnackenburg does not say), namely, the revelation of Jesus as "Savior of the world" (v 42). Theologically, these verses turn our attention from the present to the future mission of the church. V 38 thus situates the disciples in their own missionary situation; it underlines that *die Zeit Jesu* is different from *die Zeit der Kirche*, though basically both "times" form a unity, a point which Schnackenburg does not develop[29]. For him, then, the main in-terest in the passage, as indeed in the entire Gospel, is the self-revelation of Jesus, not *Missionsarbeit*, still less "eine pädagogisch-seelsorgerische Einwirkung Jesu auf die Frau" (p. 456).

Schnackerburg's emphasis on the importance of Jesus' self-revelation

---

[27]Wilkens, *Entstehungsgeschichte*, 138. Bligh ("Jesus in Samaria," 341) also emphasizes the sacramental character of the episode. But in his view, 4:32—34 parallels 6:26—35, and both are "preparatory to the explicitly Eucharistic passage in 6:51—58." See also Boismard-Lamouille, *Synopse III*, 131—132 (on the parallelism between the themes of "water" (4:10—14) and "bread" (6:33—35).

[28]Schnackenburg, *Johannesevangelium* I, 455—457.

[29]Schnackenburg, *Johannesevangelium* I, 478—488.

in the passage (and here he is supported by Fortna and Leidig) can hardly
be dispusted[30]. Unlike Bultmann, he also recognizes that thematically vv
31—38 function on a different level from vv 39—42 and the rest of the
passage. His great difficulty in integrating vv 31—38 and the missionary
theme into the whole passage is nonetheless self-evident. In reality, Schnackenburg's restriction of the mission theme to vv 35—38 (the mission of the
disciples) implies that Jesus' work from the Father is not *Missionsarbeit*.
This is most apparent in his insistence that the mission theme must not
be allowed to over-shadow the theme of Jesus' self-relevation in the passage. His own view that "relevation" (vv 1—26) and "faith" (vv 39—42)
are the two dominant viewpoints in the passage also suggests that these
are two separate or independent entities.

From the perspective of 20:30—31, however, would one not rather say
that the major theme in the passage, as indeed of the whole Gospel, is
"the relevation of Jesus as intended for faith-acceptance?" Put differently, does Jesus' self-revelation in the Gospel not have as its ultimate goal
the awakening of a faith-response in the audience (3:15—16, 36; 5:24;
6:40; etc.)? Is this revelation for faith, then, not mission work? Strikingly,
while Schnackenburg himself decries the importance of pastoral pedagogy
in the passage and denies that 4:1—26 is a conversion story, he nonetheless continually speaks of Jesus' leading the woman and the Samaritans
to faith in him ("zum Glauben führen," cf. p. 465). This notion of leading
to faith does imply a process, and, hence, a conscious methodology.
Schnackenburg himself (p. 456) cites as evidence of "die Höherführung
des Glaubens" the woman's and the Samaritans' progressive understanding
of Jesus: from "a Jew" (v 9), to a "Sir" (v 11) to one "greater than our
Father Jacob" (v 12), "a prophet" (v 19), "the Christ" (vv 26, 29) and
"the Savior of the world" (v 12).

Leidig, therefore, is right when she observes that the recognition that
Jesus is the Savior of the world is not "selbstverständlich" either to Jews
or to Samaritans. Both need to undergo an "Erkenntnisprozess." Schenke,
too, seems closer to the Johannine perspective when he states that the
purpose of the Evangelist's redaction of the original story is to show that
Jesus, the God-sent Savior of the world, brings the life-giving revelation
which human beings must receive in faith[31]. The key to the integration
of the entire passage, vv 1—30, 31—38, 39—42, one which embraces the
"independent themes" (*selbständigen Themen*, p. 457) recognized by
Schnackenburg and which may help to resolve the obvious ambivalence
in his position, may yet lie in this mission theme in all its dimensions

---

[30]Fortna, (*Gospel of Signs*, 190) holds that the question of Jesus' identity is implicitly raised
even in v 9; Leidig (*Jesu Gespräch*, 266) states: "Das erklärte Ziel jedes johanneischen Gesprächs ist
es, Jesus als den Messias zu zeigen."

[31]Leidig, *Jesu Gespräch*, 152; Schenke, "Jakobsbrunnen," 159. It is to be noted, however,
that Schenke shows very little interest in the overtly missionary section of the pericope (vv 31—
38), which section he distributes among the three redactional levels (see the chart above).

(methodology included), the importance of which Schnackenburg is so eager to deny.

Lindars, it was noted earlier, believes that the story has no historical foundation but that it was created by the Evangelist on the basis of Acts 8 and Mt 10:5; 15:34. He divides the passage into "a discourse" (vv 1—26) and "the testimony of the Samaritans and reflections on the missionary task" (vv 27—42)[32]. In contrast to Schnackenburg and Olsson in particular, Lindars maintains that the story is "more than a revelation-discourse," and sees it as a "model of the mission of the church"[33]. Its ending with the conversion of the Samaritans (v 42) shows that though the missionaries give witness to Christ, their task is not complete until the people come to personal faith in him (p. 198). The purpose of the whole story is to show that the new life in the Spirit (Jn 3) leads to fecundity and to mission which breaks out of Jewish confines and demonstrates its universal scope (p. 192).

The disciples are introduced into the story for the purpose of "dovetailing the story-discourse into the larger composition of the Gospel." Structurally, vv 31—38 are inserted to "fill in the time" of waiting for the return of the woman and the Samaritans, a well-known "sandwich" construction (or that of a story within a story) as in Mk 5:21—43 and 11:12—21[34]. Theologically, the insertion serves to "relate the story [i.e., of Jesus' encounter with the woman and the Samaritans] to the Church's missionary work, which is a continuation of Jesus' public ministry." (p. 193).

Lindars' efforts to interpret the whole story, not just vv 31—38, in terms of mission is highly laudable. But his difficulty in integrating both sections of the pericope in terms of mission is also apparent in the deliberate distinction he makes between "the ministry of Jesus" and "the missionary task of the church" (cf. pp. 175, 192, 193). For, though Lindars rightly speaks of "Jesus' mission," "the whole purpose for which he was sent," "mission in the broad sense" will only *begin* when his personal task is completed in his Passion (p. 195). So, ultimately, mission for Lindars means "the mission of the church." That he holds this is evident from his position that vv 31—38, like the farewell discourses, serve to relate Jesus' work to the mission of the church. Is this, in fact, how 4:31—38 and the Gospel view the relationship between "the work of Jesus" and "the mission of the church?" Put differently, do vv 31—38 and Jn 13—17 interpret Jesus' work from the standpoint of that of the disciples, alone properly understood as mission? Or do they, on the contrary, relate the

---

[32]Lindars, *John,* 172, 174, 192.

[33]Lindars, *John,* 192. For Schnackenburg see n. 28 above; Olsson, *Structure and Meaning,* 204.

[34]Lindars, *John,* 193. His view is shared by Fortna (*Gospel of Signs,* 194—195) who holds that in the *SQ,* the story came between Jn 11:15 and 17 and that as a conversion story, it led in the source into Jesus' ministry in Jerusalem.

mission of the disciples to that of Jesus[35]? Finally, is the distinction between "the ministry of Jesus" and "the missionary task of the church" warranted by the Gospel? In what sense can 4:1—42 be regarded as "a model of mission?"

Olsson, like Lindars, makes a consistent effort to interpret the whole of 4:1—42 from the standpoint of mission. But his confusing and often contradictory use of terminology and concepts makes it very difficult to determine his exact position[36]. Nowhere is this confusion more apparent than in his use of the terms *ergon* and *erga,* or in the meanings he attributes to Jesus' "hour," "food" and "work of harvest." For instance, Jesus' *"earthly works"* is a "phase" in the redeeming activity of the Father and Son, and this is "summed up" in *to ergon* in 4:34, 17:4 and also in *to potērion* in 18:11 (pp. 66—67); Jesus' *erga* which are God's *erga* also include the *erga* of the disciples. At the same time, the *ergon* of Jesus has two phases and includes God's work, Jesus' work and the disciples' work seen in the same perspective, with the "hour" at the center. But this "hour" which is at the center is also "the dividing line" between Jesus' earthly ministry and his work as the glorified one[37]. Furthermore, mission is "Jesus' work of harvest" and this "refers to the glorified Christ," whereas his "food," refers to "the earthly Jesus" (pp. 234, 253). Yet elsewhere we learn that Jesus' "food" in the text covers *"the whole* of Jesus' task of salvation and all that is implicit therein"[38].

Despite this confusion, however, the following two points emerge as an accurate description of Olsson's position. First, for Olsson the activity of Jesus himself, not only that of the disciples, can be viewed as mission only from the post-Easter standpoint. In other words, Jesus' work is not mission work till after his resurrection when he wins followers through the activity of the disciples. Expressions to this effect abound in his book: "the mission" is Jesus' "work after his glorification" (p. 229) when his "mission merges into that of his disciples" (p. 231); the emphasis in 4:1—42 is "on how Jesus, *after the 'hour',* receives *Samaritan* disciples, i.e., on the 'Samaritan mission'" (p. 239).

Secondly, unlike Lindars, Schnackenburg, Barrett, Odeberg and others who recognize the universal or representative aspect of the Samaritan episode, Olsson consistently and emphatically denies this universal dimension of the pericope[39]. The episode, in his view, is concerned only with

---

[35]For a different approach to the relationship between Jesus and the disciples see C.H. Giblin "The Miraculous Crossing of the Sea (John 6. 16—21)," *NTS* 29 (1983) 96—103.

[36]Olsson, *Structure and Meaning,* esp. pp. 66—67, 225.

[37]Olsson, *Structure and Meaning,* 234—235; see further his discussion of the *ergon* which begins on p. 238.

[38]Olsson, *Structure and Meaning:* compare his excursus on mission (pp. 241—248) with his interpretation of the text (pp. 250—257) or his discussion of the *ergon* (pp. 66—67, 224—225) with his treatment of the same topic on pp. 234—235, 238—239.

[39]Lindars, *John,* 192; Schnackenburg, (*Johannesevangelium* I, 478—479) sees in the harvest imagery (vv 35—37) a reference to the future mission of the church, while v 38 refers to the mis-

"the union of Judah and Ephraim." This, indeed, is the thesis or the basic standpoint from which Olsson interprets the entire pericope. Indeed, not only is "the union of Judah and Ephraim" the meaning of Jesus' *ergon* and the main theme of the two dialogues in 4:1–42, but this union provides the model for the Evangelist's conception of mission in the Gospel as a gathering of God's scattered children[40]. The specific function of "the revelation-discourse" (vv 31–38), then, is to teach the disciples "how the Samaritans are integrated into the new people of God." (pp. 241, 238).

This is not, by any means, a detailed discussion of Olsson's interpretation of 4:1–42, whose book has been abundantly reviewed[41]. But his difficulty in integrating the mission thought in the whole passage is, perhaps, more apparent than in the instances previously examined; and that is rather ironic given his basic insight that Jesus' *ergon* is the unifying theme of the Samaria text[42]. The chief difficulty with him as with Lindars lies in his explicit denial of the missionary character of Jesus' *earthly work* reported in the Gospel. Olsson's understanding of the *ergon*-concept also raises some questions. He speaks throughout of "Jesus' *ergon*" of which the *erga* of the Father and of the disciples form a part[43]. Is this in fact how the Gospel conceives the relationships in the ownership of the *ergon* and *erga*[44]? And does the Gospel justify Olsson's division of Jesus' work into "time before" and "time after" the hour, or his distinction between Jesus' "food" and his "work of harvest," the ones (i.e., "time after" and "work of harvest") considered as mission work and the others not? Finally, dissatisfaction also needs to be expressed over Olsson's virtual

---

sion in Samaria; Barrett, *John,* 229; Odeberg, *Fourth Gospel,* 190–191. See further, Bligh, "Jesus in Samaria," 333 and the authors cited in n. 18 above.

[40]Olsson, *Structure and Meaning,* 240–241, 248, 252, 277 (on the union of Judah and Ephraim) and 238, 241, 248, 251, 256 (on how this union serves as the model for mission in the Gospel).

[41]For reviews of Olsson's book see, for instance, J. Duncan Derrett (*HeyJ* 16 [1975] 442) who praises his rendering of the episode of the Samaritan woman as "magnificently handled"; Thyen ("Auf neuen Wegen des Rätsel des vierten Evangeliums auf der Spur? Überlegungen zu dem Buch von Birger Olsson," *SvEA* 40 [1975] 136–142) also sees the work as a ground-breaking one, but points out the need to develop a standard terminology for "text-linguistic" studies; R. Kieffer (*RB* 82 [1975] 464–465) says, after a careful reading, that Olsson's conclusions prove unconvincing and criticizes the work for its vague and undefined terms, its heavy analytical paraphanelia which gets in the way of "le sens," and the lack of sustained reflection on the work of the commentator or the Evangelist as the interpreter. Finally, B. Stolt (*Linguistica Biblica* 34 [1975] 110–123) finds the work pioneering but lacking in a satisfactory discussion of the representative character of the texts, a precise definition of concepts, a systematic treatment of Johannine symbolism and a clear statement about the relations between the OT events and those described in John.

[42]It is not always clear, however, whether by "Samaria text" Olsson means 4:1–42 or only vv 31–38; or whether it is the *ergon* itself or "the discusssion" of the *ergon* which plays this unifying role. See, for instance, pp. 238–239.

[43]Olsson, *Structure and Meaning,* 234–235, 250, 253; see also nn. 36 and 37 above.

[44]For our discussion of this topic see pp. 141–142 below.

dismissal of v 42 which obviously poses a problem for this thesis of the unification of Judah and Ephraim[45].

Unlike the critics discussed up to this point, *Boismard-Lamouille* attribute vv 31–34, 35–36 and 37–38 to three different redactional levels: John II-A, II-B and III, respectively. They hold that only the first two of these levels somehow deal with mission. In vv 31–34 John II-A defines the nature of Jesus' mission from the Father; in vv 35–36 John II-B introduces the harvest theme which also has a missionary perspective as in Lk 10:2 and Mt 9:37–38. The real interest of John II-B, however, remains to combat the jealousies which existed in the early church between the disciples of Jesus and those of the Baptist as 3:23–30 attests. It is for this purpose that the Evangelist presents Jesus himself recognizing the important, though relative, value of the work of John the Baptist and of his disciples who, they hold, are the "others" in v 38. But in vv 37–38 John III is no longer concerned with the Samaritan mission, contrary to Cullmann, or even with mission as such. Rather, he strives to combat "une certaine tendence des chrétiens issus du paganisme pour qui la révélation ne comcençait qu'à Jesus." The point of these verses, then, as in v 22b (also assigned to John III) is to affirm through the mouth of Jesus himself the positive role played by Moses and the OT prophets (who on the level of John III are the "others" in v 38) and of Judaism generally in salvation history[46]. Thus, if in the discussion scholars generally interpret vv 37–38 as referring to the mission of the disciples, this interpretation is rejected by Boismard-Lamouille in the perspective of the final redaction of the Gospel.

Our last major author on 4:1–42 to be mentioned is *Leidig*. However, her dissertation adds nothing positively new to the positions of scholars already discussed for the understanding of mission in 4:1–42. The work aims at showing that vv 22 is the "key verse" (*Schlüsselvers*) to the understanding of the messianic function of Jesus and for the understanding of "the Jews" in the rest of the Gospel[47]. In her view, then, mission is one of the four factors in the passage which contribute most decisively "zum Verständnis der Juden" (p. 106) in the Gospel. Hence it is not an important theme in its own right, let alone the dominant theme in 4:1–42.

More than the other scholars surveyed, Leidig emphatically insists that mission in the passage refers only to the mission of the disciples: vv 2 and 38 speak of their mission in Judea and Samaria respectively, a position

---

[45]Only about three times in this whole study does Olsson (*Structure and Meaning*, 29, 74, 277) refer to the Samaritans' confession of Jesus as "the Savior of the world" (v 42) and each time the verse is listed among other passages as evidence of a successful Samaritan mission.

[46]Boismard-Lamouille, *Synopse III*, 134 (II 5 ca, cb), 143 (III 6 c), 144 (III D 3). It is to be noted that these authors also entertain the possibility that vv 37–38 could be the work of John II-B rather than of John III, which explains why they see the "others" as both John the Baptist and his disciples (level of John II-B) and as Moses and the OT prophets (level of John III).

[47]Leidig, *Jesu Gespräch*, vii–ix.

which is a variation of Olsson's[48]. Like most of the scholars examined, Leidig does not really address the issue of the structural or functional relationship between vv 31—38 and the rest of the passage. Rather she believes that though this insertion may "appear" to depend on the dialogue with the Samaritan woman, "das stimmt aber nicht ganz." Instead, just as the discourse with the woman filled up the time of waiting for the return of the disciples, so now the discourse with the disciples fills up the time of waiting for the return of the woman and the Samaritans. So, like Roustang, Olsson, and Boers, Leidig gives an extensive list of parallels and characteristics which exist between the two dialogues. These parallels emphasize the similarities between the woman and the disciples and their differences from Jesus[49]. On the whole, Leidig seems particularly careful not to use the term mission when speaking of the activity of Jesus, but prefers, instead, to speak of Jesus' doing God's will, of his "Sendung" and of his "weltweiten Retterdienst" (pp. 152, 153, 158). Jn 4:34 appears to be no more than the Johannine version of the temptations (cf. Mt 4:1—11; Mk 1:12—13; Lk 4:1—13; p. 147). The most startling of Leidig's statements, however, is her assertion: "Nur an dieser Stelle des Johannesevangeliums [i.e., in 4:1—42] ist von Mission die Rede." She argues that this takes place among Samaritans who are not Jews (p. 107). Thus, Leidig's position even more than Olsson's ("union of Judah and Ephraim") or Robinson's much earlier view that the purpose of the Gospel is to define who is a true Jew, conceives the theme of mission both in 4:1—42 and in the Gospel as a whole in an extremely narrow way[50].

Of the other major commentaries not mentioned in the survey, *Brown* does not raise the issue of the mission theme in the passage. He refers to it merely in passing, noting that the explanation that Jesus' food is his mission (v 34) leads rather naturally into the extension of the metaphor in terms of harvest (v 35). This means that the fruit of his mission is represented by the Samaritans who are coming to him[51]. Thus, with Bultmann, Brown tends to link vv 31—38 to vv 39—42. His discussion of vv 31—38 focuses on the problematic nature of the proverbial sayings in vv 35, 37, on the issue of the mission of the disciples during the lifetime of

---

[48]Leidig, *Jesu Gespräch*, 153; Olsson, "Jesus wins people by baptism but the disciples do the baptizing." *Structure and Meaning*, 239.

[49] Leidig, *Jesu Gespräch*, 151—154, 205—207; Roustang, "Les moments de l'acte de foi," 350—353. On the whole Roustang's study is too abstract and philosophical to be of much value in this present study; Olsson (*Structure and Meaning*, 175 and 220, 193 and 233, 238) focuses his parallelism of the two sections of the episode on the linguistic forms; Hendrikus Boers, "Discourse Structure and Macro-Structure in the Interpretation of Texts: John 4:1—42 as an Example," *SBLASP* (Chico: Scholars, 1980) 159—182, esp. p. 169.

[50]Robinson, "Destination and Purpose," 122 (for John "the only true Judaism is that which acknowledges Jesus as its Messiah. Becoming a true Jew and becoming a Christian are one and the same thing."). Bowker's variation of the thesis ("The Origin and Purpose of St. John's Gospel," *NTS* 11 [1964—1965] 390—408) is that the purpose of the Gospel is to redefine the meaning of Judaism (p. 399).

[51]Brown, *John* I, 181.

Jesus raised by v 38, and, more generally, on the possible relationship between 4:1—42 and what is known elsewhere in the NT about the Samaritan mission[52]. Again, he does not raise the issue of the possible relationship in terms of mission between vv 31—38 and the rest of the episode, but, with the generality of critics, conceives of mission only from the standpoint of the post-Easter activity of the disciples.

C. The Results of the Survey

The above extensive presentation of contemporary approaches to the literary and thematic issues in 4:1—42 gives one a good feel both of the seriousness of the level on which these issues are discussed and of the peculiar refusal of the Johannine material itself to be boxed into either-or categories. While the result of the discussion is too complex to be summarized, the following important results may be noted. First, the survey amply illustrates the observation made earlier in this study that in general critics tend to restrict the notion of mission in the Gospel to the post-Easter activity of the disciples. For while a few believe that 4:1—42 deals in some way with mission, most critics hold that vv 31—38 (8, 27) stand apart from the rest of the passage, irrespective of whether they were written by the same author or were added later by another author. What distinguishes these verses from the rest is their clear focus on the disciples and on their missionary activity. Furthermore, according to Lindars, at least, it is held that this episode concerning the disciples was introduced for the purpose of integrating the main story of Jesus' encounter with the Samaritan woman and the Samaritans into the larger composition of the Gospel and in order to relate Jesus' work to the missionary work of the disciples.

A second important result is the wide disagreement which exists concerning the function of vv 31—38 in the passage as a whole or the structural and thematic relationship between these verses and vv 1—30, 39—42. Fortna and Schulz, for instance, see no intrinsic relationship whatever between these two major sections, other than in the parallelism of certain Johannine features: *double-entendre* ("water," v 10 and "food," v 32), misunderstanding (vv 11—12, 33) and the "entrance-exit" procedure which sets the stage for each of the encounters (vv 7—8, 27—28). Both Schnackenburg and Leidig believe that the mission theme is subsidiary and independent, or, at best, that it serves a much more central theme in

---

[52]For instance, the "others" are the Hellenists and Philip (pp. 183—184); 4:34, 5:36, 9:4 and 17:4 are all descriptions of the nature of Jesus' ministry; and 4:38 relates to 17:18 and 20:21 on the future mission of the disciples (p.174). For another reflection along similar lines see R. H. Lightfoot, *St. John's Gospel, A Commentary* (Oxford: Clarendon, 1956) 126.

the passage: the self-revelation of Jesus (Schackenburg) and the Jewish character of Jesus' messiahship (Leidig). Bultmann goes a step further and sees the mission theme as that which unites vv 31—38 and 39—42. On a wider scale, however, he divides the passage into vv 1—30 and vv 31—42 and holds that both are united by the theme of witness (Jesus' witness to himself, vv 1—30 and the believers' witness to him, vv 31—42) rather than by mission. The earlier critics, Wellhausen and Spitta, saw Samaria rather than mission as the unifying element of the two episodes.

Finally, though Lindars and Olsson extend their discussion of the mission theme to the whole passage, their otherwise perceptive approach is undermined by their position that Jesus' work is mission only when viewed from the post-Easter standpoint and as part of the post-Easter activity of the disciples. Their position clearly raises questions concerning both the missionary character of the pre-Easter activity of Jesus and the value of the gospel genre in which the narrative is set and which by nature focuses on the pre-Easter phase of Jesus' life and work[53]. Olsson, in particular, makes an unclear distinction between Jesus' *ergon* (his work *before* and *after* the 'hour'), his mission which is centered in the events of the hour and his "harvesting mission" (or his winning followers through the disciples "after the 'hour'").

Thus, unlike in the case of the literary criticism of 4:1—42, there appears to be no kind of consensus concerning the missionary character of the whole passage or even of the missionary perspective of vv 31—38. After the extensive survey, we are still left with the question: What exactly is happening in 4:1—42 taken as a unified pericope the unity of which is underlined not only by its geographical setting in Samaria, as noted by Wellhausen and Spitta, but by Jesus himself who is both the focus and constant character in the different parts of the episode: vv 1—30, 31—38, 39—42? While there may be no simple answer to the question, the negative results of the survey indicate the need to break out of the current cycle of approach which starts with the understanding that mission in the passage refers only or primarily to the post-Easter activity of the disciples.

---

[53]Bailey (*Traditions,* 105) contends that John's Gospel deals with the period and problems of the church "exclusively" in connection with Jesus' life, whereas in Luke, because of the existence of Acts, this is not the case. This observation is not entirely correct because of the existence of the Johannine Epistles which also deal with the problems of the church. Nevertheless, it is to be noted that the problems of the church dealt with in the Gospel are primarily concerned with the mission of the disciples: 4:31—38; 13—17; 20:10—21:25. Nils Alstrup Dahl ("The Johannine Church and History," *Current Issues in New Testament Interpretation* [eds. William Klassen and Graydon F. Snyder; London: SCM, 1962] 124—142) also considers 4:1—42 as an important and illustrative example that "the situation of the post-resurrection church is prefigured and anticipated during the earthly ministry of Jesus in Israel." (p. 127). It is, therefore, of crucial importance first of all to recognize the deliberate focus of the Evangelist on the period of Jesus' earthly life, and then to ask the by-no-means idle question why he chose to deal with the church's missionary problems within this context of Jesus' life.

D. Towards a Working Hypothesis

The foregoing survey has shown that the real problem area in the inter-pretation of 4:1–42 lies in the structural and thematic relationship between vv 31–38 and 1–30, 39–42 in their present Gospel context. The fundamental questions that need to be addressed, then, are these: First, if an episode which focuses on the disciples and their future mission (vv 31–38) was superimposed or inserted into an already existing story of Jesus' encounter with the Samaritan woman and the Samaritans (vv 1–30, 39–42), what does this insertion say about both the missionary charac-ter of the latter story itself and the relationship between the two episodes now juxtaposed? In other words, why was the episode concerning the disciples inserted in this particular story of Jesus' visit to Samaria and in this apparently disruptive order, vv 8, 27, 31–38? Is there any particular significance in the points at which these two stories intersect? And does one throw light on the other?

Secondly, if, as Lindars holds, this episode about the disciples served to integrate the Samaritan episode into the larger composition of the Gos-pel, what may be gathered from this integrating principle concerning the role played by the disciples in the conception of mission in the Gospel as a whole? In other words, why were the disciples used as the integrating factor, and precisely in their capacity as missionaries?

The scope of this last question, unlike that of the first, extends beyond the Gospel context to the missionary situation of the Evangelist. But the answer to it depends to a large extent on that of the first, namely, on whether or not the Gospel understands Jesus' work in Samaria from the standpoint of mission. Though implied but nowhere explicitly raised in the extensive literature surveyed, these questions are crucial for our fuller comprehension of the passage. They may yet hold the unifying key to its many disparate elements, both literary and thematic.

The Hypothesis

These questions, of course, can be fully answered only after a careful exegesis of the passage. Nevertheless, we deem it necessary to advance the following working hypothesis which is in effect a description of the passage as it now stands. Our hypothesis is that all of 4:1–42, not just vv 31–38 or 31–42, deals with Jesus' mission from the Father seen from three different perspectives: vv 1–26(27) deals with this mission dialogi-cally from the standpoint of the non-believer, the Samaritan woman, whom Jesus seeks to lead to faith in him; vv 31–38 deals with it didac-tically from the standpoint of the disciples whom Jesus instructs on the nature of their own involvement in the mission, and vv 28–30, 39–42 deals with it dramatically and conclusively by illustrating, on the one hand, the normative character of Jesus' mission (with regard to both its scope and method) and, on the other, the nature of the relationship which must needs exist between the disciples/missionaries and those whom they bring to faith in Jesus.

Put in rhetorical terms, we view vv 1—26(27) as the *thesis* or the *narratio* and vv 28—42 as the *consequential argument* composed of an *expositio* (vv 31—38) and a *demonstratio* (vv 28—30, 39—42). On a different level, the structural relationship between vv 1—26 and 28—42 can be compared to that which exists elsewhere in the gospel between the *sēmeion* and its relevant explanatory discourse[54]. In brief, this research views mission as the unifying theme of the entire pericope. The specific issues raised in each section will, we hope, emerge in the course of the exegesis.

Finally, the absence of the disciples during the whole of Jesus' en-encounter with the Samaritan woman raises the question of who constitutes the real audience of the episode and of the Gospel. The question again points to the need to address the issue of the missionary situation of the Evangelist and of the audience addressed in the Gospel. This will be done after we have discovered what the passage and the Gospel say concerning mission.

Exegetical Presupposition

It is well known that every hermeneutic has its underlying methodology, and every exegesis its own particular focus[55]. Hence, no one exegesis can be expected to account with equal emphasis for all the features in any given passage. Rather, once a hypothesis has been formulated, it becomes necessary to direct the exegetical focus on those features of the passages which will best enable one to test the validity of the hypothesis[56]. This means, basically, that it is the task in hand which determines

---

[54]It is disputable whether or not the Gospel sees 4:1—42 as "a sign," given v 54; but the issue lies beyond the scope of this present discussion. Here we are merely interested in pointing out a common pattern in the Johannine style which consists in first narrating an event then expounding its significance; see, for instance, 5:1—9 and (10—16) 17—47; 6:1—15 and (16—25) 26—71; 9:6—7 (8—12) and 1—5, 13—41; 13:2—11 and 1, 12—20. In 11:1—54 the narration of the event is inter-woven with the explanation of its significance. The verses given here in parentheses refer to the transitional verses.

[55]See, for instance, W.G. Doty, *Contemporary New Testament Interpretation* (Englewood Cliffs: Prentice Hall, 1972) 81; Kümmel, "Die Exegese und ihre hermeneutische Grundlagen," *Das Neue Testament: Geschichte der Erforschung seiner Probleme* (Freiburg: Karl Albert, 1958) 128—143; also *Das Neue Testament im 20. Jahrhundert. Ein Forschungsbericht* (SBS 50; Stuttgart: KBW, 1970) 63—72; Ernst Lerle, *Voraussetzungen der neutestamentlichen Exegese* (Frankfurt a/M: Lutheraner Verlag, 1951) 55, 71.

[56]See, in particular, Doty, "Exegesis: The Movement from Text to Interpretation," *NT Interpretation*, 78—81; R. Morgan ("The New Testament and Hermeneutics," *Journal of Dharma* 5 [1980] 5—19) maintains that while the best rational methods of the day are used, NT interpretation is often guided by a prior decision about their subject matter. We prefer to say "hypothesis" rather than "subject matter" since the analysis of a text, if it is conducted in close fidelity to the text itself and the intention of the author, can overthrow as well as confirm a hypothesis.

not only the choice or combination of methods, but the degree of attention paid to any features in a given passage[57].

We recall once more that the particular interest of this present investigation is to discover the interpersonal dynamics involved in the portrayal of mission in the Gospel as this concerns both Jesus and the Evangelist and their respective audience. It is also our contention that from the standpoint of Jesus and his audience the dialogue constitutes the most "visible" aspect of this missionary activity, that which best enables us to "observe" the interaction between Jesus and his audience. From the standpoint of the Evangelist and his audience, the interaction operates within the entire narrative-dialogue framework. The narrative constitutes the Evangelist's primary method of involving his audience in the dialogue between Jesus and his audience, and through which he leads this audience to be personally present at and involved in the dialogue and so come to make a personal faith response to Jesus.

It is, then, this basic interest in mission as dramatized in the narrative-dialogue framework which will guide our exegesis of 4:1—42. In other words, the exegesis will pay particular attention to the possible meanings suggested, on the one hand, by the manner of exchanges between Jesus and the woman, and, on other other, by the narrative clues offered by the Evangelist. Accordingly, all excursions into possible OT and Samaritan traditions which may underlie the passage will be entertained only if they are seen to be directly related to this basic concern with mission. Finally, it is important to recall that we are testing a method, the contextual method, which focuses on the creative work and meaning of the final redaction of the biblical text. In order to give this method a chance, other issues which could profitably be rasied in the passage will have to be held in abeyance. The validity of the exegetical focus adopted here can ultimately be judged by the fruit it produces, whether, in fact, these results do offer a satisfactory interpretation of the passage as a whole. To this exegetical task we now turn.

---

[57]For instance, Schenke ("Jakobsbrunnen," 159) recognizes that "Exegese und Exegese ist nicht dasselbe!" and so feels free to base his study of Jn 4 on his belief that there are many redactional layers in the passage, and to orientate his exegesis towards illustrating this point. The result of his analysis appears on the chart on p. 61 above.

Chapter IV

Exegesis of John 4:1−26: The Thesis

The previous Chapter presented a discussion of the different suggestions made concerning the structural and thematic scope of 4:1−42. In this Chapter we shall analyze the first part of the pericope, vv 1−26, under the following units: vv 1−6, introduction and setting, and vv 7−26, the missionary dialogue between Jesus and the woman developed in two stages: the request for a drink (vv 7−15) and the revelation of Jesus' messiahship (vv 16−26), with v 10 constituting the structural and theological watershed of the entire dialogue. Since v 8 prospectively prepares for v 27, its function will be discussed in connection with the episode concerning the disciples (vv 27, 31−38) in Chapter V.

We recall, too, that the basic interest in this present Chapter is to determine whether or not mission can be seen as the basic screen which holds together and gives meaning and coherence to the disparate literary and thematic elements of the dialogue discussed in Chapter III. In other words, can Jesus' journey through Samaria and his encounter with the Samaritan woman be interpreted from the standpont of mission? What are the specific missionary issues raised, and how does the narrative-dialogue function on the level of Jesus and the woman? Given this unified focus of the exegesis, the analytical divisions suggested here will necessarily be transcended, especially in the discussion of those concepts which belong to more than one section of the passage.

The Greek text used in the ensuing exegesis, as indeed throughout the study, is the 26th critical edition of Nestle-Aland's *Novum Testamentum Graece* (DBS, 1979). Any departure from the readings proposed by these authors will be discussed when we are dealing with the text in question. With this proviso we may now begin our exegesis of vv 1−26.

A. Introduction and Setting, Vv 1−6

1. Exegesis

a) The introduction, vv 1−3

The introductory verses 1−3 function as a link on two levels: on the literary level they link the Samaritan episode (and by this we mean the whole of 4:1–42) with 3:22–36 by recalling Jesus' baptismal activity vis-à-vis that of the Baptist (v 1; 3:22–26); on the theological level they implicitly raise the question of who Jesus is in relation, for instance, to the Baptist (v 1; 3:27–36) who publicly disclaimed that he was "the Christ" (3:28; 1:20)[1]. As Jesus' baptismal activity in the Judean territory drew crowds away from the Baptist (3:26), gave rise to the dispute between John's own disciples and a Jew concerning purification (3:25) and roused the envy of these same disciples (3:26–30), so now it stirs up the interest of the Pharisees. In any event, it rouses Jesus' awareness of the Pharisees' concern over his baptismal activity and occasions his leaving Judea for Galilee (v 3). The encounter in Samaria takes place within this context of his journey from Judea to Galilee; and the journey motif also links the Samaritan episode to the Galilean episode (4:43–52) which closes this chapter.

Westcott remarks on the unusual use of the verb ἀφῆκεν (v 3) which has the general sense of leaving a thing to itself, its own wishes, ways, and fate[2]. The Johannine usage is, however, too varied to allow such a definite interpretation to be drawn[3]. The usual interpretation given to Jesus' action here is that he wishes to avoid any premature confrontation with the Pharisees or, at least, not to be interrogated by them or their emissaries as had been the case with John the Baptist (1:19–28). The interpretation finds support in the Gospel where Jesus escapes arrest from his adversaries because "his hour" had not yet come (7:30; 8:20; cf. 12:27, 13:1; 17:1).

From the perspective of mission, the theological issue in these introductory verses centers on the scope of v 1b which speaks of "Jesus' making disciples and baptizing" and of v 2 which appears to correct this statement as well as 3:22. While scholars regard v 2 as a gloss because of its corrective tone, Hoskyns rightly points out that the view lacks the sup-

---

[1] The literarily ungainly repetition of Ἰησοῦς in v 1 may be due to the fact that the second ὅτι-clause gives the indirect form of the report which the Pharisees heard. The direct form would thus be "Jesus is making and baptizing more disciples than John." This fact also accounts for the use of the present tenses, ποιεῖ and βαπτίζει. Compare the ὅτι-clause in v 17c where Jesus repeats the woman's direct statement in v 17a. Strikingly, the Johannine account places the beginning of Jesus' ministry before the arrest of the Baptist, while in Mark (1:14) Jesus' ministry begins after the arrest. The Johannine chronology thus has the advantage of allowing the Baptist to rise to the test when Jesus actually supplants him in his baptismal career (3:22–36) as he himself announced beforehand (1:29–34).

[2] B. Foss Westcott (*The Gospel According to Saint John: The Authorized Version with Introduction and Notes* [New Impression; London: John Murray, 1919] 66–67, note on v 3) remarks that this usage is unique in the NT. See also *BAG*, 125–126. The aorist form of the verb underlines the decisiveness of Jesus' withdrawal from Judea.

[3] In the following passages the verb ἀφιέναι is used: 4:28 (the woman "left" her water pot); 4:52 (the fever "quit" the son of the officer). In other instances, the verb can mean "to leave without support" or "to abandon" (8:29; 10:12; 14:18; 16:32); "to let go" (11:44, 48; 12:7; 18:8); "to leave the world to go to the Father" (16:28); "to leave peace with the disciples" (14:27); and even to take away sins (20:23; cf. 1 Jn 1:9; 2:12; Jas 5:5).

port of manuscript evidence[4]. The parenthetical flavor of the verse admits of explanation on stylistic grounds and belongs in line with other explanatory remarks also found in this chapter (cf. vv 8, 9c). The common interpretation of v 2 is that it seems designed to avoid equating Jesus' activity with that of John (cf. 1:26, 33; 3:23) and to limit the latter to his disciples. The real issue, however, is to determine whether v 1b describes one or two different, even if dependent, activities. In other words, is the activity of "baptizing," which in the last analysis is attributed to the disciples, not to Jesus (v 2), synonymous with "making disciples"? Or is the καί in v 1b to be understood copulatively or epexegetically? We recall that both Olsson and Leidig maintain that it is indeed the disciples, not Jesus, who are actually making and baptizing disciples[5].

In the evidence of the Gospel and of the NT generally, baptizing and making disciples are not synonymous activities. For instance, there is no indication that all who flock to Jesus to be baptized (3:26) have become his disciples; the same applies to those baptized by John. For one thing, the sole purpose of John's baptizing mission was to lead "all" to believe in Jesus (1:6—8; 3:27—30) or so that he might be revealed to Israel (1:19—28, 29—34 ; 3:31—36). The Synoptics also report of Jesus' being baptized by John (Mt 3:13—17; Mk 1:9—11; Lk 3:21—22, all echoed in Jn 1:29—34), but they in no way imply that Jesus thereby became the Baptist's disciple. Similarly, though Paul claims to have "begotten" all the Corinthian Christians through the preaching of the gospel (1 Cor 4: 15), he is glad that he baptized only a few of them since Christ did not send him to baptize but to preach the gospel (1 Cor 1:13—17)[6]. Finally, it needs to be recalled that Apollos was a staunch believer and missionary even though he received only the baptism of John (Acts 18:24—28). There is ample evidence, then, that "making disciples" and "baptizing" are not identical activities[7].

The expression μαθητὰς ποιεῖ, *a hapax legomenon* in the NT, is itself very striking. A parallel expression in Mk 3:14 (ἐποίησεν δώδεκα) refers to the appointment of the Twelve for a certain function rather than to

---

[4]Hoskyns, *The Fourth Gospel,* 23. Those who see v 2 as a gloss include Bernard, *Commentary,* 133; Wellhausen, *Erweiterungen,* 33; Wilkens, *Entstehungsgeschichte,* 129. The emphasis that the disciples not Jesus baptized may also be explained by the fact that baptism in the Spirit (1:33) only takes place as the fruit of Jesus' glorification (7:37—39; cf. 3:3—14). It is not clear what function this baptism by the disciples serves; that of John serves to draw attention to Jesus as the Messiah (1:31), not for the forgiveness of sins as in Mk 1:4. Yet even in this pre-Easter perspective in which the story is set, there is the understanding that Jesus' baptism is superior to that of John (3: 25—30).

[5]See p. 72 above.

[6]Paul's attitude towards baptism here seems to imply that even in the Christian community, baptizing was viewed as an activity inferior to preaching the gospel. A similar attitude may underlie v 2, though this is not readily evident.

[7]In Mt 28:19—20 the making of disciples is clarified by two functions: that of baptizing and teaching.

making them disciples of Jesus (cf. Mk 1:7, 13). Other NT passages employ the verb μαθητεύειν either passively (Mt 13:52; 27:57) or transitively (Mt 28:19; Acts 14:21), when describing the same activity. The Johannine formulation is thus strikingly concrete[8]. Moreover, it places the emphasis on Jesus as the subject and conveys an almost causative (Hebr., hiphil) meaning which is registered in Delitzsch's translation of this passage (העם ־ ־ך, v 1b)[9]. The expression thus carries the same force as ζωοποιεῖν in 6:63. This emphasis is all the more striking in that throughout the Gospel, with very few exceptions (cf. 2:15, 16), the verb ποιεῖν is used as a technical term for God's work of salvation (the mission) done either directly by God himself or through Jesus (5:20 ; 14:10) or given to Jesus to do and complete (4:34; 17:4 ;cf. 5:30 ; 8:29 ; 10:25, 32, 37—38; 14:31). The verb further describes the specific aspects of this work done by Jesus, especially his "signs" (2:11, 23; 3:2; 5:11, 15; 6:30; 11: 37, 47). The whole debate in 5:17—45, for instance, centers on Jesus' "doing" his Father's will.

On the level of the audience, the verb describes the human participation or the lack of it in this same mission (3:21; 5:29; 6:28; 7:17; 8:38, 41, 44 ; 15:5, 21 ; 16:2, 3)[10]. These passages which describe the individual's response are mostly negative: the Jews do the work of their father, the devil, in contrast to Jesus who does the work of God, his Father (8: 38, 41, 44); Judas's "deed" consists in the betrayal of Jesus (13:31); hostile unbelievers will do evil deeds to the disciples (15:21; 16:2, 3). When positive, they emphasize that the deeds are done in or through God and Jesus (3:21; 6:28; 15:5).

The conclusion to be drawn from this evidence, then, is that while v 2 attributes the activity of baptizing to the disciples, it does not thereby attribute to them also the "making of disciples." Jesus does not win people by the baptismal activity of the disciples. In the NT evidence and general Christian practice, baptism is administered to those who believe. From the standpoint of the community, it constitutes the community's recognition of this belief and serves as an act whereby the community welcomes the believer into its "fellowship" with God (cf. 1 Jn 1:4); but baptism itself does not *cause* one to believe or become a disciple. John and the NT are agreed on this issue[11].

---

[8]The verb ποιεῖν has the primary sense of "to fabricate" or "to create" (e.g., poetry); cf. *BAG*, 485; *LSJ*, 1427. The LXX uses the verb for the Hebrew ב ר א in the creation account of Gen 1:1, for instance.

[9]Franz Delitzsch, הברית החדשה (Berlin, 1912).

[10]The use of the verb ποιεῖν to describe God's action or that of human beings in relation to his is not unique to John or the OT and Judeo-Christian traditions generally. Herbert Braun's study (*TDNT* IV, 458—484) reveals a similar emphasis in the Greek world. While the LXX uses the verb to translate a wide range of Hebrew verbs (See Hatch and Redpatch, *A Concordance to the Septuagint* [Oxford: Clarendon, 1897] 1154), a considerable number of the more than 3200 entries refers to God's action. Cf. *TDNT* IV, 459.

[11]The case of Nicodemus, for instance, illustrates that one cannot really understand or accept

Indeed, John's Gospel is particularly clear on this issue; for if the disciple is one who believes in Jesus as the Father's envoy (6:29) and who continues to remain in him and in his word (8:31; 15:4—8), then it follows that only Jesus can make disciples or draw them to the fold or to himself (10:16; 12:32). This holds true even if the word is initially spoken by the disciples (17:20). John 4:42 is a clear case in point (cf. 1:43—51). So the "making of disciples" must be seen as part of Jesus' exclusive mission from the Father (3:34; 17:2—4). Indeed, it is the Father himself who draws disciples to Jesus (4:44—45, 65; cf. 4:23c). To say that the disciples, not Jesus, baptized (v 2) may yet be another way of saying that theirs is essentially a harvesting mission as in vv 35—38. Only in this sense, too, may v 2 be seen from the post-Easter standpoint.

A last issue worth noting in these introductory verses concerns the mention of the disciples in v 2. This verse indicates that the disciples do not suddenly appear in v 8 for the first time as an after-thought. Rather, they are present in the background all the time, indeed since 3:22. Nor is this the only passage in the Gospel where the appearance of the disciples is sporadic. Hence, if they were to be considered as a later insertion in this present passage on this basis, one would have to posit the same for most of the first part of the Gospel[12]. Most importantly, it needs to be noted that from the outset the passage draws attention to the different roles of Jesus and the disciples in the missionary enterprise, a theme which is developed fully in vv 31—38.

b) The setting, vv 4—6

Verse 4 moves the story and the action from Judea to Samaria. The dispute over ἔδει centers on whether it expresses personal convenience (so the majority of scholars from Lagrange to Bultmann and beyond) or whether it expresses the divine will for Jesus[13]. The first interpretation

---

the teaching of Jesus on baptism (birth from above through water and the Holy Spirit, 3:3—10), unless one is first prepared to believe in him as the unique and authorized teacher from God (vv 11—21, 31—36). In Acts (2:37—38, 41; 9:18; 10:47—48) baptism comes afterwards and presupposes faith and repentance.

[12]One of the arguments commonly advanced in support of the theory that the disciples are a later insertion into the story is that just as Jesus started the journey alone (v 1), he continues it alone after the episode (v 43). Yet it is also to be noted that in 2:13 Jesus goes to Jerusalem alone, while in 2:17, 22 and 3:22 (long after the feast) he is said to be with his disciples. Similarly, after 4:38 the disciples disappear in the Gospel till 6:3, which episode takes place in Galilee. Yet 7:3 implies that Jesus has disciples only in Jerusalem, not in Galilee! In 12:1 Jesus is alone for the feast, but in v 4 Judas suddenly appears to object to Mary's wasteful anointing. The Gospel evidence thus shows the lack of prominence of the disciples in the fisrt part of the Gospel where the focus is on Jesus' interaction with a wide range of audiences. Indeed, only in Jn 4, 6 and 11 are the disciples more closely interwoven with the narrative. For further sporadic appearances of the disciples prior to 13—17 see 6:71—9:2; and 9:2—11:7, 8, 12, 54.

[13]Lagrange: " ἔδει n'indique pas une volonté divine, mais une convenance personnelle d'itinéraire." *Evangile de Jean* (5 ed.; EBib; Paris: Lecoffre, 1936), 103; Bultmann, *Commentary*, 176; Lindars, *John*, 178; Schnackenburg, *Johannesevangelium* 1, 458; to mention but a few.

rests on the fact that Samaria was the shortest route from Judea to Galilee
(Jos. *Ant.* 22.6.1; *BJ* 2, 232 [for which compare Lk 9:52–56]; *Vita* 269).
Hence, the quickest way for Jesus to avoid the Pharisees was to take this
route out of Judea. Cullmann and Brown, however, interpret the verb in
the theological sense, while Barrett and Haenchen see both interpretations
as possible, but lean more towards the first[14]. The theory of the shortest
route, however, does not really account for the notion of *necessity* embodied in the verb ("he had to"). Brown's observation, that since Jesus
was already by the Jordan valley it would have been quicker to go up
north from there through the Bethshan gap, does not fit the Johannine
situation which does not specify the geographical locale of Jesus' baptismal activity though it does that of the Baptist (3:23)[15]. The phrase $\epsilon i \varsigma$
$\tau \dot{\eta} \nu$ 'Ιουδαίαν $\gamma \tilde{\eta} \nu$ (3:22) means quite simply "in the Judean territory."

Josephus, too, does not support the theory of the short cut. His account concerns the pilgrimage *to*, not *from* Jerusalem. Although rabbinic
rules permitted one to take the quickest possible means to get to the
Temple or the synagogue for worship, it prohibited taking the same means
back since this proved a lack of love for God's service (*b. Ber.* 6b)[16]. Besides, Jesus remained in Judea long after the Passover feast (2:23–3:22);
hence he would not have been covered by the pilgrimage conditions
mentioned by Josephus, even if pilgrims from Galilee took the same route
back. The notion of necessity expressed in this passage, therefore, needs
to be explained on other grounds.

The first point to note is that, as it applies to Samaria from a Jewish
standpoint, $\ddot{\epsilon}\delta\epsilon\iota$ refers to the situation of open hostility which existed
between the two nations, which hostility is plainly stated in v 9 (cf. 8:
48) and for which the OT, NT and Josephus furnish ample evidence[17]. In
other words, it is because of this open hostility, not because the route
through Samaria is the shortest, that the notion of "having to" arises at
all. The meaning of vv 3–4, then, could be that Jesus is so desperate to
get out of hostile Judean territory that he was forced to go through this
enemy territory. But nothing in v 1 or in the Gospel narrative up to this

---

[14]Cullmann, *Heil als Geschichte: Heilsgeschichtliche Existenz im Neuen Testament* (Tübingen,
Mohr-Siebeck, 1965) 255; Brown, *John 1,* 169; Barrett, *John,* 230 (though in his first edition Bar-
rett was clearly of the opinion that the verb referred to Samaria being the short cut to Galilee);
Haenchen, *Johannesevangelium,* 238.

[15]Brown, *John* I, 169.

[16]The three references in Jeosephus are: $\dot{\epsilon}\nu$ ταῖς $\dot{\epsilon}$ορταῖς εἰς τὴν ἱερὰν πόλιν (*Ant.* 20.6.1,
118); $\ddot{\epsilon}\delta\epsilon\iota$ ... ταχὺ ... $\dot{\alpha}\pi\epsilon\lambda\theta\epsilon\tilde{\iota}\nu$ ... $\dot{\alpha}\pi\dot{\sigma}$ Γαλιλαίας ... εἰς 'Ιεροσόλυμα (*Vita,* 269); and πολ-
λῶν $\dot{\alpha}\nu\alpha\beta\alpha\iota\nu\acute{\sigma}\nu\tau\omega\nu$ 'Ιουδαίων $\dot{\epsilon}\pi\iota$ τὴν $\dot{\epsilon}$ορτήν (*BJ* 1.12.3, 232). Josephus never states what route
the pilgrims took on their return to Galilee. Obviously, the pressure to get to the feasts on time
made them take the unsafe route through Samaria, a journey of three days (*Vita,* 269). That they
should take the same perilous route back when the pressure was no longer there would make very
little sense.

[17]See 2 Kg 17:24–41; Neh 4:1–23; Lk 9:52–53; Jos. *Ant.* 18.2.2; 20.6.1; *BJ* 2.13.3 (see
further *Ant.* 11, 341; 12, 257). For the rabbinic literature on the subject see *T. Levi,* 7:2 and *Str-B,*
I, 538–560.

point indicates that the hostility between Jesus and the Pharisees had reached such a peak as to make this interpretation reasonable. It is only later that the hostility of the leaders towards Jesus develops and increases in intensity: first they persecute and desire to kill him (5:16, 18), then send the Temple guards to arrest him (7:32, 45–52), attempt to stone him (8:59), forbid any to confess him as "the Christ" (9:22–23), and finally decide in the Sanhedrin to get rid of him (11:47–54).

This increased hatred derives from his statements about his divine origin (5:18; 8:58; 10:33, 36), not about his making disciples. The only confrontation with the leaders up to this point is in 2:18–22 when they ask him for a "sign" as proof of his authority for upsetting the Temple commerce. So though the report in v 1 may have a part in Jesus' decision to leave Judea for Galilee, it does not fully or satisfactorily explain why he "had to" pass through Samaria. Besides, Jesus does return to Jerusalem and Judea on three other occasions prior to his final arrest (5:1; 7:10; 11: 11, 16).

This means, then, that the theological interpretation, namely, that ἔδει refers to the divine will for Jesus, cannot be rejected, especially in view of v 34 (cf. 6:38). Since Jesus lives only for the Father's will (4:34; 6:38; 17:4) and can do nothing except what he sees the Father doing (5: 19), there can be no other imperative in his life than the Father's will. Moreover, viewed positively, the situation of open hostility between Jews and Samaritans which is well exploited in the passage (vv 9, 20, 22, 27) makes his going there on mission all the more striking. Equally, the extraordinary reception given him by the woman and the Samaritans contrasts sharply with his poor reception by the Jews (cf. 2:18–3:21; 4:44).

This contrast may be deliberate since the *dispositio* forms an important part of the meaning. Against this background of hostility, too, the issue of fellowship raised negatively in vv 9, 20, 22, and positively in vv 36, 40 receives special prominence. Finally, whatever its usage in other NT or OT passages, the Johannine usage of the verb consistently refers to the eschatological necessity of God's plan of salvation executed by Jesus, either as it applies to him personally (3:14, 30a; 9:4; 10:16; 12:34; 20:9), to the Baptist, his precursor (3:30b), to the individual vis-à-vis this mission (3:7), or to the new order of worship established by his mission[18]. Consistent Johannine usage thus leads one to see ἔδει as expressing the divine

---

[18]For a discussion of δεῖ in OT, NT, Rabbinic and Hellenistic literature, see Walter Grundmann, *TDNT* II 21–25; Erich Fascher, "Theologische Beobachtungen zu δεῖ," *Neutestamentliche Studien für Rudolf Bultmann* (BNZW 21; Berlin, 1954), 228–254, esp. pp. 252–254 where he discusses the usage in John's Gospel. While Jewish tradition predicted that all nations would flock to Jerusalem for worship in the messianic era (cf. Is 2:2–3; Mic 4:1–4), Jesus declares, on the contrary, that true worshipers in this messianic era are those who worship God in spirit and in truth (v 23). Given this background, therefore, the verb in v 20 does not refer simply to the dispute over Jerusalem and Gerizim. The place where one "ought to" worship remains, in the Jewish perspective, eternally Jerusalem. Its eternal significance is here rendered null and void by Jesus.

will for Jesus. In short, his encounters in Samaria form part of his divine mission from the Father (4:23).

The second issue in this section concerns the scope of κοπιᾶν (v 6). The common view again rejects the interpretation that the term is a technical one for missionary labor as in v 38 or in the NT generally[19], and holds that it merely describes Jesus' physical exhaustion from the journey. The argument claims support from the expression ἐκ τῆς ὁδοιπορίας which appears to define, and thus delimit, the meaning of the term in v 6. A further question to be raised, however, concerns the ὁδοιπορίας itself: Is the journey through Samaria a missionary undertaking or not? The answer has partially and positively been given in our discussion of v 4. But a fuller answer must await the completion of the analysis of the entire passage.

However, it is to be noted that a special feature of this particular passage is that words function on more than one level of meaning ("water," vv 7–15; "food," vv 31–34). The same applies in this instance. Jesus' physical exhaustion derives from his obedience to the Father's will and continues throughout the entire passage: v 8 suggests that he had not eaten, since the disciples had gone to buy food — this is reinforced by his request for a drink (v 7). The disciples' urging him to eat, and their surprise that he might have been brought food by someone else (vv 31, 33) reminds the reader that Jesus still has neither eaten nor taken a drink. Hence, the reality of his physical exhaustion cannot be downplayed. On the level of Johannine symbolism, however, the physical exhaustion dramatizes very forcefully the spiritual labor involved in the mission. In 12:24 the imagery of the death of a wheat grain is used to express the same concept; in 16:21 that of a woman in labor, and in 13:1 and 15:13 that of loving unto death (cf. 2 Cor 6:3–10). Jesus' mission involves physical exhaustion in the fullest sense of the word.

On the level of approach to mission, and of Jesus' interaction with the woman, his wearied state serves another function. The fact that he is sitting down exhausted (οὕτως [v 6] is most likely a stage direction), in enemy territory, thirsty and needy, makes him not only approachable but needy and even vulnerable before the woman. By the same token, his physical condition gives the woman a real advantage over him, an advantage which she exploits fully (vv 11–12). This presentation of Jesus as weak and dependent recalls the humility traditionally associated with the missionary (cf. Phil 2:6–11; 2 Cor 8:9; Is 42:1–4), in which Hillel excelled over Shammai (*'Abot* 2, 6; *b. Šabb.* 31a), and which Paul paints so vividly in 1 Cor 4:9–13[20]. In Jesus' case, his exercise of humility is

---

[19] In addition to the commentaries, see in particular Friedrich Hauck, κόπος, κοπιάω, *TDNT* III, 827–830, especially his comparison of 4:38 with Jos. *Ant.* 2, 321, though he admits that 4:38 has the same distinctive meaning as in Paul (e.g.; 1 Cor 9:15, 18; 15:10; 2 Cor 11:23; 1 Thess 2:9; Col 1:9) and in Acts 20:35.

[20] The Rabbinic traditions cited here report the incident of three proselytes whom R. Shammai

outstanding by the fact that though he is the one with "the gift of God" to offer (v 10), he nonetheless approaches the woman as a beggar. His portrait here as a weary traveller and beggar is thoroughly at odds with Wrede's and Bultmann's image of him as a God striding the earth barely touching it[21].

The realism of Jesus' physical tiredness is further accentuated by the reference to the time of day "noon" (ὥρα ἦν ὡς ἕκτη). Some critics interpret this to mean that since the woman was a sinner, she went to the well when she was unlikely to meet anybody. This pure speculation has very little interest for the story. The reference to the time of day goes with Jesus' arrival at the well (v 6) and perhaps, too, with the reference to the disciples' having gone to buy food (v 8), but not with the time of the woman's arrival at the well (v 7). One only has to know the conditions even of today's Palestine to appreciate fully this picture of a wearied traveller sitting at a functioning well, but lacking the means with which to draw. On a stage setting, and the dramatic qualities of this episode have been repeatedly emphasized since Windisch, how very welcome the woman's arrival must appear and how very real Jesus' request for a drink[22]. That he then poses as a giver of living water rather than as one needing a drink (v 10, 13—14) must indeed surprise and intrigue the woman (vv 11—12).

A third issue in this section concerns the geographical and theological significance of the setting of the story. Critics identify "Sychar" as ancient Shechem (modern Nablus), not Askar. If this identification is correct, the city derives its importance from association with the Patriachs of whom Jacob and Joseph are explicitly mentioned (v 5)[23]. On the theological level, most critics agree that the scene evokes one or other of the OT well encounter stories: Isaac's servant and Rebekkah (Gen 24: 10—19), Jacob and Rachel (Gen 29:1—14), Moses and Zipporah (Ex 2: 15b—21). The dispute, however, centers on determining which of these stories, if any, has the richest associations with the Samaria narrative.

A close examination of these parallel stories reveals that while there are some broad similarities in all the stories combined: the meeting at

---

chased away because they laid conditions for their admission to Judaism. Hillel, however, admitted them on their own terms only gradually to lead them to the orthodox position concerning the full observance of the Torah.

[21]See p. 27 above.

[22]Windisch, "Der Johanneische Erzählungsstil," 181; Lothar Schmid, "Die Komposition der Samaria-Szene Joh 4, 1—42," *ZNW* 28 (1929) 148—158 ("ein kleines Kunstwerk," 153); Dodd, *Interpretation,* 311 ("a highly dramatic dialogue with an appropriate narrative setting"); Bligh, "Jesus in Samaria," 329 ("one of the most skilfully written passages" in the Gospel); Schnackenburg, *Johannesevangelium* I, 456 ("Der Aufbau ist fast dramatisch."); Brown (*John* I, 176) lists "various techniques of stage setting" which illustrate the Evangelist's "masterful sense of drama."

[23]Not only Jacob (Gen 33:18) and Joseph to whom the land was given (Gen 48:22), but before them Abraham (Gen 12:6—7) was in Shechem. Joseph is finally buried there and the land passes to his descendants (Josh 24:32).

the well itself, some connection with marriage, and, in the case of Jacob and Moses, a possible persecution/flight to a foreign country, there are no real parallels between the OT stories and the Samaritan narrative as it now stands. Even the careful and detailed development by Boismard-Lamouille of the analogy between this episode and the Isaac-Rebekkah story lacks convincing force, mainly because their analysis concerns the hypothetical story of Document C, not our present Gospel narrative[24]. A striking difference between the Johannine account and these OT stories lies in the centrality of marriage in the Patriarchal accounts. This is not clearly an issue in 4:1—42, even though Jesus is called "the bridegroom" in 3:29, and even though some notion of wooing (in the sense of persuading the woman) is clearly present (v 10, 21). Moreover, none of the women in the OT stories are previously married, let alone five times.

Most importantly, if John is using any of these stories, then he has radically reversed their function in a number of key issues. For instance, in the OT stories the request for a drink serves to reveal to the thirsty stranger the right woman to be sought in marriage. In John, on the contrary, the request serves towards the revelation to the woman of the stranger who is seeking for the drink (vv 10, 25—26). While Isaac's servant and Jacob are delighted with the answers to their questions, Jesus, on the contrary, finds the woman's explanation of the worth of the Patriarchal well wholly inadequate for his purposes. And the woman must herself ask for and receive in faith the "gift of God" which he brings. Whatever echos there may be, therefore, between the Johannine account and the OT stories, one must admit that the Johannine interest in the present Gospel narrative wholly transcends that of its OT counterparts.

Another ancient theory which is closely related to the martial interpretation of the setting is the view that the "five husbands" (v 18) refer to the five gods of the five nations settled in Samaria in 722 B.C. by the Assyrian king Shalmaneser (2 Kg 17:24—41), that "the sixth, not her husband," refers to the syncretistic worship of Yahweh current in the NT era. Accordingly, Jesus is here seen to be wooing the woman from this ignorant worship (v 22a) to the enlightened worship of Yahweh (vv 21, 23—24). For Origen, the five husbands represented the five books of the Samaritan Pentateuch (SP). The theory of the five gods has received its most recent and systematic defense from Boismard-Lamouille[25].

This theory has in its favor the high level of Johannine symbolism present in the Gospel and which could allow for this interpretation. On the level of *double-entendre*, it has been noted that *ba‘al* (pl. *be‘ālīm*) in Canannite language means both "husband" and "god" (or "lord"), so there could be a deliberate play on words involved in the usual Semitic

---

[24]Boismard-Lamouille, *Synopse III,* 136. The passages compared are parts of 4:6b—7 with Gen 24:43; and 4:28—30, 40 with Gen 24:28—32.

[25]Origen, *Commentaire sur Saint Jean* (SC 222, 57); Boismard-Lamouille, *Synopse III,* 137.

fashion (cf. Hos 2:16—17)[26]. A serious objection to this interpretation, also noted by Schnackenburg, is that the five gods of the Samaritans were worshiped simultaneously, not successively, as would be the case if this identification were intended in v 18[27]. Moreover, the worship of Yahweh ran parallel with these other worships (2 Kg 17:29—34, 41). Besides, the number of gods add up to seven, not five (2 Kg 17:30—31), though Josephus (*Ant.* 11.14.3, 288) reduces this number to five. Finally, even if the worship of Yahweh alone survived in the NT era, the greatest objection still remains that the theory does not account for the way the "five husbands" function in the passage. We shall return to this issue later.

If the OT well-encounter stories with the related issue of marriage constitutes an inadequate background to the Johannine account, of what significance, then, is the setting described in vv 5—6a? In our judgment, this setting is important because it introduces two of the key concepts which are operative in Jesus' dialogue with the woman, and which are important both from his and her point of view, namely, "Jacob's well" and the concept of "gift" ($\check{\epsilon}\delta\omega\kappa\epsilon\nu$). The importance of wells in drought-tormented Palestine and in the Middle East generally is common knowledge (cf. Gen 26:14—22; Ex 15:22—27; 17:1—17). For the Samaritans, however, this is not just any well. The absence of the article ($\pi\eta\gamma\dot{\eta}$ $\tauo\tilde{\upsilon}$ $\text{'}Ia\kappa\acute{\omega}\beta$) stresses its importance as a place name; it has a long ancestry dating back to Jacob. For the woman in particular, the well stands as a living testimony of their proud descent from Jacob (v 12), something, therefore, which gives her a sense of national identity. The Jacob-ancestry is very important to the woman, especially when set against the background of the contemptuous attitude of Ben Sira who views "the foolish people that dwell in Shechem" as "no nation" at all (50:25—26). By its extraordinary depth (v 11), the well, dug in alluvial soil and surrounded by abundant springs which probably fed it, lends itself to being regarded both as a $\pi\eta\gamma\acute{\eta}$ and a $\varphi\rho\acute{\epsilon}\alpha\rho$ (v 12)[28], and so fits in well with the Johannine symbolism and *double-entendre*.

Most importantly, the well is seen by the woman as Jacob's "gift" to his descendants (v 12). In this setting, Jacob is introduced as a "giver"; it is in this capacity, not as wife-seeker, that Jesus compares with and transcends him in the narrative (vv 10, 14). Noticeably, in v 5 it is the field, not the well, that Jacob gave to his son Joseph, yet except for the reference to "this mountain" (v 20), the gift of the field seems to play no

---

[26]For a detailed discussion on the subject see Brown, *John* I, 171; Boismard-Lamouille, *Synopse III*, 137.

[27]Schnackenburg, *Johannesevangelium* I, 468.

[28]The nature of Jacob's well is thus similar to that described in Gen 26:19: באר מים חיים Boers ("Discourse Structure," 167) believes in a possible reference here to the targumic tradition that Jacob did not need a bucket to draw water from the well because when he lifted up the stone the water lept to the surface and overflowed for twenty years (*Tg. Pal.* 28 [sic]:10). Boers, however, does not date this targumic material.

role in the dialogue. This further supports our view that the setting emphasizes the role of Jacob as a "giver." Boers indeed calls him a *theios anēr,* even though the validity of the concept has been cogently questioned by Holladay[29]. Indeed, the clause "which Jacob gave to his son Joseph," evokes contrastingly 3:16, the foundation text on mission: while Jacob gave the field to his most beloved son, Joseph, God gave his uniquely beloved Son to the world that it might have eternal life in him. V 10 certainly refers to this gift of salvation given through the Son, though elsewhere God's love and gift to the Son is emphasized (3:33—34; 5:20; 10: 17; 15:9; 17:23), and all in reference to the Son's mission.

Finally, this emphasis on "gift," mentioned explicitly nine times in vv 5—15, coupled with the reference to Shechem/Sychar and the statement in v 38 in particular, strongly suggests that Josh 24, more so than any of the OT well-encounter stories cited above, constitutes the most probable OT passage underlying this episode: God's innumerable free gifts to his people including a land on which they had never "labored" and a harvest they had never planted (v 13; cf. Jn 4:38), demands from them a corresponding homage of true worship and faithful service (vv 14—28; cf. Jn 4:21—24). A significant point in this inspirational passage or "type scene" as Alter would put it, would then be that ultimately, it is God, not Jacob, who gave both the land and the well to the Samaritans[30]. This point is stated explicitly with regard to Moses as the giver of bread from heaven (6:32—33), an episode which has many parallels with our present scene. The setting at Jacob's well thus porports to play an integral, visible role in the message which Jesus wishes to convey to the woman in the dialogue.

2. Summary of the Discussion Concerning Vv 1—6

The salient points in our discussion of the missionary elements in vv 1— 6 may now be summarized as follows:

(a) *General background.* Jesus' journey through Samaria and the ensuing encounter is seen as part of the divine plan for his mission. The background of hostility which exists between Jews and Samaritans and

---

[29]For Boers see n. 28 above; Carl R. Holladay (*Theios Aner in Hellenistic-Judaism: A Critique of the Use of This Category in New Testament Christology* [Missoula: Scholars Press, 1977]) has cogently demonstrated that Hellenistic-Jewish writers (for instance, Philo) never intended to divinize their biblical heroes when they applied the term *theios anēr* to them. To hold, then, that the NT authors portrayed Christ as a *theios anēr* because they borrowed this concept from Hellenistic-Judaism is to ascribe to their work the influence of a source that never existed. See further the positive review of Holladay's dissertation by Murphy-O'Connor, *RB* 88 (1981) 143—144.

[30]Robert Alter, *The Art of Biblical Narrative* (New York: Basic Books, 1981) 47—67. The Johannine scene can be compared to the type scenes described here by Alter only in the broadest terms. The well never plays as significant a role in the OT encounters as it does here in John.

which in this introductory verse is also registered by the notion of necessity (v 4) raises the issue of fellowship (a sense of belonging together) —
itself an important aspect of mission — which is developed in vv 9, 20,
23—24, 36, 40, 42. The distinction made between Jesus' activity and that
of the disciples also raises the issue of their respective roles in the missionary enterprise which is also developed in vv 31—38, 41—42.

(b) *Terminology.* In the passage the terms δεῖ and κοπιᾶν have a double
meaning. Theologically, they express, respectively, the eschatological
necessity of Jesus' mission in Samaria (cf. v 34) and the labor involved
in the execution of this mission (as in the rest of the NT). The κοπιᾶν concept also accentuates the attitude (humble, dependent, approachable)
required of the missionary in order to give the advantage to the one to be
led to faith. Noticeably, the description of the setting focuses on the
Patriarchal tradition which is of importance to the woman. On the narrative level, the portrayal of Jesus as a weary, thirsty traveller in an alien
land makes his request for a drink very real.

(c) *Concepts.* The setting introduces two important concepts: Jacob's
well seen as a source of water, and Jacob himself seen as "the giver" of
gifts (the field and the well). These concepts are of pressing importance
to the woman; Jesus recognizes this and soon employs them in his dialogue with her as the natural means of progressively leading her to believe
in him as the Messiah (v 26), as one, that is, who is greater than the revered ancestor Jacob and whose gift of water brings eternal life. From this
perspective Josh 24 (also staged in Shechem) emerged as the most fitting
OT background to the Samaritan episode. The suggestion was inspired by
the emphasis which is placed in both the OT and Johannine passages on
the absolute gratuitousness of God's gifts to his people and the corresponding demand of true worship from them. In many ways, therefore,
the introductory verses appear to be deliberately designed to prepare
integrally for the ensuing dialogue.

B. The Missionary Dialogue, Vv 7—16

The chief task, in this present section, we recall, is to examine closely
the level of interaction between Jesus and the woman, whether this is
real or whether the woman serves merely as a foil for the exposition of
Jesus' unrelated teachings concerning living water and the revelation of
himself as the Messiah. In particular, given the thematic and structural
problems raised in Chapter III, can mission be seen as the fulcrum which
holds together the different themes of living water (vv 10—15), true
worship (vv 20—24) and the revelation of Jesus' messiahship (vv 25—26)?
What new light, in brief, does attention to the central concerns of the

Evangelist and to his art of narrative-dialogue shed on our understanding of the passage?

1. The General Structure of the Dialogue

Admittedly, the dialogue lacks an easily discernible symmetrical structure. But our task as exegetes is to endeavor to make sense of the passage as it now stands. With Lindars to some extent, this present study recognizes two, not three, basic divisions in the dialogue : the theme of the gift of living water (vv 7–15) and the revelation of Jesus' messiahship (vv 16–26)[31]. V 10 embodies the *theme* of the entire dialogue, like "the text" a homily[32]. Grammatically, v 10 consists of a protasis (v 10a, 10b) and an apodosis (vv 10c, 10d) — see the outlay of the dialogue attached, p. 94. In the protasis, Jesus puts before the woman two conditions for asking and receiving the gift of "living water," namely, (i) knowledge of "the gift of God" (v 10a), and (ii) knowledge of who Jesus is who mediates this gift (v 10b).

These two points raised in the protasis are developed dialectically in the conversation, the one in terms of living water set as a contrast to the water from Jacob's well (vv 11–15), the other in terms of Jesus' prophetic and cultic knowledge set against the woman's information about her private life (vv 17–19) and contrasted with Jewish and Samaritan beliefs concerning worship (vv 20–24). It needs to be noted in this connection that the real issue in vv 20–24 is not the theology of worship as such, but that Jesus can speak so authoritatively on the subject. His doing so without first presenting his credentials to the woman further underlines the issue of his true identity (v 10b, 26) which the woman connects with that of her expected Messiah (v 25).

Verse 7 introduces the theme of living water, and vv 17b–19 lead into the discussion on Jesus' identity. This question of his identity is, however, first raised by the woman herself, σὺ Ἰουδαῖος ὤν (v 9a). It is important to note from the outset, though the point will be developed later, that the movement of the entire dialogue centers on the woman and her needs. It is for her sake that the conversation takes place in the first instance. The promise of living water is made to her; if she receives it, it will benefit

---

[31]Lindars, (*John,* 177–185, 185–191), adopts the divisions: "Living water" (vv 4–15) and "the true teacher" (vv 16–26). In this present study vv 4–6 are treated as part of the general setting of the pericope.

[32]The theory that the Gospel material may originally have existed as homilies has been repeatedly emphasized by Lindars (*Behind the Fourth Gospel,* 47, 60; *John,* 51–54) and others. The authors cited by Lindars in support of his position include Barrett, Braun, Brown, Schnackenburg, and Sanders (*John,* 51). Since the homiletic model suggests a one-sided communication, it does not entirely fit 4:1–26, which is clearly a dialogue, unless, of course, one envisages a homily in dialogue form.

her personally (vv 10d, 13—14). Also *she* determines the terms in which the issues are discussed, by the way she understands both Jesus' initial request for a drink (v 7) and his command to her in v 16. Each time, Jesus follows along her terrain, but without losing sight of his main objective, which is to bring her to that knowledge of himself which will lead her to ask and receive the gift of living water (vv 10a, b, 26). Contrary to both Leidig and Hudry-Clergeon, v 26, not v 22, is the climax of the dialogue[33].

From the woman's viewpoint, the gift of living water constitutes the salient aspect of the conversation. It is this which interests and intrigues her most (v 11). Her question centers on both the whence and means by which Jesus can provide the promised water (v 11c). Even when she resumes the issue of Jesus' identity, it is essentially in terms of what he can offer by comparison to the ancestor Jacob (v 12). Thus her attitude resembles that of the Galilean Jews who compare Jesus to Moses as the giver of bread from heaven (6:30—35)[34]. Recognizing this predominant interest of the woman, Jesus first develops the theme of "gift of God" (vv 13—14), and only when the woman brings this topic to a close (v 15) does he move the conversation back to the theme of his identity (v 16). We may now take a closer look at the manner in which these issues are discussed and at the nature of the exchanges between Jesus and the woman.

2. Exegesis of Vv 7—15: The Interaction

a) Vv 7—10: the proposition

The statement "Give me to drink" in v 7b is both a request and an offer, or better still, an offer made in the form of a request. V 10 makes this clear. The request formula is remarkably, perhaps even deliberately, vague: it does not specify "water," though given the circumstances (v 6—7a) this is the meaning which readily imposes itself. In the perspective of

---

[33]Leidig (*Jesu Gespräch*, xvii), sees v 22 as "Kulminationspunkt und Schlüsselaussage" of 4: 1—42; Hudry-Clergion ("De Judée en Galilée," 830) takes the unit of the pericope as 4:1—45, and comes through a series of chiastic structures to the conclusion that vv 20—26 constitutes the center of the pericope with v 24 (which he interprets as the revelation of God) as the climax. The rest of the passage he regards as anti-climactic.

[34]Not only the Samaritans and the Jews, but the Semitic mentality generally measures greatness very concretely: in terms of riches and military achievements; for instance, Nimrod, "the first mighty man on earth" (Gen 10:8—12), Abraham (Gen 13:2) — even his faith and love for God are measured by his willingness to sacrifice Isaac (Gen 22:9—12). The same mentality underlies the portrayal of Yahweh as "a mighty man" (גבור איש) and owner of the entire universe (cf. Ps 89:8—13).

*The Text of the Narrative-Dialogue: 4:7–15**

Jesus	*Woman*	*Evangelist*

7b
δός μοι πεῖν

8
οἱ γὰρ μαθηταὶ αὐτοῦ
ἀπεληλύθεισαν εἰς τήν πόλιν
ἵνα τροφὰς ἀγοράσωσιν.

← 9
πῶς, σὺ Ἰουδαῖος, ὢν
παρ' ἐμοῦ πεῖν αἰτεῖς γυναικὸς Σαμαρίτιδος οὔσης;
9c
οὐ γὰρ συγχρῶνται Ἰουδαῖοι
Σαμαρίταις.

10
εἰ ἤδεις τὴν δωρεὰν τοῦ θεοῦ
→ καὶ τίς ἐστιν ὁ λέγων σοι· δός μοι πεῖν,
σὺ ἂν ᾔτησας αὐτὸν
καὶ ἔδωκεν ἄν σοι ὕδωρ ζῶν.

11 κύριε, οὔτε ἄντλημα ἔχεις
καὶ τὸ φρέαρ ἐστιν βαθύ·
πόθεν οὖν ἔχεις τὸ ὕδωρ τὸ ζῶν;

→ 12 μὴ σὺ μείζων εἶ τοῦ πατρὸς ἡμῶν Ἰακώβ
ὃς ἔδωκεν ἡμῖν τὸ φρέαρ
καὶ αὐτὸς ἐξ εὑτοῦ ἔπιεν
καὶ οἱ υἱοι αὐτοῦ καὶ τὰ θρέμματα αὐτοῦ;

13
πᾶς ὁ πίνων ἐκ τοῦ ὕδατος τούτου
διψήσει πάλιν·
14
ὃς δ'ἂν πίῃ ἐκ τοῦ ὕδατος οὗ ἐγὼ δώσω αὐτῷ
οὐ μὴ διψήσει εἰς τὸν αἰῶνα,
ἀλλὰ τὸ ὕδωρ ὃ ἐγὼ δώσω αὐτῷ γενήσεται ἐν αὐτῷ
πηπὴ ὕδατος ἀλλομένου εἰς ζωὴν αἰώνιον.

15 κύριε, δός μοι τοῦτο τὸ ὕδωρ,
ἵνα μὴ διψῶ μηδὲ διέρχωμαι ἐνθάδε ἀντλεῖν.

---

* This outlay of the text indicates the manner in which the two main themes of "the gift of God" and of "who Jesus is" are picked up in the exchanges between Jesus and the woman. Clearly the question of "who Jesus is" is not developed in this first part of the conversation.

the Gospel, however, the thirst which this request implies, like the hunger implied in vv 31—33, could refer to Jesus' desire to do and accomplish his Father's will (v 34), namely, that he should give eternal life to those who believe in him (vv 10d, 13—15; 3:16—17; 6:39—40; 17:2). Indeed, critics generally interpret 19:28, 30 ("I thirst." "It is completed.") in the light of 4:7b. At any event, the explanation given in vv 10, 13—14 indicates that more than physical thirst is involved. In this explanation, the "drink" which Jesus is requesting from the woman is receptivity on her part to "the gift of God," the "living water," which he thirsts to offer. The significance of this "gift" will be discussed presently. Ironically, however, the woman is the one who needs to drink. Jesus' thirst and her as yet unrecognized thirst are thus inseparably linked.

From the perspective of the woman and in the light of her immediate concerns (she has come to draw water, v 7a), the request could only refer to physical thirst and drink. Jesus' physical condition (v 6) justifies her understanding the request in this sense. And so the oft-cited Johannine technique of *double-entendre* arises from the fact that both Jesus and the woman share in common the human experience of thirsting and drinking. The difference lies in that for Jesus this human experience also serves as a medium for conveying a reality of the spiritual order. The same applies in all the instances of *double-entendre* which underlie this episode (vv 31—34) and other passages in the Gospel (2:19—22; 3:3—10; 6:30—35). The value of the technique, therefore, is not purely or even primarily literary[35]. In this passage, Jesus' desire to do and complete the Father's work is comparable to the human experiences of thirst and hunger (vv 7, 32). That is his *raison-d'être* (v 34); and this thirst and hunger are satisfied when his hearers, in turn, thirst to receive the gift of eternal life which he brings (v 10c; 6:29; 7:37—39).

The seriousness with which the woman takes Jesus' request for a drink, physically understood, is illustrated by her great surprise and cutting rejoinder in v 9a,b. The rejoinder is tantamount to a refusal to give the drink. Her reaction is inspired by the standing hostility between Jews and Samaritans discussed earlier, a hostility to which the Jews give a socio-religious expression by not "co-using with the Samaritans" (v 9c)[36]. This

---

[35]Bultmann (*Commentary,* 135, n. 1) holds that the Johannine *double-entendre* arises from the fact that "there are concepts and statements, which at first sight refer to earthly matters, but properly refer to divine ones." Accordingly, the misunderstanding arises from thinking that the earthly meaning exhausts all the possibilities. Schille ("Das Evangelium als Missionsbuch," 8—9) most correctly sees the misunderstanding as arising from the missionary perspective. Wead (*Literary Devices,* 71—94) regards the techniques as a metaphor.

[36]Daube ("Jesus and the Samaritan Woman: The Meaning of συγχράομαι" *JBL* 69 [1950] 137—147; also *The NT and Rabbinic Judaism,* 273—382) interprets the verb in this sense. His interpretation finds support from a number of critics: Joachim Jeremias, Σαμάρεια, *TDNT VII,* 88—94, esp. p. 91, n. 25; similarly T.E. Pollard ("Jesus and the Samaritan Woman," *ExpT* 92 [1981] 147—148) who also cites Augustine's *Tractate on St. John* 15.4.11, adding that "Augustine either invented the theory or drew from tradition." Lindars (*John,* 181) disagrees with this

background of hostility also lends reality to the woman's great surprise. Given this background, that a Jew should ask a Samaritan for a drink is odd enough in itself; odder still in this instance is that the Samaritan in question is also a woman. The phrase, γυναικὸς Σαμαρίτιδος οὔσης, placed last in the sentence, is emphatic. It has rightly been interpreted in reference to the rabbinic belief that Samaritan women were by nature a permanent source of uncleanliness[37]. The woman, therefore, knows her position *vis-à-vis* the Jews (both as a Samaritan and as a woman), and is effectively asking Jesus whether he does not know the rules (πῶς σύ;).

Most strikingly, in his reply (v 10), Jesus does not debate the issue of mutual national antagonism between Jews and Samaritans. Rather, he transfers the discussion from this socio-religious context of reciprocal contempt and separatism (v 9) to the sphere of God's relationship and dealings with human beings, where the governing principle is his generous bounty or "free gift"[38]. In this concept of "gift of God,"as later in those of "true worship" (vv 20–23) and eschatological harvest (vv 36–38), existing human differences typified by the Jewish-Samaritan situation are shown to be transcended. The expressions "gift of God" and "who this is" are remarkably vague; they form part of Jesus' technique of arousing the woman's curiosity or of leading her to desire to know both him and the gift he offers. Equally, the expressions "living water" and "who this is" are in response to the woman's reply in v 9a,b: the former relates to her understanding of Jesus' request in terms of physical water, the latter to her calling him a "Jew." Jesus thus appears to be very attentive to the woman's "interpellations."

It is highly debated whether the expression "gift of God" refers to Jesus himself, his self-revelation and teaching generally, the Holy Spirit (as in Acts 2:38), the Torah (as in rabbinic and Qumran literature), Wisdom (as in the OT and Philo), or the Samaritan Pentateuch. This, again, is not the place to embark on any detailed discussion on the subject; the

---

interpretation but offers no convincing argument for his own position. That the prohibition to co-use with the Samaritans dates from 65/66 A.D. is not disputed (*b. Šabb.* 16b, 17a; cf. *t. Nid.* 5, 1); but that "tablefellowship" with Gentiles (of whom the Samaritans are the worst; cf. Jn 8: 48) was something unheard of is well attested even in the Synoptic Gospels (Mt 9:10–12; Mk 2: 15–17; Lk 5:29–32) not to mention Acts 10:1–11:18. See further J. Neusner, "The Fellowship (חבורה) in the Second Jewish Commonwealth," *HTR* 53 (1960) 125–142.

[37]For the rabbinic view that Samaritan women were menstruous from birth, hence a perpetual source of uncleanliness, see the references given in the previous note; also the extensive study in *Str-B* I, 540–560, especially on rules of purity (pp. 540–541), food laws (pp. 541–542) and worship (pp. 542–544).

[38]The word δωρεάν in v 10a is a noun; but basic to the root meaning of the term is the notion of "freely," or "for nothing" (cf. Büchsel, δωρεά, *TDNT* II, 167). The adverbial use of the term (δωρεάν) brings out this meaning very clearly. Of the NT usage, Rev 21:6 evokes this passage, while Mt 10:8 (δωρεὰν ἐλάβετε, δωρεὰν δότε) is particularly striking in that it, too, occurs in the context of the missionary charge. A good OT parallel is Is 55:1. John's Gospel emphasizes throughout the absolute gratuitousness of God's gift of salvation given through Jesus (cf. v 38; 1: 12–13, 16–17).

literature on it is abundant[39]. However, whatever possible answers may be given to the question, priority belongs to the answer which can be derived from the Johannine context itself.

In the immediate context, the "gift of God" (v 10a) is first defined in the concrete imagery of "living water" (v 10d): if the woman asks for "the gift of God" she will be given "living water." The two terms are thus synonymous. On this basis, McCool, Brown and Porsch argue that the terms refer to both the Holy Spirit and Jesus' self-revelation or teaching generally[40]. This interpretation finds its rationale in the Gospel itself which explicitly equates "the Spirit" with "rivers of living water" (7: 37—39). Moreover, the Gospel posits water and the Spirit as the conjoint medium of birth from above (3:5—8); it identifies Jesus' word as the Spirit which causes to live ($\tau\grave{o}$ $\zeta\omega o\pi o\iota o\tilde{v}\nu$, 6:63), assigns a revelatory function to the Spirit (16:12—13), and states that the Spirit will be and remain in the disciples (14:17) as will this "living water" (v 14) or Jesus' life-giving word (6:63; 15:7)[41]. In addition, both the Spirit and Jesus' word are seen as the Father's and Jesus' "gift" to the believer (14:17; 17:8), to lead them into the complete truth (16:12—13) or to life-giving knowledge of Jesus and the Father (17:3). In 19:30 Jesus "hands over" ($\pi\alpha\rho\acute{e}\delta\omega\kappa\epsilon\nu$) the Spirit and after his glorification finally bestows this Spirit on the disciples (20:22) as promised (7:37—39). There are thus sufficient contextual grounds for viewing the Spirit in his revelatory and life-giving capacity as "the gift of God."

There is, however, another much wider and all-embracing context in which the notion of "the gift of God" is to be understood in the Gospel. The key passage here is 3:16, the foundation text on mission. Here it is stated that "God's gift" to the world, freely given out of love, is his uniquely beloved Son. The purpose of the gift is so that those who believe in him may have "eternal life." A direct link is thus established between 3:16 and 4:10, 14: both passages inseparately link the "gift of God" (understood as "eternal life") with Jesus through whom this gift is given. Put differently, Jesus is God's primary gift without whom the gift of "liv-

---

[39]Origen (*Commentaire sur Saint Jean* III, 13.1.1—7, 42 [SC 222, pp. 34—35]) interprets "living water" as the gift; cf. *BAG*, 832—833; Porsch, *Pneuma und Wort*, 135—145; for the commentaries, see, in particular, Bultmann, 180, n. 4; Barrett, 233—234; Schnackenburg, I, 462—464; and Brown, I, 178—179 (who gives an extensive discussion on modern views on the subject). The numerous references in the *QL* include: 1QS 4:20—21; CD 2:12—13; 1QH 7:6; 8:17—17; 12:11; 17:25. See further Freed, *Old Testament Quotations in the Gospel of John* (Leiden: Brill, 1965) 22.

[40] F.J. McCool, "Living Water in St. John," *The Bible in Current Thought: Essays in Memory of M.J. Gruenthaner* (ed. J.L. McKenzie; New York, 1962) 226—235; Brown, *John* I, 179; Porsch, *Pneuma und Wort*, 143.

[41]The single most comprehensive treatment of the relationship between the Spirit and Jesus' revelatory word is that of Porsch, as the title of his dissertation indicates. Justin Martyr (*Apology* I.33) identifies the Spirit as the word; Leonhard Goppelt ($\mathring{v}\delta\omega\rho$, *TDNT* VIII, 322—333) sees Jesus' gift as "his word (8:37; 15:7), his Spirit (7:39; 14:17) and Himself."

ing water/Spirit/word" is impossible. This, perhaps, explains why the gift of the Spirit and the life-giving knowledge which he brings depend wholly on Jesus' glorification, or upon his unreserved giving of himself, εἰς τέλος (13:1; cf. 12:24; 15:13), and why the disciples are incapable of fully comprehending his word till they receive the Spirit, the fruit of his glorification (14:26; 16:12—13). Even in the dialogue with Nicodemus, the "new birth" through water and the Spirit (vv 3—8) is made possible only by Jesus' "being lifted up" (ὑψωθῆναι, vv 14—15; cf. 12: 23—33).

Viewed in this comprehensive perspective of the Gospel, "the gift of God" can further be defined as the gift of salvation given in and through Jesus. V 42 supports this interpretation as do also 3:17; 8:30—36. The καί in v 10b thus correlates the two main clauses, the one referring to the "gift of God," the other to Jesus, the one through whom this gift is bestowed. Both the gift and the agent are thus two sides of the same coin; the one cannot be understood or received without the other. Indeed, v 10d seems to equate Jesus with God as the giver of the gift; for in v 10a God is the giver (subjective genitive), whereas in v 10d as in v 14 Jesus himself is clearly the giver of "the living water/gift of God."

Indeed, on the understanding that Jesus and the Father are one (10:30) which means that he is God (5:18; 10:33, 36; 19:7), the Gospel presents Jesus and the Father as the joint giver of eternal life (5:21; 6:27, 32—33, 35, 52; 17:2; cf. 1 Jn 5:11, 16). Only in this all-embracing context of Jesus' life-giving mission can the Spirit and Jesus' own teaching be seen as "the gift of God" since they constitute the conjoint medium through which he actually communicates "eternal life" to those who believe in him. The overtones of the OT Wisdom motif (finding whom is finding life and God's salvation, Prov 8:35) present in this passage, as in 7:37—39, are all summed up and transcended in the person of Jesus[42]. The whole point of v 10, therefore, is that if only the woman knew it, she, not Jesus, is the beggar who needs to ask and receive from him the gift of eternal life, given freely for the asking (cf. 1:16—17; Is 55:1—2).

b) Vv 11—15: "the gift of God"

How much of Jesus' explanation in v 10 the woman has understood is registered by her reply in vv 11—12. It is obvious that the concept of "the gift of God" has completely escaped her. This is because whatever meaning the concept may have had in contemporary theology, its particular meaning in John, as something which is inseparably linked with the person of Jesus, belongs in the order of revelation and proclamation.

---

[42]For a study of the wisdom motifs in John see, for instance, Michael Theobald, *Im Anfang war das Wort: Textlinguistische Studie zum Johannesprolog* (SBS 106; Stuttgart: Katholisches Bibelwerk GmbH. 1983) esp. pp. 98—109; Freed, *OT Quotations*, 21—38; Boismard-Lamouille, *Synopse III* (see their index references to Sirach, Proverbs and Wisdom).

Therefore, it cannot be arrived at by reasoned discourse or through reflection on one's daily preoccupations. It has to be accepted in faith through the testimony of Jesus himself, even though one's daily experiences may serve as the medium in which this revelation is given. This point is made more clearly in the case of Nicodemus (3:1—21), where his rationalistic approach to knowledge of Jesus' identity (v 2) and to his teaching (vv 4, 9) are shown to be wholly inadequate for the purpose (vv 10—12). If, then, the woman fails to grasp the concept of "the gift of God," it is because at this point she does not yet know who Jesus is. This comes only in v 26, when her response to Jesus also takes a dramatic turn (v 28—29). The whole movement of the passage thus supports the view that in the Johannine perspective, knowledge of "the gift of God" and of Jesus' true identity are inseparable (cf. 17:3)

The point which really intrigues the woman in the whole of the explanation given in v 10 is the notion of "living water" which she understands naturally as "spring water" (v 11)[43]. Her curiosity thus centers on how Jesus can provide this kind of water when he lacks even the basic means (a bucket) of drawing from the deep well. It is also from this primary standpoint of "spring water" that she understands and reacts to the question of Jesus' identity, since she compares him to Jacob, the giver of the well whose water, in her view, Jesus seems to slight. Her reply in vv 11—12 is, in effect, a defense of the ancestral water.

Her approach is starkly practical. As in v 9 she draws Jesus' attention to the predicament of his own situation: he has no bucket, the well is deep, so his reaching this well water is out of the question. Given these real conditions, plus the fact that Jesus himself is thirsty, even just now asking for a drink, his offer of "spring water" must, to say the least, appear ridiculous. Her argument in v 11 is *a minori ad maius*. There is a pointed emphasis on the "whence," both by the addition of the οὖν and by its place in the sentence, with vv 11a and 11b building up to its momentum. Equally the expression τὸ ὕδωρ τὸ ζῶν is emphatic, by comparison to Jesus' ὕδωρ ζῶν (v 10d). Her question in v 11 is, therefore, undisguisedly ironic. Accordingly, the κύριε which prefaces this question

---

[43]It will be recalled that the religious meaning given to "living water" belongs to a latter OT and Jewish thought generally, starting with the Prophets and the Psalms. If the Samaritans accepted only the Torah, the woman would not have been exposed to this late Jewish interpretation. In the Torah, "living water" is required mainly for purificatory purposes (cf. Lev 14:5, 50; Num 19:9, 17). The use of "living water" in the religious sense in the OT and post-biblical literature include Jer 2:13; Is 12:3; 55:1; Ez 47:1; Zech 14:8; Ps 36:8—9; 46:4; *Ps. Sol.* 14:3; *Od. Sol.* 11:18—19; 30:1. The most developed and varied usage of the term is, perhaps, to be found in Qumran where it applies to "knowledge" (1 QH 4:11; 2:18; 1QS 10:12; 11:3); the drinkers of the waters of life are eternal trees (1QH 8:12) who become the garden of Eden (1QH 8:20; cf. 6:16), and, most importantly, the water of life is the revelation given esoterically to the community (1QS 11: 3—9). In Judaism, it is applied to the Torah (*'Abot,* 1:11). See further the discussion by H. Braun, *Qumran und das Neuen Testament* I, 114—115, 120, and the article by Goppelt mentioned in n. 41 above, esp. pp. 221—222.

is to be interpreted as "Mister" rather than as "Lord," even though the Evangelist's audience may have understood the term in this latter sense. Nonetheless, the woman has somewhat abandoned the antagonizing title Ἰουδαῖος for a more civil form of address, even if it is sarcastically intended.

Not only does Jesus' offer of living water appear ridiculous to the woman, but as far as she is concerned, no water can be better than that of Jacob's well[44]. As already noted, this is not just any well, but one that is renowned for its antiquity and whose usage goes back to the founding father himself: he, his family and all his livestock drank from it; so did generations after him. Yet despite the centuries of use, the well has neither dried up nor become exhausted. Thus, in addition to its revered ancestry, the well has a character which is almost eternal. Can Jesus, then, possibly produce anything better[45]. Strikingly, the question is put in typical Semitic fashion in terms of Jesus being "greater than" Jacob (v 12a). Since in Semitic thought greatness is measured by one's achievements, one can only demonstrate one's greatness by furnishing material proofs. It follows then that only if Jesus is greater than Jacob can he provide water better than that of Jacob's well. Her question prefaced by μή, however, implies that Jesus cannot possibly be greater than Jacob, or can he? The possibility is thus left open, for though a μή question expects a negative answer, it does not necessarily rule out a positive one. Rather, precisely because it expects a negative answer it makes a positive one all the more striking.

As in v 10 Jesus, again, does not dispute any of the issues raised by the woman: his lack of a bucket, the depth of the well, the revered traditions associated with it, and Jacob's greatness proved by the gift of the semi-eternal well. Instead he focuses on what is undoubtedly the central concern of the woman: the water itself as capable of quenching thirst. It is striking that the woman does not seem to consider any other usage of the water than that it quenches thirst (v 12b,c). This must be in response to Jesus' initial request (v 7b), after which request he seems no longer interested in the drink (v 10). In his second explanation (vv 13—14) Jesus also stays within this focus of water as that which quenches thirst. In place of v 13 (that those who drink water such as this will thirst again) Jesus might have pointed out to the woman, as he does to the Galilean Jews (6:49—51), that her ancestor Jacob and his sons and flock all drank this water and are dead, whereas the one who drinks the water he gives will never die. This, in effect, is implied in v 14. But the polemic tone which underlies the exchanges between Jesus and the Jews (5—10) is

---

[44]This may explain why the woman comes all the way to this well, even though there were, in the view of some critics, other wells closer to her home. This view, however, implies exact knowledge of the location of the woman's home in relation to this and other possible sources of water, a datum which the Evangelist is not interested in providing.

[45]See n. 28 above.

wholly lacking in this present dialogue. The reason we suggest for this is that while the former dialogues belong to the forensic type, character- ized by attack and defense, the present episode, on the contrary, may be typed as the philosophical variety of spontaneous enquiry[46].

In the Johannine adaptation, Jesus' request for a drink (v 7b) serves as the initial question; the woman's rejoinder (v 9a,b) makes her vulnerable in that she supposes Jesus to be no more than a Jew; Jesus' counter re- mark, "if you knew" (v 10), constitutes the inference drawn from the woman's reply and which brings about a new vulnerable reply from her (vv 11–12); and so the pattern continues throughout the dialogue. In the second part of the dialogue (vv 16–26), the pattern begins in v 16. Though there is adaption, the three basic components of the philosophical variety mentioned by Daube (namely, initial question, vulnerable rejoin- der, inference drawn from the rejoinder) are present in the dialogue. Furthermore, here as in the Socratic setting, the dialogue aims at instruct- ing or giving the woman information about Jesus and the nature of his mission. Thus throughout the dialogue Jesus never disputes any of the issues raised by the woman. In vv 13–14 he simply spells out for her the radical differences between "this water" (the "this" is emphatic) and the water which he gives[47].

Jesus' water differs fundamentally from the water from Jacob's well on three scores: with respect to its function, to its location and accessibility, and to its natural and intrinsic quality.

(a) Function: This water quenches thirst continually and so rules out the need for repeated drinking. V 14a ("will not thirst ever") is set in marked contrast to "will thirst again" (v 13). Here, as in Rev 7:16 (cf. 21:6; 22:17), the absence of thirst expresses the perfect happiness which God's and Christ's salvation ("living water") generates in the individual[48].

---

[46]A description of both the forensic and the philosophical variety (also known as the Socratic question) is given by Daube, *NT and Rabbinic Judaism,* 151, 154; also Quintilian, *Inst. Or.* V.xi. 3–4, 27; Cicero, *De Inv.* 1.31.51. While the setting in life of the philosophical variety is "spontan- eous enquiry," that of the forensic type involves "attack and defense." In general, the Gospel shows a preference for the forensic type (Jn 5–10). Perhaps it does so because Jesus and the Jews have enough common grounds for debating (the Law, the Prophets, a common religious heritage, v 22), which is not the case with the Samaritan woman. Lagrange (*Jean,* 109) also compares vv 17–18 to the Socratic method, a view which further supports our position spelled out here.

[47]The primary reference to "this water" (v 13) is, no doubt, the water from Jacob's well; but by extension it includes any type of physical water (spring, or well), since Jesus is ultimately con- cerned, not with physical water, but with salvation.

[48]The evidence of Rev. 21:6 and 22:17 supports the view here advanced, namely, that "the gift of God, living water" signifies the total gift of salvation. The two references are from the last chapters of the book which describe the new heaven and the new earth which God sets up defini- tively for his elect. In the P Oxy I, p. 3 (Moulton-Milligan, 165), the event of Jesus' appearance and revelation in the world spells the doom of all thirst. See further Johannes Behm, διψάω, δίψος, *TDNT* II, 226–227.

(b) Location: This water is located in the person who drinks it (v 14b), not in Sychar as is Jacob's well. Hence both repeated trips (vv 7a, 15b) and such contraptions as "bucket" (v 11a) prove entirely unnecessary. Moreover, because the water is located in the individual, it not only is accessible, but is very personal and intimate, being the unique possession of the drinker. Jacob's well, on the contrary, belonged first to Jacob and was later handed down to his descendants[49]. In addition, while the well remains the exclusive heritage of Jacob's descendants (*"our father, who gave us,"* v 12), the water which Jesus gives is open to anyone who so desires it (ὅς δ᾽ ἄν, v 14a).

This observation may offer a clue to the interpretation of the problembatic text 7:38. Do the "springs of living water" flow out of Jesus' or the believer's heart? In the light of 4:14, much will depend on whether the *origin* or the *location* of the living water is in question. If origin (or source), then it is from Jesus' bosom (like the river which flows from God's and the Lamb's throne, Rev 22:1); if location, then it is from the drinker's bosom. The same applies even if the "rivers of living water" is interpreted as the Holy Spirit, since he comes from the Father and Jesus (14:16, 26; 15:26) and "remains in" the believer (14:17). Does this mean, then, that salvation is an inalienable gift of the individual ("will never know thirst, v 14a)? The answer to the question lies in v 10a. If one really knows who Jesus is in the Johannine sense of the word (cf. 17:3), then the danger of ceasing to believe and thereby becoming a dead branch (15:6; cf. 8:31–36; 14:6; 1 Jn 2:18–19) is eliminated. The imagery of the vine and branches, in particular, underlines the indispensability of the Father's and Jesus' sustaining role in the life of the believer.

(c) Natural or intrinsic quality: The water which Jesus offers is neither a "spring" nor "flowing water" as the woman thinks, but "living water" in the spiritual sense of the word. As water which gives eternal life, it far transcends all the categories of water known by the woman[50]. Not only that, from a simple drinking portion (πίῃ ἐκ, v 14a), the water grows and becomes a "spring" of water (v 14b) which gushes forth from within, propelling the drinker towards eternal life. Thus the water which Jesus offers far surpasses the semi-eternal Jacob's well, which, its inexhaustibility and antiquity notwithstanding, remains essentially a well.

---

[49]It is striking that, unlike Jacob, Jesus does not himself drink of the water which he gives. This is precisely because the gift signifies salvation. Unlike the Gnostic redeemer figures, Jesus is not "the saved savior" (cf. Percy, *Ursprung der johanneischen Theologie,* 147–193, 194–228, 237–387), hence he himself has no need of this water.

[50]The sense of the Johannine contrast is best captured by Jer 2:13 where God is described as "the fountain of living water" (πηγὴν ὕδατος ζωῆς, LXX) in contrast to "the leaky cisterns" dug out by the people for themselves, but which are incapable of holding water. Justin (*Dialogue,* 114. 1–5) interprets 4:14 in the light of Jer 2:13, and sees this water as flowing from the "beautiful rock," "Christ."

The aorist subjunctive (πίη [ἐκ], v 14a) tends to emphasize that a once and for all drinking is envisaged.

The verbs γενήσεται and ἀλλομένου (v 14b) aptly describe both conceptually and visually the living and life-giving quality of the water. Unlike the well water which has to be drawn (vv 7a, 15b), this water wells up from within of its own accord, energizing and giving new life where there was previously none, as in the case of the two cripples cured by Peter and John (Acts 3:8) and Paul (14:10). From the evidence of these two cripples, the "leaping up" movement signifies not only life and abundance but also "joy," which is a missionary motif (3:29; 4:36; 20:20; cf. 1 Jn 1:4; Acts 5:41; 8:8, 39; 11:23). In particular, this joy is a characteristic of the messianic, eschatological age (v 36) or of definitive salvation (Rev 7:16—17; 21:4)[51]. Jesus' answer in vv 13—14 thus serves as a restatement and expansion of what he means by "gift of God," using the imagery of water and the task of water-fetching both of which are familiar to the woman.

The woman's rejoinder in v 15 shows she is impressed by Jesus' explanation, though it is debatable whether this impression is genuine or still sceptical. The answer to this depends on whether or not she has fully comprehended the explanation given by Jesus. How much of this explanation has she actually taken in? She has heard, for instance, that the water quenches thirst (her "that I may not thirst again" indicates this). Secondly, she has heard that the water is located in the individual who drinks it, hence her desire to be spared further repeated trips to the well (v 15b). Her whole reply in v 15 evokes that of the Jews in 6:34 who request to be given this bread always, without really understanding what it is all about as the sequel (vv 60—66) shows. The woman's reply, however, is not exactly identical with that of her Jewish counterparts, for unlike the Jews, she goes on to give the reasons why she wants "this water" (we note again her insistent τοῦτο τὸ ὕδωρ).

These reasons prove either (1) that she has not grasped at all the concept of "the gift of God," or (2) that she does not believe a word of Jesus' explanation in vv 13—14. In this latter case, her reply in v 15 is no more than a *reductio ad absurdum* of the lofty promise made by Jesus, her way of saying that she wants to be bothered no further on the subject. In our view, the second alternative appears to be closest to the woman's position. Her request thus has the effect of bringing the conversation to a standstill, if not to an actual close. The exchanges in vv 16a—17, which we shall examine presently, strengthen this interpretation.

---

[51]On joy as a missionary and eschatological motif, see 3:29; 4:36; 11:15; 15:11; 16:20—24 (where v 22 could be seen as fulfilled in 20:20); 1 Jn 1:4; Mt 2:10; 25:21—23; Lk 2:10; 8:13; 24: 52. In Acts both the evangelizers (5:41; 11:23) and the evangelized (8:8, Samaria; 8:39, the Ethiopian Eunuch; 15:31, the churches in Asia) rejoice. Similarly, Paul's letters abound in apostolic joy: Rom 16:19; Phil 2:19; 2 Cor 7:9, 13, 16 (which contrasts sharply with his previous disappointment with the Corinthians in the first letter). For further discussion on the subject, especially in the OT, see Conzelmann, χαίρω, χαρά, *TDNT* IX, 359—372.

As regards the first alternative, it will be noted that Jesus nowhere says that his gift of water will dispense the receiver from the need to drink water such as is provided by Jacob's well. The woman's reply, however, implies this. The intrinsic link which Jesus establishes between his water and "eternal life" should indicate to her that the water in question is not ordinary water and that it functions differently from ordinary water. This link completely escapes her. So whether one opts for (1) or for (2), v 15 indicates that the woman has not comprehended the explanation given her by Jesus. None of the conditions listed in v 10a,b has, therefore, been fulfilled. V 15 thus brings to a close, without any visible success, the first part of the conversation with its theme of "gift of God/ living water." The cycle of this first part of the conversation may be illustrated as follows:

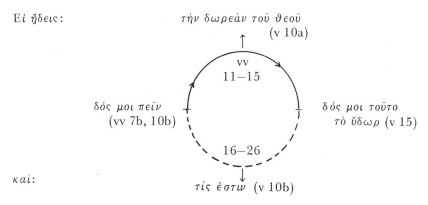

Εἰ ᾔδεις: τὴν δωρεὰν τοῦ θεοῦ (v 10a)

vv 11–15

δός μοι πεῖν (vv 7b, 10b)   δός μοι τοῦτο τὸ ὕδωρ (v 15)

16–26

καί: τίς ἐστιν (v 10b)

Jesus, the good teacher, knows that the woman has not understood his explanation concerning the gift of God. Indeed v 16 betrays a sense of frustration on his part. Nevertheless, as would a good teacher whose pupils have missed the real point of an important lesson, he starts all over again, using a different strategy and tactics. V 16 thus begins the second part of the conversation with focus on v 10b ("who this is"). For only when this second theme is properly understood will the first also be understood. Before we examine this second half of the conversation, however, it will be useful at this point to highlight the missionary significance of the motifs of thirst and of living water present in this first part of the dialogue.

c) "Thirst" as a missionary motif

On the evidence of 4:34, we noted that Jesus' thirst (v 7b) like his hunger/food (vv 31–33) signifies his longing to accomplish the Father's work. We thus compared the imperative which this longing exercises in his life to the basic human drives of hunger and thirst. Not that the Father's will is some compelling blind fate (εἱμαρμένη); rather, the natural experiences of hunger and thirst are used as powerful illustrations of the degree to which his love for the Father's will possesses him (cf. 10:17; 14:31; 15: 13), a love which is rooted in the Father's own love for the world (3:16). In short, Jesus lives for his mission. The same sentiment is expressed by Paul in 2 Cor 5:14, where his overwhelming awareness of the all-embracing reality of Christ's love bears him and his co-workers along in its own stream, impelling them to a missionary zeal which borders on madness (v 13)[52].

On the physical, non-symbolic level, hunger and thirst are common missionary motifs, hardships which the missionary must bear for the sake of the "Good News." They result mostly from the actual physical conditions of travel as is the case in this passage (vv 3—6; cf. 2 Cor 11:27). In 1 Cor 4:11, for instance, not only Paul but presumably Apollos and Cephas (v 12) also hunger and thirst for the gospel. In the Synoptics and Acts, the motif becomes a form of ascetic preparation for mission: John the Baptist exercises his mission in great austerity (Mk 1:6; Mt 3:1—4; Lk 3:2); Jesus himself fasts for forty days as a prelude to beginning his mission (Mt 4:1—11; Lk 4:1—13; cf. Mk 1:12—13); and the community in Antioch fasts and prays before sending out Paul and Barnabas (Acts 13: 3). So, too, the apostles themselves fast and pray before appointing elders for the churches they had founded (Acts 14:23)[53].

Another indication of the missionary perspective of the motifs of hunger and thirst present in 4:1—42 is that here, as in Paul (1 Cor 4:8; 2 Cor 6:10a; 11:28—29), this hunger and thirst of Jesus aims at enriching others. Indeed, Paul, too, mentions the enriching poverty of Christ (2 Cor 8:9; Phil 2:6—11). In the dialogue, Jesus' thirst, it was seen, is that the woman may receive from him living water. Similarly, his "food" consists in the completion of the Father's work which alone will enable the disciples to receive wages by entering into the eschatological harvest (vv 35—38; cf. 16:7; 20:21—22; 21) or to bear enduring fruit (15:16). In Jesus' case, the deprivation goes even unto death (10:14, 17; 12:24, 27, 32; 13:1; 15:13; 19:28—30). Because of its close link with the motif of "living water" (vv 10—15), this thirst-quenching thirst of Jesus forms an aspect of the eschatological motifs which abound in this episode, and which indicate that the missianic age has indeed been ushered in by Jesus' mission (vv 26, 42)[54]. So, although the woman does not know it, her

---

[52]Hudry-Clergion's view ("De Judée en Galilée," 820) that Jesus went through Samaria because he had "un rendez-vous à ne pas manquer," captures well the Johannine spirit since "un rendez-vous" implies a prior agreement by the parties concerned, in this instance, Jesus and his Father.

[53]The discussion on vv 1—6 highlighted some missionary motifs which John holds in common with his NT contemporaries. See further Daube, "Jewish Missionary Maxims in Paul," *ST* 1 (1947) 158—169.

[54]These eschatological motifs include the verb $\delta\epsilon\tilde{\iota}$ (vv 4, 20, 24), the gift of God seen as salvation (v 14), the "hour" which comes but now is (vv 21, 23; cf. v 35), the messianic expectation (vv 25—26; cf. v. 42), the theme of harvest/wages (vv 35—37), and that of entering with joy into the labor of others (vv 36—38).

request for "*this* water" is indeed a request for the blessings of salvation or of life promised in the messianic days (cf. Is 12:3; Zech 14:8; Ps 36: 8–10).

It needs to be recalled, too, that the basic impulse which motivated the apostolic missionary activity in the NT was the realization or conviction that in the risen Christ, eschatology had broken into history (Acts 2: 14–36; 13:32–33; 1 Cor 15:14–15, 31–32, 45–57). In John, however, the missionary activity begins with Jesus himself, with his very coming into the world, since this coming marks the dawn of eschatology (vv 21, 23, 26)[55]. Thus even what appears to be a neutral terminology (the motifs of thirst and hunger) contrived in the interest of *double-entendre* with a view to advancing the story, proves to be an integral aspect of Jesus' mission on many levels.

3. Exegesis of Vv 16–26: The Interaction

We suggested above that vv 16–26 develop dialectically the second theme of the protasis (v 10b), namely, the question of Jesus' identity, a second fact which the woman must know as the condition for asking and receiving the "gift of God." The structural difficulties inherent in the actual transition from the first to his second part of the conversation cannot, however, be minimized. In our view, this transition is established in three ways: verbally, dialectically and dramatically.

Verbally, the transition is indicated by the catchwords "come here" ($\delta\iota\acute{\epsilon}\rho\chi\omega\mu\alpha\iota, \acute{\epsilon}\lambda\vartheta\grave{\epsilon}$ $\acute{\epsilon}\nu\vartheta\acute{\alpha}\delta\epsilon$, vv 15b, 16). The impression mentioned above that the woman's reply in v 15 has the effect of bringing the conversation to a close is strengthened by the exchanges in vv 16–17a. While the woman desires to be spared all further trips to the well (v 15a), Jesus, on the contrary, asks her there and then to make this very trip twice: namely, to go home and return to the place ($\acute{\epsilon}\nu\vartheta\acute{\alpha}\delta\epsilon$) with her husband (v 16)[56]. Given the woman's wish, followed by Jesus' command, her laconic re-

---

[55]For our discussion of the Johannine eschatology see below, pp. 165–168.

[56]The woman's use of $\delta\iota\acute{\epsilon}\rho\chi\epsilon\sigma\vartheta\alpha\iota$ which contrasts with Jesus' simple $\acute{\epsilon}\lambda\vartheta\epsilon\tilde{\iota}\nu$ has the sense of "come all the way hither" (Westcott, *John*, 71), which usage draws attention to the distance to be covered. Cf. *BAG*, 194. The catchword $\acute{\epsilon}\nu\vartheta\acute{\alpha}\delta\epsilon$ (vv 15, 16), on the other hand, has the effect of sustaining and stabilizing (on the spot) the conversation which is at near breaking point. This impression of breaking point, perhaps, explains why some critics see the transition as highly contrived. The suggestion, however, is that the woman cannot leave the well because the conversation is not yet over, she does not yet know who Jesus is (v 10b). To appreciate the unified structure of the passage, one needs to dig beyond the surface. Another explanation given to v 16 is that if the woman had to receive this gift of living water, her husband would have had to be present, since women had no rights in the Semitic world. The view rests on the assumption that Jesus is speaking of ordinary water or is concerned with socio-marital issues. In particular it runs counter to his whole approach to the woman which is intensely personal throughout. V 16 is in view of vv 18 and 26.

joinder (v 17a) could be interpreted as further indication that she does not wish to be bothered further or that she desires to end the conversation.

Dialectically, the nature of the conversation itself becomes strained at this point. Unlike the woman, Jesus wants the conversation to continue, because the issue of his identity which the woman seems to have completely forgotten, has yet to be treated. If this interpretation is correct, then Jesus' continued patience with the woman heightens further the reality of his missionary labor (v 6).

Dramatically, a reversal of roles takes place. In v 7b Jesus is the beggar, the woman the one with water to give; but in v 15 the woman becomes the beggar (this holds irrespective of the seriousness of her request), and Jesus the one with water to give. Not only that; on the strength of the woman's request which Jesus takes seriously, he becomes a commander (v 16). His triple command registered by the incisive aorist imperatives contrasts sharply with his previous single request (v 7b). The contrast is all the more striking in that both these verses have a parallel structure, and each introduces the main topic of discussion in the corresponding part of the dialogue[57]. However, while the request in v 7b focuses on Jesus' own need ("give me"), the command in v 16 centers on the marital status of the woman ("your husband"). This reversal of roles thus serves as a prelude to bringing to the fore the true identity of Jesus.

a) Vv 16—19: their function

We have, then, three ways in which the second part of the dialogue is linked with the first. The real problem, however, concerns the thematic relationship of vv 16—19 to vv 20—26. The discussion in Chapter III evinced that a number of critics consider vv 16—19 as the remnant of a lost story, the primary purpose of which was to portray Jesus as a *theois anēr* or *Wundermann.* In their present context, however, these verses are seen as having no intrinsic relationship to the themes of worship (vv 20—24) and of the revelation of Jesus' messiahship (vv 25—26). Our contrary position posits that the revelation of Jesus, an issue raised in v 10b, is the central theme in the whole of vv 16—26. Consequently, it considers both the transitional verses 16—19 and the theme of worship (vv 20—24) to be in function of vv 25—26, not independent of it. In other words, the comprehensive issue is the revelation of Jesus, and the comprehensive mode in which the issue is discussed, that of Jesus' supernatural knowledge. The intrinsic link between the various sections of this last part of the dialogue is, therefore, to be sought along these lines of issue and mode of discussion. The *theios anēr* theory, if it has any value at all (see Holladay's work mentioned in note 28 above), might thus be found to confirm

---

[57]Except for ὕπαγε in v 16 which is always present (Zerwick, *Analysis,* I, *ad. loc.*) the imperatives in vv 7b and 16 are all aorist.

rather than contradict the whole movement of the dialogue in vv 16—26.

The parallelism between v 7b and 16 is not only grammatical. As v 7b introduces the key elements of the issues discussed in vv 7—15 (the notions of "gift" and "drink"), so v 16 holds the key to the mode in which the issue of Jesus' identity is discussed in vv 16—26. We approach the subject with the assumption that Jesus genuinely wants the woman to know "who he is," just as much as he wanted her to know the significance of "the gift of God/living water." Our enquiry, therefore, centers on how v 16 and its sequel vv 17—19 function in the step by step self-revelation of Jesus to the woman which culminates in v 26[58]. From Jesus' perspective, the command to call the husband (v 16) is made with the revelation in v 18 in view, even though the woman does not know this. If she did, her reply in v 17a might have been different. Put differently, when Jesus asks the woman to go and call her husband, he knows already that she has no husband, that she has been five times married, and that the man she is now living with is not her husband. The marital theme is thus introduced with a view to letting the woman know that *Jesus himself knows* about her own private life, even though he is a complete stranger from an enemy territory. V 18 thus functions in much the same way as 1:48b, where Jesus gives evidence of his divine knowledge to Nathanael by claiming knowledge of him, specifically under the fig tree, prior to his being called by Philip, and hence to their first meeting. As we shall see presently, Jesus' revelation of his divine knowledge to the woman has an effect on her similar to that which it had on Nathanael.

First, however, how is the woman's reply in v 17a to be understood? There are two possibilities: She may truly mean that she has no husband, which means that she does not consider herself married to the man with whom she is living. In this case she *is* speaking the truth, as Jesus' reply confirms (v 17b). On the other hand, she may be telling a lie either because, as Bligh maintains, she has marital designs on Jesus[59], or because, as we maintain, she really does not want to be bothered further by Jesus. Her reply in this latter case would thus aim at putting an end to the conversation. Of the two possibilities, that of marital design is the least likely; such a suggestion runs into serious conflict with v 9c ($o\dot{v}$ $\gamma\dot{\alpha}\rho$ $\sigma v\gamma\chi\rho\tilde{\omega}v\tau\alpha\iota$). Marriage in the Semitic world, in the first century A.D. as today, is a social contract, not a private one. Given the well documented mutual hatred which existed between Jews and Samaritans and of which the woman herself is fully aware (v 9a,b, 20), a marital design on Jesus on her part would be most unlikely, if not completely out of the question[60].

---

[58]Wilkens, "Stück für Stück wird die Frau zur Erkenntnis geführt, dass Jesus der Messias ist." *Entstehungsgeschichte,* 136.

[59]Bligh, "Jesus in Samaria," 335—336.

[60]For instance, the Talmudic booklet, *Masseket Kutim,* 1.3, decrees: "We do not give them wives, NOR DO WE TAKE WIVES FROM THEM" (cf. Montgomery, *The Samaritans,* 198); *Qiddushin* 75a only prohibits marriage with Samaritan women, whereas the *Kutim* here includes men.

A combination of the other possibilities, paradoxical as it may seem, is not unlikely. The woman is telling the truth, but with her tongue in her cheek, because she wants to get rid of Jesus. If so, she is caught in her own trick. Consequently, the impact of Jesus' reply in v 17b—18 must indeed be overwhelming and so prove devastating to her defensive stance sustained throughout the preceding part of the conversation. Against this background, in which the woman is speaking the truth for the wrong reason, Jesus' somewhat ironic but deeply respectful emphasis on how "well" and "truly" she has spoken ($\kappa\alpha\lambda\tilde{\omega}\varsigma, \dot{\alpha}\lambda\eta\vartheta\acute{\epsilon}\varsigma$) becomes all the more significant. This affirmation discloses his tactful manner of appealing to the woman to drop her resisting stance. The same tone of appeal continues through vv 21—24 ($\pi\acute{\iota}\sigma\tau\epsilon\upsilon\acute{\epsilon}\ \mu o\iota, \gamma\acute{\upsilon}\nu\alpha\iota$), and it finally works. Up to this point, the woman has been trying to block the conversation. In any event, her rejoinders have not revealed any genuine interest on her part in the conversation. Her questions have been calculated in the main to annoy Jesus, though in vain. Her quarrelsome attitude is evident, for instance, from the taunting question in vv 9 and 11 and from the rhetorical question in v 12. Now, however, and for the first time, she not only shows a genuine interest in Jesus' statement in v 17b—18, but actually takes the initiative in advancing the conversation (v 20).

Whatever may be said about the sincerity of her reply in v 15, there is no doubt about the genuineness of her observation in v 19; v 20 makes this clear. She is in part helped to this by the sustained sincerity of Jesus' entire approach to her. Our earlier suggestion that her request in v 15 is a *reductio ad absurdum* finds a backing in v 18c where Jesus tells the woman that in this particular instance ($\tau o\tilde{\upsilon}\tau o$) she has spoken the truth. The implication is that up to this point she had only been joking, and the only instance where this could apply is v 15. Indeed, Lagrange (*Jean*, 111) rightly points out that if the woman recognizes only in v 19 that Jesus is a prophet, her request in v 15 could not have been very serious. The woman is thus beginning to realize that Jesus is not just one of those religious impostors for which the period was notorious[61].

Concerning the issue of husbands and their meaning in this passage, one should note that Jesus refers to the woman's five husbands as the reason for his holding that the woman has indeed spoken the truth. The mention of the five husbands does not, therefore, constitute the major

---

[61]Josephus gives an extensive list of such messianic, though for the most part politically motivated, figures: the Samaritan whose projected trip to Gerizim with a crowd of followers to discover the hidden Mosaic vessels was crushed by Pontus Pilate (A.D. 35; *Ant.*18, 85—87); Theudas and his followers whose trip to the river Jordan to renew the miraculous crossing was intercepted by Cuspius Fadus (A.D. 44; *Ant.* 20, 97—98; cf. Acts 5:36); the false prophets and their followers whose trip to the desert to renew the wonders of the Exodus was stopped by Felix (A.D. 52—60; *Ant.* 20, 169—172; *BJ* 7, 437—438), Bar Koseba under Hadrian, Judas the Galilean mentioned by Gamaliel (Acts 5:37), and Simon Magus (Acts 8:9—11). When placed within the context of these spectacular messianic movements of the period, Jesus' approach to the woman as an individual and his very personal promise of "living water/salvation" stands apart distinctively.

thrust of his reply in v 17b—18; this reply focuses rather on how well and truly the woman has spoken (καλῶς, v 17b; ἀληθές, v 18c). The subtle way in which the revelation of Jesus' divine knowledge (or prophetic knowledge, as the woman understands it) is communicated must surely add to the impact of surprise which Jesus' whole reply makes on the woman.

The view is widespread that in v 18 Jesus lays bare to the woman the secrets of her own sinful life; this interpretation has been given a special existentialist coloring by Bultmann[62]. The view is interesting as a modern theologoumenon on the passage, but it is hardly the issue from the Johannine perspective. Jesus reveals to the woman nothing which she does not already know about herself. This is not to deny the sinfulness of her situation. For whatever may be said about the legitimacy of her previous five marriages, it is evident that in her present situation immorality is involved (a situation not to be taken lightly in the world of the first century). That Jewish law allowed a maximum of three marriages is also well known (*Str-B,* II, 437). But there is no indication in the passage that the Evangelist intends to present Jesus as confronting the woman with her sinful life.

Both Haenchen and Westcott are quite right on this issue; so, too, Lindars (note 62 below). For nowhere in the entire gospel tradition does Jesus *set out* to confront individuals with their sinfulness. In John there is appeal to faith, and warnings of the consequences of unbelief (8:21, 24; 9:41; 15:22, 24) and against sinning in the future (5:14; cf. 8:11), but never a confronting of individuals with their sinful life. Statements such as "yet none of you keeps the law" (7:19) need to be understood within the forensic contexts in which they occur. Indeed, it is by coming to Jesus, the light and Savior of the world (v 42; 3:19), that individuals are enabled to change from their sinful life to a life "lived in God" (3:20—21; cf. 8: 30—36).

---

[62]The sin-exposure theory characterizes most of the commentaries: Zahn, *Johannes,* 242; Lagrange (*Jean, 110*): Jesus aims at awakening in the woman "la conscience morale au contact d'un homme de Dieu"; Hoskyns (*Fourth Gospel,* 243): in the woman's sin, the sin of the Samaritans and of the world is exposed; Schnackenburg (*Johannesevangelium* I, 468): "die Frau ihrer Schuld bewusst ist"; Lindars (*John,* 185): "Jesus confronts the woman with her life-history," adding, however, that this might be "felt on other grounds to be improbable"; Barrett (*John,* 236) countering Bultmann holds that the disclosure of life theory is to be accepted "only if it refers to the effect of the revelation." Westcott (*John,* 71) holds that the point of v 18 is to show the woman that "her life was open to the speaker." Haenchen (*Johannesevangelium,* 242), however, is most emphatic that the Evangelist is not interested in the illegal marriages of the woman: "Was er zeigen will, ist das überirdische Wissen Jesu." Westcott's and Haenchen's position thus entirely agree with our own position.

Bultmann's existentialist interpretation states that "Revelation is for man the disclosure of his own life. Man is made aware of the unrest in his own life, which drives him from one supposed dissatisfaction to another, . . . Jesus shows the woman the truth of her own situation. Only by man's becoming aware of his true nature, can the Revealer be recognized." *Commentary,* 188. Basically sound as this theology is, one wonders whether the Evangelist would have readily understood the categories used or espoused the focus of concern here.

Our interpretation of v 17a leads to this conclusion (i.e., that Jesus is not interested in confronting the woman with her sinful life); it is also not supported by v 29 where the curiosity centers on Jesus as the man who has told the woman (i.e., who knows) all she ever did. The theological issue in v 18, therefore, concerns Jesus' revelation to the woman of the supernatural knowledge which he himself possesses. A comparison to the Nathanael situation again clarifies this: once Jesus mentions seeing Nathanael under the fig tree (1:48b), the incident ceases to function in the story, having served its revelatory purpose. Similarly, in this present passage, Jesus makes no further reference to the woman's five husbands. Instead, there is a further revelation (v 26; cf. 1:50–51), and a confession (v 29; cf. 1:51). This means, finally, that as v 16 is stated with v 18 in view, so v 18 itself is stated ultimately with v 26 in view. Its sequel, from the perspective of Jesus' audience, are vv 29 and 42.

If, therefore, v 18, by specifically referring to the woman's private life, is designed to let her know that Jesus possesses supernatural knowledge, then the view that the five husbands are the five gods of Samaria or the five books of Samaritan Pentateuch looses its convincing force. Long before the days of Jesus, the Jews knew that the Samaritans had five gods and that their worship of Yahweh was an aberration from the truth (2 Kg 17:24–41; Ezra 4:1–4). There would be nothing extraordinary, therefore, in a Jew telling a Samaritan this. Besides, the post-exilic events which led to the destruction of the temple on Mount Gerizim by John Hyrcanus (128 B.C.) and the contemporary event of the desecration of the Temple in Jerusalem by the Samaritans (Jos. *Ant.* 18.30; 9.288–291; 11.88, 97), sufficiently prove that the impiety of the Samaritans was no secret to any Jew. Consequently, the only interpretation which makes sense in the light of vv 19, 29 and 39 is that which takes the five husbands as five husbands, literally. This is the way in which the Evangelist intends it to be understood. If the symbolic interpretation broadens our understanding of the passage, well and good; but this secondary interpretation should not be allowed to distract from the primary one, let alone render it irrelevant[63].

---

[63]That there are overtones of the false worship of the Samaritans in the passage is undeniable, especially in the light of v 22. Also Hosea 2 compares the idolatory of Israel to the unfaithfulness of an adulterous wife. But the tendency to see the woman as purely symbolic, or in Olsson's words, "a mouthpiece of the Samaritan faith" (*Structure,* 238–256) and to read her history as purely symbolic of Samaritan history, is to overlook a very important element in the entire Johannine portrayal, namely, Jesus' focus on the woman as an individual, a point which we shall examine more closely later. In v 42, the Samaritans certainly do not see the woman as their mouthpiece, let alone a representative of their history (cf. v 28–29). Accordingly, only when the personal history of the woman is given its full significance can it then be used as an interpretative paradigm for Samaritan history or any other. While John's Gospel undeniably abounds in symbolism (e.g., light, darkness), much caution needs to be exercised in the symbolic interpretation where individuals are concerned. In their case it is better to speak of examples (παραδείγματα) rather than of symbols.

Moreover, the rhetorical dimension of the Gospel evinced in miraculous *sēmeia* demands that the woman's five husbands be taken literally, that is, that her not very laudatory marital record be given its full personal significance. This portrait of the woman, five times married, living with a man not her husband, places her in the same category as other hopeless cases which serve as the material of Jesus' "signs" in the Gospel: water destined for Jewish purificatory rites is changed into the best wine (2:1—11); a cripple who had waited thirty-eight years to be cured by the yearly stirring of the water of the pool is simply told to take up his bed and go home if he wishes to be made whole (5:1—9); a man born blind has his eyes opened (9:1—7), a thing unheard of before (v 32); and Lazarus, dead and buried for four days, is raised to life (11:38—44). Even in the miracle of the loaves, where the Evangelist follows the traditional account rather closely (6:1—15; cf. Mt 14:13—21; Mk 6:32—44; Lk 9:10b—17), he emphasizes more than the Synoptics the hopelessness of the actual situation (6:7—9)[64]. The material objects of Jesus' "signs" thus prove to be extraordinarily inadequate, and their very inadequacy throws into greater relief their "sign" value.

Given the woman's past and present history, Jesus' effort to seek her out and reveal to her the mystery of the "gift of God" and of his own identity becomes all the more remarkable. It underlines both the reality of the "gift" itself and Jesus' identity as "the Savior of the world" (v 42; cf. 1:29, 36). On the formal rhetorical level, the story of the woman, as in the "signs," functions as an argument from "unlikes" (*imparia*). Its convincing value is, therefore, great, especially since, as is generally held, the woman is here set up as a contrast to the rabbi Nicodemus[65]. The force of the

---

[64]The hopelessness of the situation is doubly emphasized by Philip: that the two hundred denarii would not suffice to buy bread for the crowd even for each person to have a little piece (v 7), and by Andrew: that the five barley loaves and two fishes are nothing among so many (v 9). In addition, only John mentions Jesus' testing the disciples since he himself knew what to do (v 6), and his explicitly asking them in the end to pick up the remnants (v 12). Moreover while in the Synoptics the people ate and were satisfied (ἐχορτάσθησαν, Mt 14:20; Mk 6:42; Lk 9:17), in John they were "filled" (ἐνεπλήσθησαν, v 12), which verb suggests maximum satisfaction. So on the whole the Johannine emphasis on the "sign value" of the miracle is more pointed. Daube (*NT and Rabbinic Judaism*, 36—51) attributes the emphasis on the plentifulness of the miracle and on the gathering up of the remnants to the influence on John of the story of Ruth and Boaz.

[65]In Hellenistic rhetoric, arguments from "unlikes" (*imparia*) are most useful in exhortation (*ad exhortationem*). For instance, since courage is more remarkable in a woman than in a man, the example of Lucretia is more persuasive than that of Cato and Scipio (Quintilian, *Inst. Or.* V.xi. 10). Again in the Johannine adaptation, the positive response to Jesus' self-revelation by someone like the Samaritan woman portrayed as a contrast to the rabbi Nicodemus, would carry most weight. The same contrast is intended between the Samaritans and the Jews (2:23—25; 4:44; 5—10). The extraordinary character of the Johannine "signs" are, perhaps, to be explained primarily on this rhetorical ground, namely, the need to present an argument which carries most persuasive weight. That the primary purpose of their portrayal is *ad exhortationem* is clearly stated in 20:20—31, a passage whose importance as the key to the rhetorical framework of the Gospel we considered at length in Chapter II.

Interestingly enough, R.J. Dillon (*From Eyewitness to Ministers of the Word: Tradition and*

argument and of the contrast would, however, be lost, unless the woman's personal marital history is allowed its full significance[66].

We may bring this part of the discussion to a close by recalling yet another similarity between vv 16—19 and the incident concerning Nathanael (1:48—49). Because Philip had already told Nathanael that Jesus was the one of whom Moses and the prophets wrote (1:43), he was able to confess straight away, after Jesus' revelation of his divine knowledge, that Jesus was the "Son of God," "the king of Israel" (1:49). The woman, however, has had no such previous information concerning Jesus. She has merely been told thus far "if you knew who this is" (v 10b); the nearest, therefore, that she can come to a confession is to call Jesus "a prophet" (v 19), and to express this as her own personal insight or discovery based on the revelation in v 17b—18. However, the conversation now develops in such a way as to bring her to the same knowledge as Nathanael had received from Philip (v 26).

b) Vv 19—26: "who this is"

Noticeably, it is the woman who introduces both the notion of "prophet" and the dispute between Jews and Samaritans concerning the right place to worship. As earlier she had implicitly raised the issue of Jesus' identity by calling him "a Jew" (v 9a) and determined the direction in which the concept of "the gift of God" was discussed by the way she understood "living water," so now her interpretation of v 18 in vv 19—20 (namely, her identification of Jesus as a prophet and her introduction of the theme of worship) determines the direction in which the issue of Jesus' identity is now discussed. Hence, as v 16 is stated in view of vv 18 and 26, so from the woman's standpoint, v 20 elaborates what she understands by προφήτης (v 19).

In v 19 the woman "perceives" (θεωρῶ) that Jesus is a prophet. This is simply an intellectual perception of a fact, not a spiritual insight into meaning, for which notion the Evangelist usually employs the perfect of ὁράω (1:34; 3:11, 32; 19:35)[67]. The question whether or not προφή-

---

Composition in Luke 24 [AnBib 82; Rome: Biblical Institute, 1978] 252) also holds that Luke portrays the Samaritans as "outcasts" to whom he accords a special status from the standpoint of the Christian mission to Samaria. He further cites Frieder Schütz (*Der leidende Christus: Die angefochtene Gemeinde und das Christuskerygma der lukanischen Schriften* [BWANT 89; Stuttgart: Kohlhammer, 1969] 119) who also sees in the Lucan accounts concerning the Samaritans a Christology of the "Savior of the outcasts." John may not, therefore, have been the only NT writer who saw a rhetorical value in the faith of the Samaritans.

66Other scholars who reject the allegorical interpretation of the five husbands include Lagrange (*Jean*, 110) who also points out v 29 as a major obstacle in the allegorical interpretation; Barrett, *John*, 235; Schnackenburg, *Johannesevangelium* I, 468; Brown *John* I, 171; Haenchen, *Johannesevangelium*, 242; and Bultmann (*Commentary*, 188, n. 3) who prefers to see the woman's history as symbolic rather than allegorical.

67In John, ἑώρακα "means the kind of 'having seen' which has produced a permanent result enabling the man that 'hath seen' to bear witness." Abbott, *Johannine Vocabulary*, 1605, p. 111;

της refers to the Samaritan *Taꞌeb* will be discussed more fully in connection with Μεσσίας, χριστός in v 25. Here it needs only be noted that προφήτης is anarthrous. The term is, therefore, to be understood in a very generic way. Besides, it is well known that the Samaritans rejected the prophetic books and that the only prophet they recognized was the one who was to return (Deut 18:15—18)[68]. In v 19, the woman simply recognizes Jesus as *a* Jewish prophet. V 20 supports this interpretation; the juxtaposition of "our fathers" and "you" shows that in the woman's mind, Jesus remains essentially a Jew, a Jewish prophet, no doubt, but a Jew nonetheless. Jesus' own remark in v 22 underscores this point.

V 20 proves to be crucial in determining the connection between the revelation of Jesus' prophetic knowledge (vv 16—19) and the discussion on true worship (vv 21—24). The important issue is to determine whether in v 20 the woman is cleverly diverting attention from her own sinful life or whether in her mind Jesus' being "a prophet" is intrinsically linked with the controversy surrounding Jerusalem and Gerizim as the right place to worship. The notion that in v 20 the woman is diverting attention from her own life rests on the interpretation that v 18 discloses to the woman her own sinful life; but we have seen that such an interpretation is unfounded in the Gospel. If v 18 does not aim at exposing the woman's sinful life, then neither can v 20 be intended to divert attention from this sinfulness. Indeed, v 29a indicates that the woman is not ashamed to talk about "all" she ever did. Wherein, then, lies the connection between vv 19 and 20?

The answer depends largely on what one understands by connection. It is important not to forget that the primary literary form of this entire section is the dialogue, not the treatise. Secondly, there are no set rules as to what may or may not come into a conversation. We recall once more that the woman, Jesus' partner in dialogue, constitutes the primary link between vv 19 and 20, to the extent that her awareness of Jesus as a prophet triggers in her mind the issue of worship which she rasises in v 20. Unlike in the previous situation concerning "living water," the woman here for the first time begins to think on the religious/spiritual plane, helped by Jesus' supernatural knowledge in vv 17b—18. As earlier she had responded to Jesus' request for a drink by raising the issue of the social enmity between Jews and Samaritans, so now her recognition of Jesus as a prophet on the basis of v 18 leads her spontaneously to raise the issue of the single most important religious dispute existing between Jews and

---

for his full discussion of the different verbs of seeing in John see nos. 1579—1611, pp. 104—111. "They have seen me" (pf.) in 15:24 stands as part of the statement of judgment pronounced against the Jews, who though they have been given enough "signs" in every sense of the word still refuse to believe in Jesus as the Father's envoy. This refusal to believe is attributed to the hardness of their hearts (cf. 12:37—43; 9:41).

[68]See Montgomery, *The Samaritans*, 243—245; MacDonald, *Theology of the Samaritans*, 204—211; Bowman, *The Samaritan Problem*, 60.

Samaritans. The woman thus proves to be remarkably in touch with the current disputes between the two nations. As for finding a topic worthy of a Jewish prophet she could do no better than raise this long-standing issue of Gerizim versus Jerusalem, a topic which is of common interest to them both[69]. Besides, are not Jewish prophets known for their championship of the cause of Yahweh's cult[70]?

The manner in which the woman frames the dispute is particularly striking: "Our fathers worshiped" (not "we worship"), but "you say." The practice of the fathers is thus juxtaposed with the dogma of the Jews, all viewed from the standpoint of the Samaritans. It is also as if the woman herself were completely neutral to the whole situation or as if she had no identity of her own. This neutrality again betrays the woman's great attachment to ancestral practices ("this well," "this mountain"), which perhaps, serve as her reassurance against the contempt of the Jews. This time, however, there is a question of authority involved, since the practice of the fathers predates by far the current dogma of the Jews.

The juxtaposition of the aorist and present tenses in v 20 draws attention to this fact. Explicitly included among the fathers are Jacob and Joseph (vv 6, 12). But according to the Samaritan tradition, Abraham also performed his greatest act of faith and worship, the sacrifice of Isaac, on Mount Gerizim. Over that mountain, the Shekina associated with the Mosaic revelation, dwells unseen with his angels[71]. The authority of the fathers thus takes precedence over the contemporary Jewish insistence that one "ought to" worship in Jerusalem, which cultic site only dates from the Davidic era (2 Sam 6). Moreover, this time the woman simply states the situation without the cutting irony of vv 9, 11—12, 15. The calm which has now descended in her attitude towards Jesus indicates a genuine respect and openness on her part.

Jesus, in turn, is aware of the change and seizes upon it to win the woman's confidence even further. We notice the formal title of respect

---

[69]When exactly the Samaritan schism started is a matter for dispute (cf. Montgomery, *The Samaritans*, 46—88); but that the Samaritans held to the sanctity of Gerizim, at least as much as the Jews held to that of Jerusalem as the place to worship, is not disputed. Belief in Gerizim formed the fourth article of the Samaritan creed (Bowman, *Samaritan Problem*, 30), and it is well known that the Samaritan Pentateuch reads "Gerizim" in place of "Ebal" in Dt 27:4. Thus not only was Gerizim the place of the sacrifice of Isaac; next to Sinai it was the mountain of revelation, the eternal hill, the point of entry into the invisible, the new Eden of the end-time (MacDonald, *Theology*, 406).

[70]The concern of the prophets for the true worship of Yahweh through fidelity to the covenant is too commonplace to need documenting. As far as the Samaritans were concerned, however, Moses' zeal on Sinai on the occasion of the golden calf would be a good starting point (Ex 32: 24—34). One is also reminded of Elijah on Mount Carmel (1 Kg 17:17—40), and Amos in Bethel (7:7—17).

[71]Montgomery, *The Samaritans*, 236—239. The strong belief in the sanctity of Gerizim explains, perhaps, why the Samaritans continue to worship on this mountain to this day (even as the Jews do outside the Wailing Wall in Jerusalem) though the temple destroyed by John Hycanus in 128 B.C. has never been rebuilt.

("woman") by which he addresses her (v 21; cf. 2:4; 19:26; 20:13, 15). In appealing to the woman to take him seriously ("believe me," v 21), something she has not done up to now, Jesus shows his usual tactful concern not to contradict her. As earlier he had refused to enter into the standing quarrel between the Jews and the Samaritans or to dispute the worth of Jacob's well (vv 9–10, 11–14), so now he transposes the issue of worship to a completely different plane, that of eschatology. In this new sphere of reality, the issue of worship centers on the right manner or true meaning of worship, not on place. In this order, both Jerusalem and Gerizim become irrelevant (v 21) since what counts is the attitude of the worshiper towards God (v 23).

This is what is meant by worshiping "in Spirit and in truth" (v 23). The fundamental meaning of the Hebrew verb השתחוה rendered by the Greek (προσκυνεῖν) is that of inclining oneself or bending towards the object worshiped. The primary meaning of the term here, then, precludes an action done on set hours, days (e.g. the sabbat) or seasons in Jerusalem or on Gerizim. It emphasizes, rather, the orientation of one's entire life towards God, such that he becomes the only imperative in one's life. A clear example of one such worshiper is Jesus himself whose sole raison d'être is to do his Father's will (v 34; 5:30; 6:38; cf. Heb 10:9). Worship "in spirit and truth" thus describes the quality of life which is proper to those who are born again of "water and the Spirit" (3:3, 5–8), or who are empowered to become "children of God" (1:12–13); for such life is impossible without the gift of the Spirit/living water, the fruit of Jesus' accomplished mission (7:37–39; 14:7)[72].

Furthermore it is the Father who "seeks" (ζητεῖ, v 23c), that is, who enables this genuine worship in the worshipers. In the Johannine perspective, the "seeking" by the Father signifies, not a passive desire on his part, but his causative action in the individual without which a genuine human response is impossible (cf. 6:44, 65; 15:1–2). Jesus' dialogue with the woman itself exemplifies the Father's seeking, since Jesus does his work (v 34). In this connection we may note the heavy emphasis on the Father in vv 21 and 23. The expression, "God is Spirit" (πνεῦμα ὁ θεός, v 24) defines not the nature of God as such but the mode of his creative, life-giving action in human beings (cf. 1:12–13; 3:3–8; 6:63). That is why the authentic response to him can only be made in the same mode, "in Spirit and in truth," and why this is stated as an eschatological imperative (δεῖ προσκυνεῖν, v 24b). Πνεῦμα describes the nature of eternal life which is given even now in Jesus (20:22–23), while ἀλήθεια in the Johannine perspective stresses the reality of this gift (as opposed to mere appearance, so Bultmann) and guarantees its permanence[73]. Though this

---

[72]For further discussion on the meaning of προσκυνεῖν in Greek and Hebrew usage see Heinrich Greeven, *TDNT* VI, 758–766, esp. 759–763.

[73]Bultmann, ἀλήθεια, *TDNT* I, 235–251, esp. 250–251. One may further compare Paul's description of life in the Spirit (Gal 5:22–26) as opposed to life in the flesh (Gal 5:16–21) where

new mode of worshiping is present here and now in Jesus, in his personal example and teaching, it is yet to come, since its full realization is bound up with the arrival of his own "hour," the "hour" of his glorification (7: 39; 16:7)[74].

The puzzling statement in v 22 is much discussed both in the commentaries and in specific studies on 4:1—42[75]. To enunciate briefly our own position: The real puzzle is v 22a, not v 22b; ἡ σωτηρία in v 22b expresses the same gift of salvation (cf. v 42) already described by Jesus in terms of "living water" (v 14). This gift, it was noted, is inseparably bound up with the person of Jesus, whose Jewish nationality is repeatedly mentioned in the dialogue (vv 9a, c, 20, 22a). If Jesus, "the Savior of the world" (v 42), is by nationality a Jew, there should be very little mystery in the statement that "the salvation" which he brings takes its earthly departure point (ἐκ), not origin (παρά), "from" the Jews[76]. In its visible historical form, salvation grows out of the Jewish milieu; the plural ἐκ τῶν Ἰουδαίων is noteworthy. Several explanations could be given for this statement: because the revelation in Christ is a continuation and the fulfilment of that given by God to the Jews (cf. 5:39—40, 45—47); because the Jews guarded this revelation in its more complete form than did the Samaritans who rejected the prophets (cf. 1:45); because the departure point of salvation is God's promise made to the Jews as in Is 9; 11; 45:8, 17 (so Lindars, *John*, 118); and, most importantly, because Jesus who brings this definitive salvation (4:10, 14; cf. v 42) is himself a Jew (vv 9, 20; cf. 7:42; Acts 13:23; Rom 1:3; Lk 1:70).

Moreover, nowhere in the whole Christian tradition is there ever an attempt to deny the essentially Jewish origin, in its human manifestation, of God's salvation. Even Paul, who teaches emphatically that Jesus has abrogated the law, makes exactly the same point as in v 22, and much more explicitly in Rom 9:4—5 (" . . . to them belong the Patriarchs, and

---

authentic human response to God is also viewed as a way of life. In Eph 2:20—22 (cf. 1 Cor 3: 16—17; 6:19; 2 Cor 6:16—7:1) this way of life is further described as spiritual worship. See further, de la Potterie, *La Vérité dans saint Jean* (2 vols. AnBib 73, 74. Rome: Biblical Institute, 1977).

[74]A fuller treatment of the issue of eschatology in the passage and the related questions (e.g., the notion of the "hour") is undertaken at the end of Chapter V, pp. 165—168.

[75]Apart from Odeberg (*The Fourth Gospel*, 170), Bultmann (*Commentary*, 189, n. 6), Bauer (*Johannesevangelium*, 67) and Haenchen (*Johannesevangelium*, 243—244), most of the commentaries also hold that "we" in v 22 refers to Christians set against Samaritans and Jews (as they believe it also does in 3:11). See Zahn, *Johannesevangelium*, 244; Lagrange, *Jean*, 122; Brown, *John* I, 171; Schnackenburg, *Johannesevangelium* I, 470; Lindars, *John*, 188; and Barrett, *John*, 237. Leidig's thesis that v 22 defines the essentially Jewish character of Jesus' messiahship would seem to put in question, and rightly so, this "Christian" interpretation of v 22.

[76]Παρά is the preposition most frequently used in John for origin or source (e.g., 1:7; 8:40 [from God]). Outside the references to places of origin (e.g., Bethsaida, 1:44; cf. 7:42; 11:1; 12: 21; 19:38), the Gospel's usage of ἀπό also implies causality or originator of the mission (3:2; 6: 38; 13:3; 16:30), whereas the primary meaning of ἐκ is "departure point," that from which separation takes place. Cf. *BAG*, 88, no. 4, 234, n. 3; *BDF*, 133, n. 3, 209; and Abbott, *Grammar*, no. 2295, pp. 231—232.

of their race, according to the flesh, is Christ."). The whole thrust of the
book of Acts is another case in point, a fact which is all the more remarkable, if, as is generally held, Luke was a Gentile[77]. V 22b, then, may be
seen as a statement concerning a well-known historical fact, which in the
passage provides an explanation (ὅτι, or as Lagrange translates it, "c'est
pour cela que") for the rather enigmatic v 22a[78]. Because God's salvation
is given through the Jews (cf. Rom 9:4—5), it can be said that the Jews
"worship what they do know."

It now remains to determine how v 22a functions in the passage.
First, it needs to be noted that the verse is not a contemptuous assertion,
of Jewish superiority. Lindars is quite right here. Nonetheless, it is not a
captatio benevolentiae as he seems to imply, namely, that if John had a
Jewish audience in mind, he would not want them to think that Jesus was
siding with the Samaritans[79]. It has been seen that throughout the dialogue Jesus never denies the reality of the socio-religious conflicts raised
by the woman, but rather transposes these issues to the eschatological
plane wherein alone they can be irrevocably resolved. This focus on the
new order does not mean, however, that Jesus is deaf to the woman's concerns.

A special feature of this second part of the dialogue is the manner in
which Jesus eagerly affirms the woman's replies. All of v 22 which is
stated in the same subtle or parenthetic style as v 18 serves as yet another
instance of Jesus' effort to affirm the woman's statements. So v 22 responds directly to the problem raised by the woman, though her categories
are transcended (not place of worship but knowledge of what one worships). Though Jerusalem and Gerizim are no longer necessary as places
of worship, the fact remains that the locus of God's formal revelation is
in Judaism; Jesus himself is the culminative proof of this[80]. The two
juxtaposed phrases: "what you do not know," "what we do know" (v
22a), thus refer to the fact of revelation which reaches its fulness in Jesus,
having passed through the prophets (1:45; cf. Acts 4:24) whom the
Samaritans refuse to recognize. Accordingly, the worship which is based
on this progressive revelation emerges as the *enlightened* worship. Moreover,

---

[77]In the well-known Lucan schema, salvation history is accomplished in Jerusalem (Lk 24:18,
27, 45—46), whence it spreads to Judea, Samaria and the ends of the earth (Acts 1:8). Similarly,
Philip proclaims "the Christ" (not the Taʾeb) in Samaria (8:5) and "Jesus" to the Ethiopian
Eunuch (8:35). We may recall, too, Peter's proclamation to Cornelius and his household (Acts
10:34—43).

[78]The ὅτι here is clearly causal, "because." See Abbott, *Grammar*, no. 2178, p. 156; Lagrange,
Jean, 112.

[79]Lindars, *John*, 186, 188.

[80]We are not suggesting here that ἡ σωτηρία is a synonym for Μεσσίας as Schnackenburg
(*Johannesevangelium* I, 470) tends to suggest. Rather, "the salvation" in v 22 is to be understood
first and foremost as "the gift of God" announced in vv 10, 14. Only insofar as Jesus is the agent
of this salvation (v 10) does the concept apply to him as "the Savior" (v 42). Jn 3:16—17 allows
for this interpretation. Compare also Rev 7:10; 12:10; 19:1; Rom 1:16; Eph 1:13.

the very fact that the woman is waiting for "Messiah" (this absolute form is striking) to resolve the issue (v 25) implies that she does not feel absolutely certain about the claims of Gerizim, whereas the Jewish position entertains no such doubt (vv 20b, and 22 ["we know"]).

Concerning the nature of the σωτηρία itself, it will be recalled that the LXX translates the two Hebrew verbs ישע (to free from bondage) and פלט (to escape) by σώξειν. Both meanings are implied in John. Negatively, "the salvation" means freedom from slavery to sin (8:34–36; cf. 1:29; 20:23); positively, it means giving eternal life (3:15, 16; 10:10); and both are made possible only through Jesus, the Son (8:31, 36). The articular form tends to emphasize the definitiveness of this salvation given in Jesus. But since sin leads to death (5:29b; 8:24), salvation also means escaping death or judgment, in the sense that one is never caught by it (5:24; 11:25–26). Fohrer is thus right in considering σωθῆναι as the natural opposite of κρίνειν[81].

Finally, it is to be noted that while the woman tends defensively to hide behind the tradition of the fathers ("our fathers/you," v 20), Jesus on the contrary addresses the present generations ("you/we," v 22). Each group, Jewish and Samaritan, needs to assume full responsibility for its current religious practices and needs to do this, not in the light of what "the fathers" did *long ago*, but in response to what "the Father" wants and what he does *now* through Jesus (vv 10, 21, 23–24). In contrast to the woman's approach, that of Jesus is throughout intensely personal and challenging. All his requests and statements are addressed to her personally (using the second person singular, σύ). If in vv 23–24 he leaves the discussion on the plural level as the woman raised it, it is because worship is also a public and communal affair. The "true worshipers" belong together (cf. v 36; 10:16; 11:52; 17:20–21; 1 Jn 1:4). Ultimately, then, as in the first part of the dialogue, Jesus' reply to the woman responds to the issues both latent and overt which she raises in v 20[82].

How much of the explanation the woman has understood is, again, debatable. What is remarkable is her refusal to be swept off her pragmatic stance even to hear a Jewish prophet state, contrary to the Jewish eschatological stance on the issue, that Jerusalem is no longer relevant as a place of worship[83]. She does seem, however, to respond, at least, to

---

[81] Fohrer, σώξειν, TDNT VII, 997.

[82] That v 22 is concerned with revelation (its certainty or knowledge of what one worships), is further indicated by Jesus' substitution of the pronoun ὅ for the woman's prepositions ἐν, ὅπου (v 20). More important than "where" one worships is "what" one worships. The woman's "I know" (v 25) would seem to indicate that she has grasped the point concerning the need for enlightened worship, where the revelation comes from an authoritative source.

[83] Vv 20–21 need not be interpreted as indication that the Temple in Jerusalem had already been destroyed at the time the Gospel was written. On the contrary, the verse would make full sense only if Jerusalem was still functioning as the center of Jewish worship. For one thing, there is no evidence that after A.D. 70 the Jews still held tenaciously to Jerusalem as the place where one ought to worship (v 20).

Jesus' appeal to her personally. For the first time she takes a personal stance "I know" (οἶδα) and no longer seems to hide behind either the tradition of the fathers or the prevailing custom (v 9)[84]. Her answer in v 25 partly indicates the reason for her neutrality noted in respect of v 20, namely, her certainty that Messiah, the one with authority, will ultimately "disclose" or "proclaim" (ἀναγγελεῖ) the truth concerning the matter of worship[85]. Despite the exaggeration, the term ἅπαντα (cf. her πάντα ὅσα, v 29) must refer primarily to the issue of worship and the points rasied by her and Jesus in connection with it. Until Messiah comes, then, she remains sceptical not only with regard to the Jewish and Samaritan claims concerning the right place to worship, but over Jesus' radically new teaching on the subject. The unasked question which must be uppermost in her mind as she listens to Jesus concerns the authority by which he says these things (cf. 2:18). That is, who is Jesus, what are his credentials, and the guarantee that what he says is true?

In raising the issue of the coming Messiah, does the woman half suspect that Jesus himself might be the one? And is she thus voicing her suspicion indirectly or subtly to see how Jesus reacts to it? Perhaps she has not, after all, completely forgotten Jesus' conditional statement in v 10b ("if you knew who this is"). If so her "I know" not only links vv 25[26] verbally with vv 22[20—24] ("you do not know," "we know,"), it also links it, and so the whole of the second part of the dialogue, with v 10b. The theme of knowledge thus brings the conversation back to its beginning, thereby establishing that the real aim of vv 16—26 is to lead the woman to know who Jesus is (v 10b).

Strikingly, the Messiah which she expects is not defined according to time, space and national descent as is that of the Jews (7:26—27, 40—42, 52) but in terms of his mission as teacher and revealer (if the term is not too technical a translation for ἀναγγέλλειν)[86]. At any event, v 25

---

[84]NA[26] prefers the reading οἶδα of the major witnesses to οἴδαμεν of the minor ones. We agree with Nestle-Aland here, not simply because οἶδα is the *lectio difficilior*, but because throughout the dialogue the woman expresses her own personal views (what she thinks about Jacob's well, for instance), and not what the Samaritans as a group would say in this particular encounter. In other words, while the issue she raises are general ones, the opinion and attitude she expresses towards them are her own. Οἶδα fits best into this general pattern. From this perspective, too, she is clearly not a "mouthpiece" of the Samaritan faith.

[85]The verb ἀναγγέλλειν meaning "to disclose, announce, teach, proclaim" is synonymous with λαλεῖν and is similar to ἀπαγγέλλειν, "to tell, proclaim, announce publicly with authority" (*BAG*, 51; *LSJ*, 602). That λαλεῖν and ἀναγγέλλειν are synonymous is well attested in 16:13 where both verbs describe the future mission of the Holy Spirit (cf. 1 Jn 1:3).

[86]The term "revealer" has in John a special connotation as applied to Jesus which it would not have had from the woman's standpoint in v 25. A good discussion of the relation between the Jewish and Samaritan messianic expectations in the Gospel is given by Bowman, *Samaritan Studies*, 60—69; and Appold, *Oneness Motif*, 64—74. From the specifically Jewish standpoint, see de Jonge, "Jewish Expectations about the 'Messiah' According to the Fourth Gospel," *NTS* 19 (1972—1973) 246—270; Schnackenburg, "Messiasfrage," 240—264; Emil Schürer, *The History of the Jewish People in the Age of Jesus Christ* II (rev. ed. Geza Vermes *et al.*; Edinburgh: T and T Clark,

reveals the woman's openness to learn. Moved by her opening disposition, Jesus, in turn, rewards her by making the astonishing self-revelation unparalleled in the Gospel for its explicitness (v 26 cf. 9:35–38). This startling revelation has the catalytic effect of making the woman abandon her water pot in order to run with speed in her eagerness to spread the news of her encounter with Jesus to her fellow Samaritans (vv 28–29).

Jesus' self-proclamation, thus, gives the woman more than the guarantee she sought. The ἐγώ εἰμι appears to be and has indeed been interpreted as a "recognition" formula, in that it identifies Jesus as the Messiah expected by the woman. In fact, however, the statement appears to be a disguised, hence all the more powerful, revelation formula. We shall attempt to explain this in the following discussion[87].

c) Vv 25–26: the messianic issue

The important questions which arise with regard to vv 25–26 concern the identity of the Messiah expected by the woman and the relationship between this Messiah and the one proclaimed by Jesus in v 26, and which the woman later proclaims to her fellow Samaritans in v 29. In other words, is this Messiah the Samaritan Taʾeb ("the one who is to return"), and does Jesus in v 26 identify himself as the Taʾeb? Which Messiah, ultimately, does the Gospel designate in v 26? These questions are important in view of the global aim of the Gospel which is to persuade its readers to believe that "Jesus is the Christ, the Son of God" (20:30–31). Ultimately, they all have to do not only with the identity of the Messiah, but also with the manner in which he can be identified both in the passage and in the Gospel as a whole. The answers to them should also indicate both the degree of Jesus' missionary success in Samaria and the force of "example" (παράδειγμα) in the woman's and Samaritans' response to him (vv 28–30, 39, 42).

Concerning the Taʾeb, since the woman is a most patriotic Samaritan (vv 9b, 11–12, 20), one would naturally expect her Messiah to be the same as that expected by her nation. Once this has been posited, however,

---

1979) 488–544; and on messianism in general see Pierre Grelot, *L'espérance juive à l'heure de Jésus* (Collection "Jésus et Jésus-Christ;" Paris: Desclée, 1978).

[87]The discussion of the ἐγώ εἰμι statements in John usually distinguishes two major categories: i) the absolute use: 6:30; 8:24, 28, 58; 13:19; 18:5, 6, 8; and ii) the use with a descriptive predicate: 6:35, 48, 51; 8:12; 10:7, 9, 11, 14; 11:25; 14:6, 15:1, 5. In the list given here, 4:26 is most noticeably missing (cf. Kysar, *The Fourth Evangelist*, 119 [-127], whose list covers research from 1963 to 1975; and Appold *Oneness Motif*, 82 [-85]. While Schweizer (*EGO EIMI*, 126) tends to consider 4:26 as a revelation formula because vv 10b and 15 depend on it, Butlmann (*Commentary*, n. 3, 225–226) denies that it is a sacred revelation formula and sees it rather as belonging to the same category as 8:5, 6, 8, which he classifies as an indentification formula. In 4:26, however, more than identification is involved. The same is true of 18:5, 6, 8; that the soldiers who come to arrest Jesus fall to the ground when he says "I am" shows that more is involved than in 9:9, for instance, where the blind man identifies himself to the questioning Jews. Our ensuing discussion of the "messianic issue," clarifies this; see also n. 97 below.

the problems only begin, not end. Intensive research to date on the Samaritan messianic expectation from Merx and Montgomery through Gaster, Bowman, MacDonald, and Meeks, to Kippenberg, Purvis and a host of others, reveals the impossibility, given existing sources, of determining accurately the features and functions of the Samaritan Taʾeb in the first century[88]. Was he, for instance, a *Moses redivivus?* a *Joshua redivivus?* or a *Henoch redivivus*[89]? Concerning his function, was he to be simply "a restorer," or a "restorer of the cultus," "a revealer of truth," "a converter of nations," "a gatherer of the scattered," "the prototype of those who return [to the Lord] and who receive compassion"[90], or a political figure in religious garb such as is described by Josephus (*Ant.* 18, 85–88)?

The problem is further complicated by the fact that not only do the earliest known written sources, the *Memar Markah (MM)*, date from the fourth century A.D., but the oldest extant manuscript of the MM itself dates from the fourteenth century[91]. That the Samaritan expectation of the Messiah dates from the earliest times is not disputed. Strikingly, Jn 4:25 and Jos. *Ant.* 18, 85–87 are often cited as the earliest evidence for this. Understandably, since the Samaritans and Jews shared the same belief in God, Moses, and the Torah, it was inevitable that their messianic figures should have similar features, or that both should draw from the same sources for their messianic beliefs. The proof-text often used for the Samaritan Taʾeb (Deut 18:15–18) quoted by Peter in Acts 3:20–24 in the Temple in Jerusalem before the "men of Israel" (v 12) is a typical example of this[92]. For our purposes, however, the one area of agreement by scholars in Samaritanism is highly significant, namely, that the term "Messiah" (מ שׁ י ח) does not occur in Samaritan sources prior to the six-

---

[88]Merx, *Der Messias oder Taʾeb der Samaritaner* (BZAW 17; Giessen: Alfred Töpelmann, 1909), 41–44; Montgomery, *The Samaritans,* 239–251; Moses Gaster, *The Samaritan Oral Law and Ancient Traditions*: I, *Samaritan Eschatology* (Great Britain: The Research Publishing Company, 1932), 221–229; Bowman, "Samaritan Studies: I, The Fourth Gospel and the Samaritans," *BJRL* 40 (1956–1958) 298–327; MacDonald, *Theology,* 262–271; Meeks, *Prophet-King,* 250–257; Kippenberg, *Garizim und Synagoge: Traditionsgeschichtliche Untersuchungen zur Samaritaninschen Religion der aramäischen Periode* (Religionsgeschichtliche Versuche und Vorarbeiten 30; Berlin/New York: Walter de Gruyter, 1971): "Der Taheb" (276–305), "Der Prophet wie Mose" (306–327); Purvis, "The Fourth Gospel and the Samaritans," 161–166, 117–190; Appold, *Oneness Motif,* 56–74; Freed, "The Fourth Gospel and the Samaritans," 245–251; de Jonge, "Jewish Expectations," 268–270; Odeberg, *The Fourth Gospel,* 181–187.

[89]For a discussion on this topic see Merx, *Messias,* 43; MacDonald, *Theology,* 262–263; and Meeks, *Prophet-King,* 253.

[90]Cf. Montgomery, *The Samaritans,* 246, n. 169; MacDonald, *Theology,* 262–263 (citing the *MM* III, 3 and *The Samaritan Chronicle,* p. 497), 364–365 (citing the *MM* IV, 12 in reference to John 4:25).

[91]MacDonald, *Theology,* 361; Kippenberg, *Garizim und Synagoge,* 276–305; Purvis, "The Fourth Gospel," 165.

[92]That Samaritans and Jews shared the same sources has been emphasized by Merx, *Messias,* 44; Bowman "Studies," 314 (who thinks they may even have had the same creed); and de Jonge, "Jewish Expectations," 268. De Jonge also cites Justin (*Apology* I.43.6) who states that both Jews and Samaritans expected "the Christ" because both had news of him from the prophets!

teenth century[93]. Since, therefore, available external evidence is not very helpful, one is forced back on the Johannine text itself for possible clues to the identification of the Messiah in v 25.

The first important point to note is that the woman uses the term Μεσσίας without the article, in contrast to Andrew's τὸν Μεσσίαν (1:41) where the term receives a further specificity from Philip in v 45. Similarly, the woman does not simply say "I know that [a] Messiah is coming," but she goes on to define "Messiah" as "the one who is called Christ." The χριστός which she gives as a synonym of Μεσσίας is also anarthrous. In 1:41 this latter term is also anarthrous, but in this earlier passage the term is an interpretation (so, too, Bultmann), which is clearly not the case here[94]. The defining terms, ὅ ἐστιν μεθερμηνευόμενον [1:41] and ὁ λεγό-μενος [4:25]) give a different quality to χριστός in each passage as it re-lates to Μεσσίας. In 1:41 the relationship between the two terms stands as "the Messiah," "the Christ," but in 4:25 as "Messiah," "Christ." The statement in 1:41 would be translated, "the Messiah, which term means the Christ," and that in 4:25, "Messiah, the one called Christ." Whether, therefore, with Bultmann following Odeberg one sees the qualifying phrase as part of the woman's statement, as we do here, or with Barrett one attributes it to the Evangelist himself on the basis of 1:41, the fact remains that "Christ" indicates how "Messiah" is to be understood in this particular passage[95].

In this context then, that is, for the woman, "Messiah" is a generic term; it lacks the specificity given to the term in 1:41[45]; in Johannine terms it would be equivalent to "one sent" since the Greek word Μεσσίας is the equivalent of the Hebrew מ שׁ י ח which noun derives from the same root as the verb מ שׁ ח. The woman's messianic or anointed figure has, therefore, no well-defined contours of nationality and descent as has that of the Jews in 7:27—36, 40—52. What matters is that he is expected and that he will teach and announce "everything." It is debatable whether ἄπαντα is to be understood in a comprehensive way or as "everything con-cerning the issue of worship," with special reference to the Gerizim/ Jerusalem controversy in which the woman is particularly interested. V 29 would support this latter interpretation, for the only thing that Jesus

---

[93] Kippenberg, *Garizim und Synagoge,* 303, n. 218; Appold, *Oneness Motif,* 70; de Jonge, "Jewish Expectations," 268.

[94] The explanatory clause in 1:41 focuses on the meaning of the term "Messiah," whereas that in 4:23 gives "Christ" as a different name for "Messiah"; it is the term most commonly used by the Jews in the Gospel; see, for instance, the debate in 7:25—44 and 10:24; 12:34.

[95] Bultmann (*Commentary,* 192, n. 2) considers ὁ λεγόμενος in v 25 to be different from the borrowed word as in 1:38 and 5:2. He cites Odeberg who holds that in the source the passage would have read "The Messiah, that is, the one you Jews call the Christ." Barrett (*John,* 239) sees no difference between v 25 and 1:38, 41. Some critics hold that the Evangelist substituted "Mes-siah" for the "Taʾeb" of the source and introduced the term "Christ." Curiously, though, the Evan-gelist himself seems to prefer the title "Jesus Christ" (1:17; cf. 20:31 [Jesus is the Christ]), which title is also used by Jesus himself (17:3) and by no one else in the Gospel.

ever told the woman concerns her marital life (vv 17b—18), not "all" she ever did in the strictest sense of the word. At any event, the most important point to note is the lack of rigidity in her messianic expectation.

The same flexibility applies to her view as painted in the hypothetical Johannine source[96]. Not only is her Messiah to be a teacher, or an announcer, but she herself manifests a willingness to be taught and is quite willing to accept the arbitration (as it were) of the Messiah. This flexibility is singularly proved in this passage by the fact that though Jesus is manifestly a Jew, yet when he does reveal himself to be the expected Messiah, the woman not only accepts it personally but proclaims it to others with great eagerness. Her readiness to accept even an enemy Jew as Messiah constitutes an implicit criticism of the Jews whose idea of the Messiah is so fixed that it blinds them to recognizing Jesus, one of their own, as the Messiah, despite the proofs (including his "signs") which he has given, and which they themselves cite (cf. 7:31; 11:47).

Does Jesus in v 26, then, identify himself as the Messiah expected by the woman? If the above interpretation is correct, then one can say that the woman's messianic figure is fluid enough for Jesus to identify himself "comfortably" with it, unlike the previous messianic titles given him which all proved to be inadequate[97]. As we noted above, however, the $\dot{\epsilon}\gamma\dot{\omega}$ $\epsilon\dot{\iota}\mu\iota$ in v 26 is not simply a recognition formula, if by this is meant that Jesus simply identifies himself with the Messiah expected by the woman understood for the most part as the Ta²eb. Our view is that as $\chi\rho\iota\sigma\tau\dot{o}\varsigma$ qualifies "Messiah" in v 25, so $\dot{o}$ $\lambda\alpha\lambda\tilde{\omega}\nu$ $\sigma o\iota$ defines $\dot{\epsilon}\gamma\dot{\omega}$ $\epsilon\dot{\iota}\mu\iota$ in v 26. By this statement, Jesus does identify himself as the Messiah, but the phrase $\dot{o}$ $\lambda\alpha\lambda\tilde{\omega}\nu$ $\sigma o\iota$ gives a specific character to this messiahship over and above what the woman might have expected. In other words, as the statement discloses to the woman that Jesus is the Messiah, it defines at the same

---

[96]This is true to the extent that the source is supposed to have read "The Ta²eb, the one you Jews call the Christ." See Odeberg, *The Fourth Gospel,* 181, 187; Bowman, "Samaritan Studies," 212–213. The woman thus appears to make no distinction between the Messiah expected by the Jews and the Samaritans. It is striking that the nationality of the Ta²eb is not discussed in the literature surveyed. However, if the story of Josephus (*Ant.* 18, 85—87) is anything to go by, the Ta²eb would, at least, have had to be someone who believed in the sanctity of Gerizim, in accordance with the fourth article of the Samaritan creed. Jn 7:27 and Justin (*Dialogue* 8.4) indicate that even in some Jewish circles the nationality of the Messiah was not fixed.

[97]Meeks (*Prophet-King,* 318, n. 1) and Appold (*Oneness Motif,* 70) both maintain that the use of Messiah/Christ by the woman evinces a "levelling of terminologies" which is very evident in the Gospel. Similarly, Origen (*Commentaire sur Saint Jean* 13.28, 163; SC 222, p. 122) once spoke of the "heterodoxy" of the woman. The expression "levelling of terminologies" could, however, be misleading, as if for the Evangelist one Christological title was just as good as another. From his perspective, however, all existing messianic titles (the prophet, Messiah, Christ) are inadequate taken singly and from the standpoint of Jesus' audience. Jesus embraces all these titles *and* transcends them. Even the specifically Johannine Christological titles ("uniquely beloved Son," "Son of God," "son of man") are inadequate taken singly. There thus appears to be no adequate title in the human language for one of whom it is said "and the Word was God" (1:1).

time the quality of his messiahship manifested in his approach to her, in the promise of living water/eternal life, in his knowledge of her own private life and in his teaching concerning worship. The verb λαλεῖν is used in the Gospel as a technical term for Jesus' proclamation, or more specifically, for his revelation of the Father, which constitutes the definitive offer of salvation (15:22)[98]. Jesus does not simply "announce" a message to the woman, he promises her eternal life and promises this as something which he has both power and authority to give (vv 10, 14)[99].

Ultimately, therefore, the Messiah with whom Jesus identifies himself in v 26 is not the Samaritan Taʾeb, nor even the nebulous figure expected by the woman, but the transcendent Johannine Christ whose true identity has already clearly been defined in the first three chapters of the Gospel, especially in the first chapter with its litany of Christological titles[100]. Most importantly, the key question which arises in this whole discussion concerns the manner in which the Messiah may be identified. It will be noted that the woman had actually met the Messiah and was indeed conversing with him without recognizing him as the Messiah. This means that the Messiah can be known only when Jesus personally identifies himself, a criterion which the Jews, especially their leaders, are unwilling to accept, even though they had the additional witness of the Baptist to help them (5:33–36; cf. 10:41).

Noteworthy also is the method by which this self-revelation and or self-identification is made. Jesus does not start by telling the woman that he is the Messiah, worthy of belief. Rather, he acts like one in his attitude towards her, in his teaching and in his supernatural knowledge of her own private life. The identification grows out of this entire revelation in action, as a process of discovery in which the woman plays an important role. The revelation of his divine knowledge in vv 17b–18 is the leading light guiding the woman in this process of discovery as v 28–29 show. The following antiphonal sketch of the second half of the conversation as it relates to the first half (where Jesus takes the lead, indicated in the sketch by the sign >) brings out clearly both the importance of vv 17b–18 as the turning point in the encounter and the leading role (indicated by the sign <) which the woman plays from this point on.

---

[98]The single most important passage which indicates that the verb λαλεῖν refers to the revelatory character of Jesus' dialogues is 15:22: "If I had not come and spoken (ἐλάλησα) to them, they would have had no sin, but now they have no excuse for their sin." See further our discussion on λαλιά in v 42; pp. 171–172.

[99]Schniewind (*TDNT* I, 61–67) points out that the object of ἀναγγέλλειν (most commonly used by the NT for ἀγγέλλειν) is usually a religious experience which one has personally witnessed (e.g., miracles [Mt 28:8; Lk 8:8; Mk 5:14] and the resurrection appearances [Mt 28:8, 10; Lk 24: 9; Mk 16:10, 13]). If so, the predominant meaning of the term when applied to others, not to Jesus, would be "to report" (cf. 1 Jn 1:1–4).

[100]See n. 97 above.

Jesus	>	*The Woman*	

10b V Εἰ ἤδεις τίς ἐστιν

R μὴ σὺ μείζων εἶ . . . ;   12

16   V ὕπαγε, φώνησον τὸν ἄνδρα
σου

R οὐκ ἔχω ἄνδρα.   17a

17bf V καλῶς εἶπας, τοῦτο ἀληθὲς
εἴρηκας.

R θεωρῶ ὅτι προφήτης εἶ
σύ.   19

<

V οἱ πατέρες ἡμῶν . . .   20

21f R πίστευέ μοι γύναι

V οἶδα ὅτι Μεσσίας ἔρχεται 25

26   R ἐγώ εἰμι ὁ λαλῶν σοι.

The revelation formula itself (ἐγώ εἰμι) looks backwards to τίς ἐστιν (v 10b) and forwards to both μήτι οὗτός ἐστιν (29b) and ὅτι οὗτός ἐστιν (v 42), thus constituting the watershed of the entire pericope. The woman's final response is also given in action: she abandons her water pot and goes into the city to spread the news of her encounter and discovery. The abandonment of her water pot which in the first part of the dialogue served as a symbol of her advantage over the Jewish beggar (v 11) actually began in vv 19—20 when she recognized Jesus as a prophet and introduced the issue of worship, concerning which she proved her neutrality more than she had done with regard to the worth of Jacob's well (vv 11—12).

If this whole interpretation is correct, then the story gains in persuasive force, especially when it is read against the background of 3:1—21 and 5—10. This persuasive force lies in its serving as an argument from *imparia* (p. 112, n. 65 above). The Samaritan woman not only has to abandon her belief in the sanctity of Gerizim, but she accepts to do this on the revelatory word of a Messiah who is a Jew by nationality. In the case of the Samaritans, the situation is further intensified by the fact that the initial bearer of the message is a woman and a sinner (vv 28—30, 39). Yet both they and the woman are able to transcend these human obstacles to receive the revelation which is essentially God's gift given through Jesus.

An important message of Jesus' approach to mission also emerges in v 22. The missionary may not compromise the truth of the revelation with regard either to its content or to its historical origins. The audience does determine the terms in which the revelation is communicated: living water, worship, this mountain versus Jerusalem. The content of the revelation, however, is not a matter for dialogue; it belongs in the order of proclamation and, therefore, has to be accepted in its entirety on its own terms. Its primary bearer is God's designated agent, the Messiah/Christ to whom others also bear witnesses (cf. vv 29—20, 39). The Christ proclaimed in the dialogue and in the Gospel is the "Son of Joseph from Nazareth," according to the flesh (1:45). Neither John nor any of the other NT writers dream of identifying him with any of the messianic figures of the many contemporary religions, not even Acts with its naturalistic approach (17:22–32; cf. vv 31–32)[101].

This may yet explain why the Gospel which evidently has some Gentile audience in mind (as witness the explanations in 1:38, 41; 4:9c; 20:16) still insists on persuading its readers to believe that "Jesus is the Christ, the Son of God" (20:31). The recognition of Jesus as a historical person constitutes an essential part of the recognition of his messiahship, even as does the recognition of his divine origin (6:60–66; 5:18; 10:22–39). The two aspects of his identity stand inseparably together. In short, the Messiah which Jesus reveals to the woman in the passage is not the "variegated" Samaritan Taʾeb, but the Son whom the Father sanctifies and sends into the world, in the historical context of Judaism, as a gift to be received in faith by both Jews and non-Jews (v 10). It is because of his divine origin that he not only transcends the messianic expectations of Jews and Samaritans but stands as the Savior of all peoples (v 42).

4. Summary of the Analysis of Vv 7–26

The main results of our analysis of vv 7–26 may be briefly summarized under the following three headings: a) the relationship between the major themes of the dialogue, b) the rhetorical devices used and, c) the important missionary features which emerged in the interaction between Jesus and the woman.

(a) The relationship between the major themes. Our exegesis highlighted two closely related major themes in the dialogue: God's gift of salvation which is free for the asking (vv 7–15) and the messianic identity of Jesus as the Christ appointed by God to dispense this gift of salvation (vv 16–26). Vv 1–9 introduced these two themes in a general way by Jesus' request for a drink ("give me," v 7b) and by the woman's identification of him as an enemy "Jew" (v 9). More specifically, v 10 embodies the double theme of the dialogue which is here set forth grammatically in terms of a protasis (vv 10a, b) and an apodosis (vv 10c,d). In the actual unfolding of the dialogue, Jesus develops first the concept of the gift of God, this being of uppermost interest for the woman (vv 11–15), then that of his messianic identity (vv 16–26). The former is done in terms of

---

101 The NT evidence on this issue is conclusive. Indeed, not only the NT, but also the evidence of the Apostolic Fathers. Their major fight against the Gnostics lay in the latter's attempt to deny the historical value of Jesus' life and of God's salvation generally. Even today, the authentic Christian missionary proclaims no other Christ than Jesus of Nazareth. Cf. 1 Cor 2:2.

the imagery of "living water," the latter in terms of Jesus' divine and authoritative knowledge demonstrated both in his "prophetic" knowledge of the woman's private life (vv 16—19) and in his radically new teaching concerning worship (vv 20—24). His subsequent identification as Messiah and Christ (vv 25—26) thus grows out of the experience of the entire dialogue.

Linguistically, the whole dialogue is held together by the key verbs "to be" ("who this is" [v 10b], "you being a Jew," "me being a Samaritan woman" [v 9], "I am" [v 26]), and "to know" ("if you knew" [v 10a], "I know" [v 25]), which verbs also look forward to the second half of the episode (vv 27—42): "could this be?" (v 29), "that this is" (v 42), "you do not know" (v 32), "we know" (v 42). These verbs thus draw attention to the central theme of the dialogue, who Jesus is and how life-giving knowledge of him may be attained, namely, through his personal revelation of himself and the Father, which is the essence of his mission (v 10; cf. 17:2—4, 6).

Theologically, the teaching on living water and true worship are closely related because both belong to the eschatological order ushered in here and now by Jesus' coming and mission. Living water, the gift of eternal life, is realized in individuals through the imparting of the Holy Spirit who is the fruit of Jesus' accomplished mission (7:37—39); it is the Spirit who also enables true worship, the personal and communal expression of this new life as it relates to God (v 24). That the issue of "living water" (Spirit, eternal life) is inseparably linked with Jesus' messiahship is further indicated in 7:37—41a. Jesus' promise of living water to believers (7:37—39) makes some of his Jewish audience declare that he is "indeed *the* prophet," and others, that "he is the Christ" (vv 40, 41a). Even so, in the dialogue with the woman, the discussion moves from the promise of living water (vv 10—15) to the identification of Jesus as "prophet" and "Messiah/Christ" (vv 19, 25—26). These two passages would indicate that John and his contemporaries saw an intrinsic connection between the promise of living water (salvation) and the Messiah. In the dialogue the connection is strengthened by the revelation of Jesus' supernatural knowledge (vv 17b—18) as it is in 6:1—15 by the miraculous multiplication of the five loaves and two fishes.

Finally, on the level of dialogue itself, the most basic link between the two sections are the dialogue partners themselves, Jesus and the woman. Jesus initiates the dialogue and introduces the themes of the conversation, but the woman determines both the order in which these issues are developed and the modes used in explaining them to her: the imagery of living water grows out of her present occupation of water-fetching; she introduces the themes of prophetic knowledge (v 19), worship (v 20) and of messiahship (v 25). The woman thus proves to be not a foil but a very active participant in the dialogue. Jesus brings the revelation but she provides the medium by which this revelation is communicated to her personally. The literary genre of the episode, that of a dialogue, not only permits genuine exchanges between Jesus and the woman but allows for the introduction of different themes all geared towards the revelation of Jesus as the Messiah and Christ (vv 10, 26)[102].

(b) Rhetorical devices. A striking feature of the dialogue noted in our analysis is that Jesus never disputes any of the issues raised by the woman, but instead transfers them to the eschatological plane where they are resolved by being given new meaning. Because of this we classified the episode as a type of the philosophical variety, as opposed to the forensic type which is characterized by attack and defense. The hortatory/persuasive approach of Jesus, especially in the second part of the dialogue, supports this classification. Specific rhetorical features highlighted include the structure of the entire dialogue in terms of a protasis and an apodosis, the argument *a minori ad maius* (vv 11—12), and the use of irony which permeats the entire dialogue, and which arises in both the woman's (vv 11—12) and Jesus' (vv 17b—18) statements[103].

More fundamentally, the whole episode was seen to be an argument from *imparia*. The Samaritan woman herself was seen as belonging in line with the characters in the Johannine "signs." That a Samaritan, a woman, five times married, and living with a man not her husband, should first be chosen by Jesus as the object of his self-revelation, and secondly, should respond positively to this revelation also leading other Samaritans to do so even though the said Messiah is an enemy Jew, emphasizes on the one hand, the gratuitous nature of Jesus' mission, and, on the other, the persuasive force of the entire portrayal. This persuasiveness of the story is further intensified by the *dispositio* whereby the response of the woman and later of the Samaritans is contrasted with the negative response from the Jews and Nicodemus (2:23—3:21; 5—10). The ultimate aim of this rhetorical portrayal, however, is to persuade the reader of the Gospel to make the same faith response to Jesus as does the woman, and later the Samaritans (20:20—31).

(c) Missionary features. The basic components of any missionary kerygma are the revelation and the language or human forms in which this revelation is communicated. It was seen that in the dialogue Jesus brings the revelation which he in no way compromised even at the risk of sounding offensive (vv 13, 22), while the woman in her particular situation and interests (water-fetching, Jacob's well, "living water," marital record,

---

[102]One may, for instance, recall Justin's *Dialogue with Trypho,* where the genre of the dialogue enables him to introduce a variety of topics in his efforts to convince Trypho of the pre-eminence of the Christian way of life.

[103]Wead, (*Literary Devices,* 47—68) studies the use of irony in the Gospel, and its relation to classical Greek usage. Of particular interest is the section, "The Irony Related to Discipleship" (pp. 66—68). In our view the most important function of irony in the Gospel is that it forms part of the rhetorical devices which the Evangelist musters to persuade his readers to believe that Jesus is the Christ, the Son of God (20:30—31).

Gerizim versus Jerusalem, and the coming Messiah) determines the categories by which the revelation is communicated. *Interdependence* thus emerges as the primary missionary feature inherent in the dialogue. Moreover, it is Jesus who throughout adapts himself to the language categories introduced by the woman whose interventions he takes most seriously. The peculiar feature of *double-entendre* illustrates the seriousness with which Jesus considers the woman's language categories and at the same time the real difficulties involved in the effort to communicate divine revelation in words which the human audience can understand.

The second important missionary feature concerns Jesus' manner and method of approach to the woman. This approach is essentially one of humility and deep respect. Though Jesus is the one with the "gift of God" to offer, he nevertheless approaches the woman as a beggar, thereby making himself most approachable, even putting himself at the woman's mercy at the start of the conversation. This humility in the exercise of mission recalled that of Hillel before his proselytes or Paul's missionary principle of "becoming all things to all peoples" in the hope of winning them to the Lord (1 Cor 9:19—23; cf. 2:2—3). Jesus' humility is further demonstrated by his readiness to let the woman dictate the terms of the conversation, even to suffer himself to be taken for a fool (vv 11—12, 15; cf. 1 Cor 4:10). Where necessary, however, he does command but only subsequently to let the woman lead, all with a view to leading her through a process of discovery to that life-giving knowledge of himself which he desires for her (vv 10, 26)[104].

In the dialogue this respect was manifested in a number of ways: by his engaging in the dialogue in the first place even though the partner is a Samaritan and a sinful woman. This respect was all the more striking in that it came to the fore (vv 21—24, 26) after Jesus had revealed to the woman his knowledge of her sinful life[105]. Jesus' consistent approach to the woman as an individual forms part of his respect for her. For while the woman thinks in broad categories (Jews against Samaritans, Jacob and his household, the fathers, Messiah will tell *us*), Jesus' message is primarily directed to her personally (if you knew, you would ask . . . he would give you; believe me, woman; I who am speaking to *you*, I am he). Moule is thus quite right in drawing attention to the individualism of John's Gospel[106]. This focus on the woman as an individual does not, however,

---

[104]Daube's studies ("Jewish Missionary Maxims in Paul," *ST* 1 [1947] 158—159, and "A Missionary Term" *NT and Rabbinic Judaism*, 336—361) considers the humility expected of the missionary from the Pauline perspective. Nevertheless, the traits he highlights here can profitably be used for the understanding of the Johannine approach as well.

[105]The same respect is shown to the woman taken in adultery (8:10—11). Though this episode is considered to be non-Johannine, it does, nonetheless, capture the Spirit of the Johannine Christ.

[106]Moule, "The Individualism of the Fourth Gospel," *Essays in NT Interpretation,* esp. 101—104. The dominance of the forms σύ, σοί and of the verbs in the second person singular draw attention to the person to person nature of the encounter between Jesus and the woman.

mean that Jesus' message to her has no universal significance. But it does mean that Jesus is not using the woman as a foil to propound his teaching. Most importantly, it illustrates that while the message has a universal appeal ("anyone who drinks the water I give," v 14), the response of faith which it seeks to elicit has to be made on an individual basis. The gift of God, of salvation, which he brings is realized in individuals, not in a cosmic vacuum (cf. 3:15, 16b, 18; 7:37—38).

Concerning Jesus' method of leading the woman to faith, we have seen that this consists in his leading her through a process of personal discovery. This process is also marked by the technique of arousing curiosity where his surprise of her rises in a mounting crescendo (give me a drink; you have had five husbands; I who am speaking to you, I am the one). The corollary of this method lies in Jesus' eagerness to confirm the statements of the woman (vv 17b—18, 21); its most outstanding feature is that the dialogue (vv 7—25) comes before the dogma (v 26). As with the missionary enterprise itself (v 6), there is nothing facile about the method used in "wooing" the audience. Jesus' patience with her highlighted in the analysis of vv 15—17a illustrates that the missionary preaching, the efforts to lead to faith, involves a real struggle. This struggle is intensified by the accompanying physical conditions of thirst and hunger, all aimed at enriching others, and which in Jesus' case goes even unto death.

Finally, two other important missionary motifs raised in the dialogue but not sufficiently developed concern the issues of fellowship (vv 9, 2) and that of salvation as "the gift of God." It is because salvation is primarily "the gift of God" that Jesus does not lord it over the woman or that he exercises his ministry with deep respect (cf. 13:1—17; 1 Cor 4:1). These issues will come to the fore in the second part of the pericope in the viewing of the disciples' mission essentially as a harvesting, where sower and reaper "rejoice together" (vv 35—38) and in the interaction between the Samaritan woman and the Samaritans (vv 39—42). From the perspective of the woman, as later of the Samaritans, the dialogue illustrates the importance on the part of the audience of openness to Jesus and his self-revelation as the condition for benefiting from his saving mission.

Our entire analysis of vv 1—26 has thus demonstrated that Jesus' encounter with the Samaritan woman can meaningfully be interpreted as a missionary undertaking. The core of the *thesis* in vv 1—26 is that Jesus is the Father's appointed agent of salvation, the Messiah or Christ. This thesis is stated not as an abstract proposition, but by portraying Jesus actively engaged in missionary work in Samaria as he communicates his message of salvation in all earnestness to the worst of sinners (humanly speaking). Our exegesis of the rest of the episode (vv 27—42) in the next chapter will develop and, hopefully, confirm this missionary perspective of vv 1—26.

Chapter V

John 4:31–42: The Consequential Argument

The hypothesis proposed earlier is that the formal relationship, literary and structural of vv 27–42 to vv 1–26 is analogous to that which exists between the σημεῖον and its explanatory discourse. Vv 1–26 dramatize the thesis, that Jesus is the Father's eschatological agent of salvation, "the Messiah" (v 26), and verses 27–42 spell out and reinforce didactically the meaning of this thesis as it applies to the disciples themselves. The present Chapter will attempt to develop and test this hypothesis. First, the whole structure of 4:1–42 needs to be more clearly delineated: All of 4:1–42 portrays Jesus' missionary work in Samaria; vv 7–26 dramatize this work as it concerns Jesus' efforts to lead the Samaritan woman, a non-believer, to life-giving knowledge of him[1]. Vv 31–38 explain to the disciples the significance of this missionary work and their own role in it. And vv 39–42, the conclusion of the entire pericope, serves as a mini-replay, still for the benefit of the absent disciples (v 8) of the key missionary issues raised both in Jesus' dialogue with the woman (vv 7–26) and in his own instruction of them (vv 31–38). The lesson in the concluding section of the story emerges in the dramatic portrayal of the interaction between the Samaritan woman and the Samaritans.

The missionary instruction of the disciples is thus doubly consolidated as in the case of witness: first by Jesus' explicit instruction of them, the *expositio* (vv 31–38), then by the missionary interplay between the Samaritan woman and the Samaritans, the *demonstratio* (vv 28–30, 39–42). This illustrative function of vv 28–30, 39–42 explains, perhaps, why the conclusion of the dialogue is held off until after Jesus' instruction of the disciples. It needs to be borne in mind, however, that the real audience of the entire episode is that of the Evangelist. The message in all of 4:1–42 is ultimately addressed to this audience. We will analyze in turn each of these interpretative sections and then attempt a synthesis of the important missionary motifs present in the whole pericope.

---

[1] Strikingly, faith is not mentioned in the dialogue till vv 39 and 42. "Believe me woman" (v 21) is more an appeal to accept the trustworthiness of Jesus' message than a formal appeal to believe in him as in 20:31, for instance. The reason for this is that up to v 26 the woman does not know who Jesus is; believing comes only through contact with the revelation of the Revealer (cf. 2:11; 3:12; 8:24; 9:35–38; 10:24–26; 20:30–31; cf. Rom 10:14–15, 17). So vv 29, 39 and 42 look back to v 10 as the successful outcome of Jesus' missionary preaching in Samaria.

A. The points of Intersection, Vv 8, 27

We saw in Chapter III that scholars generally regard vv 8 and 27 as insertions whose sole purpose is to prepare for the major insertion of vv 31–38[2]. These verses do indeed prepare for the latter episode; but is their function in the story purely or even primarily literary? If not, in what more significant ways do they prepare for the episode concerning the disciples? We noted earlier that the disciples are part of the narrative from the beginning (v 2). V 8 indicates further that when Jesus left Judea for Galilee through Samaria (v 3; cf. 3:22) the disciples also left with him. The entire dialogue with the Samaritan woman, however, takes place against the background of the absence of the disciples. The pluperfect (ἀπεληλύθεισαν) indicates that they were completely out of sight when the woman came to draw water and Jesus entered into conversation with her (v 7). The purpose of their absence is important, "to buy food."

The juxtaposition of vv 7b and 8, linked with the explanatory particle, γάρ suggests that had the disciples been present Jesus would not have asked the woman for the drink. The particle gives the reason for the request; it thus serves the same function as in vv 9c, 18, 23, 42, 47[3]. This can be interpreted in two ways: either the disciples would have drawn for Jesus to drink, or they would have been a hindrance to the request either deliberately or by their very presence. Since Jesus' request is not concerned ultimately with physical drink (v 10), the implication is that the disciples would have objected to his missionary dialogue with the woman.

This impression is confirmed in v 27. The disciples return from their food-buying and are "dumbfounded" (ἐθαύμαζον) to see Jesus speaking with the woman; so stunned, indeed, that they cannot bring themselves to ask him the meaning of it all. Bultmann and Brown, for instance, observe that the disciples are shocked not so much because Jesus is speaking with a Samaritan (as v 9 would lead one to expect) as that he is speaking with a woman; μετὰ γυναικός is absolute. Their shock is, therefore, interpreted in reference to the rabbinic rule prohibiting a man to speak with a woman in public were it his own wife (*b. Yom.* 66b; *b. ᶜErub.* 53b; *b. Qidd.* 70.1; *Str-B* II, 438)[4]. True as all this may be, it cannot be overlooked that given the geographical setting of the scene described in such detail in vv 5–6a, the woman in question would hardly have been any other than a Samaritan "come to draw water" (v 7a). Also speaking of the dramatic qualities of the scene, she would have been dressed like a

---

[2] See the discussion on pp. 59, 61 above; also Boismard, *BETL* 44, 238 and the commentaries.

[3] The use of γάρ in John is extensively discussed by Abbott, *Grammar*, nos. 2068, 2393, 2683 (pp. 102–103); for the particular usage in 4:44–45, see no. 2067 (p. 103).

[4] See further, Bultmann, *Commentary*, 193, n. 5; Brown, *John* I, 173. ʾAbot 1.5 and Sirach 9:1–9 expound extensively on the evils that come from dealing with women generally.

Samaritan woman. Equally, the question how she knew that Jesus was a Jew (v 9a) can be answered on the same grounds, by his manner of dressing[5]. The shock of the disciples, then, receives its full force when its object is seen in all its horror: Jesus' dialogue partner is a woman *and* a Samaritan and he is speaking with her in a public setting. They have every reason, therefore, to be shocked, but the deeper the shock, the more the lesson should strike home when it is given (vv 31–42).

Their reflective but unasked questions ($\tau i\ \zeta\eta\tau\epsilon\hat{\iota}\varsigma\ /\lambda\alpha\lambda\epsilon\hat{\iota}\varsigma$;) are both addressed to Jesus, not partially to the woman as some critics hold[6]. Besides, if they themselves were shocked at Jesus speaking with the woman (the subject of $\dot{\epsilon}\lambda\dot{\alpha}\lambda\epsilon\iota$ is Jesus, not the woman!) would they have indulged in the same themselves? The rabbinic prohibition applied equally to them. It would seem that here, too, a *double-entendre* is involved. At first sight it appears as if the disciples are astonished at Jesus' merely conversing with a Samaritan woman. However, in view of the weight already given to the verbs $\zeta\eta\tau\epsilon\hat{\iota}\nu$ and $\lambda\alpha\lambda\epsilon\hat{\iota}\nu$ in vv 24 and 26, more is at stake here than mere chatting.

It is uncertain whether the disciples heard the solemn pronouncement in v 26. If they did, as $\dot{\epsilon}\pi i\ \tau o\acute{\nu}\tau\omega$ suggests (and on a stage setting the disciples would be entering as the pronouncement was made), then one would have to concede that the disciples had some idea of the nature of the conversation. The imperfect $\dot{\epsilon}\lambda\dot{\alpha}\lambda\epsilon\iota$ also suggests that they were aware of a stretch of the conversation (which is not improbable since in the geographical setting of the scene, they could have seen Jesus speaking with the woman from afar). Whatever the case, there is a strong suggestion that the disciples do suspect what their master "seeks" with the woman and do not like it. A comparison of v 27 with 21:12b would support this interpretation[7]. Notably, the unasked question in 21:12b is set in the context of a meal (or of food and eating) as is the case in 4:31–34; also the question at issue in both passages is the disciples' relationship with Jesus in the missionary enterprise. In 4:31–34 the disciples found food for Jesus, but he would not eat; in the post-resurrection scene, on the contrary, Jesus himself is feeding the disciples having first helped them to catch the fish, even cooking for them. In 4:33 the disciples do not understand and are afraid to ask lest they be told too much, but they are told all the same. In

---

[5]Even today the different ethnic groups that inhabit the Holy Land are easily distinguished by their manner of dressing, be they Arabs, Jews, Druzes or Westerners.

[6]Bernard (*Commentary* 1, 152) believes, on Patristic evidence, that $\tau i\ \zeta\eta\tau\epsilon\hat{\iota}\varsigma$; is addressed to the woman. Brown (*John* 1, 173), however, believes that this evidence is probably from Tatian who, being an Encratite, might have disliked the idea that Jesus took initiative with a woman. The NAB (St. Anthony Guild's edition, 1976) attributes the "seeking" to the woman, and the "speaking" to Jesus.

[7]In 21:12b none of the disciples asked Jesus "who are you?" because they knew it was the Lord. Though no reason is given for their not asking in 4:27, the specific questions they might have asked ("what do you seek?" "why are you speaking with her?") indicate the line of their thinking and disapproval (cf. 16:5–7).

21:12b they finally understand and so ask no questions. The parallels between these two scenes with the reversal of roles: Jesus now does the feeding and the disciples finally understand, tends to support our interpretation of the disciples' activity in 4:31, 33 as symbolic of their self-assigned role in Jesus' mission.

The probable reason for the disciples' objection to the missionary dialogue lies in v 9c. But Jews not "co-using" with Samaritans is only the tip of the iceberg; the real issue is the absence of any kind of fellowship between the two nations. In Jewish view, the Samaritans are people possessed by the devil (8:48). The astonishment of the disciples thus receives its full impact when it is interpreted against this background of socio-religious enmity between the two nations.

The view that the disciples are presented in v 8 as a potential obstacle to Jesus' dialogue with the woman is strengthened further by the following facts: Their arrival effectively puts an end to the conversation which managed to reach its climax in the nick of time (v 26). It also serves as a signal for the woman to depart (v 28), her waterpot abandoned, though she returns later in the narrative with more reinforcement (v 30). Once the woman leaves, the disciples make no attempt to find out concerning the conversation but turn their attention to their pressing concern, the food which they had gone to buy for the master (v 31)[8]. One gets the impression that they wish to forget that the conversation had taken place and to return to the situation as it had been before their departure to buy food (vv 4—6, 8). Jesus, on the contrary, wishes them not to forget but positively to learn a lesson from his encounter with the woman (vv 31—38). From the perspective of the disciples, the abandoned waterpot serves as a reminder that the woman had been there, though from the woman's standpoint its abandonment signifies her eagerness to run with zeal and speed to share the news of her encounter with her fellow Samaritans (vv 28—29). Jesus' thirst remains as yet wholly unsatisfied, and to the missionary motif of thirst is now added that of hunger (vv 31—34).

The juxtaposition of vv 27 and 28 also deserves notice. Though one cannot be dogmatic about the significance of this point of intersection, it is nonetheless reasonable to say that the placing of v 27 before v 28 achieves two things: First, it makes the disciples aware with deep emotion ($\dot{\epsilon}\vartheta a\acute{u}\mu a\varsigma ov$) that the conversation had taken place, and so prepares them for the double explanation of its significance given in vv 32, 34—38 and 39—42. Secondly, it also makes the woman aware that Jesus is not alone, and that he has, if not disciples in the technical sense, at least followers.

---

[8] It may be noted in passing that, contrary to some critics, the disciples are not presented here as "food-mongers" or as a contrast to the woman said to be "spiritually minded." Nowhere in the entire dialogue is there ever a question of the disciples seeking food for themselves. Their concern is for the master, and that is important given the missionary significance attached to the motif of food in this and other passages in the Gospel. See our further discussion of this issue in Chapter VI with reference to 21: 1—14 and 6:1—13.

Moreover, even if Scroggs's suggestion, that the description of the missionary, his activity and dress (Mk 6:8–11 and Mt 10:5–15) parallels that of the wandering cynic preacher, does not apply to John, his study does show that Jesus' and the Evangelist's audience would have been aware of wandering preachers[9]. To see one such preacher, then, with a group of followers would highly enhance his credibility. At any rate, the possibility cannot be outruled that for the woman the arrival of the disciples adds further convincing weight to Jesus' ἐγώ εἰμι in v 26, even though the disciples themselves do not know this. If this is so, then the οὖν in v 28 is more than a literary device of "reprise"; it registers the double impact on the woman of both Jesus' solemn claim in v 26 and its reinforcement by the arrival of the astonished disciples (v 27)[10].

To sum up, the ways in which the disciples are introduced into the story, the points at which their introduction intersects with the main story of Jesus' encounter with the woman, highlight two facts: That, on the one hand, the disciples take exception to Jesus' missionary work in Samaria (vv 7–8, 27), but, on the other, they themselves have a positive, though relative, role to play in this missionary enterprise. Jesus' explanatory discourse in vv 32, 34–38 largely addresses these two issues. The order in which the episode concerning the disciples is interwoven into the main story indicates that vv 31–38 is related not only to vv 39–42, but also to vv 1–26. For just as the placing of v 27 before vv 28–30 links vv 31 to vv 39–42, so the reference to the disciples in vv 2, 8, 27 also links vv 31–38 to vv 1–26. This interlocking structure thus demands that 4: 1–42 be interpreted as a unified whole.

B. The *Expositio*, Vv 31–38

The whole of vv 31–38 is recognizably didactic; it focuses on the relationship between Jesus and the disciples in the missionary enterprise rather than on the relationship of "the Samaritans (the harvest)" to "the

---

[9] Robin Scroggs, "Paul as Rhetorician: Two Homilies in Romans 1–11," *Jews, Greeks and Christians: Religious Lectures in Late Antiquity. Essays in Honor of W.D. Davies* (Leiden: Brill, 1976) 271–297, esp. p. 274, n. 11.

[10] Boismard ("Un procédé rédactionnel dans le quatrième évangile: la Wiederaufnahme," *BETL* 44, 235–241) examines a number of instances where he believes that οὖν in the Gospel is a literary device (a "reprise" or "Wiederaufnahme") which serves to resume the thread of a story after an insertion by another author; for instance, 11:12; 18:37. If v 27 is a latter insertion (Boismard, 238), then the οὖν in v 38 would serve merely to resume the story from v 26 or better still from vv 18/19 seen as part of the hypothetical primitive story of Jesus' encounter with the woman. Whether or not this is true, one cannot exclude the possibility that οὖν in v 28 refers to the double impact on the woman of Jesus' solemn declaration in v 26 and the disciples' arrival, with their unconcealed surprise. That οὖν in John expresses impact stemming from preceding events is evident in 18:4, 6, 7, 11, 12, which cannot all be resumptive.

revelation of Christ"[11]. A further support of this is that the vocabulary in vv 35—36 focuses attention on the different activities of the agents at work, the sower and the reapers, not on the harvest itself. This section explains to the disciples their unasked question of what Jesus is seeking with the woman (v 27), the reason for it (v 34), and the consequences of this seeking for the disciples themselves (vv 35—38), though, ultimately, it is the Father who seeks (v 24).

Since the problem of the literary unity of vv 31—38 has already been discussed in Chapter III (pp. 58—64), we may now propose the following simple structure for this section: v 34 embodies the major statement or solemn pronouncement out of which the entire dialogue grows and from which it receives meaning; vv 31—33 provide the immediate background and context for the statement; and vv 35—38 explain progressively its significance as it applies to the disciples themselves. The explanation is given first figuratively, using the imagery of sowing and harvesting (vv 35—37), where the disciples are designated as the harvesters (v 36), then explicitly in the description of their missionary role as an entering into the labor of others (v 38). Whatever its original setting, therefore, v 38 is not an isolated statement in the passage; from the standpoint of the disciples, it constitutes the climax to which Jesus' teaching in vv 35—37 builds[12]. Viewed comprehensively, v 34 not only links vv 31—38 to vv 1—30 and 39—42, it also relates the whole of 4:1—42 to the entire Gospel which is about Jesus' mission from the Father (cf. 3:16; 17:4).

1. Vv 31—33: the Situation

Verses 31—33 introduce the situation by means of the usual Johannine techniques of *double-entendre* and dramatic irony. As in the dialogue with the woman, the terms for the discussion are furnished by the disciples themselves: food, their concern that Jesus should eat (v 31), and their unspoken fear lest someone else might have brought him food (v 33). The situation thus clearly looks back to v 8, thereby keeping in view the conversation with the woman which coincides with the time the disciples spent looking for food. Since the adverbial phrase ἐν τῷ μεταξύ looks backwards to vv 28—30 and forwards to v 39, it gives vv 31—38 the appearance of an insertion calculated to fill up the time of waiting for

---

[11]Olsson (*Structure and Meaning,* 238, 239) holds that the teaching in vv 31—38 is concerned with the relationship of the Samaritans to "the revelation of Christ," or with "how the Samaritans come to believe in Jesus," namely, through the work of the disciples in "the situation after the 'hour.'" His view that the story is "a metaphorical account" (p. 209) takes it for granted that it has no historical foundation whatever, but the issue needs to be discussed. See below, pp. 188—191.

[12]For the authors who assign vv 37—38 to the post-Johannine level see the chart on pp. 61—62 above. Of the authors here cited, Boismard-Lamouille do not rule out the possibility that these verses could have originated from the Evangelist himself on the level of John II-B (see p. 72 above).

the arrival of the Samaritans (vv 30, 39). This is the interpretation given, for instance, by Lindars, Leidig, and Schnackenburg[13]. This, however, is not entirely so; a tension is created between the two scenes (vv 31—38, and 28—30, 39—42) both by the use of the imperfect ἠρώτων (v 31) and by the manifestly different interests of Jesus and the disciples (vv 31, 33 and 32, 34): the disciples "keep urging" Jesus to eat (v 31) but he in turn keeps refusing as he awaits with longing the return of the woman and the Samaritans[14].

This tension created between Jesus' own concern and that of the disciples for him is further accentuated by the *double-entendre* concerning food and the dramatic irony in the exchanges in vv 32—33. Though the Gospel's audience and Jesus know it, the disciples do not know that the Samaritans are actually coming to Jesus (v 30), and that this coming forms part of his real food (v 32). Their lack of knowledge thus parallels that of the woman in v 10, and spells the same need for the instruction of the disciples (vv 34—38) as it had done in the case of the woman. "You do not know" (v 32) parallels "if you knew" (v 10a). Both the disciples and the woman stand in need of Jesus' revelation concerning both himself and the nature of his mission as it applies to each: the woman (vv 7—26) as a proselyte, the disciples (vv 31—38) as missionaries. Olsson is thus correct in seeing vv 31—38 as a revelation to the disciples; the problem with his thesis lies in his insistence that the revelation concerns the relation of the Samaritans to Jesus' mission. An *Erkenntnisprozess* is indeed necessary not only for the Jews and Samaritans concerning Jesus' identity (so Leidig) and the nature of his mission, but also for the disciples[15].

The obvious disappointment of the disciples (μή τις;) at Jesus' reply in v 32 is striking: if he has already eaten, are all their efforts to procure food for him then useless? have they been supplanted by another? The obvious suspect would be the woman, especially in view of the abandoned waterpot[16]. The answer to their questions is ironically both "yes" and

---

[13]Lindars, *John*, 193; Leidig, *Jesu Gespräch*, 153; Schnackenburg, *Johannesevangelium* I, 455—457, 478.

[14]The line up of the finite tenses in vv 31—34 is highly revealing: ἠρώτων (v 31) the imperfect of iterative/conative action is followed by the punctiliar aorist, εἶπεν (v 32). This implies that the disciples kept urging Jesus to eat until he finally told them he had other food to eat. Ἔλεγον (v 33) is then the imperfect of deliberative action: the disciples try to discern the meaning of the statement. The rhetorical question, μή τις heightens their reflection, while the historic present λέγει (v 34) lends life to the entire narrative.

[15]Olsson, *Structure and Meaning*, 238—239; Leidig, *Jesu Gespräch*, 152; also, Bultmann, *Johannes*, 144; and Kuhl, *Die Sendung Jesu*, 141.

[16]Brown (*John* I, 173) also sees the woman as the likely suspect. Jeremias (*TDNT* VII, 93) points out that in Lk 10:37 the lawyer also resorts to a circumlocution, "the one who showed him mercy," rather than mention "the Samaritan" expressly as Jesus does in v 34. Jn 4:33 may reflect the same attitude on the part of the disciples. Sirach 50:26 also contemptuously avoids mentioning the Samaritans by name, as he does in the case of the Edomites, though he mentions the Philistines.

"no." Yes, because the disciples do not understand the nature of Jesus' food (v 32) and because the woman has indeed brought him to eat both by her personal response and by her leading her fellow Samaritans to Jesus. No, because the woman's response, her continuing Jesus' mission into the city, does not supplant the role of the disciples rightly understood; rather, it offers them an example for their own appropriate missionary response.

If, then, one could pinpoint the issues at stake suggested by the entire portrayal of the disciples in vv 2, 8, 27, 31–33, they would be as follows: First, while the disciples baptize (that is, welcome into their fellowship) disciples drawn by Jesus from among Jews (v 2), they are on the contrary opposed (or at least, closed) to the idea of his reaching out to "foreigners" represented by the Samaritans. For, contrary to the view of some critics, vv 9, 20 and 22 make it clear that Jews and Samaritans did not see themselves as members of the same race, let alone as "half-brothers." Worse still, the literature shows that in the eyes of the Jews, the Samaritans were worse off than Gentiles. Sirach's attitude (50:25–26) is a case in point. In 8:48 the term "Samaritan" is synonymous with "devil possession." In Lk 17:18 Jesus respectfully calls the grateful Samaritan leper cured by him a "foreigner" (ὸ ἀλλογενής). So whatever modern scholars may think of the Jewish parentage of the Samaritans on the basis of 1 Kg 17 and Jn 4:12, the Jews themselves, including the disciples, thought differently.

Brown's suggestion that part of the problem in the Johannine community was the integration of new members, in particular the Samaritans, may not be totally unfounded[17]. It is disputable, however, whether the main reasons for this are theological (as Brown holds) or sociological. If the evidence of the Gospel (4:9, 27; 8:48) be taken at its face value the reasons, as it applies to the Samaritans in particular, would seem to be sociological rulings reinforced by religious ones. The NT evidence amply corroborates this[18]. Against this background, the choice of the Samaritan woman has a forceful paradigmatic and rhetorical value: Because she epitomizes the socio-religious traits which the disciples could hold in aversion, Jesus' encounter with her provides a most fitting context for bringing to the surface this attitude of the disciples and instructing them.

Secondly, there is a suggestion that the disciples are not simply passively opposed to Jesus' missionary outreach to the woman, but that they try to dictate the terms for his mission. If the missionary symbolism attached to the motifs of drink and food in the passage has any convincing value,

---

[17]Brown, *Community of the Beloved Disciple,* 43–47.

[18]Nowhere, perhaps, is this issue more clear than in the case of Cornelius, with its prelude of the "unclean food" which Peter would not eat (Acts 10:9–20) and its sequel: the opposition of the brethren in Judea (11:1–18). Worth noting is that the opposition is not so much that Peter baptized Gentiles as that he ate with them (v 3). Gal 2:11–14 shows that this social issue was not simply a Lucan invention.

then the disciples' concern to provide food for Jesus and his rejection of this offer (v 32) followed by the explanation in v 34 could be taken to mean that it is the Father, not the disciples, who determine the course and the nature of his mission. We shall return to this issue presently in the discussion on v 34. Whatever the value of these suggestions, the point emerges that the entire portrayal of the disciples reveals their lack of understanding of the true nature of Jesus' mission and their appropriate role in it. It remains to be seen whether Jesus' explicit instruction of them in vv 34—38 in any way corroborates this interpretation.

2. Verse 34: the Father's "Work"

Every word in this central verse is weighty and important. Because of its significance in the missionary perspective of the whole Gospel, we shall analyze it not only in the context of 4:1—42 but also in that of the Gospel as a whole. In its immediate context, the pronouncement states Jesus' exclusive relationship with the Father in the missionary enterprise and posits this as the basis for the disciples' relationship with him in their missionary work (vv 35—38). With regard to Jesus' relationship with the Father, the statement emphasizes, on the one hand, the centrality of the Father in the work of salvation: he owns it ($αὐτοῦ\ τὸ\ ἔργον$) and sends Jesus for its execution, and, on the other, both Jesus' uniqueness and dependence on the Father in the execution of this work — he is "one sent" and his whole livelihood consists in doing and completing this work. Ἐμὸν βρῶμα and αὐτοῦ τὸ ἔργον thus form two sides of the same coin. The possessive adjectives ("my," "his") are both emphatic and this emphasis underlines the perfect correspondence which exists between the Father's will concerning the work and Jesus' intensive desire to accomplish it.

The metaphor of food also carries with it a sense of satisfaction and delight (cf. v 36; 14:31; 15:10—11; 17:13)[19]. And because it is done freely and with love, the work also delights the Father (10:17—18). The mutual satisfaction entailed in the doing and completing of the work is recapitulated in the harvest imagery where sower and reaper rejoice together contrary to the normal practice (vv 36—37). Schrenk sees an

---

[19]This motif is a common biblical one: Judg 9:13; Qoh 9:7; 10:19; Ps 104:14—15. The biblical metaphor of food emphasizes not only sustenance and livelihood, but dependence on God who alone provides for all his creatures (Ps 104:27—29; 136:25; 145:15—16; 147:8—9). In Wis 16:25—26 and Mt 6:25—34, God's word and the seeking after his kingdom are said to nourish more than does ordinary food. These two passages come very close in spirit to Jn 4:34. Psalms 40:7—8; 119: 16, 24, 47, 92—93 also sing of the delight which derives from doing God's will or keeping his commandments. Hebrews 10:6—7 (citing Ps 40:7—8; cf. Jn 4:34), sees God himself as being delighted by Jesus' doing of his will, because it is done out of love (cf. Jn 14:31; 15:10). In our present passage, v 36 encapsulates this theme of mutual rejoicing.

exact correspondence between "doing the will" and "completing the work."[20] This is true only if "the will" is seen as referring to God's single purpose for humanity, namely, that the world might be saved through his envoy, Jesus (3:16–17). In other passages, the Father's will is described negatively as "not losing anyone" entrusted to Jesus, and positively, "that those who see the Son and believe in him may have eternal life" (6:39, 40). Jesus himself always does "what pleases" the Father (8:29), and is conscious of doing, not his will, but the Father's (5:30; 6:38).

Tò ϑέλημα in v 34, therefore, does not carry the exact connotation as τò ἔργον. It defines, rather, Jesus' obediential relationship with the Father in the missionary enterprise, and not the nature proper of "the work." The specific mention of the Father's will here may also be called for by (and hence, be a response to) the disciples' persistent urging of Jesus to eat (v 31). If so, the point made by Jesus, as we suggested earlier, is that the Father's will, not that of the disciples, constitutes the driving force of his life. A tension is thus suggested between the Father's impelling will in Jesus' life and the disciples' misplaced zeal for him. Leidig, indeed, sees v 34 as the Johannine version of the temptations[21]. While this suggestion appears a little far-fetched, her position does, nevertheless, recognize the tension inherent in the juxtaposition of vv 31, 33 and 32, 34.

Mention was made earlier of the imprecise interpretation given by some critics to the terms ἔργον and ἔργα[22]. It needs to be clearly stated, however, that the term τò ἔργον is used exclusively in the Gospel for the Father's work of salvation, given to Jesus to do and complete. Nowhere in the entire Gospel (4:34; 17:4) is ownership of "the work", attributed to Jesus, let alone to the disciples. It is always the Father's work; Jesus alone does and completes it, but he does not own it. The same applies to τà ἔργα. In vain does one search the Gospel for a passage where Jesus speaks of "my work" or "my works." He refers always to "the work" or "the works" of the Father who sent him.

Only his unbelieving brethren speak of Jesus' works (7:2). But for Jesus himself, it is always the Father who shows or gives him the works to do or who himself does them through him (5:19–20; 14:10, 11). Where Jesus presents himself as the subject who does "the work," he specifies that he does them "in his Father's name" (10:25, 32, 37, 38). Believers are promised the same works as Jesus, even greater ones (14:12). But the work of salvation (τò ἔργον) is done and completed exclusively by Jesus (4:34; 17:2–4; cf. 4:10). The Gospel evidence is thus meticulously insistent that the ἔργον belongs exclusively to the Father, and that it is given to no one else to do and complete but Jesus. This consistency can

---

[20] Schrenk, ϑέλημα, *TDNT* III, 52–62, esp. p. 55.

[21] Leidig, *Jesu Gespräch*, 148.

[22] Olsson, *Structure and Meaning*, 66–67, 225, 234–235, 238–241; see also pp. 70–72 above.

hardly be accidental and it is crucial for the proper understanding of the Johannine approach to mission not to miss the emphasis.

Equally, it should be self-evident that τὸ ἔργον and τὰ ἔργα are not interchangeable in the Gospel. The singular (τὸ ἔργον v 34 ; 17:4) refers to the totality of the work of salvation which Acts 5:38 also attributes to God. Here Gamaliel uses it of the entire Christian movement (cf. Acts 13:41, citing Hab 1:5). In instances where "the work" does not refer to the totality of the work of salvation, it is always qualified: "which of these works" (αὐτῶν ἔργον, 10:32), "for no good work" (καλοῦ ἐργοῦ, 10:33) and "one work" (ἕν ἔργον, 7:21). "God's work" (τὸ ἔργον τοῦ θεοῦ) in 6:29 refers explicitly to the faith response to Jesus' mission which God requires of any who would benefit from his saving mission, and as an indispensable condition. From the standpoint of Jesus' audience, therefore, belief in Jesus constitutes the work proper exclusively demanded by the Father. This work, like "true worship" (v 24), belongs in the sphere of God and is demanded by him; it is opposed to the human or rationalistic approach (e.g., 3:2, 4, 9–10). "The work of believing" thus constitutes the human corollary to "the work of salvation" done and completed exclusively by Jesus.

Bultmann sees the ἔγρα as referring to the whole of Jesus' activity as the Revealer and includes in it ζωοποιεῖν and κρίνειν which he considers as part of Jesus' μαρτυρία. Thus Bultmann, following Wendt, makes no distinction between ἔργον and ἔργα in the Gospel[23]. Jesus' witness does refer to the totality of his mission which is contrasted with that of the Baptist (5:36) and which is essentially to give life (3:16; 10:10) by revealing the Father (14:9–10; 17:4, 6). Since judgment is the reverse side of the "work of salvation" accomplished by Jesus, something which the individual metes out to himself or herself by his or her refusal to believe in Jesus (3:18–19, 36; 5:24), it cannot be seen as ἔργα in the Johannine sense of the word. Besides, it is stated that believers will do the same works of the Father as Jesus does, but they are never conceived of as judges in the Gospel (contrast the Synoptics: Mt 19:27–30; Lk 22:30). In the Gospel Jesus is the one and only judge precisely because he is the Son, the only way to the Father (5:22; 14:6). People stand or fall by their response to him and him alone (15:22–24). The activities by which he accomplishes the Father's work of salvation, however, are all positive; they include preaching, healing, and teaching the disciples[24].

The designation of the Father as the sender (τοῦ πέμψαντός με) refers not only to his absolute primacy as the owner and initiator of the mission, but also to Jesus as the one uniquely sent by him and totally dependent on him in the execution of "the work." As already noted, the Father's

---

[23]Bultmann, *Commentary*, 265; Wendt, *Johannesevangelium* II, 40–41.

[24]Wilkens (*Zeichen und Werke*, 30, 44–45) discusses further the demonstrative character of the "signs" and their relationship to "works"; de Jonge ("Signs and Works," esp. pp. 124–125) argues wrongly, in our view, that Jesus' words are not included in his works.

role is not restricted to his owning the work and sending Jesus (3:16) [25]
Throughout the Gospel, he is shown to be actively involved in the mission
from the standpoint of both Jesus and his audience: he does his own
works and speaks his own words in Jesus (14:10, 11), shows him the
works which he himself does (5:20), witnesses to him (5:32, 37) and puts
his authenticating seal on Jesus' mission by glorifying him (8:54; 12:28;
17:1, 5). In respect to the audience, the Father "draws" believers to Jesus
(6:44, 65; but cf. 12:32), seeks the true worshipers (4:23), prunes the
branches of the vine to make them more fruitful (15:1–2), and, as Giblin
points out, keeps the gate to the sheepfold (10:3)[26]. Thus at every turn of
"the work," the Father is actively present[27].

From the standpoint of Jesus, the phrase τοῦ πέμψαντός με, expresses
both his dependence and his uniqueness in the mission. The dependence
is demonstrated in his never claiming the ownership of any aspect of the
work, or in his seeing everything as a "gift" from the Father: the "work"
and "works" to be accomplished (5:36; 14:10; 17:4), the words he speaks
(12:49; 14:11; 17:8), and even the disciples themselves (6:37; 17:6).
Indeed Jesus' dependence is so complete that he can do nothing without
the Father (5:19, 30; 8:28b). He is in every sense of the word, the active
channel through whom the Father performs his own works. The Johannine portrayal of Jesus' role in the mission is thus very different from that
in Mt 9:37–38 and Lk 10:2 which portray him as "the Lord of the harvest." In John, the harvest is part of "the work." If then Jesus himself is
sent, is dependent, and does not own the mission, then neither do the disciples. The person who acts as the owner of the mission is a false messenger who seeks the glory for himself or herself (7:18). This point which
is raised in 4:31–38 in the context of 4:1–42 is developed at length in
Jn 5 and 7–8.

More positively, as one sent Jesus enjoys a unique and an unrivalled
role in the mission as the Father's sole executive agent, because he is the
Son (1:18; 3:35–36; 5:19–22; 8:31–36). The Baptist and the Spirit are
also sent by the Father (1:6–8, 15, 33; 14:26; 15:26); the Baptist is even
called an ἀπεσταλμένος (1:6; 3:28), a term never applied to Jesus[28]; but
while he too refers to God as ὁ πέμψας με (1:33), the designation is qualified and so delimited by βαπτίζειν. It, therefore, does not carry the same
absolute sense as it does when used by Jesus, and where it is often reinforced by πατήρ (8:16, 18; 12:49; 14:24; 20:21) which term speaks of

---

[25]See our previous survey of the ὁ πέμψας με passages, pp. 1–2 and n.4 (p. 2).

[26]C.H. Giblin, "The Miraculous Crossing of the Sea (John 6.16–21)," *NTS* 29 (1983) 96–103, esp. 100.

[27]John's portrayal of the Father's role in "the work" thus parallels that given by Paul in 2 Cor 5:18–19: God was in Christ reconciling the world to himself. Unlike Paul, however, John does not attribute to the Father the transmission of the ministry of reconcilliation to the disciples. In John, Jesus alone sends the disciples (4:38; 15:16; 20:21–23).

[28]The only possible reference to Jesus as ἀπεσταλμένος is in 9:7, where the pool of Siloam is translated "sent". But the usage here is figurative. See further, Wilkens, *Zeichen und Werke*, 46.

Jesus' exclusive filial relationship with his sender. Thus while Jesus is clearly dependent on the Father who sends and sustains him, he is equally clearly in a class all by himself, sent as no one else is sent.

Terminology apart, Jesus' mission differs essentially from that of the Baptist in that the latter's mission consists essentially in identifying Jesus as the Messiah and Son of God who is to baptize with the Holy Spirit (1: 29, 31—34, 36; 3:27—30, 31—36; 5:33, 35). But Jesus is himself the unique agent of God's salvation, the only way and access to the Father (14:6), the only door to the sheepfold (10:7). Strikingly, the Baptist himself plays no participatory role whatever in the Father's "work" given to Jesus to do and complete. Neither the concept of "the work" nor of "the works" is ever associated with him, though the latter is with the disciples (14:12). The same applies to Moses, the OT prophets and Scripture itself: they all serve to bear witness to Jesus that he is the Father's promised agent of salvation (1:45; 5:39; 6:32—33; 8:28a), but they do not themselves play any active part in his saving mission. Their role ends where that of Jesus begins (1:17; 5:39—40; 6:49—50). But while their witness terminates in Jesus, Jesus' own witness by far the greater witness (5:36), points to the Father whom he alone reveals by his entire life and work (1:18; 3:11—13; 6:46—47; 14:9) in order to give life to believers.

Concerning the Spirit, he, too, is sent, but by both the Father and Jesus (14:26; 15:26; 16:7). Like the Baptist he has a witnessing mission (15: 27) but his witness differs from that of the Baptist in that it testifies to the truthfulness of Jesus' claims and accomplished mission (16:11). The ὁ παράκλητος passages (14:16—17; 15:26—27; 16:7—15) show that the Spirit's proper sphere of action is in the disciples in the harvest or completed phase of "the work." He is their counsellor (14:16—17) and their teacher, revealer and announcer (16:12—15). There is also a suggestion that the Spirit works in some mysterious ways in the world independently of the disciples: he is their co-witness to Jesus (15:26—27) and also has the task of convicting the world (or of exposing its wrong ideas) concerning sin, righteousness and judgment (16:7—11)[29]. Unlike the Baptist, then, the Spirit plays a participatory role in Jesus' mission, first, because he himself is the fruit of this mission (7:39; 16:7a; 20:22), and, secondly, because he makes possible the witnessing/harvesting mission of the disciples (16:12—15) which we shall discuss fully in the analysis of vv 35—38[30].

---

[29]Porsch (*Pneuma und Wort,* 280) also notes that the Spirit acts directly in the world. For his full discussion of 16:7—11, see pp. 275—289.

[30]Unlike the Synoptics (Mt 4:1; 12:28; Mk 1:10—12; and especially Lk 3:22; 4:1, 14, 18; 10: 21), John does not emphasize the guiding activity of the Spirit in Jesus' mission. Rather he portrays Jesus as the one who receives from the Father the fulness of the Spirit solely in order to give it to others (1:33—34; 3:34). In contrast to the Baptist, Jesus baptizes with the Spirit (1:31—33); the bestowing of the Spirit distinctively characterizes his mission. This giving, we have already noted, depends squarely on his own departure or glorification (7:39; 16:7b). The activity of the Spirit is thus relegated to the completed phase of "the work."

Finally, the verbs "to do" and "to complete" in v 34 also underline Jesus' unique role in the Father's work. He alone does and completes this work. Only upon its completion do the disciples come in as active participants and beneficiaries. In 19:30, the perfect τετέλεσθαι, like the complexive aorists in 17:4, 6, indicates that once completed, the work stands completed. That is why all subsequent participation can only mean a harvesting or an entering into the labor of others (vv 36, 38).

The statement in v 34 thus encapsulates the key elements proper to the Johannine understanding of mission. And we may now summarize the salient points which emerged in the analysis of this verse within the Gospel context as a guide to our interpretation of vv 35–38 and 28–30, 39–42. The first important point which emerged in the discussion is that the ἔργον understood as the work of salvation belongs exclusively to the Father such that his ownership of it is total. Not only does he initiate the mission by sending Jesus, but he is actively present in its actual execution, working through Jesus and in and for his audience. Conjointly with Jesus, the Father sends the Spirit to enable the disciples to respond fully to Jesus and his mission and to testify to the world concerning the truthfulness of this mission.

Secondly, though Jesus himself is completely dependent on the Father and obedient to him as his agent, he nonetheless enjoys an exclusive role in the execution of the work. This role is not only unique and exclusive, it is irreplaceable: he alone does and completes the work; in this he has neither predecessors nor successors. Moses, the OT prophets, the Baptist, even Scripture itself, serve only to point him out as the Father's unique agent of salvation. The Spirit is the fruit of his mission while the disciples reap the fruit thereof.

If, judging from these particular emphases on the Father's exclusive ownership of "the work" and of Jesus' unrivalled role in it, a suggestion could be made concerning the missionary problems addressed, it would be that the Gospel is trying to counteract an owner attitude towards the mission on the part of the disciples. But we must await the full results of the analysis of 4:1–42 and of further Gospel material for confirmation (or contradiction) of this view.

3. Vv 35–38: the Disciples as Reapers

The basic meaning of this section, discussed partly in the previous one, is that the disciples themselves have a role to play in Jesus' mission (vv 35b). Furthermore, compared to Jesus' own mission, this mission of the disciples is essentially a harvesting/fruit-gathering one (v 36–38). This theme of the disciples' share in Jesus' mission is developed first figuratively (ἐν παροιμίαις) in terms of the imagery of "sowing and harvesting" (vv 35–37) and then overtly (παρρησία; cf. 16:25) in the explicit description of their mission as an entering into the labor of others (v 38). Our task

The Text of the Dialogue-Discourse, 4: 31—38

| *The Disciples* | | *Jesus* |

31 ῥαββί, φάγε

32 |ἐγὼ βρῶσιν ἔχω φαγεῖν
    |ἣν ὑμεῖς οὐκ οἴδατε.

33 μή τις ἤνεγκεν αὐτῷ φαγεῖν;

34 |ἐμὸν βρῶμά ἐστιν
    | ἵνα ποιήσω τὸ θέλημα τοῦ πέμψαντός με
    | καὶ τελειώσω αὐτοῦ τὸ ἔργον.

35a οὐχ ὑμεῖς λέγετε
     ὅτι ἔτι τετράμηνός ἐστιν
     καὶ ὁ θερισμὸς ἔρχεται;
35b   ἰδοὺ λέγω ὑμῖν
                             ἐπάρατε τοὺς ὀφθαλμοὺς ὑμῶν
                             καὶ θεάσασθε τὰ χώρας
                             ὅτι λευκαί εἰσιν πρὸς θερισμὸν ἤδη

36 ὁ θερίζων μισθὸν λαμβάνει
     καὶ συνάγει καρπὸν εἰς ζωὴν αἰώνιον
     ἵνα ὁ σπείρων ὁμοῦ χαίρῃ καὶ ὁ θερίζων
37   ἐν γὰρ τούτῳ ὁ λόγος ἐστὶν ἀληθινὸς
     ὅτι ἄλλος ἐστιν ὁ σπείρων
     καὶ ἄλλος ὁ θερίζων

38   ἐγω ἀπέστειλα ὑμᾶς θερίζειν
     ὃ οὐχ ὑμεῖς κεκοπιάκατε
     ἄλλοι κεκοπιάκασιν
     καὶ ὑμεῖς εἰς τὸν κόπον
     αὐτῶν εἰσεληλύθατε.

now is to examine more closely the particular way in which this message is communicated, taking into consideration the problems posed by the text for the understanding of the passage. The discussion will be conducted with reference to the above text of the discourse.

The general movement of the section is as follows: Jesus' completion of "the work" (v 34) ushers in definitively its completed phase, namely, the harvest phase (v 35). Attention then naturally shifts to the harvester and the nature of his work (vv 36—38). V 37 is transitional; it renders explicit the distinction between "sower" and "reaper" only implied in v 36. But while the terms "sower" and "reaper" look back to v 36, the distinction itself (ἄλλος ὁ σπείρων, ἄλλος ὁ θερίζων) looks forward to ἄλλοι/ὑμεῖς in v 38. The whole section thus moves climactically to v 38 which indicates beyond doubt that the section is concerned with the mission of the disciples[31].

Thüsing notes that v 35a reads like a transition from v 34 but unfortunately rejects this good insight on the grounds that vv 35–36 is still concerned with Jesus' own mission, who in Thüsing's view, is the harvester in v 36[32]. But v 35 does move the discussion from the mission of Jesus to that of the disciples. The eagerness of the disciples to provide food for Jesus (vv 31, 33) can be interpreted in Johannine symbolism (see our previous discussion on thirst and hunger as missionary motifs, pp. 104–106) as signifying their desire to participate in his mission. If so, Jesus does not completely reject this their desire; he first corrects their misunderstanding of the nature of his mission (vv 33, 34), and then proceeds to tell them wherein lies their own participation in this mission (vv 35–38)[33]. Hence, all of vv 35–38, not simply vv 37–38, expands the meaning of Jesus' mission (v 34) seen from the perspective of the disciples. The explanation is called for by the disciples' genuine but mistaken concern for Jesus (vv 31, 33) as he carries out his Father's mission in Samaria. And the harvest imagery appears to relate to their present concern with food (vv 8, 31) and their expectation of the coming harvest (v 35a).

Verse 35

From their first appearance on the scene, the disciples are portrayed as a reflecting, questioning group (vv 27, 33). In v 35 Jesus seizes upon this natural disposition to invite them to an even deeper reflection on the current situation. The question formula in v 35a (οὐχ ὑμεῖς λέγετε) is emphatic given the position of ὑμεῖς ("Do not you yourselves say?"). Moreover, in contrast to the questions introduced by μή (vv 12, 33) it expects a positive answer. But the *non-sequitur* in v 35b heightens the contrast between Jesus' position and that of the disciples. As earlier in vv 17b–18, the main purpose of v 35a is to bring to the surface a situation in the disciples own experience, which acknowledged situation is then used as the shared premises for instructing them. The technique is a common rhetorical one; it consists in leading the dialogue partner to concede a point from which inference is then drawn or on which a further argument is then built. Indeed v 35 may be considered as an expanded *enthymeme*: "a reflection drawn from contraries," or "a conclusion based on a denial

[31]Boismard-Lamouille's position (*Synopse III*), that v 37 belongs to v 38 and not to v 36 overlooks that the themes of "sower and reaper" in v 36 are carried over into v 37.

[32]Wilhem Thüsing, *Die Erhöhung und Verherrlichung Jesu im Johannesevangelium* (NTAbh 21. Münster, Westfalen: Aschendorffsche Verlagsbuchhandlung, 1959/1960), 53–54.

[33]Do we have here an echo of the technique highlighted by Giblin, "Suggestion, Negative Response and Positive Action in John's Portrayal of Jesus" (*NTS* 26 [1980] 197–211)? See esp. pp. 202–211.

of consequents" (you say, but in this case it does not follow)[34]. According to Quintilian, this deliberative approach, one of the three classes of
rhetoric, is particularly apt for the purposes of instruction ; hence its
suitability for the present didactic section[35].

The first major problem which arises concerns the identity of ὑμεῖς in
v 35a. Does this refer exclusively to the disciples addressed and from
whom Jesus dissociates himself or to humanity in general? In other words,
is the view expressed in v 35a that of the disciples themselves based on
their own calculation at the time of the conversation (so Hoskyns), or is
it a common proverbial saying concerning the normal interval between
the sowing and harvesting seasons (so Brown, Barrett, Giblin and
others)[36]?

The major objections to the proverbial interpretation are first, that the
interval between the sowing and harvesting seasons is generally six, not
four months, though much would depend on the nature of the crop. The
evidence of the Gezer Calendar often cited in support of the theory is
not conclusive[37]. Schnackenburg's suggestion that the interval is calculated from the waiting time of the farmer, the period between the sowing
and reaping, not from the total interval needed for the crop to grow,
introduces another problem of how this period of waiting may be accurately determined given the variables recognized by Schnackenburg
himself[38]. The keen expectation of the harvest (v 35a) could occur at
any point in the interval depending on the situation of the one thus consciously expecting; for the saying expresses a sense of need that the har-

---

[34]Quintilian, *Inst. Or.* V.x.1−2; VIII.v.9; see also V.viii.5; and xi.3−5.

[35]Quintilian, *Inst. Or.* VIII.*Praef.*6. The other two classes of rhetoric mentioned here are the
demonstrative and the forensic.

[36]Hoskyns, *The Fourth Gospel,* 246; Brown, *John* I, 174 (his main reason being that the saying
is short enough to be a proverb); Barrett (*John,* 241) maintains that on the lack of evidence that v
35a is a proverb, the statement should be understood as based "on the common reckoning";
Giblin, "Miraculous Crossing," 99. Other supporters of the proverbial interpretation include Olsson, *Structure and Meaning,* 62; Lagrange, *Jean,* 119. Those who are undecided include Thüsing,
Die Erhöhung, 53; Schnackenburg, *Johannesevangelium* I, 482. Bultmann, *Commentary,* 197.

[37]The Gezer Calendar dates from the 10th century B.C., and is thus pre-exilic. For an extensive discussion on the issue see *Str-B,* II, 431−440; Lagrange, *Jean,* 119; Barrett, *John,* 241; Bultmann, *Commentary,* 196 n. 4; F.M. Braun, *RB* 62 (1955) 26. A.W. Argile, ("A Note on John 4:
35" *ExpT* 82 [1970−1971] 247−148), argues that v 35a is a quotation from Greek poetry as is
Acts 17:28, for instance, because the verse falls into iambic lines. Did the interval between sowing
and reaping in Greece also take four months? Argile does not say.

[38]Schnackenburg, (*Johannesevangelium I,* 482−483). In fairness to the author, it must be
noted that he himself admits that the statement could be provoked either by the occasion or by a
proverb; also he appears not to be fully satisfied with his own explanation. A clear indication of
this is his admission that though the interval took six months, the sowing could have been delayed
by rains and that the harvesting could have come at the end of April or the beginning of May; the
answer in his view, then, does not lie in the way the statement is formulated. This, to us, is an implicit admission that the interval between sowing and harvesting or the period of waiting could not
be fixed with the degree of certainty implied either by the proverbial interpretation or by Schnackenburg's own position. This is so because of the undeniable variables (e.g., the late rains) involved.

vest should come. Secondly, no evidence has been found for the existence of such a proverb (cf. *Pal. Taʿan* 1, 64a), while the contrary is true of v 37 which the passage clearly identifies as a proverb ὁ λόγος (Hebr., המשל)[39]. Finally, ἔτι embodies the notion of "remaining" time in reference to a process already begun[40]. Therefore, it cannot embrace the notion of a complete interval between sowing and reaping on which the proverbial interpretation rests.

On the other hand, Hoskyns' view that v 35a records a saying of the disciples themselves at the time of the conversation has the following internal evidence in its favor: Firstly, Jesus' dialogue partners throughout vv 31—38 are exclusively the disciples; the four ὑμεῖς in vv 32, 35b and 38ab are indisputably addressed to them. Given this exclusive focus on the disciples, it is highly improbable that ὑμεῖς in v 35a should suddenly be addressed to a generic "you yourselves" among whom the disciples are included. Such an interpretation also goes against the evidence of the Gospel which consistently makes a clear distinction between the disciples and others[41]. It seems best, then, to see v 35a as a saying of the disciples themselves. Their quest for food makes this not an improbable interpretation[42]. Besides, the proverb in v 37 is expressed in an impersonal, not personal manner as is v 35a.

Moreover, the antithetical structure of v 35 coupled with the exclusive focus on the disciples in the whole vv 35—38 demands a unity of reference for ὑμεῖς in both vv 35a and 35b. Besides, only the disciples present can perform the actions commanded in v 35b. The contrast between

---

[39]Such is Delitzsch's Hebrew translation of ὁ λόγος. W.G.E. Watson ("Antecedents of a New Testament Proverb;" *VT* 20 [1970] 368—370) compares 4:37 to an Ugaritic letter fragment from Ras Shamra (p. 369) and concludes that the point of the proverb in John is to emphasize that sower and reaper are different persons. Though no exact biblical parallel is found to John's form of the proverb in v 37, the passages suggested include Deut 20:6; 28:30; Mic 6:15; Job 15:28 (LXX); 31:8; Mt 25:24; Lk 19:21. Both Amos (9:14b) and Isaiah (62:8—9; 65:21—25) reverse the sense of the proverb: you shall sow and reap, in the time of restoration. Isaiah (65:24—25) also connects the reversal with fellowship. For further discussion see Bauer, *Johannesevangelium*, 74.

[40]Consistent Johannine usage supports the view that ἔτι refers to "remaining time" in a process already begun: 7:33; 11:30; 12:35; 13:33; 14:19; 16:12; 20:1. The use of ἔτι/καί in v 35a is particularly comparable to that in 14:19 where the meaning is reinforced by the use of οὐκέτι. See further *BAG*, 315—316, who cites *PPar* 18: ἔτι δύο ἡμέρας ἔχομεν καὶ φθάσομεν εἰς Πηλοῦσι, where the issue is the time "remaining" before arrival at Πηλοῦσι; also *LSJ*, 592, nos. 3 and 4; Moulton-Milligan, *Vocabulary*, 258; Bultmann, *Commentary*, 196.

[41]This is true even when the same saying is addressed to the disciples and to others: compare 7:34—36; 8:21—24 with 13:33—36.

[42]The disciples are absent prior to and all throughout vv 1—26 (cf. v 2, 8, 27); nor must one forget that there were no ready supermarkets in those days. In the Synoptic Gospels the disciples satisfy their hunger by plucking and eating heads of grain from the fields (Mt 12:1; Mk 2:23; Lk 6:1). Even if they had no right to do the same in foreign Samaritan territory, it would not have taken them so long to find food, were this the harvesting season. Moreover, granting that their absence till v 27 is deliberately contrived by the narrator, such a contrivance would lose its verisimilitude were the scene set in the harvesting season when it was possible to buy food easily. In today's Palestine food is still sold everywhere along the streets during the harvest season.

Jesus' position and that of the disciples is first introduced by the juxta-position of the negative οὐχ with the demonstrative particle but its con-tent is embodied in the two ὅτι -clauses (ὅτι ἔτι ... ἔρχεται, ὅτι ... εἰσιν/ ἤδη). What counts is not what the disciples say (v 35a) but what Jesus says to them (v 35b). This is the fundamental understanding on which the instruction in vv 35—38 is based. The demonstrative particle not only introduces a new situation and arouses the attention of the disciples to this new situation; it also emphasizes the importance of this new situa-tion[43].

The question whether ἤδη belongs with 35b or with v 36 cannot be resolved on the basis of punctuation alone, especially since the ancient witnesses are equally divided on the issue, though a good argument could be deduced from these witnesses in favor of v 35b[44]. The solution seems to lie, rather, in the antithetical structure of v 35 and in the general thrust of the entire section. Brown's view that v 36 makes more sense if ἤδη is placed with it is very attractive; this, too, is Giblin's reading and that of the majority of scholars[45]. But we tend to agree with Lagrange that given the constrastive structure of vv 35a, and b, ἤδη belongs with 35b rather than with v 36. The real contrast to v 35a ("the harvest is *yet to come*") is not that "the laborer is already receiving wages" (v 36), but that "the harvest is *already here*:" the fields are ripe, waiting for (πρός) the harvest-ing (v 35b). This means in effect that the laborers are not yet at work. V 36 is not part of the antithetical ὅτι -clause of 35b, but introduces a new idea: the harvester and his work. The movement of thought from v 35b to v 36 may thus be compared to the situation in the Synoptics where the recognition that the harvest is great spells the urgent need to send laborers into the harvest (Mt 9:37—38; 10:1; Lk 10:2, 3). The urgency of the situation in John is registered by both the aorist impera-tives and by the emphatic position of ἤδη placed last in 35b[46].

---

[43]On this significance of ἰδού see *BAG*, 370—371. Striking Synoptic parallels include Mt 2:1, 9, 13, 19; 12:41, 42; Mk 10:33; Lk 2:10, 48. Other Johannine passages are 12:15; 16:32; 19:5.

[44]Of the witnesses cited by NA[26] nine place ἤδη with v 35 (P[75] C[3] 083 f[1.13] 𝔐 lat; Or Cyr) and nine place it with v 36 (ℵ C*D L (W) Ψ 33 pc it). Six others have no punctuation mark and NA[26] cite them in support of their own position which places ἤδη with v 36 (P[66] ℵ* A B Θ al). But these undecided witnesses could equally be cited in favor of placing ἤδη with v 35, all the more so in that two of them (A Θ) join six other witnesses who have the disjunctive καί at the be-ginning of v 36 (C[3] f[1.13] 𝔐 lat sy[h]). Given the statistics, one can say that the majority of witnesses favor placing ἤδη with v 35, even though most modern scholars take the opposite view. Lagrange (*Jean*, 120), however, prefers to place the adverb with v 35, for the reason that it marks an opposi-tion between "un temps assez long et 'désormais,'" and because v 36 is absolute in character and does not, therefore, depend on time.

[45]Brown, *John* 1, 182; Giblin, "Miraculous Crossing," 99.

[46]The reason cited by modern scholars for placing ἤδη with v 36 is the "Johannine usage" attested to in 4:51; 7:14; 11:39; 14:3. Cf. Barrett, *John*, 241. But none of these passages contains an antithetical structure. So the position of ἤδη in v 35 is unique. Besides, 1 Jn 4:3 also places ἤδη last in the sentence, and from the context of the passage, one would say that this placement is also emphatic. Bultmann (*John*, 197, n. 3) holds that it makes no difference whether ἤδη goes

The interpretation proposed here, namely, that v 35b means that the fields are already ripe, waiting for the harvesting, finds support in the triple call to the disciples to be aware of this fact ($i\delta o\acute{v}$, $\dot{\epsilon}\pi\acute{\alpha}\rho\alpha\tau\epsilon$, $\vartheta\epsilon\acute{\alpha}$-$\sigma\alpha\sigma\vartheta\epsilon$ are all authoritative aorist imperatives). Such a call could be meaningless if the disciples, the harvesters (v 38), were already engaged in the harvest and receiving wages. Moreover, the disciples addressed are not sent in John and do not take any substantial active part in the mission of Jesus till after the resurrection (20:21—22) when the work is completed and the harvest ushered in definitively. Vv 2 and 38, all critics admit, are written from the post-Easter perspective. Furthermore, the tenor of vv 35—38 is decidedly didactic; placing $\mathring{\eta}\delta\eta$ with v 36 makes this verse descriptive and so weakens its didactic force.

Does the statement in v 35b, then, coincide with the end of the four-month remaining interval such that this statement can be used to determine the time of year in which the scene took place[47]? If it did, v 35a would simply mean that the disciples are four months out in their calculation, and that Jesus (v 35b) is simply alerting their attention to this error in their calculation. Such an interpretation would make little sense, not only of the whole of v 35 with its emphatic contrasts, but also of v 35a in particular which, we have seen, indicates that the disciples are actively counting the time remaining before the arrival of the harvest. If v 35b does not coincide with the arrival of the harvest expected by the disciples, how then is the whole of v 35 to be understood? What is the point of the juxtaposition of v 35a and 35b?

Giblin sees v 35b as a prophetic correction of v 35a, which he interprets as a proverb, the meaning of which is that one must wait for the harvesting after the work of sowing is done. The point of v 35b then is that the harvest has been anticipated. A parallel situation, though of a different order, is 6:21 where Jesus' presence with the disciples in the boat eliminates the remaining distance to the shore. On the external level one may cite in support the midrash on Canticles 8:14, where it is stated that if Israel is good, Yahweh will hasten the harvest, if not, the harvest will come at its usual time[48]. So there is a solid basis for viewing v 35b as a chronological correction of v 35a.

The basic problem with the interpretation, however, is that "harvest" in v 35a and 35b functions on two completely different levels of meaning: The disciples are expecting an agricultural harvest, while Jesus is concern-

---

with v 35 or with v 36 since the notion of "already now" is embodied in both verses. But if v 36 is absolute in character, as we and Lagrange maintain, then this notion does not apply to v 36.

[47]For a discussion on this issue see Brown, *John* I, 174; Lindars, *John*, 195; Bultmann, *Commentary*, 196, n. 4. Barrett (*John*, 241) like Bultmann, argues that the Evangelist is not interested in chronology.

[48]Giblin, "Miraculous Crossing," 99. See Rabbi H. Freedman and Maurice Simon (eds.), *Midrash IX* (London: Soncino, 1961[3]), last page, where the "harvest" is a symbol for Israel's redemption or greatness.

ed with the eschatological harvest. V 36 makes this plain: the fruit gathered in from the harvest is for "eternal life." So v 35b cannot be the hastening of a harvest with which it is not concerned. The midrash on Canticles does not apply to John either, since in John, the harvest (the giving and receiving of eternal life, 4:10, 14) is wholly and essentially a *free* gift (1:17; 3: 16; 4:10a, 36a, 38) as we shall see presently, something, therefore, which is not given as a reward for moral goodness.

In our view, the juxtaposition of v 35a and 35b is to emphasize that something entirely new is taking place. The disciples urgently need to be alerted to this fact, as the woman had been earlier concerning the issue of worship (vv 20—24). V 35b does just this. For as in v 31, 33 the disciples were shown seeking the wrong type of food for Jesus, so in v 35a they are shown to be expecting the wrong kind of harvest; like the woman they operate wholly within the natural order while Jesus operates within the spiritual, eschatological order. Perhaps the closest parallel to v 35 is the situation in vv 25—26: the woman is expecting the Messiah when he is already there speaking with her. In their concern for the distant harvest, the disciples are completely unaware that a new kind of harvest is already in progress. As in v 31—33, their zeal and focus are misplaced. Hoskyns may thus be right in seeing in v 35a another instance of the misunderstanding of the disciples, though the technical *double-entendre* does not apply here[49]. If it does, then it is much more subtle in vv 35a and 35b than in the case of water (vv 7—15) and food (vv 31—34).

Jesus' corrective in vv 35b and 36 as in vv 32, 34 bears upon this misplaced focus of the disciples. As earlier the human realities of water and food had been used to explain the significance of Jesus' mission for the woman (vv 10—15) and for Jesus himself (vv 31—34), so here the human realities of sowing and harvesting are used to ennuciate the arrival of the eschatological era, and the role of the disciples in this era. Jesus' first step is to awaken the attention of the disciples to the new order (v 35b); hence the force of the demonstrative particle ($i\delta o\acute{v}$) reinforced by the aorist imperatives. In the Gospel the raising up of the eyes means awareness of the current situation; it serves as a prelude to action (6:5)[50]. So personal awareness on the part of the disciples is the first and indispensable step to their proper involvement in the mission of Jesus (vv 36—38). In the passage this call to awareness is visually heightened by the scene of the approaching Samaritans, who in this concrete situation represent the fields ripe for the harvesting (v 30, 39) at which the disciples are asked to look[51].

---

[49]Hoskyns, *The Fourth Gospel,* 256.

[50]The only other instance in John is 17:1, which marks the beginning of Jesus' prayer to the Father. That the raising up of the eyes leads to action is true not only in John but also in Luke (6: 20; 16:23).

[51]This is the common interpretation among modern scholars; cf. Bultmann, *Commentary,* 197; and the other commentaries.

The approach of the Samaritans further confirms the view that the issue in v 35b is not agricultural harvest, but God's definitive work of salvation, the dawn of the end-time, symbolized in biblical thought by the harvest imagery[52]. Bultmann and Bligh have both suggested that the issue at stake in the Johannine community voiced in v 35 is a missionary lethargy on the part of the disciples, a tendency to stand by idle (Bligh) or to postpone action on the grounds that the time has not yet come (Bultmann)[53]. However, it needs to be noted that the attitude which underlies the statement in v 35a is that of a person who owns the field, and who, therefore, has the right to expect the harvest. This holds true in the normal order of things, not in the parabolic sense cited in v 37 (Is 5:1—7; Mt 21:33—46; Mk 12:1—12; Lk 20:9—19; Jn 15:1—16). If such is the underlying attitude of the disciples as already suggested in their seeking food for Jesus and objecting to what he seeks with a woman (vv 27, 31, 33), then the whole purpose of the otherwise "disjointed" vv 36—38 is to correct this attitude of the disciples. The correction is done first, by describing objectively and in general terms the harvester's work in this new order (vv 36—37), and then by applying this specifically to the disciples themselves (vv 37—38).

Vv 36—37

Because the eschatological harvest is of a completely new order, it operates according to norms which are wholly different from the natural harvest, even as the water promised the woman (vv 13—14) and worship (vv 21—24) have their own unique, non-natural modes of operation. First, the harvesting work itself is seen as a "receiving" (λαμβάνειν), not as the reward of one's own sowing. Unlike Mt 20:1—16, the receiving of wages is put first because the harvester's work *is* a receiving of wages. Μισθὸν λαμβάνειν and συνάγειν καρπόν are almost synonymous terms: "fruit-gathering" describes the content proper of the harvester's work, but this work is also seen as its own reward (μισθόν λαμβάνειν). This interpretation is made possible on both grammatical and theological grounds.

---

[52]See Joel 3 (esp. v 13) = LXX 4; Is 27:11—12; 4 Ezra 4:28; 9:17, 31; 2 Baruch 70:2; Mt 13: 30, 39; Mk 9:29; Rev. 14:15. It is to be noted, however, that while the harvest theme in these passages emphasizes definitive separation and judgment, the Johannine eschatological harvest emphasizes definitive unification (v 36b). The same emphasis is placed in 10:16; 11:52 and particularly in Jn 17 where the arrival of Jesus' hour, the harvest phase of "the work," calls forth an intensified prayer from him for the unity of all his followers. Not that the theme of judgment is missing in John, nor is the theme of gathering in absent in these biblical passages. But for John, the definitive separation began with Jesus' entry into the world (1:5) and took effect in humanity's response to his mission (9:41; 15:22). All who are in him, therefore, and continue to remain in him, are *ipso facto* separated from the world (17:16). What matters now is that they remain united in order to testify to the world concerning the reality of the eschatological harvest brought about by Jesus' accomplished mission (13:35; 17:20—23).

[53]Bultmann, *Commentary,* 196: the delay may be caused by indolence: "Tomorrow, tomorrow, but never to-day." Bligh, "Jesus in Samaria," 342.

Grammatically, the word μισθός (Hebr., פעל ה‎) means both work and reward, the result of the work done[54]. A similar double meaning is embodied in the verb κοπιᾶν (vv 6, 38). In its noun form (κόπος, v 38c) the word describes the tedious nature of the work itself, and in its verb form (vv 6, 38a,b) the resulting tiredness experienced by the one who so engages in this difficult labor[55]. Jesus' physical exhaustion in v 6 was seen to be the result of his laborious missionary journey (p. 86). By comparison to his, the missionary activity of the disciples is essentially a "receiving of wages" (v 36, 38). The reward-aspect of the work is reinforced by the "joy" which the harvester experiences with the sower (v 36b).

Theologically, not only is salvation seen in the Gospel as the gift of God (3:16; 4:10a), but the personal mission of each agent is viewed as a gift: that of John the Baptist (3:27—30), of Jesus himself (5:36; 17:4) and of the Holy Spirit (16:13—15). The same applies in v 36 in the mission of the disciples. Not only is their mission described as a "receiving" of wages (the same verb λαμβάνειν is used of the missions of the Holy Spirit and of the Baptist [16:15; 3:27]), it is also understood that this mission benefits them personally. The point is emphasized in v 38 where the mission of the disciples is described first negatively (οὐ κεκοπιάκατε), then positively (εἰσεληλύθατε). The gift and rewarding nature of the mission of the disciples receives added weight when vv 36 and 38 are read against the OT context of the entry into the promised land, Josh 24, a passage which in our view constitutes the most appropriate OT background to 4:1—42. When the Israelites harvested the produce of the land, this harvesting was itself "work"; but the work was, nonetheless, Yahweh's "free gift" to them (Josh 24:13).

In NT traditions, it is understood that the missionary receives physical sustenance from his or her mission (Lk 10:7; Gal 6:6; 1 Cor 9:11, 14), even as the OT priests did from their temple service (Nu 18:8, 31; Deut 18:1—3; cf. 1 Cor 9:13). In Wisdom 5:15, the reward received by the righteous for his labors (v 1c) is also eternal life with God. John, however, does not emphasize the material aspect of the reward, nor does his concept of "eternal life" mean the kind of immortality envisaged by the Wisdom of Solomon. He focuses rather, on the present new order, on a "realized eschatology"[56], expressed concretely in v 36b and throughout

---

[54]See H. Preisker's extensive article on μισθός, *TDNT*, IV, 695—728: in general usage (pp. 695—706) in late Judaism (712—714); in the NT (pp. 714—728); and in the OT (pp. 706—712) by E. Würthwein. See, further H. Loewe, "The Ideas of Pharisaism," in *Judaism and Christianity*, I—III (W.O.E. Oesterly, H. Loewe and J.J. Edwin, eds., New York, Ktav Publishing House, 1969), II, pp. 1—58, esp. p. 17.

[55]See our previous discussion on v 6, pp. 86—87.

[56]The term, "realized eschatology," is here understood in the Johannine sense of the word, namely, that Jesus' coming into the world and his accomplished mission mark the dawn and definitive establishment of the end-time in human history. Consequently, those who believe and are

the Gospel in terms of "fellowship": the fruit gathered in by the harvester results in his rejoicing together, at the same time and in the same place with the sower (ὁμοῦ)[57]. Indeed, this is the whole purpose of his work (ἵνα). The point is stated even more explicitly in 1 Jn 1:1–4: The preaching of the word aims at bringing the hearer into the all-embracing fellowship with the Father, and the Son and the preachers (v 3), but has as its ultimate purpose the utter completion of the preachers' joy (ἡ πεπλη-ρωμένη, v 4). Put differently, the eternal fellowship which results from the mission is the cause of the mutual rejoicing of sower and reaper.

This is precisely because the work of sower and reaper operate in view of the same goal and reality, eternal life. The sower gives this life (3:16; 10:10; 4:10, 14); the reaper both receives and gathers in its fruit (4:14, 36a,b). To gather fruit for eternal life means essentially to bring "together" (σὺν-ἄγειν) into lasting fellowship. In 15:16 the same concept is expressed in terms of "bearing fruit which endures." In this connection it is worth recalling our earlier discussion on the significance of the baptizing role of the disciples (pp. 81–83). Here too, the fruit-gathering activity of the disciples flows from and is defined by Jesus' own missionary activity: both are in view of eternal life lived out in fellowship and mutual rejoicing (cf. 15:11; 17:13; 16:21–22).

The importance of fellowship is heightened by the background of socio-religious separatism in which both the woman and the disciples are caught up (vv 9, 20, 27). The need for fellowship inspires the fundamental conception of mission in the Gospel as a "gathering in" (v 36b; 6:44; 10:16; 11:52; 12:32; 21:5–11). The same basic conception of mission is expressed visually in the imagery of the sheepfold (10:1–16); of the vine and the branches (15:1–18), of the one boat and unbroken net (21:2–8) and conceptually/liturgically in the Lord's prayer for the all-encompassing unity of believers, present and future (17:11–23)[58]. Given this emphasis on fellowship and on the joy which it generates, it is not surprising that those passages which emphasize mission as a "gathering in" carry an equally strong emphasis on the necessity of mutual love (15:9–17; 17:24–26) or on love as the motivating force of the missionary endeavor (10:17–18;

---

in him are transferred even in this life from the realm of darkness and death (the realm of unbelief) to that of light and eternal life (1:12–13; 3:21). See further, pp. 165–168 below.

[57] The adverb embodies all three notions (together, at the same time and in the same place); see *BAG*, 599. All three concepts are also present in 21:2 where the disciples' togetherness results in a fruitless catch until Jesus appears among them (vv 1, 4, 14). In the kindred expression συνάγειν εἰς ἕν (11:52; cf. 10:16) unity rather than physical togetherness is emphasized, as in 17:9–23, the ἕν indicating the "place" to which the scattered children of God are to be led.

[58] The unity is "all-embracing" because it encompasses the vertical dimension, with Jesus and the Father (17:23), the horizontal dimension, unity among the disciples themselves in the Father and Jesus (v 21), and the temporal dimension, unity of believers of all ages (v 20). To see, then, "the union of Ephraim and Judah" as the inspiration behind John's "account of the gathering of the new people of God" (Olsson, *Structure and Meaning*, 248), seems like putting the cart before the horse.

13:1; 21:15–17; 3:16), even when such love results in death for oneself (13:1; 15:13; 12:24–26; 21:18–29)[59].

Fellowship as the ultimate goal of mission also explains the importance attached to community in the Gospel (1:12–13, and the farewell discourses), why 1 John emphasizes *ad nauseam* love of the brethren and sees it as the criterion for knowledge of God (1 Jn 4:7–8), why John sees the treachery of Judas in a worse light than the Synoptics (13:21–30; cf. Mt 26:21–25; Mk 14:18–21; Lk 22:21–23), and why the departure of some of the brethren is proof for 1 John that they never belonged to the group in the first place (2:19)[60]. Finally, the importance placed on fellowship explains the second unique characteristic of the eschatological harvest described in v 37.

This second unique characteristic is that the harvesting task itself inaugurates a wholly new relationship between the sower and reaper. The bitter edge of the proverb v 37 is eliminated, or better still, replaced by mutual rejoicing. For the experience whereby one sows for another to reap arises either from lack of fellowship, and so is given as a punishment (Deut 28:30; Lev 26:16; Mic 6:15; Job 31:8–18), or from the simple fact that the present life is not eternal, since the sower dies before the harvest (Deut 20:6–7). In John both obstacles are overcome: instead of enmity and punishment, there is lasting fellowship and mutual rejoicing in the completed task, a rejoicing made possible because both sower and reaper have the same goal and objective (v 36), the promoting of eternal life in the believer (the fruit) through a life-giving faith in Jesus (3:16; 6:40; 10:10; 20:30–31). Even the believer, the fruit, shares in the same goal and objective (6:47). The second obstacle, death, is definitely overcome by the fact that the new life engendered by the sowing/harvesting task is "eternal" ($\epsilon\grave{\iota}\varsigma$ $\zeta\omega\grave{\eta}\nu$ $\alpha\grave{\iota}\acute{\omega}\nu\iota o\nu$, vv 14d, 36b).

---

[59]Jesus' self-sacrificing love (13:1; 15:13) is rooted in the Father's own love for the world, even as it constitutes the concrete manifestation of this love (1 Jn 4:10, 19). In the Father's case the depth of this love is manifested in his giving up his uniquely beloved Son, loved as no one else is loved ($\tau\grave{o}\nu$ $\upsilon\grave{\iota}\grave{o}\nu$ $\tau\grave{o}\nu$ $\mu o\nu o\gamma\epsilon\nu\tilde{\eta}$) in order to save the world (3:16; 1 Jn 4:9; cf. 3:34; 15:9). This same self-giving, self-costing love is given as "a new command" to the disciples (13:35; 15:12–17; 1 Jn 3:11, 23; 4:11–21). The insistence that Jesus' and the Father's love for the world is to be the measure of the disciples' love for one another (the $\kappa\alpha\vartheta\acute{\omega}\varsigma$, $\kappa\alpha\acute{\iota}$ motif underlies these passages whether expressly stated [13:34; 15:12; 1 Jn 3:23; 4:17] or not), is rooted in the fact that one cannot be in them and yet not love as they love (17:21–23; 15:35; 1 Jn 2:5–6). To refuse to love in this way is to be like the dead branch which is cut off from the life-giving nourishing vine (15:6; cf. 1 Jn 2:4, 9, 11; 1:6). The individual concretely manifests this love in service, the kind of service which a slave performs for his master — one that is all-inclusive, and is based on the deepest respect for the one served (13:12–17, to be read against the background of 13:1–11).

[60]Judas, like the apostates in 1 Jn 2:19, never really belonged to the group (6:70–71; 13:2, 27). Furthermore, only John mentions that Judas kept and stole from the common purse (12:6; 13:29); and thrice, that he belongs to the devil (6:70–71; 13:2, 27); that it was "night" when Judas left Jesus, the light and life of the world (1:4–5; 8:12; 11:10; 12:35, 46; 1 Jn 2:1, 11) to do the work of the devil his father (3:19–20; 8:40–41a, 44; 1 Jn 3:8, 10, 15), and that Jesus was deeply troubled in spirit at the thought of Judas's coming betrayal (13:21), though he seems greatly relieved by his departure (13:31).

Strikingly, both Isaiah and Amos saw the end-time as the period when the sad human experience of one sowing for another to reap would be reversed (Amos 9:14b; Is 62:8–9; 65:21–23). But in these OT passages, sower and reaper are one and the same person, whereas in John they are decidedly different (ἄλλος/ἄλλος, v 37b, 38). The all-embracing reason in John for the mutual rejoicing between sower and reaper is the joint ownership by the Father and Jesus of everything, including the disciples, the harvesters (16:15; 17:9–10). Given this claim, that Jesus and the Father own *everything* in common, this one exception becomes all the more striking: that Jesus never claims ownership of "the work." On the other hand, neither the disciples nor the Holy Spirit are said to own anything; knowledge of everything, yes (15:15; 16:12–14), but never ownership. Nevertheless, all concerned work concertedly towards the same goal; there is, to use a modern idiom, a real team-spirit. This notion of team-spirit should shed light on the import of the last two verses of this section (vv 37–38).

Before we analyze these verses, however, the following observation should be made concerning our discussion of vv 35–37 up to this point. Just as the socio-religious problems raised by the woman (vv 9, 20) were transferred to the eschatological plane by Jesus and resolved there (living water, true worship), so, too, the relational problems inherent in human sowing and harvesting (vv 35a, 36b–37) are raised to the eschatological plane (vv 35b, 36) where they are definitively resolved[61]. The emphasis on fellowship which has been amply highlighted above makes sense not only in the context of the general enmity between Jews and Samaritans (v 9c) but also proves to be particularly relevant to the disciples themselves, who are shown to be the discriminating group (v 27b). It is not strange, therefore, that their task should be seen essentially as a gathering in (v 36). Their difficulty can be overcome if they learn to view life in the same eschatological lens as Jesus. The whole point of vv 35–37 is to impress upon the disciples that a new order of reality has come into existence, that they are part of this reality and that it is one marked by grace, fellowship and mutual rejoicing, not by enmity and separatism, still less is it achieved by one's own efforts.

Vv 37–38

It is most striking that while the cutting edge of the proverb (v 37) is eliminated, the distinction of roles between sower and reaper is not only maintained, but doubly emphasized (ἄλλος/ἄλλος, v 37; ἄλλοι/ὑμεῖς, v 38). Indeed, the proverb is true only in respect of this particular aspect

---

[61]The view that v 35b means the elimination of the interval between sowing and reaping, or of the period of waiting (Schnackenburg, *Johannesevangelium* I, 483; Lindars, *John,* 195; Giblin, "Crossing," 99) runs into conflict with the repeated emphasis in the Gospel that Jesus has to wait for his hour which ushers in the harvest (2:4; 7:30; 8:20; cf. 12:23, 27; 13:1; 17:1). Not only

($\dot{\epsilon}\nu$ $\tauο\dot{\upsilon}\tau\omega$), namely, in the separate identity of sower and reaper, not in respect to its penal aspect especially as stated in Mic 6:15[62]. The word is true in the first place because Jesus and the Father, the sowers, do not personally benefit from the completed work. The accomplished work of salvation is their gift for humanity. Secondly, the statement emphasizes that the disciples are not the sowers but the reapers. Theirs is essentially a harvesting/fruit-gathering mission; it is further underlined that the fruit they gather is that of others' labor, not of their own (v 38)[63]. This point is stated first negatively, "you have not labored," then positively, "you have entered into their labor." Similarly, the work of these others is also doubly emphasized: it is difficult in itself ($\kappaóπον$) and exacting of the laborer ($\kappa\epsilon\kappaοπιάκασιν$). Thus a very clear distinction obtains between the laborious and ground-breaking work of "the others" and the much easier and self-benefiting activity of the disciples.

The meaning of v 38 is thus almost self-evident. The major problems in the verse, however, concern the scope of $\dot{\alpha}πέστειλα$ and the identity of the $\dot{\alpha}λλοι$ (the "others"). Since the disciples are not sent in the Gospel till after the resurrection, is the aorist in v 38a (as in 17:18) to be understood as proleptic (spoken in anticipation of the actual sending in 20:21–23) or as prophetic (that Jesus' intention to send the disciples is indeed tantamount to his actually sending them)? In the vision of the Gospel, both interpretations are possible[64]. Indeed, the election and call of the disciples is inseparable from their mission (15:16), and the first activity of the disciples consisted in leading others to Jesus (1:40–42, 45–46).

A further problem which arises, however, is this: if the aorist is proleptic, what becomes of the perfects in v 38b? Both Abbott and McKay have drawn attention to the high consistency in which the significance of the perfective aspect is used in John (and in the NT generally)[65]. In the light of this grammatical diagnosis v 38b implies, then, that those ad-

---

Jesus, but also believers have to wait for the arrival of this hour to receive the promised gift of the Spirit (7:37–39). Also in John the disciples do not engage in the harvesting task till after the resurrection (Jn 21). V 35b, then, is not concerned with correcting a proverb, but with pointing out didactically (hence proleptically) the reality of the eschatological harvest which demands the attention of the disciples.

[62] It is worth noting that in most of the examples cited (Deut 6:11; Jos 24:13; Mt 25:26; Lk 19:21) only one or other aspect of the proverb is emphasized. Similarly, v 37 emphasizes only one aspect of the proverb but the other aspect forms the background for v 36; the explanatory $\gamma\dot{\alpha}\rho$ relates to this.

[63] In this idiomatic sense, "fruit" means the outcome of one's own labor or conduct (Mt 7:16–20; Lk 6:43–44; cf. Gal 6:7–9). Such an understanding is ruled out by 4:36–38. Even where the disciples are seen as those who bear fruit, it is made plain that this fruit can be borne only in Jesus (15:1–8, 16).

[64] Zerwick (*Analysis* I, 297) combines both: "spoken in anticipation with prophetic utterance."

[65] Abbott, *Grammar*, nos. 2442–2443, pp. 324–326; nos. 2473–2477, pp. 344–347; K.L. McKay, "On the Perfect and Other Aspects in New Testament Greek," *NovT* 23 (1981) 289–329. See, further, J.H. Moulton and N. Turner *Grammar of New Testament Greek* III: *Syntax* (Edinburgh: T and T Clark, 1963) 5, 67–69.

dressed are already engaged in missionary work. Whether or not they are aware that others started laboring *before* and are *still* working with them (κεκοπιάκασιν) is another matter. The reprimanding tone of v 38 implies that they are not so aware of the role of these "others," hence, their need for the strong reminder (v 38b).

It seems best, then, to view all of v 38 as clearly reflecting the post-Easter standpoint from which the Gospel is written. The verse implies that those so addressed need to be reminded that they are not the principal agents at work in the missionary enterprise. Quite the contrary, they are merely appropriating the fruit of others' labor without doing any work themselves (εἰσεληλύθατε)[66]. Joshua 24 again comes readily to mind. Written long after the entry into the Promised Land, the passage no doubt reflects the actual experience of the author and of his audience, even while embodying traditions that go back to the period of entry. The same applies to 4:1–42; v 38 more than any other verse in the entire pericope clearly reflects the post-Easter perspective of the Evangelist and his audience. This is the only experience which makes complete sense not only of the aorist in v 38 but also of the perfects. It is also the experience which helps to account for the reprimanding tone of the verse, as also of v 42[67].

This interpretation is strengthened by the fact that neither the disciples, nor later the woman (v 42) have visibly done anything which merits this reprimand. All the disciples have done in this passage is show a genuine concern for Jesus (v 31) and object, as would any conscientious Jew of the period, to his speaking publicly with a woman (v 27). Though these apparently innocent actions symbolize their misunderstanding of the nature of Jesus' mission and their role in it, in the woman's case, the passage reports of no action which could merit her the reaction of her fellow citizens in v 42. Even if one considers the general picture of the pre-Easter activity of the disciples reported in the Synoptics (Mt 10:1–42; Mk 6:7–11; Lk 9:1–6; 10:1–20), one would still not be able to justify the tone and thrust of vv 38 and 42 in terms of the pre-Easter missionary activity of the disciples alone. These verses, therefore, furnish a special clue to the understanding of the missionary situation of the Evangelist and of his community.

Ἄλλοι, *v 38*. The identity of the ἄλλοι (sowers) in v 38b is one of the most hotly debated issues in the whole passage. Every possible suggestion has been made, and from every possible angle. The following listing gives

---

[66]According to *BAG*, 761, this is the primary meaning of the proverb in v 37. In v 38 this meaning is reinforced by the notion of "entering into" the labor of others. The disciples are the lucky ones!

[67]It is possible to see an echo of 4:38 in Lk 10:17–20. Jesus was present, watching while the disciples cast out devils (v 18); but they are to rejoice not because of what they have been able to achieve, for the power to cast out demons is itself a gift (vv 19–20a), but rather because their names are already registered in heaven (v 20b).

a synthesis of these suggestions from the different perspectives in which these suggestions are made:

1.   *From the literary/contextual level,* Jesus and the woman, as contrasted with the disciples.

2. *From the literary/geographical level,* John the Baptist and his followers who exercised their baptismal ministry at Aenon near Salim, prior to the ministry of Jesus and his disciples (3:23). In this instance, Jesus and the disciples are the reapers from their labor.

3. *From the OT historical level,* the OT prophets, God's messengers who preceded Jesus, and into whose labor he and the disciples have now entered.

4. *From the NT historical level,* either (i) the first disciples whose work, grounded in that of Jesus, preceded that of their successors, or (ii) Philip and the evangelizers of Samaria among whom is to be numbered the author of the Gospel, as contrasted with people like Peter and John who went to Samaria after them (Acts 8:4—25).

5. *From the universal/existentialistic level,* any predecessors of any missionary work.

6. *From the structural and theological levels,* Jesus and the Father as contrasted with the disciples[68].

The most challenging of these suggestions is the last one made from the structural and the theological viewpoints. Thüsing and Schnackenburg both consider v 36 in isolation from v 38. In this structural context, then, both authors see the Father as "the sower" and Jesus as "the reaper" in v 36; their reason being that Jesus continues and completes the work of the Father (v 34). Their view is shared by both Olsson and Kuhl (though these latter do not isolate v 36 from v 38). However, while Thüsing further identifies the "others" in v 38 as Jesus and the Father, Schnackenburg denies this completely and opts with Cullmann for Philip and the evangelizers of Samaria. Giblin disagrees with both Thüsing and Schnackenburg concerning their interpretation of v 36, on the grounds that this introduces a double typology foreign to the Gospel. He agrees, however, with Thüsing against Schnackenburg that the "others" in v 38 refer to

---

[68]*1.* Bernard, *Commentary* I, 159; Olsson, *Structure,* 233; Hoskyns, *The Fourth Gospel,* 247. *2.* Bultmann, *Commentary,* 199, n. 2 (if v 38 is pre-Johannine); J.A.T. Robinson, "The 'Others' of John 4, 38. A Test of Exegetical Method," *SE* I (= TU 73; 1959) 510—515; Bligh, "Jesus in Samaria," 342; *3.* Lagrange, *Jean,* 121 (following the Fathers of the Church); F.M. Braun, *Jean le théologien* II, 24; Odeberg, *The Fourth Gospel,* 190; Lindars, *John,* 197; Boismard-Lamouille, *Synopse III,* 144 (or classify under no. 2 above if attributed to John II-A, p. 143); *4.* (i) Spitta, *Johannesevangelium;* 102—103; Wellhausen, *Johannis,* 21; Wilkens, *Entstehungsgeschichte,* 136, n. 502; (ii) Cullmann, "La Samarie et les origines de la mission chrétienne, 3—12; *Johanneische Kreis,* 16, 51—52; Bligh, "Jesus in Samaria," 344; Jürgen Becker, *Johannes,* 182; Schnackenburg, *Johannesevangelium* I, 486—487. *5.* Bultmann, *John,* 199; Heanchen, *Johannes,* 247—248; *6.* Zahn, *Johannes,* 263; Thüsing, *Die Erhöhung,* 57; Giblin, "Crossing," 99—100.

Jesus and the Father. Giblin thus sees Jesus and the Father as both the "sower" in v 36 and the "others" in v 38[69].

The variety of suggestions outlined above demonstrates the complexity of the problem concerning the identity of the "others" in v 38 as well as the key importance of this identification for the understanding of the passage. Thüsing's and Schnackenburg's position countered by Giblin raises the further question whether "sower" and "reaper" in v 36 are to be identified with ἄλλοι and ὑμεῖς in v 38, respectively. In order to determine with some degree of certainty which of these various suggestions is the most probable, the following clarifications need to be kept in view: First, the focus of concern in vv 35–38 is the mission of the disciples as this relates to that of Jesus (v 34). The vocabulary of harvesting in vv 36–38 applies first and foremost to the disciples. But this focus on the disciples as the harvesters does not mean that others are excluded from the harvesting work[70]. Indeed, the perfect in v 38b implies that these "others" are still at work with the disciples even in the harvesting phase of the enterprise. All that is emphasized in v 38, then, is that the disciples' role in the missionary work not only is extremely easy, compared with that of the "others," but that this very role benefits them personally[71].

Secondly, the thrust of the whole section is didactic; hence, the concepts "sower" and "reaper" as well as "fruit" (all singulars) are used didactically, not prescriptively. This means that "sower" and "reaper" in v 36 refer to categories of workers, not to individuals on a one to one basis. These concepts, however, receive their specific application in v 38. V 38, therefore, furnishes the key as to how the general reference in vv 36–37 is to be understood. If the disciples are the "reapers" in v 38, and this can hardly be disputed, then they must also be the reapers in v 36. So Giblin is right against Thüsing and Schnackenburg that the reapers in v 36 are the disciples, not Jesus. As we also maintained earlier against Thüsing, the focus on Jesus' mission ends in v 34 not in v 36; v 35 marks the transition to the mission of the disciples (p. 147). This structural line up of vv 34–38 should also help to determine the identity of the "others" in v 38, who must also be the "sower" in v 36. The diagram attached on the following page helps to illumine the movement of thought in this whole section.

---

[69]For the references to Thüsing, Schnackenburg, Olsson, Cullmann and Giblin see the previous note; Kuhl, *Die Sendung,* 141.

[70]The proverb, v 37, never means that the sower cannot reap. Cf. *BAG,* 761; 1 Cor 9:7; Gal 6: 7, 8; 2 Cor 9:6. Indeed, the criticism of the third servant in the parable of the pounds (Mt 25:24, 26; Lk 19:21–22) implies that the master should reap only where he sowed.

[71]This meaning is made explicit in 15:1–8, 16: the disciple who has an abiding faith in Jesus (vv 4–6; cf. 8:31–32) receives personal nourishment from him and the Father and is caused by them to bear fruit. The very choice and election of the disciples is in view of their missionary fruitfulness, the result of their being in Jesus (v 16).

Diagrammatic Illustration of the
Movement of Thought in vv 34—38

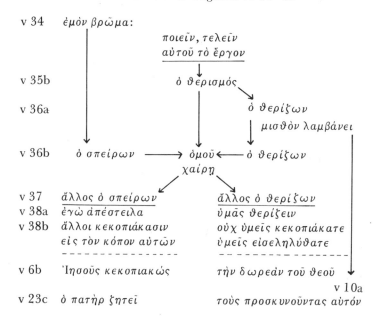

v 34	ἐμὸν βρῶμα:	
		ποιεῖν, τελεῖν αὐτοῦ τὸ ἔργον
v 35b		ὁ θερισμός
v 36a		ὁ θερίζων
		μισθὸν λαμβάνει
v 36b	ὁ σπείρων ──→ ὁμοῦ ←── ὁ θερίζων	
	χαίρῃ	
v 37	ἄλλος ὁ σπείρων	ἄλλος ὁ θερίζων
v 38a	ἐγὼ ἀπέστειλα	ὑμᾶς θερίζειν
v 38b	ἄλλοι κεκοπιάκασιν εἰς τὸν κόπον αὐτῶν	οὐχ ὑμεῖς κεκοπιάκατε ὑμεῖς εἰσεληλύθατε
v 6b	Ἰησοῦς κεκοπιακώς	τὴν δωρεὰν τοῦ θεοῦ
		v 10a
v 23c	ὁ πατὴρ ζητεῖ	τοὺς προσκυνοῦντας αὐτόν

This structural pattern and movement of thought in vv 34—38 reveals that Jesus must be one of the "others" (v 38b) and "sower" (v 36). The first contextual clue to this is that the verb κοπιᾶν which describes the labor of the "others" is already used to describe Jesus' present missionary journey to Samaria (v 6; pp. 86—87 above). In both these verses, the tense of the verb is the perfect. The second contextual clue is v 34: Jesus alone *does* and *completes* the sending Father's work; and it is the completion of this work which alone makes possible the harvesting mission of the disciples. Though κόπος is not identical with ἔργον, it describes the laborious and costing nature of this work.

It was seen too in the analysis of v 34 within the Gospel context that "the work" belongs exclusively to the Father who is depicted not as an absentee landlord but as one who is present and active at every phase of "the work." The Father does not simply own the work, he is always at work (5:17). His active seeking of the believer, for instance, is mentioned in this very pericope (v 23c). So both language and context lead one to conclude that the "others" in v 38 are both the Father and Jesus. This contextual evidence is further strengthened by the theological perspective already discussed, namely, that "the work" is done and completed by none other than Jesus and the Father. Indeed, their oneness is not only one of congruency in action (*Deckungsgleichheit in der Aktion*), but also ontological (*Wesensidentität der Gottesnatur*, 1:1c; 5:18; 10:33, 36; 20:

28)[72]. Ultimately, then, it is radically impossible to separate Jesus' activity from that of the Father.

Thüsing's objection that Jesus cannot be the sower in v 36 because the Father owns and begins the work by sending him can be met by this observation: A crucial distinction needs to be made between the Father's exclusive ownership of "the work" and the activity by which this work is done and completed. All the vocabulary of sowing and reaping in vv 36–38 describe activity, not ownership. The Father's ownership of the work does not preclude Jesus' working conjointly with him in its operation (v 34; 5:17; 17:4). Indeed, it is only in the Son that the Father's activity can be seen and felt by those for whose sole benefit this work is undertaken (14:9–11). On this level of visibility, it is true to say that the Father can do nothing without the Son (cf. 1:18; 14:8–9). Jesus sows with the Father as his unique agent of salvation or there is no sowing. Equally, Schnackenburg's position that the term sower is unbecoming of the Father runs into serious conflict with the Gospel's own portrayal of the Father. For in the Johannine conception of mission, unless the Father sows with the Son there is also no sowing or harvesting (cf. 5:19; 14:10; 15:1–8). We have already seen the different fundamental activities which the Gospel attributes to the Father.

To sum up our discussion, then, the Johannine language and theology of mission demand that only the Father and Jesus be seen as the "sower" and "others" in vv 36 and 38. Theirs is the conjoint activity by which "the work" is done and completed. John the Baptist and the OT prophets are excluded; theirs, as we have seen, is essentially a witnessing role to the effect that Jesus is the expected end-time Messiah. Both the woman and the first disciples, including Philip and the evangelizers of Samaria are also excluded. For the woman and the disciples of all times reap the fruit of Jesus' accomplished mission, first for themselves and then through witnessing to this God-given salvation by leading others to Jesus (gathering in the fruit; 4:28–29, 39, 42; 15:16; 21:1–14). For the fruit of this work is bestowed as a gift to both would-be converts and prospective missionaries (vv 36, 38). The mission of the disciples is modeled, no doubt, on that of Jesus, but only with respect to the dependence on the sender; crucial aspects of Jesus' mission are necessarily closed to them. Jesus' glorification, accomplished once for all (19:30; cf. Heb 10:12, 14) is the definitive act whereby the work is completed once for all, the drawing/gathering activity is programmatically achieved (12:32; 10:16; 11:52), and the disciples themselves receive the Spirit/power to become both children of God (1:12–13; 7:37–39) and fruitful participants in the harvesting of "the work" (15:1–17; 20:21–23; 21).

Not only, therefore, is Jesus' and the Father's the basic groundwork and *sine qua non* of the missionary activity of the disciples, objectively

---

[72]The debate on this issue is discussed above, p. 25.

achieved once for all, but also both Jesus and the Father are actively present at each instance nourishing the disciples themselves and enabling their missionary fruitfulness (15:1—5; 21:6, 12—13). Furthermore, their activity precedes that of the disciples in each individual fruit gathered in: Jesus knew and saw Nathanael before Philip led him to Jesus (1:46, 48); the Greeks already know of Jesus before they ask Philip for an audience with him (12:20—22); Jesus himself predicts and prays for all future converts as he does for the disciples present (17:20—23), while none can come to him unless they are drawn by the Father (6:44, 65) while he himself also draws them (12:32).

Κεκοπιάκασιν aptly describes the antecedent and abiding activity of the Father and Jesus in the entire missionary enterprise. Far from Jesus' mission achieving meaning through the activity of the disciples, therefore, the disciples' own mission is set squarely within the context of Jesus' mission, and receives its meaning only as an aspect of it[73]. The concept of "reaping" doubtless applies primarily to the disciples in vv 36—38, to emphasize the relative nature of their mission. But while they help to gather in the harvest, they are not the only ones at work, nor do they usher in the harvest (v 35b). For the activity of reaping is not to be equated with the harvest itself which is brought about by Jesus' completed mission (v 34; 17:4; 19:30).

Finally, Bultmann's universal, existentialistic identification of the "others" is ruled out. This may hold as a theologoumenon; it is even the view of Paul (1 Cor 3:6; 4:15; 9:1d); but it is essentially not that of John. In the Johannine conception, every missionary endeavor of every age means essentially and fundamentally a harvesting, a reaping of the fruit of the work of salvation accomplished definitively by Jesus and the Father. This holds regardless of whether one is a predecessor or a successor in the mission field. Indeed, strictly speaking, there are only two predecessors, both acting conjointly and simultaneously, and whose role in the missionary enterprise is primary and irreplaceable, namely, Jesus and the Father. All others are successors who are enabled by them to reap the fruit of their work.

Given this unmistakably clear conception of mission in the Gospel, the intriguing question is why the Evangelist took such pains to relativize the missionary role of the disciples. But this question must await our completion of the analysis of the conclusion of the pericope (vv 28—30, 39—42). Before we move to this last section, however, this seems an appropriate place to consider briefly the relationship between the various terms which kept recurring in the foregoing sections of our discussion, but which have hitherto not received adequate treatment. These terms are the ἔργον, eschatology, "the hour," "sowing" and "the harvest."

---

[73]See our previous discussion of Lindars' and Olsson's position concerning this issue, pp. 69—72 above.

4. Johannine Eschatology and Related Concepts

The first point to note is that the terms ἔργον and eschatology are comprehensive categories, while the terms "sowing," "harvest" and "the hour" denote particular perspectives of these comprehensive categories. The term ἔργον it was seen, designates the totality of the work of salvation done and completed conjointly and exclusively by Jesus and the Father. This work inaugurates and establishes definitively a new order in humanity's relationship with God, one which is marked by grace (free gift) and truth (1:17b; 3:16; 4:10, 24)[74]. In its unfolding, this ἔργον has a pre- and a post-Easter phase. The pre-Easter phase is the sowing phase during which only the Father and Jesus are at work. This is the phase in which the objective work of salvation is accomplished. It is also the period during which the Spirit is not given because Jesus has not yet been glorified (7:39).

The post-Easter phase constitutes the harvesting phase, or the completed phase of the work; this phase is ushered in definitively by Jesus' glorification (3:14; 8:28; 12:28, 34; 17:4—5; 19:30)[75]. This is the phase during which the Spirit, the indispensable agent of the new life (6:63; 16:7) is actually given to believers (20:22) to enable them to become the children of God (1:12—13; 3:3—8, 21), to receive the promised gift of eternal life (4:14; 7:37—38), to perform the worship in spirit and in truth (4:21—24), to grasp fully Jesus' teaching (14:25—26; 16:12—15) and participate actively in Jesus' mission of gathering in and reconciliation (15:26—27; 4:35—38; 20:21, 23; 21). This, in short, is the phase when the fruit of Jesus' accomplished mission is actually reaped by all believers[76].

The term "harvest" in John, thus covers only the post-Easter phase of Jesus' mission; it does not, therefore, include the period of his earthly life as it does in Matthew (9:37—38; 21:33—46) and Luke (9:2). John's

---

[74]The prologue (1:16—17) indicates that the notion of gift in such passages as 3:16 and 4:10 is to be understood as something absolutely free and unmerited (χάριν ἀντὶ χάριτος), given exclusively through Jesus. "Truth" also refers to the real (as opposed to the symbolic or the shadow) also found in Jesus (cf. 4:13—14; 5:39; 6:32—33, 48—51, 55—58). See, for instance, Bultmann, ἀλήθεια, *TDNT* I, 238—251. De la Potterie's objection (*La Vérité*, II, 702) that truth refers to Jesus himself rather than to the reality of these values (worship, bread, life, etc.), tends to introduce an unnecessary problem since these values cannot be found in their true form apart from Jesus, and since Jesus' self-revelation is precisely in view of his self-communication.

[75]The terms ὑψωθῆναι, δοξασθῆναι describe the same reality of Jesus' passover to the Father (13:1), namely, his passion, death and resurrection. In the light of 8:28, ὑψωθῆναι describes this reality from the standpoint of the Jewish leaders, while δοξασθῆναι describes it from that of the Father and Jesus (8:54; 11:4; 12:23, 28; 13:31—33; 17:1, 4, 5).

[76]The debate whether salvation is accomplished by the incarnation or the passion/resurrection (pp. 25—26 above) seems unwarranted by the Gospel. The ἔργον is conceived of as a single unbroken movement from beginning to end (4:34; 17:4). Put differently, the work of salvation is accomplished by Jesus' uninterrupted journey from the Father into the world and back to the Father (16:28; 13:1). In other words, salvation is accomplished by his incarnation, life, passion, death and resurrection, by the sum total of his life on earth.

position is, perhaps, closer to that of Mark (4:26–29). This distinction again underlines Jesus' exclusive role in the missionary enterprise as the one who alone sows with the Father.

As ἔργον describes the new world order brought about by Jesus' mission, so *eschatology* describes the new time order in which this new world order operates. The eschaton signifies the "end-time" foretold by the prophets (Is 2:2; Joel 3:1–3). But unlike in the OT and NT (Mt 13:30–39) the eschaton in John is not synonymous with the harvest period traditionally seen as the period of judgment or of prophetic utterance (Acts 2: 17–21). In John, on the contrary, the eschaton is a reality which spans both the sowing and harvesting phases of "the work." This eschatological era began with Jesus' coming into the world (1:5, 14) and perdures with the completed phase of "the work." Its impact is experienced as "life" by believers and as "judgment" by non-believers (3:18–21, 36; 5:29). The arrival of this end-time carries with it certain non-negotiable imperatives (δεῖ) for Jesus himself (3:14, 30a; 4:4; 9:4; 10:16; 12:34; 20:9), for his audience (3:7; 4:24), and for his precursor (3:30b).

Strikingly, the missionary activity of the disciples is never seen as an eschatological necessity, though the self-effacing mission of the Baptist is (3:30b), and though new birth and true worship on the part of believers are (3:7; 4:24). This is because Jesus' mission necessarily includes that of the disciples. Their harvesting mission (4:36, 38; 21:2–14) can be viewed as an eschatological imperative only insofar as this mission is already achieved in Jesus' programmatic gathering of all to himself (10:16; 12: 32). Similarly, the consideration of the Baptist's self-effacing mission as an eschatological necessity (3:30b) underlines again Jesus' unrivalled status as the Father's sole agent of salvation (3:31–36)[77].

From Jesus' own perspective, this eschatological necessity has two dimensions: first, it applies to him personally since it spells the necessity of his glorification, the Father's last seal on his self-giving mission (3:14, 30a; 12:34; 20:9); secondly, it applies to his missionary activity as he reaches out to a wide range of audiences (4:4; 9:4; 10:16). It is, however, through his coming, his outreach to his audience and his glorification that he establishes definitively the new order of reality known as the eschatological order.

In its pre-Easter phase, and from the standpoint of Jesus' own audience, this eschatological era is described as both *"the hour"* which "now is" (4: 21, 23; 5:25) and which "is coming." The former statement is proclamatory in nature: it simply alerts the attention of the hearer to the fact that the messianic era has indeed dawned with Jesus' coming into the world (cf. 4:25–26), and to their need to become aware of the consequences

---

[77]We have discussed elsewhere in detail the particular ways in which the Baptist's witness (3: 27–31) testifies to Jesus' uniqueness as God's sole agent of salvation: T. Okure, " 'How Can These Things Happen?' A Study of Jn 3:1–21 in Context" (*Mémoire* for the Ecole Biblique et Archéologique Française, Jerusalem, 1982) pp. 23–24, and nn. 48–48a, p. 79.

which this coming has for them personally. Jesus' presence and missionary activity constitute the most visible aspects of this "hour which now is." The latter statement, "the hour is coming," refers, from the standpoint of Jesus' audience, to the moment of Jesus' glorification when the promises of new birth (3:3–8), everlasting life (4:10–14; 6), true worship (4:21–24) and victory over death (5:24–29) are fulfilled and made possible for believers. From the perspective of Jesus' audience, therefore, the expression ὥρα νῦν ἐστιν does not refer to the hour of fulfilment. Its perspective, set in the context of the deliberative type of rhetoric, is essentially futuristic (4:35b)[78]. For its actuality for them coincides with the hour of Jesus' own glorification (7:37–39) and is thus identical with Jesus' personal "hour" (7:30; 8:20; 12:23, 27; 13:1; 17:1). In its post-Easter phase, and from the standpoint of the Evangelist's own audience, "the hour" is never "coming"; it always "is" (ὥρα νῦν ἐστιν). This is so because from their perspective Jesus' mission is accomplished and its fruit and promises are permanently made available to anyone who so desires to reap it.

However, while eschatology pinpoints the advent of the new world order, it does not eliminate the natural order with its needs and demands: for instance, the need for drinking water such as this (4:13), for expecting the natural harvest (4:35a), and even for physical death (16:2b; 19:30; 21:19, 23). Believers remain in the world (17:11), even though they are not of the world (15:18–19; 17:14; 1 Jn 3:1, 13; 4:4, 7; 5:4), and their mission is to the world (17:18–23; 1 Jn 4:17). They are, therefore, subject to the demands of the natural order. However, because of their faith in Jesus, death can no longer be seen as a termination; rather it constitutes the final step in the process of passing over from death to life through believing in Jesus (5:25, 28–29; 11:25–26). Eventually, the natural world order itself will be terminated (1 Jn 2:17). The "last day" in John (6:39, 40, 44; 11:24; 12:48; cf. 5:28–29) refers to this end of the natural world order, what Revelation calls "the harvest of the earth" (14:16). It is the day of the final victory of the believer over death, when he or she enters definitively into the complete possession of eternal life already begun here and now, and in the fellowship of Jesus and the Father (16:22–23a).

Johannine eschatology, then, is essentially realized eschatology in the most fundamental sense of the word: it is realized in Jesus' mission, realized in both believers (as life) and unbelievers (as judgment). Consequently, it is incorrect to speak of present ("realized") and futuristic eschatology in John as if these were two different theological concepts

---

[78]We had earlier identified vv 31–38 as the deliberative type of rhetoric (p. 148). Now, this deliberative type is not only suitable for didactic purposes, but, according to Wuellner ("Paul's Rhetoric of Argumentation in Romans: An Alternative to the Donfried-Karris Debate over Romans," *CBQ* 38 [1976] 330–351), it is concerned with the judgment about the value of an issue "which is emerging in the future" (p. 342); see also Quintilian, *Inst. Or.* III.viii.6.

attributable to two different authors — the "realized eschatology" to the Evangelist, and the futuristic eschatology to the ecclesiastical redactor[79]. In John, there is only one type of eschatology, realized eschatology. But this one eschatology has both a present and a future perspective: the present perspective lies in the new life begun here and now through faith in Jesus and through the imparting of the Holy Spirit (3:3—8; 4:10, 14; 7:37—39; 10:10; 20:30—31). It is lived out through active fellowship in the community of believers (13:32—35; 1 Jn 3:14), and it sets believers apart from the world (1:12—13; 15:18—19; 17:14, 16; 1 Jn 1:3, 13; 4:4, 7; 5:4). The future perspective is the hour of victory over and through death, that day when believers will know fully the reality of their relationship with Jesus and the Father and of Jesus' own unique relationship with the Father (14:20; 1 Jn 3:2). For unbelievers, the future perspective means the day of definitive judgment (5:29b; Rev 20:13—15).

This brief discussion on Johannine eschatology and its related concepts further underlines the point highlighted in the analysis of 4:1—38, namely, that Jesus' teaching to the woman and the disciples makes sense only when viewed as realities of the eschatological order where everything is a gift to be received in faith. These realities, therefore, transcend those of the natural order with its socio-religious and political problems and predicaments. Jesus' mission from the Father is the exclusive means by which this new order and its realities are brought into existence. The rest of the episode which we will now examine further underscores this point.

C. The *Demonstratio*, (27)28—30, 39—42: Jesus, the Missionaries and the Evangelized

Verses 28—30, 39—42, the conclusion to the preceding dialogues with the Samaritan woman (vv 1—26) and the disciples (vv 31—38), succinctly recapitulate and affirmatively dramatize the major missionary issues raised in each of these dialogues. The thesis of the narrative, that Jesus, the Messiah, is the sole agent of God's salvation who alone does and completes his work (vv 1—26, 34) is antithetically elaborated in vv 35—38: the disciples are not sowers, but reapers of the fruit of Jesus' missionary labor. The conclusion, then, is that, though the disciples, represented by the Samaritan woman, have an important role to play in the harvest phase of "the work," symbolically represented by the Samaritans, they in no way stand on a par with Jesus (vv 28—30, 39—42). The issue of fellowship raised negatively in vv 4, 9, 20, 22 and positively in vv 36—37 is re-

---

[79]Bultmann, *Commentary*, 261—262 (where he holds that the ecclesiastical redactor introduced 5:28—29 in order to correct the Evangelist's view in v 24).

solved in the narrative in v 40. Also like the woman, the Samaritans manifest the need for openness to Jesus' mission as the condition for benefiting from his saving mission. Finally, the importance of method in approaching the audience is again displayed in the interaction between the Samaritan woman and the Samaritans. The ensuing analysis will attempt to highlight the particular ways in which these themes are demonstrated in vv 28–30, 39–42.

Crucial to our understanding the scope of mission in this section is the manner in which the woman's response in vv 28–30 is to be interpreted. Is this response one of scepticism, of half-belief or of complete faith that Jesus is the Christ (v 26)? The problem rests on the cautious note which colors the woman's statement in v 29b. Because this statement is prefaced by $\mu\acute{\eta}\tau\iota$ it is taken to mean either "he is not the Christ, is he?" or "could he possibly be the Christ?" In the first interpretation the woman is said to be wholly sceptical of Jesus' self-revelation in v 26, since $\mu\acute{\eta}\tau\iota$ is equated with $\mu\acute{\eta}$ which expects a negative answer[80]. In the second, she is said to be doubtful, cautious or only half-believing since "elle doit déférer au jugement des personnes compétentes"[81]. Westcott, Morris and Becker, however, tend to see the woman's response in v 29 as one of complete belief in Jesus[82]. This, too, is our view, because the text itself furnishes sufficient grounds for interpreting the woman's response in vv 28–29 as one of complete belief in Jesus as the Messiah (v 26).

This contextual evidence bears upon the progressive movement of the woman's response to Jesus, especially from v 17b onwards where she listens more and speaks less than she did in vv 7–17b, and on the testimony of both the Evangelist and the Samaritans (vv 39, 42). The woman's progressive openness to Jesus moves from an attitude of hostility ("you a Jew," v 9) through that of scepticism (vv 11–12, 15–17a), to one of real curiosity ("a prophet," vv 19–20). It was earlier suggested (p. 120) that the woman herself first suspected that Jesus might be the Messiah and so sought (v 25) and received from him confirmation concerning this (v 26). Given this progressive openness on her part, it would be out of character if her response in vv 28–29 were a sudden reverting to her initial scepticism rather than a step further in her taking Jesus seriously. The turning point of her response which began in v 19 thus reaches its climax in vv 28–29. Her psychological abandonment of the waterpot (v 19) be-

---

[80] See *BDF*, no. 427, 2; Westcott, *John*, 163; Lagrange, *Jean*, 116; Brown, *John* I, 173.

[81] Lagrange, *Jean*, 116. This indeed is the majority view shared, for instance, by Barrett, *John*, 240; Haenchen, *Johannesevangelium*, 246; Lindars, *John*, 193; for Schnackenburg (*Johannesevangelium* I, 478) conclusions as to the woman's own belief are irrelevant; Brown (*John* I, 173) sees the woman's faith as "incomplete," but holds that she expresses a "shade of hope"; Olsson (*Structure and Meaning*, 152) is insistent that the Evangelist is not interested in the woman's own belief since she is only a mouthpiece of the Samaritans.

[82] Westcott (*John*, 163) citing Chrysostom calls her an "apostle commissioned by faith"; for Morris (*John*, 275) though a negative answer is expected, a positive one is hoped for; Becker, *Johannes*, 183.

comes a physical reality in v 28 as she runs with eagerness into the city to call her fellow Samaritans, a dramatic gesture all the more striking given her previous complaint about the distance from the city to the well (v 15b)[83].

The second evidence is that the Evangelist himself considers the woman's report in v 29 to be the word of a witness (τὸν λόγον τῆς γυναι-κὸς μαρτυρούσης) on the grounds of which some of the Samaritans first believed (v 39). It is highly unlikely that the mere report of Jesus' knowl-edge of her private life would have awakened faith in her fellow citizens (vv 39, 42) when the revelation itself failed to awaken faith in her, the reporter, for whose sole benefit the revelation was initially made. It is generally noted that v 39 is a discrepancy introduced by the Evangelist into a lost primitive story of Jesus' encounter with a woman[84]. But when this has been observed, we are still left with the task of understanding the Evangelist's intention whose work (not the hypothetical primitive story) is the only sure evidence we have, and whose audience would have been expected to make sense out of the story as it now stands. In this present context, v 39 placed before vv 40—42 indicates that the Samari-tans believed *because of* the woman's word[85]. If she is not a believer from the outset, Bultmann's view that she represents the disciples, the messengers, makes no sense[86].

The woman's *witness,* therefore, needs to be taken seriously, not only because witness is a technical term in the Gospel, but because her report meets the criterion for authentic witness in the Gospel[87]. The content of her report is what she first heard and personally experienced from Jesus himself. Her word in v 29 is based not only on vv 17b—18 ("all I ever did"), but also on vv 25—26 ("the Christ")[88]. In John the true wit-ness reports on what he or she has seen and heard. This is true of the Bap-tist's witness (1:31—34), of the Beloved Disciple's witness, whose singular authority lies behind the Gospel (19:26—27; 20:2, 8; 21:7, 20—24). It is true of the joint witness of the disciples (15:27; cf. 1 Jn 1:1—3) and of the Holy Spirit (16:13). It is true, above all, of Jesus' exclusive witness to the Father (1:18; 3:11—13, 32; 5:36; 6:46; 7:29; 8:38).

Moreover, the purpose of the woman's witness, like that of these other witnesses, is to lead the listener to believe in Jesus as the Christ. This is

---

[83]The woman's zeal in vv 28—29 is noted by Bultmann, *Commentary* 193, n. 1; Lagrange, *Jean,* 193 (citing Θ which actually adds "running"); Haenchen, *Johannesevangelium,* 246.

[84]Redactional approach holds that after v 30 the story continued in v 40. See the discussion above, pp. 58—64, esp. the chart, pp. 61—62.

[85]This, too, is Olsson's view, even though he holds that the woman's personal faith is unimpor-tant (n. 81 above).

[86]Bultmann, *Commentary,* 201; also Westcott, *John,* 163. In John only the believer can be-come a messenger or witness (15:27; 17:8, 18).

[87]See pp. 3—4 and note 8 (p. 4) above.

[88]Similarly Schnackenburg, *Johannesevangelium* I, 478. It is, therefore, inaccurate to hold that v 29 takes no account of vv 20—26 but is concerned only with vv 17—18; and to cite this as proof that vv 20—26 is a latter insertion which has not been integrated into the passage.

the primary, even exclusive function of witness in the Gospel[89]. Verse 41 mentions "many more" who believe in Jesus through personal contact with him during his two days' stay. The issue is the "increasing number of believers," not the "quality" of faith of these believers[90]. This means that the believers in v 39 are to be taken seriously. The speakers in v 42 are this first group of believers, not the "many more" who believe because of Jesus' own word (v 41). So terminology apart, the woman's report in v 29 stems from her personal experience of Jesus' self-revelation, reveals her faith in that revelation and inspires the same faith in her hearers. In the terms of the Gospel, it qualifies as a true witness.

The third and final evidence is that the Samaritans themselves recognize the woman's testimony as the initial grounds of their belief in Jesus (v 42). Bultmann's position that λαλιά means mere chatter as opposed to Jesus' substantial λόγος runs into conflict with the evidence of the Gospel itself which uses λαλιά and, copiously, the verb λαλεῖν as a technical term to describe Jesus' own proclamation. The references are too many to be listed here and may easily be verified from the concordance. But Jn 3:11 and 8:43, which Bultmann says have a different meaning, deserve special attention[91].

In 3:11 the expression   ὃ οἴδαμεν λαλοῦμεν
is synonymous with   ὃ ἑωράκαμεν μαρτυροῦμεν
and its content is described as   τὴν μαρτυρίαν ἡμῶν.

So λαλεῖν like μαρτυρεῖν describes the activity known as μαρτυρία. In 8:43 τὴν λαλιὰν τὴν ἐμὴν is juxtaposed with τὸν λόγον τὸν ἐμόν. Two interpretations are possible: either hearing Jesus' "word" is seen as a prerequisite for knowing his "speech" (if the leaders do not know Jesus' speech it is because they do not even hear his word), in which case λαλιά is rated higher than λόγος; or λαλιά is meant as a synonym for λόγος. The second alternative is the more likely interpretation, given the whole context of 8:43 and the significance attached to Jesus' λόγος in the Gospel. In 8:31 Jesus' plea to his audience to remain in his "word" comes after his speech (ταῦτα αὐτοῦ λαλοῦντος, v 30) which led many to believe in him. Λόγος (8:31) and λαλιά (8:43) are thus interchangeable and both describe the content of μαρτυρία. The woman's λαλιά in 4:42 is, therefore, not mere chatter any more than is Jesus' λαλιά in 8:43. Rather, the term describes her "word of witness" (v 39). It is not without reason that some witnesses have substituted μαρτυρία for λαλιά in v 42[92]. For it is this witness which first led some of the Samaritans to believe in Jesus.

---

[89]Even in the negative instances where Jesus testifies against the world (4:44; 7:7; 13:21; cf. 2:23–25) or where the Spirit does so (16:8–11), it is always in reference to the world's or the individual's refusal to believe in him and live. Thus, the Johannine conception of witness differs radically from the purely forensic or halakhic type.

[90]So, too, Becker, *Johannes*, 182–183; Olsson, *Structure*, 158–159.

[91]Bultmann, *Commentary*, 201, 210, n. 3.

[92]The following witnesses are noted by NA[26]: ℵ* D b l r[1].

This interpretation is reinforced by the thrust of v 42 which is concerned, not with the *quality* of the faith of the Samaritans, but with the *grounds* of that faith (οὐκέτι διά). The Samaritans do not disparage the quality of the woman's proclamation; all they say is that they *no longer* believe *because of her witness*. It is the same faith of the same group of people based on different grounds (vv 39, 42). In brief, the Samaritans who first believed in Jesus because of the woman's word now have a more solid basis for the same *faith*, their personal contact with Jesus during his two days' stay. There is even a suggestion that their initial "faith" in Jesus through the woman's word now becomes "knowledge" (οἴδαμεν) through their personal contact with Jesus himself. Faith as the basis of knowledge is well attested to in the Gospel, as de la Potterie points out (6:69; 8:31, 32; 10:38)[93]. But there is no suggestion whatever that their initial faith is not real. This "knowledge of faith," as Bultmann puts it, expresses itself here as elsewhere as confession (οὖτός ἐστιν, cf. 1:34; 6:69; 11:27)[94].

In this connection, αὐτοῦ rather than αὐτοί is the preferred reading in v 42. Αὐτοί lays the emphasis on "the hearers" of the word: You heard him, we, too, have heard him, so we both stand equal. This smacks of triumphalism and competition, a spirit wholly lacking in John (cf. 1 Cor 3: 3, 18—23), even if it reigned among the members of the Asclepius cult[95]. Αὐτοῦ on the contrary, shifts the issue from the comparative merits of the hearers of the word to that of the missionaries themselves. The question, then, becomes, not who has heard Jesus (first hand or second hand), for here second and first hand hearers are the same people in that order, but who is the primary evangelizer, the real converter of the Samaritans, Jesus or the woman[96]? The answer, obviously, is Jesus, even when in all appearances the woman first led them to him. This we have seen to be a key issue not only in vv 31—38 but throughout the Gospel wherever there is a reference to the mission of the disciples (15:1—8, 16; 17:18—

---

[93]De la Potterie, "la foi est le moyen de parvenir à la connaissance." *La Vérité* II, 553—558 (citation 553). This is true not only in those passages where the order is explicitly "faith" then "knowledge" (8:31—32; 6:69; 10:38), it is also what separates the Baptist, for instance, from Nicodemus (1:31—34; 3:2—10), as we have elaborated in " 'How Can These Things Happen?' " 14—19, esp. pp. 17—18.

[94]Bultmann, *Commentary*, 201.

[95]So Bultmann, *John*, 202, n. 1. Even if such a spirit existed among his audience, the Evangelist would hardly endorse it; his understanding of salvation as a pure gift rules out all boasting whether of the evangelizers or of the evangelized.

[96]As Bultmann himself (*Commentary*, 200, n. 5) acknowledges, he borrowed the concept of first-hand and second-hand hearers from Kierkegaard (*Philosophische Brocken*, esp. ch. 5), whose modern existentialistic outlook could not have influenced the Evangelist. As we noted in Chapter II (pp. 45—48, esp. p. 46), the ancients gave the same weight to a message, whether heard directly from the speaker or reported by a reliable witness. Contrary to Bultmann (p. 201), the Samaritans do not "criticize" the woman's proclamation. Haenchen, (*Johannesevangelium*, 248) also rejects Bultmann's view; but his reason that both the woman and the Samaritans first believed in Jesus as a "Wundermann" is equally debatable, especially in the light of v 25.

23; 21) or to the primary drawing/gathering activity of Jesus and the Father (6:44–45; 10:16; 11:52; 12:32). While the Samaritans acknowledge the initial and tantative role of the woman in inspiring their faith, they make it quite plain that Jesus, not she, is ultimately their evangelizer. In this they themselves confirm Jesus' point about the nature of the missionary role of the disciples in v 38. The Samaritans do not merely believe through Jesus, as they believed through (διά) the woman, the believe him to be the only Savior of the world (ὅτι). Therein lies the crucial difference, the faith that results in eternal life (20:31), and which the Samaritans share equally with the woman (vv 10, 13–14, 42).

Another important problem which arises still in connection with the reading αὐτοῦ or αὐτοί is the scope of ἀκηκόαμεν. What exactly have the Samaritans heard? If αὐτοῦ is adopted, then what they have heard is Jesus himself during his two days' stay with them. For as is well known, ἀκούειν not only takes the genitive of the person heard, but also refers to direct audition or hearing with the ears[97]. The context indicates that it is this direct audition which contrasts with the woman's report about Jesus and constitutes the firm basis of belief. But if αὐτοί is adopted, then the object of ἀκηκόαμεν cannot be Jesus himself but the same ὅτι-clause as that of οἴδαμεν. This alternative which is the generally accepted reading gives as the object of ἀκηκόαμεν the post-Easter proclamation of Jesus by the disciples, as in Acts 8:5–25[98]. So what the Samaritans hear, then, is not Jesus himself, but the report about him by people like Philip, Peter and John.

This interpretation obviously makes Jesus' two days' stay in Samaria completely insignificant in the story. V 42 thus grows, not out of the Samaritans' own experience of Jesus, but of some nebulous report about him. This view needs to explain how this later report about Jesus is different from that of the woman since both qualify as "hearsay". What sense would it make to reject the woman's report about Jesus as insufficient grounds for belief only to replace it by another report from some unspecified witnesses? Clearly the whole build-up in vv 39–42 militates

---

[97]This, according to *BDF*, no. 731 and Moulton, *Grammar III. Syntax* 161, is the classic rule. Also in cases of indirect audition, the genitive is used when a report is involved which one has received from the speaker "in any way at all" (*BAG*, 32, n. β). This consistent grammatical usage reinforced by the theological one would seem to favor the reading αὐτοῦ.

[98]The reading αὐτοί is adopted not only by NA[26] and most of the major commentaries, but also by some of the translations, e.g., RSV: "for we have heard for ourselves." The JB, however, has "we have heard him ourselves"; so, too, Olsson, *Structure,* 125. Most commentaries do not address the problem posed by the reading αὐτοί. Others attempt explanations which are contradictory but serve to show they are aware of the problem. Thus, Schnackenburg (*Johannesevangelium* I, 490) who believes that what the Samaritans hear is the whole Gospel, also holds that the saying concerns the impression (*Eindruck*) which Jesus' words made on the Samaritans; similarly, Lagrange: "ils sont entendu et ils savent, par la clarté qu'a faite en eux cette parole et cette présence" (*Jean,* 122). Haenchen (*Johannesevangelium,* 248) believes the Samaritans hear the Lord's own words in the message of the preachers.

against such an interpretation. The contrast is not between one missionary disciple and another but between all missionary disciples (represented by the woman) and Jesus himself whose mission is constitutive of all other missionary endeavors. The object of ἀκηκόαμεν must, therefore, be Jesus himself (αὐτοῦ)[99]. It is worth recalling, too, that the *demonstrative* type of oratory (under which we have classified vv 28—30, 39—42) is concerned primarily with the present situation.

The post-Easter proclamation of the disciples does not render Jesus' own proclamation irrelevant; so the hearing motif in the Gospel cannot be relegated to the post-Easter era only. If Jesus said anything at all during his life time, he must have done so in order to be heard by his own audience. Indeed, the degree to which his own audience listens to him determines the measure of attention which his disciples can hope to receive from their own audience (15:18—21; 17:14). Jesus' repeated complaint against his Jewish audience is that they do not listen to or accept him and his word (5:43; 8:43, 51, 52, 55; cf. 1:11). In Samaria, on the contrary, his word finds favorable reception by both the woman and the Samaritans. The Samaritan woman, in turn, serves as his initial witness to her fellow citizens (vv 28—30). This means that she herself is a believer since only believing witnesses can inspire faith in others (17:8, 20; 20:8, 30—31), and rightly so, because the ultimate goal of the witness is fellowship in Jesus between the witnesses and those who receive their witness (v 36; 1 Jn 1:1—4).

While the woman's response in v 29 is not indicative of her incomplete faith in Jesus, the cautious note in her statement registered by μήτι still needs to be accounted for. Bultmann rightly maintains that the question in v 29b is put from the viewpoint of the addressee. His view is shared by Moulton who cites 21:5 in support[100]. In our view, then, v 29b is a veiled confession couched in the form of a question in order to appeal to the personal judgment of the Samaritans, get them to reflect, and so arouse their interest in Jesus. In short, the "caution" forms part of the woman's technique of arousing the curiosity of her fellow Samaritans in order to lead them to Jesus: "Elle intrigue les gens au point qu'un groupe sort avec elle de la ville: ils vont à Jésus, déjà à demi-gagnés"[101]. This technique the woman first learnt from Jesus himself (vv 7, 10) and it may be compared to 1:46 where Philip repeats to Nathanael the words of invitation he first learnt from Jesus, "come and see" (1:39). Indeed, the parallels, as well as

---

[99]We are well aware that only minor witnesses (D a sy[c]) favor the reading αὐτοῦ. But our argument here as throughout the study is based not primarily on the weight of the witnesses but on the general thrust of John's theological viewpoint. Ultimately, it is the Evangelist's consistent theology which should judge the extant witnesses, not the reverse.

[100]Bultmann, *Commentary*, 193, n. 3 (citing Jn 7:26; Mt 12:23; Lk 3:15 as further evidence); Moulton, *Grammar I*, 170, n. 1.

[101]Louis Bouyer, *Le quartrième évangile* (Paris: Editions Maredsous, 1955), p. 109. See also Bultmann, (*Commentary*, 193), who remarks on the woman's method of arousing curiosity.

the differences, between Jesus and the woman in the missionary situation in Samaria are too striking to go unnoticed as the *chart* below reveals.

Item	*Jesus*	*The Woman*
Objection by others: the external impetus motivating the missionary undertaking	The Pharisees hear of the success of Jesus' disciple-making activity (v 1)	The disciples return and are shocked to see Jesus conversing with the woman (v 27)
Description of the initial missionary response	ἀφῆκεν, ἀπῆλθεν . . . λέγει αὐτῇ ὁ Ἰησοῦς (vv 3, 4)	ἀφῆκεν, ἀπῆλθεν . . . λέγει τοῖς ἀνθρώποις ἡ γυνὴ (v 28)
Method of engaging the partner by appealing for help	δός μοι πεῖν (v 7)	δεῦτε ἴδετε ἄνθρωπον, κτλ. (v 29a)
and arousing curiosity	εἰ ᾔδεις τίς ἐστίν (v 10)	μήτι οὗτός ἐστιν ὁ χριστός; (29b)
The encounter leads to the knowledge desired for the partner	ἐγώ εἰμι ὁ λαλῶν σοι (v 26)	οὗτός ἐστιν ὁ σωτὴρ τοῦ κόσμου (v 42)
The encounter is followed by a commentary on the missionary task	λέγει αὐτοῖς ὁ Ἰησοῦς ἄλλοι κεκοπιάκασιν	ἠρώτων αὐτὸν μεῖναι οἱ Σαμαρῖται αὐτοῦ ἀκηκόαμεν
with focus on the disciples' role	ὑμεῖς εἰσεληλύθατε (vv 31-38)	οὐκέτι διὰ . . . πιστεύομεν (vv 39-42)

Whether consciously intended by the Evangelist or not, the parallelism here highlighted gives the woman's missionary activity the character of a diptych of Jesus' own mission, but with the obvious difference that the woman cannot lay claim to Jesus' ἐγώ εἰμι. She leads her fellow citizens, not to herself, but to Jesus so that they can make their own personal discovery of him; the success of her method she owes to Jesus himself. Her fellow citizens press the point by confessing Jesus not her, as the sole "Savior of the world". The successful missionary not only witnesses to Jesus' deeds, he or she uses Jesus' method in approaching the audience because it is Jesus' mission still. He inspires every aspect of the disciples' mission.

The debate whether the title ὁ σωτὴρ τοῦ κόσμου is Hellenistic (as applied, for instance, to Roman emperors since the time of Hadrian) or

Jewish can never be resolved on this external level[102]. Bultmann is right that the title states what it is that "the believer knows"[103]; and all one can safely say regarding the meaning of the title outside the Gospel context is that the Samaritans themselves knew what they meant when they used it. The meaning intended by the Evangelist for his audience, for whose sake alone the Gospel was written, is also clearly indicated in the book. If Jesus is sent to "save" ($\sigma\omega\zeta\epsilon\iota\nu$) the world (3:16—17; 5:24; 12:47), to take away its sin (1:29), to be its light (8:12; 9:5; 12:46) and bread of life (6:33, 51), then it should come as no great surprise that he be confessed as the "Savior of the world." Jn 4:22 and the Gospel as a whole provide sufficient grounds for the use of the title. As noted in the commentaries, the title occurs only in one other passage in the whole of the NT, 1 Jn 4:14 ($\sigma\omega\tau\tilde{\eta}\rho\alpha\ \tau o\tilde{v}\ \kappa\acute{o}\sigma\mu ov$, cf. v 9), a work generally attributed to the same author as that of the Gospel, and where the emphasis on the world-dimension of Jesus' mission is equally outstanding. In the Gospel, this is yet one more title given to Jesus, God's end-time Messiah (1:9) not only in 4:1—42 (see vv 9, 15, 19, 25—26, 31 for the many titles given to Jesus in this passage), but also in the whole of chapters 1—4. These first chapters of the Gospel contain a display of Christological titles, none of which is considered adequate in itself[104].

Most importantly, the title in v 42 grows out of the Samaritans' personal experience of Jesus as the universal Messiah whose saving mission transcends Jewish national boundaries bolstered by socio-cultic practices (vv 9, 20, 22). Salvation does indeed take its departure point from the Jews, but it does not end with the Samaritans. The fruit of Jesus' mission is offered to any ($\pi\tilde{\alpha}\varsigma\ \acute{o}$) who are open enough to receive it (vv 13—14)[105]. In the Gospel as we now have it, there is not a more appropriate context to attribute this title to Jesus than in Samaria and by the Samaritans themselves. For it will be recalled that in the references cited earlier concerning the mutual hatred between Jews and Samaritans (pp. 84, and n. 17, 95—96 and nn. 36, 37) it is the Jews who prove to be the superior and contemptuous group (see, in particular, Sir 50:25—26). The same is true of the way the problem is formulated in vv 9, 20, 22[106]. That the

---

[102]For the discussion on this topic see *Str-B* I, 67—70; Delitzsch translates the title: הַמָּשִׁיחַ מוֹשִׁיעַ הָעוֹלָם on the basis of vv 22 and 25. See further Foerster/Fohrer, $\sigma\omega\tau\acute{\eta}\rho$, *TDNT*, VII, 1009—1021; Barrett, *John*, 244; Becker, 184, Brown, *John* I, 175; Haenchen, *Johannes-evangelium*, 248; Morris, *John*, 284.

[103]Bultmann, *Commentary*, 201.

[104]The inadequacy of these titles derives from the fact that Jesus is not simply "the Messiah/ Christ" (1:41; 4:25), the royal son of David and "king of Israel" (1:49), "a teacher from God" (3:2), or "a prophet" (4:19), but "God" (1:1), and, therefore, Son in the ontological sense of the word (1:18; 3:16; 5:18; 10:33, 36). So the Gospel seeks to evoke belief in him as "Christ *and* Son of God" (20:31).

[105]The emphasis on the individual permeates the Gospel: 3:16, 18, 20—21; 5:24; 8:51; 10:9; 12:47; 14:22—23; cf. Moule. "The Individualism of the Fourth Gospel," *Essays*, 91—109.

[106]In v 9a,c the Jews are in the nominative case, and the woman's surprise lies in the fact that

Samaritans themselves should then spontaneously confess Jesus as "the Savior of the world" through their own personal experience of him means that Jesus is "indeed" (ἀληθῶς) a Savior, not patronizing or condescending but setting free and bringing into fellowship (v 40; cf. 1:12—13; 8:34—36)[107]. Jesus' courtesy towards the Samaritans as earlier towards the woman (v 21) is revealed in his waiting patiently to be invited into the city and in his gracious acceptance of the invitation (v 40) despite the situation described in v 9c.

Jn 4:39—42 may look to a situation years later, and the possibility cannot be denied, though it cannot be proved. That, however, does not invalidate the meaning which the Evangelist wishes to convey by the way he has chosen to tell the story. We recall that our primary concern in this study is with the message which emerges from the way the story is told[108]. In the demonstrative type of rhetoric, the speaker is the educator and the concern is with the present situation[109]. In the story, the Samaritans are primarily addressing the woman in v 42, even as they address Jesus in v 40. The Johannine audience may then get the message by identifying with the different characters in the story. But the message lies in the way the story is told.

The confession of the Samaritans is public as is that in 1:34; 6:69; 11:27; and it grows out of the joint witness of Jesus and the woman. This is the central confession sought in the Gospel (20:31) and whatever form it takes, it always focuses on what Jesus' mission means for the audience who so confesses him[110]. In the case of John the Baptist, the confession (1:34) is preceded and followed by a public denial that he himself is the Christ (1:20; 3:23), a denial which is all the more striking given the positive way in which the question is put to him by the envoy of the Pharisees (1:19)[111]. Only the hardened hearer asks "who are you"

Jesus is the one making the request, contrary to Jewish practice (v 9c); in v 20, the harmless practice of the fathers is set against the eschatological dogma of the Jews (δεῖ). V 22 needs little comment, even though it is stated factually, not injuriously; 8:48 is the clearest case of all.

[107]The adverb in v 42 emphasizes not only the reality of Jesus' universal messiahship, but conviction of this fact on the part of the Samaritans themselves. See pp. 117—119 above on the meaning of salvation in John. Reconciliation is part of the setting free, such that those saved can now speak of "we" (cf. 1 Jn 3:1, 13; 4:17; 5:4) united with Jesus against the unbelieving world (cf. 1: 12—14), and no longer of "we," "you" (vv 9, 20, 22).

[108]Alter (*The Art of Biblical Narrative,* 179) notes that the "complexly integrated ways in which the tale is told" "requires us to learn new modes of attentiveness as readers." This, it must not be forgotten, is what we are trying to do in this study, using the contextual approach (pp. 50—51 above).

[109]Cf. Wuellner, "Paul's Rhetoric," 342. This is so since this type deals with praise or blame. Quintilian, *Inst. Or.* III.iv.9.

[110]The confessional passages (1:34, 49; 4:29, 42; 6:69; 11:27; cf. 9:38) are the human corollaries to Jesus' own "I am" (4:26; 6:35, 41, 48, 51; 8:12, 24, 28, 58; 10:7, 9, 11, 14; 11:25; 12: 19; 14:6; 15:1, 5).

[111]John's reply is striking in that the denial "I am not the Christ" is a most unexpected answer to the question "who are you?" (1:19—20).

(8:25) in an attitude of unbelief (οὐκ ἐπίστευσαν). This unbelief rests on satisfaction with own self-acquired knowledge (οἴδαμεν, 6:42; 7:27, 41; 9:24, 29; 3:2), with its resulting blindness to and rejection of Jesus' life-giving knowledge (5:39—40). In this passage, the confession of the Samaritans, like that of the woman, is shown to be a response to Jesus' own self-revelation, given as a gift (v 10). The following diagram illustrates this.

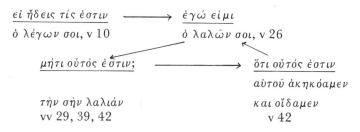

εἰ ἤδεις τίς ἐστιν ⟶ ἐγώ εἰμι
ὁ λέγων σοι, v 10   ὁ λαλῶν σοι, v 26

μήτι οὗτός ἐστιν; ⟶ ὅτι οὗτός ἐστιν
                                    αὐτοῦ ἀκηκόαμεν
τὴν σὴν λαλιάν   καὶ οἴδαμεν
vv 29, 39, 42   v 42

Like the woman, John the Baptist, Martha, and Peter, the Samaritans are open to the revelation of Jesus, and this openness leads to their recognizing and confessing him as the "Savior of the world." In the vision of the Gospel, the cycle of faith is incomplete without this open confession by the believer, a confession which, in turn, becomes a witness to its hearers. Indeed, genuine belief in Jesus is inseparable from a missionary impetus (cf. 1:38—46; 15:16). Since the purpose of the missionary enterprise is to give life to the full (10:10), restated in Peter's case as feeding the flock (21:15—17), the missionary (represented by the woman) does not lord it over those whom he or she evangelizes. Nor in the last analysis, are the evangelized indebted to him or her (v 42a) since both parties share in the same gift, the fruit of Jesus' mission (vv 10, 36, 38). Furthermore, the evangelized show the maturity of their faith by themselves revealing new dimensions of the shared faith in Jesus' inexhaustible revelation (v 42; cf. 16:12—14).

This point is made in many different ways in the Gospel. Jesus must go if the Holy Spirit is to come to the disciples and make them mature witnesses (16:7); John the Baptist must decrease if Jesus is to increase, and if he himself is to remain faithful to his mission given him from above (3:27, 30); Peter is given charge of the sheep, but himself remains Jesus' follower to the end, and has no say in the individual fate of the sheep (21:18—22); believers will do even greater works than Jesus himself (14: 12). The conclusion is obvious: as far as knowledge of Jesus is concerned the "more" is always yet to come (1:51; 16:12—15). If this is so, then no one has the final word about Jesus' revelation. Jesus himself lives on, the primary evangelizer of both individuals (14:21—23) and the community and continues to instruct ("sanctify in the truth") both present and future believers (17:19—20) or the Spirit does so in his name (16:12—15). Little wonder, then, that the Samaritans' knowledge of Jesus should surpass that of the woman. Yet both have this in common, that unlike the Jews (6:42, 52, 60, 66; 7:27, 40—51; 8:48—59; 9:24, 29; 10:20, 24—39), they are ready to accept Jesus' self-revelation, even though this revelation transcends their own previous expectations[112].

The issue of fellowship raised in vv 4, 9, 20, 22, 27 is resolved practically in vv 40–42 as it was conceptually in v 36. By accepting the invitation of the Samaritans and remaining with them two days, Jesus himself proves to be non-discriminating (for remember, it was the Jews who kept aloof from the Samaritans, not the other way around). His two days' stay also lends practical weight to his teaching that his mission is for all (vv 10, 13–14, 21–24). According to *Didache* (11, 5), two days was the traditional length of stay in any one place expected of the genuine missioanary/prophet. It was also not uncommon for converts to request their evangelizers to stay with them as proof that these missionaries really believed in the genuineness of their conversion (Acts 16:14–15). As we know from other sources, the issue of fellowship was the single most important social problem facing the early Christians (Gal 2: 11–15; Acts 10:9–11:18; Eph 2:13; 3:3–6). It is inconceivable then that the audience of the Gospel would have heard the story of Jesus' missionary activity in Samaria and yet not make any associations between this activity and their own experiences of mission, especially since Jesus is here presented as *the* evangelizer of Samaria.

This brings us to the final important issue raised in these concluding verses, namely the relation between the woman and the Samaritans or between the evangelizer and the evangelized in the context of Jesus' mission (v 42). Here we meet with the same puzzle as we did in v 38. These two statements seem uncalled for by the action either of the woman or of the disciples in the story, and read rather like meteors from the sky of the Johannine community. The intriguing question is why the Samaritans felt the need to tell the woman that they no longer believed because

---

112Research on the precise nature of Samaritan messianic expectation is so far very inconclusive (pp. 121–123 above). It is, however, highly improbable that the woman would ever have expected to meet the Messiah at a well as a wearied, thirsty, traveling Jew begging her for a drink. Moreover, in the light of her statement in v 20 and of her rejoinder in v 25 which is a response to Jesus' explanation in vv 21–24, the Messiah she is expecting is more an arbiter over the controversy surrounding Jerusalem or Gerizim as the right place to worship, than a teacher of "all things" in the strict sense of the word. Her ἅπαντα (v 25) is as gross an exaggeration as is her πάντα ὅσα (v 29). The former relates to the single issue of worship in much the same way as the latter refers to her marital history which is all that Jesus ever told her about her life (vv 17b–18).

Whatever the historical nature of the Samaritan messianic expectation, Haenchen (*Johannesevangelium*, 248, 256) contends that like the woman, the Samaritans initially went to see a "Wundermann" but only later came to recognize Jesus as the Savior of the world. Haenchen's position does not give adequate recognition to the second part of the woman's statement (v 29b). Besides, if v 29 were all that the Samaritans had to go by, Haenchen's position would be plausible. But the narrative economy or the necessarily summary nature of vv 28–30, 39–42 allows us to presume that the woman narrated her whole encounter with Jesus (vv 7–26). Still v 42 shows that their personal encounter with Jesus meant a consolidation of their faith in and knowledge of him first gained from the woman. The title "Savior of the world" may also have a reference to the issue of fellowship: Jesus did not come for a privileged few but for all peoples.

of her testimony. Was she boasting of her role in having led the Samaritans to Jesus or did the first group of Samaritans who believed because of the woman's testimony (v 39) feel inferior to the "many more" who believed through direct contact with Jesus (v 41)? Or is v 42a yet another indication of the common view that John's Gospel discredits the value of *signs* to awaken faith and gives this value to Jesus' *word* instead[113]? Does the statement then mean that the Samaritans believe not because of Jesus' "sign" reported to them by the woman (vv 17b—18, 29a) but because of his "word" ($\dot{\alpha}\kappa\eta\kappa\dot{o}\alpha\mu\epsilon\nu$)?

The hypothesis that v 42a stems from an inferiority complex on the part of the first group of believing Samaritans can be ruled out completely, for the Gospel gives no grounds for such a view: We saw this in discussing the choice between $\alpha\dot{v}\tau o\acute{\iota}$ and $\alpha\dot{v}\tau o\ddot{v}$ (pp. 173—174). The alternative view that Jesus' *word* is set against his *signs* as alone capable of awakening faith is much more complex and calls for a thorough discussion which is beyond the scope of the present study. Our view on this whole question, however, is that to date no scholar has offered any convincing proof that John's Gospel views Jesus' "signs" pejoratively[114]. Besides, the Samaritans did not personally hear vv 17b—18; they simply took the woman's vague word for it (vv 29—30, 39), such that whether it be with regard to Jesus or the woman, their response of faith is based on the "word" heard (vv 39, 42). Moreover, it is disputable whether vv 17b—18 count among the Johannine "signs."

With these two alternatives eliminated, we are left with the first hypothesis that the woman is probably boasting of her role in having led the Samaritans to believe in Jesus. This view finds support in the discovery that a polemic against the missionary disciples heavily underlies the Gospel. The whole point of v 42, then, as with v 38, is to emphasize the uniqueness of Jesus' role in the missioary enterprise. This point is first made covertly in vv 39—41: as soon as the Samaritan woman successfully leads out the Samaritans, the narrative shifts attention from her to Jesus; she fades into the background till v 42a when her role is relativized. The Samaritans' interaction with Jesus dominates the whole scene. While the woman's testimony is not rejected, the Samaritans own that they are ultimately not indebted to her for their belief in Jesus. The implication of v 42 with its emphasis on $\sigma\dot{\eta}\nu$ seems to be that whether spoken by Jesus himself or reported through the witness of others (vv 29, 39; cf. 17:20), Jesus' deed and word, the composite activity by which he accomplishes his Father's work, is the basis of belief (15:26—27; 20:30—31; 21:24). In 20:24—29 Thomas is upbraided by Jesus for not having believed the word

---

[113]See for instance, Boismard-Lamouille, *Synopse III*, 48—49; Haenchen's position (previous note) also implies this.

[114]De Jonge, ("Signs and Works in the Fourth Gospel", *Jesus, Stranger,* 117—140, esp. pp. 117—118), also challenges this interpretation of "signs" in the Gospel.

of his fellow disciples that they had seen him. Ultimately, the word of the disciples on mission is Jesus' word, just as Jesus' own word is that of the Father who sent him (14:10–12; 17:14, 20). This further indicates that the distinction between the λαλιά of the preacher and the λόγος of Jesus is alien to the Gospel. The woman reaps from Jesus both the content and method of her mission to her fellow citizens[115]. That the newly converted Samaritans can reveal to her a new dimension of Jesus' messiahship underscores the fact that she does not own the mission[116].

These, then, are the major missionary issues raised in vv 1–26, 27, 31–38 and recapitulated in vv 28–30, 39–42: method in approaching the audience, openness on the part of the audience, fellowship as the goal of the mission, the centrality of Jesus' role in the missionary enterprise and, correspondingly, the essentially subordinate and dependent nature of the disciples' mission. Of these, the last point is the most important as it was in vv 36–38. V 42 like v 38 grows out of the missionary situation of the Johannine community or audience and calls for an examination of the missionary *Sitz-im-Leben* of this audience as the external stimulus which shapes the Evangelist's understanding and approach to mission. This we shall undertake in the next Chapter after we have summarized the results of our exegesis of 4:1–42 and, in keeping with our contextual approach, sought corroborative evidence in the rest of the Gospel for its emerging missionary issues.

D. Summary of the Exegesis of 4:1—42

A detailed summary of the main missionary issues highlighted in the analysis of the setting (vv 1–6) and of each of the three main parts of the pericope (vv 7–26; 27, 31–38; 28–30, 39–42) is given at the end of each of these sections or parts thereof. The primary purpose of this present summary is to correlate the overall results of the exegesis of Jn 4:1–42

---

[115]Some scholars believe that the woman is not sent by Jesus, while others interpret her action in vv 28–29 as the fulfilment of Jesus' command in v 16. Whether or not this last point should be pressed, the fact remains that Jesus awaits the woman's return with the Samaritans and, furthermore, uses her missionary endeavor as the basis for his missionary instruction of the disciples (vv 31–38). Chrysostom and Westcott (n. 82 above) actually call her "an apostle".

[116]Is v 42, set against v 29, proof that the higher Christology in John came from the second generation of believers, notably the Samaritans? (So Brown, *The Community of the BD,* 28; cf. Cullmann, *Johanneische Kreis,* 45). The Gospel evidence in no way points in this direction. We have seen that the title "Savior of the world" grows out of the fundamental conception of Jesus' mission as being universal in scope; also, this conception is attributed to Jesus himself (3:16–18;

with the working hypothesis proposed at the end of Chapter III. This hypothesis, it will be recalled, is that the whole of 4:1–42, not merely vv 31–42, deals with mission, Jesus' mission from the Father, and that when viewed from this missionary perspective the episode forms a recognizably literary and thematic whole. Better to achieve this purpose, the present summary will focus on structure, setting and method of approaching the audience as the unifying elements of the pericope. Individual themes such as the importance of "gift" and "fellowship" as the goal of mission will be treated under one or other of these three headings. The summary will end with an attempt to assess the historical worth of the Samaritan episode.

1. Structure

Our analysis of Jn 4:1–42 revealed three distinct moments in the missionary enterprise: Jesus and the Samaritan woman (vv 1–26), Jesus and the disciples (vv 27, 31–38) and the Samaritan woman and the Samaritans *vis-à-vis* the mission of Jesus (vv 28–30, 39–42). Fundamentally, however, there is only one all-embracing theme in the whole passage, the mission of Jesus from the Father seen from the perspective of the non-believer (vv 1–26) and of believers in their capacity as missionaries (vv 27–42). The central thesis of the entire pericope is that Jesus is the sole eschatological and irreplaceable agent of God's gift of salvation who alone does and completes his work (vv 10, 25–26, 34, 42). Consequently (argument ἀκόλουθα)[117], all believers who receive Jesus' mission do but reap its fruit, whether they respond to it personally (vv 7–28) or lead othes to do so (vv 29–42). The inter-weaving of the main story (vv 1–26, 28–30, 39–42) with the missionary instruction of the disciples (vv 27, 31–38) underlines the essential unity of the conception of mission in the passage, the fact that the mission of the disciples is itself an integral part of Jesus' own mission.

This *thesis* and its *consequential argument* is developed contrastively in a series of orchestrations: in the *narratio* (vv 1–26), in the *expositio* (vv 31–38) and in the *demonstratio* (vv 28–30, 39–42). In the *narratio*

8:12; 9:5, 39; 10:36; 12:31, 46–47). In 4:1–42, the woman and the Samaritans are contemporaries, they both meet Jesus during the same trip through Samaria. In the Gospel, one and the same group of disciples is promised a fuller insight into Jesus' previous teaching (14:25; 16:4) as well as knowledge of as yet unrevealed truths (16:12–15). This acquisition of full knowledge about Jesus is attributed to the Holy Spirit, not to the Samaritans. Besides, 4:22 precludes any attempts to cut the Johannine Christology from its Jewish moorings. Georg Richter (*Die Fusswaschung im Johannesevangelium: Geschichte ihrer Deutung* [Regensburg: Friedrich Pustet, 1967] 288–295) also emphasizes the rootedness of the Gospel and its community in a Jewish milieu rather than in Samaritanism.

117Quintilian, *Inst. Or.* V.x.76.

the thesis is presented without comment in the narrative plot: Jesus and the Father are the only ones involved in the effort to lead the woman to a life-giving knowledge of Jesus (vv 10, 23). The disciples are absent throughout the conversation looking for food (vv 8 [pluperfect] 27). There is even a suggestion that had they been present Jesus' conversation with the woman might not have taken place. The exclusiveness of Jesus' and the Father's role in the missionary enterprise is also thematically illustrated in the discussion of the "gift of God" (gift of salvation, vv 10—15) and on true worship (vv 21—24), both eschatological realities which are brought about by Jesus' messianic mission (vv 10, 26) actively willed by the Father (vv 23—24). The thesis is also hinted at in the use of the verbs κοπιᾶν and ζητεῖν (vv 6, 23) which look forward to κοπιᾶν and κόπος in v 38.

In the *expositio* the thesis is expressed summarily in the concept of the Father's "work" given exclusively to Jesus to do and complete. Not only does the concept exclude all God's messengers who preceded Jesus, it makes the missionary participation of the disciples possible only at its completed or harvest phase. Consequently, the missionary participation by the disciples can be nothing other than a reaping of fruit or a receiving of wages (v 36). The point is reinforced by the contrasting imagery of sower and reaper applied to the Father-Jesus and the disciples, respectively, where the activity of the disciples is seen as no work by comparison to that of Jesus and the Father, or positively, as an entry into their labor (vv 37—38).

In the *demonstratio* the centrality and all-embracing nature of Jesus' mission is dramatized by both the woman and the Samaritans. The woman receives from Jesus both the content and the method of her proclamation to her fellow citizens (vv 28—30). The Samaritans, in turn, demonstrate both by their attitude (vv 40—41) and by their open confession (v 42) that Jesus, not the woman, is their primary evangelizer, the grounds or foundation of their faith.

Our analysis of 1:1—42 set against the positions of scholars extensively surveyed in Chapter III has indeed shown that the whole pericope can be reasonably comprehended in its literary and thematic unity when viewed from the standpoint of mission. Furthermore, the thematic structure and development of the passage clearly demonstrate that Jesus' mission from the Father is the standpoint from which the mission of the disciples is understood, not the reverse, as was regularly maintained in previous studies (cf. pp. 64—65). Far from relating Jesus' work to the mission of the church (Lindars, p. 69 above) or seeing his work as mission only from the standpoint of the post-Easter missionary activity of the disciples (Olsson, p. 70), the passage presents the mission of the disciples as an integral and very dependent part of Jesus' own mission. Not only is Jesus' mission constitutive of that of the disciples, but the whole conception of mission in 4:1—42, as indeed in the entire Gospel, takes its point of departure from Jesus' mission from the Father; it is sustained by it and culminates in it.

2. Setting

The prevailing trend in previous studies was to explain the significance of the setting of the episode in Samaria in terms of the legitimization of the Christian Samaritan mission (p. 65). Our analysis has shown, on the contrary, that the primary significance of the Samaritan setting lies in its rhetorical or persuasive and exemplary (παράδειγμα) force. Equally, the setting lends great weight to Jesus' teaching on the universality of his mission (vv 13–14, 21–24), on the gift-nature of this mission (vv 10a, 36a, 38) and on the importance of fellowship as the goal of the missionary enterprise (v 36b).

The rhetorical rule of the thumb is to choose the most representative case and leave the rest to interpretation and inference (20:30–31, cf. p. 46). Because of her sex, nationality and deplorable marital history (vv 9, 17b–18, 27), the woman represents the lowest grade of humanity to whom Jesus' mission of salvation could be directed. If such a woman, then, can be deemed worthy of Jesus' self-revelation, then nobody can be excluded from his saving mission. He is indeed "the Savior of the world" (v 42). Conversely, the favorable response given to Jesus' mission by the Samaritan woman and the Samaritans contrasts sharply with the unbelief of Nicodemus (3:1–21) and the Jews (2:13–25; 5–10) and so serves as a powerful appeal to the audience of the Gospel to believe in Jesus (pp. 112–113 and nn. 64, 65; 129).

On the theological level, the choice of the Samaritan woman and the Samaritans underlines the gift nature of Jesus' mission. Not only does his mission exclude no one (vv 13–14, 21–24, 42; cf. 14:23–24), it is in every sense of the word a "gift" (cf. 3:16–17) something which is wholly unmerited; not gained as patriarchal inheritance (vv 11–12, 20a), still less imposed (δεῖ) as superior theology (vv 20b, 22). Moreover, the free gift is not offered with indifference to any who are willing to receive it, it is made attainable by the Father's active seeking of such recipients through Jesus' mission and the imparting of the Holy Spirit (v 23; cf. 6:37, 44, 65; 12:32; 16:12–13; 20:22). From the perspective of the disciples, the gift nature of their mission (vv 36–38) is underscored both by the OT background evoked (vv 5, 38; Josh 24) and by the fact that, given the enmity between them and the Samaritans, they would hardly make it a point of achievement to bring the Samaritans and their like into their fellowship. Only on the level of grace (v 36, 38) is such mission made possible. Hence the glory of the mission cannot be accredited to them as missionaries (v 38).

The Samaritan setting is finally significant because the background of political (v 4), social (v 6) and religious (vv 20, 22) enmity which exists between Jews and Samaritans accentuates the importance and the reality of the fellowship which Jesus' mission establishes. The teaching on fellowship is given both conceptually (vv 21–24, 36) and practically (vv 7, 40–42). Conceptually, the eschatological realities of eternal life, true worship and missionary harvest which Jesus' mission brings unite into one lasting fellowship all those who receive this mission. This is because the operative norms of these realities differ radically from what obtains in the normal order: life-giving water opposed to water from Jacob's well; worship in spirit and in truth where the Father does the seeking of the worshipers, as opposed to Jerusalem-Gerizim controversy as the right place to worship ; the sad experience of one sowing for another to reap is replaced by mutual rejoicing precisely because the purpose of Jesus' and the Father's joint sowing is so that others may reap eternal life (v 36 ; cf. 3:16; 10:10). So all competition and complexes (superiority and inferiority) are eliminated because these gifts are offered on a non-exclusive non-competitive basis and because all recipients (both evangelizers and evangelized) work towards the same goal of eternal life (vv 10, 13—14, 36). On this level, all segregating barriers typified in the Samaritan/Jewish relationship disappear.

On the practical level, the importance of fellowship is highlighted first by Jesus' requesting a drink of water from the woman (v 7) and secondly, by his being invited and accepting the invitation of the Samaritans (v 40), which invitation fundamentally contradicts the experience of v 9. Jesus' two days' stay in Samaria, the increasing number of believers among the Samaritans (v 41) and the recognition by the Samaritans themsevles that Jesus is "indeed" the Savior of the world (v 42) all illustrate the reality of the eschatological joy brought about by Jesus' mission (v 36). Seen in this light, the setting in Samaria gives a deeper, wider and more unifying significance to the missionary thrust of the entire pericope than does the theory of the union of Ephraim and Judah or the legitimization of the Samaritan mission of which we found little evidence in our analysis[118].

3. Method in Mission

An essential aspect of the missionary undertaking is the interaction between the one sent and his audience, especially since the sole purpose of this undertaking is to evoke from the audience a faith-response to the divine agent and his message (pp. 4—6). Our extensive survey of previous studies on mission in the Gospel (Chapter I) evinced a serious lack of effort to explore this aspect of mission (see summary, pp. 34—35). Furthermore, while Jesus' preferential use of the dialogue as a means of communicating with his audience is self-evident, the real significance of this dialogue form as a means of mutual exchange or of promoting mutual

---

[118]It needs to be borne in mind that the weight of the argument advanced for seeing Jn 4:1— 42 as a legitimization of the Christian Samaritan mission rests on the assumption that "others" in v 38 refers to the evangelizers of Samaria (cf. Cullmann, *Johanneische Kreis,* 16, 51, 79—80). But we saw that both the contextual and theological meaning of the term precludes such an interpretation.

understanding between him and his dialogue partners was seen to be rendered practically *null* and *void* by the oft-cited feature of *double-entendre* (a feature whereby Jesus understands a reality of the supernatural order while his interlocutors understand one of the natural order). A further complication of the problem was the image of the Johannine Christ projected by Wrede, Bultmann and Käsemann, namely, that of a divine being who strides the earth barely touching it (p. 27). The total impression conveyed by both these theories was that the audience is of little consequence in the missionary enterprise since what matters is the Revealer and his message. Since this impression ran counter to the whole hortatory/persuasive thrust of the Gospel (20:30–31) and cast a serious doubt on both Jesus' and the Evangelist's declared evangelistic purpose, it demanded that the significance of the *double-entendre* and the whole portrayal of Jesus in the Gospel be critically re-evaluated.

Our analysis of 4:1–42 revealed that the dialogical exchanges between Jesus and his audience, the woman in particular (vv 7–26), were genuine exchanges. It showed to what lengths Jesus went out of his way to meet the situation of the woman, using her immediate concerns (water-fetching, Jacob's well, the issue of worship) as well as his own physical predicament as a thirsty traveler as the starting point. Not only did the conversation develop along lines in which the woman understood Jesus' initial request for a drink, but the woman herself determined throughout the conversation the categories used in communicating the revelation (pp. 128–131)[119]. The same applied in the case of the disciples: both the food and harvest imagery used (vv 32, 34, 35–37) were taken from their immediate concerns. Indeed the whole corrective tone of vv 31–38 seemed called for by their misplaced zeal (vv 27, 31, 33).

Another real advantage of the dialogue form itself is that it allows for the introduction of different topics: living water, marital history, worship, food and harvest, all of which are geared towards the intended message in each section of the conversation (vv 26, 38). Moreover, though these topics appear to be unrelated, they are in effect united by the background of eschatology ushered in by Jesus' mission, of which they convey different aspects (eternal life, true worship, missionary harvest) and which is the only context in which the whole pericope makes sense (Eschatology, pp. 165–168 above).

Jesus' genuine interest in the audience is further shown in his humble approach which gives the advantage to the dialogue partner, in his deep respect for the woman, in his deference for her views and that of the disciples, in his gracious acceptance of the invitation of the Samaritans, and in his leading both the woman and the disciples each in her/their own way through a process of discovery. Not only Jesus, but the woman, in

---

[119]These pages refer only to the brief summary of our analysis. But the reality in the exchanges permeates the whole dialogue, vv 7–26.

turn, employs relevant aspects of the same method in her approach to the Samaritans. The reality of the missionary undertaking is also underscored by the difficulty Jesus experiences in convincing the woman; the disciples, too, stand in need of his reorientation, and it took two days before the Samaritans ventured a personal confession of Jesus (v 42). Interest in the audience, however, rules out compromising the message of the revelation; it leads rather to emphasis on the radical newness of the realities established by Jesus' mission.

Far from betraying a lack of interest in the audience, the feature of *double-entendre* arises from a genuine interest in the situation and values held highly by the audience. It reveals the inevitable consequence of trying to convey realities of the heavenly realm in human language (cf. 3: 12), the only language meaningful to the audience. The feature in its most comprehensive form in the Gospel is "the Word become flesh" (1:1, 14), which fact causes not only misunderstanding among the audience, but is interpreted as blasphemy (5:18; 10:33, 36). Nevertheless, there is a real correspondence between the human categories used and the heavenly realities they are intended to convey: living water signifies eternal life in abundance (v 14; 10:10), harvest as a reaping of what is already sown conveys the notion of the fruit-gathering mission of the disciples (where Jesus and the Father do the sowing), physical birth evokes birth as children of God (3:3—7; 1:12—13), bread as that which sustains life illustrates the truth that Jesus is the very life of those who believe in him (6:26—58; 14:6; 5:39—40). So, despite its inadequacy, the human language remains the only cogent means of conveying the meaning of the life-giving message of Jesus' mission.

If, however, misunderstanding arises, it is not from a desire to confound the audience or overstress the importance of the message and the Revealer to the detriment of the audience. Rather, the lack of understanding underscores on the one hand, the need for revelation and on the other, that, ultimately, response to the message must rest on faith, not on human reasoning. For even after the further explanation given, the audience still fails to understand or grasp the import of the message (4:15; 3:9; 6:34, 41, 52, 60). The importance of faith as the condition for grasping the message is revealed in the openness to Jesus' message on the part of both the woman and the Samaritans in contrast to the incredulity of Nicodemus or the outright refusal to believe on the part of the Jews and, most especially, of their leaders (5—10; 12:37—42).That is why, in the Gospel, faith remains a permanent condition for discipleship (8:31—32; 15:1—8; 2: 22; 20:9).

Concerning the Evangelist, his interaction with the audience lies first of all in the use of dialogue the significance of which he obviously shares with Jesus, even if he did not actually invent this form as Jesus' preferential mode of addressing his audience[120]. Most specifically, however, the narra-

---

[120]The composition of the dialogues is generally attributed to the Evangelist. Though he may

tive is the means whereby the Evangelist generates and sustains the audience-involvement in the events portrayed and by which he gives this audience clues as to how the exchanges between Jesus and his audience are to be understood. A striking feature of his method in 4:1—42 is that almost all of his narrative sections and asides deal with the different situations of conflict, missionary (vv 2, 8, 27, 39—41) and social (v 9c, 27), which underlie the passage, and which evidently relate to the *Sitz-im-Leben* of the Evangelist and his audience. His interventions must, therefore, be seen not only as a means of getting his audience involved in Jesus' dialogue with his audience, but also of leading this audience to relate the issues raised in the dialogue to its own living situation. The Evangelist is, therefore, not only an exegete but a pastor. His narrative emphasis corroborates in many ways the message which Jesus himself emphasizes in the dialogue: the primacy of Jesus' role in the mission (4: 1—6, 26, 34) and the essentially harvesting nature of the disciples' missionary enterprise (4:2, and 4:36—38). So here again, Jesus' self-witness is reinforced by that of the Evangelist and the latter's distinctive contribution to the understanding of mission in the Gospel is, perhaps, to be sought in these areas of double-emphasis.

E. The Historical Question

The flavor of 4:1—42 is admittedly literary, to the extent that the episode is one of those chosen and carefully presented by the Evangelist in his "book" in order to bring out the significance of Jesus' mission and so persuade his audience to believe in Jesus (20:30—31). But to say that the story is a literary portrayed "example" of the dynamics and truths about Jesus' mission does not necessarily mean that it has no basis in history. Quite the contrary, for, according to Quintilian, for example to be convincing, it must be based on facts, not on fiction, since it is "impossible to prove what is doubtful by what is no less doubtful"[121]. A fictitious account of a faith-response to Jesus by the woman and the Samaritans would hardly persuade the living audience of the Gospel to make a

---

have given them their present Gospel form, one would be hard put to prove that Jesus did not use dialogue in addressing his Palestinian audience. The Synoptic Gospels abound in instances where he dialogues with a wide variety of people. For instance, Martha and Mary (Lk 10:38—42); the centurion (Mt 8:5—13); the father of the epileptic boy (Mk 9:14—29); the Syrophoenician woman (Mt 15:21—28; Mk 7:24—30); the rich young man (Mt 19:16—22); the two blind men (Mt 9:27—31); the Baptist (Mt 11:2—6); the Pharisees (Mt 9:1—12; 12:1—8, 22—45; 15:1—20); the seventy-two disciples (Lk 10:17—24); the disciples (Lk 9:10—20, 21—28; Mt 16:5—12, 32—39), and so forth.

[121] Quintilian, *Inst. Or.* V.xii.2. Lagrange also asks those who view the story as merely symbolic, or expressive of dogma: "Mais depuis quand est-il interdit au génie de s'appuyer sur la realité? Pourquoi ne lui emprunterait-il pas les traits qui signifient, qui expriment la verité?" *Jean*, 101.

true faith-response to him. Besides, interpretation presupposes the prior existence of the events interpreted (pp. 46—47). So Schnackenburg and those who share his view are right that the story has a basis in history[122]. It is, however, impossible to determine categorically from our extant sources the precise contours of this historical basis. Among other things, the portrayal of the woman coupled with the Evangelist's knowledge of the scene is too true to life to be a mere invention[123].

Luke 9:51—56 and Matthew 10:5 are often cited as proof against the historicity of Jn 4:1—42. None of these passages, however, as Jeremias also points out, supports this view[124]. "A village in Samaria" (Lk 9:52) is not synonymous with the whole of Samaria. Josephus shows that some villages were more open to jews than others[125]. According to Lk 9:56, Jesus turned to "another village" ($\dot{\epsilon}\tau\dot{\epsilon}\rho\alpha\nu\ \kappa\dot{\omega}\mu\eta\nu$), not to "another route" ($\dot{\epsilon}\tau\dot{\epsilon}\rho\alpha\nu\ \dot{o}\delta\dot{o}\nu$) after his rejection by one Samaritan village. Since Jesus was already in the Samaritan region (by the West Bank) he would have had to pass through Samaria somewhere to get to Jerusalem short of going all the way back to the region of Galilee to take either the coastal route or that by the Jordan valley[126]. The Lucan account, which also speaks of one continous journey to Jerusalem and the general conditions of travel which obtained in Palestine under Roman rule, lead one to conclude that "another village" (Lk 9:56) must mean "another *Samaritan* village." So Lk 9:51—56 does not rule out the possibility of the Samaritan mission of Jesus, Jn 4:1—42.

The Matthean evidence (10:5), in turn, concerns a one-time mission of the disciples during the lifetime of Jesus, not the mission of Jesus himself as is the case in 4:1—42. In the episode the disciples play no active part whatever in Jesus' interaction with the woman and the Samaritans, and their presence is very much kept in the background. Besides, the parable of the Good Samaritan (Lk 10:30—37) and the story of the one grateful leper out of ten (Lk 17:11—19) testify that Jesus did have contacts with the Samaritans during his lifetime. So the encounter in Jn 4:1—42 is neither historically nor theologically improbable.

A final objection to the historicity of the episode is that a "mass con-

---

[122]Cf. p. 67 above. Sharers of this view include those who hold that the Evangelist took over the story from the *Grundschrift* (p. 61 above) or that the story was preserved in Samaritan circles (pp. 10—11).

[123]Lagrange, founder of the Ecole Biblique in Jerusalem, notes, concerning the Johannine account, how struck one is, the more one gets to know the land, by "la parfaite exactitude des moindres circonstances." *Jean*, 101.

[124]Joachim Jeremias, Σαμάρεια, Σαμαρίτης, *TDNT* VII, 88—94, esp. 92—93 and n. 31.

[125]The same applies to present day Palestinian Arabs who, perhaps, are the modern counterparts of the biblical Samaritans, while the handful of modern Samaritans in Shechem are more friendly with the Jews than were their first century counterparts.

[126]It needs to be borne in mind that the journey was done on foot and that the mountainous terrain put limits to the routes that one could reasonably take. Cf. Jos. *BJ* 2.12.3—6 on the geography of Samaria and Judea.

version" of the Samaritans during Jesus' lifetime is highly unlikely, especially given the fact that there is no follow up to this conversion in the Gospel. Two observations need to be made concerning this objection. First, the idea of "mass conversion" is something imposed upon rather than attested to by the passage. The narrative speaks simply of an unspecified number of Samaritans who followed the woman out of the city (and there could not have been very many of them, given the circumstances) and came to believe in Jesus (v 30, 39, 42) and then of an additional number ("many more") who later believed as a result of Jesus' two days' stay in the city (v 41). It gives no indication, however, as to the precise number of these believers, nor does it imply that Jesus went outside the one city of Sychar which had invited him to seek converts (vv 40, 43). His missionary activity in Samaria is, therefore, much more restricted than that exercised later by Philip, Peter and John (Acts 8:4—25). Besides, it must not be forgotten that Palestine of this period was seething with messianic figures who had their ready followers, and Samaria was no exception (Jos. *Ant.* 18, 85—87; cf. n. 61, p. 109 above). So even within this historical context a large following of Jesus by the Samaritans would not be improbable.

The second observation is that the confession of the Samaritans belongs in line with that of Nathanael (1:49), Peter (6:68), the man born blind (9:38) and Martha (11:27). In all these cases, the practical follow-up of the confession must await the resurrection only after which believers are given the Holy Spirit (7:37—39; 20:22—23) and know experientially the significance of their belief in Jesus. The Samaritans are no exception to this general rule. All this is not to deny that the Johannine account may evoke echoes of the known historical development of the church, where persecution in Judea (Acts 8:1—3) leads to a very fruitful missionary endeavor in Samaria (8:4—25). Indeed some scholars have compared the progression of Jesus' missionary movement in John (from Jerusalem after the passover feast [2:13—3:22] through Samaria [4:1—42] to Galilee [4:43—54:6]) to the Lucan schema in Acts 8:1[127]. Ultimately, however, there is no documentary evidence for rejecting the basic historicity of the Johannine account in 4:1—42.

Concern with the historicity of the episode must not, however, distract from the Evangelist's primary focus in telling the story. His primary concern in the narrative is to project the all-embracing character of Jesus' mission. In this passage, this missionary activity is directed towards both non-believers (vv 1—26) and believers (vv 27—42). It brings about eschatological realities in the order of life, worship, and missionary partici-

---

[127]Strictly speaking, the Lucan schema is Jerusalem, Judea, Samaria and the ends of the earth (Acts 1:8), rather than Judea, Samaria and Galilee. Acts 9:31 places Galilee alongside Judea before Samaria. It is more likely that the mission was preached in Galilee first before Samaria, since the first disciples were almost all Galileans (Jn 7:52).

pation and aims at creating a lasting fellowship among all its recipients. Jesus' role in the missionary enterprise is unique, primary and irreplaceable. This last point is stated polemically in our passage, in the deliberate attempt to relativize the missionary role of the disciples (vv 38, 42). The core of the Johannine approach to mission lies precisely here and is rooted in his fundamental missionary hermeneutic that God's work of salvation done and completed once and for all by Jesus is essentially and in every respect a gift (3:16). While his narrative and narrative-dialogue section underscore this fact (vv 1–6, 39–42), his best approach is to let Jesus himself comment on roles and relationships in the missionary enterprise (vv 31–38), for, what "carries greatest weight in deliberative speeches is the authority of the speaker" coupled with his own "excellence of character" (Quintilian, *Inst. Or.* III, viii. 12).

The treatment of the missionary role of the disciples, in our view, holds a special clue to the missionary *Sitz-im-Leben* of the Evangelist and his audience. We shall examine this situation in Chapter VII after we have sought corroborative evidence in the Gospel (Chapter VI) for the key missionary issues highlighted in the analysis of 4:1–42.

Chapter VI

John 4:1−42 in its Gospel Context

The twofold purpose of this present study, it will be recalled, is to highlight the Evangelist's approach to mission and, as far as possible, to discover the actual living situation which could have forged his conception of mission. Salient features of his approach emerged in our analysis of the basic text, 4:1−42. But before these features can be regarded as characteristically Johannine and, consequently, be used as the basis of an enquiry into the missionary situation of the Evangelist and his audience, the results obtained from 4:1−42 need further to be substantiated with supportive evidence from the rest of the Gospel. Accordingly, this present Chapter will attempt to place within the wider context of the Gospel the leading missionary features highlighted in 4:1−42. On the basis of this wider Gospel evidence, Chapter VII will initiate a discussion on the possible missionary *Sitz-im-Leben* of the Evangelist and his audience.

A. Salient Features of the Johannine Approach

The major results of our analysis of 4:1−42 came under four headings: 1) the structural and thematic unity of the passage, 2) the methodological dynamics involved in the actual execution of the mission, 3) the theological issues of salvation seen as God's gift and of fellowship seen as the goal of the missionary endeavor, and 4) the issue of the relationship between Jesus and the disciples in the missionary enterprise. Concerning no. 2, we saw that Jesus' interaction with his audience permeated the whole of 4: 1−42. In order, therefore, to determine adequately whether or not a similar interaction occurs in Jesus' dialogue with his other partners in the Gospel (for instance, Nicodemus, 3:1−21, the Jews and their leaders, 5−10), we would need to subject these other dialogues to the same thorough scrutiny as was conducted in the case of 4:1−42. Since such an undertaking would be impractical at this juncture, we will defer the analysis of these other dialogues for a future undertaking. Their character and importance, however, should at least be acknowledged here.

These *forensic passages* are particularly important, and so deserve a treatment of their own, not only because they portray a different style of Jesus' interaction with his audience, but also because of the problem posed by their very polemic character. It will be recalled that the polemic element in these dialogues, as in the treatment of the Baptist's mission, constitutes for many scholars the single most important reason why John's Gospel cannot be viewed as a missionary document (pp. 14—15 above). Our firm conviction, however, is that when the forensic element itself is viewed as part of the general rhetorical framework which underlies the Gospel, the missionary character of these passages will emerge in a positively new light. It is almost phenomenal that, its great significance for the understanding of the Gospel notwithstanding, this rhetorical character has received to date next to no attention in Johannine studies[1]. Since the forensic type is rhetoric at its best, we feel justified in leaving aside these passages for a separate study[2].

Of the remaining three issues, the question of Jesus' relationship with his disciples in the missionary enterprise proves to be the most crucial for our present purposes. Not only does this topic promise to hold the key to the understanding of the Johannine approach to mission and to the missionary situation of the Evangelist and his community but this missionary situation itself may have played a determinative role in the Evangelist's whole presentation of Jesus' life and work (the Gospel) from the primary standpoint of mission (pp. 1—7 above). Our examination of the Gospel material will, therefore, focus on this issue (no. 4) and the other two issues (nos. 1 and 3) will be discussed in relation to it. In other words, our ensuing examination of the Gospel material will focus on the ways in which the Evangelist underlines the respective roles of Jesus and the disciples in the missionary enterprise.

Our discussion of the *thematic and structural unity* of 4:1—42 revealed that the whole episode is concerned with Jesus' mission from the Father viewed from three different but successive perspectives: the *narratio,* Jesus and the non-believer on the level of missionary dialogue (vv 1—26), the *expositio,* Jesus and the disciples on the level of missionary instruction (vv 31—38) and the *demonstratio,* the disciples and other believers on the level of missionary interaction (vv 28—30, 39—42). The significance of the pattern lies in its emphasis on the all-embracing nature of Jesus' mission, which, ultimately, is the one and only mission in the Gospel; all the other missions are in function of it. The same structural pattern with obvious modifications underlies the Gospel viewed from the perspective of mission[3], and the parallelism between our basic text and the Gospel may be mapped out as follows:

---

[1] A fuller consideration of the significance of the rhetorical framework for the understanding of the Gospel is offered in our concluding chapter, pp. 306—310 below.

[2] For descriptions of the forensic type of rhetoric see Quintilian, *Inst. Or.* III.ix.1—9; V.*Praef.* 5; VI.iv.1; VIII. *Praef.* 11; and Aristotle, *Rhet.* 1.2.; 1.3.3.

[3] Different structual approaches to the Gospel were mentioned earlier (p. 52, n. 43). Also worth noting is Giblin's recent suggestion ("Miraculous Crossing," 103, n. 41) that the Gospel has a tri-

	Basic Text	Gospel
exordium	4:1—6	1:1—51
narratio	4:7—26	2—12
expositio	4:31—38	13—17
probatio	(4:34)	18—20
demonstratio	4:28—30, 39—42	21:1—25

In both cases, the *exordium* introduces Jesus as God's sole agent of salvation, even the one who wins followers from the Baptist (4:1; 1:29—51; cf. 3:22—36)[4]. The *narratio* centers on his interaction with a variety of interlocutors with a view to eliciting from each a faith response to him. The *expositio* embodies his personal commentary on the missionary enterprise, his explanation to the disciples of the meaning of his mission and of the nature of their participation in it. The *probatio*, the crowning point of Jesus' mission, his ὑψωθῆναι/δοξασθῆναι, is only announced in 4:34b (cf. 19:30)[5]. But this very glorification (18—20) constitutes the definitive proof that he alone is the Father's eschatological agent of salvation (3:13—17; 8:28, 30—36; 12:32). In the Gospel, then, as in 4:1—42, only when Jesus' mission has been completed (1—20), and the disciples themselves have been instructed about it (13—17) and equipped for it by the giving of the Holy Spirit (20:22; cf. 7:37—39; 14:16—17, 25; 15:26—27; 16:7—15) do they actually begin their fruit-gathering, fish-catching mission (4:36; 21; cf. 6:1—15).

Most strikingly, the treatment of the thesis and of its consequential argument also follows the same pattern in the body of the Gospel as in 4:1—42. Jesus' personal commentary on the missionary task (13—17), given after his dialogue with a variety of people (2—12), is followed by the Evangelist's dramatic portrayal of the central issue embodied in the commentary. Jn 21 thus serves the same function as 4:28—30, 39—42; it dramatically portrays in the actual exercise of mission the disciples' dependence on Jesus spelled out in detail in the farewell discourses, especially in Jn 15 and 17. As in 4:31—42, the lesson concerning their dependence is doubly consolidated, by Jesus' instruction and by the Evangelist's dramatic portrayal. The illustrative function of Jn 21, like that of 4:39—

---

partite structure based on geographical units: 1) 1:19—4:54; 2) 5—10; and 3) 11—20, with 1:1—18 and 21:1—25 as the "prologue" and "epilogue," respectively. Important as the question of structure is for the understanding of the Gospel, this issue cannot be treated as an isolated topic, since the *dispositio* is in function of the argument. To be of value, therefore, any structures proposed must needs be integrated into the central concern of the Evangelist as stated in 20:30—31. The structure we have highlighted here grows out of our present approach to this concern. Other approaches to the issue will, no doubt, reveal other structural patterns.

[4] In " 'How Can These Things Happen?' " 10—14, 19—21, we demonstrated in some detail that the Baptist's witness in 3:27ff. ends, not in v 30, as is held by most critics, but in v 36. His witness has a double dimension: personal, vv 27—30 and kerygmatic, vv 31—36. Our suggestion was viewed favorably by Boismard, the modern expert on the Johannine redaction.

[5] It is also worth noting that 19:28—30 looks back not only to 4:34 (the reference to the "completion" of the work) but also to 4:7—15, the motif of "thirst."

42, perhaps explains why this chapter has the character of an epilogue. From the Evangelist's approach to mission, however, it forms an integral part of the Gospel narrative[6]. The core of the lesson in both 4:1–42 and in the Gospel centers upon Jesus' primary, causative and irreplaceable role in the missionary enterprise, as a result of which the disciples' mission is essentially derivative, dependent and self-benefiting (4:38, 42; 15:1–8, 16; 17; 21)[7].

The whole Gospel thus has a unified view of mission understood exclusively from the standpoint of Jesus, not that of the disciples. In other words, the Gospel does not try to contain Jesus' all-encompassing mission, summed up in the ἔργον except (4:34; 17:4), within the restricted category of the disciples' mission, best understood as an entering into the labor of others (4:38). Moreover, Jesus' mission is seen as a continuum from the incarnation to the glorification (16:28), where the glorification constitutes its final and abiding phase (19:30), the phase when the Spirit enables both believers and prospective missionaries actually to reap its fruit[8].

The dominant tone in the whole portrayal of the disciples' mission in the Gospel as in 4:38, 42 is polemical (13:14; 15:5, 16; 21:21–22). The polemic overtone is perhaps less marked in the farewell discourses than in 4:38, 42, but its very presence in this overtly hortatory section of the Gospel is all the more striking. This polemic thrust reveals itself in the consistent effort throughout the Gospel to emphasize the disciples' total dependence on Jesus both for their personal life and their missionary fruitfulness (15:5, 16; 17:19; 21)[9]. We shall examine first the treatment

---

[6]The relation of Jn 21 to the rest of the Gospel is a much debated issue because of the apparently concluding nature of 20:30–31. Minear's recent article ("The Original Functions of John 21," *JBL* 102 [1983] 85–98) is fundamentally right in re-emphasizing that Jn 21 belongs to the same hand as the body of the Gospel. But few would endorse his position that "the signs which Jesus worked" (20:30) refer only to the resurrection appearances. This interpretation runs into a number of contextual problems which we cannot go into here. The whole issue of the relationship between 20:30–31 and 21:1–25 merits further discussion in the light of the significant findings of this present research, in particular, the rhetorical framework of the Gospel.

[7]These structural and theological parallels between 4:1–42 and the body of the Gospel, perhaps, justify the view of those scholars who believe that 4:1–42 was composed as an independent unit and inserted later into the Gospel. Whether or not this is true, the similarities we have highlighted here between our basic text and the rest of the Gospel seem to arise from a common theological approach to the same missionary problem rather than from a conscious effort to reproduce an already existing pattern. The author's method of approach thus reveals itself not only in the macrocosm of the Gospel but also in the microcosm of 4:1–42. See pp. 41–42 above.

[8]Jesus' giving up the Spirit (19:30) indicates not only an act of death, but also his transmission of the Spirit of life (6:63) to believers. This interpretation is grounded in 7:37–39 and 16:7 which specifically link the giving of the Spirit to Jesus' glorification/departure (cf. 20:22). See further pp. 97–98 and 165 above.

[9]The disciples' need for dependence on Jesus is also emphasized in Jn 6 which is discussed below in connection with Jn 21. Though Jn 6 is addressed to the crowd, the message that Jesus is the bread of life applies also to the disciples; vv 67–71 make this clear. Jesus' mission is to give life to "all flesh" (17:2–4); 15:1–8 drives home the importance of this point for the disciples themselves.

of this central issue by Jesus himself in the farewell discourses, then its dramatic and summative portrayal by the Evangelist in the concluding chapter of the Gospel (Jn 21).

1. The *Expositio*: Jesus' Commentary on the Missionary Task, Jn 13–17

a) Central themes

The farewell discourses lend themselves to a number of interpretative approaches, both thematic and redactional[10]. But in keeping with our general policy in this study, we shall approach them in their final Gospel form. Our interest centers on the different ways in which Jesus ennunciates for the disciples the significance of his mission as this pertains to them personally. To facilitate our task, we shall focus on the following three topics which seem to encapsulate the missionary lessons given to the disciples in these discourses. These are humility in the exercise of mission, the universal scope of Jesus' mission, and fellowship viewed from the specific standpoint of mission. Since these lessons are summed up conceptually and liturgically in Jn 15 and 17, respectively, we shall pay special attention to each of these passages.

It is worth noting in passing that a number of the motifs and sayings found in the Matthean and Lucan missionary discourses occur in John, and at times verbatim, in these farewell discourses[11]. One cannot but wonder whether these discourses might not be the Johannine version of the Synoptic missionary charge (Mt 10; Lk 9:1–6; 10:1–25). If this is so, then it is also striking that John places this charge as close as possible to the conclusive event of Jesus' mission, namely, his glorification (Jn 18–20). This placement, which differs markedly from that of the Synoptics (the *dispositio* is very much part of the argument), again underlines his position that Jesus alone does and completes the Father's work (17:4)[12]. This argument gains in force when it is remembered that, unlike the Synoptics, John records no missionary undertaking of the disciples during

---

[10]Outside the commentaries, the most recent comprehensive bibliography on Jn 17 and the farewell discourses is that of Ritt, *Das Gebet zum Vater*. Substantial works which have appeared on these discourses since the publication of Ritt's book include the dissertations by D. B. Woll, *Johannine Christianity in Conflict: Authority, Rank and Succession in the First Farewell Discourse* (SBLDS 60; Chico: Scholars Press, 1982) and G.C. Nicholson, *Death As Departure: The Johannine Descent-Ascent Schema* (SBLDS 63; Chico: Scholars Press, 1983). See also Segovia, "John 15:18–16:4a: A First Addition to the Original Farewell Discourse?" *CBQ* 45 (1983) 210–230.

[11]We may, for instance, compare the following Johannine and Synoptic passages: Jn 13:16; 15:20 and Mt 10:24; Jn 13:20 and Mt 10:40; Jn 15:21 (1 Jn 3:13) and Mt 10:22; Jn 15:23 and Lk 10:16; and Jn 16:2 and Mt 10:17, 21. The predominance of the Matthean material in these parallels would indicate that the tradition does not derive from Q, if such a source ever existed in a single version.

[12]On the importance of the *dispositio* for the argument see, for instance, Quintilian, *Inst. Or.* III.ix.1; IV.iii.15; and all of VII.

Jesus' lifetime, even though he regards their missionary fruitfulness as an integral part of their call (15:2, 16).

In general the farewell discourses propose Jesus as the model for the disciples to follow in their exercise of mission (13:15); but striking exceptions to their imitation of him shall emerge in the course of our analysis. Indeed, the καθὼς ἐγώ, καὶ ὑμεῖς motif receives its most appropriate rhetorical application in respect to Jesus and the disciples in these farewell discourses[13]; of this the footwashing (13:1–11, 12–17) constitutes the most vital visual and conceptual symbol.

Humility in the exercise of mission

The evidence of 4:38–42 allows us to infer that the basic problem with the missionary disciples addressed lies in their tendency to forget that they are sent by Jesus and to appropriate the glory of the missionary enterprise[14]. The double reminder that they do but reap the fruit of Jesus' and the Father's labor (v 38) and that the faith of believers is not accredited to them (v 42) makes sense against this background which betrays an attitude of pride and boasting on the part of the missionary disciples. This same warning against the spirit of self-aggrandizement is registered proverbially in 13:16, and in 15:16 (cf. 12:26). In place of this attitude, Jesus seeks to inculcate in the disciples a spirit of humility. He does this both by his own personal example of washing their feet (a social action assigned to slaves, as explained in vv 12–17) and by his intense prayer to the Father from whom he received the mission (17:4) and on whom he depends for its final accomplishment, his glorification (v 1; cf. 8:54, 12:28). Since these two actions (the footwashing and the prayer) open and close the discourses, Jesus' missionary instruction of the disciples is thus placed squarely within the context of humility exercised towards both the human audience (the disciples themselves, 13:1–17) and the sending Father (Jn 17)[15].

In rhetorical terms, 13:1–17 may be described in Daube's words as a perfect example of the "mystifying action of the master" (vv 1–8), which causes "perplexity" in the "circle of disciples" (vv 9–11) as a pre-

---

[13]See our earlier discussion on the καθὼς, οὕτως motif, p. 54, n. 49 above.

[14]We recall Fridrichsen's view (p. 28, n. 88 above) that the Gospel was written from the standpoint of a very successful Christian mission. V 38 certainly gives this impression. Nonetheless, it needs to be borne always in mind that missionary success need not be confined in John to outreach to non-believers. The believer's faith itself is a reaping of the fruit of Jesus' and the Father's labor.

[15]The Synoptics also present Jesus as a model of humility and service for the disciples to follow: he came "not to be served but to serve" (Mt 20:26–28; Mk 10:42–45); or is among the disciples "as one who serves" (Lk 22:24–27). In Matthew 18:2–4 the disciples are told to imitate the humility of a child if they wish to be the greatest in the kingdom of heaven. The same emphasis on humility is underlined in 23:8–12 put in the context of the "woes" against the Scribes and Pharisees whose oppressive authority the disciples are not to imitate. See further 2 Cor 8:9 on the enriching and imitable poverty of Christ.

lude to a lesson given in the "explanation of the action" (vv 12–17). Jesus' action, however, is more than a mere rhetorical exercise. The foot-washing, as Richter rightly observes, illustrates the true nature of his mission, namely, life-giving service (3:16–17; 4:10, 14; 10:10; 17:2–4)[16]. The force of the example lies in that the master is the one washing the feet of his disciples, yet the disciples are exhorted thereby to wash, not the feet of their slaves, but one another's feet (13:16). Strictly speaking, then, they cannot imitate the depths of Jesus' humility; even here he surpasses them. No wonder their imitation of him is seen as a "beatitude" (v 17), which motif evokes grace and gift rather than merit (cf. 1:16–17)[17].

Finally, Jesus' humility, exercised concretely in the slave-like service of the disciples, forms part of the manifestation of his utmost love, the bedrock on which mission rests (3:16; 13:1). In his case, this love is literally carried to the extreme (εἰς τέλος, 13:1) in his physically laying down his life for his friends (cf. 10:15; 12:24; 17:19), the disciples themselves (15:13–14). The disciples may imitate him in this extreme love (12:25–26; cf. 15:12–13, 17; 21:18–19); even then, they do but "follow," his example (12:25–26; 13:16; 21:19b–22), and are personally honored for it (12:26b).

The scope of the mission

Though historically Jesus exercised his mission in Palestine, the scope of this mission is the whole world (1:9, 10a; 3:16–17; 16:28), and its destined audience, "all flesh" (17:2; cf. 12:32). He is in the world (1:10a), "speaks in" (λαλῶ ἐν, 17:13) and "to" (λαλῶ εἰς, 8:26; 18:20) the world. Palestine like Samaria serves a paradigmatic function. As Jesus' immediate audience in Galilee (1:29–2:12; 4:44–54; 6:1–7:9; 21), Jerusalem (2:13–3:21; 5; 7:10–10:39; 11:55–57; 12:12–20:31), Judea (3:22–36; 11:1–54; 12:1–11) and Samaria (4:4–42) were challenged to respond to him, so are all peoples of the world challenged to make the same faith response to the same mission of Jesus accomplished once for

---

[16]For a detailed description of this rhetorical type, see Daube, *NT and Rabbinic Judaism*, 183. Strangely enough, Daube does not mention Jn 13:1–17 among the NT references he cites here. Richter (*Fusswaschung*, 288), like Thüsing (*Erhöhung*, 133, n. 42), sees the footwashing as a "sign" comparable to other "signs" in the Gospel. For him the sign character of the footwashing lies in its soteriological and Christological significance; it points to Christ's salvific death on the cross, the conclusive proof that he is the Messiah (pp. 287–300).

[17]Jn 13:17 and 20:29 are the only two instances where the adjective μακάριος is used in the Gospel. In both passages, the notion of "being blessed" has a soteriological significance; this is most obvious in 20:29. That this is also true of 13:17 is indicated in 13:6–8: partnership with Jesus involves serving as he serves, and this partnership comes as a gift from Jesus (v 7). Hauck (μακάριος, *TDNT* IV, 369–370) holds that in the NT the motif of blessedness "refers overwhelmingly to the distinctive religious joy which accrues to one from sharing in the salvation of God's kingdom." Cf. Rev 1:3; 22:7.

all during his earthly sojourn in Palestine. Whether personally proclaimed by him or reported later by his disciples (17:20; 20:30—31; 21:24—25; 1 Jn 1:1—3), Jesus' self-revealing mission, which is in effect the revelation of the Father (1:18; 17:6), constitutes the one and only saving mission for the world[18].

In the Gospel, the world in the literal sense (as a cosmic entity) needs, of course, to be distinguished from the world in the metaphorical sense (as the sphere of unbelief). The former is God's creation (1:3, 10b), the object of his love even unto salvation (3:16, 17; 12:47; cf. 1:29; 4:42; 1 Jn 2:2; 4:9, 14), both effected through Jesus as "Word" and "Son." The latter designates the world of sin and darkness which rejects Jesus, the light (1:5, 10c—11; 3:19—20) and "hates" both him and the Father and those who belong to him (7:7; 15:22—23; 15:18—19; 17:14a; 1 Jn 3:1, 13). This is the world for which Jesus does not pray (17:9), and to which he cannot reveal himself because of its very resistance to him and his Spirit (14:17, 22—24). This is the world from which Jesus dissociates himself and his followers (8:23; 17:14, 16; 1 Jn 2:16; 4:17), a world which has its own prince (12:31; 14:30; 16:11), prophets, followers and value systems (7:7; 8:44; 1 Jn 4:1, 5; 2 Jn 7), and which Jesus' followers must not love (1 Jn 2:15)[19]. But since belonging to the world is a matter of personal choice, not of ontological dualism as at Qumran[20], Jesus' accomplished mission abides, despite its rejection, as a permanent offer of salvation to this very world (14:23; cf. 1:5; 16:33). To this end the disciples and the Spirit remain in the world (17:15, 18—23; 16:8—11; 13: 35), though Jesus himself no longer remains visibly in the world (14:33; 17:11).

Strictly speaking, therefore, unlike the successors of the halakhic messenger, the disciples do not continue Jesus' mission beyond the geograph-

---

[18]The universal focus of Jesus' mission so pervades the Gospel that it is wholly unconvincing to seek to relegate this mission to the confines of Judaism, Diaspora or otherwise. Cf. Robinson, *Redating*, 293. Even more strange than Robinson's position is Martyn's view (e.g., *Gospel in History*, 66, 120) that "the world" refers to the "Jewish Quarter" in the Evangelist's city. It is equally unsatisfactory to attribute this world-focus of Jesus' mission in the Gospel to a secondary redactor. For when this focus is eliminated what we are left with is a completely different Gospel, in which case the issue seems hardly relevant to the discussion of the present "book."

[19]The injunction in 1 Jn 2:15 not to love the world is interpreted as evidence of the author's pessimistic attitude towards the world as evinced, for instance, in 2:17 and 5:19. But when this "world" is understood as that which deliberately rejects its maker (Jn 1:10—11) and is bent on its own pursuit of pleasure, then one can at least sympathize with the author's stance. His approach to the world is perhaps much more uncompromising than is ours today. It is to be noted, however, that the author never counsels his audience to nourish "everlasting hatred" of those outside the community, as does Qumran (1QS 9:21; Vermes, *The Dead Sea Scrolls in English*, 88 and n. 20 below).

[20]Vermes (*The Dead Sea Scrolls*, 51) rightly sees the whole of the War Scroll (1QM) as a theological treatise concerning the struggle of the "Sons of Light" (the members of the Qumran sect) against "the Sons of Darkness," particularly the Kittim (the Gentiles). See further 1QS 3:13—4: 25.

ical limits reached by him. This would be the case if, as Borgen maintains, Jesus were portrayed as a halakhic agent[21]. Whatever may be said about the influence of the halakhic principle on the Johannine portrayal of Jesus as "one sent," there is this fundamental difference between the Johannine Jesus and the halakhic agent: theologically, the disciples do not continue Jesus' work "beyond the limitations of his work in Israel" as Borgen maintains. The reasons are as follows: first, though the events narrated in the Gospel take place in Palestine, the Gospel makes it quite plain, right from the outset, that Jesus' mission is to the world (1:9–10; 3:16–17; 10:36; 12:47b; 17:18a). Secondly, the disciples themselves are sent to the same world as Jesus himself was sent by the Father (17:18b), so their spheres of action are not lineo-spatial but identical. Thirdly, the completion of Jesus' work necessarily includes expansion beyond Israel (12:32, to be read within the context of the coming of the Greeks, 12:20–36; cf. 7:35). Fourthly, while Jesus co-opts the disciples into his mission, he is not replaced by them; rather, he continues actively to work in them such that without him they can do nothing (15:5). The disciples' mission, then, is not successive to that of Jesus but concurrent with it in its completed phase, the harvest phase.

Therefore, though the disciples are sent to the same world and in the same way ($\kappa\alpha\vartheta\dot{\omega}\varsigma$) as Jesus himself was sent by the Father (17:18; 20:21), they are not sent on equal terms as obtains in halakhic situations. Their mission consists exclusively in witnessing to the reality of God's salvation (15:27; 1 Jn 1:1–3; 4:9, 14) accomplished exclusively in, with and through Jesus (4:34; 17:4; 19:30). They do this both by their life of mutual love and service in community (13:35) and by proclaiming to others the knowledge of Jesus' life and work as they had personally witnessed it (17:20; 20:30–31; 21:24). In essence, however, their mission adds nothing to the mission of Jesus. Once completed (19:30), "the work" stands completed in all its dimensions, and the disciples reap the fruit thereof[22].

The only real points of comparison between Jesus and the disciples as those sent lie in the attitude and method which must needs obtain in the exercise of mission as well as in the type of response which they can hope to receive from their hearers. The attitude entails, on the one hand, complete dependence on the sender and, on the other, humility towards the human audience (13:1–17). The human response to be expected in-

---

[21]Borgen ("God's Agent," 143) holds on the evidence of *Qidd.* 41a that upon his return to the sender the agent was free to appoint others on the same terms as he himself had been sent to continue his work beyond the geographical limitations of his own mission; but he also notes that *Giṭ.* 3.5–6, 29b puts limits on the practice.

[22]Thus the Pauline notion of making up what is wanting in the sufferings of Christ for the sake of his body the church (Col 1:24) is wholly missing in John. The verb $\pi o\iota\epsilon\tilde{\iota}\nu$ in 4:34 and 17:4 has the sense of to execute thoroughly (esp. since it is reinforced by $\tau\epsilon\lambda\epsilon\tilde{\iota}\nu$ in both instances) so nothing is wanting to the Father's work completed by Jesus. See further *BAG*, 72, 809–810 and 849.

evitably entails rejection by the world (1:10–11; 15:22–16:4), though there is also promise of a positive response (1:12–13; 17:20) because of Jesus' victory over the world (1:5; 16:33; 1 Jn 5:4)[23].

Concerning dependence on the sender, Jesus' complete dependence on the Father was discussed at length under the aspects of "the work" and of the expression, "the Father who sent me" (pp. 140–145). The disciples' need for dependence on Jesus was also ennunciated in 4:31–38, particularly in the description of their mission as a harvesting or an entering into the labor of others (4:36, 38). In the farewell discourses, their dependence is underlined in a variety of ways: in the description of the disciples themselves as branches who depend on the vine and the gardener for their sustenance and missionary fruitfulness (15:1–8, 16), in the promise of the gift of the Holy Spirit who alone will give them full understanding of Jesus' teaching, comfort and strengthen them personally and enable them to be Jesus' courageous witnesses (14:16–17, 26; 15:26–27; 16:7–15), in Jesus' intense prayer for them, and in such explicit statements as 13:16 and 15:5, 16[24].

Moreover, if the disciples succeed in leading others to believe in Jesus (17:20), it is because Jesus and the Father have already drawn such believers through their joint accomplishment of "the work" (pp. 162–163), by their continued activity in the believer (6:44–45, 65; 10:16; 14:23) and by their active presence enabling the missionary fruitfulness of the disciples themselves (15:1–8; 21). Finally, there is a hierarchy in the sending process: the Father sends Jesus who enjoys a unique relationship with him; Jesus and the Father send the Holy Spirit (14:16; 16:7, 15); but only Jesus sends the disciples (4:38; 17:18; 20:21) such that ultimately they are wholly responsible to him. The Father's demands from them point them to Jesus (6:29; 1 Jn 3:23) and his love for them is determined by their response to Jesus (16:27; 14:21). Any sense of equality with Jesus is thus completely outruled. The disciples' mission is thus embraced wholly in that of Jesus, as an aspect of it.

These points are summed up in the ὑψωθῆναι/δοξασθῆναι motif. Once lifted up, like the Mosaic serpent (3:13–15; 12:32; cf. Num 21:8–9), Jesus stands as the Father's definitive "sign" and exclusive agent of salvation for all peoples, such that without him it is forever impossible for anyone either to know the Father or be saved (15:22–23; cf. 8:28, 30–36; 14:6)[25]. The coming of the Greeks in 12:30 forcefully illustrates

---

[23]The believer's faith which overcomes the world (1 Jn 5:4) is precisely faith in Jesus as God's victorious agent of salvation (1 Jn 3:16, 23). Hence believing in Jesus is rightly seen as *"the* work" which God expects from Jesus' human audience (6:29).

[24]In John, the Holy Spirit is in every way a gift. The disciples are not even asked to pray for this gift as they are in Lk 11:13; they do not even seem to be aware that they need this gift. Jesus freely promises it to them, then personally departs so that the Spirit may come upon them (16:7–15). Though he prays the Father to send the Spirit, he himself is a co-sender with the Father (16:7); after the resurrection, he personally imparts the Spirit to his disciples (20:22).

[25]In 17:3 eternal life consists in the joint knowledge of Jesus and the Father, a knowledge

this point. Their coming is seen by Jesus himself (12:23) as the event which ushers in his long-expected "hour" (7:30; 8:30; cf. 2:4), the "hour" of his glorification (13:1; 17:1), or of the completion of his mission (19:30). This, too, is the "hour" when he definitively draws "all" to himself (12:32). Jn 12:20—32 thus indicates that Jesus' personal mission is not accomplished (his "hour" not yet come) until the Greeks (the Gentiles), like the Jews and the Samaritans, are drawn to him. The desire of the Greeks to see Jesus matches that of Andrew and his unnamed companion (1:37—39), of Simon (1:41), of Nathanael (1:45) and of the Samaritans (4:29—30, 40). Their coming completes the universal cycle, lends full force to the πάντας in 12:32 and ironically illustrates the truth in the fear of the Pharisees (12:19)[26].

Some scholars have argued that Greeks in 12:20 are Hellenistic Jews, not Gentiles since they were in Jerusalem for the Jewish Passover. Such a view, however, lacks the backing both of the Johaininne context and of the NT evidence which consistently distinguishes between Jews (regardless of their Palestinian or Hellenistic origin) and Greeks. Usage by Josephus reveals the same[27]. The channel by which Jews, Samaritans and Greeks come to Jesus is itself remarkable. John the Baptist introduces the first disciples to Jesus (1:29—26), then the disciples introduce their Jewish

---

which can only be gained by accepting Jesus' revelatory mission (cf. 9:41; 15:22; 17:6—8). Though not specially called a "sign," Jesus' "being lifted up/glorified" is the "sign of signs" in the Gospel. This is clear from such passages as 2:18—22, 3:14—15 (especially when read within the context of the Jews' and Nicodemus' quest for signs, 2:23—3:2, 4, 9) and 8:28. It is also evident when one recalls the OT passage which underlies 3:14—15, namely, Num 21:4—9. Similarly in the Synoptics, the only sign given the Jews is that of Jonas, whose three days in the belly of the whale evoke the three day event of Jesus' passion, death, and resurrection (Mt 12:38—40; Lk 11:16, 29—32). The motif of "looking upon" in 19:35 may yet be the last reference in the Gospel to Num 21:8—9 as the OT background for understanding the "sign" character of Jesus' glorification.

[26]For a comparison of the Johannine schema with that of the Synoptics and Acts see in particular Aileen Guilding, *The Fourth Gospel and Jewish Worship: A Study of the Relation of St. John's Gospel to the Ancient Jewish Lectionary System* (Oxford: Clarendon, 1960) 50—51.

[27]The argument that the "diaspora of the Greeks" (7:35) refers to the Jews of the Diaspora is wholly unconvincing. Though the Greek word διασπορά came (in Jewish and Christian writings) to be associated with the Jews who lived outside Palestine, there is no evidence that this was the exclusive meaning of the term even in Jewish circles. The term applies primarily to *the area outside Palestine* where the Jews are scattered, not to the Jews so scattered (cf. *LSJ*, 359). Besides, 7:35 explicitly says: "the Diaspora of the Greeks to teach *the Greeks*" (not "to teach the Jews"). Any one familiar with Jewish mentality would know that under no circumstances would a Jew refer to other practicing Jews as "Greeks" (that is, "Gentiles"). John 7:35 gives no indication that, if Jews are meant, these are not practicing Jews. Even Qumran with all its sectarianism still distinguished between Jewish apostates (since "all Israel" would be saved at the last day) and the Gentiles, the Kittim, who would definitely be destroyed. Cf. Vermes, *The Dead Sea Scrolls*, 182—186. Concerning Gentiles going to Jerusalem to worship, one needs only recall that "the court of the Gentiles" in Herod's Temple was not a mere decoration. Besides, Josephus (*Ant.* 11, 329—339, esp. 336) narrates how Alexander the Great sacrificed in the Temple guided by the priests (the understanding being that the Macedonian performed the sacrifice himself); he states further that "all peoples" were allowed to worship together with the Jews (*Ant.* 11, 87). Finally, the whole Jewish understanding was that all nations *should* worship in Jerusalem (Jn 4:20).

companions (1:41, 45). On the whole Jesus moves freely among his Jewish audience and is readily available to them, even at night (3:2). But it is
Jesus himself who seeks out the Samaritans since they would not have
come to him otherwise, given the perennial enmity between them and the
Jews (pp. 84, 95—96, 133). The Greeks come to Jesus of their own accord, but timidly: they need Jesus' friends to introduce them.

Does this mean that the Gentiles were converted by the disciples, not
by Jesus himself? On a large scale, yes, since the Gentile mission proper
belongs to the post-Easter phase of Jesus' mission, the harvest phase. But
it is not improbable that the Gentiles who lived in Palestine or came from
outside to the feasts heard Jesus and so were in effect his converts when
they later joined the group of believers (cf. Mt 27:54; Mk 15:39; Lk 23:47).
In this connection it needs to be recalled that in John the sentence of
Jesus' "crime" is written in the three languages of the contemporary
world, Hebrew, Latin and Greek (19:20). John might have said of Pilate
that "he wrote this not of himself, but being the representative of the
world ruling power at the time was moved by God to write in this way
since Jesus is king not only of the Jews, but of Romans and Greeks as
well" (cf. 11:51—52).

There is a careful and consistent effort, then, to relativize the mission
of the disciples, even if the harvest (what modern scholarship understands
as "mission proper") is gathered in through them. In modern idiom, the
disciples' mission is one of raising their own and others' consciousness, as
well as welcoming others into the fellowship of believers. Their task is to
help others become aware of and know what God has already given to
them in Jesus (20:30—31; 1 Jn 1:1—3). In their method of preaching they
do not talk about Jesus; they simply lead others to him so that they can
hear him for themselves (1:29—36, 41, 45 ; 12:22; 21:8, 10—11). This
means, in effect, that they do not come between Jesus and the believers,
who find life, not in them, but in Jesus (20:31; 1 Jn 4:9; 5:11—13). Their
joy, the reward proper to their mission (1 Jn 1:3—4), consists in welcoming the believer into the fellowship with the Father and with his Son,
Jesus Christ (17:20—23).

This welcoming into fellowship is described in the Gospel as baptizing
(4:2; pp. 81—82), gathering in fruit (4:36), dragging in the fish-filled
net (21:8) and, possibly too, forgiving sins (20:23), since sin constitutes
the basic barrier between human beings (4:9, 20, 22; 8:44—48) and between human beings and God (8:30—36). Ultimately, however, only
Jesus forgives sins and so enables this fellowship of the children of God to
take place (1:29; 8:30—36; 1 Jn 3:5)[28]. When the disciples welcome into

---

[28]In 1 Jn 3:4—6, the community of believers is a sinless group, not because its members are
incapable of sinning (1 Jn 1:6, 8—10) but because God's "spark of life" lives in them. This means
that sinlessness is attributed to God's incessant action in the individual, not to anything that the
individual does by himself or herself (1 Jn 1:7; cf. 17:19). That is why sinlessness is ultimately
synonymous with belonging to God as opposed to belonging to the devil (8:44; 1 Jn 3:8, 10). See

fellowship, therefore, they are only making visible (13:35) the reality of God's definitive offer of salvation accomplished once and for all through Jesus. Those who hear them have the freedom either to accept their witness in faith and so join the fellowship (17:20—23 ; 1 Jn 1:3—4) or to reject it and so pronounce their own death sentence (3:18—19; 5:29; cf. Rev 20:13—15). Both believers and missionaries rejoice together in their new God-given identity as children of God (1:12—13). Thus both the acceptance of the word and the missionary preaching itself mean an entering into the labor of Jesus' accomplished mission (4:10, 14, 21, 23—24, 38, 42; 21:9—13).

Fellowship in mission

The treatment of fellowship in Jn 4:1—42 focused on the transcending of socio-political and religious barriers. In the farewell discourses the theme is given a specifically missionary thrust under the aspects of mutual love and corporate action. By their self-sacrificing love for one another (13:12—17; 15:9—17; 1 Jn 3:16), the disciples continue to convince the world of the reality of Jesus' mission from the Father (13:35). An essential aspect of Jesus' mission is that he be physically seen by his audience (6:40; 12:45; 14:9; 1 Jn 1:1—3); it is for this purpose that he "became flesh and pitched his tent among us" (1:14, 18). Jesus thus reveals the Father by his incarnation and visible presence, that is, by his entire life and work as a human being (10:38; 14:8—11), even if this revelation meets with rejection (15:22—25; cf. 9:41; 10:25—26; 12:37—50). It follows, then, that the group of believers who conjointly, not individually, constitute the *alter Christus* (imagery of the wine and branches, 15:1—8) must needs continue to make Christ visibly present in and to the world by their life of mutual love and service[29]. Their love for one another constitutes both their claim to authenticity as Christ's followers (13:34—35; 15:9—17) and the proof to the world that God's salvation accomplished in Jesus is genuinely actual (17:20—23).

The Johannine notion of fellowship, therefore, is not something which believers aspire to in the next life; it defines the reality of their Christian existence here and now. A theological idea of belonging to Christ was translated into a program of action, characterized by mutual love and service, on the one hand, and missionary preaching, on the other. The μένειν motif in John is neither gnostically nor "aposynagogically" intended, but theologically and socially, with allegiance to Jesus as the determinative factor[30]. To believe in Jesus is to remain with the authentic

---

further E. Malatesta, *Interiority and Covenant: A Study of εἶναι ἐν and μένειν ἐν in the First Letter of Saint John* (AnBib 69; Rome Biblical Institute, 1978) 247—250.

[29]Strictly speaking, the term *alter Christus* has no place in the Johannine vision. For Jesus is never replaced either by the individual or by the group of believers. The imagery of the vine and the branches (15:1—7) underscores this point.

[30]For a further discussion of the μένειν motif along these lines see Schnackenburg, *Die Johan-*

group of believers who keep his commandment, (13:34; 15:9—17) and abide by his teaching (8:30—36; 10:3—4, 16). Conversely, failure to believe in Jesus entails physical separation from the group of believers or from Jesus' company (6:60—66; 8:35; 13:30 [Judas]; 15:2; cf. 1 Jn 2:19)[31].

This conception of fellowship as something that has to be socially and concretely expressed is itself an aspect of the Johannine eschatology (pp. 165—168). For if those who believe in Jesus are transferred here and now from death to life (5:24) or from the sphere of this world and its values to that of Christ (3:18—21), then the reality of this Christian existence demands that such believers, who though separated from the world yet remain in the world (17:11—16), stick together, encourage and support one another along this new way of life. Murphy-O'Connor has amply demonstrated the existence of the same notion in Paul[32]. Indeed, with due allowance made for the differences in terminology and imagery (e.g., the vine and its branches in John [15:1—8], the body and its members in Paul [1 Cor 12:12—31]), this author's insightful commentary on 1 Corinthians could serve equally for John's Gospel on a number of key missionary issues[33]. Luke's account of the life of the early Christian community (Acts 2:44—47; 4:32—37) is rooted in the same conception that the call to the Christian life entails, on the one hand, separation from the world, and on the other, the creation of a new community marked by mutual giving and receiving[34].

---

nesbriefe (HTKNT 13/3; 4th ed; Freiburg: Herder, 1970) 66—72 and Malatesta, *Interiority and Covenant*, esp. chapter 5, "Interiority and Fraternal love," (pp. 263—282) where he emphasizes the essentially socio-communal aspect of belonging to Jesus.

[31]In 1 Jn 1:3c the idea of physically belonging to Jesus and the Father is underscored by the very terminology used: κοινωνία ἔχειν as opposed to κοινωνεῖν (2 Jn 11). In the Epistle the concept is negatively intended: "have nothing to do with" (cf. Brown, *Epistles*, 691—692). The concreteness of the Johannine formulation may reflect a Semitic influence. If so it needs to be recalled that in Semitic thought "fellowship" (especially as practiced by Qumran and the Pharisees, cf. Neusner, "Fellowship," p. 96, n. 36 above) was not a vague theological concept but a rigorous program of action which embraced the social aspects of life as well. The Semitic concept is thus very different from the Roman idea of *societas* (cf. Pheme Perkins, "Koinonia in 1 John 1:3—7: The Social Context of Division in the Johannine Epistles," *CBQ* 54 [1983] 631—641). Its most perfect social expression is the concept of "table-fellowship"; this further explains the heinousness of Judas' crime (13:26—30; cf. Mt 26:21—30, 47—49; Mk 14:18—26, 43—46; Lk 22:21—23, 47—48).

[32]Jerome Murphy-O'Connor, *1 Corinthians* (New Testament Message 10; Wilmington: Michael Glazier, 1979 [1982]) esp. pp. 9—35.

[33]Specific points of comparison include fellowship as the goal of the mission (1 Cor 1:9) of which all the other calls to peace (1 Cor 7:17; Col 3:15), to freedom (1 Cor 7:22; Gal 5:13) and to sanctification are different facets (p. 5); the dependence of the preachers on their sender (p. 10), and the need for mutual love and service (pp. 23, 25):

[34]In Acts, too, the group of believers are united not only doctrinally and liturgically (in their belief in Jesus, in the prayers and in the breaking of the bread, 2:46—47; 4:32a) but also in their common ownership of material goods (2:45; 4:32b, 34—37). Fellowship for this group was materially costly; for some like Barnabas it entailed a decline in social status for the sake of the common good (4:36—37). In John the risks involved are even more radical since it entails a readiness to lay down one's life for Jesus (12:24—26) and for the brethren (15:13; cf. 1 Jn 3:16).

Contrary to Meeks, then, the Johannine community arose, not as a counter-reaction to external, negative forces — social alienation and expulsion from the synagogue, but from a positive commitment to Jesus understood as God's eschatological agent of salvation, whose mission ushers in and establishes a new world order to be lived out here and now[35]. In other words, the primary impetus and determining factor in the creation of the new community is allegiance to Jesus and his new order of reality (his kingdom is not of this world, 18:26; cf. 3:18—21; 12:31; 16:11), not social and religious alienation. Furthermore, the community does not simply form around Jesus as people form around a hero, it lives in and by him, and is thus by its very nature separated from the world (1:5; 3:21; 11:36; 15:19; 17:14—16; 1 Jn 1:5—7; 2:9—10, 16; 4:17). It is also worth recalling that the idea of religious fellowship lived out socially was not a unique conception of the Johannine and NT Christians; it was practised with equal intensity by other contemporary religious groups notably, Qumran and the Pharisees[36].

Equally, Martyn's "highly imaginative" thesis, that the portrait of the Johannine community painted in the Gospel betrays the actual trauma of the post-Jamnia ejection from the synagogue, has rightly been rejected by a number of eminent scholars, despite Brown's favorable acceptance of it[37]. Likewise unsatisfactory is his view, similar to that of Meeks cited above, that the dualistic patterns of thought and of "the world-foreignness" present in the Gospel were fully developed in this period of social and religious dislocation from the synagogue and the world[38]. The basic problem with this entire approach lies in its understanding that the identity of the Johannine community was determined by external, hostile forces and that the resulting experiences of this community, in turn, shaped those of Jesus narrated in the Gospel, such that the Gospel is in fact an account of the life of the community read into that of Jesus. Yet

---

[35]Meeks, "The Man from Heaven," esp. pp. 70—71. His basic thesis is that social alienation and ejection from the synagogue led the Johannine group to develop a myth explaining its origin from above, as a group different from the rest of humanity. In other words, they developed a theology of "fellowship" and of other-worldly destiny to compensate for their rejection by both Jews and Gentiles. As in the all too humanistic approach to the Johannine situation, Meeks' view attributes little or no significance to the formative influence which Jesus' own identity and life must have exercised on the Johannine community. Was Jesus a myth for the Evangelist or did he really believe that Jesus came from the Father, from above (16:27; 18:8) and that if believers belonged to him, then their ultimate destiny lay with that of the Master (1:12—13; 14:1—3; 17:24)?

[36]The concrete form of the expression φέρειν καρπόν (15:2) as opposed to the more common καρποφορεῖν (cf. Mt 13:23; Mk 4:20, 28; Lk 8:15; Rom 7:4, 5; Col 1:6, 10) is again striking. Jn 15:2 thus looks back to 4:36 (συνάγει καρπόν). As in n. 31 above a Semitic influence may underlie this formulation.

[37]The whole thrust of Martyn's thesis (*History and Theology, passim.*) again is that the Gospel is based on a two level drama in which the experiences of the community is projected into that of Jesus. In other words, the historicity of the events narrated in John's Gospel begins and ends with that of the Evangelist's own day. The approach again regards the historicity of Jesus' own life narrated in the Gospel as virtually non-existent and of no value.

[38]Martyn, "Glimpses into the History of the Johannine Community," *BETL* 44, esp. 160—174.

our present contextual research up to this point furnishes no basis for such a projection theory.

From the historical and theological standpoints of the Gospel, Jesus' experiences and his exclusive meaning in God's plan of salvation determine and shape the identity and experiences of the disciples, not the reverse. The idea of separation from the world did not necessarily arise from persecution; Paul counsels the same to his Corinthians and his converts generally, though using a different set of terminology (life according to the Spirit and life according to the flesh) and there is no evidence that the Corinthian community addressed was subject to persecution from the synagogue and the world[39]. In brief, the community's understanding of itself as a group apart from the world finds its primary and determinative origin in its allegiance to Christ as God's end-time Messiah. The goal of Jesus' mission is to bring believers into lasting fellowship with himself and the Father, and the existence of a visible Christian community, whose way of life is different from that of the world, constitutes part of the eschatological reality of this mission. Persecution may indeed ensue as a result of the community's witnessing allegiance to Jesus; it may even strengthen this allegiance (16:1–4; 17:14; 1 Jn 3:13–14; cf. Acts 4:23–37), but it does not cause it to come into existence[40].

Paradoxically, while the disciples are exhorted to mutual love and service in the community, they are equally alerted to the hatred of the world. Put positively, the hatred of the world itself constitutes a sign that believers do not belong to the world, anymore than Jesus belongs to the world (17:14, 16; 1 Jn 2:16; 4:17). For the world loves its own (15:19) even as Jesus loves his own (10:11, 15, 17–18; 13:1; 15:14). One's allegiance is revealed by what one knows and loves (3:19–20; 8:42; 12:42; 13:35)[41]. The disciples reveal their love for Jesus, not in words (1 Jn 3:18; cf. Jas 1:22), but concretely and visibly (1 Jn 4:20) in their love for one another, received and carried out as a command (13:34; 15:12, 17; 1 Jn

---

[39]Cf. 1 Cor 1:26–30 which sets the tone for the letter or gives the rationale behind Paul's entire position; see also Gal 5:16–25.

[40]There is a need to distinguish between the historicity of Jesus' life and suffering and the process through which the disciples came to a full understanding of the meaning of that life and suffering. Their own experiences may ultimately have helped them to remember and fully to understand the meaning of Jesus' life and the teachings he gave them (cf. 16:4). But it strains all credibility to hold or give the impression that nothing happened during Jesus' own lifetime, that the disciples made it all up from their own experiences. Strangely enough, while certain scholars find no problem accepting that the disciples suffered for Jesus' sake, they think it inconceivable that Jesus himself did suffer and that he predicted the same suffering for his followers (even as the prophets before them had suffered). The crucifixion was not an invention of the Johannine community, nor did it come out of the blue. As all the Gospels testify, it must have formed the climax of a series of conflicts between Jesus and the Jewish leaders who rejected him.

[41]Again we are reminded here of the impossibility of separating one's religion from one's life. The separation of church and state, of religion and life, was a notion wholly alien to our NT authors and their audience.

3:11, 23; 4:21; 5:1—2). To love in this way is, in effect, to participate in the Father's and Jesus' own love for the world, also expressed in action (3:16, 35;10:17; 13:1)[42].

Belonging to Jesus, then, is not a vague theological concept, but a reality which permeates the disciple's daily living and which is both experienced in one's personal relationship with the Father and expressed socially in one's love and service of other believers. Henceforth, all the socio-political and religious barriers shattered by Jesus' mission are replaced by one eschatological barrier defined in terms of one's response to Jesus. Henceforth, humanity *in toto* is divided into those who love/believe in Jesus/the Father and those who hate/reject him (15:22—24; 16:3 ; 1 Jn 2:22—24; 2 Jn 9), namely, believers and the world (17:25—26; 1 Jn 4: 5—6). The term "world" in the farewell discourses, seen as a contrast to "believers," is thus apocalyptically/eschatologically intended and belongs to the same apocalyptic terminology in the Gospel as "light/darkness," "truth/falsehood," and "life/death" (cf. 1:5; 3:19—21;5:24;12:35—36). In the Gospel these terms are not cosmic powers as they generally are in apocalyptic literature; rather, they receive their concrete meaning in reference to Jesus of Nazareth, God's eschatological agent of salvation (1: 41, 45; 5:29, 45—47; 7:25—29, 40—44 ; 8:21—29;10:22—29; 11:27;12: 12—16)[43].

Johannine dualism is thus as unequivocal as it is radical. It is rooted in John's perception of the finality of Jesus' role in human history. Henceforth, Jesus himself becomes the great divide: people stand or fall, live or die (3:18; 4:24—29; 6:53—57; 8:24—36), see or remain blind (9:41) by their acceptance or rejection of him. That is why all peoples, Jews, Samaritans and Greeks, have to be given the opportunity to hear and respond to his mission. For though Jesus draws all to himself by his glorification (12:32), this does not happen automatically; individuals still have to respond freely to this offer of life in fellowship with him and the Father (14:23).

---

[42]The Father manifests his love for the world by sending his uniquely beloved Son (3:16) and for the Son by giving everything into his hands (3:35; cf. 5:20); Jesus, in turn, manifests his love for the Father by doing his will or what pleases him (5:30; 6:38; 15:10) and for the world by laying down his life for his sheep (10:17) which includes his disciples (13:1;17:19; cf. 1 Jn 3:16a) whom he no longer calls slaves but friends and to whom he, too, reveals everything he has learnt from the Father (15:13—15). Loving in words has no place in Johannine thought (14:15;1 Jn 3: 18), for that is a lie (1 Jn 1:6; 2:9—11;4:20).

[43]The direct link established in 1:41, 45 and 5:45—47, for instance, between Jesus of Nazareth and Moses would indicate that ultimately John is not concerned with Gnostic speculation or apocalyptic futurism but with God's action as it actually takes place here and now in human history in the person of Jesus as it had done earlier through the agency of Moses. The Gospel gives concrete physical examples of how Jesus gives life (Jn 5, 11) and serves as the light of the world (Jn 9). The response which this action of God demands of the individual also needs to be concretely/ physically expressed in one's whole way of life; walking in the light, for instance (12:35; 1 Jn 1: 7), has nothing to do with the possession of a secret Gnostic illumination but with loving as God loves (1 Jn 2:6, 9—11). Without this love one cannot claim knowledge (experience) of God (2:4).

The very presence in the world of the group of believers bonded together by mutual love and service constitutes the visible proof of the reality of this offer (13:35; 15:19). The missionary preaching, in turn, serves to strengthen this reality (17:20–23); for if there is no fellowship to bring one into, then the whole theology of mission and the missionary enterprise itself lose their meaning and purpose (4:36; 10:16; 11:52; 1 Jn 1:3–4). By the same token, to withdraw into self and barricade self against the world because of persecution or ejection from the synagogue is equally self-defeating. If Jesus did not give up in face of death (14:31), then neither should his followers (16:1–4). Indeed the need for witnessing to Jesus is made all the more imperative by such persecution since Jesus' coming into the world necessarily involves a standing combat with the value systems of this world (1:5)[44].

Given the importance attached to the community as the visible locus of the reality of Jesus' mission and to mutual love and service as the authenticating marks of this community, the worst that could happen would be for the disciples to love the world or assimilate its evil ways (17:14–16; 1 Jn 2:15–17). Worse even than this would be the presence of disunity and lack of love within the community itself; for then this community would betray itself and, if it were possible, make nonsense of Jesus' mission[45]. This explains why Jesus' prayer for his missionary disciples (17:18) is in effect a prayer for their "oneness" ($\H{\iota}\nu\alpha\ \H{\omega}\sigma\iota\nu\ \H{\epsilon}\nu$), a oneness modeled on and rooted in Jesus' own oneness with the Father (17:21, 22, 23; cf. 10:16); this also explains why this "oneness" is explicitly cited as proof to the world that the Father sent Jesus (17:22, 23) and loves the disciples themselves as much as he loves him (17:23)[46].

It explains, too, why Judas' betrayal is seen as a source of deep affliction for Jesus himself (13:18, 21–30; cf. 6:70–71). Judas, called "a devil" by Jesus (6:70) and "a thief" by the Evangelist (12:6), may yet have been seen at the time of the Evangelist as the prototype of the de-

---

[44]The juxtaposition of the present ($\varphi\alpha\acute{\iota}\nu\epsilon\iota$) and the complexive aorist ($\kappa\alpha\tau\acute{\epsilon}\lambda\alpha\beta\epsilon\nu$) in 1:5 would indicate that the world was doomed to defeat from the start (cf. 16:11, 33c; 1 Jn 5:4). Unlike the Synoptics (Mt 10:17–20; Mk 13:9–11; Lk 21:12–15) and Acts (9:14–16), John does not explicitly state that persecution constitutes the opportune moment for witnessing to Jesus. Nonetheless, it needs to be noted that the one explicit statement in the Gospel about the witnessing role of the disciples (15:27) occurs in the section which deals with Jesus' and their rejection by the world and the synagogue (15:22–16:4). In the Lucan evidence (Acts 8:1–40) persecution proved to be the catalyst which launched the Christian mission in full scale outside the confines of Judea.

[45]Cf. Murphy-O'Connor, *1 Corinthians*, 27 ("Worse than those who build with defective materials are those who would attempt to destroy the unity of the community"; cf. 1 Cor 3:17). This is precisely because the community is the locus where the reality of Christ's mission and the Christian faith are made visible (13:35).

[46]Short as this passage (17:20–23) is, its concentration on the theme of oneness is most striking. Not only is this theme mentioned in every successive verse (twice in v 22), its importance is also reinforced by the citation of the unity between Jesus and the Father as the model for the unity of "all" Jesus' disciples of all ages (v 21) and by the phrase of fulfilment (v 23).

partees who were really "never one of us" (1 Jn 2:19), "the anti-christs," "the liars" and "the false prophets" (1 Jn 2:18, 22; 4:2, 3; 2 Jn 7) who are also typified by the "thieves and brigands" in Jn 10:8, 10a. All these "anti-christ" figures have one thing in common: they plunder, scatter and lead astray the flock which Jesus gathers into a unity (10:1—18; 1 Jn 2:26 —27; 3:7); in brief, they destroy the community, and its witness to Jesus. Judas, for instance, attacked Mary of Bethany for her wasteful annoint-ing of Jesus (12:4—6), disturbed the peace of the community at the anti-cipated Paschal meal (13:2, 21—31), and ended up betraying Jesus himself (18:2—6). In the face of such a threat from within, it becomes particular-ly necessary to focus on the community and to emphasize its missionary and eschatological significance.

The focus on the disciples as a group further underlines Jesus' unique-ness in the missionary enterprise. For while he single-handedly does and completes the Father's work (4:34; 17:4), the missionary effectiveness of the disciples resides in their corporate action. This emphasis on corporate action with regard to their witnessing mission differs sharply from the very personal approach to the individual with respect to the faith response solicited to Jesus' mission (e.g., 4:7—26)[47]. In the discourses as in 4:31— 38, the focus is on the disciples as a group: the disciples as a group are designated as reapers (4:36—38), as witnesses (13:35; 15:27; 17:20—23), as those chosen and set up to bear lasting fruit (15:16), as preachers (17: 20) and as fishers (21:1—14). This emphasis on the corporate action of the missionary disciples achieves three things: Firstly, it spotlights the fact that the mission is entrusted to the group, not to individuals, so its truthfulness can be objectively verified (20:30). Even when the individual acts alone, there is always a reference to a "we" (1:45). Philip and Andrew, the paradigms of missionaries, never act alone (12:21—22; cf. 6:7—8)[48]. Equally, 1 Jn 1:1—5 speaks of "we" witnesses, though it is clearly an individual (an "I") who writes the letter (2:1, 7, 12—14, 26; 5: 13).

Secondly, and bearing on the first, the group approach draws attention to Jesus as the only leader and shepherd of the flock (10:6; 12:32); for whether the disciples love one another unto death (15:12—13; 1 Jn 3:16) or are themselves hated to death by the world (15:18—21; 16:1), they do no more than follow Jesus' own example (10:4, 15, 17—18; 12:24—26, 32—33; 15:22—24; 21:19), and are sustained by him at every stage (15:

---

[47]We discussed at length in Chapter IV Jesus' very personal approach to the woman and also cited Moule's article, "The Individualism of the Fourth Gospel." John's Gospel emphasizes both individual response and corporate action.

[48]In 1:41 Andrew simply finds his brother Simon and leads him to Jesus, but he is designated as "one of the two" who first went to stay with Jesus (1:37—40). Moreover, while the BD is the revered witness behind the Gospel (21:24), it is equally understood that Jesus' "signs" recorded in the Gospel were worked "in the presence of his disciples" (20:30; cf. 15:27). Jesus' revelation is, in fact, not a Gnostic secret confided to the initiated few, but a message which he speaks openly in the world "for all to hear" (18:20—21).

5; 21:5—6, 9—13). As the way, the truth and the life (14:6), he counsels them nothing which he himself has not personally experienced. The Gospel is thus very consistent about the normative role which Jesus' life plays in the life and experiences of the disciples.

Finally, the focus on the group reduces the risk of individuals behaving as if they owned the mission, thereby appropriating the glory of the enterprise (4:38, 42). This glory belongs only to the Father (15:8 ; 17:4, 22) who alone glorifies, in turn, those who obey him (8:54; 11:4; 12:28, 43; 13:31—32; 17:1, 5). To seek one's own glory is to fail to recognize that one is sent and that everything is consequently a gift (5:41—44; 7: 18; 8:50, 54). Against this spirit of self-glorification, which in the Gospel is typified by the Pharisees (5:41—44), Jesus himself and the Baptist stand out as exemplary models[49]. It is of the nature of the one sent to seek the glory of the sender. To act otherwise is to falsify one's own identity and betray one's mission. This central issue and all the important missionary lessons given to the disciples in the discourses are summed up in Jn 15 and 17.

b) Jn 15:1—18, 16: the need for dependence

The imagery of the vine and branches visually encapsulates the central theme highlighted in the foregoing discussion concerning the centrality of Jesus and the disciples' all-round dependence on him. In addition to the points already discussed in reference to Jn 15, the following may further be noted. Firstly, the disciples, the branches, receive their identity from Jesus, the vine. The question of identity is very important in Johannine thought[50]. The same point is made in 1 Jn 2:20, 26 in terms of having/receiving the χρῖσμα[51]. The very life and missionary fruitfulness of the branches depend entirely on their "remaining in" the vine (v 5). For once cut off from the vine, the branches cease to exist (v 6). The disciples' role is, no doubt, important since only the branches bear fruit[52].

---

[49]The Baptist's humility in the exercise of his mission manifests itself in his disclaiming to be the Christ; he does so thrice: before the emisaries of the Jewish authorities (1:19—28), before the crowd (1:29—26) and before his own disciples (3:27—36). His entire attitude summed up in 3:30 stems from his recognition that as one sent he can lay claim only to what God gives (3:27). This recognition is the bed-rock of humility, the attitude proper to the missionary.

[50]Schnackenburg (*Johannesevangelium* 1, 457) rightly observes that Jesus' identity constitutes the central theme of every episode in the Gospel. Consequently, the identity of the Baptist (1: 6—8, 19—28; 3:26—30), of Moses (5:45—47; 6:32) and of Jesus' human audience also becomes an issue, namely, where does each person stand in relation tò Jesus (cf. 1:12—13; 3:19—21; 8:37—47; cf. 1 Jn 3:1—3; 4:5—6; 5:1—5)?

[51]There is, perhaps, an intended play on words in the line up of the terminology in 1 Jn 2: 18—22: ἀντίχριστοι, ὁ χριστός and χρῖσμα ἔχετε where the "anti-christs" are those who do not belong with the group of believers (v 19), because they refuse to acknowledge that Jesus is the Christ (v 18).

[52]See further, Murphy-O'Connor, *1 Corinthians*, 23—24 (on the importance of the missionaries in Pauline thought — though God has no need of human agents, he decides to use intermed-

Nevertheless, without the tending care of the Father (vv 1—2) and the nourishing activity of Jesus, neither life nor fruit-bearing is possible for the disciples (vv 4—5). Jesus sustains and sanctifies them by his word of revelation (vv 3—4), by personally serving them (13:10), by laying down his life for them (17:19) and by giving them the Spirit as their abiding comforter and teacher of truth (14:17, 25—26; 16:12—14; 20:23; 1 Jn 2:27; 5:6c). Consequently, Jesus'activity and that of the Father are conjointly seen as the primary and enabling activity (cf. 4:38); all the disciples have to do is bear fruit. The expression $\kappa\alpha\rho\pi\grave{o}\nu$ $\varphi\acute{e}\rho\epsilon\iota\nu$ (vv 4, 16), recalls $\sigma\upsilon\nu\acute{a}\gamma\epsilon\iota$ $\kappa\alpha\rho\pi\acute{o}\nu$ (4:36), and both describe the essentially harvesting nature of the disciples' mission[53].

Secondly, the fruit-bearing role itself is a gift by Jesus' own choice and election, not a role given directly to the disciples by the Father (v 16). The disciples are, therefore, wholly accountable to Jesus in their missionary activity, even as Jesus is accountable in his to the Father who sent him (Jn 17). Again, this hierarchy in the sending process is consistently sustained in the Gospel (4:38; 13:16; 15:16); nowhere is it stated or suggested that the Father sends the disciples. The perfect $\check{e}\vartheta\eta\kappa\alpha$ (v 16) has a causative sense as does $\zeta\omega\sigma\pi\sigma\iota\epsilon\hat{\iota}\nu$ in 5:21 and 6:63. It expresses the outward missionary thrust while $\dot{e}\xi\epsilon\lambda\epsilon\xi\acute{a}\mu\eta\nu$ (aorist[1]) expresses the inward personal relationship with Jesus (cf. 6:70). Both the election and the sustaining in fruitfulness stem from Jesus' love for the disciples (vv 8—17)[54].

The same point is made in the passage on the bread of life (6:56—57), in the distinction between "remaining in" Jesus (the personal dimension, v 56) and "living because of him" (the missionary dimension, v 57). The missionary scope of v 57 is indicated by the $\kappa\alpha\vartheta\dot{\omega}\varsigma/\kappa\dot{\alpha}\gamma\dot{\omega}$, $\kappa\alpha\grave{\iota}/\kappa\dot{\alpha}\kappa\epsilon\hat{\iota}\nu\sigma\varsigma$ structure of the verse where $\dot{a}\pi\acute{e}\sigma\tau\epsilon\iota\lambda\acute{e}\nu$ $\mu\epsilon$ $\dot{o}$ $\zeta\hat{\omega}\nu$ $\pi\alpha\tau\acute{\eta}\rho$ is the common term of reference. As Jesus lives by the Father by doing and completing his work (4:34; 17:4), so the disciples live by him by their abiding faith in him (6:29, 67—70) and by keeping his commandments (15:10—17); these are the conditions by which they are enabled to bear fruit or serve as his witnesses (15:27)[55].

Missionary fruitfulness, then, in whatever way it is understood, forms an essential aspect of the Johannine conception of discipleship. For not only is nourishment by the vine the condition for bearing fruit (vv 4—6),

---

iaries). This need for human intermediaries in no way constitutes the grounds for pride; it should rather bring home to all concerned the reality of God's love further manifested in his free desire to involve human beings in the harvesting task of his saving work.

[53]See n. 36 above on the possible Semitic influence underlying this Johannine formulation.

[54]The aorist[1] emphasizes Jesus' choice of the disciples for himself in much the same way as formerly God chose the fathers for his own possession (Acts 13:17; Deut 4:37; 10:15 [LXX]; cf. Jn 6:13; 13:18). By this election the disciples are entitled to have a part in him (13:8b), a point which is developed at length in 15:1—8.

[55]Lagrange (*Jean*, 185—186) also interprets 6:57 from a missionary perspective: "en s'unissant au Fils de Dieu l'homme apprend à lui consacrer son service." He cites Augustine and Aquinas as supporters of his position. See also Hoskyns, *The Fourth Gospel*, 299.

but fruit-bearing itself is the only condition for remaining in the vine (v 2a). Personal sanctity and missionary fruitfulness are thus inseparable. One cannot remain in Jesus, the Father's envoy, or be "christened" ($\chi\rho\bar{\iota}\sigma\mu\alpha$ $\check{\epsilon}\chi\epsilon\iota\nu$) and yet not be sent along with him. "Partnership" with Jesus (13:8a) entails a loving service of all the brethren (13:12—17; 15: 9—17); this, too, is viewed as missionary activity (13:34—35; 15:12—17), as obedience to the sender (15:9—11)[56]. Finally, the perfect in v 16, like the descriptive presents in vv 1—7, emphasizes that while the disciples bear fruit, they themselves remain the work of Jesus and the Father. Hence the glory of their fruitfulness is accredited not to them but to the Father (15:8)[57]. On the other hand, it is nowhere suggested that the Father works in Jesus for his (i.e., Jesus') own good. All his conjoint activity with, in, and through the Son is for the benefit of the disciples[58].

c) Jn 17: Jesus' missionary prayer

Hubert Ritt's monograph on Jn 17, *Das Gebet zum Vater,* offers a comprehensive survey of important works done on this chapter and analyzes the prayer itself from different perspectives[59]. Our concern here is simply to highlight the nature of the prayer and its function within the whole context of Jesus' mission as portrayed in the Gospel.

The scope of the prayer

The prayer begins by announcing the arrival of "the hour" when, having completed the Father's work (v 4), Jesus needs to be "glorified" by the Father himself (v 1). It also ends with a reference to this work as an activity which he will continue to carry out in the disciples (v 26). Said publicly, the prayer is in effect Jesus' public report back to the Father of the work which he gave him to do (v 4). It may be seen, then, as a descriptive summary of Jesus' mission, with respect both to its content and method. The prayer focuses on Jesus' attitude as one sent (vv 18a, 21c, 23c). This summary is done in the form of a prayer; the form is important.

As in 4:34, the prayer attributes to the Father complete ownership of

---

[56]The Apostolic Exhortation of Paul VI, *Evangelii Nuntiandi* (*AAS* 68 [1976] 69) also sees a missionary significance in a loving Christian (specifically religious) community. John, however, is concerned with the witness of *all* believers, not simply of religious.

[57]The use of the aorist ($\dot{\epsilon}\delta o\xi\dot{\alpha}\sigma\vartheta\eta$) in 15:8 is interesting. The sense could be proleptic as in v 6 ($\dot{\epsilon}\beta\lambda\dot{\eta}\vartheta\eta$, $\dot{\epsilon}\xi\eta\rho\dot{\alpha}\nu\vartheta\eta$), so Zerwick, *Analysis* 1, 332. But is there not a hint that the disciple's fruitfulness, both personal and communal/missionary, is already included in Jesus' accomplished mission?

[58]If Jn 15:1—8, 16 is the Johannine version of the unfaithful vine dressers (Mt 21:33—46; 25: 14; Mk 12:1—12; Lk 20:1—19; Is 5:1—7), then the Johannine account underlines the fact that the Father and Jesus, his last and unique messenger, do not simply turn up at the harvest to claim the fruit of the vine. Rather, both are continually at work enabling the life and fruitfulness of those who bear fruit.

[59]See the extensive review of Ritt's book by Giblin, *JBL* 101 (1982) 460—463.

the work and underlines Jesus' role in it as its sole executive agent (vv 2, 4). The purpose of this work is to give life to "all flesh" (v 2; cf. 3:16—17; 4:10—15; 10:10). Since eternal life consists in the joint knowledge of the Father and his sole executive agent (v 3, which recalls 4:10), revelation of the name (vv 6, 26) by transmission of the word (v 8) is rightly seen as the activity by which this life is communicated to believers who are here represented by the disciples. This transmission of "the word," however, is not to be understood as being exclusive of his "deeds" since it is by his entire life as a human being that Jesus reveals the Father (1:18; 5:36; 10: 38; 12:45; 14:8—11).

This motif of giving life through revelation is very evocative of the OT Wisdom traditions (Prov 8:22—36; Sir 24:1—29) as are indeed those of existence before creation (v 5; Wis 9:9) and of the "word" as the unfailing accomplisher of God's purpose (v 4; Is 55:10—11). That the Gospel associates Jesus with OT Wisdom/logos traditions hardly needs debating[60]. But neither can the crucial differences between the Johannine Jesus and his OT counterparts (God's agents) be overlooked. We have already underlined this point in respect to the prophetic messengers in our discussion of 4:34 (pp. 140—145, esp. 143—145). As for Wisdom, she is said to be a creature, the first, no doubt, but a creature nonetheless (Prov 8:22—23; Sir 1:4, 9; 24:8—9). Above all, she is clearly identified with "the book of the covenant," the Mosaic law (Sir 24:23; cf. vv 8—12), which Jesus declares to be a mere witness to him, but which, unlike him, is incapable of giving life (5:39—40); its very significance ends with Jesus' own entry into human history (1:17—18). Similarly, though God's "word" comes down to earth and unfailingly accomplishes his designs (Is 55:10—11; cf. Jn 16:28 read in the context of the accomplished work, 17:4; 19:30), Isaiah nowhere suggests that "the word is God" (Jn 1:1c) or that it became a human being (1:14). In brief, in whatever way it is conceived, the OT Wisdom/logos figure has no identity outside the Mosaic law and outside God's activity accomplished in the history of the chosen people prior to the coming of Jesus. It is precisely at this point that this figure and Jesus of Nazareth part company (1:17)[61].

The way God speaks, that is, reveals himself through Jesus, is thus radically different from the way he spoke formerly through his OT agents:

---

[60]The most comprehensive study of the OT background underlying John's Gospel outside the commentaries is perhaps that of Günter Reim, *Studien zum alttestamentlichen Hintergrund des Johannesevangeliums* (SNTMS 22; Cambridge: University, 1974) esp. pp. 191-205 on John and the apocryphal wisdom literature, and the bibliography, esp. pp. 285—293; see also André Feuillet, *Le Prologue du quatrième évangile: Etude de théologie johannique* (Paris: Desclée de Brouwer, 1968) and the bibliography, pp. 289—294, esp. pp. 290—292.

[61]The same applies to Philo's Logos and to Wisdom as portrayed in the Wisdom of Solomon (7: 22—81). This figure is linked essentially with God's work in creation and the history of the chosen people. In other words, the concept may be Hellenistic but the reality behind it is essentially God's power at work in history up to the time of the author. The Johannine notion of Son is lacking in these portrayals.

In Jesus God himself becomes ontologically and humanly his own spokes-man (1:18; 5:18; 10:30—33; 14:8—11). The title "Son" or "uniquely beloved Son" (μονογενής [1:18], ὁ υἱὸς ὁ μονογενής [3:16]) under-scores this point (cf. Heb 1:1). Jesus is not a divine power at work in the world from creation through the history of the Jewish people to the days of the wisdom writers, nor is he simply a personified emanation of God's glory (Wis 7:25; cf. 7:22—8:1). He is God's ontological and uniquely beloved Son (1:18; 3:16; 5:30; 10:33, 36), one who shared the glory with the Father from before creation (17:5), but who has now become a human being (1:14) in a recognizable historical context (1:41, 45; 2:1—5, 12; 6:41—42; 7:27, 41, 52; 19:19) in order to reveal both his glory and that of the Father (1:14, 18; 2:11; 14:9).

Unlike all his OT counterparts, therefore, Jesus is ontologically a person from both the divine and the human perspectives. Believers receive God's own word when they receive Jesus of Nazareth as his unique spokesman and agent of salvation (17:8)[62]. They see God and his glory when they see him (1:18; 14:9). That is why in the Gospel knowing Jesus is synonymous with knowing the Father (5:37—38; 12:45; 14:9; cf. 17:3) who is in him (10:38; 14:10—11, 20; 17:21, 23). That is why, too, "remaining in Jesus" and "remaining in his/God's word" (5:38; 14:24b; 17:8, 14, 17) are the same (8:31; 15:4—7)[63]. If even these great OT figures do not compare with Jesus, then neither can his disciples who depend on him for everything (4:38; 13:16; 15:5, 16)[64].

The prayer also recapitulates Jesus' fundamental attitude of humility and dependence on his Father in the exercise of mission. As in previous passages (pp. 142—143), the prayer emphasizes the gift-nature of every aspect of Jesus' mission: the work now done and completed (v 4; cf. 4:34; 9:4; 10:37; 14:10), the words spoken (vv 8, 14, 17; cf. 3:34; 5:24; 7:16; 12:49—50; 14:24) and even the disciples themselves (vv 2, 6, 9, 12, 24; cf. 6:37, 39, 44, 65; 10:29; 18:9). Jesus' spirit of dependence stands out particularly in the prayerful attitude itself, in his interceding both for himself (vv 1—5) and for his disciples (vv 6—26; cf. 11:41—42;

---

[62]Robinson (*Redating,* 289) thinks it a "crude anachronism" that the phrase "Jesus Christ" should be put on the lips of Jesus in 17:3; consequently he considers this verse to be a gloss. The use of the term here may, however, be deliberate: to underscore the point that the Christ in ques-tion in whom life is to be found is none other than Jesus of Nazareth. In the Gospel the stumbling block for Jesus' audience is neither his humanity nor his divinity taken separately, but that he a man should claim to be God (5:18; 10:33; 19:7). The confession formula in the Gospel, that Jesus is "the Christ, and Son of God" (cf. 11:27; 20:31), may yet have a special reference to this very problem. We shall consider this question in detail in our next chapter.

[63]To "remain in" Jesus' word, or in him and to "keep" his word are synonymous expressions (cf. 5:47; 8:51, 52, 53; 14:23, 24; 15:20; 17:6). Both refer to a life commitment to or a lasting faith in Jesus, the Son (cf. 8:30—36).

[64]The so called Johannine polemic is never directed against any of these OT figures; on the contrary, they are seen as faithful witnesses (5:39, 45—47) as is also the Baptist (5:33—35) and even Abraham (8:39). The issue rather is the refusal of Jesus' Jewish audience to accept the cum-ulative testimony offered by these figures (5:46—47; 7:19; 8:40).

12:28). In the Synoptics, the disciples are asked to pray the Lord of the harvest to send laborers into the harvest (Mt 9:37—38; Lk 10:2). Also in the Synoptics, Jesus thanks the Father for his action in the disciples (Mt 11: 25—26; Lk 10:21). Here in John he prays not only for the disciples, but also for his own glorification. This public prayer for his own glorification confirms his oft-repeated claim that as one sent he does not seek his own glory and that only the sending Father glorifies his agent (5:41, 44; 7:18; 8:50, 54; 12:28; 13:31—32). This emphasis is all the more striking in this passage seeing that Jesus shared the glory with the Father before the world began (17:5). On the whole, the prayer for his glorification recalls the attitude attributed to him in Phil 2:6—11 and Heb 5:5[65].

More than ever before, the prayer also brings out Jesus' pastoral concern for his disciples, a concern which grows in depth and urgency because of his pending departure (vv 11—13) and which, consequently, centers on their needs during this period of his physical absence from them (v 11; cf. 14:16—17). The prayer thus leaves no doubt that the disciples are squarely part of Jesus' own mission, whether it be before or during its completed phase. Strikingly, the needs of the disciples for which Jesus prays are the same as those which had previously formed the subject of his instruction, namely, the consciousness of their separation from the world, the courage to face the world's hatred which must ensue because of their belonging to him (vv 6—19; cf. 15:18—16:4), and the need for mutual love and unity as a witness to his mission (vv 11, 20—23; cf. 13: 34—35; 15:9—17). Joyful fellowship with Jesus and the Father is also cited as the ultimate goal of the mission (vv 3, 24—28; cf. 14:3; 15:11; 16:22—24). By transforming these issues into prayer Jesus again *doubly* underscores their importance for the disciples.

Like the good shepherd (10:1—6), Jesus has watched over the disciples so that none is lost, except Judas who belongs to the destroyer (v 12; cf. 6:70—71). His total commitment of himself by the laying down of his life is "for" the disciples (ὑπὲρ αὐτῶν, v 19; cf. 10:15, 17—18). He does this so that, separated from the world (vv 14—16), they, too, in their mission to the world (v 18), may be totally committed to the truth, God's word spoken by him (vv 17, 19b)[66]. Put on Jesus' lips, the motif of vicar-

---

[65]It is striking too that, though Jesus claims to be a co-witness to himself with the Father (8: 17—18), he never claims to co-glorify himself with the Father (8:50, 54). It is always the Father who glorifies (12:28b) or who is asked to glorify both his name (12:28a) and the Son (17:1). Such NT passages as Phil 2:6—11; 2 Cor 8:9; Mt 11:29 and Heb 5:5 corroborate the Johannine portrait of Jesus as one who was truly humble in his attitude towards both his Father and his human audience. Strangely enough, this humble side of Jesus is hardly ever stressed in contemporary NT Christologies.

[66]For a discussion of the meaning of ἁγιάζειν and its OT background see Procksch, *TDNT* I, 111—112. Procksch, however, does not bring out the specific meaning of the word in John 17. The context of vv 17 and 19 strongly suggests that from the perspective of the disciples the word carries, on the one hand, the sense of separation from the world (that is from falsehood) and, on the other, confirmation or consecration in the truth, Jesus' word spoken to them. Jn 17:19 and

ious suffering, which is not peculiar to John (cf. Mk 14:24; Lk 22:19, 22; Rom 5:6–8; 1 Cor 11:24; 15:3; Col 1:24), becomes particularly forceful, especially when read in the contexts of 10:17–18; 12:24–32; 13:1 and 15:13[67]. The net result of this entire portrayal is that the disciples do not simply reap the fruit of Jesus' mission; they are themselves the first-fruits of this mission (vv 6–8, 20; cf. 10:16).

The function of the prayer

The prayer is addressed to the Father and is, therefore, seriously intended. As prayer, it constitutes an earnest handing back into the Father's hands of Jesus' accomplished mission. Yet this prayer is said publicly (17:13); in the light of 11:42 and 12:30, the purpose of this public recital must be for the benefit of the attending disciples, so that they may hear and learn to believe that the Father did indeed send Jesus (11:42). Jn 20:30 draws attention to the fact that Jesus' "signs" were done "in the presence of his disciples." It needs to be recalled, however, that at this point the disciples themselves are still very much half-convinced believers (16:29–33), and that Jesus' prayer begins precisely at the point where he makes them aware of their weak and vulnerable faith (16:31–32). The prayer has a bearing on this weak faith by its counteracting assurance of Jesus' own victory over the world (16:33; cf. 1:5). In Luke 22:31–33 Jesus prays only for Peter; in John he prays for all the disciples of all ages (v 20). The prerogative of strengthening the disciples belongs exclusively to him; and he shares this with the Holy Spirit (14:22–30; 16:7, 12–15, 21–41), not with Peter (cf. Lk 22:32).

What, then, are the specific lessons embodied in the prayer? In what ways does it exhort or strengthen the disciples? First to be noted is the contrast between 16:31– 32 and 17:6–8, 25. In the former passage Jesus predicts his abandonment by all the disciples, an action which betrays the unreliability of their professed faith in him (v 31). In the latter, on the contrary, he singles out for praise the disciples as those who have kept the Father's word revealed to them by him (vv 6, 25) and who, receiving the word, know and believe *truly* (ἀληθῶς) that he was indeed sent by the Father and that all he has comes from the Father (vv 7–8). The rest of this prayer thus rests on this premises that the disciples are those who have truly believed in Jesus' mission from the Father, a fact which 16:31– 32 seems to contradict.

10:15, 17–18 clearly refer to Jesus' vicarious offering of himself for his disciples. In both passages Jesus' is concerned with the disciples' ability to discern the truth: in Jn 10 it is a question of knowing and following Jesus, the true shepherd, as opposed to following the thieves and brigands; in Jn 17 it is a question of knowing and keeping Jesus' word/ways as opposed to allowing self to be seduced by the ways of the world (vv 14, 15).

67The motif of vicarious suffering is generally associated with Paul (e.g., Rom 8:27; 1 Cor 1: 13; Gal 1:4; 2:20; 3:13; Tit 2:14; cf. 1 Pet 2:21; 3:18). But this conception, which is Jewish rather than Hellenistic in origin (the classic text is Is 53), is equally prominent in the Johannine theology: cf. 6:51; 10:11, 15, 17–18; 11:50 [=18:4]; 11:51; 13:37, 38; 15:13; 17:19; 1 Jn 3:16.

This apparent contradiction can be explained by bearing in mind that 17:6—8 forms part of the prayer. As prayer, these verses express Jesus' earnest desire that his disciples come to the "complete knowledge of faith" in him as the Father's agent and *persevere* in that knowledge. From the disciples' standpoint, their being singled out serves as an invitation/ exhortation to them to recognize their need for an ever-deepening faith in Jesus and to strive to grow in the same. From the Father's standpoint, therefore, these verses are intercessory, but from that of the disciples who are listening they are hortatory. The same applies throughout the prayer; its efficacy rests in the person praying and in the promised gift of the Holy Spirit, not in the merit of the disciples. From Jesus' own standpoint, the disciples' faith is also important since his glorification is bound up with or includes their abiding fidelity to him (17:2—3, 9—26). This means that the completion of Jesus' mission includes the existence of a visible community of believers since the word does not return empty but accomplishes that for which it was sent (3:16; 10:10; 17:4; cf. Is 55:10—11).

Secondly, the prayer also gives the disciples an insight into the secret of Jesus' unique relationship with the Father as his pre-existent Son (v 1) and exclusive agent of salvation (vv 2—3). This uniqueness is also underlined by the manner in which immediate relationships are paired in the prayer; this may be schematized as follows:

"*you—me,*" "*I—them/others,*" "*they/others—me,*" "*I—you.*"

The cycle of relationship thus begins and ends with the sending Father, while Jesus constitutes the indispensable mediator between him and the disciples; for whether they turn to the right or to the left they cannot by-pass Jesus to reach the Father (vv 6—26). Not only is salvation accomplished once for all by him (19:30), he remains always the sole access to the Father (v 2; 14:6). In this respect, the prayer may also be seen as Jesus' final appeal to the disciples to *continue* to believe in him and in his messianic claims. Moreover, since they were with him from the beginning (15:27; cf. 1:29—51; 2:1—11) and witnessed the entire execution of his mission (20:30), they can now judge for themselves whether the public report back to the Father corresponds with the deed. The prayer thus underlines the truthfulness of Jesus' words and claims. Its particular effectiveness to convince this time lies in its being addressed directly to the Father whom it is impossible to deceive (cf. 7:18; 8:46; 18:37; 1 Jn 2:21, 27).

To sum up, in terms of his effort by speech actively to persuade his audience to believe in him, Jn 17 constitutes the crowning point of Jesus' missionary activity; the glorification (18—20) marks the Father's authenticating seal on this mission (12:28; 17:2, 5)[68]. Jn 17 thus forms an integral part of the Johannine conception of mission. Central to this concep-

---

[68]Käsemann (*Testament*, 7) calls this chapter a postscript; Nicholson (*Death as Departure*, 164) sees the prayer as the end of Jesus' mission. But his glorification (18—20) is very much part of his mission, even as is his enabling activity in the disciples (Jn 21).

tion is the understanding that the whole missionary enterprise stems from and terminates in the Father, such that its glory belongs wholly to him and is his alone to confer on his agent. The prayer underlines this point by demonstrating Jesus' humble, dependent and prayerful attitude towards the Father who sent him, this despite both his divine origin (v 5; cf. 1:1; 10:36) and his exclusive role in the work (17:2–3)[69]. By the same token it underscores the totality of the disciples' dependence on Jesus both by its hierarchical thrust and by the force of example: if Jesus cannot appropriate the glory of the completed work, least of all can the disciples glory in their limited participation in the mission (15:8); whatever glory they may hope to have comes as a gift, as a sharing in Jesus' own glory (17:22, 24–26).

The prayer thus embodies the same missionary emphases as is present in the rest of the Gospel. If it was added latter as Käsemann and others maintain, then it must have been added by the Evangelist himself or by one who thoroughly grasped his distinctive approach to mission. This approach is so deeply embedded in the Gospel that it requires the closest attention to recognize it.

2. The *Demonstratio* by the Evangelist, Jn 21

In the concluding chapter of the Gospel, Jn 21, as in 4:39–42, the Evangelist summarily dramatizes the central points made in the discourses concerning the disciples' relationship with Jesus, namely, their need for total dependence on him both for their personal life and missionary fruitfulness[70]. The theme of the whole episode is best summed up in 15:5c: "without me you can do nothing." The narrative purports to illustrate the "manner" (οὕτως) of Jesus' self-revelation to his disciples after his resurrection (vv 1, 14). The use of the verb φανεροῦν rather than ὁρᾶν/

---

[69]Critics generally see v 3 as a gloss. Boismard-Lamouille, for instance (*Synopse III*, 393, 400), attribute this verse to John III, the final editor of the Gospel. In their view this verse (like 14:28b) betrays John III's attempt to tone down the high Christology of the Evangelist (John II) in order to placate the Jews who might find the suggestion of polytheism intolerable. He does this by emphasizing that there is only one God. But would John III not have achieved his purpose more effectively by deleting "Jesus Christ" altogether from 17:3 and by surpressing those passages in the Gospel which state unequivocally that Jesus is God (1:1; 5:18; 10:33, 36; 19:7; 20:28) and that eternal life is to be found only in him (3:15–17;5:24–25;6:47–51, 53–58; 7:27–28, 39; 8:24, 51; 15:22–25; 20:31)? The mere addition of "one true God" cannot reduce the impact on the reader of all these other passages. Jn 17:3 fits in well with this overwhelming emphasis on Jesus' divinity and on his being God's sole agent of life. In our view, the reference to "the one true God" underlines that the only authentic authority behind Jesus' mission is the God ("the only true God") whom the Jews do not know (cf. 8:47, 55). Their ignorance of God reveals itself in their refusal to accept Jesus as his unique Son and Messiah (8:19; 15:21; 16:3; cf. 14:7).

[70]Lightfoot (*John*, 159), Giblin ("Crossing," 101) and Ruckstuhl ("Zur Aussage und Botschaft von Johannes 21," *Kirche des Anfangs*, 329–262, esp. p. 345) also note that the accounts in Jn 6 and 21 emphasize the disciples' dependence on Jesus.

ὤφθην as in the Synoptics (cf. Mt. 28:7, 10; Mk 16:7; Lk 24:23, 34) is particularly striking. What is at stake here is not physical sight as in 20: 14—29 (the disciples saw but did not recognize Jesus straight away [v. 4], and Jesus does not identify himself this "third time" as he did in previous appearances), but insight into the way in which Jesus continues to be present with the disciples and work through them. The recognition that "It is the Lord," comes from the Beloved Disciple as a result of the miraculous catch (vv 6—7).

The whole account is highly symbolic, in many ways evocative of 6:1— 21, 67—71, and is, perhaps, the only truly symbolic passage in the entire Gospel. It is important to distinguish between the paradigmatic and the symbolic in John's Gospel. In the former, characters like Nicodemus, the Samaritan woman, the man born blind and the Jews serve as typical examples of audience-response to Jesus. In the latter, the terms used stand for something else; for instance, the fishing expedition represents the disciples' missionary activity (cf. Mt 4:9 ; Mk 1:17; Lk 5:10), "night" smybolizes the realm of darkness which is opposed to or marks the absence of Jesus, the light (vv 3, 4; cf. 3:2, 19b, 20; 13:30), the "unbroken net" (v 11) is traditionally interpreted as symbolizing the unity of the Church (not, incidentally, of the Johannine community)[71], and the number of fish (153), the number of Christian churches in existence at the time of the Evangelist[72]. Other symbolic elements will emerge in our brief analysis of the episode.

The first part of the fishing incident deals with the conditions necessary for the missionary fruitfulness of the disciples (vv 1—8), the second part (vv 9—14) and the rest of the chapter (vv 15—19, 20—23, 24—25) with the personal relationship of the disciples with Jesus, also set within the context of mission; for in the Johannine vision personal call and missionary fruitfulness are inseparable (15:16).

a) Conditions necessary for missionary fruitfulness (vv 1—8)

The fishing incident is placed within the completed phase of "the work." It contrastively illustrates the result of the disciples' missionary efforts first without Jesus (vv 2—3), then with him (vv 4—8). Upon Peter's initiative, a group of seven disciples decide to go fishing. This project represents missionary activity and is a community undertaking (ὁμοῦ, v 2; cf. 4:36; Acts 2:1). Noticeably, the project takes place at

---

[71]In Lk 6:2 the nets were breaking because of the weight of the catch so Peter and his companions called to the sons of Zebedee for help. A number of scholars believe Jn 21:1—14 is the Lucan account which John has turned into a post-resurrection episode.

[72]In the common view, the 153 fishes symbolize the totality and fulness of Christian churches that would come into existence through the apostolic preaching; the unbroken net is said to symbolize the unity of these churches. (cf. Boismard-Lamouille, *Synopse III,* 484—485). See Brown, *John* II, 1074—1076 for a full discussion of the theories advanced on this topic. This figure (153) may simply represent the total number of churches in existence in the Evangelist's own day.

"night," that is, in the absence of Jesus. Moreover, the disciples undertake the project without any reference to Jesus: "I am going fishing," "we are going with you" (v 3). As might be expected, the whole night's toil proves abortive (v 3b)[73].

At dawn (which here symbolizes the beginning of Jesus' self-revelation, v 4), Jesus arrives at the shore, awaits the disciples as they return with their empty boat, draws from them a personal admission of their fruitless toil and on the basis of this admission personally directs them to fish in the right way (εἰς τὰ δεξιὰ μέρη, vv 4—6a), that is, at his instructions and under his enabling presence. The disciples obey (v 6b) and a double miracle occurs, the catch itself and the unbroken net (v 11). The abundance of the catch made at Jesus' single instruction contrasts sharply with the fruitlessness of the previous night-long toil, and so drives home the lesson given in 15:5c. The lesson is further accentuated by the fact that the "abundant fruit" borne by the disciples as a result of Jesus' enabling presence (v 11; cf. 15:2, 8) renders their boat inadequate. Unable to *draw* the net into their boat, they drag it along with them to Jesus on the shore (v 8)[74].

This impossibility of dragging the net into the boat also underlines the helplessness of the disciples in the missionary enterprise. They do not contain the enterprise but serve it and so need always to be aware of the greater laborer whose toil sustains theirs and to whom they must direct the fruit of their undertaking (cf. 4:38; 15:16). For as Jesus never lost sight of the Father who sent him in exercising his mission (14:10), so neither should the disciples lose sight of Jesus who sent them (21:4b, 7a, 12b). Finally, if traditionally the boat, "Peter's bark" (Lk 5:3—5), represents the Church into which all are gathered, this symbolism is totally discarded in John. Unlike in Luke 5:3—5, Jesus does not enter the boat but directs the operation from the shore. In the parallel incident at sea in 6:16—21 the Johannine account does not specify the owner of the boat. The entire portrayal again underlines the disciples' total dependence on Jesus.

---

[73]We say "as might be expected" because "night" for the Evangelist represents the sphere of darkness, unfruitfulness and inactivity (3:2, 19b, 20; 8:12b; 12:35c, 46c; 9:4; 11:10a; 13:30). It is the opposite of Jesus, the light (1:4, 5, 9; 3:19, 21; 8:21a,c; 9:5; 12:46a), from whom comes life and all fruitfulness (1:4; 11:9—19; 12:25—36) and without whom the disciples can do nothing (15:5).

[74]The disciples' inability to draw the net into their boat may be intended in this very symbolic passage as a contrast to the drawing activity of Jesus and the Father (6:44; 12:32). These are the only three occasions where the verb ἐλκύω is used in the Gospel in a specifically missionary context: the Father draws followers to Jesus (6:44); Jesus draws all peoples to himself by his "being lifted up" (12:32) but the disciples cannot draw to themselves the fruit of their own missionary labors (21:6c); instead, they draw it to Jesus who alone enables them to bear fruit. The Father's name, not theirs, is glorified if they bear abundant fruit (15:8).

b) Personal relationships (vv 9—14, 15—23, 24—25)

The second part of the fishing incident (vv 9—14) illustrates that the disciples' personal nourishment comes from Jesus (vv 5, 9, 13), and the rest of the episode, that he, too, decides their personal destinies. The whole section recalls the intimate relationship which exists between the vine and its branches, the sustaining role of the vine, and the need for the branches to continue to remain in the vine if they are to have life and bear fruit (15:1—8, 16). As the vine nourishes the branches not from a distance but with its own sap, so does Jesus nourish the disciples with his own life and from his own hands. The gestures in v 13 are charged with Eucharistic overtones (cf. 6:11). Though John does not record the actual institution of the Eucharist, he emphasizes more than the other Evangelists the importance for the individual of eating Jesus' flesh and drinking his blood (6:53—58)[75].

Jesus' primary concern is for the disciples, whether or not they have something to eat (v 5); even before they make their catch, he already has fish roasting for them, of his own provision. When the disciples arrive at the shore, they simply enter into his labor (cf. 4:36). Moreover, the fruit they *gather in* serves as their *reward* (cf. 4:36) since they also eat of their catch (vv 10—13). The dependence of the disciples is further underlined by their receiving the food as a gift from Jesus' hands (v 13). Finally, it will be noted that while Jesus feeds the disciples he does not himself eat with them; rather he sustains them on their mission while his own food/mission is to do and complete his Father's work (4:34), namely, to give fulness of life to those who believe in him (3:16; 10:10)[76].

Jn 6:1—21. Though set within the sowing phase of "the work," 6:1—21 illustrates the same need for the disciples' total dependence on Jesus. This is the only occasion in Jesus' life time when the disciples actually take part in his mission (4:2 is proleptic), and most strikingly, the participation is wholly one of service, carried out to the minutest details according to Jesus' instructions (vv 10—13), in contrast to the Synoptic accounts (Mt 14:13—21; Mk 6:32—44; Lk 9:10—17). In John the initiative comes from Jesus (v 5), not from the disciples themselves as in the Synoptics (Mt 14:15; Mk 6:35—36; Lk 9:12); Jesus' question to Philip is a test, since he himself knew what to do (v 6). Both Philip and Andrew admit the impossibility of the situation, and thereby their complete helplessness (vv 7—

---

[75]Jn 6 is commonly viewed as the Johannine version of the institution of the Eucharist. If so, then it is worth noting that his account emphasizes not the rite of the institution (Mt 26:26—29; Mk 14:22—25; Lk 22:16—20), but its meaning for Jesus' audience (v 51, 53). The Johannine "Last Supper" (13—17) brings out further the life-giving nature of Jesus' mission (cf. 17:19).

[76]Ruckstuhl ("Zur Aussage und Botschaft von Johannes 21," esp. pp. 346—347) also notes the Eucharistic overtones present in v 13, and the fact that Jesus nourishes the disciples with his own life. He observes further (p. 347) that while the feeding in 6:1—14 is seen as a "sign," the Eucharistic meaning of which is explained in 6:32—35, the feeding in 21:12—13 signifies the Eucharist itself.

9; cf. 21:5b). The five loaves and two fishes which Jesus blesses and *gives* to the disciples to distribute to the crowd is furnished not by the disciples (v 9; cf. Mt 14:17—18; Mk 6:38; Lk 9:13), but by a little boy in the crowd (vv 10—11); the disciples *receive* the food from Jesus' hands and give it to the crowd (vv 10—11). After the feeding, Jesus again orders them to gather up and save the remnants (v 12; cf. Mt 14:21; Mk 6:43; Lk 9:17). The disciples then gather together (συνήγαγον) and fill twelve baskets (v 13).

Thus in contrast to the Synoptic account, the Johannine report emphasizes Jesus' initiative at every turn of the episode. Again, these marked differences between John and the Synoptics in the handling of this traditional material can hardly be accidental. The disciples' role is made extremely easy for them by Jesus: all they have to do is distribute the food provided by him and gather up the surplus. Though no mention is made of their partaking of the food in this instance, one cannot help wondering what they did with the twelve baskets, and whether this might not be for them[77]. Unlike the Synoptics, John associates only two disciples, Philip and Andrew (vv 5b, 8), with Jesus' quest for food for the crowd. "The Twelve" are mentioned only later in the context of Judas' betrayal (vv 67, 70, 71). Interestingly, Philip and Andrew are again the pair who inform Jesus of the coming of the Greeks in 12:20—22. Earlier, Andrew had brought his brother, Simon Peter, to see Jesus, and Philip, Nathanael (1: 40, 45). These two thus stand out in the Gospel as paradigms of missionaries (cf. 17:20).

The episode at sea which follows after the feeding underlines the need for dependence (6:16—21). The disciples' hard labor in the *dark* against the storm and the length of the sea comes to a "sudden" end the moment Jesus arrives, reveals himself to them and enters into the boat. Most strikingly, once Jesus enters in, the boat becomes irrelevant as a means of transportation (v 21). If, as Giblin cautions, this sea-crossing should not "be pressed to refer specifically to the mission of the disciples"[78], it does, nevertheless, look forward to Jn 21; the disciples themselves are part of Jesus' own mission and his missionary effort is directed as much towards them as towards the crowd. Verses 67—71 make this clear: despite their special election (v 70; cf. 15:16), the disciples have to meet the same chal-

---

[77]The Synoptics also mention the "twelve baskets" (Mt 14:20b; Mk 6:43; Lk 9:17b); and Luke 9:12, in particular, emphasizes the initiatory role of "the Twelve" ("the disciples" in Mt 14: 15; Mk 6:35) in the concern for the crowd. Robinson (*Redating,* 293) believes that the twelve baskets in John refer to the "fulness of Israel" still to be gathered in after the Judeans (the Jews in Palestine) had eaten. This is clearly one of those instances where the exegesis is conditioned by "a prior decision" concerning the subject matter (cf. p. 77, n. 56 above); for Robinson's interpretation derives from his sustained theory that the Gospel is written to win the Jews of the Diaspora. But can we honestly attribute to John's Gospel a marked interest in the salvation of the Jews seen as a group distinct from other ethnic groups? In reality, the Jews, specifically those in Palestine, are presented as the only representative group which rejects Jesus' testimony.

[78]Giblin, "Crossing," 103, n. 31.

lenge of faith which God requires of all Jesus' followers (6:29) and which
is the sole condition for both personal and missionary partnership with
him (6:56—57; 15:1—8)[79].

Finally, not only do the disciples come under Jesus' mission in terms
of their personal nourishment and missionary fruitfulness, but their personal destinies are wholly determined by him (21:15—23). Peter's triple
confession of love given in response to Jesus' question (vv 16—18) is generally interpreted as a reinstatement of Peter after his triple denial of
Jesus during the Passion (18:17, 25, 27). Significant, however, is the fact
that the triple charge given to Peter to feed the flock does not rest on
merit, but constitutes the proof of Jesus' total forgiveness of Peter and of
his acceptance of Peter's profession of love: the proof that you love me
is that you will feed my flock, for in the Gospel, love is expressed by
action (14:15; 15:10). By this acceptance of Peter's confession of love,
Jesus also confers on him the power to live out his previous lip-service
boast that he would lay down his life for Jesus (v 18; cf. 13:37). The difference is that this ability, also previously promised by Jesus (13:36), is
now given to Peter as a gift, as an act by which he will glorify God, not as
something which Peter demonstrates by his own strength and which
gives him advantage over the others[80].

Though Peter is given charge to feed the flock, the flock remains
Jesus' property: "my lambs," "my sheep" (vv 16—18); for there is only
one shepherd whose role is non-transferable (10:1—16; cf. 17:2, 9, 10).
All the disciples form part of the flock whose proper duty is to follow the
shepherd (12:26; 21:20) and that includes Peter himself (21:19; cf. 1
Jn 3:16). Besides, the charge is primarily one of service, not of authority,
a service based on Jesus' own example of feeding the disciples. That is
why Peter can exercise no jurisdiction over the destiny of another sheep
(vv 20—21). The fate of the individual sheep is strictly a matter between
Jesus and the sheep concerned. The fundamental Johannine conception
of one flock, one shepherd or of the vine and the branches underlines
Jesus' irreplaceable role within the community of believers. If the charge
does carry some notion of authority, this authority is understood primarily in terms of self-sacrificing love (vv 18—19); it is essentially a pastoral
authority[81].

---

[79]The order of events in Jn 6 and 21 is reversed: in Jn 6 the miraculous feeding on land pre-
ceeds Jesus' self-revelation at sea; in Jn 21 the self-revelation at sea precedes the feeding on land.
Both passages thus emphasize "the sea" as the locus of Jesus' revelation to the disciples of their
need for dependence on him. Without him they are literally and metaphorically at sea!

[80]The phrase "more than these others" probably echoes the tradition found in Mt 26:33—35
and Mk 14:29—31 where Peter boasts that even if all the other disciples deny Jesus he will not.

[81]Though we cannot go into a detailed discussion on this issue, in our view, the terminology
of the charge to Peter in vv 15—17 emphasizes more the notion of "taking care of," feeding and
tending (βόσκειν), than of "governing and ruling" (cf. Brown, *John* II, 1112—1117). The designation of the flock as "lambs," "shearlings" and "little sheep" (πρόβατία, diminutive form in certain
MSS) underlines this point. To use a human analogy, the notion of "ruling and governing" usually

Is the portrayal of Peter in Jn 21, then, not an attempt by the ecclesiastical redactor to reinstate the Petrine authority and so bring the Johannine account in line with orthodox traditions[82]? It would seem not; the general portrayal of Peter here is consistent with the policy in the Gospel to relativize the role of all the disciples. Unlike the Synoptic accounts, Jesus nowhere commits either to Peter or to the Twelve the keys of the kingdom of heaven (Mt 16:19) or the power to judge the twelve tribes of Israel, seen as a reward for abiding with Jesus in his trials (Mt 19:28; Lk 22:28–30). In John, their being with Jesus from the beginning entitles the disciples to be his witnesses (15:27), while all judgment is committed exclusively to the Son (5:22).

The difference between John and the Synoptics is all the more striking if Jn 21:16–19; 6:67–71 and 20:20–23 are the Johannine versions of Mt 16:13–20; 16:18–19 and 19:27–30 (= Lk 22:30), respectively. In Jn 21:15–17 Peter's triple confession of love is followed not by a conferring of powers to lose and bind, or by making him the foundation of the church, but by the charge to feed the flock even unto death (vv 18–19). Similarly, his confession of faith in 6:68–69 calls forth not a praise of blessedness (Mt 16:18–19), but a reminder of the election of the Twelve and of the fact that one of them is a devil; the integrity of the group is at stake (6:70–71). Finally, in 20:23 the role of the disciples consists in forgiving sins (not in judging the twelve tribes of Israel, Mt 19:27–30; Lk 22:30) which commission, as already noted, has a reference to bringing into fellowship, or to persuading others by the witness of the preacher's life to believe and find life in Jesus.

Indeed, the Gospel is not unaware of the traditional leadership role usually assigned to Peter (cf. 20:5–6; 21:2, 11). But precisely because of this his traditional role, Peter becomes the most fitting figure through whom to illustrate the lesson of the disciples' need for dependence on Jesus. His authority is one of pastoral service, not of ownership. That is why his interference with the destiny of another sheep is rejected in no uncertain terms (21:21–22). As in the rest of the Gospel, this final chapter plays down Peter's role, not, incidentally, in favor of the BD but of Jesus himself. Neither Peter nor the BD pose as Jesus' rival. For Jesus alone is the way to the Father and the life (14:6), the only door to the sheepfold (10:17).

---

applies in respect to adults, not to babies and little children. The latter need tender loving care, not government. Peter is given the charge to tend and look after the flock as a concrete expression of his avowed love for Jesus. While the notion of ruling and governing is present in the use of the shepherd imagery in the OT, NT and extra biblical literature (cf. Brown, *John* II. 1114), it is not readily evident that the Johannine usage of this traditional imagery emphasizes the same notion of authority (cf. Jn 10, set against the background of Ez 34:1–16, 23; 37:24).

[82]For a discussion of the "rehabilitation" theory see, for instance, Brown, *John* II, 1110 (strongly in favor); and Schnackenburg, *John* III, 362 (moderately in favor). Brown cites Spitta, Gougel and Bultmann as among those who reject this theory.

The BD figures, then, not as Peter's rival in terms of authority (cf. 20: 5—6) but as the embodiment of the ideal of discipleship envisaged by the Gospel, one characterized by a close personal relationship with Jesus (13:23—26; 18:26—27), by a faith-oriented attitude (20:8; cf. 2:22; 12: 16), and by self-effacing witness (19:35; 20:30—31; 21:24—25). His witnessing role, like Peter's pastoral service, draws attention not to himself but to Jesus (20:30; cf. 21:7), nor does it constitute him Peter's rival. We do not even know his name while we know that of Peter and of a few others. Indeed, the BD does not even rival Peter in terms of personal love for Jesus (21:15—18); his being loved by Jesus is a grace (1:16—17; cf. 13:23, 25—26; 18:26—27), not something, therefore, which can be accredited to him. Like the genuine witness, the BD does not seek his own glory (7:18; 5:41, 44; 8:54)[83].

Peter and the BD thus typify, each in his own way, the meaning of discipleship in the Gospel, namely, utter dependence on Jesus which rests on faith in the revelation of his love given and received as a gift and exercised in mutual service. In this respect, they both unite; they do not rival one another since both are called to the same following of Jesus (21:19b, 20—22), even if the personal manner of this following is different in each case (vv 22—23). If, then, there is any suggestion of rivalry in the Gospel, such rivalry is between Jesus and Peter (cf. 21:21—22) or to put it more broadly, between Jesus and the disciples. This consistent effort throughout the Gospel to subordinate *all* the disciples (not only Peter) to Jesus calls for some explanation.

B. Summary of the Gospel Evidence

The results of the analysis of the farewell discourses and of Jn 21 have largely confirmed those obtained in the analysis of 4:1—42 concerning the Johannine approach to mission. This joint evidence of both our basic text and the discourses demonstrates that the salient features of the Johannine approach concern the centrality of Jesus in the missionary enterprise, the essentially dependent nature of the disciples' mission, fellowship as an essential aspect of mission and method in the exercise and portrayal of this mission. In the discourses as in 4:1—42, the theme of Jesus' uniqueness is underlined by the ἔργον concept, by the statement that he is the only way to the Father (14:6), and by the emphasis on his ontological divine sonship. Though mutely expressed in 4:34, this last point is brought to the fore in the discourses in the motif of pre-existence

---

[83]The personal character and attitude of the Beloved Disciple will emerge even more clearly in our discussion in Chapter VII; see esp. pp. 238 and 252 below.

(16:28; 17:1), as it was earlier both in the ὁ μονογενής passages (1:14, 18; 3:16, 18) and in Jesus' whole debate with the Jews, Jn 5—10. Jesus' ontological divine sonship is portrayed throughout the Gospel as an inalienable aspect of his messiahship or saving mission from the Father. We shall say more on this issue in the next chapter.

Equally, the theme of the disciples' dependence on Jesus in the discourses undergoes a development from 4:1—42. Not only do they depend on him for their missionary harvesting, but they cannot at any moment or in any capacity by-pass Jesus to reach the Father. Jesus' mediation remains always a *sine qua non* for the disciples with respect to their personal life, missionary fruitfulness and access to the Father. In the discourses this dependence of the disciples is underlined in the imagery of the vine and the branches, in the promise of the Holy Spirit seen as a gift, in Jesus' pastoral prayer for his disciples of all times and in the whole narrative in Jn 21.

The important issue of fellowship also takes on the character of a new command to love and serve one another after Jesus' own example. This mutual love constitutes the authentic identity of the new, eschatological community brought into existence by Jesus' accomplished mission. The missionary purpose it serves is reinforced by active missionary preaching on the part of the disciples (15:27; 17: 20; 21). In other words, the eschatological community defines itself both by the mutual love and service of its members in community and by its active efforts to make Jesus known so that others may be drawn into the fellowship with Jesus and the Father, a fellowship lived out visibly here and now in the community of believers.

Finally, with regard to method, the discourses and Jn 21 also reveal that the above points are made in a highly polemical or corrective manner as in 4:1—42; the discourses, in addition, witness to a marked persuasive and hortatory thrust. A most important feature of the evangelist's method is that he presents Jesus himself personally dialoguing with his audience either in order to bring this audience to believe in him or in order to comment on the missionary task itself. In brief, in the Johannine conception of mission, Jesus is central not only with regard to the meaning and content of mission, but also with regard to its method of approach.

If the net-result of our entire analysis is correct, namely, that there is a systematic effort on the part of the Evangelist to subordinate the disciples to Jesus in every aspect of their life and mission, then this self-evidence of the Gospel calls for a revision of the modern approach whereby the mission of the disciples is said to have constituted the basic inspiration for the understanding of the mission of Jesus. Not only does mission in John cover more than the post-Easter activity of the disciples, but this post-Easter activity itself is seen to be derivative of Jesus' own mission and wholly dependent on it. The revision also calls for a new effort to understand why the Evangelist took such pains to relativize the missionary role of the disciples. To this task we now turn.

Chapter VII

The Social Context

The consistent portrait of mission which has emerged in the foregoing analysis of Jn 4:1–42; 13–17 and 21 furnishes us with a firm basis for an enquiry into the missionary situation of the Evangelist and of his audience. The central and ever-recurrent questions raised by the results of the analysis are these: What concrete historical circumstances could have brought forth from the Evangelist his unmitigated emphasis on the all-pervading significance of Jesus in the missionary enterprise, with its corresponding spotlight on the disciples' all-round dependence on him? In what known historical situation, if any, can we reasonably situate this Johannine conception of mission with its distinctively polemical and hortatory thrust aimed at the disciples themselves? In brief, what specific historical circumstances could have shaped the Evangelist's total conception of mission which has emerged in our foregoing analysis with regard to both its content and method? On a secondary level, can we infer from this missionary situation the probable date of the Gospel as we now have it?

Our intention here is not to explore in any detail the specific nature of the missionary issues raised in the Gospel as these concern the Evangelist and his audience. Still less do we intend to join in the current heated debate on the general *Sitz-im-Leben* of the Johannine community[1]. Our aim, quite simply, is to try and relate the portrait of mission which has emerged from this study to some kind of life-situation which could have formed the living inspirational context of the Evangelist's approach. The need to relate the Gospel evidence (the literary dimension) to the social context (the audience-dimension) is called for by both our contextual

---

[1] Studies in the situation of the Johannine community outside the commentaries include: Brown, *The Community of the Beloved Disciple;* Cullmann, *Der johanneische Kreis;* Martyn, *History and Tradition; The Gospel of John in Christian History: Essays for Interpreters* (New York: Paulist, 1978), esp. pp. 55–89; "Glimpses into the History of the Johannine Community from Its Origin through the Period of Its Life in Which the Fourth Gospel Was Composed," *BETL* 44, 149–175; Culpepper, *The Johannine School*; Rigaux, "Die Jünger Jesu"; W. Wiefel, "Die Scheidung von Gemeinde und Welt im Johannesevangelium auf dem Hintergrund der Trennung von Kirche und Synagoge," *TZ* 35/4 (1979) 213–227. Indeed one might say that the situation of the Johannine community currently constitutes the most intriguing and the most discussed area in Johannine studies. The issue is also related to the question of the Johannine redaction since each redaction was supposedly destined to meet the needs of a particular audience.

method and John's Gospel itself. From the standpoint of the contextual method, the audience forms an integral part of the context of any NT work whose fundamentally pastoral or missionary character none disputes[2]. From the perspective of the Gospel, the declared intention of "the book" (20:30—31) makes the audience-dimension all the more significant (cf. pp. 48—49 above). For if the Gospel is consciously addressed to a living audience in order to persuade this audience to believe that Jesus is the Christ, the Son of God, then the situation of this audience and the possible influence it might have exercised on the formulation of the message constitute an integral dimension of the Gospel's total meaning[3].

In keeping with our contextual approach, we will conduct our enquiry within the Johannine corpus itself, with particular attention to the Epistles which, unlike the Gospel with its more universal and elusive background, clearly address a specific historical situation. No scholar would dispute this fact, even if 1 John is seen more as a tractate than a letter[4]. The question of date, also an important aspect of the historical/social context, will be briefly considered after we have gained a better insight into the nature of the missionary situation presupposed by the Gospel. To facilitate the enquiry, the ensuing discussion will be organized under the following headings: 1) the missionary situation of the Evangelist and of his audience based on the evidence of the Gospel, 2) the relationship between John's Gospel and Epistles and the light which this throws on the missionary situation of the community, 3) the implications of this relationship for the understanding of the Johannine approach to mission, and 4) the probable date of the Gospel in the light of the contextual evidence highlighted in this investigation.

---

[2] The pastoral/missionary dimension of the NT works hardly needs documenting. The point is most clear with respect to Paul's letters and the epistles generally which constitute the bulk of the NT literature. The Gospels are "the good news of Jesus Christ" proclaimed to the nations (Mt 28: 19—20; Mk 16:15—16; Lk 24:46—49; Jn 20:30—31; cf. Acts 1:1—8). Revelation is a set of letters addressed to the seven churches of Asia Minor also depicting the practical consequences for individuals and nations who accept or reject the message.

[3] Murphy-O'Connor's *St. Paul's Corinth: Texts and Archaeology* (Good News Studies 6; Wilmington: Michael Glazier, 1983) has recently brought to light the intrinsic influence which the socio-cultural and religious situation of the Corinthians exercised on both the content and language of Paul's letters addressed to them. Similar documentary studies yet remain to be conducted with respect to other addressees of the Pauline and NT works. The contribution of the audience to the formation of the NT is today one of the most neglected areas in NT studies; yet strangely enough, were it not for the different audiences and their respective needs we would probably not have had a single work in the NT canon.

[4] 1 John is considered as a tractate because it lacks the usual salutation or address, the identification of the author and of those addressed, and the final greeting (cf. Rom 1:1—7; 16:17—23). See further Bruce, *Epistles*, 25; and the comprehensive description of the epistolary form by Brown, *Epistles*, 788—795; cf. *Community*, 94.

A. The Missionary Situation from the Gospel Evidence

1. The Community's Interest in Mission

Our first step in discussing the missionary situation of the community presupposed by the Gospel is to address the fundamental question raised in the survey in Chapter I, namely, whether the Evangelist and/or his community were interested in mission. For obviously if neither of them was, then the problem of mission is not an issue for them, and this whole section of the study becomes irrelevant. The position of scholars on this issue was extensively discussed in the survey (pp. 7–34). For easy reference, we list here the major positions taken with regard to the author and community of the Gospel in its present final form[5]. First, the Evangelist was not concerned with mission, understood exclusively as outreach to non-believers, but rather with strengthening the faith of believers against the onslaught of persecution by both world and synagogue. This, we recall, was the majority view (pp. 11–12). Second, the Evangelist/community was interested in mission and these missionary efforts were directed towards converting Jews, Gentiles, Samaritans or any of the three combined (pp. 9–11). Third, the Evangelist, not the community, was interested in mission (Painter), or conversely, the community more so than the Evangelist was interested (Schnackenburg) (p. 32).

We may now put the question quite simply thus: In the light of our foregoing analysis of the Gospel material, were the Evangelist and/or his community interested in mission? The answer in the light of this analysis is that both the Evangelist and some, at least, of his community were interested in mission, otherwise, the entire missionary emphasis of the Gospel makes no sense. Concerning the community, or the disciples, we noted that the emphasis does not point in the direction of urging them on to missionary activity as would have been the case had there been a marked anti-missionary attitude among them. Rather, the emphasis reveals a consistent attempt to remind the disciples that Jesus and the Father, not they, are the real agents at work. In brief, the emphasis focuses on *the right attitude* which should animate the disciples *in the exercise of mission,* namely, that though sent, they are wholly dependent on Jesus.

Mention was made earlier of Bultmann's and Bligh's view that 4:35 addresses a missionary lethargy on the part of the disciples (p. 153). Our close analysis of the whole of 4:35–42 revealed, however, that the central issue in the passage is not so much the delay of missionary action on the part of the disciples as it is their need to recognize both the advent

---

[5]By "author" here we mean the Evangelist, not the modern critic's final redactor, editor or John III. The overall result obtained in our analysis of the literary layers of 4:1–42 applies on a larger scale to the Gospel; for most literary critics would view the bulk of the Gospel as the work of one author, though they may differ as to whether this author wrote his work in one or many editions.

of the eschatological harvest ushered in by Jesus' completed mission and the operational relationship which this completed mission establishes between them and Jesus in the missionary enterprise. The whole passage seemed destined to correct a possessive attitude towards the mission on the part of the disciples and a tendency to come between Jesus and those brought to faith in him (4:38, 42).

Equally, it might be argued that 15:2, 6 suggests an anti-missionary attitu'de on the part of the disciples, in the reminder that missionary fruitfulness is the condition for remaining in Jesus. If these verses were ever intended in this sense, such is not their primary meaning in this present Gospel context[6]. The whole passage rather emphasizes the need for continued belief in and dependence on Jesus as the sole condition for remaining alive. Missionary fruitfulness understood here primarily as selfless love of the brethren after the example of Jesus' own love for the disciples (15: 12—17) constitutes the concrete proof that one is alive in Jesus. So we may conclude that the Gospel passages we have examined give no evidence of an anti-missionary attitude on the part of the disciples or the community addressed by the Gospel. What they understood by mission and how they carried out their missionary activity are, however, a different matter.

That the Evangelist himself was interested in mission seems hardly questionable. The conception of the Gospel from the fundamental standpoint of mission is to be attributed to him, the author who has left his own distinctive stamp on the Gospel. His missionary interest is too deeply ingrained in the fabric of the Gospel to be assigned to a mere redactional layer. As we saw in the introductory survey of the Johannine data itself (pp. 1—7), the missionary interest in the Gospel reveals itself in the portrayal of Jesus' life on earth from the standpoint of mission: he is the one sent by the Father to give eternal life to believers through the joint revelation of himself and the Father. We noted it, too, in the positive and negative portrayal of other important characters in the Gospel from the standpoint of mission, positively, John the Baptist and the Holy Spirit, and negatively, the Pharisees who are the paradigms of the anti-sent (5: 41—44). Even the call of the disciples in John has a missionary perspective, one which in essence defines the whole nature of their future missionary task, and which consists in leading others to see and believe in Jesus (compare 1:40—49 and 4:28—30', 42; 17:20).

To the Evangelist, too, we attribute the distinctive features of the

---

[6]Critics generally regard 15:1—17 as part of the original Gospel material in contrast to 15:18—16:4 which is said to be a late insertion. Cf. Painter, "Glimpses of the Johannine Community in the Farewell Discourses," *NTS* 27 (1981) 525—543; and Segovia, "The Theology and Provenance of John 15:1—17," *JBL* 101 (1982) 115—128; also "Original Farewell Discourse," p. 196, n. 10 above. While Boismard-Lamouille (*Synopse III*, 366—367) assign vv 1—17 to John II-B, they allege on the evidence of Mt 3:19 that vv 1—2 and 5—6 are older material which the Evangelist has incorporated. These authors do not, however, discuss the meaning of these verses in their original context.

Johannine approach to mission which has emerged from this study. This approach we know by now consists in presenting Jesus himself actively engaged in mission in dialogue with a variety of interlocutors and also personally commenting on the missionary task. But if we were to pinpoint even more closely the particular character of this approach it would be in terms of his emphasis on Jesus' uniqueness in the missionary enterprise (*the thesis*) and the corresponding insistence on the essentially dependent, derivative and self-benefiting nature of the disciples' mission (*the consequential argument*). Not only, then, is the Evangelist interested in mission, but the consistent and corrective approach aimed at the disciples themselves is to be attributed to him.

Our evidence thus leads us to conclude that both the Evangelist and his community were interested in mission. The problem seems to lie rather in their different understanding of mission, especially on the issue of Jesus' and the disciples' respective roles in the missionary enterprise. This brings us back to our central task, that of determining, if possible, the nature of the circumstances which might have brought about the difference between the Evangelist and some of his community in their approach to mission. What was happening on the missionary scene at the time the Gospel was written?

2. The Missionary *Sitz-im-Leben*

The Gospel evidence taken by itself suggests that the basic missionary problem in the Johannine community lay in the tendency on the part of some, at least, of the missionary disciples to set themselves against Jesus by claiming for themselves the glory of the missionary enterprise, thus forgetting that they were sent, which means dependent. This Christ-rivalry, it would seem, went hand in hand with a lack of love and fellowship within the community, which lack of fellowship threatened the very significance of the community as an eschatological group of believers who witness to the reality of Jesus' life-giving mission from the Father.

The specific form which this rivalry took is not readily discernible in the Gospel, nor are its real causes. For instance, was the rivalry the by-product of the lack of love and fellowship within the community, manifested in the resistance to admitting certain groups of believers into the community, for example, the Samaritans? Did the rivalry itself cause the lack of fellowship by splitting up the community because of disagreements over the newly introduced "high Christology" brought by the new arrivals[7]? Or did the rivalry and lack of fellowship stem from two different causes, even though both affected the community adversely?

---

[7] Brown (*Community*, 43–47) holds that the crisis in the Johannine community started when the Hellenists (Jews with anti-Temple views) and the Samaritans (with a high "Moses piety") joined the community. The theological ideas brought by these new arrivals formed the "*catalyst*"

Woll's dissertation on 13:31—14:26 is commendable for its primary insight that a Christ-rivalry reigned among the disciples themselves, and consequently, that a polemic is directed against them[8]. But his identification of this rivalry as one of charismatic leadership according to which, on the basis of Mk 13:5, 6, some of the disciples may have actually claimed to be Christ himself lacks convincing force. Nor is Woll alone in holding this view[9]. For one thing, the Marcan passage deals with people who at the end of time (the Parousia) claim to be Christ himself returned, whereas John's Gospel deals with disciples who, for one reason or another, usurp Christ's unique place in the community. The ones are "false" Christs ($\psi\epsilon\upsilon\delta\acute{o}\chi\rho\iota\sigma\tau o\iota$), the others "anti-christs" ($\grave{\alpha}\nu\tau\acute{\iota}\chi\rho\iota\sigma\tau o\iota$)[10].

In addition to the disciples who usurp Jesus' role in the missionary enterprise, there are those who stop believing and cease to be Jesus' disciples for doctrinal reasons (6:60—66; 8:30—59)[11]. Their ceasing to remain Jesus' disciples is important because of the threat it poses to those who remain with Jesus. In 6:60—66 the unbelieving disciples do not simply part company with Jesus (v 66); they declare that since his is a hard word nobody can be expected to listen to him (v 60). Jesus' question to

---

which inspired the development of the Johannine "high christology." This development, in turn, brought about suspicion of the group by the more orthodox Christian Jews of Baptist descent. Curiously enough, Brown himself (*John* I, 172—173, 175) accords no "high" Christological status to the confession of the Samaritan woman (4:29; cf. v 25) and the Samaritans (4:42) which passages constitute the only solid evidence we have in the Johannine corpus for a "Samaritan" Christology.

[8]Woll, *Johannine Christianity,* esp. pp. 128 and 176, n. 79.

[9]See, for instance, Brown, *Epistles,* 680—690; Robinson, *Redating,* 286—287; Dodd, *Epistles,* 149—150; Marshall, *Epistles,* 21—22. Rigaux ("Die Jünger Jesu," 202—213) sees the Johannine group not so much as "advanced Christians," as an "elite community of prophets" who in fidelity to Jesus' teaching had formed around a charismatic leader in opposition to persecution and false teaching.

[10]The Marcan passage concerns people who come in the last days claiming to be "the Christ," and saying, "I am he." The Johannine position, on the contrary, deals with people who "deny" that Jesus is the Christ. The primary meaning of $\grave{\alpha}\nu\tau\acute{\iota}$ is not "identification with" but "opposition to." Walter Grundmann ("Antichrist," *TDNT* IX, 571—572) rightly holds that the idea of opposition is the most dominant in the Johannine use of the term, in contrast to its usage in other NT writings (cf. Mk 13:14—27; 2 Thess 2:3—10; Rev 13). See further, *BAG,* 76; Plummer, *Epistles,* 57, 63.

[11]Jesus' address to those "who *had believed* in him" (8:31) extends to v 59, since no change of audience is indicated; throughout he is speaking with "the Pharisees" (v 13) or "the Jews" (vv 31, 48, 52, 57). Zerwick (*Analysis* I, 312) regards the perfect participle in v 31 as a pluperfect but believes that it indicates an "enduring action." Abbott (*Grammar,* 2506, pp. 365—366) also regards the perfect in v 31 as a pluperfect adding that "As there is no pluperfect active participle, John, like other authors, employs the perfect participle as an equivalent." But unlike Zerwick, he argues rightly that "the context excludes the notion of completeness," and that "there is no intention to imply perfect belief." On the contrary, the context indicates "transition from belief to the bitterest enmity." V 31b (that true discipleship demands "remaining in" Jesus' word and for ever; cf. v 36) and v 59 (the sequel of the conversation) prove conclusively that the context precludes the notion of enduring belief and that the author has no intention to imply "perfect belief." The situation in this chapter thus parallels that in 2:23—25 and in 6:60—66. In each case, the faith of the audience lacks depth and lasting conviction.

the Twelve (v 67) aims at making them take a stand in this crisis of faith. Yet while they choose to stay out of a public faith rather than of rational conviction (vv 68—69) they are reminded in the person of Judas that the threat to faith remains a constant reality (vv 70—71; cf. 16:31—33).

With the disciples in 8:30—59, the problem is also doctrinal not persecution or ejection from the synagogue. While those in 6:60—66 find both his teaching on the Eucharist and his claim to heavenly origin impossible to accept, these latter contest his claim to divinity (vv 56—59) and in particular his suggesting that they who had never been enslaved, being born of God and of Abraham, should ever be thought of as sinners (vv 33, 39, 41, that is, equated with people who do not know Yahweh)[12]. The doctrinal aspect involved in the disciples' reaction to Jesus is, therefore, important; but in no case is there a suggestion directly or indirectly that the disciples in question are actually claiming to be Jesus. The insistence in the discourses that neither the disciples nor anyone else can come to the Father except through Jesus (14:6; 17:2—3) need not be taken as implying that some of the disciples actually believed they could dispense with Jesus in their ascent to eternal life and the Father[13]. In 5:39—47, for instance, Jesus' unbelieving Jewish opponents hold that their self-acquired knowledge of the Scriptures and their trust in Moses are adequate means to eternal life, such that they have no need of Jesus. In the case of the disciples, it is one thing to believe that Jesus is the Savior of the world and God's sole agent of salvation (4:42; 6:68—69) and quite another to act accordingly or not to claim the glory for self (4:38, 42; 13: 17; 15:8, 16)[14].

---

[12]In Jewish mentality, Gentiles are by nature sinners since they do not know Yahweh or the Torah. This attitude is summarily expressed by Paul in Gal 2:15; 4:8—9; see further Eph 1:12; 4: 17—18. Qumran regarded all outsiders, both Jews and Gentiles, as sinners (1QS 1:10; 2:4—5; 3: 18—25; 1QM 1:1; 1QpPs 37:2—5), though it also believed in the ultimate conversion of "all Israel," when the rest of Israel, men, women and children, would join the Sons of Zadok, the Qumran sect, and be taught the Torah (1QM 1:1—6; 1QSa). In Johannine thought *all* are sinners, whether they be Jews, Gentiles or believers; hence all stand in need of God's free redemption given in and through Jesus to be received in faith (cf. 1:12—13, 17, 29, 36; 3:16—17; 8:31—36; 13:10; 15:3; 1 Jn 1:8—2:2). This view that all stand in need of God's redemption given through Jesus is, however, not exclusively Johannine (cf. Rom 1:18—3:31; Gal 2:15—21). In Jn 8:30—59, as in all his debates with the Jews, Jesus tries to get his Jewish audience to see that they, in fact, do not know God since they reject him and the life-giving knowledge of God which he brings. Their capital sin lies precisely in their blinding claim to knowledge of God and to sinlessness (8:21, 24; 9:41; 15:22, 24).

[13]The questions put to Jesus by the disciples: Thomas (14:4), Philip (14:8) and Judas not Iscariot (14:22), would indicate that the disciples who continued to believe in Jesus did not see him as wholly irrelevant in their efforts to ascend to the Father. They simply wanted something more: to get to the Father himself. The whole situation indicates that they had not sufficiently grasped how total and complete was Jesus' representation of the Father (14:9—11).

[14]Adolf Schlatter (*Die Briefe und die Offenbarung des Johannes* [Stuttgart: Calwer, 1964] 44) vividly depicts the "antichrist" as one who behaves *as if* he had won his own salvation by his own "might" (*Kraft*); he concludes that the apostle saw many such people in his own day. One can be an "antichrist" as much by one's attitude of pride in one's religious achievements as by one's out-

What seems clear then, from the evidence of the Gospel, is that the problem has to do with the fact of Jesus' identity and mission from the Father, and with the practical implications which this revealed identity had for non-disciples and disciples alike. Was Jesus or was he not God's divine and sole eschatological agent of salvation from the Father such that he had neither predecessors (the OT, Moses, John the Baptist) nor successors (the disciples themselves)? And such that there were no alternatives to the way of salvation which he offered (8:24; 14:6; 17:2–3)? What did believing in him mean in terms of the inter-personal relationship of believers here and now? Beyond these central observations we cannot convincingly say more concerning the missionary situation of the Johannine community on the evidence of the Gospel alone. The Johannine Epistles may yet shed light on this issue.

B. The Gospel and the Johannine Epistles

That John's Gospel and Epistles are closely related writings is disputed by none. Equally no critic would dispute Bultmann's position that the question of the relationship of John's Gospel to the Epistles is essentially the question of the relationship of the Gospel to 1 John[15]. Widely disputed, however, are the questions of authorship, chronology and the specific nature of the relationship between the two works. Are both works directed against the same or different fronts — the Gospel against the world and 1 John against believers[16]? Again, according to Lightfoot following the Muratorian Canon, was 1 John written as a companion volume to the Gospel and intended to be circulated with it[17]? Or, according to Robinson and Brown, was 1 John written a decade or so after the Gospel either to correct errors caused by the misinterpretation of the Gospel (Brown) or to defend the truth of the Gospel against those who would

---

right denial that "Jesus is the Christ." Thyen ("Entwicklungen innerhalb der johanneischen Theologie und Kirche im Spiegel von Joh 21 und der Lieblings jüngertexte des Evangeliums," *BETL* 44, 249–299) says, for instance, that of Diotrephes (3 Jn 9) the Evangelist would have said "er hat Gott nie gesehen" (p. 298). The same would apply to the "advanced Christians" in 2 Jn 9.

[15]Bultmann, *The Johannine Epistles: A Commentary* (Philadelphia: Fortress, 1973) 1. This, of course, does not mean that 2–3 John are not equally important for the situation of the community as our ensuing analysis will show.

[16]This, for instance, is the view of Bultmann, *Epistles,* 1 (citing Haenchen, "Neuere Literatur," 35–36); Brown, *Community,* 23, 97; and Robinson, *Redating,* 290. For Robinson the Gospel is not so much directed "against" the world as it is intended to convert the Jews of the Diaspora.

[17]Lightfoot (*Biblical Essays,* 198) holds that the author of the Canon regarded 1 John as "an epilogue" to the Gospel. Plummer (*Epistles,* xlv) strongly shares this view. Boismard-Lamouille (*Synopse III,* 68–69) on their part believe that the Evangelist wrote 1 John during the same period that he wrote his second redaction of the Gospel (John II-B, ca. A.D. 90).

distort its meaning (Robinson)[18]? Finally, while Bultmann and Brown among others attribute the Gospel and 1 John to different authors, Westcott, Lightfoot, Boismard-Lamouille, Robinson and a host of other authors attribute it to the same author[19]. This, too, is our view and the reasons for our adopting this view will become apparent in the ensuing discussion.

The questions of the chronological and situational relationship between the Gospel and 1 John are crucial to our discussion of the missionary situation of the Johannine community. For if, according to Brown's systematically sustained thesis, the misunderstanding of the Gospel caused the situation dealt with 1 John, then we obviously cannot use the Epistle written *post-eventum* to elucidate the living situation of the community presupposed by the Gospel[20]. Equally, if the priority of the Gospel to the Epistle "falls short of proof," though it is now generally assumed, we cannot with any degree of probability, let alone with certainty, argue the situation of the Gospel from that of the Epistles[21]. Our first important task, then, is to address the issue of the chronological relationship between the Gospel and 1 John as the basis for using the Epistle to elucidate the situation of the Gospel. In keeping with our contextual method, we will scrutinize the texts themselves for possible contextual clues to these issues[22].

1. The Chronological Relationship

The Gospel makes no reference to any work outside itself (20:31). The author of 1 John, however, speaks of itself as "a repeat" of a former work ($\pi\acute{\alpha}\lambda\iota\nu$ $\gamma\rho\acute{\alpha}\varphi\omega$, 2:8), one which deals with the same issues and rests on

---

[18]Robinson, *Redating*, 290; Brown, *Community*, 23, 93–114; and *Epistles*, 35, 73–86.

[19]Brown (*Epistles*, 19–30) offers a comprehensive survey of the discussion concerning the relationship of the author of the Gospel to that of 1 John. Most of the arguments he presents are against the oneness of authorship based on differences in style (pp. 21–25), in thought (pp. 25–28) and in life situation (pp. 28–30). The few arguments advanced in favor of the oneness of authorship rest on similarities in style (pp. 20–21). Brown himself (*Epistles,* 35) regards the unity of authorship as "likely, but not certain." For further surveys on this discussion see Marshall, *Epistles,* 32-42; Plummer, *Epistles,* lxvii–lxxiv (himself strongly in favor of the unity of authorship), and Schnackenburg, *Johannesbriefe,* 28–32 (also strongly in favor on the basis of similarities in language [pp. 29–30] and in theological outlook [pp. 30–32]). The view that favors the unity of authorship is more ancient and has more supporters than that which opposes it. The Canon, for instance, dates from ca. A.D. 190; see also Eusebius, *H.E.* 8.25.18–21.

[20]Brown not only sustains this thesis in his *Community of the Beloved Disciple,* his whole commentary on the Johannine Epistles is written from this fundamental standpoint.

[21]See, for instance, Robinson, *Redating,* 290; Westcott, *Epistles,* xxxi; Schnackenburg, *Johannesbriefe,* 32–33; and the good summary by Brown, *Epistles,* 32–35.

[22]Our approach here differs from the current practice whereby the Gospel alone is viewed as the determinative document for comprehending and dating the Epistle. Yet a few scholars do hold that a proper understanding of the Epistles must start with the Gospel; thus Plummer, *Epistles,*

the same presuppositions as the previous work $(2:7-8, 12-13, 14)^{23}$. This present work, 1 John, is further distinguished from the previous work by the juxtaposition of the present and aorist tenses of the verb $\gamma\rho\dot{\alpha}\varphi\epsilon\iota\nu$; as the $\gamma\rho\dot{\alpha}\varphi\omega$ passages (2:1, 7, 12, 13) refer to the present work, so the $\check{\epsilon}\gamma\rho\alpha\psi\alpha$ passages (2:14a,b,c 21, 26; 5:13) refer to the previous work[24]. Moreover, the author insists that this present work contains nothing new, only what the audience knows already (2:7, 21, 24; 3:11; cf. 2 Jn 5), and it knows this from Jesus himself, their evangelizer and teacher (2:25, 27), not from the author. The author's aim in this present writing, then, is simply to draw the attention of his readers to this their already acquired knowledge, which, presumably, is also the subject of the first work. The question now is to determine whether this first work is 2 or 3 John which Robinson, for instance, believes were written before 1 John, and in that order, or whether it is the Gospel[25]. Again we must seek the answer to this question by delineating as far as possible the character and scope of this work as it is described in 1 John itself.

From the central $\check{\epsilon}\gamma\rho\alpha\psi\alpha$ passages (2:21–27; 5:13) we gather the following information concerning the subject matter, method, purpose and content of the previous work. The *subject matter* of this first work is described globally as "the message" ($\dot{\epsilon}\pi\alpha\gamma\gamma\epsilon\lambda\dot{\iota}\alpha$, 2:25) or teaching ($\delta\iota\delta\dot{\alpha}\sigma\kappa\epsilon\iota\nu$, 2:27; cf. 2 Jn 9) which those addressed are said to have received from the beginning of their conversion ($\dot{\alpha}\pi'$ $\dot{\alpha}\rho\chi\tilde{\eta}\varsigma$, 2:7, 24) from Jesus himself ($\alpha\dot{\upsilon}\tau\dot{o}\varsigma$ $\dot{\epsilon}\pi\eta\gamma\gamma\epsilon\dot{\iota}\lambda\alpha\tau o$ $\dot{\upsilon}\mu\tilde{\iota}\nu$, 2:25)[26]. This message ($\tau\dot{o}\nu$ $\dot{\alpha}\pi'$ $\dot{\alpha}\rho\chi\tilde{\eta}\varsigma$, 2:13a, 14b) already known to the audience and received from Jesus himself is the same as that which the author and his co-eyewitnesses also received from Jesus himself (1:1–3, 5). So though the readers are said to have received the message from Jesus himself, in actual fact this message was transmitted to them, the audience addressed, by the author and his co-eyewitnesses (1:1–4)[27]. This means then that though the author and his

---

xlv, xlvii; and T.W. Manson, *On Paul and John* (London, 1963) 87–88 (cited by Bruce, *Epistles*, p. 30, n. 10).

[23]These "presuppositions" are given in 1 Jn 1:12–13a (expressed in the present tense) and vv 13b–14 (expressed in the past tense). The previous work, of course, need not be the Gospel except that but for the closeness of the Epistle to the Gospel the debate would probably not have arisen in the first place.

[24]Some critics see the use of the aorist in these passages as merely a stylistic variation or the epistolary aorist, while others take it as a regular aorist. The issue is, however, not conclusively resolved in favor of either position. See the summary of the discussion by Plummer, *Epistles*, 45–47. Our ensuing discussion brings to light substantial reasons for viewing the aorist as a regular one.

[25]Robinson, *Redating*, 288; see further, Marshall, *Epistles*, 42–48; and Brown, *Epistles*, 14–19.

[26]Bultmann (*Epistles*, 1–2) believes that $\dot{\epsilon}\pi\alpha\gamma\gamma\epsilon\lambda\dot{\iota}\alpha$ like $\mu\alpha\rho\tau\upsilon\rho\dot{\iota}\alpha$ refers to "the proclamation." Brown (*Epistles*, 192–194) also holds that $\dot{\alpha}\gamma\gamma\epsilon\lambda\dot{\iota}\alpha$ is the word technically used by John for the more traditional $\epsilon\dot{\upsilon}\alpha\gamma\gamma\dot{\epsilon}\lambda\iota o\nu$, a term never used by John (see also Schniewind's article cited on p. 125, n. 99 above).

[27]Bultmann (*Epistles*, 2) rightly holds that $\dot{\alpha}\pi'$ $\dot{\alpha}\rho\chi\tilde{\eta}\varsigma$ in 1 Jn 1:1 refers to the time when the

co-eyewitnesses actually proclaimed the message, and though this present author actually wrote about it, he in effect sees Jesus as the real teacher and evangelizer of the audience.

We are here reminded of Jn 4:42 (αὐτοῦ ἀκηκόαμεν) and of our whole previous discussion to the effect that the Gospel envisages no intermediary, strictly speaking, between Jesus and the believer, even though the disciples may serve as the visible agents for drawing such believers to Jesus (17:20). We are not surprised, then, that in keeping with this Johannine approach, the author not only sees Jesus as the evangelizer and teacher of the audience addressed but regards him as the one who "christened" them (2:20), taught and continues to teach them by his anointing/Spirit given to them as the abiding teacher of truth (2:21, 27; 3:24; 4:13; 5:6b; cf. 2 Jn 9–11). This view that Jesus and the Spirit exercise a permanent teaching role among the believers is also that of the Gospel (14:16–17, 23, 26; 16:7–15). The Epistle further insists that because of this permanent teaching role, the audience addressed has no need at any point of another teacher (2:20, 27). This teaching received from Jesus himself is to be used as the yardstick by which to measure the veracity of any other teaching that is offered (2 Jn 7–11).

The author's *attitude and approach* towards his work and audience thus parallel those of the Evangelist in the Gospel. This approach, we remember well, consisted in his allowing Jesus himself to interact directly with his audience through the use of dialogues, while the Evangelist's narrative effort served merely as a reinforcing postscript to the points already made by Jesus in the dialogues. In this respect, then, we may say that 1 John is to the Gospel as Jn 4:28–30, 39–42 is to 4:7–26, 31–38 or as Jn 21 is to Jn 13–17 (cf. pp. 193–195). In both works, the author takes the back seat or sees himself only as Jesus' mouthpiece. In the Epistle this approach is all the more striking since the author and his co-eyewitnesses actually evangelized the audience addressed, and since he continues to exercise a special pastoral responsibility towards the group as the letter itself testifies. His entire approach indicates that in his mind, Jesus' role is irreplaceable.

Thirdly, *the purpose* of the previous work (ταῦτα ἔγραψα ὑμῖν, ἵνα, 2:26; 5:13) is, on the one hand, to warn the audience against deceivers (2:26; cf. 3:7; 4:6c; 2 Jn 7) and, on the other, more positively to exhort them to "remain in" or continue in the teaching which they had initially received from Jesus (2:24)[28]. This message is that Jesus is the Christ, the

---

witnesses first had contact with Jesus, that is, from Jn 1:29 onwards (cf. 15:27); so, too, Brown (*Epistles,* 155–158, esp. pp. 157–158). Bultmann, further holds correctly that the ἀπ' ἀρχῆς in 1 Jn 2:7, 24 and 3:1 refers to the beginning of the proclamation of the word by the witnesses to the converts addressed in the Epistle. Brown (*Epistles,* 265) tends to reject this distinction or at best sees it only as "a second option."

[28]Malatesta (*Interiority and Convenant,* 27–36) studies the motif of "remaining in" as used in both Gospel and Epistles.

Son of God, and that eternal life is to be found only in him (5:13).
Again we are reminded of the declared purpose of the Gospel (20:30–31),
a connection also noted by a number of critics, though they overlook
the persuasive hortatory thrust of both passages[29]. The "things" (ταῦτα)
said to have been written in the previous work (2:26; 5:13) refer to the
total content of the work, "the message." The Gospel describes the same
content summarily as "the signs" which Jesus worked (20:30–31),
"signs" here being a reference to the demonstrative character of the message, that Jesus is the Christ. The use of the third person perfect passive
of the verb γράφειν in the Gospel as opposed to the first active in the Epistle seems to underline the fact that the real author of the events narrated
in the Gospel is Jesus himself, not the Evangelist[30]. But in the Epistle, as
in the more narrative sections of the Gospel, the author comes to the fore
to interact more directly (*viva voce*) with his audience, though always in
order to redirect their attention to their real teacher, Jesus himself, and to
the teaching which they had already received from him.

The author's insistence that, even in the previous work as in the Epistle,
he is not teaching them anything new (2:7–8, 21) forms part of his per-
suasive/hortatory approach. Notably, the author does not refute the errors of his opponents by arguing with them, he simply recalls his readers
to the truths already received (2:26–27). What he does, in effect, is to
appeal to their own common sense and better judgment. The readers
already know the truth about which he tells them (1 Jn 2:21), and tells
them not only in the Epistle and previous work but from the very beginning of their conversion (1 Jn 2:7, 12–14). All they have to do now is to
abide and live by this truth (the message), and not allow themselves to be
swept off their feet by false teachers (1 Jn 2:26). In the previous work,
then, as in the Gospel and Epistle, the author aims at persuading his audience to continue to believe in Jesus as the Christ and Son of God, in
whom alone is eternal life (2:25; 5:13; Jn 20:31).

The similarities noted here between the Gospel and the previous writing
described in 1 John lead us to conclude tentatively, at least, that the work
in question is the Gospel, not 2 or 3 John. This conclusion finds further
support in the fact that the Epistle itself claims to treat the same issues as
those treated in the first writing. A close look at these *issues* in 1 John
leads us not to 2 and 3 John but to the Gospel. Westcott, Boismard-Lamouille, Plummer and Brown have taken pains to document some of the
striking similarities between the Gospel and 1 John[31]. We may cite here

[29]See Robinson, *Redating,* 290; and Plummer, *Epistles,* xlv.

[30]The passive tenses of γράφειν in 20:30–31 are usually explained on the grounds that the
Gospel in its present form is the work of a Johannine school (or of different redactors), not that of
an individual. The impersonal ὁ γράψας in 21:24 is also explained on the same grounds. Our explanation here fits in with the clear tendency on the part of the Evangelist to direct attention away
from himself to Jesus. His tendency to anonymity is evident in both the Gospel (he is simply "the
disciple whom Jesus loved," 21:24) and the Epistle.

[31]The parallelisms between the Gospel and the Epistles, especially 1 John are spelled out in

some of those similarities which are most pertinent to our discussion or touch upon issues which we have already discussed in the Gospel.

Chief among these are the questions of Jesus' messiahship (1 Jn 2:22; 5:1), his divine ontological sonship (4:15// Jn 5:18; 10:33, 36), or his being "sent" by the Father as the sole Savior of the world (4:9—10, 14 // Jn 3:16—17; 4:42; 17:2); both works deal with the abiding significance of his mission as the only means of eternal life and of the forgiveness of sins (5:11—12 // Jn 5:39—40; 8:24—36); both work on the understanding that the acceptance or rejection of the Son is acceptance or rejection of the Father (2:22—23; 4:15; 5:10 // Jn 5:23; 15:23—24). From the standpoint of Jesus' audience both works emphasize the need to believe in Jesus, which is ultimately to believe in God's witness to his Son (5:9—10; 3:23 // Jn 5:37—38; 6:29; 8:18), and also the importance of living out here and now the fellowship with the Father and his Son (1 Jn 1:4 // Jn 1:12—13; 4:36) in the practical keeping of the new law of brotherly love (1 Jn 1:6—10; 2:7—11; 3:11—18; 4:7—13, 19—21 // Jn 13:12—17, 34—35; 15: 9—17).

This list is by no means exhaustive. But these major similarities between the Gospel and 1 John cannot convincingly be swept aside in favor of the minor differences between them[32]. Indeed, not only does 1 John deal with some of the major issues treated in the Gospel, but the ἔγραψα passages in particular seem to presuppose whole chapters of the Gospel. Even though some critics argue that the aorist in 2:21, 26 cannot refer to the Gospel, the same cannot be said for 5:13. The argument with regard to 2: 21, 26 holds only when one overlooks the fundamental similarity in the method of the author in both the Gospel and 1 John, namely, his deep awareness that Jesus, not he, is the anointer, sanctifier and teacher of the audience (cf. Jn 13:8b, 10; 15:3; 17:19). So rather than argue against it, the whole context of 2:21—27 points us back to the Gospel. With 5:13, the issue is even more striking. For the whole discussion which precedes this verse evokes the discussion in Jn 5:36—44 and 8:17—36: there is the emphasis that we ought to prefer God's witness to human witness, that in this witness of the Father the life he has given us is to be found only in his Son, and that, consequently, only the Son can set free from sin. Indeed, the fact that both the Gospel and 1 John were intended to circulate as companion volumes may yet explain the curious phenomenon noted by Brown and other critics, namely, the absence of any direct quotation from the Gospel in the Epistle[33]. Whatever the case, we have here sufficient

---

Westcott, *Epistles,* 30—34; Plummer, *Epistles,* l-lii, lxxii—lxxiv; Boismard-Lamouille, *Synopse III,* 69 and Appendix I; and Brown, *Epistles,* Appendix I, Chart II, 757—759.

[32]Brown's entire reconstruction of the situation of the Johannine community rests on the assumption that the Gospel and Epistles are the works of two different authors. The grounds for this lies not in "the major stylistic and theological similarities" between the two works but in "the minor differences" between them (*Community,* 95).

[33]Brown (*Epistles,* 33) finds it "a surprising fact, if 1 John was written after" the Gospel, that

contextual grounds for siding with those scholars who argue in favor of the chronological priority of the Gospel to 1 John, even if the interval between the two works yet remains to be discussed[34].

2. The Situational Relationship

Once we have established with reasonable certainty that the Gospel antedated the Epistle, our next important task is to determine whether both works are concerned with the same or different situations within the community. Though scholars differ concerning the precise purpose of the Gospel, the majority agree that both works deal with two completely different situations. We have already cited the representative views of Bultmann, Brown and Robinson who hold either that the Gospel is directed against the world and the Epistle against believers (Bultmann, Brown), that the Epistle is intended to correct errors caused by the misinterpretation of the Gospel (Brown) or that while the Gospel aims at converting Jews of the Diaspora the Epistle sets out to defend the truths of the Gospel against those who would distort its meaning (Robinson)[35]. The specific error allegedly combated by the Epistle is generally agreed to be some form of Docetism, as it is described, for instance, by Ignatius of Antioch (A.D. 110) or later by Irenaeus and Epiphanius[36]. 1 Jn 4:2 and 2 Jn 7 are cited as the internal evidence for this docetic interpretation. W. Grundmann, for instance, entertains the possibility that the heresy might be Ebionism, rather than Docetism, but he personally settles in favor of the more common docetic interpretation[37].

A few voices, however, seem to disagree with this docetic interpretation, and, consequently, with the view that both works deal with two completely different situations. Lightfoot's view that the Epistle was

---

"no passage in any of the Epistles is a direct or certain quotation" from the Gospel. Eusebius (*H.E.* 3.38.1—2) implies that a work was cited only if it was not contemporary with the citing author. He mentions that Clement of Rome cited the letter to the Hebrews in his letter to the Corinthians thus indicating that Hebrews is "not a recent writing." If then 1 John does·not cite the Gospel, it might be because both works belong together (as "epilogue" and "body of the text") or because they are clearly contemporary.

[34] Very few scholars dispute this order; see the summary of the discussion by Brown, *Epistles,* 32—35. Brown himself accepts the priority of the Gospel to the Epistles and both his *Community of the Beloved Disciple* and his commentary on the Epistles are based on this premises.

[35] Robinson, *Redating,* 292—307, where he also refers to his earlier work: "Destination and Purpose," 292.

[36] Ign. *Trall.* 9—10; *Smyr.* 2; *Eph.* 7 (cf. Polycarp, *Phil.* 2); Irenaeus, *Adv. Haer.* I.26.1; Epiphanius, *Haer.* 28.1. These last two witnesses focus on the Cerinthian type of Docetism, the Christological heresy which postulates two separate identities for Jesus Christ, namely, "Christ," the divine principle who descended into Jesus at his baptism and departed before the passion, and "Jesus," the human being, who was born of Mary and died on the Cross.

[37] Grundmann, χριστός, κτλ., *TDNT* IX, 570—571; see further Brown's summary of the discussion of this issue, *Epistles,* 333—337.

intended to be circulated with the Gospel as a kind of postscript implies
that both works deal with the same situation. In this particular article
Lightfoot does not discuss the nature of the heresy, but the pains he takes
to document the Jewishness of the Gospel with particular focus on the
messianic ideas, would lead one to conclude that in his view the heresy
combated in 1 John is Ebionism (to which he refers in another context)
rather than Docetism[38].

Another notable departure from the docetic interpretation is the position of Boismard-Lamouille. These authors hold, on redactional basis,
that 1 John in particular is the work of John II-B, the author who wrote
the bulk of the present Gospel. He wrote both works towards the end of
the first century when he moved from Palestine to Ephesus[39]. The enemies he encounters at Ephesus and whom he attacks in both the Gospel and
Epistles are certain Jewish-Christians whose false teachings (2 Jn 7—11)
cause divisions within the community (3 Jn 9—10). They deny the reality
of the incarnation (1 Jn 4:2; 2 Jn 7), the divinity of Jesus (1 Jn 2:22—23)
and his messiahship (1 Jn 2:22, 5:1). In Boismard-Lamouille's view, these
adversaries of the Evangelist may even have protested that Jesus in fact
did not present himself the way the Evangelist does, an objection which
John II-B meets by appealing to the Holy Spirit who was to lead the slow-
learning disciples into the complete truth (16:12—15; cf. 2:22; 12:16; 14:
26).

Furthermore, Boismard-Lamouille consider certain characters described
in the Gospel to be a projection of those whom John II-B encounters in
his own community as these are described in the Epistles. Thus the Jews
who had believed in Jesus (8:31a, 37—47) and the defecting disciples (6:
60—66) represent the departees from the community (1 Jn 2:19) who,
like the Pauline adversaries in Galatia (3—4), are more Jewish than Christian in their approach to Christ[40]. Similarly, Jesus' unbelieving brethren
who are loved by the world (7:7) typify the false teachers in the Epistles
whom the world loves and to whom it listens (1 Jn 4:4—6; cf. 3:13—14).
In short, the overall position of these two authors is that both the Epistles
and the Gospel at the level of John II-B deal with the same opponents who
refute Jesus' messiahship and divinity either for doctrinal reasons or because they are faced with a choice between Jesus and ejection from the
synagogue[41].

---

[38]Lightfoot, *Biblical Essays*, 23—26, 198. His reference to Ebionism is on p. 7; see also Plummer, *Epistles*, xxvi.

[39]Boismard-Lamouille, *Synopse III*, 59.

[40]These authors do not actually regard the Johannine adversaries as Judaizers. Rather, they see them as Jewish Christians who become disenchanted with their belief in Jesus and return to Judaism (*Synopse III*, 59, 242—244); these departees thus share with the Pauline adversaries a strong inclination towards Judaism.

[41]Boismard-Lamouille, *Synopse III*, 213—214. These authors, then, believe that John II-B pro-jected his life situation into that of Jesus depicted in the Gospel.

Their conclusion is all the more significant because they are not directly concerned with establishing the chronological relationship between the Gospel and the Epistles, a relationship they say is difficult to establish, given the possibility that the Epistles, like the Gospel, may have undergone many redactional stages. Brown and Kümmel, among others, completely reject the idea of layers in 1 John[42]. Yet this difficulty notwithstanding, Boismard-Lamouille nevertheless conclude on "undeniable" stylistic grounds that both the Gospel and the Epistles are written by the same hand. They then argue from this unity of authorship to the unity of situation on the level of John II-B. Though these authors find few supporters for their theory concerning the four levels of the Johannine redaction, they are not alone in suggesting that the Epistles deal with the same situation as the Gospel[43].

We thus have two clearly opposed views concerning the nature of the situation in 1 John and its relation to that of the Gospel. The majority view considers the situation in the Epistles to be docetic and gnostic and, therefore, different from that of the Gospel. The minority views the same situation as Judaic, possibly Ebionite, and, therefore, similar to that of the Gospel. Which of these two assessments of the situation is closest to the Johannine evidence itself? Does the majority carry the vote? We think not. The single most important argument adduced in favor of the majority position is the denial in the Epistles of the reality of the incarnation or of the humanity of Christ, as the case may be (1 Jn 4:2; 2 Jn 7)[44]. In the Gospel, it is noted, the situation is quite the reverse. Jesus' humanity is so well recognized by his opponents that his claim to divinity is treated as blasphemy (5:18; 8:57—59; 10:33, 36; 19:7). His humanity, too, with its Galilean rather than Judean origin, consitutes the major obstacle to accepting his claim to be the Christ (6:41—42; 7:40—44, 52b). If, therefore, the schismatics in the Epistles deny the reality of the incarnation, they cannot be equated with Jesus' opponents in the Gospel for whom Jesus' divinity, not his humanity, poses a problem. Brown sums up the whole docetic in-

---

[42]Brown, *Epistles,* 57; *Community,* 103, n. 201. Kümmel (*Einleitung,* 439—400) considers unproved the supposition that there was a Vorlage for 1 John. Bultmann (*Epistles,* 2—3) believes that the author used sources. See Brown's reconstruction of the Bultmannian Source (*Epistles,* Appendix I, Chart III, 760—761).

[43]Wurm (*Die Irlehrer im ersten Johannesbriefe* [Freiburg, 1903] cited by Schnackenburg [*Johannesbriefe,* 14—15] and Marshall [*Epistles,* 16]) and O'Neill (*The Puzzle of 1 John: A New Examination of Origins* [London: SPCK, 1966] 2—70) both hold this view. O'Neill's theory is criticized by Bultmann (*Epistles,* 2), Bruce (*Epistles,* 32, n. 8), Marshall (*Epistles,* 30) and Brown (*Epistles,* 45—46).

[44]The branch of Docetism which here recommends itself most is the Cerinthian type described in n. 36 above. Central to this heresy is the denial of the divinity of Jesus of Nazareth. The dualism posited between "Christ" and "Jesus" is only an attempt to get around this denial. Unlike Cerinthus, the Jews in the Gospel make no attempt to get around the issue (5:18; 10:33; 19:7). See further Westcott, *Epistles,* xxxiv; and Brown, *Epistles,* 65—68 and Appendix II, 766—771 (on Cerinthianism in Patristic literature).

terpretation thus: In the Gospel the argument is that "Jesus is *the Son of God*;" and in the Epistles, that "*Jesus* is the Son of God"[45]. The issue thus seems to settle itself.

But does it? What exactly is denied or affirmed in 1 Jn 4:2 and 2 Jn 7, the humanity of "Christ" seen as a separate being from Jesus of Nazareth or the divinity of Jesus of Nazareth seen as "Jesus Christ" or Son of God? These are not idle questions. All we want to point out is that difficult as the issue is, the docetic/gnostic interpretation does not adequately account for all the elements embodied in these two key passages, let alone in the rest of the Epistles. As far as we can make out, the line of argumentation seems to run as follows: First, it is posited on the basis of 1 Jn 4:2 and 2 Jn 7 that the heresy in question in the Epistles is some form of Docetism. Secondly, because of 1 John 2:22 and 5:1, the specific branch of Docetism involved must be the Cerinthian type (which regards Jesus and Christ as two separate beings), not the fantom type (which holds that Jesus only *appeared* to be human). Thirdly, therefore, 1 Jn 2:22 and 5:1 must be a reference to some form of the Cerinthian denial that Jesus, the human being, is not "the Christ," the divine principle which is said to have descended upon him at his Baptism and to have left him just before the passion. Fourthly, this identification of the heresy as Cerinthianism now helps to explain 1 Jn 4:2 and 2 Jn 7, the meaning of which is that Christ, the divine principle, did not become a human being in the person of Jesus of Nazareth. Fifthly and finally, 1 Jn 4:3 refers, on the basis of this identification, to those who "negate the importance of Jesus," or who consider the earthly career of Jesus to be of no salvific value[46].   Thus all the major elements in the opponents' position seem to be well accounted for.

That a vicious circle underlies this whole argumentation process is self-evident. It will be noted, too, that the docetic interpretation of 1 Jn 4:2 and 2 Jn 7 focuses only on the complement, ἐν σαρκί, but tends to ignore both the subject which in each instance is Ἰησοῦς Χριστός not simply Χριστός and the predicate which in each case is expressed in a perduring aspectual form: ἐληλυθότα (perfect participle, 4:2) and ἐρχόμενον (present participle, 2 Jn 7). Thirdly, the docetic interpretation draws its strongest evidence from external Patristic sources cited in note 36 above, especially from the letters of Ignatius of Antioch. Brown's high profile of the secessionists, in particular, leans heavily on these letters on the grounds that the Johannine Epistles (which he dates to ca. A.D. 100) and the letters of Ignatius (ca. A.D. 110) were only a decade apart and came from the same geographical area of Asia Minor. Yet it is to be noted, too, that Brown also dates the Gospel to a decade before the Epistles (ca. A.D. 90). On the other hand, Robinson's latest challenge of the dating of NT works

---

[45]Brown, *Community,* 111.

[46]This outline of the situation is based mostly on Brown's description of the position of the secessionists, *Epistles,* 49–68; and *Community,* 94–95, 101–123.

deserves serious consideration (cf. n. 103 below). Yet even if Brown's dating of these works is correct, one sees no reason why the letters of Ignatius should have priority over the Gospel on temporary grounds, since both were equidistant, timewise, from the Epistles. Besides, Boismard-Lamouille also date the Johannine works at about the same period as Brown, but they assign a very different interpretation to the Johannine heresy, one which is much closer to the situation in the Gospel than to the docetic, Ignatian evidence[47]. So an important part of Brown's premises, chronological proximity to Ignatius of Antioch, does not go unchallenged.

The question to be asked, though, is whether, if we never had the Patristic evidence cited above, we would ever have been tempted to interpret 1 Jn 2:22; 5:1 and 4:2; 2 Jn 7 in the Cerinthian/gnostic sense rather than in the Johannine (Gospel) sense. Brown, for instance, rightly rejects Käsemann's docetic interpretation of the Gospel, even as he rejects the view of those who regard Jn 1:14 as anti-docetic[48]. But his entire version of the tenets of the secessionists in the Epistles raises far more questions than it resolves. For instance, it is not readily clear how the *denial* that "Jesus Christ has come in flesh," or the refusal to *confess* "Jesus Christ come in flesh" would mean that the opponents "accepted the reality of the incarnation" but simply "believed that the human existence of Jesus, while real, was not salvifically significant." And are we wholly satisfied that by *denying* "Jesus is not the Christ" (2:22, the term "denying" is crucial) the adversaries are hereby so stressing "the divine principle in Jesus that the earthly career of the divine principle is neglected?" Finally, if what mattered to the opponents "was that eternal life had been brought down through a divine Son who passed through this life" why then does the author of 1 John insist that if we accept human witness, all the more reason why we should accept the Father's witness to his Son, which witness is that he, the Father, has given us life and that this life is in his Son (1 Jn 5:9—12)[49]? How does this Johannine appeal *a minori ad maius* differ from the position of the enemy as Brown reconstructs it? Does this appeal to the Father's witness not rather point us back to the whole discussion in Jn 5:18—47[50]?

More could be said concerning Brown's high profile of the secessionists. Forestell, for one, considers this to be the chief weakness of Brown's commentary on the Epistles[51]. All we want to point out is that the doce-

---

[47]Boismard-Lamouille (*Synopse III*, 68) date both the Gospel (on the level of John II-B) and 1 John to ca. A.D. 95—100; Brown, *Community*, 23, 178—179.

[48]Brown, *Community*, 16, n. 17.

[49]These citations from Brown are from his *Community*, 112, 114.

[50]The Father's witness to his Son that we know of is that given in the Gospel, and it concerns Jesus of Nazareth whose divine sonship the Jews deny outright (cf. 10:33—39). Indeed, they are prepared to accept that he might be the Christ (v 24) but that he might be the Son of God, never (vv 33, 39; cf. 8:58—59).

[51]J.T. Forestell, *CBQ* 45 (1983) 679—681, esp. pp. 680—681.

tic reconstruction of the heresy supposedly found in the Epistles far out-
strips the internal evidence of the text itself. Even Brown himself admits
as tenuous the evidence on which his portrait of the schism is based[52]. If,
then, a choice has to be made between the external Patristic or hypothetical evidence and the internal Johannine (Epistles and Gospel) witness,
we do not hesitate to give logical priority to the self-evidence of the Johannine texts themselves, at least until convincing reasons have been prof-
fered to the contrary. For none would deny that the Epistles and Gospel
are closer companions than are the Epistles and the letters of Ignatius.
Besides, if it is possible that the opponents in the Johannine Epistles
misread the Gospel, might it not be equally possible that the adversaries
mentioned by Ignatius also misread 1 Jn 4:2 and 2 Jn 7, even as we
are still inclined to do today? Whatever the case, the dissatisfaction
generated by the current docetic/gnostic interpretation of the position of
the opponents in the Johannine Epistles forces us back on the Johannine
texts themselves and challenges us to seek within their contexts alternative interpretations to this all-important, but difficult issue[53].

a) 1 Jn 4:2 and 2 Jn 7

First we examine what is denied or confessed in both 1 Jn 4:2 and 2 Jn 7:

$$\text{Ἰησοῦν Χριστὸν ἐν σαρκὶ ἐληλυθότα (1 Jn 4:2)}$$
$$\text{Ἰησοῦν Χριστὸν ἐρχόμενον ἐν σαρκί (2 Jn 7).}$$

In both verses, the complement ἐν σαρκί is anarthrous, meaning "in flesh,"
rather than "in the flesh." In Jn 1:14 the word flesh, also used absolutely,
designates "a human being," the same as in 17:2 where it occurs in the
collective sense with the adjective πᾶς ("all"). So the expression ἐν σαρκί

---

[52]Brown himself (*Epistles,* 366) states: "The few lines of 2:19 constitute *most* [italics mine] of
our historical knowledge about the Johannine schism." One may also recall his earlier preference
(n. 32 above) for the "minor" differences over against the "major" similarities as the grounds for
rejecting the unity of authorship for the Gospel and the Epistles.

[53]It needs to be emphasized that Brown himself (*Epistles,* 67), and other critics recognize that
the situation described by Ignatius of Antioch is more fully developed than is supposedly found
in the Epistles. Schnackenburg (*Johannesbriefe,* 22) goes further to declare that 1 John represents
a type of heresy we cannot identify and that the Johannine opponents are not Docetists in any of
the forms we know today; see also Marshall, *Epistles,* 17—22; Bruce, *Epistles,* 17, n. 11; and de
Jonge, "The Use of the Word χριστός in the Johannine Epistles," *Studies in John, Fs. J.N. Sevenster* (Leiden: Brill, 1970) 66—74. Bultmann (*Epistles,* 38—39) regards it immaterial whether or not
we can identify the heresy, "the decisive point," in his view, is that the passage testifies to "the
inability of Gnostic thought to comprehend the offense" of the Christian revelation, "namely,
the paradox that a historical event . . . is the eschatological event." Thus the premises that 1 John
is dealing with a form of docetic or gnostic heresy clearly constitutes a major problem for the comprehension of the passage. In the ensuing discussion, we shall steer away both from this apparently
deceptive premises and from the basic assumption that all the errors corrected in the Epistles reflect the tenets of the "antichrists" (1 Jn 2:18—19). Whither this new approach leads remains to
be seen, but it should, at least, be given a chance.

here must mean "as a human being"[54]. Secondly, the subject of the complement in each case is "Jesus Christ," not simply "Christ" or "Jesus." What then does the designation "Jesus Christ" mean for the author of the Epistles? His consistent usage clearly indicates that the term is synonymous with "Son of God" (1 Jn 1:3; 3:23; 5:20; 2 Jn 3). The same meaning underlies the rare use of the term in the Gospel (1:17; 17:3, which last passage merits comparison with 1 Jn 5:20)[55]. Placed once at the beginning (1:17), and next towards the end (17:3) of the Gospel, the term "Jesus Christ" receives its contextual meaning from the entire Christological debates conducted in the Gospel, where the issue is whether or not Jesus is *the Son* of God, the Father's sole revealer, life-giving agent and judge (see in particular 1:18; 3:16−21; 5:18−47; 8:30−36; 10:10, 37−39; 15:22−25). It hardly needs to be emphasized that Jesus' ontological divine sonship constitutes the central issue in both Epistles and Gospel and that this issue is inseparably linked with the question of his messiahship (5:18−47; 10:22−39; 19:7; 1 Jn 2:23−24; 3:8; 4:9, 10, 14; 5:9−12, 13; 2 Jn 9).

Concerning the predicates ἐληλυθότα (pf. ptc.; 1 Jn 4:2) and ἐρχόμενον (present ptc.; 2 Jn 7), it will be recalled that the verb ἔρχομαι in John has a specifically missionary perspective, being the active counterpart of Jesus' view of himself as "one sent" (p. 3 above). Martha's confession is a striking witness to the messianic, missionary use of the verb: I have believed that you are the Christ, the Son of God, come into this world (εἰς τὸν κόσμον ἐρχόμενος, 11:27). And she is here speaking to Jesus of Nazareth whose claims to divine sonship and messiahship constitute the standard theme of debate in the Gospel. Yet Martha's situation (and that of

---

[54]The significance of the anarthrous forms is discussed in *BDF*, no. 253 (2) and (3). The anarthrous use of "sea," "earth" and "heaven," is said to express the characteristic or specific quality of these objects. Following on this principle, Giblin ("Three Monotheistic Texts in Paul," *CBQ* 37 [1975] 527–547) sees the expression ἐν κόσμῳ in 1 Cor 8:4b as conveying "the notion of reality in terms of created existence, probably that sphere of created existence in which men operate" (p. 531, n. 20). Other Pauline passages which he cites include Rom 5:13; 1 Cor 14:10; Phil 2:14; see also Col 1:20. In this light the anarthrous expression ἐν σαρκί must express the characteristic of what it is to be human (Hebr., בָּשָׂר, Gen 2:2, 12; Is 40:6).

[55]See n. 62, p. 215 above on the discussion of the term "Jesus Christ" in 17:3 and on the possible influence of 1 Jn 5:20 on this passage. A possible contextual objection to our messianic interpretation of the tenets of the antichrists might be 1 Jn 5:6−8 which many critics regard as strong evidence that the issue in question is some form of *docetic* Christology. While we cannot go into the details of the argument here, we agree wholly with Brown (*Epistles*, 595) first, that 1 Jn 5:6−8 is obscure to *us* today (not to the author and his audience; see Brown's lengthy discussion of the many interpretations given to this passage, *Epistles* 577−585); secondly that the issue in this passage is not Docetism whether this be understood in the classic sense or in the sense in which Brown himself interprets it (pp. 595−599). If, following Brown's own example, we were to give to the passage an "explanation which makes the most sense" to us (p. 595) we would approach the passage as a digression, or a citation of a known liturgical or catechetical formula, which bears on the author's thesis that salvation is given in and through the life and death of Jesus Christ, the man from Nazareth, the Son of God. These three terms: the Spirit, the water and the blood, also have a sacramental/soteriological reference in the Gospel; cf. 3:3−8; 19:34−37.

the Gospel generally) in no way suggests that two beings are involved, Christ (the divine principle) and Jesus.

The statement "Jesus Christ has come in flesh," then, seems to mean no more than that "the Son of God has become [and remains, pf. tense] a human being in the person of Jesus." It is another way of saying that "Jesus," is "the Son of God" (1 Jn 4:15; 5:5; 2 Jn 3). The statements in 1 Jn 4:2 and 2 Jn 7 cannot, therefore, be taken in isolation from these other passages, nor from those passages where it is equally emphasized that "Jesus is the Son of God" (1 Jn 1:7; 5:5). The issue thus proves to be the same as in the Gospel, and the shift of emphasis noted by Brown (n. 45 above) is not readily apparent.

b) 1 Jn 2:22 and 5:1

Next we examine the counter statements in 2:22 and 5:1:

ʼΙησοῦς οὐκ ἔστιν ὁ χριστός / ʼΙησοῦς ἐστιν ὁ χριστός

The first point to note is that the word χριστός is a title, not a proper name[56]. This would indicate that the question at issue is Jesus' messiahship, rather than the separate identities of "the Christ," the divine principle, and of "Jesus," the man from Nazareth. In the Johannine corpus, "Jesus" is a name, while ὁ χριστός and ὁ υἱὸς τοῦ θεοῦ are predicates of this name. Where "Christ" is intended as a name rather than a title, it appears mostly in the form "Jesus Christ" (Jn 1:17; 17:3; 1 Jn 1:3; 2:1; 3:23; 4:2, 15; 5:6, 20; 2 Jn 3, 7)[57].

As predicates in John, "Christ" and "Son of God" are both intrinsically related, but they are not exactly synonymous as some critics hold[58]. The title "Christ" speaks to Jesus' role as the Messiah, the anointed end-time prophet promised by God and expected by all Judaism (cf. Deut 15:15–18). The primary reference of this title, then, is to Jesus' mission of salva-

---

[56]NA[26] distinguishes between the name and the title by writing the former with a capital X (cf. 2 Jn 9) and the latter with a small x.

[57]The use of "Christ" as a proper name is most frequent in Paul (1 Cor 3:12–20, 22–23, 30), though he appears to have received this usage from tradition (1 Cor 15:3). See also Heb 3:6; 1 Pet 1:11, 19; Eph 1:4, 10, 12, 20. Elsewhere we find the forms "Jesus Christ" (Mt 1:1, 18; Mk 1:1; Rom 1:1, 4; Acts 9:34; 10:36, 48; Eph 1:5; Rev 1:1, 2, 5; etc.), "Christ Jesus" (Rom 2:16; 6:11; 8:1; Phil 1:1; Col 1:1; Eph 1:1), "Christ the Lord" (Lk 2:11, 26) and "the Lord Jesus Christ" (Phil 4:23; Eph 1:2, 3; Col 1:3). Schnackenburg ("Messiasfrage," 240–264) regards the designation "Jesus Christ" in 1:17 and 17:3 as an official title in contrast to "Christ" which refers to the Jewish/Samaritan Messiah. Cf. 1 Mac 4:46; 14:41.

[58]See, for instance, de Jonge, "χριστός in Johannine Epistles," 68, 69. For him the two terms "Christ and Son of God" are not only closely linked, but synonymous and interchangeable. Jn 20:31 taken by itself would support this interpretation. But the rest of the evidence in the Gospel (see n. 59 below) suggests a shade of difference between the two terms. Grundmann (*TDNT*, IX, p. 571. n. 495) also sees "Christ" and "Son" as interchangeable, but he rejects the idea that "Jesus Christ" is a double name. Rather, he sees "Christ" as a "sobriquet qualifying Jesus" such that "Jesus Christ" in 1 Jn 5:5 means "Son of God." (p. 571, n. 500)

tion[59]. "Son of God," on the other hand, refers to his divine origin and identity as God's ontological Son on the basis of which he not only is the Messiah expected, but surpasses by far all the different messianic expectations of his audience. Jesus' uniqueness as Son is given a special accent by the designation, ὁ μονογενής, which designation occurs only in the Johannine corpus (Jn 1:14, 18; 3:16, 18; 1 Jn 4:9). In other words, in the Johannine vision, Jesus' ontological divine sonship is an inalienable aspect of his messiahship.

It is precisely because of his unique relationship with the Father that Jesus alone can reveal the Father (1:18; 14:9) and be his most perfect representative (*Wesensidentität* and *Deckungsgleichheit*, 5:19—20; 8:28; 14:10—11). It is for this reason, too, that Jesus has neither predecessors nor successors, and that his coming as Messiah/Savior of the world is simply it (8:24, 28a; 9:39; 15:22—24; 1 Jn 4:14—15; 5:9—13). It will be noted, too, that all of Jesus' saving activity is done precisely in his capacity as *Son*: the Son gives life (3:16—17; 5:19—21, 24—26; 1 Jn 5:11—13), judges (3:18—19; 5:22—23, 27—29); saves and sets free (8:34—36; 1 Jn 3:8; 4:9, 14). Understandably, then, confession of Jesus as "the Christ" means confession of him as "the Son of God" (1:29; 11:27; 20:28), and persuasion to believe in Jesus as "the Christ" is also persuasion to believe in him as "the Son of God" (20:31; 1 Jn 2:22—23; 4:14; 5:1, 5).

It is not surprising, then, that both the Gospel and Epistles take great and consistent pains to emphasize that the response given to Jesus, the Son, is also the response given to the Father: hatred of the Son is hatred of the Father (3:36; 15:23—24), acceptance of Jesus and his teaching is acceptance of the Father and his teaching or witness (5:43; 6:29, 40 [= 1 Jn 3:23] ; 7:16—17; 1 Jn 5:10), honor done to the Son is honor done to the Father (5:23), denial of the Son is denial of the Father (1 Jn 2:22), possession of the Son is possession of the Father (1 Jn 2:22—24), and knowledge of the Son is knowledge of the Father (14:7—11, 20, 23) which conjoint knowledge means life (17:3; 1 Jn 5:12—13). Such an emphasis on the divine sonship of Jesus in both the Gospel and Epistles makes sense only where this idea of divine sonship (ontologically understood) is rejected outright in any of its forms (and this includes that of the divine principle)[60]. It needs to be emphasized that the issue of divinity in the Gospel is not simply that of Jesus' divine origin, or of the divine au-

---

[59]The Gospel makes this particularly clear in the question put to the Baptist and his reply (1:20, 25), in the Baptist's confession (3:28), in the debate of the Jews (7:26—41) and their final question to Jesus himself (10:24). See further 4:25, 29. In the OT Is 61:1 might be cited in support of the view that the designation "Christ" refers primarily to Jesus' role as one "anointed" and "sent" on mission (LXX ἔχρισέν με εὐαγγελίσασθαι; Hebr., מ שׁ ח אתי לבשׂר).

[60]The Johannine emphasis on the Father/Son relationship constitutes another marked difference between the Johannine presentation of Jesus and the halakhic agents of Merkabah mysticism. Jesus is not simply a representative; he is the Son, and, consequently, the most perfect and complete revealer of the Father; one who is radically different from Moses and the Prophets (1:17—18; cf. Heb 1:1—2; 3:1—6).

thority behind his mission (the OT angels were divine beings, and the Baptist is said to have been sent by God, 1:6). The issue is his claim to an exclusive filial relationship with the Father (10:36).

This whole evidence, then, leads us to conclude that the statements of 1 Jn 2:22 and 5:1 are to be understood in the messianic, not docetic sense, the same as is issue in the Gospel. This conclusion is reinforced by the name which is given to Jesus' opponents in the Epistles. These receive their fundamental designation ἀντίχριστοι (2:18; 4:3; 2 Jn 7) from their central tenet: Ἰησοῦς οὐκ ἔστιν ὁ χριστός (1 Jn 2:22; cf. 5:1). Grundmann has remarked on the peculiarity of this formulation found only in the Johannine Epistles, even though the idea is a common one in the NT (cf. Mt 24:11, 24; Mk 13:5, 6, 22; 1 Tim 4:1; 1 Thess 3:5)[61]. It is not improbable, however, that the Johannine Epistles mean something very different from the other NT works. All these antichrist figures are, no doubt, end-time prophets, but their activities are different. In the Johannine Epistles, the "antichrist" is literally one who opposes Jesus, the Christ, or puts himself in his place by denying and refusing to believe and confess Jesus as the Christ, and Son of God. The designation "antichrist," is thus etymologically intended and most appropriately so. The other epithets given to these figures, "deceivers" (1 Jn 2:26; 3:7; 4:6; 2 Jn 7–8), "liars" (1 Jn 2:22) and "false prophets" (1 Jn 4:1), all derive from their central anti-messianic tenet ("Jesus is not the Christ") and their missionary activity. For not only do they themselves refuse to believe that Jesus is the Christ, the incarnate Son of God, but they also strive to dissuade others from believing (1 Jn 2:26; 3:7; 4:1; 2 Jn 8, 10).

To counteract their deceptive activity, the author of the Epistles exhorts his audience to hold on to the message they received from Jesus himself, and to *believe* and *confess* that he is the Christ. His exhortation is rooted in his own personal belief, and that of his fellow eyewitnesses, that the Father did send his Son to give life to the world (1 Jn 1:1–3; 4: 14–15). The truthfulness of this teaching is certified by the Father's own witness to the Son (1 Jn 3:23; 5:9–11) and is permanently guaranteed by the abiding teaching role of the Spirit (1 Jn 2:20, 27; 3:24; 4:2, 13).

The Epistles thus present two diametrically opposed lines of response to Jesus. On the part of the antichrist, the response is marked by *denial, disbelief* and *refusal to confess*; and on the part of the believer, by *acceptance, belief* and *confession*. The former derives its inspiration from the deceiver (1 Jn 4:3, 6), the world (4:4) or from itself (2 Jn 9); the latter receives his from God's Spirit (4:2) who points the believer back to Jesus' teaching and the Father's witness transmitted by the eyewitnesses (1 Jn 1:1–3, 5; 2:24–27; 5:9–12; 2 Jn 9a). The object of the controversy is Jesus, and what is denied or affirmed about him is also set forth antithetically: "He is not the Christ" (2:22), "he is the Christ" (5:1). "He is

---

[61] For Grundmann's position see n. 10 above.

not the Son of God [Jesus Christ] come in flesh" (4:2; 2 Jn 7), "he is the Son of God come in flesh" (4:15; 5:5). To say that he is the Son of God "come in flesh" means that he has been sent by the Father to give eternal life to those who believe in him (4:9–10, 14, 16; 5:13; cf. Jn 17:3). However, the only way of testing the truthfulness of the claims made for Jesus is to believe in him. Thus, as in the Gospel, believing and confessing constitute the only means of gaining access to the life-giving knowledge of God which Jesus brings. That is why faith alone constitutes the believer's victory over the world (5:4; cf. 4:4; Jn 16:33). For it is this faith which sets the Christian community apart from the world, whether or not the world knows it (3:1, 13–14; 4:5–6).

It needs to be emphasized, however, that the antichrists are not the opponents of the author of the Epistles, but of Jesus himself, the Christ. Not only do these opponents deny that he is the Christ, but they vie with him in teaching the people and gaining their allegiance (2:26; 3:7; 4:5; 2 Jn 7–10). Because of this, the author rightly presents Jesus as their protagonist, the only true teacher whose teaching is to be used to test the authenticity of all other teaching (2 Jn 8–10). Ultimately, the readers have to choose, not between the author and the opponents, but between these latter and Jesus. Here again, Brown and other critics tend to overplay the rivalry between the author of the Epistles and the secessionists. The Epistles themselves furnish very little evidence for such a rivalry, 3 Jn 9 and 12 being the only possible passages. The author certainly does not see himself as the rival of the secessionists, the antichrists proper; for as Brown himself would admit, Diotrephes is not one of them[62].

Nevertheless, there is a level at which the antichrists are set over against the believing community (not just against the author) whose relationship with Jesus is also etymologically construed, χρίσμα ἔχετε (2:20). By refusing to believe, the antichrists alienate themselves *ipso facto* from this community, and become thereby classified with the world (4:5). 1 Jn 2:19 need not be seen as physical separation from an enclosed community. Belief in Jesus determines one's allegiance no matter where one is placed geographically (Jn 4:23–24). However, since the fellowship with Jesus and the Father is expressed practically in daily living, and since partnership with Christ and partnership with the world are mutually exclusive, believers are enjoined to have nothing to do with this antichrist (2 Jn 11). This injunction receives its particular poignancy from the crisis situation: physical contact with these deceivers might resullt in a loss of faith (2 Jn 8)[63].

---

[62]Brown (*Epistles*, 673–674) disagrees with those who stipulate that Diotrephes holds the same tenets as the secessionists. We shall see presently the contrast between the attitude of the author and that of the antichrists and of disciples like Diotrephes.

[63]Similarly, in 1 Cor 5:9–13 Paul enjoins on the Corinthians to have nothing to do with the immoral Christian (not with the immoral of this world). At Qumran, expulsion from the community for any number of reasons was a common feature. See Vermes, *The Dead Sea Scrolls*, 92–95; and *The Dead Sea Scrolls in English*, 84–86.

It would be wrong, however, to limit our understanding of the "anti-christ" to those who refute Jesus' messiahship and divinity. The community situation is quite complex. In addition to the antichrist proper, the schismatics (2:18—19), there are others within the community who are given to self-aggrandizement, or who behave as if they owned the mission. We know of at least one such character in the Epistles, Diotrephes who "loves to make himself first" (φιλοπρωτεύων αὐτῶν), and who seems to be a law unto himself (3 Jn 9—10). Gaius, on the other hand, is his anti-thesis (3 Jn 1—8, 11). In the author's own vision, people like Diotrephes would be classified as antichrists in their own way[64]. In contrast to them, the author deliberately refuses to impose himself, despite his evidently authoritative standing in the community (1 Jn 2:7, 12—14, 18; 5:21; 2 Jn 12; 3 Jn 9—10, 12—14). If he imposed himself, he would be usurping Christ's place in the community, an action against which he preaches. By his very attitude he acts like a true missionary eyewitness, one who seeks, not his own glory, but the glory of his sender. His attitude thus becomes a perfect and consistent imitation of that of Jesus, the Father's envoy, as this is portrayed in the Gospel.

Finally, it appears that in the community are also people who are neith-er like the schismatics nor like Diotrephes. These are believers who pride themselves on their belief in Jesus, and consider themselves as sinless be-cause of this belief, without bothering to live out its practical implications, summed up in the new law of love. The heavy ethical emphasis in 1 John (1:10; 2:3—11, 29; 3; 4:7—21; 5:1—3, 21) seems to be called for by and aimed at this group. By far the greater portion of the letter is devoted to this one issue of love of the brethren or of the need to "walk as Jesus walked" (1 Jn 2:6; 3:16; 4:11). Given this proportional emphasis, one could say that this issue was most important for the author. And rightly so, because without this love, the claim to believe in Jesus constitutes a lie (1:6—7; 2:4; 3:7—10; 4:8; cf. Jn 13:34—35). The activity of the anti-christs no doubt caused disturbances and disunity in the community, but it would be wrong to interpret all this ethical emphasis as a reaction against their errors[65].

The author is not simply exhorting his readers to an abstract, theolog-ical belief in Jesus but to a living faith which expresses itself in active living. 1 Jn 3:18 is the key text here, "Let us not love in word and talk but in deed and in truth." To claim to have fellowship with Jesus and the Father while refusing to love the brethren is merely to deceive oneself (1: 6; 2:4; 3:7—8, 10, 12, 14—15, 17; 4:20). Faith in Jesus and love of the

---

[64]We recall Thyen's view (n. 14 above) that the author of 1 John would regard people like Diotrephes as if they had never seen God. The same verdict applies to those who refuse to walk in the law of love.

[65]Galatians and Hebrews also deal with false teaching, but both contain injunctions concern-ing ethical conduct which have no direct relation with the doctrines condemned (Gal 5:13—6:11; Heb 13).

brethren are thus two sides of the same coin. So we are not surprised that the author's efforts to persuade his readers to believe in Jesus and remain in his teaching go hand in hand with an even greater effort to persuade them to mutual love. Brown rightly recognizes that everything the author says need not be interpreted as inspired by the secessionists, adding that the author may have used the occasion to correct errors no matter who held them[66]. All the more reason, then, why we should be very cautious against reading too much into the Epistles concerning the ethical values supposedly denied by the secessionists. The necessity of loving the brethren is too central to Johannine (and NT) thought (cf. 1 Cor 13:1–13; Jas 1:22) for emphasis on it to be seen as called for by the activity of non-believers, who are clearly regarded as "not of us" (1 Jn 2:19)[67].

Moreover, the way the issues are stated in the Epistles and their contexts should serve as a guide for determining whether or not they stem from the position of the opponents or from the believing community itself, regardless of the activity of the opponents. The theological errors corrected seem to be linked in each case with such expressions as denying/believing, confessing and refusing to confess (1 Jn 2:22; 4:2–6, 15–16; 5:1, 9–11), even as they are backed by explicit warnings against deceivers (2:26; 4:1; 5:21; 2 Jn 7–11)[68]. Ethical issues, on the other hand, are presented as something which believers themselves hold ("if we say," 1:8), to which they need to pay attention, or about which they need have no illusions. In brief, it would seem that neglect in this area was not caused by the opponents. It is not unlikely that among the community were some like those at Corinth who thought believing in Christ and being endowed with charismatic gifts was enough to make them holy while they neglected the fundamental law of love. A situation in the community not unlike that at Corinth may yet account for the strong reminder that all are sinners standing in need of God's forgiveness (1 Jn 1:8–2:3; 4:9, 14). For though believers have in them God's life principle which keeps them from sinning (3:6, 9), they cannot claim to belong to God unless they love as God loves (1 Jn 2:2–6; 3:16–18). Everything the author of the Epis-

---

[66]Brown, *Epistles,* 48. Similarly, Marshall (*Epistles,* 15) sees the ethical issues cited as part of the tenets of the heretics. But Plummer (*Epistles,* 95) holds that the false prophets need not all be identified with the antichrists; his view allows for a complexity in the situation addressed in the Epistles. In Dodd's view (*Epistles,* 65) all of 2:29–4:12 deals with the central theme that Christians are children of God; he considers 4:1–6 as the only possible return to the false teaching of the antichrists, the denial of the incarnation.

[67]The examples given in the letter to illustrate the lack of brotherly love: hating, killing, closing one's heart to the needs of a brother (3:15–17), can hardly be interpreted as mere "indifference to ethical values." Equally, the Corinthians did not simply refrain from loving; they indulged in the most atrocious immorality (1 Cor 5:1–13; 6:1–11, 12–20; 11:17–22; 12:14–31). See further Murphy-O'Connor, *1 Corinthians,* 39–54.

[68]The warning in 3:7 can be interpreted impersonally, as meaning "make no mistake about it." It need not, therefore, imply that someone is teaching the addressees that loving in action is unnecessary. V 18 (let us not love in word and mere talk but in deed and in truth) would support this interpretation.

tles says, therefore, need not be interpreted from the primary standpoint of the opponents. Brown is entirely right on this issue.

We may now *summarize* our discussion up to this point concerning the relationship between the Gospel and the Epistles. The discussion reveals a very close relationship between both works. On the doctrinal/Christological level, the question at issue in both works is Jesus' messiahship and divine sonship. Is he or is he not as he claims to be "the Christ, the Son of God?" The centrality of this question in the Gospel hardly needs to be documented. It is the central theme of each chapter, or as Lightfoot puts it, "the one standard theme of conversation"[69]. Moreover, the purpose of the whole book is to persuade its readers to believe in this truth (20:30—31). The centrality of this question is also reinforced by the confession formulae in the Gospel, all of which have or imply the double predicate "Christ, Son of God"[70]. In the Epistles the centrality of the theme is accentuated by the tenet of the antichrists that "Jesus is not the Christ, the Son of God, come in flesh." It is reinforced by the very etymological designation of these opponents as the *antichrists,* and by the counter confession of the author and his exhortation of his readers to continue to believe and live out their faith in Jesus as "the Christ, the Son of God."

Secondly, the thesis or central issue is treated forensically or polemically in both works. Jesus' claim to be the Christ, the Son of God ($\dot{\epsilon}\gamma\dot{\omega}\ \epsilon\dot{\iota}\mu\dot{\iota}$), is refuted or denied by his opponents ($o\dot{\nu}\kappa\ \ddot{\epsilon}\sigma\tau\iota\nu$); in the Gospel the refutation is not simply verbal (5:18; 6:42, 52, 60; 7:25—27, 40—43, 45—52); it entails physical attack (6:66; 7:30, 32; 8:59; 10:31). In the Epistles, the refutation is accompanied by active campaigns to dissuade others from believing (1 Jn 2:26; 4:1; 2 Jn 7—8, 10—11); this activity strongly echoes Jn 9:22 (cf. 7:13; 19:38). The denial is further met on Jesus' part by a reassertion of the claim (cf. 5:19—30; 6:61—62; 7:33—34, 37—39; 8:24, 28; 9:5, 39—41; 10:25—29, 32, 34—38; 12:44—50), and on the part of the favorable audience by belief and confession: $\sigma\dot{\nu}\ \epsilon\dot{\iota}$ (1:49; 6:69; 11:27; cf. 9:38; 20:28), and $o\dot{\nu}\tau\dot{o}\varsigma\ \dot{\epsilon}\sigma\tau\iota\nu$ (4:29, 42; 1:34; cf. 3:27—30; 20:31; 1 Jn 4:3, 14—15; 5:1, 5).

On the level of the community, both works are united in their emphasis that belief in Jesus must manifest itself concretely in the keeping of his new law of love even unto death (Jn 13:34—35; 15:13; 1 Jn 3:16; 4:11—12). Put differently, since love is the distinguishing mark of the community, born of God who is love (1 Jn 3:7—8), fellowship with Jesus and the Father involves the commitment of one's entire life to walking as Jesus did (Jn 13:12—17; 1 Jn 2:6), loving as he loved (Jn 13:1; 15:13—15; 1 Jn

---

[69]Lightfoot, *Biblical Essays,* 24.

[70]The confession formula in 11:27 and 20:31 specifies "the Christ, the Son of God." The worshiping of Jesus by the man born blind (9:38) and by Thomas (20:28) also implies a recognition of divinity. Nathanael's confession (1:49) rests on the level of the Davidic Messiah, and understandably so since this is his first contact with Jesus. Peter's confession (6:68—69) must be read within the context of the whole discussion in Jn 6 of Christ's divine origin.

3:16). Both works are united, too, in their recognition of the centrality and irreplaceability of Jesus' teaching role within the community and on the resulting need for the disciples to be humble and recognize their total dependence on Jesus. We have discussed these points amply in respect to the Gospel. In the Epistles, the need for dependence with regard to one's personal holiness is even more emphatically stated: if we say that we have no sin, we deceive ourselves and the truth is not in us (1:8); worse still, we make God a liar (1:10). Christ's blood alone cleanses us from our sins (1:7) and he is both our ransom and our advocate with the Father (2:1—2).

The need for the exercise of humility with regard to mission is illustrated in the author's attitude towards his audience: he does not in any way impose on them or pose as their teacher (1:1—5; 2:21, 27); whatever action has to be taken against a brother must be taken by the community (3 Jn 9—10). His sole purpose in writing is to enhance the mutual joy which he and other believers share (1:4; 2 Jn 12). The need for humility is illustrated, finally, in the juxtaposition of Gaius and Diotrephes, the former outstanding for the praiseworthy truthfulness of his life and genuine service of the brethren, including strangers (3 Jn 1—8), the latter notorious for his egocentric pomposity and bigotries (3 Jn 9—10). The former is helpful to the missionary cause, the latter, harmful (3 Jn 5—8, 10).

Finally, both works are united with regard to the author's personal approach or treatment of the issues raised. In both works, the author first allows Jesus to interact directly with his audience, then adds his own persuasive efforts to that of Jesus. In the Gospel, Jesus' interaction takes place in the dialogues and discourses, the author's persuasive efforts, in the narrative sections. In the Epistles, Jesus' interaction takes the form of a reminder to the audience that Jesus was and remains their primary teacher, while the author's persuasive efforts lie in the reminder itself, in the whole hortatory thrust of the Epistles and in the warning against deception of any kind, whether by self or by the antichrists. On a wider scale, then, the Epistles stand to the Gospel as the narrative sections of the Gospel stand to the dialogues and discourses.

Given these similarities in theme, in the manner in which these themes are handled and in the author's personal attitude towards his work, we cannot but conclude that both the Gospel and Epistles stem from the same hand and deal with the same situation. This situation is marked on the part of the antichrist by the refutation of Jesus' claim to be the Messiah and Son of God, and on the part of faithful disciples by a high tendency to neglect mutual love and forget their all-round dependency on Jesus. This means, in effect, that the situation in the Epistles is much closer to that of the Gospel than to that of Ignatius of Antioch. Or if we insist that the situation in the Epistles is docetic/gnostic, then we will have to posit the same for the Gospel, a viewpoint which only Käsemann, perhaps, would endorse[71]. How this situation may have come about, its

---

[71]Käsemann (*Ketzer und Zeuge: Zum johanneischen Verfasserproblem,* ZKT 48 [1951] 292—

effects on the formation of both the Gospel and Epistles and its implications for the mutual understanding of both these works, will form the focus of the next section of our discussion, which, for brevity's sake, we will simply entitle "implications of the relationship."

C. The Implications of the Relationship

1. Our Position

We begin this section by stating more clearly our own position concerning the relationship between the Gospel and the Epistles. If the result of the above discussion is correct, namely, that the Gospel and Epistles stem from the same hand and deal with the same complex situation where the issues are in the order of Christology, community and personal belief all set within the overall context of Jesus' mission from the Father, then one conclusion readily imposes itself. It is this, that the Gospel did not cause the disturbances and departures reported in 1 John, nor are the Epistles correcting errors supposedly caused by the misinterpretation of the Gospel. On the contrary, we will have to posit that the troubles existed within the community *before* either the Gospel or the Epistles were written. Rather than occasion the crisis, therefore, the Gospel in its present final form, was, like the Epistles, written as a result of the crisis and in response to it.

This means that both the Gospel and the Epistles are to be seen as the author's double response to the activity of the antichrists and the behavior of certain disciples. In the Gospel he first presents Jesus as both the defender or champion of his own cause against the counter tenets of the antichrist, and the exemplary instructor of the disciples on the need for mutual love and for humility in the exercise of mission. Then in the Epistles, he draws his readers' attention to Jesus' teaching embodied in the Gospel (the ἔγραψα passages), while at the same time reminding them that they already know these truths from the beginning of their conversion. Thus, in both the Gospel and Epistles the author has the one aim in view: to urge his readers *to continue to believe* that Jesus is the Christ and Son of God in whom alone eternal life is to be found (20:30–31; 1 Jn 2: 26; 5:13). This means in effect, that but for the crisis within the group of believers, the Gospel and the Epistles in their present form would probably never have been written.

To say that the Gospel was written as a result of the crisis does not, however, mean that its contents date from the crisis. Quite the contrary,

---

311, also in *Exegetische Versuche und Besinnungen* [Göttingen: Vandenhoeck und Ruprecht, 1960] I, 168–187) believes that the author of both the Epistles and the Gospel was himself a docetic Gnostic whom Diotrephes dismissed from the community because of his false teaching.

the traditions incorporated into "the book" (20:30) existed from the beginning and were taught or handed down as from Jesus himself (1 Jn 1:1–3, 5; 2:24–25). They may have been passed on either orally or in some written form. The latter possibility cannot be outruled, though there is no way of conclusively proving it[72]. The pre-existence of the material or traditions is stated by the author himself who concedes that his works contain nothing new to his audience (1 Jn 2:7, 21). Because of the crisis, however, these traditions are now cogently and persuasively written down to sustain the readers' faith against the onslaught of the antichrists. It is not unlikely, therefore, that the crisis played a major role in shaping the present Gospel with its markedly forensic, polemical and hortatory thrusts[73].

The need to persuade the readers to continue to believe that Jesus is the Christ, the Son of God, (20:30–31) is rendered acute by the contrary activity of the antichrists (1 Jn 2:26; 5:13). But if the antichrists could deny these claims it is only because the claims had first been made for Jesus. For if in forensic cases the denial of charges constitutes the strongest line of defense (cf. Jn 8:48, 49)[74], then in a situation where a claim is refuted the reassertion of the claim must also constitute the strongest line of defense (cf. 10:33, 34–38). So the denial by the antichrists is met by an even stronger reassertion in both Gospel and Epistles that Jesus is the Christ. In the Gospel this claim is doubly defended, first by Jesus himself (the defendant) who cites in support of the claim the witness of the Baptist, of the Father, of the Scriptures, of Moses (5:31–47), of his words and works and of his indisputably sinless life (8:46). The claim is also indirectly defended by the believing audience: the Samaritan woman and the Samaritans (4:29, 42), Nathanael (1:49), Peter (6:68–69), Martha (11:27), the man born blind (9:38), and even the once doubting Thomas (20:28). Above all it is defended by the Beloved Disciple whose witness is the entire Gospel (21:24–24). Given this crowd of witnesses, the truthfulness of the claim cannot be easily refuted (cf. 7:17), unless, of course, one chooses to "remain blind" (9:40–41) to this preponderant evidence (cf. 10:32; 12:37; 15:22, 24).

It needs to be noted, too, that in forensic situations the judge constitutes the primary audience whom each of the protagonists seeks to influence since ultimately he has to decide which of them is right[75]. In the

---

[72]In addition to Lindars' extensive description of the pre-Gospel forms of the Gospel material, *Behind the Fourth Gospel*, see also the more recent article by M.D. Goulder, "The Liturgical Origin of St. John's Gospel," *SE* 7 (1982) 205–221.

[73]The "disputations" in the Gospel are, then, not simply part of the Evangelist's "style of story telling about Jesus in his homilies" (Lindars, *John*, 52); they have some reference to the actual life situation of the Evangelist and his audience. Lindars, of course, is rightly reacting against Martyn's position that the debates have no historical value on the level of Jesus but simply reflect the arguments which were actually taking place between the church and the synagogue in the Evangelist's own day.

[74]Quintilian, *Inst. Or.* III.vi.10.

[75]Quintilian, *Inst. Or.* III.ix.7.

Johannine situation, the primary audience of both the Gospel and the Epistles are those whom the author seeks to sustain in their faith in Jesus, but whom the antichrists also seek to dissuade from believing. In the Gospel the Evangelist makes the greater part of his appeal through Jesus, presented in dialogue with his audience, and using two major rhetorical modes, the forensic (3; 5—10) and the deliberative (4:31—38; 13—17). Jesus thus becomes as it were the Evangelists' spokesman[76]. The Evangelist himself supplements Jesus' persuasive efforts by interweaving Jesus' persuasive dialogues with his own narrative and demonstrative art (e.g., 4:1—6, 28—30, 39—42; 21).

Does this mean, then, that the Gospel is merely a parable designed to teach the Evangelist's audience, or that it presents nothing more than a projection of the situation of the Evangelist into that of Jesus? In other words, are the stories of Jesus' encounter with his audience in the Gospel meant to be taken seriously at their own level or do they function merely on the Evangelist's level as capable of persuading his audience to his viewpoint? If the latter were the case, then the whole undertaking would be doomed to failure since "it is obviously impossible to prove what is doubtful by what is no less doubtful"[77]. For one thing, the question at issue on the level of Jesus and his audience (the Gospel) and that of the Evangelist and his audience (the Epistles) is exactly the same. The audience changes but Jesus and his claims remain the same, so, too, the refutation of these claims. In the most fundamental sense of the word, therefore, Jesus' situation constitutes the all-inclusive paradigm for the situation of the Evangelist and of his audience. So the arguments used by Jesus to convince his audience apply most appropriately as "proofs" capable of convincing the Evangelist's audience.

Here again we turn to Quintilian for technical support, and can do no better than cite him fully. After noting that "example" which is a type of *proof* applies "most appropriately to historical parallels," he continues thus:

> The most important of proofs . . . is that which is most properly styled example, that is to say the adducing of some past action real or assumed which may serve to persuade the audience of the truths of the point which we are trying to make. We must therefore consider whether the parallel is complete or only partial, that we may know whether to use it in its entirety or merely to select those portions which are serviceable (*Inst. Or.* V.xi.6).

Do we not find here a convincing rationale for the Evangelist's entire approach in the Gospel as illustrated in his key statement (Jn 20:30—31)? He maintains that he is not recounting Jesus' life in its entirety, for there are many other signs which he did (20:30; 21:25), still less then is he re-

---

[76]Porsch (*Pneuma und Wort,* 2, and n. 15, p. 42 above) states that Jesus and all the characters in the Gospel speak the Johannine language. From the rhetorical/paradigmatic perspective, however, it is the Evangelist who speaks the language of Jesus.

[77]Quintilian, *Inst. Or.* V.xii.3.

counting fables. Rather, he deliberately *selects* from events in Jesus' life only those incidents which *parallel his own situation* which can therefore *serve to persuade* his readers to believe in Jesus. In other words, he narrates from Jesus' situation only those events or issues which help his readers to cope with their own similar situation.

Ultimately, then, the needs of the Johannine audience and the particular problems they face determine what is selectively told about the life of Jesus. Since his messianic and divine identity stand at the heart of every episode in the Gospel, we are right in claiming that this, too, is the central issue in the Johannine situation. Connected with this issue are the obstacles to believing, the kind of attitude which fosters belief and the practical results which must accompany belief on the personal, communal and missionary levels, without which results (fruit which endures) the claim to believe in him is only a lie. We may say, then, that there is a projection of the Evangelist's situation into that of Jesus. This projection, however, is not primarily in terms of persecution from the synagogue; still less is it in terms of making the Evangelist's situation the model for understanding that of Jesus. On the contrary, the Evangelist seeks to understand his own situation and problems in the light of Jesus' own situation. The projection is in terms of "example." What he narrates about the paradigmatic situation, Jesus' situation, gives us a special insight into his own time, as a hermeneutical process, not as a recreation of the past in the light of the present[78].

Still in the light of this principle that historical parallels are chosen because of their similarity to one' own situation, we may infer that the primary causes which led to departures from the Johannine community were internal and doctrinal rather than external and social, for instance, ejection from the synagogue. In 3:1—21, for instance, Nicodemus finds Jesus' teaching on birth from above an impossibility ($\pi \tilde{\omega} \varsigma \ \delta \acute{u} \nu \alpha \tau \alpha \iota$; vv 4, 9). In 6:26—66 the Galilean Jews react in exactly the same way to his teaching on the Eucharist ($\pi \tilde{\omega} \varsigma \ \delta \acute{u} \nu \alpha \tau \alpha \iota$; v 52; cf. v 60). The issue in both situations is of the sacramental order, and each audience seeks convincing signs, its own way, rather than faith proposed by Jesus (cf. 3:2; 6:30—31)[79]. In the debates with the leaders in Jerusalem (5; 7—10; 12), the issue centers on Jesus' messiahship and divine sonship, where the claim to divine sonship clearly constitutes the chief stumbling block (5:18; 8:35, 56—59; 10:30—39; cf. 19:7). Among this group we meet half-believers or people who waver between belief and disbelief (7:31; 8:30; 10:42; 11:45;

---

[78]For the interpretative nature of the Gospel see n. 10. p. 41 above; also Smalley, *John: Evangelist and Interpreter* (Greenwood: Attic, 1978) esp. pp. 191—242. Interpretation is, however, different from the projection of the present into the past such that the past receives its existence for the first time only from what is happening in the present.

[79]In " 'How Can These Things Happen?' " (pp. 14—19) we discussed in detail Nicodemus' fundamental attitude of unbelief and the antithetical parallels between him and the Baptist in their response to Jesus.

12:11, 42; cf. 2:23—25). Jesus' last appeal in 12:44—50 is addressed to these wavering believers as well as to those who do not believe at all. To the wavering disciples, too, is addressed the lesson concerning the dead branches which must needs be cut from the vine (15:6).

Against this background, we may infer that certain Jews of the Evangelist's day first became disciples when they heard it preached that Jesus was the Messiah. But after they had had time to "look into the matter" (cf. 7:52), decided that Jesus did not meet the Scriptural and traditional criteria set for the Messiah (7:25—27, 40—44, 52; 12:34). Most importantly, these people appear to have found the teaching on Jesus' ontological divine sonship, the mystery of the incarnation, the most difficult to accept (cf. 6:41—42; 5:18; 8:56—59; 10:33—39; 1 Jn 4:2, 15; 5:1, 5; 2 Jn 7)[80]. It is not unlikely, then, that these people would either completely part company with Jesus or develop their own Christology which saw him as no more than an exceptional human being and prophet. This last option, we know, was adopted by the Ebionites, who may yet be the main trouble-makers described in the Johannine Epistles, especially in 1 Jn 4: 2 and 2 Jn 7.

That the complete rupture with Jesus was caused by fear of ejection from the synagogue is not readily evident from the text. If the Johannine evidence be taken at its face value, the fear of ejection from the synagogue is seen as the reason for remaining a crypto-Christian, a hidden confessor of Jesus (9:22; 12:42—43; 19:38), not for refusing to believe in him. Complete rupture and refusal to believe, on the other hand, rest squarely on doctrinal grounds (cf. 6:41—42, 60, 66; 8:30, 56—59). Besides, would one fear to be ejected from the synagogue who truly believed, in the Johannine sense of the word, that Jesus was the Christ, the Son of God? If one did, then that would be a sure sign that one did not really believe in the first place (cf. 2:23—25; 6:64, 66; 8:30—31; 1 Jn 2:19). As in the Gospel, the departees in 1 Jn 2:19 did not suddenly wake up one fine morning and decide to part company with Jesus and his group of disciples. There must have been debates, discussions and scrutiny of the Scriptures similar to that reported in the Gospel (7—9) prior to the definitive break, at which point rational arguments, not faith, gained the upper hand[81].

Martyn is thus right up to a point when he views the debates in the

---

[80]It is most difficult for us today fully to appreciate how very testing Jesus' claim to divine sonship must have been to the Jew of the first century who had been brought up in a strong tradition of monotheism. As noted in the previous chapter, the personifications of Wisdom and the logos were simply that, personifications. The Johannine notion of "the Son of God" (ontologically understood) who in addition becomes fully a human being finds no antecedents or parallels in Jewish (or Hellenistic) theology.

[81]For the Evangelist, rationalistic arguments are totally inadequate as means of knowing and accepting Jesus' self-revelation. Not only that, rationalistic approach is shown to be a positive hindrance to this knowledge (3:9—12; 5:39—41; 9:41).

Gospel as actual disputations in the Evangelist's day[82]. But the protagonists in the Evangelist's day need not necessarily be seen as hardline synagogue Jews set against convinced Christians. The contenders are more likely convinced believers (among whom is the author) and wavering Christians. Nor must we forget that even at Jesus' own level the debates were wholly an in-house affair, since Jesus was debating with his fellow Jews. Also as in the Gospel, the debates may have taken place in different areas and among different classes of people. 1 Jn 2:18 need not, therefore, be seen as proof for the existence of a Johannine school, which is not to deny that such a school might have existed. Strikingly, though, the author of the Epistles acts in an individual capacity (1 Jn 2:1, 7−8, 12, 14, 21, 26; 5:13; 2 Jn 1, 4, 12; 3 Jn 1−15)[83], even though he functions within the context of a local church (2 Jn 13), and recognizes other co-eyewitnesses (1:1−5).

The picture of the community projected in the Epistles is that of a widespread group of believers rather than of a tightly-knit and enclosed group. Were the community not so wide-spread, there would have been no need to send letters. 1 John, traditionally classified as a "catholic epistle," (Eus. *H.E.* 3.24) is the most universal of the three letters, while 2 John is addressed to an individual church and 3 John to an individual, Gaius. Whether or not Gaius belongs to the church addressed in 2 John (cf. 2 Jn 12 and 3 Jn 9−10) or to a different church is not very clear in the texts. The evidence of traveling missionaries both orthodox (3 Jn 3, 5−8) and heterodox (1 Jn 4:1; 2 Jn 7−11), and the expressed intention of the author to visit the church and Gaius (2 Jn 12; 3 Jn 13−14), indicate that the community in question consisted of a group of believers spread over a wide area. So whether we think of the different activities of the group addressed in the Epistles (the different errors corrected and the praise offered by the author) or of the geographical spread of this group, the situation of the Johannine community appears to have been a very complex one, but one whose implications for the understanding of the Gospel is not negligible[84].

---

[82]Martyn, *History and Tradition*, 69.

[83]That 1 John is the work of an individual is indicated not only in the γράφω and ἔγραψα passages but in the whole style of the author where there is only one speaker throughout. The "we" passages refer either to the eyewitnesses among whom is the author (1 Jn 1:1−5; 4:14, we are not told whether these witnesses are dead or alive) or to the "we" believers which includes the author and his audience (1 Jn 1:6−10, 23; 3:19−24; 4:6, 19; 5:2, 9−11, 14−15, 18−20). The same individualism lies behind the witness of the Gospel (19:35; 21:24).

[84]We would like to emphasize the complex nature of the Johannine situation. In our view the single most important source of confusion in the whole discussion of this situation lies in the assumption that all or most of the errors corrected in the letter are to be seen as the tenets of antichrists (1 Jn 2:18−19). Though in theory Brown, for instance, does not hold this view, in practice he works on this basis. Marshall's remark (*Epistles*, 17) on the "elaborate way" in which 1 John deals with the Christological heresy of his opponents rests on the same assumption. Yet the various brands of Gnosticism (cf. Marshall, *Epistles*, 14−22) appear much more elaborate than 1 John.

2. The Implications

Once the relationship between the Gospel and the Epistles highlighted in all of the preceding discussion has been recognized, then a whole new light is lit for the understanding of the Gospel and for the Johannine approach in particular. In general the recognition that both works stem from the same crisis and are written by the same author to meet this crisis means that the Epistles can be used more positively to elucidate the Gospel, contrary to the current practice whereby only the Gospel is used to elucidate the Epistles on the grounds that the Gospel antedated the Epistles by a span of about ten years[85]. For our immediate purposes, this relationship of both works helps us to understand the key features of the Johannine approach which emerged in the form of questions at the end of the double survey in Chapter I, namely, what does the Evangelist himself understand by mission? Why did he choose mission as the leitmotif of his Gospel and how does he conceive the exercise of mission?

First, what does the Evangelist understand by mission? It is obvious from his goal in both works that mission for the Evangelist means fundamentally persuading his readers to believe that Jesus is the Christ, the Son of God, the giver of eternal life. This is the activity in which both he and Jesus are engaged in their interaction with their different audiences. The practical living out of this faith on both the personal and the missio-communal levels constitutes an integral aspect of believing in Jesus. This means that from the Johannine perspective mission is not restricted to winning converts once for all to a more of less theoretical faith in Jesus. The missionary undertaking includes both the initial efforts at converting unbelievers and the continued effort to sustain these believers in their faith, warn them against all sorts of deception and hold them personally responsible for it. The reminder of the personal responsibility occurs, for instance, in 1 Jn 2:21; 4:1 and 2 Jn 8. For the Evangelist himself, the primary focus of his missionary work in both the Gospel and the Epistles is the sustaining of the faith of his audience. This focus is rendered necessary by the contrary missionary activity of the antichrists. His immediate audience, therefore, are believers who stand in danger of losing their faith or of making that faith a lie. But his concentration on believers does not necessarily exclude the possibility of a non-believer reading his work, especially the Gospel, and being converted thereby. Besides, the content of the Gospel is seen as the "message" which the audience addressed received from the beginning of their conversion (1 Jn 2:7, 24; cf. 1:1—3).

Second, why did the Evangelist choose mission as the leitmotif of this Gospel? This choice seems to be largely determined by the situation ad-

---

[85]Using the Epistles to interpret the Gospel would, for instance, shed light on what is meant by walking or not walking in the light (3:19—21; 12:35) and by being children of the light (3:21; 8:12; 11:10; 12:36, 46) or of God (1:12—13). In brief, the Epistles reveal the essentially social character of these expressions.

dressed. By denying that Jesus is the Christ, the Son of God, the antichrists are in effect denying that he is sent by God or comes from the Father (cf. Jn 9:28–29). If Jesus' opponents could have had the type of proof they sought that Jesus was sent by God (cf. 2:18; 6:30) or could have induced him to be the type of Messiah they expected (6:14–15; 12:34), they would have had no problem with his claims. So the whole controversy hangs on whether or not Jesus was sent by the Father. This situation sheds lights on the dominance of the "sending" motif in the Gospel with focus on the *Father* as the "sender" (pp. 1–7)[86]. Strikingly enough, the "sending" motif has a reference to Jesus as "the Christ," while the term "Father" has a reference to the issue of his being ontologically "Son of God." So even the sending terminology most frequently used by Jesus himself (ὁ πέμψας με πατήρ) epitomizes his central claims. We meet the same in 1 John in the author's repeated witness that the Father sent his Son (4:9, 14) and that acceptance of this witness is in fact acceptance of the Father's own witness (5:9–11; cf. Jn 5:37; 8:18; 12:28–30).

As God's Son anointed and sent by the Father (10:36), Jesus represents the Father in an absolute and exclusive capacity (5:19, 30). He derives full authority from him in every respect, or better still, the Father himself lives and acts in him (14:10–11). It is futile, therefore, to continue to believe in Moses and the OT Scriptures whose sole function was to point to Jesus (5:39–44), or worse still, to continue awaiting the Messiah (8:24, 28; 15:22, 24). Even Gentiles who do not expect the Messiah in the Jewish and Samaritan sense, must be drawn to Jesus, the only way to the Father and life for all flesh (14:6; 17:2–3). The finality of Jesus' mission is thus total and all-embracing.

The tenets and activity of the antichrists also help to explain why in the first part of the Gospel Jesus not only appears in predominantly forensic situations (Jn 5–10, 12), but makes it his major concern to reveal himself as the Messiah and Son of God[87]. Since these are the claims refuted by his opponents, it stands to reason that in his defense he should stay within the terms of the debate, focus on the question at issue, and prove at every turn the validity of his claims. The Gospel genre superbly allows Jesus to make his own defense, not as an *apologia*, but as revelation and proclamation (cf. 15:22; 17:13; 18:20). So John's Gospel deserves indeed to be called "the Gospel of Jesus Christ" (both objective and subjective genitive). But Jesus' self-preaching is not for his own sake, only so that his audience may believe and find in him the life which the Father sent him to give (3:16; 10:10). Thus the situation of the audience helps to explain not only the

---

[86] See the description of "The Johannine Data," esp. pp. 1–4.

[87] We recall in this connection Bultmann's position (p. 26 above) that Jesus reveals nothing other than that he is Revealer. This situation of conflict and the focus on Jesus' indentity which it necessitates may also help to explain the fundamental and oft puzzling difference between John (with its focus on "who Jesus is") and the Synoptics (with their focus on "his teaching").

conception of the Gospel from the predominant standpoint of mission, but also the presentation of this mission from a basically forensic, combative setting (cf. 1:5, 10—11).

Third, how does the Evangelist conceive the exercise of mission? Here we come to the heart of the question concerning the Johannine approach. The question needs to be answered on two levels: the level of the attitude and approach of the one sent towards his sender, his mision and his audience, and the level of the' rhetorical/persuasive techniques mustered for the purpose of persuading the audience to believe in Jesus. Concerning the attitude of the one sent, we saw that this is characterized, in regard to the audience, by humility, deep respect for the person and efforts to meet the situation of the interlocutor; and in respect to the sender, by a spirit of total dependence and a quest of the sender's glory. In the Gospel passages examined, this attitude was amply illustrated by Jesus himself in his interaction with the Samaritan woman and the Samaritans (4:6—26, 40—41), in his instruction of the disciples (4:31—38; 13—17), and in his entire attitude towards his Father as epitomized in 4:34 and in Jn 17. It was emphasized, too, in the Evangelist's narrative account of the interaction between the Samaritan woman and the Samaritans (Jn 4:28—30, 39—42) and in the whole of Jn 21. We discovered that in the Epistles the author himself manifests the same spirit of humility in his approach to his readers (he is not teaching them anything new, they know the truth aleady), and in his conviction that Jesus is their only and irreplaceable teacher. We thus have enough consistent evidence for holding that humility in the exercise of mission is an important characteristic of the Johannine approach.

While this characteristic is theologically integral to the Johannine (and indeed NT) conception of mission[88], its pointed emphasis in both the Gospel and Epistles may very well have been influenced by the contrary attitudes of people like Diotrephes and those believers who gloried in their own sinless status while neglecting the fundamental law of love. Not only does the former love to be first, he is also projected as one who lords it over others, thereby obstructing the progress of the mission: he rejects what the author has written to the church, refuses himself to welcome missionaries and excommunicates those who do (3 Jn 9—10). Such behavior betrays the attitude of a master rather than of a servant (cf. Jn 13:12—17) and, no doubt, hurts the witness of the eschatological community (13: 34—35)[89].

---

[88]Not only John but the NT as a whole underlines the need for humility in the exercise of mission (Mt 11:29—30; Lk 10:20—21; cf. Is 42:1—4; 1 Cor 2:1—5; 3:5—9; 4:4, 11—13); see our previous discussion, pp. 86—87, 91, 130, 143 above.

[89]The reasons for Diotrephes' behavior are not stated in the letter. Brown (*Community*, 99, 133, n. 260) believes that he wishes to play it safe by steering clear of both heterodox and orthodox missionaries. Strangely enough, heterodox missionaries are not mentioned in connection with him, and his excommunication of those who welcome the orthodox missionaries can hardly be

The composite activities of the antichrists, of Diotrephes and of those whom we might call "phony" charismatics leads one to conclude that pride in a variety of forms constituted a special weakness of the community addressed by the Evangelist. It is not surprising, therefore, that he should lay special stress on the need for humility on the personal and missio-communal levels. The lesson is given both verbally and by his own personal example or by citing the witness of people like Gaius (3 Jn 1–8) and Demetrius (3 Jn 11–12). But the embodiment of this virtue and its exemplary teacher is, of course, Jesus himself as he is portrayed by the Evangelist in the Gospel.

Concerning the rhetorical techniques mustered in persuading the audience to believe in Jesus, we tentatively suggested at the beginning of this study that Jn 20:30–31 holds the key not only to the evangelistic purpose of the Gospel but also to its underlying rhetorical framework (pp. 41–49). Our subsequent investigation of the Gospel material has amply confirmed this hypothesis, to our great delight. Throughout the study, we have attempted to highlight the formal rhetorical traits present in the Gospel, and which constitute part of the Evangelist's persuasive approach to his audience (cf. pp. 101, 102 [n. 65] and 177). More needs to be said on the great significance of this new discovery for the understanding of John's Gospel in general. For the moment, however, we want to point out that the use of the rhetorical framework itself is to a great extent inspired by the life situation addressed by the Evangelist. The denial by the antichrists that Jesus is the Christ, and their efforts to dissuade others from believing call forth a contrary effort on the part of the Evangelist on behalf of the same audience. So the use of rhetoric is determined by the need to persuade the audience to faith[90].

Of the range of definitions of rhetoric offered by Quintilian (*Inst. Or.* II.xv.10–38), the most appropriate from the Johannine perspective is that which defines rhetoric as "the leading of men by the power of speech to the conclusion desired by the orator" (II.xv.10). Do we not have here a major reason, one rooted in life, why Jesus' encounters with his audience take the form of dialogues and discourses? It seems more satisfactory to attribute the Johannine discourses to the need to persuade a living audience than to see them as rooted in some hypothetical Gnostic *Offenbarungsreden*. Or if we must posit the Johannine use of the *RQ* model and source, then we still have to enquire whence these Gnostic writers derived their inspiration in the first place[91]. We need only recall the dialogues of

---

interpreted as a matter of personal indifference. It seems best to believe with the author that Diotrephes is acting in character, using the crises to make his importance felt.

[90]Persuasion to believe that Jesus is the Christ, the Son of God, means, of course, that those addressed are capable of holding an entirely different view on the matter. Indeed persuasion as an art makes sense only where different options are possible.

[91]One is often struck by the ease with which critics allow unquestionable originality to the contemporaries of the NT authors, while at the same time giving the impression that the NT au-

Plato or of Justin Martyr or the speeches of Cicero to be convinced that dialogue and speech generally constituted recognized modes of persuasion in the ancient world. In the Johannine situation, not only does Jesus dialogue with his different audience, but the Evangelist's letter is itself a form of direct address, a kind of speech, with a predominantly homiletic flavor[92].

We need to emphasize that the real audience of Jesus' dialogues/discourses, of the Evangelist's narrative in the Gospel and of his Epistles, is the same group of people whom the antichrists seek to dissuade from believing or whose behavior as Christians leaves much to be desired. In the forensic situations, this audience serves as the judge whom both Jesus and the antichrists seek to win (p. 251), but in the Gospel they are paradigmatically represented by Jesus' interlocutors. As judge, the audience intervenes only where it has an objection to make or requires the speaker to clarify a point just made. Otherwise its role consists in listening to the speakers then giving the judgment after the cases have been heard out. This may yet explain the seemingly passive role played by Jesus' audience in the Gospel[93]. But far from being artificially contrived to help the speakers/Jesus make a theological point, these interpellations constitute an integral and formal part of the argumentation process in the forensic setting (cf. 3:4, 9; 6:28, 30—31, 34, 41—42; 7:15, 20, 25). The same applies in the deliberative cases where the one instructed asks genuine questions (cf. 14:5, 8, 22). In 4:7—26 which we have classified under the type of philosophical variety of spontaneous enquiry (p. 101), the situation is different. For in this type the exchanges between the interlocutors are more substantial than in the forensic and deliberative types. But whether forensic, deliberative or philosophical, Jesus' dialogues/discourses with his audience have the same end in view: to persuade his and, consequently, the Evangelist's audience to believe and find life in him (cf. 7:37—38; 8:24; 9:41; 12:44—50; 20:30—31).

---

thors had everything to borrow from their non-Christian environment and nothing original to report about Jesus. It is possible that the Evangelist borrowed from foreign sources in writing his account of "the signs which Jesus worked." But such external (non-Christian) sources would have to be documented first independently of the Gospel and NT generally before they can be considered as possible sources which could have influenced the Evangelist. In discussing this whole issue it might also be salutary to bear in mind Jn 4:22 and 5:39—40. Would the Evangelist who believes that salvation "is from the Jews" and who holds that even the divinely revealed Scriptures are inadequate by comparison to Jesus (cf. 1:17) have fallen victim to subjecting Jesus to pagan ideas? This is not a rhetorical question; the Evangelist's own stance must needs serve as a crucial guide in this whole question of possible external influences on his work. In other words, we need to catch not simply the echoes in language or terminology (the cultural dimension) but also the similarities or dissimilarities in content and meaning (the theological dimension).

[92] We say "homiletic" in the sense that the primary thrust of the Epistles, like that of the Gospel, is pastoral rather than aesthetic. See Lindars, *John*, 51—54.

[93] See Dodd's classic description (p. 37, n. 1 above) of the passive character of Jesus' interlocutors in the Gospel.

In the use of persuasive techniques in the Gospel, therefore, the Evangelist's method and that of Jesus dovetail. For as Jesus' interlocutors exemplify different members of the Evangelist's community, so Jesus' efforts to persuade his own audience also represent the Evangelist's efforts to persuade his audience to faith. But Jesus' efforts do more than represent that of the Evangelist. Since he is the real protagonist of the antichrists as well as the only teacher of the believers addressed, he does in a very real way become present to the Johannine audience, who like the true flock must listen to his voice, not that of the antichrists (cf. 10:1– 16; 1 Jn 1:20–21; 2 Jn 9–11). So though stylistically Jesus may speak the Johannine language, in terms of meeting the needs of his audience, it is the Evangelist who speaks the language of Jesus. As one of Jesus' flock, he does no more than help his readers to listen to Jesus and apply his teaching to their particular situation. He does this, as we have seen, both in the narrative sections of the Gospel and in the Epistles where the interaction with his audience is more pronounced[94].

We may thus conclude that in its *theological conception,* the Johannine approach to mission, marked by humility on the part of the one sent, is inspired and shaped by the Evangelist's central belief in Jesus as God's unique Son and definitive agent of salvation ("the Christ"), whose role in the entire missionary enterprise can never be by-passed or replaced. Once completed the work stands completed while missionaries and believers alike enter into his labor (4:38; 15:16). Jesus is indeed the sole evangelizer (1 Jn 2:2), christener (1 Jn 2:20, 27), and teacher (1 Jn 2:27; 2 Jn 9) of the audience addressed in both the Gospel and Epistles. Believers owe to him both their initial call to holiness and their permanent capacity for leading a sinless life, one which is contrary to the world's way of life (cf. 1 Jn 5:19). For the call to holiness and to ontological fellowship with God as his children (1:12–13; 1 Jn 1:1–3, 9) is a pure gift given through Jesus (Jn 1:16; 1 Jn 3:1), while the capacity for sinlessness is made possible both by remaining in him (Jn 15:3–4; 1 Jn 3:6) and by Jesus' continued advocacy with the Father (1 Jn 2:1–2). Without Jesus, the disciples can indeed do nothing (15:5).

On the *literary/rhetorical level,* the Johannine approach to mission is shaped primarily by the situation of the audience and the task to be accomplished. The need to impress on the audience the importance of humility and dependence is met first and foremost by the presentation of Jesus as the model missionary (4:34; 17) and exemplary teacher of these virtues (4:31–38; 13:1–17; 15:1–17). The need to sustain the faith of the readers against the activities of the antichrists is equally met by presenting Jesus as the victorious defender of his own cause and claims — the

---

[94]The interaction with the audience is more pronounced in the Epistles than in the Gospel in the "I/You" relationship in 1 Jn 1:7–14, for instance. The author also interacts with his readers by citing their views ("if we say") and commenting on them.

definitive victory, of course, lies in his glorification by the Father and is recognized through faith. There is thus a perfect correspondence between the approach and method used and the task or goal to be accomplished. This means that the Evangelist's entire approach to mission arises from and is in function of his one desire to lead his readers to continue to believe and find life in Jesus (20:30–31; 1 Jn 5:13), with a faith similar to his own (19:35; 1 Jn 4:14–16).

To sum up, such, then, are some of the major implications which the recognition of the relationship between John's Gospel and Epistles holds for our understanding of the Gospel and, in particular, of the Johannine approach to mission. The situation helps a long way in explaining the Gospel's emphasis on Jesus as one sent by the Father; it throws light on why the debate in the Gospel centers around Jesus' identity as the Messiah (Christ) and Son of God and why these issues are discussed in a predominantly forensic setting, while the intention is hortatory and persuasive. From the perspective of the believers, the relationship between both works helps us to understand the polemic directed against the disciples themselves especially in their capacity as missionaries, the stress on the need for total dependence on Jesus, and the importance attached to mutual love and fellowship as the distinguishing marks of the eschatological community. Other important issues which might be considered in the light of this relationship but which lie outside the scope of the present undertaking include the way in which this established relationship might affect current theories on the origins of the Johannine Christology. In other words, if the Johannine Christology did not cause the crisis but, on the contrary, was reaffirmed in spite of the crisis, what may we conclude about the author's statement that this Christology was received from Jesus himself? And let us bear in mind that the audience addressed are expected to know and believe his word that this is the truth. Secondly, are the Christology, pneumatology, eschatology and ethics of the Gospel all that different from those of the Epistles?

On the level of composition the proposed relationship between the Gospel and the Epistles (that both stem from the same hand and deal with the same crisis) may help to explain both the seemingly unpolished structure of the Gospel and the striking difference between the grammar of the Gospel and Epistles noted by critics[95]. If the Gospel in its present form was

---

[95]Brown (*Epistles,* 152–154) finds the grammar of the Epistles poor and difficult to translate by comparison to that of the Gospel, a fact which in his view argues against the unity of authorship of both works. Houlden (*Epistles,* 19) finds the author of the Epistles to be poor not only grammatically (or as a writer generally) but also theologically: he is less penetrating and vigorous in mind than the Evangelist, is much more limited in range of thought and imagery, has a very poor Christology and did not exploit the Christology of the Gospel. This type of criticism is highly misleading as it is no longer concerned with the work but with the author as a person. In contrast, Brown (*Epistles,* 154) leads the exegete along the right track when he remarks that despite the poverty of grammar the author had his own sense of organization which we as members of the Johannine community must try to discover.

written in a critical and urgent situation, then the apparent literary seams and unsynchronized transitions between chapters (for instance the order of chapters 4, 5 and 6) would be explained by the pressure of the circumstances[96]. On the other hand, the superiority of the grammar of the Gospel to that of the Epistles would be explained by the fact that the Gospel contains material which had been received from tradition, discussed, taught and so polished by usage (liturgical? homiletic? catechetical?), while the Epistles contain mostly the author's own words spoken off the cuff, as it were, and which (more so than the Gospel) are colored by the flavor of his own situation[97].

Finally, the apparent lack of thematic coherence which critics find in 1 John may be attributed to the fact that having made his major case in the Gospel, the author now offers mainly random reflections on the Gospel themes. So 1 John does indeed have the character of an epilogue or of a footnote to the Gospel. 2 and 3 John on the other hand, seek further to apply the message of the Gospel and 1 John to particular cases. The author's missionary and pastoral efforts, like those of Paul, embrace both the pen and personal visits. His placing the issues first in their universal context (the Gospel and 1 John) before taking them up in their individual cases would indicate that the real issue for him is not the conflict between him and Diotrephes but how both of them and their audience stand in relation to Jesus' mission.

The intimate relationship established here between the Gospel and the Epistles is not entirely new. Previous scholars noted a close relationship between the two works, and Boismard-Lamouille actually saw reflected in the Gospel some characters in the Evangelist's own day. What is new in this study is that we have attempted cogently to illustrate that the Gospel and Epistles deal with the same situation, that both works grew out of the same crisis, that the author's manner of approach is fundamentally the same in both works, and that this approach in its rhetorical dimensions was greatly influenced by his own living situation. The arguments put forward here in this regard are by no means exhaustive. Nevertheless, the discussion has demonstrated that the theory, at least, deserves to be given

---

[96]Westcott (*Epistles,* xxxi) attributes the differences in language and in the treatment of common topics to the differences in genre (the gospel and the epistolary genres). He adds, "We have every reason to believe the Gospel was shaped by the Apostle in oral teaching long before it was committed to writing." This view goes back to Eusebius (*H.E.* 3.24) who records that John taught orally for a long time before he committed his teaching to writing. Curiously enough, R. Whitacre, *Johannine Polemic: The Role of Tradition and Theology* (SBLDS 67; Chico: Scholars, 1982) holds that both works deal with different situations because they belong to different genres! He subscribes to the view that the Gospel deals with the situation of ejection from the synagogue, and the Epistles, with its aftermath.

[97]If the Gospel narrative in any way reflects what Jesus himself actually said and what tradition said about him, then the differences in style between the Gospel and the Epistles might further be explained on the grounds that in the Epistles more so than in the Gospel the author is more completely the *auctor* of his thoughts and language.

as much hearing and consideration as has been given to other theories (that of ejection from the synagogue, for instance) which attempt to explain the situation of the Johannine community as this relates to both the Gospel and the Epistles. Our rejection of the docetic interpretation and that of the post-Jamnia trauma grows out of a closer scrutiny of the evidence of the texts themselves and from the deeply underlying current of the author's unified approach in both Epistles and Gospel to the central issue raised in both works. Though we approached the issue from a different perspective, our study has confirmed the view of Boismard-Lamouille, for instance, who argue strongly on undeniable stylistic grounds in favor of the unity of authorship for both the Gospel (level of John II) and the Epistles. More astonishing discoveries may yet await us in this terrain if we but follow it systematically and give it a chance to yield its own fruit. For the present we will bring this whole discussion on the missionary situation of the Johannine community to a close by briefly discussing the probable date and possible geographical setting of the Gospel.

D. The Date and Provenance of the Gospel

The dating of the Gospel is complicated by questions raised by source and redaction criticism. Not only may the Evangelist have used sources, the *SQ*, the *RQ*, the OT, the Synoptic Gospels and Paul's letters, but the composition of the Gospel may itself have undergone different redactions[98]. The dates suggested for the redaction and composition of the Gospel range from A.D. 30/40 to even A.D. 180. A most vibrant discussion of this whole issue of dating is offered by Robinson[99]. We are here concerned, however, with the probable date of the Gospel in its present final form. Even here the dates suggested range from about A.D. 60 to A.D. 120. An overwhelming majority of scholars favor the dates A.D. 90 to A.D. 100, while a striking minority favor the period prior to the destruction of the Temple of Jerusalem in A.D. 70[100].

The major reasons offered in favor of the late dating (the majority

---

[98]The discussion on the literary levels of 4:1–42 (pp. 61–63 above) applies on a larger scale to the whole Gospel. It is to be borne in mind that most literary critics assign an early date to the *Semeia Evangelium*, the *Grundschrift* or, in the case of Boismard-Lamouille, Document C and the work of John II-A, that is, to a substantial part of the traditions embodied in the Gospel.

[99]Robinson, *Redating*, 256–288.

[100]In addition to Robinson's discussion on the question of dating, Kysar's survey (*The Fourth Evangelist*, 166) reveals a growing tendency in favor of an early date for the Gospel, though those who hold this view are still a minority. Strikingly, W.H. Brownlee ("Whence the Gospel According to John?" *John and Qumran*, 182–183) argues on the evidence of the *Birkat ha-Minim* for an early rather than a late date for the Gospel. He believes that Jn 12:42 describes an earlier situation such as called forth the curse. See also n. 103 below.

view) in the early part of the century included the Johannine dependence on the Synoptics. If the Synoptics were completed at about A.D. 80, John's Gospel would then have been written in the last decade of the century. Secondly, it was posited that the Evangelist used the Gnostic Revelation Discourses (*RQ*) as a possible source. Since these discourses date from the end of the century, John's Gospel must, therefore, belong to the same period. Though today the theory of the Johannine use of the *RQ* has been almost completely discarded, the dating towards the end of the century is still strongly maintained for another reason. On the theory that 9:22, 12: 42 and 16:2 refer to the ejection of Christians from the synagogue following on the introduction of the *Birkat ha-Minim* at Jamnia (A.D. 90), a number of critics date the Gospel from that event as the *terminus a quo.* The *terminus ad quem* resides in the newly discovered Papyrus Egerton 2 and P^{52} found in Egypt, both of which date from A.D. 125. Currently, the introduction of the *Birkat ha-Minim* at the council of Jamnia stands as the strongest evidence on which the majority of critics favor a date between A.D. 90 and A.D. 100.

It will be noted, however, that none of the three hypotheses mentioned above as criteria for the late dating of the Gospel goes unchallenged. We have already mentioned the almost universal rejection of the *RQ* , thanks largely to the discovery of the Dead Sea Scrolls. As far as the Johannine use of the Synoptic Gospels is concerned, critics have yet to decide whether he used the finished Gospels or the traditions common to the Synoptics. As for the theory of ejection from the synagogue, we simply recall the strong case put against it by Robinson, Hare and Cohen, or Kümmel's summative remark that Martyn's thesis has not been proved[101] . Moreover, one gets the impression in some cases that the late dating is influenced consciously or unconsciously by the critic's theory concerning the stages of development of the Johannine community. Hence not only are the criteria used objectively questionable, in some cases they are subjective and arbitrary.

Another important internal evidence adduced in favor of the late dating of the Gospel is its "high Christology." Since such a Christology required time to develop, the Gospel which embodies it could not possibly have been composed early. John's Gospel marks the quintessence of the Christian reflection on the person of Christ; it must, therefore, belong to a later period in the development of the NT literature. The argument is reinforced by the testimony of Eusebius (*H.E.* 3.24) that John wrote to supplement what was omitted by the other three Evangelists, the implication

---

[101]See p. 14, n. 39 above on the position of these authors; also Robinson's discussion of the problem, *Redating*, 273–275. 1Qs 5:10; 6:24–7:25; 8:16–17, 22–23; CD 9:28 and Josephus, *BJ* 2.143 (on the Essenes) indicate that expulsion from the group existed in Judaism long before the NT. Indeed such expulsions arose from the notion of fellowship physically understood: if one no longer shared the life and beliefs of the group, one had no right to remain socially within that group (cf. Jn 15:6).

being that his is the last of the four Gospels. That Johannine Christology is the most highly developed in the NT is not open to dispute. But that such a development could take place only at the end of the century (A.D. 90–100) is most arbitrary and simply cannot be proved. The Evangelist attributes the disciples' full insight into the divine identity of Christ to the teaching and guidance of the Holy Spirit (cf. 16:12–13), but nowhere is there a suggestion that the Holy Spirit needed more than half a century to bring about such insight in the disciples.

Moreover, we must not confuse the time at which the disciples gained full insight into the meaning of Jesus and his mission with the time in which Jesus could have made those claims for himself in one way or another. The Gospel also speaks of the Holy Spirit *reminding* the disciples of what Jesus had previously taught them (14:26). Neither in 16:12–13 (the imparting of new knowledge) nor in 14:26 (the reminding of previous teaching) is the content of the teaching specified. Hence if 16:12–13 can be cited as proof that the divine Christology developed after Easter, one sees no reason why 14:26 cannot be read as proof that the reminder and fuller insight concerned claims which Jesus had personally made during his lifetime. Indeed, 2:22; 12:16 and 20:8–9 seem to imply that the knowledge reflectively gained by the disciples after Easter bore precisely upon claims which Jesus had personally made or which had been made for him during his lifetime, but whose significance they had not fully grasped at the time. Nor must we forget that according to the same testimony of Eusebius (*H.E.* 3.24) John taught orally "for a long time" before he finally committed this teaching to writing. If our theory that the Gospel and the Epistles grew out of the same situation is correct, then the Johannine "high Christology" must have existed "from the beginning," (1 Jn 1:1) before the actual time in which the Gospel was written. So Johannine high Christology cannot be used as a valid and conclusive criterion for the late dating of the Gospel.

Besides, the NT evidence taken at its face value offers strong indications that a high Christology existed quite early outside the Johannine corpus even if this Christology was not always expressed as clearly and as explicitly as in John's Gospel (cf. Phil 2:6–11; Gal 4:4; 2 Cor 8:9; Col 1:15–21; Heb 1)[102]. John's Gospel undoubtedly offers the most sustained defense of a divine Christology in the NT, but that belief in such a Christology was unique to him would be impossible to prove. The development of the Christology in the NT is, in our view, one of the key areas where

---

102The "high" Christology of these early NT passages is naturally disputed. But the issue is by no means definitely resolved. In our view, the whole question of the development of Christology in the NT needs to be reexamined and considerations other than linguistic or the thrust of isolated passages need to be brought to bear on the issue. This is particularly necessary in respect to Paul whose knowledge of the divinity of Jesus is seriously questioned by some critics. See, for instance, Murphy-O'Connor, "Christological Anthropology in Phil., II:6–11," *RB* 83 (1976) 25–50.

ongoing research is needed; the presuppositions on which theories of this development are based also need to be critically reexamined. So much for the arguments advanced for the late dating of the Gospel (the majority view).

The minority view which favors dating the Gospel before A.D. 70 leans heavily for support on the internal evidence of the Gospel. This evidence includes in general, the author's first-hand knowledge of the religious, political and geographical conditions which obtained in Palestine and in Jerusalem prior to A.D. 70. It is noted too that the Gospel contains early source material some of which may even predate the Synoptics. Mention is made, for instance, of "John's antequated theology" which views Christ as prophet (4:19; 9:17), as prophet-king and Davidic Messiah (1:49; 6: 14—15; 6:40—42) and as teacher (3:21; 20:16). Most importantly, the historical accuracy of the Johannine passion account is increasingly being regarded as more reliable than that of the Synoptics; John, for instance, places the crucifixion on the eve of the Passover rather than on the feast itself as do the Synoptics (13:1; 19:14, 31; Mt 26:17; 27:62; Mk 14:12; 15:42; Lk 22:1, 7; 23:54)[103].

On the whole, as Robinson notes, the Johannine portrait presupposes a well-organized and self-possessing Judaism which was not the case in Palestine after A.D. 70[104]. So the question arises whether John's Gospel which is clearly rooted in Jewish Palestinian traditions which antedate A.D. 70 could have been written after A.D. 70, when the organzied Judaism it projects was no longer in existence. The same question is raised in connection with the dating of the letter to the Hebrews which contains striking similarities to John's Gospel[105]. Secondly, could the tensions be-

---

[103]In the Johannine schema, the Passover falls on the sabbath, which explains why he calls it "a great one" (19:31); that sabbath was a double solemnity. In the Synoptics the two feasts fall on two consecutive days such that the Passover serves as the "Day of Preparation" for the sabbath. One of the clearly emerging areas of consensus among scholars is that historically the Johannine account of the passion is more accurate than that of the Synoptics. See, for instance, the papers given at the symposium which met to discuss Robinson's thesis on the redating of the NT: *Die Datierung der Evangelien: Symposion des Instituts für Wissentschaftstheoretische Grundlagenforschung vom 20. -23. mai 1982 in Paderborn* (ed. R. Wegner; Tonbandnachschrift; Paderborn: Deutsches Institut für Bildung und Wissen, 1982) esp. Robinson's own paper (pp. 231—233) where he argues for the priority of the Johannine passion account. See further the report on this symposium by J. Ernst, "Datierung oder Rück-Datierung des Neuen Testaments: Ein Bericht," *TGI* 72 (1982) 384—402. Ernst reports on two significant results of the symposium: agreement on the priority of the Johannine passion account and the need to approach the whole issue of the dating of the NT more cautiously. It says much for Robinson's position that the symposium was ever held in the first place. R.J. Campbell ("Evidence for the Historicity of the Fourth Gospel in John 2: 13—22," *SE* 7 [1982] 101—102) also argues in favor of an early dating for the Gospel as a whole.

[104]Robinson (*Redating*, 272—278) describes the situation in Judaism at this period. It will be recalled that Titus captured Jerusalem at the end of a seven-month seige at the orders of his father Vespasian and destroyed all but a few monuments in the city (August 10, A.D. 70; cf. Josephus, *BJ* 7.1—2). Hadrian finally razed the city to the ground (A.D. 135) and rebuilt it as Aelia Capitolina.

[105]See, for instance, C. Spicq, *L.Epitre aux Hébreux* (2 vols; Paris: Lecoffre, 1952) 1, 109—138.

tween Jews and Christians said to be reflected in the Gospel have taken place after A.D. 70 when the Jews themselves were undergoing persecution[106]? The crux of the Johannine problem thus appears to be, as Robinson notes, "the undeniable early source material of the Gospel and the presumption of its late composition"[107]. His personal view is that unless one *begins* with a late date for the Gospel, there is no reason for reading the events of A.D. 85—90 into 9:22 than for seeing a reference to the Bar Cochba revolt (A.D. 135) in 5:45. His extensive discussion of this whole issue leads him to date the final redaction of the Gospel to ca. 65 A.D., and the Epistles to 60—65 A.D.[108]. Incidentally, Boismard and Lamouille also date the first redaction of the Gospel by the Evangelist (John II-A) to the same period, A.D. 60—65[109]. The years 60—65 thus appear to be favored as a date for the writing of a substantial part of the Gospel, though these critics differ on what version was written at this period and where[110]. Robinson's position finds support in Leon Morris who, seven years earlier (1969), having examined the reasons offered for the late dating of the Gospel, came to the conclusion that nothing demands a date later than 70 A.D. and personally doubted "whether we can go much beyond that"[111].

On the external level the Dead Sea Scrolls first discovered in 1947 furnish clear evidence that Johannine thought patterns existed in Palestine even before the NT era. Hence the assumption that this language could derive only from Gnostic patterns of thought which began to blossom at the end of the first century died a natural death. A most challenging external argument is, perhaps, that championed by Robinson. If, he questions, John's Gospel and any of the NT works were written after A.D. 70, why is it that none of them mentions the destruction of the Temple, which event would have strongly supported their central hermeneutic that Jesus did fulfil and transcend the OT Scriptures and the religion attached to them? Whether or not one accepts Robinson's thesis so meticulously argued out in his *Redating of the New Testament,* one cannot deny that

---

[106]One does not normally become a persecutor when one is undergoing persecution oneself. The devastating impact on Judaism of the events of A.D. 70 cannot be overestimated. Cohen's view that Jamnia was intended more as a rallying point for Judaism itself than as a witch hunt for crypto-Christians deserves serious consideration.

[107]Robinson, *Redating,* 269.

[108]Robinson, *Redating,* 273, 307.

[109]Boismard-Lamouille, *Synopse III,* 68.

[110]Robinson dates the first edition of the present Gospel to A.D. 50—55 and the final redaction to A.D. 65; he situates both editions in Asia Minor. Boismard and Lamouille on their part date the first edition (John II-A) to A.D. 60—65 and situate this in Palestine; the second edition (John II-B) dates from A.D. 90—100 and originates in Asia Minor. All three authors agree that the proto-Gospel or Document C originated in Palestine around A.D. 30—50, that a substantial part of the Gospel was written around A.D. 60—65, and that the final redaction of the Gospel was undertaken in Asia Minor by the same author.

[111]Leon Morris, *Studies in the Fourth Gospel* (Grand Rapids: Wm. B. Eerdmans, 1969) esp. pp. 283—292 and 292 (his own conclusion).

the central point he raises deserves special consideration. The argument from silence in this particular instance may yet prove to be a valid and important criterion.

The above survey of the reasons offered for the early or late dating of the Gospel reveals that this whole topic cannot be considered in isolation from other issues. But those issues which relate directly to the internal evidence of the Gospel must claim priority over external ones, especially where the external criteria used are highly hypothetical and tenuous. Equally, it needs to be emphasized that precise dating of the Gospel on the basis of our extant sources is impossible. The best we can do at this point, therefore, is to relate this whole question to the major missionary issues raised in this present investigation. Do these issues and the relationship established between the Gospel and the Epistles give us any clues as to the probable date of the Gospel?

At the heart of the missionary issues raised in this study stands the question of Jesus' messiahship and his divine ontological sonship. Our investigation also revealed that on the level of the Evangelist these claims are disputed not by unbelieving Jews (as most scholars tend to think) but by disenchanted disciples. Is it likely, then, that such an internal (or even external) battle would have raged over Jesus's messianic identity as late as A.D. 90—100, the dates which most scholars favor for the final composition of the Gospel? It needs to be recalled that by this time the Christians as a group separate from Judaism had undergone at least one major persecution, that of Nero (ca. 66 A.D.) if not two or three[112]. If by this time, the last decade of the century, the messiahship of Jesus was not sufficiently established among believers, something must have gone very wrong in the evangelization process[113].

On the other hand, it could be argued that the threat posed by these persecutions caused some believers to question whether or not Jesus was really the Christ, eventually came to the conclusion that he was not, and

---

[112]After Nero (A.D. 54—68), Domitian (A.D. 81—98) and Trajan (A.D. 98—117) also persecuted the Christians, though on a lesser scale than Nero. The famous letter of Pliny the Younger to Trajan asking whether or not Christians should be sought out and destroyed would indicate that the persecution of Christians was not restricted to Rome (cf. Eusebius, *H.E.* 3.19.1—23.4). The Jewish persecution of Christians started even before Paul's conversion (Acts 4:1—3; 5:17—42; 6: 8—8:3; 9:1—2).

[113]Murphy-O'Connor (*St. Paul's Corinth,* 132) notes that Christianity had spread to all points of the empire in the first part of the century: to Damascus as early as A.D. 33, to Cyprus, Phoenicia, and Antioch in the same decade (A.D. 30—40), and to Rome by the end of the 30's. He adds that evidence disqualifies the view of small scale expansion of Christianity in the first half of the century: "What is certain is that, from the beginning, believers were inspired to carry their new faith abroad" (pp. 132—133). It is worth recalling, too, that Paul received orders to persecute Christians living outside Palestine and that at Damascus Ananias only "heard reports" of Paul's persecution (Acts 9:13). This means that he himself was not living in Jerusalem when the Pauline persecution started. The Lucan account of the spread of the Church (according to which believers did not move outside Jerusalem till after Stephen's death, Acts 8:1—2) is perhaps highly schematized.

so left the community. Ancient literature is not lacking in evidence for apostates[114]. Such a situation is possible; the major difficulty in this case is that 1 John which is supposed to post-date the Gospel by a span of years, gives no impression that the community addressed is in any danger of persecution. Even if critics sense an air of persecution from Jews and Gentiles in the Gospel, this would fit better the period before rather than after A.D. 70. For at this time organized Judaism was still very much in control, right up to the time of its first revolt against the Romans under Nero (A.D. 66–70). Also the intense missionary activities of both or-thodox and heterodox teachers reported in the Epistles would fit better this earlier period[115].

The other important issues raised do not preclude an early date either: the boasting of the disciples whether as missionaries or as charismatic individuals, the tendency to grab opportunity for self-aggrandizement or the neglect of mutual love within the community. For specific examples in these cases we will limit ourselves to Paul whose letters fall before A.D. 66, when he suffered martyrdom under Nero. Indeed, the letter to the Corinthians furnishes us with most of these examples. The Corinthian sit-uation amply testifies that a spirit of rivalry and power struggle existed among the believers in the context of mission from the early days. Not only are the Corinthians divided along missionary party lines (1 Cor 3:1–10), but Paul himself feels that as their founding father he deserves their special allegiance more than do their countless guides (1 Cor 4:15). He insists that the Corinthians follow his ways in Christ (1 Cor 4:17). We re-call too Paul's special resentment over the fact that the title of apostle was denied him despite his hard work (1 Cor 9:1–16; cf. Gal 2:6, 9). We also know that during Paul's imprisonment opportunists tried to make most of the situation to enhance their status as preachers and thus to spite Paul (Phil 1:15–18). Diotrephes was not, apparently, a unique character in this respect. John may indeed be reacting against this kind of power struggle in all its forms when he insists that Jesus is the only evangelizer of his followers and that all missionaries simply enter into his labor (4:38, 42). Paul's authoritative standing in the community clearly contrasts with that of the author of 1 John. While the one will deal harshly with the arrogant during his visit (1 Cor 4:18–21), the other will merely bring up the doings of Diotrephes (3 Jn 9–10). It is ironic, therefore, that

---

114The children of the Shepherd, Hermas, for instance, were apostates (*Hermes, le Pasteur,* SC 53, Vis. 2.2.5–8), not to mention the notorious Julian the Apostate (A.D. 361–363). Within the NT canon one may think of Simon Magus and the whole problem grappled with in Hebrews.

115According to Josephus the period preceding the destruction of Jerusalem was marked by intense and atrocious strife within the Jewish community itself (*BJ* 4.3.2–4.7.2), which strife seems to have been the chief cause for the Roman intervention (*BJ* 4.6.2–3; 4.7.3). The general picture of Christian missionary activity projected at the end of the first century (for instance, in the *Didache,* 11) is on a much lower key than is that in the Epistles. One gets the impression that impostors were now trafficking on being missionaries such that their length of stay in a given place had to be restricted to two days (*Did.* 11.5).

critics should discern in John a power struggle between the Beloved Disciple and Peter or between the author of the Epistles and Diotrephes.

The boasting of the Corinthians on personal grounds has almost become proverbial (1 Cor 4:7; 5:6). It rings as loud and phony as their empty gongs and clanging cymbals (13:1). Murphy-O'Connor attributes this boasting to their central belief that as Christians "they were definitely fixed in the state of salvation"[116]. The belief resulted in their giving way to licentiousness of all sorts (cf. 6:12–20) and called forth a strong reminder from Paul that believing was not enough any more than it was enough for the Israelites to have been under the cloud (1 Cor 10:1–14). The whole situation again parallels that of John with its reiterated emphasis that if we say we have no sin we merely deceive ourselves. Indeed the "advanced Christians" of 2 Jn 9 may not have been very different from those Corinthians who sought to "go beyond what is written" (1 Cor 4:6).

Finally, though the Corinthians are called by God into the fellowship of his Son (1 Cor 1:9), their interpersonal relationship in the community is a far cry from the witness demanded by this fellowship. They quarrel (1 Cor 1:1–10), have lawsuits against each other (6:1–7), indulge in the worst type of fornication (5:1–5), and subject the celebration of the *agape* to the utmost contempt (11:17–33). This whole situation calls forth two of Paul's most beautiful passages in the letter, the one on the unity of the body (12:12–31), the other on the excellence of love (13:1–13). On this question of fellowship practically lived out, perhaps the situation in the Johannine community was not very different from that of Corinth since equal emphasis is laid on the need for unity (the vine and the branches; Jn 17) and for brotherly love (especially 1 John). The parallels here highlighted between the missionary situation of the Johannine and Pauline communities are by no means exhaustive. But they do indicate that language and style and concrete examples apart, the Johannine missionary situation is fundamentally not very different from that of Paul. Hence if we are to use these issues as a guide for dating the Gospel, they would not necessarily demand that we date it to the last decade of the first century[117].

The parallelism highlighted above between the Johannine and the Pauline missionary situations indicate that the Johannine situation could be reasonably placed in the early part of the century but they offer no conclusive evidence against placing it in the later part of the century (after A.D. 70). The relationship we established between the Gospel and the Johannine Epistles may throw further light on this issue. According to 1

---

[116]Murphy-O'Connor, *1 Corinthians*, 46.

[117]A comparative study of the Johannine and Pauline approaches to mission might prove very rewarding indeed. NT scholarship has done much research on the NT authors and missionaries but very little on their different audiences. A much neglected but important area of research concerns the contribution which the audience brought to bear on the message itself; see n. 3 above, and our further comments on this issue in our concluding chapter.

Jn 2:12–14, the community addressed by the author includes little children, fathers and young men. Critics debate whether these terms cover two or three generations or age groups among the audience. Since the term "little children" ($\tau\epsilon\kappa\nu\iota\alpha$) is used frequently in the letter (1 Jn 2:1, 28; 3:7, 18; 4:4; 5:21) for the whole group addressed, it seems best to regard this as a term of endearment (cf. 13:33; Gal 4:19), rather than as a designation of a particular age group. The terms "fathers" and "young men" would then indicate that the group addressed embraces two generations.

This argument, however, does not lead very far when it is remembered that whole households were converted in early Christianity (1 Cor 1:16; Acts 10:44–48; 16:14–15). So the composition of the group according to age gives us no indication of the length of time that the community had been in existence. Equally, it cannot be denied that the community had existed for some time prior to the writing of the letter; the reference to the message they received "from the beginning" (1 Jn 2:7, 27) makes this clear, though how long ago this "beginning" took place cannot be determined from these verses alone[118]. Of utmost significance, however, is the author's claim that he was personally an eyewitness of Jesus and his ministry (1 Jn 1:1–3, 5). Brown holds that the author is not actually an eyewitness but that he claims to be one merely because he had seen those who had seen the Lord, in a kind of "chain reaction"[119]. This view runs into serious conflict with the great emphasis which the author places on this fact of eyewitness (using almost all the five senses, 1:1–3) and the persuasive importance which he attaches to it, both as the prologue to his letter and the basis for his preaching witness (1:5; 4:14). Moreover, why would the "chain reaction" suddenly stop with the author and not extent to his own audience especially since this audience is said to have been evangelized by Jesus himself (1 Jn 2:21, 25, 27)? Given the importance which the ancients attached to this whole issue of eyewitness (15:27; Lk 1:2–3; Acts 2:21–22; Heb 2:3; 2 Pet 1:16–18) and the fact that the author makes this claim in a time of crisis as the basis of his exhortation, we must at least accept his word that he personally witnessed Jesus' ministry, and proceed from there[120].

---

[118]Faced with the threat of the Judaizers, Paul also reminds his audience of the faith which they had first received (Gal 1:6–9; 4:8–10; similarly Heb 10:32–35); but the activity of the Judaizers did not come decades after the evangelization of Galatia.

[119]Brown, *Community*, 100; *Epistles*, 161.

[120]The NT evidence appears to be conclusive that the early Christians did not claim the status of eyewitness unless they had actually seen the Lord. Thus Luke makes it clear that he himself was not an eyewitness though he clearly saw people who had seen the Lord (Lk 1:1–4); so, too, the author of the letter to the Hebrews (2:3). Paul had a problem defending his "apostleship" precisely because he had not been one of the eyewitnesses of Jesus' earthly life (Gal 2:6–9; see also the opening of most of his letters, e.g., 1 Cor 1:1; 2 Cor 1:1; Rom 1:1). The choice of Matthias to replace Judas is determined by his sustained physical contact with Jesus from the time of his baptism to his ascension (Acts 1:21–22). In the sub-apostolic era we find the same importance

To say that the author was an eyewitness does not necessarily mean that he was John son of Zebedee. The question of the identity of the Beloved Disciple needs to be kept separate from that of his status as an eyewitness, and the evidence for each issue needs to be weighed carefully before the two are brought together. If then the author personally witnessed the events of Jesus' life, and if among his audience were still alive people whom he and his co-eyewitnesses first evangelized (the "fathers"), then this evidence would lead us to date the Gospel to a generation or at most two, after A.D. 30, the Easter event. We are not unaware of the tradition that the Beloved Disciple lived to a great old age (cf. 21:23)[121]; but the tradition does not claim the same privilege for his audience, some of whom (the "fathers") would have been adults at the time of their conversion[122].

So while it may not be possible to assign a precise date to the Gospel and Epistles, none of the evidence examined here would militate against our placing these works in the Pauline or sub-Pauline era as a parallel tradition to the works composed by the apostle of the Gentiles (Gal 2:8–9). Our cumulative evidence would support rather than argue against this dating. Boismard-Lamouille, for instance, hold that the Evangelist, John II, knew Paul's letters both when he wrote his first edition in Palestine

---

attached to the status of eyewitness physically understood (whether it be of the Lord or of those who had seen him). Thus Polycarp, called "the companion of the Apostles," is not included among the "eyewitnesses and ministers of the Lord" (Eus. *H.E.* 3.36.1); yet in Brown's theory of "chain reaction" he certainly would have qualified since he had seen John the Apostle and had been his close disciple. Similarly, in the preface to his treatises, Papias takes pains to underline that he himself had not personally seen the apostles (Eus. *H.E.* 3.39.2–3). Perhaps in John more so than in any NT work the question of eyewitness is preeminently important since Jesus is presented as the Father's witness par excellence, the only human being who has seen the Father and who, consequently, can reveal him perfectly and in an exclusive manner (1:18; 3:13). Equally the disciples addressed in the farewell discourses are able to serve as Jesus' first witnesses because they had been with him from the beginning (15:27). This overwhelming evidence weakens the convincing force of the theory of "chain reaction."

[121] If our entire argument is correct that an eyewitness, called the Beloved Disciple, wrote both the Gospel and the Epistles, then 21:23 cannot mean that he is dead at the time the Gospel is written. See the detailed arguments on this issue by Robinson (*Redating*, 298–311) and the eminent scholars who support this view. On the contextual level, all the references to the Beloved Disciple as witness of the Gospel events are either in the perfect tense (19:35) or in the present (21:24). Whatever the case, we find unconvincing the arguments put forth in support of the view that the witness is dead at the time the Gospel is written. Besides, the tradition which attributes longevity to the Beloved Disciple (Eus. *H.E.* 3.18–20) goes back to the Gospel itself (21:23); hence it cannot be totally unfounded historically.

[122] Robinson (*Redating*, 262) cites Irenaeus (*Adv. Haer.* 2.22.5) in support of the view that "old age" was for anybody over 40 or 50. According to tradition Paul died ca. A.D. 66 in Nero's persecution. If he was "a young man" (Acts 7:58) at the time of Stephen's death (ca. A.D. 30–33), at most in his 20's, he could not have been more than 60 at the time of his own death. Yet in his letter to Philemon dated to his house arrest in Rome (ca. 61–63 A.D.), he explicitly refers to himself as "an old man" (πρεσβύτης, Phlm 9), which term applied to people between the ages of 50 to 56 (cf. Philo, *Op.M.* 105; *BAG*, 700 and the references given there to Hyppocrates and Dio Chrysostom).

(ca. A.D. 60–65) and when he wrote his second edition some thirty years later in Ephesus[123]. Our author may not actually have known Paul's letters in the 60's, but he may have been dealing with a missionary situation similar to Paul's, though from a predominantly Jewish rather than Gentile perspective. The similarity in situation may account for the fundamental similarities in the comnunal issues which they raise.

The Identity of the Audience

This last observation brings us to a brief consideration of the identity of the author and of his audience. Few critics would dispute today that the author of the Gospel is a Palestinian Jew. The author's claim to be an eyewitness is, perhaps, the most conclusive evidence for this[124]. From the standpoint of the Epistle, O'Neill has gone so far as to argue that the letter was originally a Jewish document which a Jewish-Christian convert then adapted to Christianity and used as a missionary document to win his fellow Jews. O'Neill sees great similarities between 1 John and the *Testament of the Twelve Patriarchs*[125]. Though Bultmann rejects O'Neill's source theory, he praises the work for the light it throws on the essentially Jewish *Weltanschauung* of the letter[126]. But if the author is Jewish, can the same be said of his audience? At this stage of our investigation, we should discard the view that the Gospel was written to win unbelieving Jews of the Diaspora to faith in Jesus[127]. For, as we have seen, both Gospel and Epistles aim at sustaining believers in their faith. But given the specificity of the key issues discussed: Jesus' messiahship and his divine ontological sonship, his mission from the Father seen in relation to that of the Baptist, the OT prophets, Moses and the Scriptures, plus the fact that the Jews in the Gospel find Jesus' claims the most difficult to accept, one would have to posit that a substantial portion of the audience addressed is Jewish. For to Jews would the question whether or not Jesus was the Messiah be of utmost interest. The antichrists would certainly be of Jewish origin.

It would be wrong, however, to see the group addressed as exclusively Jewish. Gaius is a latin name, while Diotrephes and Demetrius are Greek. This, of course, says nothing about the nationality of these people. In the Gospel Philip is a Greek name, so is Nicodemus, and both are as Jewish as are Simon and Nathanael. It seems best, then, to posit a mixed audience

---

[123] Boismard-Lamouille, *Synopse III,* 242–244.

[124] The Beloved Disciple is not only presented as the eyewitness of the Gospel narrative, he is also portrayed as Jesus' most intimate disciple (13:23). Origen long ago compared his intimacy with Jesus, symbolized by his reclining on Jesus' breast, to Jesus' own intimacy with the Father also described in terms of his being in the Father's bosom (1:18).

[125] O'Neill's book is available to us only through the secondary sources cited in n. 43 above.

[126] Bultmann, *Epistles,* 1; so, too, Marshall, *Epistles,* 30, n. 62.

[127] Robinson appears to be the only persistent champion of this view. See his *Redating,* 285, 292–298, and our earlier discussion on the missionary nature of the Gospel, pp. 9–11 above.

for the immediate group addressed, bearing in mind the undeniably cosmic dimensions and setting of the Gospel. It may even be possible that the errors corrected ran along ethnic lines. For while the Jews would be more likely to question Jesus' claim to messiahship, the Gentile Christians who were "once sinners" (unlike the Jews; cf. Gal 2:15) but have since found pardon (1 Pet 1:18; Col 3:5–7; Eph 2:1, 11–12) would be more likely to push this their new found identity to the extreme as did the Corinthians, than would Jews who from the outset were already considered "holy." This, no doubt, is only a suggestion, but it would be worth inquiring into whether Gentile converts were more prone than Jews to charismatic errors because of their previous religious upbringing.

Concerning the place from which these works originated most critics prefer Asia Minor, in particular, Ephesus. This view has a strong backing in tradition and one 'sees no convincing reason for rejecting it[128]. The problem addressed may also have originated there, but given the fact that the Christians of the first century were not provincial in their outlook, movements or mentality, we have no reason to surmise that either the works or the problems addressed were restricted to the geographical area from which they originated[129].

E. Recapitulation: The Evidence of Hebrews

By way of bringing to a close this whole discussion on the missionary situation of the Johannine community, we may seriously question again the probability of the thesis sustained in this chapter, especially in relation to the interpretation of 1 Jn 2:22; 4:4; 5:1 and 2 Jn 7. Is it conceivable that a Jewish-Christian would have come to doubt that Jesus was really the Messiah and Son of God and eventually be led to give up his or her faith? In answering this question affirmatively, we centered our argument on the internal evidence of the Gospel, noting in particular the evidence of the departing disciples (6:66; 8:30–59), of a character such as Judas (13:30), the visual symbolism projected in the dead branch which is severed from the vine (15:6), and, we must not forget, the whole emphasis in the Johannine works on the need to "remain in" Jesus (physically understood). We argued, too, that a situation such as this most satisfac-

---

[128]Eusebius (*H.E.* 3.20) holds that after his banishment to Patmos during the persecution by Domitian (A.D. 81–96) John settled at Ephesus. Ephesus is generally accepted as the provenance of the Gospel, whether or not critics attribute its authorship to John the Apostle.

[129]The Johannine Epistles project a picture of missionaries both orthodox and heterodox. The oldest extant MS of the Gospel, P[52], dated ca. A.D. 125, was discovered in Egypt. Eusebius (*H.E.* 3.24) narrates that in his day John's Gospel was read in all the churches under heaven.

torily explains both the concentration in the Gospel on Jesus' divine sonship and messianic identity (that he is sent by the Father) and the entire persuasive and rhetorical thrust of the Gospel itself (20:30–31). If this whole procedure smacks of circularity (though we think not), we have yet one reliable, external and NT evidence to back our thesis.

This evidence is the *Letter to the Hebrews*. Interestingly, some critics believe that this letter was destined to the Christians of Ephesus or of the region of Asia Minor and offer the strongest arguments for dating it before A.D. 70[130]. Tempting as the project is and highly informative as the result may prove, we do not intend here to embark on a comparative study of the situation of the Johannine community highlighted in this chapter and that projected in the letter to the Hebrews. We simply want to note at this juncture that the letter to the Hebrews offers us an indisputable evidence that to the Jewish-Christians of the NT era the temptation to apostatize was neither inconceivable nor remote[131]. The whole purpose of the letter (13:22), like that of John's Gospel and Epistles, is to exhort the readers to remain faithful to Jesus and hold fast to their common "confession" ($\delta\mu o\lambda o\gamma\iota\alpha\varsigma$, 4:14). Negatively, the letter warns in the strongest possible terms against the danger of "apostasy" ($\dot{\alpha}\pi o\sigma\vartheta\tilde{\eta}\nu\alpha\iota$, 3:12; 12:25) or of rejecting the witness of salvation which God offers through Jesus his Son and which has been preached to them by Jesus' witnesses and the Holy Spirit (2:3). In the author's view, to reject this witness after having first accepted it is to crucify God's Son anew and hold him in contempt (6:4–6; 10:29), to commit the unforgivable sin (10:26–29), or to pass from life to death (cf. 3:12)[132].

To get his point across, he adopts the same hermeneutical process as we met in John of citing historical examples pertinent to the situation of his audience. Paul, we saw above, uses the same argumentative process with the Corinthians (1 Cor 10:1–14). For the author of Hebrews, the rebellious Israelites who left Egypt but never entered the promised land serve as a powerful warning against the danger of apostasy or of withdrawing and perishing (10:39; 2–3). "Examples" of those who believed and

---

[130]Spicq, *L'Epître aux Hébreux*, 1, 252–259; also Westcott, *The Epistle to the Hebrews* (Grand Rapids: WM. B. Eerdmans, 1955) xxxix. Naturally the exact destination of the letter is disputed. But the strongest evidence in favor of a date prior to A.D. 70 is the pains taken by the author to demonstrate that Jesus has transcended the OT priesthood with its accompanied sacrifices. Had the Temple been destroyed at the time he wrote, he would certainly have cited this as conclusive evidence for his argument. See further Myles Bourke, "The Epistle to the Hebrews," *JBC* 2, 382, no. 5, who personally favors a date prior to A.D. 70.

[131]Schnackenburg (*Johannesbriefe*, 16) and Marshall (*Epistles*, 16–17) contend against Wurm that while Jewish opponents might deny the messiahship of Jesus this cannot be true of the opponents in 1 Jn 2:18 since these were once Christians. The issue, though, is that from the standpoint of 1 John they were never really Christians.

[132]Hebrews 6:4–6 and 10:26–29 might shed some light on the meaning of the unforgivable sin in 1 John 5:16. One is also reminded of Judas (13:30) and of the dead branches cut off from the vine (15:6).

persevered to the end go all the way back to prehistory (Abel) through the whole of the OT to Jesus himself and the evangelizers of the audience addressed (11:1–12:3; 13:7). The entire hermeneutical process underlines the point that hearing the good news avails nothing unless one believes and perseveres in it to the end (4:2; cf. Jn 15:22).

Spicq believes the danger of apostasy is rooted in the fear of an impending persecution of a political nature, possibly related to the Jewish revolt against Rome (A.D. 66–70)[133]. This may well be. But equally the letter squarely grounds this danger in its audience's disenchantment with their Christian faith. Their lethargy and loss of fervor (10:32–36; 12:12) is matched by a corresponding leaning towards the Mosaic religion (13:9–10). As in the Johannine situation, the real reasons for the loss of faith are doctrinal rather than political; there is a warning against false teaching (13:9–12). At the center of the doctrinal issues stands the question of Jesus' ontological divine sonship and of the significance of his mission by comparison to that of Moses (3:1–6) and the Mosaic, Levitical cult (7:1–10:25). Though as God's messenger Jesus may be compared with the OT prophets (1:1–2), Moses (3:5–6) and even the ministering angels (1:4–14), he is radically different from and superior to them because he is a "Son" (1:2, 5, 8; 3:6), while these others are merely "servants" (1:7; 3:5). By the same token, his sacrificial offering made once and for all (7:27) achieves the sanctification of all by contrast to the ineffective offerings of the Levitical cult (7:11) which was only a "shadow" of the true order or worship established by Jesus (10:1–5).

As in the Johannine situation, other doctrinal issues disputed appear to be of the sacramental order (6:2a); or they bear upon the resurrection·from the dead and eternal judgment (6:2b), both of which issues also. figure in John (5:24–29)[134]. A final comparison with the Johannine situation is that even this overtly hortatory work also contains advice on ethical conduct (12:14–17; 13:1–7) in which the call to mutual love and hospitality figure prominently (13:1–2). There is even a reminder as in John that believers do not belong to this world (13:14).

This comparative list is by no means exhaustive; it may also be supplemented with the more general list drawn up by Spicq[135]. We do not, of course, imply that the Johannine works and the letter to the Hebrews are dealing with one and the same situation. More research would be needed before any judgment could be made along these lines. The point we are simply making is that the situation of the audience addressed by the letter to the Hebrews makes it quite plain that the temptation to stop believing

---

[133]Spicq, *L'Epître aux Hébreux* 1, 257–257; also pp. 235–236, 241. Strikingly, the author considers the impending ordeal, whatever its nature, to be nothing compared with those of the former days (10:32–35).

[134]In Jn 6 the issue is Jesus' teaching on the Eucharist, his claim to be the indispensable bread of life; the issue of true worship is raised in 4:20–24; cf. Heb 13:9–12.

[135]Spicq, *L'Epître aux Hébreux*, 109–138.

in Christ and return to Judaism was not an unreal possibility for the Jewish-Christian of the NT era. The great value of the corroborative evidence of the letter lies in the fact that like the Johannine works (and unlike the letters of Ignatius of Antioch) it belongs to the NT canon, and, in the view of some critics, at least, was destined to readers in the same region of Asia Minor. As in Hebrews, the Johannine situation in both the Gospel and Epistles deals with believers who are strongly tempted to reject Jesus' messiahship through the lure of false teaching rooted in and oriented towards Judaism. Both works deal in the same way hermeneutically with this same problem. In the Johannine situation there is an additional tendency on the part of believers to falsify this Christian belief on both the personal and missio-communal levels. The efforts of the Evangelist to sustain his readers in their belief and keep them faithful to it count as a missionary endeavor, especially since his efforts are pitted against the contrary activities of the antichrists.

The above review of the evidence of Hebrews brings to an end our discussion on the missionary situation of the Johannine community. This, in turn, marks the completion of the main task which we set out to accomplish in this study. In the first place we examined our basic text, Jn 4:1—42, from the standpoint of contemporary scholarship (Chapter III). On the basis of the problems raised by this scholarship we analyzed the text itself with a view to highlighting its missionary significance both from the standpoint of Jesus and an unbelieving audience (the *narratio* or thesis, vv 1—26 [Chapter IV]), and from the standpoint of Jesus and prospective missionary disciples (the *expositio* and *demonstratio* or the consequential argument, vv 27—42 [Chapter V]). In order to determine whether the missionary issues and approach highlighted in the basic text could truly be described as characteristically Johannine we placed these issues within the overall context of the Gospel (Chapter VI). And since the missionary undertaking necessarily involves a living audience and context, we devoted some time in this present Chapter VII to discussing the probable missionary situation which could have formed the living inspirational context of the Evangelist's work and influenced his entire approach to mission. Our remaining and final task now is to consider the general conclusions which may be drawn from this entire investigation and to highlight its significance for future Johannine studies.

Chapter VIII

Summary and Conclusion

Review of Significant Results

The task of this present investigation was to discover the different facets of the Johannine approach to mission as this relates to the living inspirational context of the Evangelist's work. The study began with a description of the Johannine data concerning his notion of mission and, in dialogue with the current state of Johannine research on mission, raised some fundamental questions concerning these data (Chapter I). It proposed that the questions raised would best be answered by efforts to delineate the Evangelist's own notion of mission, and, in particular, by close attention to his unique method of handling the issue. The contextual method, essentially a listening approach, was deemed the method best suited to the task since it would best enable us to observe the Evangelist at work and allow him to dictate his own hermeneutical norms (Chapter II).

To facilitate this task, we proposed to center our enquiry on Jn 4:1–42, a passage universally recognized as being the most overtly concerned with mission in the Gospel, even though critics differ concerning the scope and extent of mission in the passage (Chapters III, IV, V). On the basis of the findings in this episode, findings whose validity as characteristics of the Johannine approach would be tested and controlled by an examination of further Gospel material (Chapter VI), we were to initiate a discussion on the possible missionary situation of the Evangelist and of his community (Chapter VII). Such was the general design of the study.

The major questions raised to guide the investigation came under three basic headings. *The first set of questions* dealt with the rationale behind the Evangelist's choice of mission as the fundamental hermeneutic or leitmotif of his Gospel. What did he understand by mission? Why is there such an unmitigated emphasis in the Gospel that Jesus is the Christ, the ontological Son of God, sent by the Father? And why are all other important characters in the Gospel presented either positively or negatively from the standpoint of mission? Why, most importantly, is the whole subject of Jesus' mission from the Father treated in a predominantly forensic and polemical manner, such that all other missions are judged and evaluated by his own mission?

The second set of questions concerned the interpersonal relationships and methodological dynamics involved in the exercise of mission. As one sent, what is Jesus' attitude towards his sender, his mission and his audience? In particular, how genuine is the interaction between Jesus and his various audiences? Do his interlocutors play an essential role in the missionary enterprise or do they merely serve as foils? What hermeneutical principles governed the Evangelist's selection of events in Jesus' life for presentation to his own audience, and how does his method of persuading his audience relate to that employed by Jesus in respect to his own audience in the Gospel?

The third set of questions concerned the missionary scope of our basic text, 4:1–42, and of the Gospel as a whole. Does all of 4:1–42 deal with mission or is the missionary theme restricted only to vv 31–38 or 31–42 (Chapter III)? On the Gospel level, was the "book" a missionary document (*eine Missionsschrift*) designed to win non-believers to faith in Jesus? Or was it a community document (*ein Gemeinde-Evangelium*) destined to strengthen believers' faith in Jesus (20:20–31)? And finally, bearing on this issue, was the Evangelist or his community or both interested in mission? Thus, the research started out with questions for which to seek answers rather than with a thesis to prove.

The answers to the first set of questions (concerning the rationale for the Evangelist's choice of mission as the leitmotif of the Gospel) emerged *implicitly* in the detailed exegesis of 4:1–42 and in the examinnation of 13–17 and 21, and *explicitly* in the whole discussion of the missionary situation of the Evangelist and of his audience (Chapter VII). In the first place our examination of these Johannine passages revealed a deliberate, sustained and consistent effort on the part of the Evangelist to emphasize Jesus' unique and exclusive role in the missionary enterprise and, correspondingly, the essentially dependent and self-benefiting nature of the disciples' mission.

In 4:1–42 this emphasis was communicated in a variety of ways. First by the dramatic narrative technique whereby the disciples were deliberately kept off the scene during Jesus' entire dialogue with the woman (vv 2, 8, 27), in which dialogue he revealed himself to her as the Messiah (vv 16 –26) and giver of living water/eternal life (vv 7–15). The absence of the disciples thus implicitly underlined the fact that Jesus and the Father (vv 10, 23, 26) are the real laborers at work in the missionary enterprise. The thesis, that Jesus is the Father's exclusive agent of salvation (vv 1–26), was then explicitly explained to the disciples in vv 28–42, first by Jesus himself, the *expositio* (vv 31–38), then by the Evangelist, the *demonstratio* (vv 28–30, 39–42). In the explanatory section, vv 28–42, the lesson consequent upon the thesis was seen to be encapsulated in the three key verses 34, 38 and 42: in v 34 by the ἔργον concept (Jesus alone does and completes the Father's work of which the dialogue with the woman forms a part); in v 38 by the reminder that though sent, the disciples do no more than reap the fruit of Jesus' and the Father's labor; and in v 42 by the Samaritans' claim that Jesus, not the woman, is their real evangelizer. Thus Jesus' mission in all its scope was seen to be the unifying theme of the entire pericope.

Structurally, the episode was also seen to possess a formal rhetorical structure which we described in terms of the *narratio* (vv 1–26), the *expositio* (vv 31–38) and the *demonstratio* (vv 28–30, 39–42). Similarly, vv 1–26 whose literary and thematic unity is greatly disputed was seen to cohere by means of its structure (the manner in which the topic is set [v 10] and then developed) and by its genre as a dialogue in which the interests of the interlocutors determine the content. The double theme of the dialogue embodied in v 10 was seen to be developed in two parts: v 10a in vv 11–15 and v 10b in vv 16–26. The whole episode was further seen to be held together by the eschatological background in which the narrative is set. As the Messiah or God's eschatological agent of salvation, Jesus imparts eternal life to all who believe in him whether these be prospective believers or future missionaries. He exercises an exclusive and abiding role in both the sowing and harvesting phases of "the Father's work."

The central findings in 4:1–42 concerning Jesus' unique role in the missionary enterprise and the resulting dependence of the disciples on him were further seen to be developed in the farewell discourses and in Jn 21. In these passages, Jesus demonstrated himself as the one who sustains the disciples in their personal life (the imagery of the vine and the branches, and the feeding after the miraculous catch), renders fruitful their mission (by sending them the Holy Spirit, praying for them and personally enabling their miraculous catch, symbolic of their missionary fruitfulness) and serves as their model of humility in the exercise of mission. Thus the καθὼς ἐγώ, καὶ ὑμεῖς motif which dominates the farewell discourses was interpreted as having a particular reference to the need for the disciples to imitate Jesus both in his humble service of the disciples themselves (a lesson summed up in the footwashing) and in his attitude of total dependence on the Father who sent him (a lesson summed up in his prayerful attitude in Jn 17).

The conclusion drawn from the total evidence of the Gospel was that the disciples addressed by the Evangelist must have stood in special need of being reminded of Jesus' uniqueness as God's eschatological agent of salvation (the Christ and Son of God) and of the resulting need for their total dependence on him. The missionary emphases in the Gospel suggested that an attitude of boasting, a tendency to behave as if they owned the mission, and pride in a variety of forms must have constituted a special weakness of the Johannine audience. The lessons given directly to the disciples concerning Jesus' exclusive role in the missionary enterprise (4:34; 17:4) and concerning the need for humility on their part as missionaries (4:38, 42; 15:16; 21) were seen to be indirectly reinforced by the negative portrayal of the Pharisees as the anti-type of those sent, and by the positive portrayal of the Baptist, Moses and the Scriptures as reliable agents whose mission gives faithful witness to Jesus. The whole portrayal of Jesus' relationship to other missionaries in the Gospel thus emphasized that as God's Messiah, sent by him to give life to the world (3:16; 17:2–3), Jesus has neither predecessors nor successors. All the lessons on mission expressed in a variety of ways in the Gospel were, however, seen to be intended for the benefit of the disciples themselves, the Johannine audience for whom the Gospel was written, rather than as a polemic against Moses and the Baptist, or any of the OT messengers[1].

The conclusions arrived at on the basis of the Gospel evidence concerning the missionary situation of the Evangelist and of his audience were explicitly confirmed by the discussion in Chapter VII. The relationship established between the Johannine Epistles and the Gospel led to the discovery that the missionary situation of the Johannine audience was marked on the one hand by defecting disciples who denied Jesus' messiahship and his ontological divine sonship and sought to persuade others to do the same, and, on the other, by disciples who either acted as if they owned the mission (e.g., Diotrephes) or behaved as if they had no need of continued dependence on Jesus for their personal holiness, their assumption being that their mere belief in Jesus constituted them in a permanent state of sinlessness.

Evidence for the attitude of the latter group was found in their claim that they had no sin, in their neglect of mutual love, and in the strong reminder by the author that to claim knowledge of God and of Jesus while refusing to walk as Jesus walked is simply to deceive oneself. Conversely, the defecting disciples who contested Jesus' claim to be the Christ and Son of God were seen to be reflected in the Gospel by the disciples who ceased permanently to walk in Jesus' company (6:66; 8:30—31), by Judas (13:30), by the dead branches cut off from the vine (15:2, 6), and by the Jews whose fickle faith Jesus would not trust (2:23—25). The recurrent motif of $\mu \acute{e} \nu \epsilon \iota \nu$ in the Gospel was seen as having a particular reference to this situation where believers stood in real danger of ceasing to "remain in" Jesus, that is, of discontinuing to believe in him (cf. 6:67—71) and so have a part in him.

The situation of the Johannine audience as evinced by both the Gospel and the Epistles helped to explain many of the otherwise puzzling missionary features in the Gospel: Jesus' reiterated claim that he is the Christ and Son of God, uniquely sent by the Father, was seen to be in response to the denial by the antichrists that he is not the Christ and Son of God; the emphasis on the need for mutual love as the concrete expression of discipleship of Jesus and the distinguishing mark of the eschatological community was, in turn, seen to be called for by the disciples' tendency to rely on faith alone; the insistence that the disciples do no more than enter into the fruit of Jesus' and the Father's labor was intended to serve as an antidote against all forms of self-aggrandizement as exempli-

---

[1] Our discussion on the situation of the Johannine community revealed that those who contest Jesus' messiahship are not *unbelievers* but apostate Christians who now renounce their discipleship of Jesus (6:66; 8:30—31) in favor of that of Moses (9:28—29). If the followers of the Baptist ever claimed that their master was the Messiah, the evidence for this is very slim indeed, as far as the Gospel is concerned, Jn 3:25—26 being the only remote evidence that could be alleged in support.

fied by Diotrephes[2]; and the fundamental conception of the missionary activity as a gathering into a unity where Jesus and the Father do the initial drawing (6:44; 12:32) received new light when set against the background of the disruptive activities of the antichrists (typified in the Gospel by the thieves and brigands, 10:7—10) and even of a Diotrephes (3 Jn 9—10).

The situation of the Johannine audience also helped to explain the predominantly forensic, polemical and hortatory thrust of the Gospel. For while Jesus defends his claims against those who contest them, his real purpose is to bring his audience to judge rightly and so come or continue to believe in him (8:48; 10:37—38). On the paradigmatic/rhetorical level, Jesus' efforts to persuade his audience serve indeed as the Evangelist's efforts to persuade his own audience to continue to believe that Jesus is the Christ and Son of God (20:30—31). Thus the rationale for the choice of mission as the fundamental hermeneutic or leitmotif of the Gospel proves to be deeply rooted in the situation of the audience addressed by the Evangelist. The needs of this audience also determine the choice of events in Jesus' life recorded in the Gospel. The findings in Chapter VII concerning the situation of the Johannine audience received external support from the situation in 1 Corinthians and from the letter to the Hebrews. Hebrews, in particular, served as a good example that the Johannine situation and the hermeneutical procedures adopted to meet this situation were living realities in the life of the NT Christians.

The answers to the second set of questions (concerning the interpersonal relationships and methodological dynamics involved in the exercise of mission) emerged chiefly in our exegesis of 4:1—42 — in Jesus' interaction with the Samaritan woman (vv 7—26) and the disciples (vv 31—38), and in the interaction between the Samaritan woman and the Samaritans (vv 28—30, 39—42). The attempts made by Jesus and the woman to engage their partners in dialogue were revealed among other ways in the efforts to meet the situation of the audience, to arouse curiosity, and on Jesus' part in particular, by his allowing the woman to dictate the terms of the conversation while not losing sight of his primary objective (v 26). His attention to the situation of the audience was also displayed in the case of the disciples in the description of Jesus' mission from the Father as his food (vv 31—34) and of the disciples' mission as a harvesting (vv 35—38), both "food" and "harvest" being of special concern to the disciples at the time of the dialogue. Hence the feature of *double-entendre* which underlies Jesus' dialogue with the woman and the disciples appeared to be not merely a literary technique designed to advance the narrative but something rooted in Jesus' genuine effort to communicate to his audience the

---

[2]It is important to remember that Diotrephes' actions had adverse effects which extended beyond him as an individual to the local community at large, and even to traveling missionaries, including the author of the Epistles (3 Jn 9—10).

true meaning of his divine mission using the concepts familiar to his human interlocutors (living water, food, the harvest).

The results of our investigation thus proved as misleading the position of a number of critics who hold that in 4:1–26 Jesus is not interested in the techniques of convincing preaching, but only in his self-revelation or that his audience serve mainly as foils for him to expound his teaching. On the contrary, the techniques of convincing preaching were seen to constitute an essential aspect of this rhetorical Gospel, which deliberately sets out to convince its readers to believe that Jesus is the Christ and Son of God. By the same token, Jesus' interlocutors are not treated as foils, any more than are those of the Evangelist whom he genuinely seeks to persuade to believe in Jesus. From the standpoint of the interlocutors themselves, their apparent passiveness was explained either on the analogy of the role of the judge in forensic situations or on the part of pupils in a learning situation. In both cases, the apparent passiveness was seen to be the natural outcome of the rhetorical method chosen by the Evangelist as his fundamental method of approach. Both Jesus' and the Evangelist's concern for their audience thus confirmed the importance of the ἴνα-clause highlighted in the examination of the Johannine data at the beginning of the study, namely, that the entire missionary enterprise is for the benefit of the audience. This remains true whether we think of Jesus' audience or of the Evangelist's own audience whose needs, we have seen, determined both the selective content of the Gospel and the rhetorical/persuasive method of its presentation.

Concerning the attitude of the one sent, humility in the exercise of mission emerged clearly as the attitude proper to the missionary. This attitude was exemplified by Jesus himself in his complete orientation towards his Father (4:34; 17) whose sole glory he sought and on whom he depended for every aspect of his mission including his glorification (17:1), this despite the fact that as God (1:1) and Son he shared the glory with the Father from the beginning (17:1). Given Jesus' fundamental attitude of complete dependence on the Father, his reiterated claim that as Son and one sent he can do nothing except what he sees the Father doing is not to be interpreted exclusively in terms of his equality with the Father (so Bultmann), but also as expressive of the genuineness of his obediential dependence on the sending Father (so Haenchen). This is particularly true since he proposes his attitude of dependence as the model for the disciples to imitate in their relationship with him as their sender (15:5, 16).

Jesus' humility in approaching his audience was also seen in his deep respect for the Samaritan woman despite her sex, personal history and nationality, and in his deference to the Samaritans whose invitation he patiently awaited and graciously accepted. The importance attached by the Evangelist to this attitude of humility was further demonstrated in his own personal approach in the Gospel and Epistles. He approached his audience by appealing to them and resisted the temptation to impose on them or usurp Jesus' role as the primary and abiding evangelizer and teacher of the community. This humble attitude was also clearly illustrated in the person of John the Baptist (1:29—36; 3:27—30). For this particular issue, therefore, the Gospel and Epistles conjointly present, not the usual two, but three witnesses, thus strongly underscoring its importance for the audience addressed by the Evangelist.

Concerning the audience itself, its role is not restricted to determining the language and method used in mission. Our investigation revealed that the primary and active contribution of the audience lies in the readiness to be open to Jesus' self-revelation, which openness is defined summarily as believing in the one sent by the Father (6:29; 20:31). For without this belief it is impossible to receive the gift of eternal life which the Father sent and authorized Jesus to give (3:16; 10:10; 17:2—3; 20:31). The Gospel emphasizes the importance of faith not only by contrasting it with self-acquired knowledge, but rhetorically by the *dispositio* whereby the Samaritan woman and the Samaritans are set against the incredulous Nicodemus on the one hand (3:1—21), and against the sign-seeking, Scripture- and tradition-searching Jews on the other (5—10). Initial faith in Jesus, however, is not enough. Believers are urged to remain in this faith all through life and are commanded to make it a living reality by transforming it into a program of action defined by mutual love and service. It is this love alone which constitutes the authentic witness of the believing community to the reality of the new order brought into existence and definitively established by Jesus' accomplished mission.

This importance attached to mutual love and service was seen to be an integral aspect of the Evangelist's theology of mission; but the emphasis he places on it both in the Gospel and in the Epistles was seen to be largely inspired by the *Sitz-im-Leben* of his community as depicted in the Epistles. So in whatever way it is viewed, the Johannine approach to mission derives its distinctive character from the situation of the audience which the Evangelist seeks to meet (20:30—31). The importance of this audience for the understanding of the Gospel can, therefore, never be over-emphasized.

Such, then, are the major results of our investigation concerning the rationale for the Evangelist's choice of mission as the leitmotif of his Gospel and for the theological and methodological dynamics involved in his portrayal of Jesus' mission from the Father. This very portrayal also serves as a missionary activity on the part of the Evangelist himself in respect to his own audience (20:30—31). But fundamentally, the Gospel knows of only one mission, that of Jesus; all other missions portrayed in the Gospel are in function of his one saving mission from the Father. Once completed, his mission stands completed such that the disciples do no more than reap its fruit. Under no circumsatnces, therefore, can it rightly be said that the Gospel presents Jesus' mission from the standpoint of that of the disciples. For not only does the mission of the disciples form an integral part of Jesus' mission, but the disciples themsevles remain always the sheep of his flock such that his pastoral concern for them can never be dispensed with any more than the vine can be dispensed with in the life of the branches.

Whatever projection there is, then, of the situation of the Evangelist into that of Jesus belongs in the order of hermeneutics, that of choosing from historical parallels (events in Jesus' life) those examples which best correspond to the situation of the audience addressed, and which can help this audience to cope with its own situation. To view otherwise the relationship between Jesus' mission portrayed in the Gospel and that of the Evangelist and his community is to misconstrue the evidence of the Gospel itself, and, ultimately, to obscure the Evangelist's distinctive understanding of mission and his contribution to the missionary perspective of the NT.

The answers to the third set of questions (concerning the missionary scope both of 4:1–42 and of the Gospel as a whole and the bearing which this has on the missionary attitude of the Evangelist and of his community) emerged in our whole discussion on the meaning of mission in the Gospel. Strictly speaking, these are problems raised by contemporary scholarship, not by the Johannine data themselves; and they arise because of the restricted meaning attached to mission in modern times, that is, primarily as outreach to non-believers in "the Third World." We have already reviewed the question of the missionary scope of 4:1–42 by showing that Jesus' mission in all its aspects (directed towards both non-believers and believers) constitutes the unifying theme of the episode. Seen from his perspective, the whole of 4:1–42 is concerned with mission. The problem of the missionary character of the passage arises only where mission is understood exlcusively from the standpoint of the post-Easter activity of the disciples, a conception which is certainly not Johannine. On the issue of the missionary attitude of the Evangelist and his community our findings were that both were interested in mission, but that they differed (the Evangelist and some of the disciples, at least) in their understanding of the role of the disciples in this missionary enterprise.

Concerning the missionary scope of the Gospel (20:30–31), our research confirmed that the "book" is addressed primarily to believers. It does not thereby follow that the Gospel is not a *Missionsschrift*. The modern distinction between *Missionsschrift* and *Gemeinde-Evangelium*, or the view that missionary activity applies only in respect of non-believers is simply alien to the Gospel; Jesus' normative missionary activity embraces both believers and non-believers, and the Evangelist's efforts to persuade his already believing audience to continue to believe in Jesus are indeed missionary work. Nor is this comprehensive view of mission (as something directed towards believers and non-believers) peculiar to John. The same obtains in the whole of the NT. For to the NT authors, to John certainly, initial conversion marked the beginning, not the end, of missionary activity, since believers had constantly to be urged to live out their belief practically. Moreover, given the constant threat to faith from an unbelieving majority, the world, believers needed to be constantly sustained in their belief and held personally responsible for it[3]. The Gospel itself and the letter to the Hebrews witness to this fact. We may also recall that all the letters of Paul, the great missionary of the Gentiles, are addressed to believers; and that but for these believers and their problems we would probably not have had any of Paul's letters, Romans being a possible exception[4]. Equally, though the book of Acts embodies samples of apostolic preaching to non-believers, it itself is addressed to a believer (1: 1). Whether or not Theophilus is a real or fictitious character does not alter the fact that Luke approaches him as a believer.

The Johannine (and NT) conception of mission thus proves to differ radically from that of the twentieth century. In the Johannine vision the missionary field is the whole world (3:16) and believers themsevles are strangers in this world (17:14). As long as they remain in the world, they need to be constantly *kept from* this world and from the evil one (17:15), but *kept in* God's word spoken by Jesus (14:1; 17:11) till Jesus returns and takes them to himself and the Father (14:2—3). Meanwhile their manner of life in community constitutes their authentic witness to the world of the reality of life which they possess in Jesus (4:14; 20:31). The joy of the eschatological harvest (4:36; 17:13) begins here and now in the mutual love and support which believers give to and receive from one another (1 Jn 1:4). At no point in one's life, therefore, is one dispensed from the need of believing; for the believer who apostatizes or plays false to his or her Christian belief is worse off than a person who never believed in the first place[5]. For these personal and communal reasons the activity directed towards believers, especially during a crisis of faith (1 Jn 2:26), becomes the most important missionary activity of all. As the good shepherd distinguishes himself by staying with the flock when the wolf threatens its life, so the Evangelist, the spokesman for Jesus, directs all his missionary energy to sustaining the faith of his fellow Christians threatened by the antichrists and to exhorting them to give flesh to their belief in Jesus[6].

---

[3]It needs to be remembered that Christians in general, not only "Johannine" Christians, were a minority in the first century A.D. Not till Constantine (A.D. 306—337) made Christianity the state religion did Christians become the majority. Brown's view (*Epistles*, 106) that 1 Jn 4:5 means that the secessionists are the majority and are winning more followers than the author of the Epistles finds no support in this passage. For as Brown himself later admits, "world" here designates the sphere of hostility to God (*Epistles*, 498), not the ratio of apostates unbelievers.

[4]Paul's Epistles as a rule grow out of the problems and needs of his communities. Romans, however, is written not in response to any specified pastoral problem but out of the obligation he feels towards them as the "apostle of the Gentiles" (Rm 1:10—14). This lack of practical reference may yet explain why the letter poses such difficulties for the interpreter.

[5]See, in particular, Heb 10:26—29 which we suggest might shed light on the "unforgivable sin" in 1 Jn 5:16. *The Shepherd of Hermas* is even more emphatic on the impossibility of repentance after apostasy: Vis. 1.3; 2.5—8 (*SC* 53, pp. 82—83). In the Gospel those who hear but refuse to believe are said to be equally without excuse (15:22—25).

[6]Paul would describe the same efforts in terms of being in labor again with his little children till Christ be formed in them (Gal 4:19).

Ultimately, therefore, the debate on whether or not the Gospel was a missionary or community document seems uncalled for by the Gospel. In Johannine terms the Gospel is a missionary document, *precisely because it is a community document.* Nor must it be forgotten that for the Evangelist Jesus' missionary activity with respect to both the individual and the community lasts till after death: he calls and chooses to bear lasting fruit (15:16), evangelizes (1 Jn 2:20, 25), teaches (1 Jn 2:27), sustains the believer in life and death (4:14; 6:47–51; 21:12–13, 18–21), intercedes for his own with the Father (17:9–26; 1 Jn 2:1) and raises them up on the last day (5:24–25; 6:40; 11:25–26). By far the greater part of his life-giving missionary activity (3:16) is thus directed toward the believer. The missionary disciple merely helps to lead others to recognize and receive Jesus' gifts within the believing community constituted by Jesus' living presence.

Schille's view that mission is constitutive of the Church thus holds when it is understood that the Church's missionary activity is not directed exclusively toward non-believers[7]. The epoch-making missionary encyclical of Paul VI, *Evangelii Nuntiandi* (*AAS* 68 [1976] 1–76) also sees mission as constitutive of the Church in an all inclusive sense: preaching, teaching, ministering the sacraments, serving as the channel of grace (n. 14). John would see Jesus himself, not the disciples or the ministerial Church, as the one who continues to do all these activities, even though visibly he works through the disciples. It is a question of a different theological focus, perhaps, but one which has enormous ramifications on the Church's attitude towards its ministers, its ministries and those to whom it ministers (cf. 4:42).

Similarly, for the encyclical Jesus' mission seems to end with the resurrection and the sending of the Holy Spirit (nos. 8–12) while the Church continues his mission in history. But in the Johannine model Jesus is never replaced and he personally continues his mission in history and in the Church itself, working through believers to draw others to himself. It is again a difference of focus, but one which profoundly affects the attitude of the missionary towards his or her work and audience. It would seem that the Johannine model of Church and mission has yet to be recognized and be allowed to penetrate the Church's way of life and approach to "mission." In the current revival of interest in mission both in the Church and in the field of NT and biblical studies generally, John's Gospel has something new and unique to offer, as we have discovered in this investigation[8]. Our investigation, itself a new approach to John's Gospel, also

---

[7]Schille, "Das Evangelium als Missionsbuch," pp. 1–3.

[8]The need to reconsider the missionary dimension of the NT writings has been emphasized lately by E.S. Fiorenza, "Miracles, Mission and Apologetics: An Introduction" *Aspects of Religious Propaganda in Judaism and Early Christianity* (Fiorenza, ed.; Notre Dame: University of Notre Dame Press, 1976), pp. 1–25, and Donald Senior, "The Struggle to be Universal: Mission as Vantage Point for New Testament Investigation," *CBQ* 46 (1984) 63–81. It is not simply the missionary dimension of the NT that needs to be reviewed, but the whole conception of mission today.

sheds light on new directions which future Johannine research could profitably take. We will now attempt to highlight some of these new directions.

Directions for Future Research

At various points in this study issues came up which could not be given adequate attention in this present work either because they were too major to be dealt with here or because their scope lay outside our immediate focus. An outstanding example of the former concerns the whole question of the missionary perspective of the forensic passages in Jn 3:1– 21 and 5–10. Among the latter we saw the need critically to review contemporary theories on the origins of the Johannine Christology in the light of the relationship which emerged in this study between the Gospel and 1 John. Such a review would include a thorough examination of the presuppositions on which current theories on the origins of the Johannine Christology are based. Another issue which arose concerned the need to examine the different ways in which Jews and Gentiles responded to the Christian revelation and the influence which their cultural outlook and previous religious beliefs might have exercised on this response. We are, of course, aware of the undesirability of speaking of "Jewish Christianity" and "Gentile Christianity" as if these were different entities streamlined along national or geographical boundaries[9]. The question, rather, has to do with the relationship between culture and the Christian revelation in the NT perspective. How did the former hamper or help the individual's response to Jesus, the Christ and Son of God? From this historical paradigm we may consequently gain some insight into the negative and positive effects which cultural influences today exercise on the Christian's response to Jesus who remains still as the Christ and Son of God.

We noted, for instance, that in John the Samaritan woman and the Samaritans are more readily receptive to Jesus' messianic claims and mission than are Jesus' Jewish audience who find his claims impossible on the grounds of Scripture and tradition. Equally, the Greeks (the Gentiles, 12:20) ask to see Jesus of their own accord (and they remind one of Cornelius sending for Peter, Acts 10). Not only does Jesus' Jewish audience reject his claims, but it finally succeeds in putting him to death because of these claims (19:7). Is there more substance to this whole portrayal of the Jews in the Gospel (and in the NT) than mere Christian propaganda or "anti-Jewish polemic" seen as a retaliatory measure against the Jewish ejection of Christians from the synagogue? Viewed objectively, what specific difficulties did Jewish and Gentile Christians meet in their efforts to respond to the revelation of Jesus, and what part did their cultural backgrounds play in these difficulties? To give a serious and objec-

---

[9]See, for instance, Brown, "Not Jewish Christianity and Gentile Christianity but Types of Jewish/Gentile Christianity" *CBQ* 45 (1983) 74–79.

tive attention to these questions is to recognize that the Christian message was intended to be lived, and that believers (Christians) are not disembodied spirits who try to live out this message. The different cultural conditionings need to be exposed or held up to the searching light of the Gospel and to be discarded or retained as they hinder or help one's response.

The third and most important issue highlighted in this study concerns the need systematically to review the whole question of the missionary perspective of John's Gospel and of the NT generally, and to do this from the first not twentieth century understanding of mission. Our survey of contemporary approaches to mission in 4:1–42, in particular (Chapter III), and our subsequent findings concerning the Johannine position on the issue (Chapters IV to VII) proved clearly that modern approaches to the passage were greatly conditioned by the contemporary understanding and practice of mission. The near universal agreement that the Gospel views Jesus' mission from the standpoint of that of the disciples, when the Johannine evidence itself indicates quite the contrary, can only be attributed to the unconscious influence of the modern understanding and practice of mission.

Fiorenza's and Senior's efforts to draw the attention of biblical scholarship to the missionary perspective of the NT writings are highly commendable. But their fundamental starting points which view these writings either as "propagandistic-missionary" works (Fiorenza) or as concerned primarily with "the Gentile question" or the Church's "universal mission" (Senior), in our view beg the question[10]. The central questions that need to be asked in this whole issue is whether to the NT Christians mission meant no more than outreach to non-believers, be they Jews or Gentiles, and whether "the Gentile question" was the only serious missionary problem they faced. It is our contention that any serious attempt to come to grips with the missionary perspective or horizons of the NT must start by a reexamination of the categories currently used, and by a serious effort to understand what the NT authors themselves understood by mission. The question is all the more important since our own twentieth century understanding of mission appears to differ greatly from that of the NT[11]. Also we might discover that there are as many approaches to mission in

---

[10]See note 8 above. While Senior rejects Fiorenza's "propagandistic" approach, he himself assumes a distinction between the needs of the believers, "the insiders," and their external need to be aware of the missionary dimension of the Church. Thus the view that mission means outreach to non-believers dies hard in modern scholarship.

[11]To the modern mentality missionary endeavor is almost synonymous with efforts to meet the needs of "the Third World," a kind of substitute for their lack of technological development. The general impression given then is that those in the "developed countries," have no need of missionary activity, or of evangelization. To this way of thinking the author of 1 John would probably say ψευδόμεθα, καὶ ἑαυτοὺς πλανῶμεν (1:6, 8). For his schema recognizes two, not three, basic worlds, the world of *light* to which all believers belong, regardless of nationality and social status, and the world of *darkness* to which unbelivers belong, also regardless of nationality and

the NT as there are Christologies. A further question would then be to discover where possible the influences which the different living situations exercised on each of these approaches.

These then are some of the important questions which this study has raised: the origins of the Johannine Christology, the cultural influence on believers in their response to Jesus' revelation, and the whole question of the way NT authors understood and exercised mission. This list is by no means exhaustive and our attentive readers will no doubt notice other issues. But we will now end this investigation by devoting some time to considering what appears to us to be the most significant outcome of this research as far as future Johannine studies are concerned. The issue hinges on the question of *methodology*, with respect both to our own contextual method applied in this study and the Evangelist's own rhetorical method which underlies the entire Gospel.

The Contextual Method

A detailed description of the characteristics of the contextual method was given at the beginning of this study (pp. 50—51). It is only natural that at the end of the research we should undertake some evaluation of the usefulness of this method. As mentioned above, this study started out with questions for which to seek answers rather than with a thesis to prove. Because of this absence of a preconceived thesis, the contextual method became the one constant or guiding principle in the research. The practical result of this was that the scope of each succeeding chapter (from Chapters IV to VII) was determined by the findings in the preceding one. This, in effect, means that the research was written the way it developed.

The procedure was undoubtedly risky in the sense that we had no control over the outcome of the research; and there were moments when we seriously feared whether the dissertation would have a thesis to offer in the end or whether it would turn out to be no more than a series of exegeses of unrelated Johannine passages. Yet the attraction of the method lay in the fact that it allowed the text to disclose its own underlying structure and meaning. Judging from the significant discoveries made in this investigation, concerning the problematic passages in 4:1—42, the underlying rhetorical framework of the Gospel, and the whole question of the relationship of the Gospel to the Epistles, we feel that the risk of the contextual method was worth taking. For whether or not one accepts our interpretation of the missionary features which emerged in the study, one cannot deny that these features are there. For our part, we can safely say that were it not for the contextual method adopted a number of these features would never have been discovered. The contextual method

---

social status (3:19—21). As long as believers live, then, they need all the evangelization they can receive if they are not to be won over by the unbelieving world (17:15; 1 Jn 5:18—21).

brought to light the existence of certain recurrent patterns and characteristics as we moved from one section of the study to another. Our major
conclusions .concerning the Johannine approach to mission were then
based on the evidence of these recurrent features.

If the study can be said to have started out with any working presuppositions, it assumed that since the Gospel was addressed to a living audience (20:30–31), the situation of this audience must somehow have
influenced the way the book was written, especially because of its declared hortatory thrust. But that the key to the situation of the audience
would lie in the relationship between the Gospel and the Johannine
Epistles was a possibility we never entertained, first because of the current
belief that the Evangelist is fighting synagogue Jews, and secondly because of the dominant view that the Epistles were written long after the
Gospel and as a response to the disciples' various misinterpretations of
the Gospel. It is most curious, however, that while a great majority of
scholars believe that the Gospel was written for insiders (believers themselves) no serious or consistent attempt was ever made to see the Christological and messianic issues raised in the Gospel as possible problems
which these insiders themselves might have had. We, too, might not have
come to this conclusion had we not been led to it by the internal evidence
of the texts themselves. Our contextual clue lay, in particular, in the similarities in the messianic questions asked concerning Jesus' claim to be
the Christ *and* Son of God, as well as in the author's approach to his audience and his unified method of handling these issues in both the Gospel
and Epistles.

Aristotle states that a speech has three parts: the speaker, what he says
and those to whom he speaks[12]. Since the Gospel may be considered as a
kind of extended speech in the light of the address in 20:30–31, studies
in the Gospel which take little or no account of the audience ignore a
third of the dimension of its meaning. Our experience again proves that had
we not pressed on to consider the living dimension of the Johannine audience, we would never have gained as clear an insight into the issues
treated in the Gospel as we gained from our whole discussion in Chapter
VII. The particular merit of the findings in this study concerning the situation of the Johannine community lies in the fact that this issue was not
considered as an isolated topic but in relation to the outcome of the missionary emphases which emerged from the study of the Johannine texts
themselves. So we may further state that the value of the contextual
method lies in its comprensiveness, its seeking to establish the relationship
between the author, his work and his audience.

Another presupposition of the study was that it took seriously the Evangelist's claim that his work was a "book" (20:30). From this the inference
was drawn that the full meaning of each theme treated in the book would

---

[12] Aristotle, *Rhet.* 7.3.1.

lie in the scope of the book as a whole, not in isolated passages. A further merit of the contextual method is that it enabled us to pursue the theme of mission through the whole book, guided by the Evangelist's declared intention that he aims at persuading his readers to continue to believe and find life in Jesus. Perhaps for John's Gospel more so than for any other NT work, the contextual approach is particularly necessary if we are to get a comprehensive view of his meaning through a sustained appreciation of his distinctive way of handling issues. The cumulative style of the Evangelist has long since been recognized. What is needed is a serious effort to reckon with the implications which this cumulative style has for our full understanding of his book. In the Gospel each verse and episode sheds light on the rest and is in turn illumined by the whole.

Our final positive appraisal of the contextual method concerns the light which it sheds on the choice to be made between the variant readings, and on the significance to be attached to the Evangelist's precise use of terminology. With regard to the variant readings, by focusing our attention on the consistent theological viewpoint and stylistic traits of the Evangelist, the contextual method led us to decide in favor of adopting οἶδα rather than οἴδαμεν in 4:25, to choose αὐτοῦ rather than αὐτοι in 4:42 and πιστεύητε rather than πιστεύσητε in 20:31, and to place ἤδη with 4:35b rather than with 4:36a. While no general conclusions may be drawn from these few examples, these concrete cases do, nevertheless, indicate that wherever possible the context should be given priority as a criterion for deciding between variant readings. By "context" here we mean both the immediate context of a given passage as well as the general theological and stylistic characteristics of a given author[13]. The advantage of using context as a criterion is that it is more solidly based in the work itself and so can be more readily controlled than can such external and somewhat arbitrary criteria as *lectio difficilior* or the general rating accorded to the various MSS[14].

---

[13]The importance of context cannot be overemphasized, for it would seem that, contrary to the modern Western mind, the ancients attached far more importance to meaning, the matter, or that which is expressed, than to form, the words, or that which expresses (*Inst. Or.* III.v.1). Quintilian is particularly insistent on this issue, "give them any name you please, as long as the meaning is clear" (*Inst. Or.* III.vi.6; V.ix.9). And again, *the nature of the case* determines what parts of rhetorical art should be employed or omitted in a given case, as well as the *order* in which the questions are to be treated (II.xiii.5—6) — the "nature of the case," incidentally, includes the audience. Whether or not one shares Quintilian's view on the primacy of meaning over words, one cannot dispute that in any given situation and for any word the "clarity of meaning" resides first and foremost in the context.

[14]A full description of the criteria currently used in choosing between variant readings will be found in Bruce M. Metzger, *A Textual Commentary on the Greek New Testament* (3rd. ed., London: United Bible Societies, 1975), xxv—xxxi. Speaking for the editorial committee of the UBS Greek New Testament, Metzger recognizes the impossibility of finding criteria which can be based on grounds other than "probabilities," counseling that each variant reading "be considered in itself" and not merely by a set of rules. Though "immediate context" and "the style of the author" figure under those criteria concerned with "Intrinsic Probabilities" (pp. xxv, xxvii—xxviii), no

Concerning the issue of terminology, while it may be regrettable that, unlike the Synoptics, John's Gospel lacks a parallel voice in the NT against which we can compare and assess his redactional achievements, the Gospel does, nevertheless, provide its own interpretative norms which give us special insight into his own distinctive theology. One such norm which emerged in this study concerns his careful use of words and concepts. An outstanding example here concerns his use of the term ἔργον. Contrary to the impression which one gains from a cursory reading of the Gospel and despite the interpretation given to this term by such scholars as Olsson and Nicholson, we were able to perceive, thanks to the contextual method, that nowhere in the Gospel does Jesus claim ownership of the ἔργον or ἔργα but that he consistently attributes this ownership to the Father. That such a careful and consistent use is not accidental became all the more striking when we noticed further that the Gospel contrasts the "work" and "works" of God with the "works" of the devil. There is, of course, no parallel on the devil's side to the ἔργον understood as the work of salvation[15].

Behind this whole terminology of ἔργον and ἔργα lies the issue of one's identity and affiliation. Jesus comes from the Father and so does the "work" and "works" of the Father (4:34; 17:4). The unbelieving Jews, on the other hand, belong to their father the devil and so do his works (8:44). Believers, in turn, do "the work of God" which in their case consists not in the work of salvation, for Jesus alone does and completes that, but fundamentally in the work of faith, in believing in Jesus as the Father's exclusive agent of salvation (6:29; 1 Jn 3:23). This work of God enables them in turn to receive the gift of sonship, to become the children of God (1:12–13), and accordingly to do the same works of God which Jesus does, as proof that they belong to God (3:21; 14:12).

Another outstanding example of the way the Evangelist's treatment of issues gives us special insight into his theology concerns his whole presentation of the disciples' mission in total subjection to that of Jesus. While arguments from silence are undesirable, one cannot help wondering whether, given the systematic subordination of the disciples to Jesus set against the background of their tendency to pride and boasting, the omission of such Synoptic material as Mt 16:19; 19:28 and Lk 22:19–23 might not be deliberate. Not only are these passages omitted, but they are matched by the distinctive Johannine emphasis on the commandment of mutual love and service (13:1–17, 34–35; 15:9–17), by the emphasis

---

reference is made to the general theological outlook of the author, and understandably so; for this outlook emerges only through a sustained contextual approach to the work in question whereas elements of style can easily be recovered through a concordance type of approach.

[15]The closest antithetical parallel, perhaps, is Jn 8:44 where the devil is termed a "man-killer" (ἀνθρωποκτόνος) from the beginning (cf. 1 Jn 3:8, 10). He is thus contrasted with Jesus and the Father who possess life in themselves (5:26) and give it to others (cf. 3:16–17; 4:10,14; 10:10; 1 Jn 5:11–13).

on the essentially witnessing character of the disciples' mission (15:27; 1 Jn 4:14) and by the charge to Peter to pasture the flock even unto death (21:15—18).

There is then in the Gospel a built-in system of Johannine redaction which transcends the redactional layers often noted by the literary critics. The more the differences between John and the Synoptics are recognized, the more we should seek to explain these differences, and even the similarities, in terms of the Evangelist's total theological standpoint. It is our firm conviction that the contextual approach can cogently help us to appraise this distinctive standpoint of the Evangelist, and so have a more solid basis for assessing his relationship with the Synoptics[16].

The overall advantage of the contextual method, then, over that of pure word-study lies in the fact that this method relates the use of words and concepts to the total theological viewpoint and general concerns of the author. In other words, its distinctive merit lies in its particularity (it has a keen eye to details) and its comprehensiveness (it bears always in mind the global position of the author and of his audience). Many a "Johannine problem" might indeed be resolved by paying closer and greater attention to what the Evangelist is *actually* saying and how he says it, than to what critics want it to say, often in favor of preconceived theories. A keen attention to the text through a rigorous and exacting exegesis can be just as demanding as are efforts to discern the compositional layers of the texts or the sources the Evangelist may have used. We are not, of course, disparaging the value of studies in Johannine source and redaction criticism. The latter, in particular, draws attention to problematic areas where the exegete needs to expend his or her exegetical skill, and our exegesis of 4: 1—42 was greatly challenged by the redactional studies done on this particular passage (Chapter III).

The point we wish to make is simply that, at best, Johannine source and redaction criticism merely raise questions concerning the Gospel in its *present final form*, but in themselves they are incapable of furnishing solutions to these problems from the standpoint of *the finished Gospel*. And always there is a question mark attached to the results of their find-

---

[16]The question of the relationship between John and the Synoptics is constantly undergoing a shift in focus. Eusebius believed the Evangelist wrote to "supplement" the Synoptics concerning the first part of Jesus' ministry (*H.E.* 3.24). In the early part of this century, Windisch (*Johannes und die Synoptiker* [Leipzig, 1925]) advanced the view that the Evangelist wrote to "supplant" the Synoptics with a theology which was more in accordance with his own beliefs. In the height of the historical-critical method, the issue was to determine whether or not John's Gospel had any historical value or whether, in contrast to the Synoptics, it was pure interpretation, "a spiritual Gospel". Since redaction criticism came in vogue, the question now centers on whether or not John knew or was dependent on the Synoptics. Thus the most recent works by de Solage and Neirynck concentrate on demonstrating the presence or absence of Synoptic material in John. What we envisage, however, is a step beyond this. It would be a question of studying any given theme in each of the Gospels (Mt, Mk, Lk, and Jn) within the context of each work, and then comparing the results. The results might yield more surprises than we could have anticipated.

ings, since there is no way of objectively proving that this, in fact, is how
the Gospel came to be. These studies can, therefore, be seen as helpful
preliminaries to the exegesis of the extant text. But they cannot be seen
as a substitute for the synthetic approach, let alone as an invalidation of
it. Perhaps, after almost a century of concentration on Johannine source
and redaction criticism the time has come systematically to test these
theories through an enlightened and enriched return to the synthetic
approach to the text. For when all is said and done, the text remains the
only concrete evidence we have, disjointed or not, and all theories should
ultimately be judged by it, not vice versa[17].

We are not alone, of course, in advocating the need for a return to the
synchronic approach to the text. Nor must we forget Childs' view mentioned earlier in this study that the final canonical text exercises "a critical function" over the earlier versions, a view with which no serious writer
should have problems[18]. To this call to return to the study of the text as
it now stands, we would simply add with equal emphasis the need to give
serious consideration to the audience-dimension of the NT works. For in
our view this is one of the most neglected areas in NT studies. The importance which the situation of the audience holds for the understanding of
NT works, because of the influence which this situation exercised not
only on the problems treated but on the very language used, has recently
been brought to light by Murphy-O'Connor's pioneer work, *St. Paul's
Corinth*[19]. In our view it is in giving serious consideration to the audience
that the *contextual approach* gains most over classical exegesis, or can
indeed be termed *classical exegesis brought up to date*.

So far we have been focusing on the positive aspects of the contextual
method which emerged in this study. A possible criticism of the method
would be that it focuses too much attention on the Gospel and so fails to
take sufficiently into account the possible contacts which the Gospel may
have had with the OT, Qumran, rabbinic, Jewish and Hellenistic religious

---

[17]One cannot help resonating with Robinson (*Redating*, 310) who feels more baffled by the
"self-created aporiai" said to be discovered in the Gospel than by the "breaks and discontinuities"
in the Gospel "at which critics balk." The monumental works by J.H. Bernard, *A Critical and
Exegetical Commentary on the Gospel according to St. John* (2 vols. ICC. Edinburgh: T. and T.
Clark, 1928) and Boismard-Lamouille, *Synopse III* (published a year after *Redating*), mark the beginning and the end of some 50 years of research on Johannine redaction (1928—1977).

[18]Increasingly, NT critics are advocating a return to the synchronic approach to the text, an
emphasis which goes hand in hand with criticism of the weaknesses of the historical-critical method.
Summaries of these works are given in the recent issues of the *NTA* under "Interpretation." Noteworthy also is the presidential address delivered at the *SBL* annual meeting in 1982 by Lou H. Sil-
berman, "Listening to the Text," *JBL* 102 (1983) 1—26.

[19]*St. Paul's Corinth: Texts and Archaeology*. The highly appreciative "Introduction" by John
H. Elliott (pp. xiii—xvii) and the author's own "Foreword" (pp. xix—xxi) give ample description
of the scope of the book and its significance for understanding the letters to the Corinthians. The
documentary evidence of this book does indeed confirm Aristotle's statement that the audience
constitutes a third of the meaning of any speech. In the letters, Paul is addressing the Corinthians
using their own language.

literature generally. This obejction can be met in two ways. First, we are well aware that many studies, and even substantial dissertations, have been .done on this particular topic, precisely from the standpoint of mission in the Gospel, as we tried to indicate in our survey in Chapter I, "The Quest for Models" (pp. 16—22). It seemed to us, therefore, a waste of valuable research time and effort to keep rehearsing issues which have already been well documented in more than one work and from more than one perspective[20].

Secondly, the heavy concentration on the Johannine material was called for by our very topic. If we were to discover the Evangelist's own theology and approach to mission, we could do no better than watch him closely at work and listen to him very attentively. Watching him at work necessarily entailed shutting out other perspectives which are legitimate in themselves. Our firm conviction, also shared by Thyen, is that in many respects Johannine studies have actually been hampered rather than enhanced by heavy allusions to the hybrid of models and sources which are supposed to have influenced the Evangelist[21]. Often ideas and concepts are imported from other works and imposed on the Gospel with results that are detrimental both to the Gospel and to the parent work from which the ideas were culled. For in these instances the meaning of these concepts are hardly ever thoroughly verified first in their own contexts, the *theios anēr* theory may be cited as an example here. The worst result of the approach, in our view, is that the Gospel is never heard out on its own terms but is always viewed through the spectacles of some other work from which it is supposed to have borrowed. In consequence, the Evangelist's own originality of approach and of theological stance gets blurred, if not actually lost, in the confusing picture of Hellenistic and Jewish missionary propaganda.

An outstanding example of the way in which appeals to foreign models have conditioned Johannine studies lies in the Gnostic *RQ* influence posited by Bultmann and used as the basis for his commentary. Not only is Johannine Christology said to be marked by the descent/ascent motif, derived from the influence of the Gnostic redeemer figures, but the Johannine dialogues themselves are said to derive from this *RQ*. As a result of this basic starting point, "the Revelation" and "the Revealer" are seen as constituting the main interest of the Johannine projection; the audience become mere foils while the dialogical dimension of the Johannine dialogues, the exchanges between Jesus and his interlocutors and the positive contribution of the audience, are almost totally ignored. Though today the Bultmannian *RQ* model is almost completely discarded, as we noted in the survey in Chapter I, the studies by Miranda, Borgen, and Bühner, for instance, still follow the basic terrain set by Bultmann, in that they accept

---

[20]See, in addition, the critical survey of studies concerning "The Intellectual Milieu of the Evangelist" in Kysar, *The Fourth Evangelist*, 102—146.

[21]Thyen, "Aus der Literatur zum Johannesevangelium," *TRu* 39 (1975) 49—50.

as a basic starting point that the Evangelist was influenced by models, their main concern then being to determine which model was most influential on the Evangelist[22].

The central question, though, is why it must be posited as a basic starting point that the Evangelist had everything to borrow from his contemporary authors and nothing to offer himself. Could not his descent/ascent Christology, for instance, have grown out of his own personal experience of Jesus and his firm belief that "the Father sent his Son into the world" (3:16–17; 1 Jn 4:9–10, 14)? And might not his *emphasis* on the descent/ascent Christology also be explained in terms of the counter denial of the antichrists that Jesus was sent by the Father? We recognize, of course, the value of comparative studies; these can be done between works that are centuries apart. The question of influence is, however, a wholly different matter, especially when we are dealing with as syncretistic a culture as that of the Hellenistic-Roman world of the first century. Discussing influences in this type of world is like arguing which came first, the chicken or the egg.

The whole discussion is further flawed by the fact that often no solid attempts are made to address the many variables involved in this issue of influence, for instance, the date of the material from which the influencing model is drawn, the purpose of these works in terms of their own living audience or their relationship to life generally, and the possible channels through which these works could have influenced the Evangelist. In general, one is left with the impression that the writers of the first century world were highly endowed with originality, except the Evangelist and his NT colleagues. The event of the historical Jesus (and by this we mean that he really did exist) appears to have been incapable of inspiring the disciples with any Christology since all their inspiration came from outside: Samaritanism, Moses piety, Jewish halakhic messengers, the Qumran *maskil*, Jews with anti-Temple views and Hellenistic Gnostic revealers. Baffled by this array of possible inspirational sources, one is left wondering at times why the Father bothered to send his Son in the first place, or whether Jesus' life on earth had any intrinsic significance of its own.

It was in order to avoid both the pitfalls of what is often described as the anthological approach and the impression that the Evangelist's approach to mission had nothing distinctively original to offer that we felt it necessary to concentrate on highlighting his own unique approach as illustrated in his work, also seeking in the living situation of his aud-

---

[22]Johannine studies in particular need to remain alert to the confusion generated by the practice of building a hypothesis on a previously unproven hypothesis. For the Greeks, a *hypothesis* became valid only if it were backed by the *peristasis* (a collection of facts to substantiate the hypothesis). But we tend to go from one hypothesis to another, regardless of the lack of sound evidence to back them.

ience the primary impetus which could have motivated and so influenced this approach. From this standpoint we disagree with Barrett that the Evangelist wrote merely to please himself and that he never intended his work to be published[23]. Efforts to compare the Evangelist's work with that of his contemporaries should be undertaken after, not before, the position of each work has been thoroughly appraised in its own terms, that is, in its own context. And studies which seek to delineate the stance of a given author as this has come to us in the extant literature should be accorded as equal importance in NT studies as are those which seek to establish possible contacts between the NT writers and their contemporary Hellenistic-Jewish authors.

Of the many possible contacts which the Evangelist could have had with his contemporary world, the OT Jewish contact stands in a class apart. If one takes seriously the fundamental, all-embracing NT hermeneutic that Jesus fulfilled the Law and the prophets (Jn 1:45; 5:39, 46; cf. Lk 24:27), the question whether or not these writers were influenced by OT ideas in their portrayal of Jesus should not really be an issue, but, on the contrary, should be taken for granted. The real issue, however, should be to determine the ways in which these writers use the OT concepts in their work, each in his own particular way, and where possible the reasons for the distinctive hermeneutical stance of a given author. Do they, for instance, view Jesus' relationship to the OT merely in terms of fulfilment or of fulfilment *and* transcendence? John's Gospel leaves no doubt whatever concerning its own stance on this issue. For while the Evangelist may have used OT concepts and ideas of God's messengers to describe the mission of Jesus: for instance, the *logos* (1:1–18) whose descent/ascent motif (Is 55:10–11) is picked up in 16:28 (cf. 3:13), a prophet like Moses (6:14, Deut 15:15–18), the Davidic King (1:49), the Messiah (1:41; 4:25) and Wisdom, the distributor of gifts (7:37–39; cf. Is 55:1ff.), he makes it equally clear that all these OT figures serve merely as witnesses to Jesus (5:39, 46). Jesus' uniqueness as God's agent lies squarely in that he is both Son and God (1:1, 18; 5:18; 10:33, 36; 19:7). And as we have seen in the study this is the crucial area of Jesus' messiahship which his Jewish audience simply cannot accept. Since all contemporary Jewish ideas concerning the Messiah or other divine messengers derive from the Scriptures, the Johannine judgment in 5:39 would apply equally to them[24].

---

[23]Barrett, *John,* 134–135.

[24]The critic would be hard put to find any Jewish messianic idea which did not take its departure point from God's promises to Israel in the Law and the Prophets, and was not in function of these promises. Indeed, the first level at which the NT Christians themselves understood the identity and mission of Jesus was in terms of his fulfiling these OT promises (Jn 1:41; Lk 4:16–30; 24:27; Acts 2:14–36; 13:13–41). Knowledge of his divine ontological sonship only dawned on them later, which is not to deny that this knowledge could have been received in some form or other from the historical Jesus himself.

This means, ultimately, that after all its possible contacts with the OT have been recognized, the Johannine portrayal of Jesus' mission can be fully understood only on its own terms. If the contextual approach enables us to discover his distinctive presentation, so much the better. Hopefully, the critic will judge this study on its own terms. It is our conviction that if the contextual method has achieved no other purpose in this study, it has raised questions concerning the presuppositions on which some NT methodologies and interpretations are based, those pertaining to John's Gospel in particular. Above all, we strongly believe that the method was largely responsible for our discovering what we consider to be the most significant feature of the Johannine approach itself, namely, the essentially rhetorical character of his method, the significance of which we will now briefly consider.

The Rhetorical Framework

Perhaps the single most important and commendable methodological outcome of this investigation as far as Johannine research is concerned lies in the discovery of the essentially rhetorical character of the Gospel. This discovery promises to have far-reaching consequences not only for the understanding of the Johannine approach to mission but for the interpretation of the Gospel as a whole. Indeed, if this rhetorical framework does not actually turn out to be the long sought key to the mystery of John's Gospel, the elusive "operative fundamental of his thought," it is, nonetheless, one which no Johannine exegete can afford to continue to ignore[25]. For the rhetorical approach is a vital characteristic of the Evangelist's own method.

We suggested at the beginning of this study that Jn 20:30–31 might hold the key not only to the evangelistic thrust of the Gospel, a fact which is generally recognized, but also to its formal rhetorical character. This suggestion was initially prompted by the similarity we noted between the description of the Gospel material as selective in nature (20:30) and selectivity seen as a principle in both Jewish hermeneutics and Hellenistic rhetoric. Our primary interest in raising this rhetorical issue lay initially in the hope that it might help us to discover the hermeneutical principles which governed the Evangelist's choice of events narrated about Jesus. This principle, we have since discovered, lay in the parallelism (hence their paradigmatic function) between the events chosen and the actual problems faced by the Evangelist's own audience. But that the whole Gospel would prove to be seething with formal rhetorical traits is a possibility we never entertained. Indeed, the discovery of this aspect of the

---

[25]Kysar, *The Fourth Evangelist,* 279. McPolin ("Mission in the Fourth Gospel") also emphasizes the need to discover fluid categories for comprehending the Evangelist's thought. It is our contention that the rhetorical category in all its *"infinite variety"* (Quintilian, *Inst. Or.* VII.*Praef.* 4) does provide the needed fluidity.

Gospel rather imposed itself than was a focus we deliberately sought after in the research. The ever-recurrent and cumulative presence of these traits in passage after passage finally forced upon us the awareness that rhetoric is an all-embracing characteristic of the Evangelist's method.

Several of the traits highlighted in this study include the philosophical variety (4:7–26), and the deliberative (4:31–38; 13–17) and demonstrative (4:28–30, 38–42; 21) types aimed at instructing. Included in the latter type was the mystifying action of the master which causes perplexity in the circle of disciples as a prelude to a lesson bearing on the significance of the action (13:1–17). In addition, the whole structure of 4:1–42 itself was explained in terms of a thesis (vv 1–26) and its consequential argument (vv 27–42), even as the structure of vv 10–26 also proved to be that of a thesis (vv 10a, b) developed in two parts: vv 11–15 and 16–26. A variation of the same pattern occurs in the dialogue with Nicodemus as we discovered in a previous study[26]. We noted, too, that the primary significance of the story of the Samaritan woman as told in the Gospel lies in its paradigmatic character, and that it has a reference to the rhetorical principle which stipulates that arguments from *imparia* wield a most efficacious convincing power. We also related the portrait of the Samaritan woman to the equally extraordinary cases of the Johannine "signs," which in our view also serve a rhetorical and paradigmatic function. With regard to rhetorical details, arguments *a fortiori* were ironically employed by the woman (4:11–12) and *a minori ad maius* (or the *qal wahomer*) both by Jesus (10:34–36; 13:14) and by the Evangelist/author of 1 John (5:9–11)[27].

The most obvious evidence of the rhetorical framework of the Gospel lies in the forensic passages (5–10). Though these passages have been postponed for a latter study, their array of rhetorical vocabulary is too impressive not to be cited here, for instance, witness, advocate, accuser, and judge. Indeed once the rhetorical framework of the Gospel, its essentially persuasive and argumentative thrust (20:30–31) has been recognized, one cannot help but become alert to the rhetorical apparatus which this thrust necessarily carries with it. Not only the individual passages, but the entire Gospel seems to possess a markedly rhetorical structure complete with *proem* (1:1–18) and epilogue or peroration (21:1–25). Many a Johannine

---

26 This point was developed at length in our "How Can These Things Happen?" particularly in "Part III: The Literary Structure and the Thematic Unity of Jn 3:1–21," pp. 40–68, with the corresponding notes, pp. 83–89. The gist of this discussion is that Nicodemus' statement in v 2 embodies the theme of the entire dialogue. In vv 3–12 Jesus acts out Nicodemus' "belief" that he is a teacher from God (v 2a), while in vv 13–21 he demonstrates both how true knowledge of him may be acquired, namely, through his personal self-revelation, not via rationalistic deduction (v 2b), and the consequences for the individual who professes knowledge of him. At the time the *Mémoire* was submitted, however, we were not yet aware of the rhetorical framework of the Gospel, an awareness which would have greatly strengthened our argument.

27 The woman's argument (4:12) is *a fortiori* only ironically since in her view Jacob is greater than Jesus. She is yet to be proved wrong (vv 26, 29, 42).

problem often attributed to the different levels of composition and redaction may yet receive new solutions when they are viewed from the standpoint of the essentially rhetorical method of the Evangelist.

It is indeed most curious that while the importance of rhetoric has been particularly emphasized in recent years, little or no attempt has been made to apply this category in any systematic way in the interpretation of John's Gospel[28]. Yet this Gospel, more so than any other book in the NT canon openly declares itself in rhetorical terms (20:30—31). The reason for this "oversight" lies, perhaps, in the fact that Johannine studies in this century have concentrated for the most part on source and redaction criticism, with the result that this concentration has unconsciously conditioned approaches to the Gospel. If followed critically and objectively, the rhetorical element in the Johannine method should offer a much needed breakthrough in Johannine studies.

In case we give the impression of wishing to substitute the rhetorical mode for current models used in interpreting the Gospel, we wish to emphasize that we do not view the rhetorical mode as something pursued by the Evangelist for its own sake. The basic genre of his book is the gospel genre and his major concern is pastoral, not aesthetic. The import of the rhetorical framework in which his Gospel is cast lies in its being rooted in life. In other words, it reflects a way of thinking which characterized the world in which both the Evangelist and his audience lived. As a recognized persuasive tool it constituted the method best suited to the Evangelist's hortatory purpose (20:31). The very use of rhetoric, in our view, argues

---

[28]Daube was not the first, of course, to note the rhetorical dimension of the NT works. One thinks, for instance, of J. Weiss, *Beiträge zur Paulinischen Rhetorik* (Göttingen: Vandenhoek und Ruprecht, 1897) and Bultmann's *Der Stil der Paulinischen Predigt und der kynischstoischen Diatribe* (Göttingen: Vandenhoek und Ruprecht, 1910); nor must one forget the voluminous works by H. Strack and P. Billerbeck (*Str-B*). Daube's contribution lies in the fact that he popularized this concept both in his lectures and in his works, in particular, *The NT and Rabbinic Judaism;* "Rabbinic Methods of Interpretation and Hellenistic Rhetoric," *HUCA* 22 (1949) 237—264. However, as Scroggs ("Paul as Rhetorician: Two Homilies in Romans 1:11," *Jews, Greeks and Christians,* 271—297, esp. p. 273—274, n. 11) points out, while the importance of rhetoric in the Graeco-Roman world has "long been known . . . it is surprising how little use has been made of this knowledge."

In no case is Scroggs' statement more true than in John. Works in the rhetorical background of Paul's writings abound — see for instance the recent dissertations by Stanley K. Stowers, *The Diatribe and Paul's Letter to the Romans* (SBLDS 57, Chico: Scholars Press, 1981) and B.H. Brinsmead, *Galatians: Dialogical Response to Opponents* (SBLDS 65, Chico: Scholars Press, 1982), and the bibliography given there. For the Synoptics one may mention J.W. Doeve's dissertation, *Jewish Hermeneutics in the Synoptic Gospels and Acts* (Assen: van Gorcum, 1954), also with bibliography; and the more generalized work by Amos N. Wilder, *Early Christian Rhetoric: The Language of the Gospel* (Cambridge: Harvard University Press, 1971); and finally C.G. Montefiori, *Rabbinic Literature and the Gospel Teachings* (The Library of Social Studies, New York: Ktav, 1970) which focuses on Matthew and Luke. But to our knowledge, there is a dearth of works on John on this topic, though one may mention E.A. Nida's very recent five-page article, "Rhetoric and Translator: With Special Reference to John 1," *Bib Trans* 33 (1983) 324—328.

for the pastoral/missionary concern of the Evangelist; and recognition of this fact might help to *degnosticize* and demythologize our approaches to the Gospel. Another great advantage of using this rhetorical approach in interpreting the Gospel is that sources cited for formal examples lie wholly outside the Gospel, and are independent of the NT traditions; hence whatever formal rhetorical traits one purports to discover can be objectively and scientifically verified in a process which precludes any kind of circularity[29].

Finally, it needs to be noted that while our *formal identification of the rhetorical framework underlying the Gospel is new,* individual rhetorical traits have often been noted in the Gospel, even if these traits were not always identified as rhetorical or seen as aspects of the *Grundkonzeption* of the Evangelist's style. Borgen, for instance, has emphasized the forensic character of the Johannine dialogues in 5—10 but has viewed this from the halakhic standpoint rather than directly from the rhetorical one of which the halakhic constitutes an aspect. We may recall, too, the recognition of the dramatic character of the Gospel first systematically emphasized by Windisch — it is common knowledge that drama was the handmaid of rhetoric in Hellenistic schools. Lindars, too, has drawn attention to the "emotive" or aesthetic aspects of the Johannine style without again linking this to the general rhetorical framework of the Gospel[30]. Indeed his valiant apology for the seeming lack of morality on the part of the Evangelist who attributes to Jesus speeches of his own composition becomes completely unnecessary when this very practice is seen as a recognized hermeneutical and rhetorical principle which the Evangelist

---

[29]In this study we have for the most part limited our citations of rhetorical references to Quintilian's *Institutio Oratoria*. The reason, as mentioned in Chapter II (pp. 45—46), is that this author is the closest contemporary to the Evangelist since his dates span the years A.D. 34—100. In addition, he cites, critically reviews, and builds on the earlier works of the Greek and Roman rhetoricians. Whether the rhetorical influence on the Evangelist came through contacts with Hellenism or Judaism would be impossible to say, given the syncretistic culture of the period. We recall that Hillel (10 B.C.—A.D. 10), for instance, learnt his principles of hermeneutics from the Alexandrian proselytes, Shemaiah and Abtalion (*b. Yoma* 71b; *b. Giṭ.* 57b). These authorities must have been highly respected in Jewish circles for Hillel to cite them in defense of his own hermeneutical practices (*b. Pesaḥ.* 66a; *y. Pesaḥ.* 33a). Indeed Hellenistic influence on rabbinic exegesis seems to date as far back as 100 B.C. (Davies, *HUCA* 22, pp. 240—241; cf. n. 28 above). Hengel's *Judaism and Hellenism* (2 vols. Philadelphia: Fortress, 1974) offers a comprehensive study of the interpenetration of Hellenistic and Jewish cultures dating as far back as 360 B.C. See further G. Kennedy, *The Art of Rhetoric in the Roman World* 300 B.C. to A.D. 300 (Princeton: Princeton University, 1972). Most importantly, we need to recall that the language of the Gospel tells us more about the situation of the audience whom the Evangelist seeks to convince than about his own origins. A long standing tradition accepted by the majority of scholars situates this audience in a Hellenistic environment, namely, in Asia Minor (Eusebius, *H.E.* 3.23.1—4).

[30]The aesthetic aspects of rhetoric are well underlined by Quintilian: rhetorical features give the "impression of grace and charm" (*Inst. Or.* II.xiii.11); the art has to do essentially with "eloquence" (II.xiv.2); the aim of rhetorical speech is "to instruct, move and charm the audience" (III.v.2).

held in common with his audience (see pp. 45–49 above)[31]. Lagrange's commentary on the Gospel also notes the presence of the Socratic method here and there. Nor must we forget that the interpretative and skilful art of the Evangelist was recognized from the very earliest days[32]. The novel in our discovery, then, lies in the formal identification of a comprehensive category which embraces all these individual rhetorical traits, and many more besides, capable of shedding significantly new light on our understanding of the Gospel.

In this respect as in the application of the contextual method, this present study is only a seminal one. But we trust that it has cogently demonstrated that a rich but as yet unsystematically explored territory awaits the curiosity and expertise of Johannine exegetes. To discover the treasures buried ever so deeply in the Gospel, the exegete needs to dig deep in the terrain where the Evangelist has chosen to plant his "book." The "Johannine approach" was adopted as the topic of yet another dissertation on mission in his Gospel. But if this approach is viewed seriously as the methodological key furnished by the Evangelist himself for understanding his Gospel (20:30–31), it may yet unlock many a door which till now have defied the detective skill of Johannine scholars. This key can also prove to be a valuable tool for reassessing the validity of many hypotheses advanced in the efforts to comprehend the Gospel. In whatever direction the research is focused, a full appreciation of the Evangelist's work calls for a special attentiveness to his method of handling issues. It also presupposes a recognition that he is dealing with real people, in real life situations and in a real world, his world of the first century, not ours of the twentieth century.

By the same token, there appears to be no justification for assuming as a basic starting point that this world of the Evangelist was closed, esoteric and isolated from the rest of humanity. Or, that proud of its "high Christology," the Johannine community showed a contemptuous front not only to synagogue Jews and hostile Gentiles but also to "orthodox Christians" whose Christology happened to be too low by Johannine standards. Such a portrait of the Johannine community imputes to it a triumphalism which both the Gospel and Epistles, our exclusive source for the portrait of the Johannine community, expressly reject, and which is the very opposite of the Johannine approach highlighted in this study. Moreover, while Christian "communities" today can exist happily in near total isolation from one another, each parish and diocese and religious community guarding jealously its territorial and jurisdictional integrity, we have no evidence that such, in fact, was the status quo among the Christian communities of the NT era; the Johannine community gives no evidence of

---

[31]Lindars, *John,* esp. pp. 152–153.

[32]Eusebius (*H.E.* 3.24.3) suggests that, unlike the other three Evangelists, John represented the teachings of Jesus "in persuasive or artistic language."

being an exception here. Separation from apostates who pose a threat to one's faith in Jesus is a different matter. Nor was the Johannine community the only one exhorted to take such a stance[33].

Finally, a full comprehension of the Evangelist's approach demands from the exegete a deep appreciation of the spirit of faith and commitment to Jesus in which the Gospel was written (cf. 2:11, 18; 20:8) and which it seeks to inculcate in its readers (20:31). Without this appreciation Johannine scholarship risks becoming the victim of an all too literary, all too rationalistic approach. Such an approach would be more akin to the spirit of Nicodemus and of the unbelieving Jews, one which prides itself in its own self-acquired knowledge (οἴδαμεν), than it would be to the confessional stance of Nathanael, the Samaritan woman, the Samaritans, Peter, Martha and the Beloved Disciple himself (πεπιστεύκαμεν). In the Gospel the faith-stance is the only stance which enables the audience to gain an evergrowing knowledge of Jesus and of the significance of his mission. Without this faith-stance Johannine scholarship risks missing the whole point of the Evangelist's "book" or the whole purpose of his missionary undertaking, which is to sustain his readers in a faith-anchored, life-centered and life-giving knowledge of Jesus as the Christ and Son of God.

---

[33]For contemporary Christian and Jewish practice of expulsion see 1 Cor 5:9–13; 1QS 6:27→ 7:2, 16; 8:21–24; Justin, *Dial.* 38.1 and Ign. *Eph.* 7:1. As Brown (*Epistles,* 691–692) notes, avoiding contact with deviating brothers was heightened by the missionary situation.

Selected Bibliography

The bibliography offered here is by no means exhaustive. Rather, as in the study itself (cf. pp. 7—8 above), this *selection* is intended to reflect the range of issues which have been taken into consideration in the line of approach adopted in this research. With very few exceptions, the many authors cited in the *Theological Dictionary of the New Testament* (=*TDNT*), as indicated in the appropriate footnotes, are not included in this bibliography. The system of abbreviations is that already described on p. xiv above. See also Joseph Fitzmyer, *An Introductory Bibliography for the Study of Scripture*. Revised Edition. Subsidia Biblica 3. Rome: Biblical Institute, 1981.

A. Texts and Translations

1. Biblical and Related Fields

Aland, Kurt. *Synopsis Quartuor Evangeliorum. Locis Parallelis Evangeliorum Apocryphorum et Patrum Adhibitis.* 5th ed. Stuttgart: Württembergische Bibelanstalt, 1968.

Aland, Kurt., and Aland, Barbara., eds. *Novum Testamentum Graece. Nestle-Aland.* 26th ed. Stuttgart: Deutsche Bibelstiftung, 1979.

Carmignac, J.; Cothenet, E.; and Lignée, H., eds. *Les Textes de Qumran. Traduits et annotés.* 2 vols. Autour de la Bible. Paris: Létouzey et Ané, 1963. Vol. 2 by J. Carmignac and P. Guilbert, 1961.

Charles, R. H., ed. *The Apocrypha and Pseudepigrapha of the Old Testament in English.* 2 vols. Oxford: Clarendon, 1968.

Cohen, A., ed. *The Minor Tractates of the Talmud. Massektoth Ḳeṭannoth.* 2 vols. London: Soncino, 1965; 1971.

Delitzsch, Franz. הברית החדשה . Berlin, 1912.

Dupont-Sommer, A. *Les Ecrits esséniens découverts près de la mer Morte.* Paris: Payot, 1961. (*The Essene Writings from Qumran.* Translated by Geza Vermes. Gloucester, Mass.: Peter Smith, 1973.).

Elliger, K., and Rudolph, W., eds. *Biblia Hebraica Stuttgartensia.* Stuttgart: Deutsche Bibelstiftung, 1967/1977.

Epstein, Rabbi I., gen. ed. *The Babylonian Talmud.* 35 vols. London: Soncino, 1935—1960.

Freedman, Rabbi H., and Simon, Maurice., eds. trans. *The Midrash IX.* 3rd ed. London: Soncino, 1961.

Lohse, Eduard. *Die Texte aus Qumran. Hebräisch und deutsch mit Massoretischer Punktuation, Ubersetzung, Einfuhrung und Anmerkungen.* München: Kösel-V., 1971.

Martin, Victor., ed. *The Papyrus Bodmer II [= P66]. Evangile de Jean.* Cologny-Genève: Bibliotheca Bodmeriana, 1956.

––. *The Papyrus Bodmer XIV–XV [= P75]. Evangiles de Luc et Jean.* Cologny-Gèneve: Biblio-theca Bodmeriana, 1961.

Rahlfs, Alfred., ed. *Septuaginta. Id Est Vetum Testamentum Graece Iuxta LXX Interpretes.* 2 vols. Stuttgart: Privilegierte Württembergische Bibelanstalt. 1935.

2. Ancient Authors

Aristotle. *The "Art" of Rhetoric.* With an English Translation by John Henry Freese. The Loeb Classical Library (= LCL). London: Heinemann, 1926.

––. *Aristote, Rhétorique I, Texte et Traduction,* by Médéric Dufour. Paris: Les Belles Lettres, 1938.

Cicero, Marcus T. *De Inventione de Optima Genere Oratorum Topica.* With An English Translation by H. M. Hubbell. LCL. London: Heinemann, 1960.

––. *De Oratore.* 2 vols. With an English Translation by H. Rackham. LCL. London: Heinemann, 1960.

––. *Pro T. Annio Milone.* With an English Translation by N. H. Watts. LCL. London: Heinemann, 1964.

––. *Ad C. Herennium Libri IV. De Ratione Dicendi.* With An English Translation by Harry Cha-plan. LCL. London: Heinemann, 1964.

Eusebius of Pamphili. *Histoire Ecclésiastique I–V.* SC 31. Translated by Gustave Bardy. Paris: Cerf: 1955.

Ignatius of Antioch. *Epistolae.* Patrologia Graeca 5. Edited by J.-P. Migne, 643–728.

Joly, R., trans. *Hermas le Pasteur.* SC 53. Paris: Cerf, 1958.

Josephus, Flavius. *Jewish Antiquities.* 8 vols. LCL. London: Heinemann and Cambridge: Harvard University, 1930–1965.

––. *Guerre des Juifs. Texte établi et traduit.* 2 vols. By J. Pelletier. Paris: Les Belles Lettres, 1975, 1980.

––. *The Life. Against Apion.* With an English Translation by H. St. J. Thackeray. LCL. London: Heinemann, 1924.

Justin, Martyr. *Apolgia I & II pro Christianis.* Patrologia Graeca 6. Edited by J.-P. Migne, 326–472.

––. *Dialogi cum Tryphone Judaeo.* PG 6, 470–799.

Origen. *Commentaire sur saint Jean.* 3 vols. *I: Livres I–V.* SC 120. *II: Livres VI et X.* SC 157. *III. Livres XIII.* SC 222. Translated by Cécil Blanc. Paris: Cerf, 1966, 1970, 1975.

Quintilian. *De Institutio Oratoria.* 4 vols. With An English Translation by H. E. Butler. LCL. Lon-don: Heinemann, 1921–1933.

Rordorf, Willy, and Tuilier, André., trans. *Didache. La Doctrine des douze apôtres.* SC 248. Paris: Cerf, 1978.

B. Reference Works

Abbott, Erwin A. *Johannine Vocabulary: A Comparison of the Words of the Fourth Gospel with Those of the Three.* London: Adam and Charles Black, 1905.

––. *Johannine Grammar.* London: Adam and Charles Black, 1906.

Arndt, William F., and Gingrich, F. N. *A Greek-English Lexicon of the New Testament and Other Early Christian Literature. Second Edition Revised and Augmented by F. Wilbur Gingrich and Frederick W. Danker from Walter Bauer's Fifth Edition 1958. (=BAG).* Chicago: University of Chicago, 1979.

Blass, F., Debrunner, A.; and Funk, Robert W. *A Greek Grammar of the New Testament and Other Early Christian Literature. A Translation and Revision of the Ninth-Tenth German Edition Incorporating Supplementary Notes. (=BDF).* Chicago; University of Chicago, 1961.

Brown, F.; Driver, S. R.; and Briggs, Charles A., eds. *A Hebrew and English Lexicon of the Old Testament with an Appendix Containing the Biblical Aramaic Based on the Lexicon of William Gesenius as Translated by Edward Robinson.* Oxford: Clarendon, 1975.

Davidson, B. *Analytical Hebrew and Chaldee Lexicon.* London: Samuel Bagster and Sons, 1959.

Even-Shosan, Abraham., ed. *A New Concordance of the Bible. Thesaurus of the Language of the Bible: Hebrew and Aramaic Roots, Words, Proper Names, Phrases and Synonyms.* Jerusalem: "Kiryat Sepher" Publishing House, 1982.

Hatch, E., and Redpath, H. A., eds. *A Concordance to the Septuagint and the Other Greek Versions of the Old Testament.* 2 vols. Oxford: Clarendon, 1897.

Kittel, Gerhard., and Bromley, G. W., eds. *Theological Dictionary of the New Testament (= TDNT).* 10 vols. Grand Rapids: Wm. B. Eerdmans, 1964–1974. Vol. 10, Index Volume Compiled by R. Pitkin, 1979.

Koehler, Ludwig., and Baumgartner, Walter., eds. *Lexicon in Veteris Testamenti Libros.* Leiden, E. J. Brill, 1958.

Liddell, H. G., and Scott, R. *A Greek-English Lexicon.* New ed. rev. by S. H. Jones. Oxford: Clarendon, 1961. (=*LSJ*).

Metzger, Bruce M. *The Text of the New Testament. Its Translation, Corruption and Restoration.* 2nd ed. Oxford: University, 1968.

––. *A Textual Commentary on the Greek New Testament.* 3rd ed. London: United Bible Societies, 1975.

––., for the RSV Bible Committee. *A Concordance to the Apocrypha/Deutero-Canonical Books of the Revised Standard Version Derived from the Data Bank of the Centre Informatique et Bible Abbey of Maredsous.* Grand Rapids: Wm. B. Eerdmans, 1983.

Morton, A. Q., and Michaelson, S., eds. *A Critical Concordance to the Gospel of John: The Computer Concordance,* Vol. 5. Wooster, Ohio: The Bible Research Associates, 1974.

Moule, C. F. D. *An Idiom Book of New Testament Greek.* Cambridge: University, 1953.

Moulton, James H. *A Grammar of New Testament Greek Based on W. F. Moulton's Edition of G. B. Winner's Grammar.* 4 vols. *I: Prolegomena. II: Accidence and Word Formation with an Appendix on Semitisms in the New Testament. III: Syntax;* and *IV: Style* both by Nigel Turner. Edinburgh: T and T Clark, 1906, 1963, 1975.

Moulton, J. H., and Milligan, G. *The Vocabulary of the Greek Testament Illustrated from the Papyri and Other Non-Literary Sources.* London: Hodder and Stoughton, 1949.

Moulton, W. F.; Geden, A. S.; and Moulton, H. K. *A Concordance to the Greek New Testament According to the Texts of Westcott, Hort and Tischendorf and the English Revisers.* 5th ed. Edinburgh: T and T Clark, 1978.

Mussies, G. *The Morphology of Koine Greek as Used in the Apocalypse of St. John: A Study in Bilingualism.* Leiden: E. J. Brill, 1971.

Schürer, Emil. *The History of the Jewish People in the Age of Jesus Christ.* 2 vols. Revised and edited by Geza Vermes, Fergus Millar and Matthew Black. Literary Editor, Pamela Vermes. A New English Edition. Edinburgh: T and T Clark, 1979.

Strack, H. L., and Billerbeck, P. *Kommentar zum Neuen Testament aus Talmud und Midrasch.* 4 vols. (=*Str-B*) München: Oscar Beck, 1922–1928.

Zerwick, Marx. *Graecitas Biblica Exemplis Illustrata.* 4th ed. Rome: Pontifical Biblical Institute, 1960.

Zerwick, M., and Grosvenor, Mary. *A Grammatical Analysis of the New Testament. I: Gospel-Acts. II: Epistles-Apocalypse.* Rome: Biblical Institute, 1974, 1979.

C. Commentaries

1. John's Gospel

Barrett, C. K. *The Gospel According to Saint John: An Introduction with Commentary and Notes on the Greek Text.* 2nd ed. London: SPCK, 1978.

Bauer, W. *Das Johannes-Evangelium.* HNT 6; 3 Aufl. Tübingen: Mohr/Siebeck, 1933.

Becker, J. *Das Evangelium nach Johannes. Kapitel 1—10.* Ökumenische Taschenbuchkommentar zum Neuen Testament, Vol. 4/1. Würzburg: Echter-Verlag, 1979.

Bernard, J. H. *A Critical and Exegetical Commentary on the Gospel According to St. John.* The International Critical Commentary. 2 vols. Edited by A. H. McNeile. Edinburgh: T and T Clark, 1928.

Boismard, M.-E., and Lamouille, A. *Synopse des Quatre Evangiles en Français. III: L'Evangile de Jean.* Paris: Cerf, 1977.

Brown, R. E. *The Gospel According to John.* The Anchor Bible. Vols. 29 and 29a. Garden City: Doubleday, 1966 and 1970.

Bultmann, R. *Das Evangelium des Johannes.* MyerKom 11. Göttingen: Vandenhoeck und Ruprecht, 1941; 19th ed. 1968.

——. *The Gospel of John: A Commentary.* Oxford: Basil Blackwell, 1971.

van den Bussche, H. *Jean. Commentaire de l'Evangile Spirituel.* Bruges: Desclée de Brouwer, 1967.

Dodd, C. H. *The Interpretation of the Fourth Gospel.* Cambridge: University, 1953, 1960.

Haenchen, Ernst. *Johannesevangelium. Ein Kommentar.* Tübingen: Mohr/Siebeck, 1980.

Holtzmann, Oscar. *Das Neue Testament nach dem Stuttgarter griechischen Text übersetzt und erklärt II. V: Das Evangelium des Johannes.* Giessen: Alfred Töpelmann, 1926.

Hoskyns, E. *The Fourth Gospel.* Edited by F. N. Davey. London: Faber and Faber, 1940.

Lagrange, M.-J. *Evangile selon Saint Jean.* EB. 5th ed. Paris: Lecoffre, 1936.

Libermann, F. M. P. *Commentaire de Saint Jean.* Les Grands Mystiques: Collection publiée sous la direction du R. P. Cayre. Paris: Desclée de Brouwer, 1958.

Lightfoot, R. H. *St. John's Gospel: A Commentary.* Oxford: Clarendon, 1956.

Lindars, B. *The Gospel of John.* New Century Bible. London: Oliphant, 1972.

McPolin, J. *John.* NT Message 6. Wilmington: Michael Glazier, 1979.

Morris, Leon. *The Gospel According to John. The English Text with Introduction, Exposition and Notes.* The New International Commentary on the New Testament. Grand Rapids: Wm. B. Eerdmans, 1971.

Odeberg, Hugo. *The Fourth Gospel. Interpreted in Its Relation to Contemporaneous Religious Currents in Palestine and the Hellenistic Oriental World.* Uppsala: Almqvist and Wiksells, 1929.

Sanders, J. N., and Mastin, B. A. *A Commentary on the Gospel According to St. John.* Black's New Testament Commentaries. London: Adam and Charles Black, 1968.

Schlatter, Adolf. *Der Evangelist Johannes. Wie er spricht, denkt und glaubt. Ein Kommentar zum vierten Evangelium.* Stuttgart: Calwer, 1930.

Schnackenburg, R. *Das Johannesevangelium.* 4 vols. *I: Einleitung und Kommentar zu Kap. 1—4. II: Kommentar zu Kap. 5—12. III: Kommentar zu Kap. 13—21. IV: Ergänzende Auslegungen und Exkurse.* HTKNT IV/1—4. Freiburg: Herder, 1968, 1971, 1975, 1984.

Schulz, Siegfried. *Das Evangelium nach Johannes.* NTD 4. 2nd ed. Göttingen: Vandenhoeck und Ruprecht, 1975.

Spitta, F. *Das Johannes-Evangelium als Quelle der Geschichte Jesu.* Göttingen: Vandenhoeck und Ruprecht, 1910.

Wellhausen, Julius. *Das Evangelium Johannis.* Berlin: Reimer, 1908.

Wendt, Hans H. *Das Johannesevangelium. Eine Untersuchung seiner Entstehung und seines geschichtlichen Wertes.* Göttingen: Vandenhoeck und Ruprecht, 1900.

Westcott, B. Foss. *The Gospel According to Saint John: The Greek Text with Introduction and Notes.* Michigan: Wm. B. Eerdmans, 1954.

2. The Johannine Epistles

Brown, R. E. *The Epistles of John: Translated with Introduction, Notes and Commentary.* The Anchor Bible 30. Garden City: Doubleday, 1982.

Bruce, F. F. *The Epistles of John.* London: Pickering and Inglis, 1970.

Bultmann, R. *The Johannine Epistles.* Hermeneia: A Critical and Historical Commentary on the Bible. 2nd ed. Philadelphia: Fortress, 1973.

Dodd, C. H. *The Johannine Epistles.* The Moffat New Testament Commentary. New York: Harper and Brothers, 1946.

Houlden, J. L. *A Commentary on the Johannine Epistles.* Harper's New Testament Commentaries. New York: Harper and Row, 1973.

Marshall, I. H. *The Epistles of John.* The New International Commentary on the New Testament. Grand Rapids: Wm. B. Eerdmans, 1978.

Plummer, Alfred. *The Epistles of St. John.* Grand Rapids: Baker Book House, 1980.

Schlatter, Adolf. *Die Briefe und die Offenbarung des Johannes.* Stuttgart: Calwer, 1964.

Schnackenburg, R. *Die Johannesbriefe.* HTKNT 13/3. Freiburg: Herder, 1953.

Westcott, B. Foss. *The Epistles of St. John. The Greek Text with Notes and Essays.* Grand Rapids: Wm. B. Eerdmans, 1955.

D. On Jn 4:1—42 (outside the commentaries) and on Samaritanism

Bligh, John. "Jesus in Samaria." *HeyJ* 3 (1962) 329—346.

Boers, Hendrikus. "Discourse Structure and Macro-Structure in the Interpretation of Texts: John 4:1—42 as an Example." SBLASP 19 (1980) 159—182.

Bowman, John. "Early Samaritan Eschatology." *JJS* 6 (1955) 63—72.

——. "Samaritan Studies. I: The Fourth Gospel and the Samaritans." *BJRL* 40 (1958) 290—308.

——. *Samaritanische Probleme. Studien zum Verhältnis von Samaritanertum, Judentum und Urchristentum.* Franz Delitzsch-Vorlesungen, 1959. Stuttgart: Kohlhammer, 1967.

——. *The Samaritan Chronicle.* BZAW 107. Berlin: Alfred Töpelmann, 1969.

——. *The Fourth Gospel and the Jews.* Pittsburgh: Pickwick, 1975.

——. *Samaritan Documents Relating to Their History, Religion and Life.* Pittsburgh: Pickwick, 1977.

Braun, F. M. "Avoir soif et boir (Jn 4, 10—14; 7, 37—39)." In *Mélanges bibliques en hommage au R. P. Béda Rigaux.* Edited by A. Descamps and A. de Halleux, 247—258. Gembloux: Duculot, 1970.

Buchanan, G. W. "The Samaritan Origin of the Gospel of John." In *Religions in Antiquity. Essays in Memory of Erwin Goodenough Studies in the History of Religions.* Supplement to Numen, 14. Edited by J. Neusner, 114—175. Leiden: E. J. Brill, 1968.

Bull, R. J. "An Archaeological Footnote to 'Our Fathers Worshipped on This Mountain' John iv. 20." *NTS* 23 (1977) 460—462.

Coggins, R. J. *Samaritans and Jews: The Origins of Samaritanism Reconsidered.* Oxford: Basil Blackwell, 1975.

Cullmann, O. "La Samarie et les origines de la mission chrétienne. Qui sont les ἌΛΛΟΙ de Jean IV, 38?" In *Annuaire de l'Ecole Pratique des Hautes Etudes,* 3—12. Paris, 1954—1955.

——. "L'Opposition contre le Temple de Jérusalem. Motif commun de la théologie johannique et du monde ambiant." *NTS* 5—6 (1958—1960) 157—173.

——. "Von Jesus zum Stephanuskreis und zum Johannesevangelium." In *Jesus und Paulus. Fs. für Werner Georg Kümmel zum 70. Geburtstag.* Edited by E. E. Ellis and E. Grässer, 44—56. Göttingen: Vandenhoeck und Ruprecht, 1975.

Daube, Davies. "Jesus and the Samaritan Woman: The Meaning of συγχράομαι." *JBL* 69 (1950) 137—147.

Delcor, Mathias. "Vom Sichem der hellenistischen Epoche zur Sychar des Neuen Testaments." *ZDPV* 78 (1962) 43–48.

Freed, E. D. "Samaritan Influence in the Gospel of John." *CBQ* 30 (1958) 580–587.

——. "Did John Write His Gospel Partly to Win Samaritan Converts." *NovT* 12 (1970) 241–256.

——. "*Egō Eimi* in Jn 1.20 and 4.25." *CBQ* 41 (1979) 288–291.

Gaster, Moses. *The Samaritans: Their History, Doctrines and Literature.* The Schweich Lectures 1923. London: British Academy, 1925.

——. *The Samaritan Oral Law and Ancient Traditions. I: The Samaritan Eschatology.* London: The Research Publishing Company, 1932.

Hall, D. R. "The Meaning of συγχράομαι in John 4, 9." *ExpT* 83 (1971–1972) 56–57.

Hudry-Clergion, C. "De Judée en Galilée. Etude de Jean 4, 1–45." *NRT* 103 (1981) 818–830.

Janssens, Yvonne. "L'épisode de la Samarie chez Héracleon." *Sacra Pagina*, BETL 12–13 (1959) 77–85.

Jeremias, Joachim. Σαμάρεια, Σαμαρίτης, Σαμαρῖτις. In *TDNT* VII, 88–94.

Kilpatrick, G. D. "John IV 41 ΠΛΕΙΟΝ or ΠΛΕΙΟΥΣ." *NovT* 18 (1976) 131–132.

Kippenberg, H. G. *Garizim und Synagoge. Traditionsgeschichtliche Untersuchungen zur Samaritanischen Religion der aramäischen Periode.* Religionsgeschichtliche Versuche und Vorarbeiten 30. Berlin: W. de Gruyter, 1971.

Leidig, Edeltraud. *Jesu Gespräch mit der Samaritanerin und weitere Gespräche im Johannesevangelium.* Theologischen Dissertationen 15. Basel: Friedrich Reinhardt, 1979.

Lowry, S. *Principles of Samaritan Bible Exegesis.* Leiden: E. J. Brill, 1977.

MacDonald, John. *The Theology of the Samaritans.* The New Testament Library. London: SCM, 1964.

——. "The Beginnings of Christianity According to the Samaritans." *NTS* 18 (1971–1972) 54–80.

Merx, Adalbert. *Der Messias oder Taʾeb der Samaritaner.* BZAW 17. Giessen: Alfred Töpelmann, 1909.

Montgomery, J. A. *The Samaritans. The Earliest Jewish Sect: Their History, Theology and Literature.* Philadelphia: John C. Winston, 1907.

Neyrey, J. H. "Jacob Traditions and the Interpretation of John 4:10–26." *CBQ* 41 (1979) 419–437.

Olsson, Birger. *Structure and Meaning in the Fourth Gospel: A Text-Linguistic Analysis of John 2:1–11 and 4:1–42.* Coniectanea Biblica. New Testament Series 6. Lund: CWK Gleerup, 1974.

Pollard, T. E. "Jesus and the Samaritan Woman." *ExpT* 92 (1981) 147–148.

Pummer, R. "The Present State of Samaritan Studies." I: *JSS* 21 (1976) 39–61. II: 22 (1977) 27–47.

——. "Antisamaritanische Polemik in jüdischen Schriften aus der intertestamentlichen Zeit." *BZ* 26 (1982) 224–242.

Purvis, J. D. *The Samaritan Pentateuch and the Origin of the Samaritan Sect.* HSM 2. Cambridge: Harvard University, 1968.

Radermakers, J. "Mission et apostolat dans l'évangile johannique." *SE* 2 (= TU 87; 1964) 100–121.

de Robert, Philippe. "Les Samaritains et le Nouveau Testament." *ETR* 54 (1970) 179–184.

Robinson, J. A. T. "The 'Others' of John 4, 38. A Test of Exegetical Method." *SE* 1 (= TU 73; 1959) 510–515.

Roustang, F. "Les moments de l'acte de foi et ses conditions de possibilité." *RechSR* 46 (1958) 344–378.

Schenke, Hans-Martin. "Jakobsbrunnen-Josephsgrab-Sychar. Topographische Untersuchungen und Erwägungen in der Perspektive von Joh. 4, 5.6." *ZDPV* 84 (1968) 159–184.

Schmid, Lothar. "Die Komposition der Samaria-Szene Joh. 4,1–42. Ein Beitrag zur Charakteristik des 4. Evangelisten als Schriftsteller." *ZNW* 28 (1929) 148–158.

Schottroff, Luise. "Johannes 4, 5–15 und die Konsequenzen des johanneischen Dualismus." *ZNW* 60 (1969) 199–214.

Scobie, Charles H. H. "The Origins and Development of Samaritan Christianity." *NTS* 19 (1972–1973) 390–414.

——. "The Fourth Gospel and the Samaritans." *NovT* 17 (1975) 161–198.

——. "The Use of Source Material in the Speeches of Acts III and VII." *NTS* 25 (1978–1979) 399–421.

Tal, A. "The Samaritan Targum to the Pentateuch. Its Distinctive Characteristics and Metamorphosis." *JSS* 21 (1976) 26—38.

Wallis, Gerhard. "Jerusalem und Samaria als Königsstädte. Auseinanderseztung mit einer These Albrecht Alts." *VT* 26 (1976) 480—496.

E. General

Albright, W. F. "Recent Discoveries in Palestine and the Gospel of John." In *Background of the New Testament and Its Eschatology*. Edited by W. D. Davies, 153—171. Cambridge: University, 1956.

Alter, Robert. *The Art of Biblical Narrative*. New York: Basic Books, 1981.

Appold, Mark L. *The Oneness Motif in the Fourth Gospel: Motif Analysis and Exegetical Probe into the Theology of John*. Tübingen: J. C. B. Mohr, 1976.

Bailey, J. A. *The Traditions Common to the Gospels of Luke and John*. NovTSup 7. Leiden: E. J. Brill, 1963.

Bauer, Walter. "Johannesevangelium und Johannesbriefe." *TRu* 1 (1929) 135—160.

Baumeister, T. "Der Tod Jesu und die Leidensnachfolge des Jüngers nach dem Johannesevangelium und dem Ersten Johannesbrief." *Wissenschaft und Weisheit* 40 (1977) 81—99.

Becker, Jürgen. "Beobachtungen zum Dualismus im Johannesevangelium." *ZNW* 65 (1974) 71—87.

——. "Aus der Literatur zum Johannesevangelium, 1978—1980." *TRu* NF 47 (1982) 279—301.

——. "J 3, 1—21 als Reflex johanneischer Schuldiskussion." In *Das Wort und die Wörter. Fs. Gerhard Friedrich zum 65. Geburtstag*, 85—95. Edited by Horst Balz and Siegfried Schulz. Stuttgart: Kohlhammer, 1973.

Becker, H. *Die Reden des Johannesevangeliums und der Stil der gnostischen Offenbarungsreden*. Göttingen: Vandenhoeck und Ruprecht, 1956.

Benoit, P. "Qumran and the New Testament." In *Paul and Qumran*, 1—30. Edited by J. Murphy-O'Connor. London: Chapman, 1968.

Berger, K. "Jüdisch-hellenistische Missionsliteratur und apokryphe Apostelakten." *Kairos* 17 (1975) 232—248.

Bergmeier, Roland. *Glaube als Gabe nach Johannes*. BWANT 6/12. Stuttgart: Kohlhammer, 1980.

Beutler, Johannes. *Martyria. Traditionsgeschichtliche Untersuchungen zum Zeugnisthema bei Johannes*. Frankfurt a/M: Josef Knecht, 1972.

Bieder, W. *Gottes Sendung und der missionarische Auftrag nach Matthäus. Lukas, Paulus und Johannes*. Theologische Studien 82. Zurich: EVZ-Verlag, 1965.

Blank, Josef. *KRISIS. Untersuchungen zur johanneischen Christologie und Eschatologie*. Freiburg i/B: Lambertus, 1964.

Blinzler, J. *Johannes und die Synoptiker. Ein Forschungsbericht*. SBS 5. Stuttgart: Katholishes Bibelwerk, 1965.

Böcher, Otto. "Wasser und Geist." In *Verbum Veritatis. Fs. für Gustav Stählin zum 70. Geburtstag*. Wuppertal: Rolf Brockhaus, 1970.

Boismard, M.-E. "De son ventre couleront des fleuves d'eau (Jo., VII, 38)." *RB* 65 (1958) 523—546.

——. "Saint Luc et la rédaction du quatrième évangile (Jn iv, 46—54)." *RB* 69 (1962) 185—211.

——. "Aenon, près de Salem (Jean III, 23)." *RB* 80 (1973) 218—229.

——. "Un procédé rédactionnel dans le quatrième évangile: la Wiederaufnahme." In *L'Evangile de Jean. Source, rédaction, théologie*, 235—241. (=*BETL* 44). Edited by M. de Jonge. Leuven: Leuven University, 1977.

Bonsirven, J. *Textes rabbiniques des deux premières siècles chrétiens pour servir à l'intelligence du Nouveau Testament*. Rome: Pontificio Istituto Biblico, 1955.

Borgen, Peder. *Bread from Heaven: An Exegetical Study of Manna in the Gospel of John and in the Writings of Philo*. NovTSup. 10. Leiden: E. J. Brill, 1965.

——. "God's Agent in the Fourth Gospel." *Religions in Antiquity. Studies in the History of Religions* 14, 137–148. Edited by J. Neusner. Leiden: E. J. Brill, 1958.

——. "Some Jewish Exegetical Traditions as Background to the Son of Man Sayings in John's Gospel (Jn 3, 13–14) and Context." In *L'Evangile de Jean*, BETL 44, 243–258.

Bornhäuser, K. *Das Johannesevangelium: Eine Missionsschrift für Israel.* BFCTh 2/15. Gütersloh: C. Bertelsmann, 1928.

Bowker, J. W. "The Origin and Purpose of St. John's Gospel." *NTS* 11 (1965) 398–408.

Braun, F. M. *Jean le théologien.* EB. 3 vols. *1: Jean le théologien et son évangile dans l'église ancienne. 2: Les grandes traditions d'Israël et l'accord des Ecritures selon le quatrième évangile. 3/1: Sa théologie: le mystère de Jésus-Christ. 3/2: Sa théologie: le Christ notre Seigneur hier, aujourd'hui, toujours.* Paris: Lecoffre, 1959, 1964, 1966, 1972.

——. "La Réduction du pluriel au singulier dans l'évangile et la première lettre de Jean." *NTS* 24 (1977) 40–67.

Braun, Herbert. *Qumran und das Neue Testament.* 2 vols. Tübingen: Mohr/Siebeck, 1966.

Brown, R. E. "The Kerygma of the Gospel According to John: The Johannine View of Jesus in Modern Studies." *Interpretation* 21 (1967) 387–400.

——. *The Community of the Beloved Disciple.* New York: Paulist, 1979.

——. "The Relationship of the Fourth Gospel Shared by the Author of 1 John and His Opponents." In *Text and Interpretation: Studies in the New Testament Presented to Matthew Black,* 57–68. Edited by Ernest Best and R. McL. Wilson. Cambridge: University, 1979.

——. "Not Jewish Christianity and Gentile Christianity but Types of Jewish/Gentile Christianity." *CBQ* 45 (1983) 74–79.

Brownlee. W. H. "Messianic Motifs of Qumran and the New Testament." *NTS* 3 (1956–1957) 12–30, 195–210.

Bultmann, R. "Die Bedeutung der neuerschlossenen mandäischen und manichäischen Quellen für das Verständnis des Johannesevangeliums." *ZNW* 24 (1925) 100–146.

——. "Die Theologie des Johannes Evangeliums: Die Sendung des Sohnes." In *Theologie des Neuen Testament,* 385–422. 3rd ed. Tübingen: Mohr/Siebeck, 1958.

Bühner, J. A. *Der Gesandte und sein Weg im 4. Evangelium. Die kultur- und religionsgeschichtlichen Grundlagen der johanneischen Sendungschristologie sowie ihre traditionsgeschichtliche Entwicklung.* WUNT 2/2. Tübingen: Mohr/Siebeck, 1977.

Campbell, R. J. "Evidence for the Historicity of the Fourth Gospel in John 2:13–22." *SE* 7 (1982) 101–120.

Carson, D. A. "Current Source Criticism of the Fourth Gospel." *JBL* 97 (1978) 411–429.

Charlesworth, James H. "Qumran, John and the Odes of Solomon." In *John and Qumran,* 107–136. Edited J. H. Charlesworth. London: Geoffrey Chapman, 1972.

Cohen, Shaye J. D. "Yavneh Revisted: Pharisees, Rabbis and the End of Jewish Sectarianism." *SBLASP* 21 (1982) 45–61.

Collins, R. F. "The Representative Figures of the Fourth Gospel." *Downside Review* 94 (1976) 2–46, 118–132.

Connick, C. M. "The Dramatic Character of the Fourth Gospel." *JBL* 67 (1948) 159–169.

Conzelmann, Hans. *Grundriss der Theologie des Neuen Testaments.* München: Chr. Kaiser, 1967.

Cribbs, F. L. "A Reassessement of the Date of Origin and Destination of the Gospel of John." *JBL* 89 (1970) 38–55.

Cullmann, Oscar. *Heil als Geschichte: Heilsgeschichtliche Existenz im Neuen Testament.* Tübingen: Mohr/Siebeck, 1965.

——. *Der johanneische Kreis. Sein Platz im Spätjudentum, in der Jüngerschaft Jesu und im Urchristentum. Zum Ursprung des Johannesevangeliums.* Tübingen: Mohr/Siebeck, 1975.

Culpepper, R. A. *The Johannine School: An Evaluation of the Johannine-School Hypothesis Based on an Investigation of the Nature of Ancient Schools.* SBLDS 26. Missoula: Scholars, 1975.

Dahl, Nils Alstrup. "The Johannine Church and History." In *Current Issues in New Testament Interpretation. Essays in Honor of Otto A. Piper,* 124–142. Edited by W. Klassen and G. F. Snyder. London: SCM, 1962.

Daube, David. "Jewish Missionary Maxims in Paul." *ST* 1 (1947) 158–159.

——. "Rabbinic Methods of Interpretation." *HUCA* 22 (1949) 239–264.

——. *The New Testament and Rabbinic Judaism. Jordan Lectures in Comparative Religion II.* London: Athlone, 1956.

Dibelius, Martin. *Die Formgeschichte des Evangeliums.* 4th ed. Tübingen: Mohr/Siebeck, 1961.

Dillon, R. J. *From Eyewitness to Ministers of the Word. Tradition and Composition in Luke 24.* AnBib 82. Rome: Biblical Institute, 1978.

Dodd, C. H. *Historical Tradition in the Fourth Gospel.* Cambridge, University, 1963.

Doeve, J. W. *Jewish Hermeneutics in the Synoptic Gospels and Acts.* Assen: van Gorcum, 1954.

Doty, William G. *Contemporary New Testament Interpretation.* Englewood Cliffs: Prentice Hall, 1972.

Driver, G. R. "Covenant and Testament." In Driver, *The Judean Scrolls*, 517—584. New York: Schocken Books, 1965.

Dulière, W. L. *La haute terminologie de la rédaction johannique. Les vocables qu'elle a introduits chez les Gréco-Romains: Le Logos-Verbe, le Paraclet-Esprit-Saint et le Messias-Messie.* Collection Latomus 117. Latomus: Revue d'Etudes Latines, 1970.

Dupont, Jacques. "La persécution comme situation missionaire (Marc 13, 9—11)." *Kirche des Anfangs. Fs. für Heinz Schürmann*, 97—114. Edited by R. Schnackenburg, Josef Ernst and Joachim Wanke. Freiburg: Herder, 1978.

Elliott, J. K., ed. *Studies in New Testament Language and Text. Essays in Honour of George D. Kilpatrick on the Occasion of His Sixtieth Birthday.* Leiden: E. J. Brill, 1976.

Ellis, E. E. "Dating the New Testament." *NTS* 26 (1980) 487—502.

Fascher, Erich. "Theologische Beobachtungen zu δεῖ." In *Neutestamentliche Studien für Rudolf Bultmann zu seinem 70. Geburtstag am 20. August 1954.* BZNW 21, 228—254. Edited by Walter Eltester. Berlin: Alfred Töpelmann, 1957.

——. "Christologie und Gnosis im vierten Evangelium." *TLZ* 93 (1968) 721—730.

Feine, Paul. *Theologie des Neuen Testaments.* 21st ed. Berlin: Evangelische Verlagsanstalt, 1953.

Fenton, J. C. "Towards an Understanding of John." *SE* 4 (=TU 102; 1968) 28—37.

Festugière, André-Jean. *Observations stylistique sur l'évangile de Jean.* Paris: Klincksieck, 1974.

Feuillet, André. *Le prologue du quatrième évangile.* Paris: Brouwer, 1968.

Finkel, Asher. *The Pharisees and the Teacher of Nazareth.* AGJU IV. Leiden: E. J. Brill, 1964.

Fiorenza, Elizabeth Schüssler. "Miracles, Mission and Apologetics. An Introduction." In *Aspects of Religious Propaganda in Judaism and Early Christianity*, edited by E. S. Fiorenza. Notre Dame: University of Notre Dame, 1976.

Fortna, Robert. *The Gospel of Signs. A Reconstruction of the Narrative Source Underlying the Fourth Gospel.* SNTSMS 11. Cambridge: University, 1970.

——. "From Christology to Soteriology. A Redaction Critical Study of Salvation in the Fourth Gospel." *Interpretation* 21 (1973) 31—47.

——. Christology in the Fourth Gospel. Redaction Critical Perspective." *NTS* 21 (1975) 489—502.

Freed, E. D. *Old Testament Quotations in the Gospel of John.* Leiden: Brill, 1965.

Fridrichsen, Anton. "La pensée missionaire dans le quatrième évangile." In *Arbeiten und Mitteilungen aus den Neutestamentlichen Seminar zu Uppsala VI.* Edited by Anton Fridrichsen. Uppsala, 1935.

Fuchs, A. *Jesus in der Verkündigung der Kirche. Studien zum Neuen Testament und seine Umwelt.* Vol. 1. Linz, 1976.

Georgi, D. *Die Gegner des Paulus im 2.Korintherbrief: Studien zur religiösen Propaganda in der Spätantike.* WMANT 11. Neukirchen-Vluyn: Neukirchener Verlag, 1964.

Giblet, J. "Les promesses de l'Esprit et la mission des apôtres dans les Evangiles." *Irenikon* 30 (1957) 45—72.

Giblin, C. H. "Suggestion, Negative Response and Positive Action in St. John's Portrayal of Jesus (John 2.1—11; 4.46—54; 7.2—13; 11.1—44)." *NTS* (1980) 197—211.

——. "The Miraculous Crossing of the Sea (John 6.16—21)." *NTS* 29 (1983) 96—103.

de Goedt, Michel. "Un schème de révélation dans le quatrième évangile." *NTS* 8 (1962) 142—150.

Grässer, Erich. "Die antijüdische Polemik im Johannesevangelium." *NTS* 10 (1964—1965) 74—90.

Grelot, Pierre. *L'Espérance juive à l'heure de Jésus.* Collection "Jésus et Jésus-Christ" 6. Paris: Desclée de Brouwer, 1978.

Guilding, Aileen. *The Fourth Gospel and Jewish Worship. A Study of the Relation of John to the Ancient Jewish Lectionary System.* Oxford: Clarendon, 1960.

Grundmann, Walter. "Verkündigung und Geschichte in dem Bericht vom Eingang der Geschichte Jesu im Johannes-Evangelium: Der historische *Jesus* und der kerygmatische *Christus.*" In *Beiträge zum Christusverständnis in Forschung und Verkündigung,* 289–309. Edited by H. Ristow and K. Matthias. Berlin: Evangelische Verlagsanstalt, 1960.

Haenchen, Ernst. "Aus der Literatur zum Johannesevangelium, 1929–1965." *TRu* N. F. 23 (1955) 295–335.

——. "'der Vater der mich gesandt hat.'" *NTS* 9 (1963) 208–216.

Hahn, F. *Das Problem der Mission in der sonstigen nach paulinischen Tradition und den johanneischen Schriften: Das Verständnis der Mission im Neuen Testament.* WMANT 13. Neuchirchener-Vluyn: Neukirchener Verlag, 1963.

Hare, Douglas R. A. *The Theme of Jewish Persecution of Christians in the Gospel According to St. Matthew.* SNTSMS 6. Cambridge: Cambridge University, 1967.

van Hartungsveld, L. *Die Eschatologie des Johannesevangeliums. Eine Auseinandersetzung mit Rudolf Bultmann.* Assen: Van Gorcum, 1962.

Hengel, Martin. "Die Ursprunge der christlichen Mission." *NTS* 18 (1971) 15–38.

——. *Judaism and Hellenism. Studies in Their Encounter in Palestine during the Hellenistic Period.* 2 vols. Translated by John Bowden. Philadelphia: Fortress, 1974.

Holladay, Carl R. *Theios Aner in Hellelistic-Judaism. A Critique of the Use of This Category in New Testament Christology.* SBLDS 40. Missoula: Scholars, 1977.

de Jonge, Marinus. "The Use of the Word χριστός in the Johannine Epistles." *Studies in John Presented to Professor Dr J. N. Sevenster on the Occasion of his 70th Birthday,* 66–74. NovTSup 24. Leiden: E. J. Brill, 1970.

——. "Jewish Expectations about the 'Messiah' According to the Fourth Gospel." *NTS* 29 (1972–1973) 246–270.

——. *Jesus Stranger from Heaven and Son of God. Jesus Christ and Christians in Johannine Perspective.* Edited and Translated by J. E. Steely. SBLSBS 11. Missoula: Scholars, 1977.

——. "Signs and Works in the Fourth Gospel," *Miscellanea Neotestamentica.* NovTSup 48, 107–125. Edited by T. Baarda, A. F. J. Klijn, and W. C. van Unnik. Leiden: E. J. Brill, 1978.

——. "The Beloved Disciple and the Date of the Gospel of John." In *Text and Interpretation: Studies in the New Testament Presented to Matthew Black,* 99–114. Edited by E. Best and R. McL. Wilson. Cambridge: University, 1979.

Käsemann, Ernst. "Ketzer und Zeuge: Zum johanneischen Verfasserproblem." *ZKT* 48 (1951) 292–311. Also in Käsemann, *Exegetische Versuche und Besinnungen* I, 168–187. Gottingen: Vandenhoeck und Ruprecht, 1960.

——. *Jesu letzter Wille nach Johannes 17.* 3rd ed. Tübingen: Mohr/Siebeck, 1971 (1966).

Kossen, H. B. "Who Were the Greeks of John 12.20?" In *Studies in John. Fs. J. N. Sevenster.* NovTSup 24, 97–110. Leiden: E. J. Brill, 1970.

Kraft, E. "Die Personen des Johannesevangeliums." *EvT* 16 (1956) 18–32.

Kümmel, W. G. "Die Exegese und ihre hermeneutische Grundlagen." In Kümmel, *Das Neue Testament. Geschichte der Erforschung seiner Probleme,* 128–143. Freiburg: Karl Alber, 1958.

——. *Die Theologie des Neuen Testaments nach seinen Hauptzeugen. Jesus. Paulus. Johannes.* Grundriss zum Neuen Testament. NTD Ergänzungsreihe 3. Göttingen: Vandenhoeck und Ruprecht, 1969.

——. *Das Neue Testament im 20. Jahrhundert. Eine Forschungsbericht.* SBS 50. Stuttgart: Katholisches Bibelwerk, 1970.

——. *Einleitung in das Neue Testament.* 17th ed. Heidelberg: Quelle und Meyer, 1973.

Kuhl, Josef. *Die Sendung Jesu und der Kirche nach dem Johannesevangelium.* Studia Instituti Missiologica Societatis Verbi Domini 11. St. Augustin: Styler, 1967.

Kysar, Robert. *The Fourth Evangelist and His Gospel: An Examination of Contemporary Scholarship.* Minneapolis: Augsburg Publishing House, 1975.

——. "Community and Gospel: Vectors in Fourth Gospel Criticism." *Interpretation* 31 (1977) 355–366.

Lagrange, M.-J. "Notes sur le messianisme au temps de Jésus." *RB* 14 (1905) 481–514.

Leal, Juan. "El clima de la fe en la Redaktionsgeschichte del IV Evangelio." *Estudios Biblicos* 22 (1963) 141—177.

Légasse, S. "Le baptême administré par Jésus (Jn 3, 33—26; 4, 1—3) et l'origine du baptême chrétien." *BLE* 78 (1977) 3—30.

Leistner, Reinhold. *Antijudaismus im Johannesevangelium? Darstellung des Problems in der neueren Auslegungsgeschichte und Untersuchung der Leidensgeschichte.* Bern and Frankfurt a/M: Herbert Lang, 1974.

Léon-Dufour, Xavier. "Autour du *Sēmeion* johannique." In *Kirche des Anfangs*, 363—378.

——. "Bulletin de littérature johannique." *RechSR* 68 (1980) 271—316.

——. "Towards a Symbolic Reading of the Fourth Gospel." *NTS* 27 (1981) 439—456.

Lerle, Ernst. *Voraussetzungen der neutestamentlichen Exegese.* Frankfurt a/M: Lutheraner Verlag, 1951.

Leroy, Herbert. *Rätsel und Missverständnis: Ein Beitrag zur Formgeschichte des Johannesevangeliums.* BBB 30. Bonn: Hanstein, 1967.

——. "Das johanneische Missverständnis als literarische Form." *BibLeb* 9 (1968) 191—207.

——. "'... dass Jesus der Christus, der Sohn Gottes ist.' Eigenwart und Herkunft des Johannesevangeliums." *BK* 30 (1975) 114—117.

Lightfoot, J. B. *Biblical Essays.* Grand Rapids: Baker House, 1979.

Lindars, B. *Behind the Fourth Gospel.* Studies in Creative Criticism 3. London: SPCK, 1971.

——. "Discourse and Tradition: The Use of the Sayings of Jesus in the Discourses of the Fourth Gospel." *JSNTS* (1981) 83—101.

Lindemann, A. "Gemeinde und Welt im Johannesevangelium." In *Kirche. Fs. G. Bornkamm zum 75. Geburtstag*, 133—161. Edited by D. Lührmann and G. Strecker. Tübingen: Mohr/Siebeck, 1980.

Loewe, H. "The Ideas of Pharisaism." In *Judaism and Christianity.* 3 vols. in 1. *II: The Contact of Pharisaism with Other Cultures*, 1—58. Edited by H. Loewe. New York: Ktav Publishing House, 1969.

Lütgert, Wilhelm. *Die johanneische Christologie.* 2nd ed. Gütersloh: Bertelsmann, 1916.

——. *Die Liebe im Neuen Testament. Ein Beitrag zur Geschichte des Urchristentums.* Leipzig: A. Deichert, 1905.

MacNamara, Martin. "The Ascension and the Exaltation of Christ in the Fourth Gospel." *Scripture* 19 (1967) 65—73.

——. "Logos of the Fourth Gospel and Memra of the Palestinian Targum (ex 12.42)." *ExpT* 79 (1967—1968) 115—117.

MacRae, George W. "The Fourth Gospel and Religionsgeschichte." *CBQ* 32 (1970) 13—24.

——. "The Ego-Proclamation in Gnostic Sources." In *The Trial of Jesus. Cambridge Studies in Honor of C.F.D. Moule*, 123—139. Studies in Biblical Theology 2/13. Edited by Ernst Bammel. London: SCM, 1970.

McKay, K. L. "On the Perfect and Other Aspects in New Testament Greek." *NovT* 23 (1981) 289—329.

Malatesta, E. *St. John's Gospel, 1920—1965. A Cumulative and Classified Bibliography of Books and of Periodical Literature on the Fourth Gospel.* AnBib 32. Rome: Pontifical Biblical Institute, 1967.

——. *Interiority and Covenant. A Study of εἶναι ἐν and μένεω ἐν in the First Letter of Saint John.* AnBib 69. Rome: Biblical Institute, 1978.

Martin, Ralph P. "Approaches to New Testament Exegesis." In *New Testament Interpretation. Essays on Principles and Methods*, 220—281. Edited by I. H. Marshall. Exeter: Paternoster, 1977.

Martyn, J. L. *History and Theology in the Fourth Gospel.* New York: Harper and Row, 1968.

——. "Glimpses into the History of the Johannine Community. From Its Origin through the Period of Its Life in Which the Fourth Gospel Was Composed." BETL 44, 149—175.

——. *The Gospel of John in Christian History. Essays for Interpreters.* Theological Inquiries. Studies in Contemporary Biblical and Theological Problems. New York: Paulist, 1978.

McCool, F. J. "Living Water in St. John." In *The Bible in Current Catholic Thought: Essays in Memory of M. J. Gruenthaner*, 226—235. Edited by J. L. McKenzie. New York: Herder, 1962.

McPolin, John. "Studies in the Fourth Gospel: Some Contemporary Trends." *IrBibSt* 2 (1980) 2–26.

––. "Mission in the Fourth Gospel." *ITQ* 36 (1969) 113–122.

Meeks, Wayne. "Galilee and Judea in the Fourth Gospel." *JBL* 85 (1966) 159–169.

––. *The Prophet-King: Moses Traditions and the Johannine Christology.* NovTSup 14. Leiden: E. J. Brill, 1967.

––. "Moses as God and King." In *Religions in Antiquity. Essays in Memory of Edwin Goodenough.* Studies in the History of Religions 14, 346–371. Leiden: E. J. Brill. 1968.

––. "The Man from Heaven in Johannine Sectarianism." *JBL* 91 (1972) 44–72.

––. "'Am I a Jew?' Johannine Christianity and Judaism." In *Studies in Judaism in Late Antiquity. 12: Christianity. Judaism and Other Greco-Roman Cults. Part One: The New Testament. Studies for Morton Smith at Sixty,* 163–186. Edited by J. Neusner. Leiden: E. J. Brill, 1975.

––. "The Divine Agent and His Courterfeit in Philo and the Fourth Gospel." In *Aspects of Religious Propaganda in Judaism and Early Christianity,* 43–67. Edited by E. S. Fiorenza. Notre Dame: University of Notre Dame, 1976.

Meinertz, Max. *Jesus und die Heidenmission.* NTAbh I. 2nd rev. ed. Munster i. W: Aschendorf, 1925.

––. *Theologie des Neuen Testaments.* 2 vols. Bonn: Hanstein, 1950.

Michel, Otto. πατήρ. In *Exegetische Wörterbuch zum Neuen Testament* III, Lieferung 1/2, Spalte 1–256, cols. 125–235. Stuttgart: W. Kohlhammer, 1982.

Minear, P. S. "The Audience of the Fourth Evangelist." *Interpretation* 31 (1977) 339–354.

Miranda, J. P. *Der Vater der mich gesandt hat.* EHS 23/7. Frankfurt a/M: Lang, 1972.

––. *Die Sendung Jesu im vierten Evangelium: Religions- und theologiegeschichtliche Untersuchungen zu den Sendungsformeln.* SBS 87. Stuttgart: Katholisches Bibelwerk, 1977.

Moloney, F. J. "From Cana to Cana (Jn 2:1–4:54) and the Fourth Evangelist's Concept of Correct and Incorrect Faith." *Salesianum* 40 (1978) 817–843.

Morris, Leon. *Studies in the Fourth Gospel.* Grand Rapids: Wm. B. Eerdmans, 1969.

Moule, C. F. D. "The Individualism of the Fourth Gospel." In Moule, *Essays in New Testament Interpretation,* 91–109. Cambridge: Cambridge University, 1982.

Murphy-O'Connor, J. "An Essene Missionary Document? CD II, 14-VI, 1." *RB* 77 (1970) 201–229.

––. *1 Corinthians.* 2nd Printing. NT Message 10. Wilmington: Michael Glazier, 1982.

––. *St. Paul's Corinth: Texts and Archaeology.* Good News Studies 6. Wilmington: Michael Glazier, 1983.

Neirynck, Frans. *Jean et les synoptiques: Examen critique de l'exégèse de M.-E. Boismard.* BETL 49. Leuven: Leuven University, 1979.

––. "L'épanalepsis et la critique littéraire. A propos de l'évangile de Jean." In *Evangelica: Gospel Studies – Etudes d'Evangile. Collected Essays.* BETL 60, 143–178. Edited by F. van Segbroeck. Leuven: Leuven University, 1982.

Neugebauer, Fritz. *Die Entstehung des Johannesevangeliums.* Arbeiten zur Theologie 1/36. Stuttgart: Calwer, 1968.

Neusner, Jacob. "The Fellowship (חבורה) in the Second Jewish Commonwealth." *HTR* 53 (1960) 125–142.

Nicholson, G. C. *Death as Departure. The Johannine Descent-Ascent Schema.* SBLDS 63. Chico: Scholars, 1983.

Nicol, W. *The Sēmeia in the Fourth Gospel: Tradition and Redaction.* NovTSup 32. Leiden: E. J. Brill, 1972.

Oehler, Wilhelm. *Das Johannesevangelium: Ein Missionsschrift für die Welt, der Gemeinde ausgelegt.* Gütersloh: Bertelsmann, 1936.

––. *Zum Missionscharakter des Johannesevangeliums.* BFCTh 42. Gütersloh: Bertelsmann, 1941.

Okure, Teresa. "'How Can These Things Happen?' A Study of Jn 3:1–21 in Context." A *Mémoire* of the Ecole Biblique and Archéologique Française. Jerusalem, 1982.

O'Rourke, John J. "Asides in the Gospel of John." *NovT* 21 (1979) 210–219.

Painter, John. "Glimpses of the Johannine Community in the Farewell Discourses." *AusBR* 28 (1980) 21–38.

—. "The Farewell Discourses and the History of the Johannine Christianity." *NTS* 27 (1981) 525–543.

Panikulam, George. *Koinōnia in the New Testament: A Dynamic Expression of Christian Life.* AnBib 85. Rome: Biblical Institute, 1979.

Parker, P. "Two Editions of John." *JBL* 75 (1956) 303–314.

Percy, Ernst. *Untersuchungen über den Ursprung der johanneischen Theologie. Zugleich ein Beitrag zur Frage nach der Entstehung des Gnostizismus.* Lund: Gleerup, 1939.

Perkins, Pheme. "*Koinōnia* in 1 John 1:3–7: The Social Context of Division in the Johannine Letters." *CBQ* 45 (1983) 631–641.

Porsch, Felix. *Pneuma und Wort: Ein exegetischer Beitrag zur Pneumatologie des Johannesevangeliums.* Frankfurt a/M: Josef Knecht, 1974.

de la Potterie, I. *La Vérité dans saint Jean.* 2 vols. AnBib 73, 74. Rome: Biblical Institute, 1977.

Price, James L. "Light from Qumran upon Some Aspects of Johannine Theology." In *John and Qumran*, 9–37. Edited J. H. Charlesworth. London: Geoffrey Chapman, 1972.

Reim, Günter. *Studien zum alttestamentlichen Hintergrund des Johannesevangeliums.* SNTSMS 22. Cambridge : At the University, 1974.

Richter, G. *Die Fusswaschung im Johannesevangelium: Geschichte ihre Deutung.* Regensburg: Friedrich Pustet, 1967.

Riesenfeld, Harald. "Zu den johanneischen ἵνα-Sätzen." *ST* 19 (1965) 213–220.

Rigaux, B. "Die Jünger Jesu in Johannes 17." *TQ* 150 (1970) 202–213.

—. "Les destinatires de IVᵉ Evangile à la lumière de Jn 17." *RTL* 1 (1970) 289–319.

Rissi, Mathias. "Der Aufbau des vierten Evangeliums." *NTS* 29 (1983) 48–54.

Ritt, Hubert. *Das Gebet zum Vater. Zur Interpretation von Joh 17.* Forschung zur Bibel 36. Würzburg: Echter Verlag, 1979.

Robinson, J. A. T. "The Destination and Purpose of St. John's Gospel." *NTS* 6 (1959–1960) 117–131.

—. *Redating the New Testament.* London: SCM, 1976.

Robinson, J. M. "The Johannine Trajectory." In *Trajectories through Early Christianity*, 232–268. Edited by J. M. Robinson and Helmut Koester. Philadelphia: Fortress, 1971.

Rokeah, David. *Jews, Pagans and Christians in Conflict.* Leiden: E. J. Brill, 1982.

Ruckstuhl, Eugen. *Die literarische Einheit des Johannesevangeliums: Der gegenwärtige Stand der Einschlägigen Forschung.* Freiburg in der Schweiz: Paulusverlag, 1951.

—. "Johannine Language and Style. The Question of Their Unity." In *L'Evangile de Jean.* BETL 44, 125–147.

—. "Zur Aussage und Botschaft von Johannes 21." In *Die Kirche des Anfangs. Fs. Für Heinz Schürmann*, 339–362. Edited by R. Schnackenburg, Josef Ernst and Joachim Wanke. Freiburg: Herder, 1978.

Schille, Gottfried. "Bemerkungen zur Formgeschichte des Evangeliums. III: Das Evangelium als Missionsbuch." *NTS* 5–6 (1958–1960) 1–11.

Schnackenburg, R. "Die Messiasfrage im Johannesevangelium." In *Neutestamentliche Aufsätze. Fs. Für Josef Schmid zum 70. Geburtstag*, 240–264. Edited by J. Blinzler, O. Kuss and F. Mussner. Regensburg: Friedrich Pustet, 1963.

—. "Das Johannesevangelium als hermeneutische Frage." *NTS* 13 (1966–1967) 199–210.

—. "Zur Herkunft des Johannesevangeliums." *BZ* 14 (1970) 1–23.

Schottroff, Luise. *Der Glaubende und die Feindliche Welt: Beobachtungen zum gnostischen Dualismus und seine Bedeutung für Paulus und das Johannesevangelium.* WMANT 37. Neukirchen-Vluyn: Neukirchener-V., 1970.

Schulz, Siegfried. *Untersuchungen zur Menschensohn-Christologie im Johannesevangelium. Zugleich ein Beitrag zur Methodengeschichte der Auslegung des 4. Evangeliums.* Göttingen: Vandenhoeck und Ruprecht, 1957.

—. *Komposition und Herkunft der johanneischen Reden.* BWANT 81. Stuttgart: Kohlhammer, 1960.

Schweizer, E. *EGO EIMI: Die religionsgeschichtliche Herkunft und theologische Bedeutung der johanneischen Bildreden, zugleich ein Beitrag zur Quellenfrage des vierten Evangeliums.* FRLANT 56, NF 38. Göttingen: Vandenhoeck und Ruprecht, 1939.

Selected Bibliography 325

——. "Der Kirchenbegriff im Evangelium und den Briefen des Johannes." *SE* 1 (= TU 73; 1959) 363–381.

——. "Zum religionsgeschichtlichen Hintergrund der 'Sendungsformeln' Gal 4.4f; Rom 8.3f; Joh 3.16f; 1 Joh 4.9." *ZNT* 57 (1966) 119–210.

Scroggs, Robin. "The Earliest Christian Communities as Sectarian Movement." In *Studies in Judaism in Late Antiquity. 12: Christianity, Judaism and Other Greco-Roman Cults. Part Two: Early Christianity.* 1–23. Leiden: E. J. Brill, 1975.

——. "Paul as Rhetorician: Two Homilies in Romans 1–11." In *Jews. Greeks and Christians. Religious Lectures in Late Antiquity. Essays in Honor of William David Davies,* 271–297. Leiden: E. J. Brill, 1976.

Segovia, F. F. "The Love and Hatred of Jesus and Johannine Sectarianism." *CBQ* 43 (1981) 258–272.

——. "The Theology and Provenance of John 15:1–17." *JBL* 101 (1982) 115–128.

Senior, Donald. "The Struggle to Be Universal. Mission as Vantage Point for New Testament Investigation." *CBQ* 46 (1984) 63–81.

Seynaeve, J. "Les verbes ἀποστέλλειν et πέμπειν dans le vocabulaire théologique de Jean." In *L'Evangile de Jean.* BETL 44, 385–389.

Smalley, Stephen. *John: Evangelist and Interpreter. History and Interpretation in the Fourth Gospel.* Greenwood: Attic, 1978.

——. "The Signs in John XXI." *NTS* 20 (1974) 275–288.

Smith, D. M. *The Composition and Order of the Fourth Gospel. Bultmann's Literary Theory.* New Haven: Yale University, 1965.

——. "Johannine Christianity: Some Reflections on Its Character and Delineation." *NTS* 21 (1974–1974) 222–248.

——. "The Presentation of Jesus in the Fourth Gospel." *Interpretation* 31 (1977) 367–378.

Smith, T. C. *Jesus in the Gospel of John. A Study of the Evangelists's Purpose and Meaning.* Nashville: Broadman, 1959.

Solages, B., and Vacherot, J.-M. "Le Chapitre XXI de Jean est-il de la même plume que le reste de l'Evangile?" *BLE* 80 (1979) 96–101.

de Solages, Mgr. *Jean et les synoptiques.* Leiden: E. J. Brill, 1979.

Spicq, C. *L'Epître aux Hébreux.* 2nd ed. EB. Paris: Gabalda, 1952.

Stanley, David. "The Purpose of the Fourth Evangelist and the 'Trinification' of the World." In *Trinification of the World. A Festschrift in Honor of Frederick Crowe in Celebration of His 60th Birthday,* 259–278. Edited by Thomas A. Dunne and Jean-Marc Laporte. Toronto: Regis College, 1978.

Stauffer, Ethelbert. *Theologie Des Neuen Testaments.* Gütersloh: Bertelsmann, 1948.

Tcherikover, Victor. *Hellenistic Civilization and the Jews.* New York: Atheneum, 1975.

Teeple, H. M. "Methodology in Source Analysis of the Fourth Gospel." *JBL* 81 (1962) 279–286.

——. *The Literary Origin of the Gospel of John.* Evanston: Religion and Ethics Institute, 1974.

Theobald, Michael. *Im Anfang war das Wort: Textlinguistische Studie zum Johannesprolog.* SBS 106. Stuttgart: Katholisches Bibelwerk, 1983.

Thüsing, Wilhelm. *Die Erhöhung und Verherrlichung Jesu in Johannesevangelium.* NTAbh 21, 1/2. Münster: W. Aschendorf, 1960.

Thyen, Hartwig. "Aus der Literatur zum Johannesevangelium," *TRu* 39 (1975) 289–330; 42 (1977) 211–270; 43 (1978) 328–359.

——. "Einwicklungen innerhalb der johanneischen Theologie und Kirche im Spiegel von Joh 21 und der Lieblingsjüngertexte des Evangeliums." In *L'Evangile de Jean.* BETL 44, 249–299.

Trites, A. A. *The New Testament Concept of Witness.* SNTSMS 31. Cambridge: Cambridge University, 1977.

van Unnik, W. C. "The Purpose of St. John's Gospel," *SE* 1 (= TU 73; 1959) 338–358.

Vermes, Geza. *The Dead Sea Scrolls: Qumran in Perspective.* Philadelphia: Fortress, 1981.

Vincent, J. J. "Pluralism and Mission in the New Testament." *Studia Biblica* 111 (1978) 391–402.

Vouga, François. *Le Cadre historique et l'intention théologique de Jean.* Paris: Beauchesne, 1977.

von Wahlde, Urban C. "The Witnesses to Jesus in Jn 5:31–40 and Belief in the Fourth Gospel." *CBQ* 43 (1981) 383–404.

——. "The Johannine 'Jews': A Critical Survey." *NTS* 28 (1982) 33—60.

Wead, D. W. *The Literary Devices in John's Gospel.* Basel: Friedrich Rienhardt, 1970.

Wegener, R., ed. *Die Datierung der Evangelien. Symposion des Instituts für wissenschaftstheoretische Grundlagenforschung vom 20.—23. mai 1982 in Paderborn.* Tonbandnachschrift. Deutsches Institut für Bildung und Wissen. Paderborn, 1982.

Weinel, Heinrich. *Grundriss der theologischen Wissenschaften. Biblische Theologie des Neuen Testaments. Die Religion Jesu und des Urchristentums.* 5th ed. rev. Tübingen: Mohr/Siebeck, 1928.

Wellhausen, J. *Erweiterungen und Änderungen im vierten Evangelium.* Berlin: Georg Reimer, 1907.

Westcott, B. F. *The Epistle to the Hebrews.* Grand Rapids: Wm. B. Eerdmans, 1955.

Wiefel, Wolfgang. "Die Scheidung von Gemeinde und Welt im Johannesevangelium auf dem Hintergrund der Trennung von Kirche und Synagoge." *TZ* 35 (1979) 213—227.

Wilder, Amos N. *Early Christian Rhetoric: The Language of the Gospel.* Cambridge: Harvard University, 1974.

Wiles, Maurice. *The Spiritual Gospel. The Interpretation of the Fourth Gospel in the Early Church.* Cambridge: At the University, 1960.

Wilken, Robert L., ed. *Aspects of Wisdom in Judaism and Early Christianity.* Studies in Judaism and Early Christianity 1. Notre Dame: University of Notre Dame, 1975.

Wilkens, Wilhelm. *Die Entstehungsgeschichte des vierten Evangeliums.* Diss. Basel. Zollikon: Evangelischer Verlag, 1958.

——. *Zeichen und Werke: Ein Beitrag zur Theologie des 4. Evangeliums in Erzählungs- und Redestoff.* ATANT 55. Zurich: Zwingli, 1969.

Wind, A. "Destination and Purpose of the Gospel of John," *NovT* 14 (1972) 26—69.

Windisch, H. "Der johanneische Erzählungsstil." In ΕΥΧΑΡΙΣΤΗΡΙΟΝ. *Studien zur Religion und Literatur des Alten und Neuen Testaments. Fs. Hermann Gunkel zum 60. Geburtstag.* FRLANT 19, 171—312. Göttingen: Vandenhoeck und Ruprecht, 1923.

Woll, D. B. "The First Farewell Discourse in the Gospel of John." *JBL* 99 (1980) 225—239.

——. *Johannine Christianity in Conflict: Authority, Rank and Succession in the First Farewell Discourse.* SBLDS 60. Chico: Scholars, 1981.

Wuellner, Wilhelm. "Paul's Rhetoric of Argumentation in Romans: An Alternative to the Donfried-Karris Debate over Romans." *CBQ* 38 (1976) 330—351.

Zahn, Theodor. *Grundriss der neutestamentliche Theologie.* Leipzig: D. Werner Scholl, 1920.

Zimmermann, H. "Das absolute ἐγώ εἰμι als die neutestamentliche Offenbarungsformel." *BZ* NF 4 (1960) 54—69, 266—276.

Index of Selected Passages

1. New Testament

2. Old Testament

3. Greek and Roman Literature

4. Palestine and Jewish Literature

Index of Ancient and Modern Authors

Index of Greek Words

Index of Subjects

Wissenschaftliche Untersuchungen zum Neuen Testament

Herausgegeben von Martin Hengel und Otfried Hofius

18 Peter Lampe
Die stadtrömischen Christen
in den ersten beiden
Jahrhunderten
2. Auflage 1989. Ca. 490 Seiten.
Fadengeheftete Broschur.

19 Scott J. Hafemann
Suffering and the Spirit
1986. VIII, 258 Seiten. Fadengeheftete Broschur.

20 Hans F. Bayer
Jesus' Predictions of
Vindication and Resurrection
1986. X, 289 Seiten. Fadengeheftete Broschur.

21 Reinhard Feldmeier
Die Krisis des Gottessohnes
1987. XII, 292 Seiten. Fadengeheftete Broschur.

22 Axel von Dobbeler
Glaube als Teilhabe
1987. XIV, 348 Seiten. Broschur.

23 Peter Marshall
Enmity in Corinth: Social
Conventions in Paul's
Relations with the Corinthians
1987. XVI, 450 Seiten. Fadenge-
heftete Broschur.

24 Wolf-Dietrich Köhler
Die Rezeption des Matthäus-
evangeliums in der Zeit vor
Irenäus
1987. XVI, 605 Seiten. Fadengeheftete Broschur.

25 Günter Röhser
Metaphorik und Personifika-
tion der Sünde
1987. VIII, 218 Seiten. Fadengeheftete Broschur.

26 Wolfgang J. Bittner
Jesu Zeichen im Johannes-
evangelium
1987. XI, 334 Seiten. Fadengeheftete Broschur.

27 Jörg Büchli
Der Poimandres – ein
paganisiertes Evangelium
1987. XI, 232 Seiten. Fadengeheftete Broschur.

28 Karl-Wilhelm Niebuhr
Gesetz und Paränese
1987. IX, 275 Seiten. Fadengeheftete Broschur.

29 Migaku Sato
Q und Prophetie
1988. XIII, 437 Seiten. Fadengeheftete Broschur.

30 William L. Schutter
Hermeneutic and Composi-
tion in First Peter
1988. Ca. 320 Seiten. Fadengeheftete Broschur.

31 Teresa Okure
The Johannine Approach to
Mission
1988. XX, 342 Seiten. Fadengeheftete Broschur.

32 Matthias Klinghardt
Gesetz und Volk Gottes
1988. VIII, 371 Seiten. Fadengeheftete Broschur.

33 Joel B. Green
The Death of Jesus
1988. XVI, 351 Seiten. Fadengeheftete Broschur.

J.C.B. Mohr (Paul Siebeck) Tübingen